EUROPEAN DEMOCRACY BETWEEN THE WARS

KARL J. NEWMAN

# European Democracy Between the Wars

Translated by KENNETH MORGAN

UNIVERSITY OF NOTRE DAME PRESS

FIRST PUBLISHED IN 1970
© *George Allen & Unwin Ltd 1970*

First American Edition 1971
University of Notre Dame Press
Notre Dame, Indiana 46556

SBN 268–00426–9

Library of Congress Catalog Card Number: 70–98904

PRINTED IN GREAT BRITAIN

# FOREWORD

The totalitarian movements of the twentieth century have grown out of the very soil of democracy itself. They are a perversion of the democratic constitutional state. It is now generally acknowledged that in many countries after the First World War, especially Germany, democracy made a suicidal contribution to its own fate.

The great merit of Professor K. J. Newman's book is the way he has traced these connections in all their complexity and clarified their probable relationships. The interweaving of ideology and practice, of thought and action is constantly being demonstrated in a multitude of examples. The learned author brings a vast fund of historical knowledge to bear on this important analysis: he has shown the greatest skill in organizing the formidable mass of material according to theoretical aspects which originate in political theory. His particular asset is his penetrating assessment of developments in Austria and the Danubian countries generally. This is a particular merit of this important analysis.

After his intensive and generally objective survey of totalitarian systems Professor Newman nevertheless takes a hopeful, albeit cautious view of the future prospects for democracy. This, I believe, is a particularly gratifying addition. One can only hope that his book will reach a very wide circle of readers in addition to interested specialists.

CARL J. FRIEDRICH

# CONTENTS

CHAPTER I

# Autocracy and Democracy in Central Europe

Democracy cannot win a war. It is all talk and half-measures but no decisive action. Incompetent by nature, it is incapable of adapting itself to new ideas. In assuming the perfection of the adult human being it is based on a myth. It means the rule of the masses and thus spells the decline of civilization. It can flourish only in small communities in which the size of the population excludes military strength. On the other hand mechanization of government is the inevitable result of an increase in population.

These few sentences epitomize the widespread, seriously discussed arguments levelled against democracy between 1918 and 1939. They were also advanced against Greek democracy, particularly by Plato, and some modern advocates of tyranny have adapted them to contemporary conditions. Their opportuneness for tyranny was a real one: for in the third and fourth decades of this century, under the influence of the prevailing social conditions, many of the underlying assumptions of Plato's doctrine seemed to have come true.

As an important American writer observed in the year in which the Second World War broke out, the 'new despotism' – fascism – rejected all ideas of political freedom and equality, the doctrine of the necessary consensus between the governed and the government, and the usefulness of political discussion. The 'new despotism' proclaimed an unlimited state absolutism which would control all social life, concentrated all authority in the hands of a few autocrats, proclaimed the doctrine of the superiority of force in all internal and inter-state relations, rejected the sanctity of the rights of man and the inviolability of treaty obligations. All this amounted to autocracy within the state and anarchy in international relations.

Finally, the 'new despotism' strove to substitute an appeal to the (irrational) urges of racial and tribal ties, in place of the belief in the rule of reason and intellect.[1] There is even today a compelling logic about Plato's cycle of ever-deteriorating forms of government.[2] Even today – one might agree with the theorists of the totalitarian state on this point – democracy can destroy itself by virtue of its own innate laws and tendencies. Yet the Platonic theorem is valid only for the initial democracies. At the present time these are the developing countries; at that time it was Greek democracy – which was not allowed to develop beyond its initial stages – and later the early stages of the democracies of continental Europe before and after the First World War.[3]

If one overlooks the flaws in these theories they do, in fact, produce a convincing argument, and it seems that a Pericles must inevitably be succeeded by a Cleon, a Stresemann by a Hitler, a Demosthenes be defeated by a Philip and a Kerenski by a Lenin. French radical democracy, bordering on anarchy, led to de Gaulle's presidential constitution, and the internecine factions of the Roman Republic to military imperialism. A Dionysius must always enslave a Plato and, just as a reading of Aristotle's works led to Alexander the Great's world empire, so Marx's works led to Stalin's and Mao's reign of terror.

Yet it was only when they were torn out of their context that Plato's teaching could become the intellectual instrument of the total state. Thus Popper,[4] for example, overlooks the fact that for Plato totalitarian elements play a rather secondary role since they serve him as a means for ennobling man's soul. Only in connection with the materialism which goes back to the sceptics – and to Thomas Hobbes in particular – was it possible for the arguments not only of Pareto, Mosca, Maurras, Sorel, Lenin, Spann and Schmitt but also of Mussolini and Hitler to threaten the respect for human values embodied in the democratic form of state. This materialism stressed the animal-inhuman elements in human nature – the 'natural' man in the Pauline sense. By denying the 'divine spark', in the Stoics' sense, materialism degraded the individual human being by equating him with the molecules of Cartesian-

---

[1] Charles Edward Merriam, *The New Democracy and the New Despotism*, New York 1929, p. 217. To Carl J. Friedrich, however, must go the credit for having pointed out, even before Merriam, the dangers which arise for the future democracy from the misguided practice in central Europe. Cf. *Foreign Policy in the Making*, New York 1945, and *New Belief in the Common Man*, Brattleboro 1942; in German, *Die Demokratie als Herrschafts- und Lebensform*, Heidelberg 1959.

[2] Plato, *The Republic*, Books VIII and IX.

[3] Cf. Karl J. Newman, *Entwicklungsdiktatur und Verfassungsstaat*, Frankfurt am Main 1963. It is not always developing countries, in the economic sense, which are concerned, although countries like Poland, Hungary and Romania almost come into this category. Nevertheless all these post-war states can be described as initial or developing democracies, as they suddenly switched from an authoritarian or, as in Germany, from a semi-authoritarian form of state to parliamentary democracy.

[4] Karl Popper, *The Open Society and its Enemies*, London 1948; cf. Chap. 2, para. 3.

Newtonian scientific theory.[1] But by comparing the State with the human organism, Hobbes merely substituted theorems and a play upon words for the 'fictions' of natural rights. Rousseau was not uninfluenced by this sort of thinking. That is evident in his weakness for mob rule by means of the plebiscite,[2] leading to Caesarism, and in his glorification of the barbaric morality of natural tribes, and advocation of the despotic subjection of the individual fate to the general will.[3]

Why were Hegel[4] and Marx able to mislead so many people who had grown up in the best traditions of European humanism? Because their theories, which started out from Rousseau's pseudo-humanitarian premises and, taking a devious route via Hegel's historical-metaphysical witch's kitchen, thus finally arrived at totalitarian conclusions, were, in the nineteenth century, clouded by the phraseology of progress.

That for the former the state and for the latter the proletariat represents the *summum bonum* is largely immaterial. The racism of national socialism represents a misapplication of biological-scientific problems of human life and, in particular, of human organization. In post-war communism, Marxism once again moved nearer to Hegel, for after the end of the Second World War Stalinist communism became the most important driving force behind the world-wide development of nationalism. We are today witnessing the division of the globe into an ever-increasing number of intensely nationalistic states. At the same time communism, as Yugoslavia, Albania and Red China show, has already partly lost its unifying power. That national socialism, fascism and other authoritarian movements in Central Europe were set in motion by the results and the technique of the Bolshevik Revolution of 1917 is hardly likely to be disputed today.[5] In particular national socialism – but not only national socialism – was the attempt of those social groups badly hit by the events of 1918–1923 to come to terms with the repercussions of the impact of the revolution by partly adopting the Bolshevist mentality and techniques.[6] Conversely, after the Second

[1] A. D. Lindsay, *The Modern Democratic State*, New York 1962, p. 81. Michael Oakshott, however, in his introduction to *Leviathan*, Oxford 1957, does not agree with this view. He sees Hobbes as the continuation of a sceptical branch of the late scholastic tradition, p. LIII.

[2] *Social Contract* II, 3 and III, 15.

[3] Ibid., 1, II, 3, IV, 1, IV, 2.

[4] On the relationship between Rousseau and Hegel cf. R. M. Maciver, *Community*, London 1928, Appendix B, pp. 423–33.

[5] Bullock starts from the assumption that Hitler's only motive was a desire for personal power. Even if that be granted in the case of Hitler, it certainly does not apply to the not inconsiderable masses in the Nazi movement who firmly believed in its ideology. Allan Bullock, *Hitler*, Düsseldorf 1960, p. 383.

[6] Otto-Ernst Schüddenkopf, *Linke Leute von rechts*, Stuttgart 1960.

World War, communism took over much of national-socialist fascist thinking, technique, strategy and tactics.[1]

The totalitarian dictatorships can be shown to have developed a larger number of variations of the classical arguments. They were able to profit by the childish ailments which the post-war democracies, erected on the top of the social structure of absolutism, were bound to suffer. They derived no small advantage from the fact that the forces of democracy were novices in practising the dynamics of political power, with the result that the new liberal states treated totalitarian movements and the democratic parties as equals. This was bound to prove suicidal. At the same time an irresponsible pacifist policy on the part of the Western Powers – which could easily be misconstrued as weakness and was in fact explained as such – was a contributing factor in the underestimation of democratic military capability.

Democracy, it was said, has become an *ancien régime* and, in the feebleness of its old age, incapable of solving the problems of the modern industrial age and its economy.[2] The critics soon went over to a frontal attack on the basic ideas of the democratic state. This, so the argument ran, always found itself in a catastrophic dilemma: either the state is a genuine democracy – which, according to Rousseau and his spiritual heirs such as Carl Schmitt, it can only be when it is direct democracy – which governs itself with the help of a plebiscite and leads to Caesarism,[3] or government must be entrusted to representatives. But then it cannot be just to the claims of mass democracy. If for practical and technical reasons deputies are elected to act on behalf of the people, should not single representatives be chosen to act on behalf of that same people?[4] In the former case it is in fact not the people who govern but the party bosses,[5] i.e. people out for wealth and power, to whom the public good is a matter of utter indifference. Such a system is, it was alleged, really an oligarchy in which the voter, as Rousseau had already stated, is free only at election time; in between elections however he is a slave. Or it is a 'plutocracy', in which corrupt and incompetent parliamentarians become lackeys of the money bags. In our time,

---

[1] The establishment of communist power in east Europe, and especially the Czechoslovak coup in 1947, were accompanied in many respects by a faithful reproduction of the techniques developed by national socialism, e.g. in the case of Austria.

[2] Oswald Spengler, *Der Untergang des Abendlandes. Umrisse einer Morphologie der Weltgeschichte*, 2 vols., Munich 1918–22.

[3] In the sense of Plato's *Republic*.

[4] Carl Schmitt, *Die geistesgeschichtliche Lage des heutigen Parlamentarismus*, Berlin 1926.

[5] Heinrich Triepel, *Die Staatsverfassung und die politischen Parteien*, Berlin 1928, p. 33; quoted by Karl-Dietrich Bracher in *Die Auflösung der Weimarer Republik*, Villingen 1960, p. 41. In his second chapter Bracher gives a short but highly informative survey of the agitation against the party state and the Weimar Republic.

the dictators in the developing countries base their rejection of parliamentary government on almost identical arguments.[1] Once again the lack of understanding about the real nature of the democratic party has given fresh life to the Platonic dictum about the eternal and destructive disputes between parties.[2] Because of this misconception, opposition is interpreted fundamentally as enmity.[3] The opponents of parliamentary government do not understand, or rather pretend not to understand, that a dialectical system is involved in the relationship between government and opposition, presupposing a fundamental consensus of agreement, in which the two groups carry out a ritualized and institutionalized shadow fight. One group has the task of seeing that the pace of national progress is not too slow, and the other that it is not too fast.[4]

It is a well-known sociological fact that social structures and patterns are vertically transmitted from the upper to the lower social strata. Since in both pre-war Germany and pre-war Russia the bureaucracy was respected as a competent, socially superior element which was continually extending its power and influence – irrespective of whether it was respected or feared – the political parties, especially Social Democracy, which were fighting bureaucracy had also to organize themselves in a bureaucratic way. But since the civil service tends to submit to the orders of authority and to discourage individual initiative, this was bound to result in a leadership crisis in both the Weimar Republic and the short-lived Kerenski period. It was not just in Germany that the post-war generation felt most acutely the lack of a purposeful democratic leadership.

This partly explains why people turned to Caesarism. Thus the former Austrian Chancellor, Kurt von Schuschnigg, held the view that party democracy presupposes 'an imperceptible, decisive corrective force, borne by representatives of the people . . . in the person of the head of state, the president, or the monarch', who by virtue of his prerogative could intervene to set things right and in an emergency

---

[1] Cf. K. J. Newman, *Entwicklungsdiktatur und Verfassungsstaat*, loc. cit.

[2] Hermann Heller held the view that the turning to Caesarism and the call for the strong man gave expression to the sense of despair felt by the middle class, which sees its position of power threatened by the working class. Heller also pointed out that Oswald Spengler is in fact 'at once the most typical German representative of both the religion of force and superman and of dictatorial thinking'! The middle class really feared that its world would come to an end (H. Heller, *Rechtsstaat oder Diktatur*, Tübingen 1930, pp. 17 ff., quoted by Dr Christian Graf von Krockow, in *Die Entscheidung*, Stuttgart 1958, p. 42).

[3] Cf., for example, the friend-foe principle in Carl Schmitt, *Der Begriff des Politischen*, Hamburg 1933.

[4] Cf. R. G. Collingwood, *The New Leviathan*, Oxford 1942, pp. 210 ff. and Rudolf Smend, *Die Verschiebung der konstitutionellen Ordnung durch die Verhältniswahl*, Bonn 1919.

decide in an authoritarian manner.[1] So in the case of the Weimar Republic this 'non-party' power had in fact contributed to the victory of national socialism; a further proof of how the Hegelian idea of 'monarchic power' still pervaded political thought.

In the same book Schuschnigg makes a number of criticisms of parliamentary democracy in Austria. The most important of his arguments are worth repeating here, especially as the complaint generally levelled against parliamentarianism in central Europe between the wars originates here from a moderate authoritarian source. According to Schuschnigg, Austria lacked the great English parliamentary tradition. He maintains that the Austrian parliament was power-drunk and had over-estimated its own importance. Delegates had behaved irresponsibly and abused their parliamentary immunity. The result, in practice, had not been parliamentary government, but party factionalism leading to 'stasis'. Schuschnigg argues further that the community had been split by the two big, almost equally strong parties – the Christian Socialists and the Social Democrats. Such views show the intensity of traditional beliefs about the role of monarchy which then still prevailed in central Europe. They are typical of communities which have lived for a long time under a 'dyarchic' system. This also explains why today in the developing countries almost identical arguments are advanced against the parliamentary system by the opponents of the constitutional state.[2]

In the course of the elections, Schuschnigg continues, the parties had accustomed the electorate to irrelevant arguments, which were then turned against the parties themselves. Party rule had therefore amounted to nothing less than rabid demagogy in the elections and in parliament itself, while 'horse-trading' had been common practice in the parliamentary committees. The electoral system had made it impossible for any party to form a majority – which then made co-alition governments necessary. But coalition governments can rule only with the aid of compromises and cannot solve really vital problems. No wonder that the people considered professional politicians to be dishonest. Although the accusation of personal corruption was unjustified, party coalitions led to phenomena approaching or resembling it – because these dishonest compromises justified suspicions in the minds

[1] Kurt von Schuschnigg, *Dreimal Österreich*, Vienna 1937, p. 137.
[2] Cf. K. J. Newman, 'The Dyarchic Pattern of Government and Pakistan's Problems', in *Political Science Quarterly*, New York 1960. The term 'dyarchy' first appeared in connection with the 'Government of India Act' of 1919, by which, in the Indian provinces, cabinets responsible to provincial legislatives were introduced, the most important residual ruling powers remaining however in the hands of Viceroy and Governors. The dyarchic system introduced by the British as a transitional form in political education for responsible government led however to a diminished sense of political responsibility.

of the people. A continual pressure applied in the civil service by parliamentarians on behalf of their party friends also gave rise to the charge of favouritism. The Austrian socialists had been playing with the thought of the dictatorship of the proletariat; on the other hand the Socialist Party had not been a genuine workers' party and workers had also been members of the Christian-Social People's Party. Finally, Schuschnigg repeated Mussolini's argument that democracy may perhaps be useful in western Europe, but it was not a suitable article for export.

The striking feature of Schuschnigg's apology for the authoritarian system is the great similarity which exists between these charges and those which are now being advanced in the developing countries against the Western constitutional state. The author has discussed these accusations in detail elsewhere.[1] However, to enable the reader to make a comparison, they may be briefly recapitulated here. The opponents of democracy in the new states of Asia and Africa put forward the following arguments: parliamentary democracy was forced on the developing countries by the colonial powers and is essentially alien to them. The population is not educated enough to work the democratic form of state. In order to capture their votes irresponsible politicians hoodwink the poverty-stricken masses with slogans and pseudo-programmes which cannot possibly be carried out. The intellectuals under the influence of foreign ideas are a small group only interested in debating and making inflammatory speeches. The destructive and irresponsible criticism of the government by politicians hinders the smooth despatch of government business. The political parties are a clique of rapacious, egoistical, self-perpetuating politicians, theorists and unemployed lawyers, whose intrigues reduce national stability to a mockery. This unbridled activity leads to frequent changes of government; on the other hand, the same faces always reappear in the various governments. Ministerial office is used by the politician – the word becomes almost a term of abuse – only as an opportunity for personal enrichment and boundless corruption. Also, in the parliamentary system the constant inter-party quarrels lead to a state of profound disintegration in the nation. Even state defence and national independence are used as mere playthings. President Sukarno has declared that the idea of an active opposition is alien to the Indonesian way of life,[2] and Alexander Adande of Dahomey has said that behind an idealistic mask each party represents a definite class and a definite economic interest. Parties are quite prepared to tell lies, to compromise and to act in a demagogic and

[1] K. J. Newman, *Entwicklungsdiktatur und Verfassungsstaat*, op. cit., pp. 13 ff.
[2] Cf. *Major Governments of Asia*, Ed. George McT. Kahin, New York 1958, pp. 565 ff.

corrupt fashion.[1] Just as was the case previously in central Europe, the functional significance of political parties and of the part played by the opposition in forming the political will is not understood.

The question now arises whether these things are symptomatic of young democracies whose peoples lived for a long time under an autocratic administration and then opted for a democratic-parliamentary system of government too suddenly.

It may not be possible in the case of Germany to speak of a developing country in the economic sense, although this description was to some extent applicable to the Hungarian half of the Habsburg monarchy and the Balkans. But one can certainly speak here of developing countries in the political sense since the population of these countries were only partly educated in politics – as in the case of Germany, Austria and Czechoslovakia – or almost totally untrained, as in the case of Serbia, Poland and Hungary. The comment by the Pakistan Prime Minister, Choudhury Mohammed Ali, was not inappropriate: that democracy, like the art of balancing a bicycle, is an art which must be learned gradually – this also applies to central Europe. It takes time to learn the right balance between order and freedom. The schools in which this experience is gained are free elections. Free inter-party discussion is the teaching method employed in these schools. The modern world possesses no better method for training in politics.[2]

Othmar Spann's idea of the élite,[3] which found its clearest expression in the Sudeten-German *Kameradschaftsbund*, the *Ordensburg* ideas of the SS and the claim to rule made by the *Politbüros* of trained professional politicians, have repeatedly paid tribute to Plato's concept of the threefold division of society (into rulers, warriors, workers and peasants). Correlated to the absolute claim to rule on the part of a leading élite is the anarcho-nihilistic rejection of the social hierarchy and of all legitimate authority based on traditional right, which springs directly from the phenomenon of the masses. The contradiction between these two extremes is only apparent. As even Georg Simmel knew, complete equality only exists under an absolute monarchy,[4] for only where the one is all powerful are the others equal because they are powerless.

---

[1] Cf. Rupert Emerson, *From Empire to Nation. The Rise of Self-Assertion of Asian and African Peoples*, Cambridge (Mass.) 1960, p. 187.

[2] Choudhury Mohammed Ali's answer to the Pakistan Constitutional Commission questionnaire, Dacca, Karachi, June 17, 1960.

[3] Cf., for example, *Der Wahre Staat*, Leipzig 1921.

[4] Cf. Georg Simmel's statements about 'Nivellement' in his *Soziologie*, Berlin 1923, p. 113.

## Democracy's Advance and Retreat

The republican-democratic form of state came to central Europe in 1918 in the wake of the defeat of the Central Powers. To say that democracy or republicanism was imposed on the nations concerned would not be quite accurate. They were, however, undoubtedly recommended to them in Wilson's Fourteen Points. Moreover the psychological impact of the collapse of the Russian Tsarist Empire and the victory of the Western Powers, achieved as a result of a crushing superiority in strategy, raw materials and weapons, gave rise to conclusions about the superiority of democratic rule over monarchic and military states. There had been an indigenous and strongly-rooted tradition of liberalism and constitutionalism both in Germany and the western part of the Danube monarchy which was under Austrian administration, as well as in Italy. But there were only rudimentary traces of the constitutional system in those parts of east and south Europe which had for centuries been under influence of the Ottoman and Tsarist empires.

The multilingual Habsburg monarchy with its strong tradition of tolerant coexistence and gradual education towards self-government was the first to succumb to the democratic principle of the right to national self-determination.[1]

The deposing of the Tsar in 1917 had set in motion an anti-monarchist wave which then, in the following year, swept over Germany and Austria as well. Under the shock of defeat, a republic was probably desired by the majority of the people in these countries. But, as Max Weber observed even in the summer of 1918, it was more than doubtful whether any genuine, firm wish to adopt the democratic type of state really existed there at that time.[2] In the other countries of central Europe, none of which had known universal franchise, the switch to parliamentary republicanism came even more abruptly.

Nor was the anti-democratic reaction long in coming. It began five years after the democratic revolution, actually in Italy[3] which had fought on the side of the Western Allies in the First World War. Yet if fascism had not found such a strong response far beyond Italy's

[1] Oskar Jászi, *The Dissolution of the Habsburg Monarchy*, Chicago 1961.

[2] Bismarck left behind him a nation completely lacking in any sort of political education, one which was far below the level it had reached in this respect twenty years earlier, and above all a nation without any kind of political will whatever, accustomed to having the great statesman at its head look after politics for it . . . and, in the name of 'monarchial rule', accustomed to endure fatalistically whatever decisions were taken about it – Max Weber, 'Parlament und Regierung im neugeordneten Deutschland' in *Gesammelte Politische Schriften*, Tübingen 1958, p. 307.

[3] Erwin von Beckerath, *Wesen und Werden des faschistischen Staates*, Berlin 1927.

frontiers, who knows whether it would not have remained one of those lively, but transient *intermezzi* which are not infrequently to be met with in the history of the Latin races? But after Italy three new constitutional states, namely Poland[1] (1938), Yugoslavia[2] (1929) and Romania[3] (1930) went over to the authoritarian system. The liberal parliamentary state had already met an early death a short time before in Hungary (March 1919). There it was taken over by Béla Kun's communist republic, which once again was ousted by a right-wing authoritarian dictatorship under Admiral Horthy.[4]

In Germany the situation was different. It was only after a long, ruthless struggle that national socialism, exploiting the world economic crisis of 1933, was able to gain a decisive victory over the democratic forces inside the state which the Weimar Republic had built up and sought to defend, albeit with unsuitable means but with great self-sacrifices.[5] In the following year autocracy spread to Austria.[6] It was obvious that the already existing autocracies such as Poland, Hungary, Romania and Yugoslavia thus received a new and more powerful stimulus from this extension of authoritarian elements. The time came when fascism spread to western Europe and was even able to exert some influence in staunchly democratic countries like Great Britain, France, Belgium and Norway. As dictatorships can act more ruthlessly, they often achieve surprising initial successes. It looked as though they were in a position to be able to combat the consequences of the world economic crisis far more effectively than the democracies in which a free and often unrestrained press was free to exaggerate the shortcomings of freely-elected rulers.

## In Quest of Democracy for the Large-Scale States

In the course of their development the states of the Western world were repeatedly confronted with the problem of spatial expansion with the

[1] Malbone W. Graham, 'Polish Politics, 1918–1939', in Bernadotte E. Schmitt (ed.), *Poland*, Berkeley, Los Angeles 1945, pp. 136 f.; Forst de Battaglia, *Zwischeneuropa*, Frankfurt 1954, pp. 59 f.

[2] Maček, *In the Struggle for Freedom*, New York 1958; see also *Ost-Europa Handbuch*, Yugoslavia, published by Werner Markert, Cologne, Graz 1954; also Hugh Seton-Watson, *Eastern Europe between the Wars*, Cambridge 1962, pp. 225 f.

[3] Cf. H. Seton-Watson, op. cit., pp. 203 f.

[4] Forst de Battaglia, op. cit., pp. 331 f.; cf. also Miklos Horthy, *Ein Leben für Ungarn*, Bonn 1953; Wenzel Jaksch, *Europas Weg nach Potsdam*, Stuttgart 1955, pp. 220, 221, 259; H. Seton-Watson, op. cit., pp. 187 f.

[5] Cf. bibliography on the history and constitutional history of the Weimar Republic at the end of the book.

[6] Karl Renner, *Österreich von der Ersten zur Zweiten Republik*, Vienna 1953; *Geschichte der Republik Österreichs*, published by H. Benedikt, Munich 1954.

ensuing consequences, both negative and positive, to their political structure. They either succeeded in maintaining their simple popular institutions in a small area (for example, the people's assemblies of individual Swiss cantons which had evolved out of the old Germanic democracy) to which these peoples owe their original vigour; or they formed a large unit, in which the voice of the individual was necessarily overwhelmed. These great states were certainly able to raise sufficient soldiers and war materials; it was, however, all too easy for the political organization to become a mechanical bureaucratic system in which little regard was paid to the individual as such.[1]

But even long before the industrial revolution and the dawn of mass society, democracy had evolved two techniques to overcome its spatial limitation, creating the democratic form of representative government at the centre and local self-government at the periphery – though these institutions which had emerged in antiquity and in western Europe, since the early Middle Ages, had always served the constitutional state (as for example the Reichstag of the old Empire and other representative assemblies based on the estates of medieval Europe), but, not always democracy. As instanced by Magna Charta they served the feudal nobility and urban patricians against the monarchy. Only much later did the Third Estate and the working class find them useful in the course of the fight for democracy in Britain and on the Continent.

The existence of these possibilities for realizing large-scale democracy was recognized as early as the time of the French Revolution. In the first place it was the enthusiasm for this revolution which spread the *idea* of democracy over the whole continent. But just as the representatives of this revolution overlooked the fact that democracy *as a way of life* presupposes self-discipline and tolerance and can only be realized in political institutions, they also overlooked the significance of the most important democratic institution, namely local self-government. Every large state, whatever its type, needs government at its basic level. 'No Bishop, no King', King James I of England had exclaimed. Where there are no departmental prefects there are also no military emperors, it could be said of France. The type of local administration which befits a democracy is not a prefect dependent on the central government but an elected local self-government educating the citizens for responsibility. There can be no doubt that the adoption of a system of *elected* administrative officers plays a most vital part in the process of overcoming the heritage of autocracy.

[1] Charles Horton Cooley, *Social Organization*, New York 1962, pp. 91 f.; cf. also Jacob Burckhardt, *Weltgeschichtliche Betrachtungen*, Berlin, Stuttgart 1910, Ch. II, p. 32.

After the First World War there appeared in large parts of central Europe first signs of a developing technological and mass society. This was bound to have an unsettling effect on rural communities. The influence emanating from the town was at once confusing and exciting. It resulted in that decline in the standard of thinking and taste and loosening of ties which de Tocqueville and Ostrogorski had already observed. The masses seemed to become more susceptible to political slogans and headlines. Along with all this went a noticeable lowering of critical power. Real political interest did not come into it. Thanks to the experience gained in developing countries we now know more about these phenomena. The new democracy had suddenly brought millions of people face to face with politics, many of whom were neither used to political thinking nor to political responsibility;[1] in the monarchic state they had relied on to the privileged classes. In addition, large sections of the central-European masses were still under the sway of dynastic, religious and patriotic sentiments. Because of this split consciousness, parties whose ideological programmes played up to these mass feelings were likely to dominate the political spectrum of the post-war period.[2]

Much in these symptoms can be traced back to the immediate effects of industrialization. Yet these phenomena are also consequences of the spatial expansion of society which accompanies industrialization. People were no longer confined to the closed society of the village: they now quickly spilled beyond its borders, but could not digest and master the new impressions flooding in on them from outside with the same speed. Sudden radical changes of this sort inevitably entail a weakening or partial collapse of social controls, particularly of the *mores*. The development of mass society resulted thus in a decline in moral and intellectual standards.

But for these social and socio-psychological conditions the astounding success of modern dictatorship would be inconceivable. Karl Jaspers then put forward the thesis that the phenomenon of demagogues intoxicating the masses to be ruled by military oligarchies is the result of modern technology and economy. Thus social evolution engenders tendencies which threaten to destroy the state. The dictatorial restoration of unity, authority and obedience is then a reaction on the part of the state.[3]

The expansion of community has been referred to as causing political

---

[1] Cf., for example, Milan Hodža, *Federation in Central Europe*, London, New York, Melbourne 1942, pp. 184 ff.

[2] Cf. Eschenburg's theory of the 'Substitute Emperor' in *Die improvisierte Demokratie der Weimarer Republik*, Laupheim 1955, p. 38.

[3] Karl Jaspers, *Die geistige Situation unserer Zeit*, Berlin, Leipzig 1931, p. 84.

life to be intensified. Democracy is inconceivable without a sober discussion of political day-to-day problems.[1]

But how can discussion of this sort be reconciled with the realities of mass society? Political propaganda, carried on with the means and methods of modern psychology,[2] increasingly excluded the critical, factual discussion of political issues. In the twenties political rivalry was confined to the meeting hall or the open-air meeting. There discussion and protest were possible. With the arrival of radio, amplifiers and television the human voice acquired such a vast range that about the year 1930 indoor political meetings began to lose their importance.

The democratic governments and parties were slow to adapt themselves to these new circumstances. Aristotle thought that the number of citizens in a state must be small enough for all to be able to hear the herald's voice. This meant that every citizen should publicly be able to take a stand on political issues. Let us consider the role played today by mass communications where public opinion is concerned. It can then easily be perceived that democracy must take the utmost care to prevent these highly effective means of exerting influence from becoming the monopoly of a single political party. Without some vigilance these means are far more useful to the rule of one than of the many.[3]

In the past tyranny imposed over large areas had always involved considerable risks for the ruler. The King of Persia would find it hard to control his satraps. Today the dictator can give his orders from thousands of miles away and make instantly sure that they have been carried out. The possibilities for high-speed communication of information were developed round about 1920. Radio programmes began to be broadcast daily. Newspapers increased their circulation beyond anything ever known before. The opportunities and possibilities for political parties which had no access to radio and press inevitably

[1] 'The extremely critical position of parliamentarism today is due to the development of modern mass democracy which has made public discussion and argument a formality.' Carl Schmitt, op. cit., p. 10.

[2] Statistics for Poland, Czechoslovakia, Austria, cf., for example, Forst de Battaglia, op. cit., p. 73. In 1932, out of 1,000 inhabitants in each country, 26 in Poland, 92 in Austria, 99 in France, 122 in Switzerland, 136 in Germany, and 182 in England owned a radio set. In 1936 Poland had 743 cinemas with a seating capacity of 273,000. Czechoslovakia had 1,608 cinemas, Germany, with twice the population of Poland, had 54,000.

[3] 'As long as democracy was only a pseudo-democracy, in the sense that it granted political power at first only to a small, propertied and educated group, and only gradually to the proletariat, it led to the growth of rationality even when in fact this amounted to no more than the rational representation of its own interests. But since democracy became effective, i.e. since all classes played an active part in it, it has been increasingly transformed into what Max Scheler called a "democracy of emotions".' Karl Mannheim, *Man and Society*, London 1940, p. 45.

deteriorated. The media for influencing public opinion became concentrated in the hands of the few.

This period had also seen a significant increase in political activity. In the dynastic state the capital was generally also the seat of the court, the natural centre of politics. Even the French Revolution was fought and won for the whole of France in the streets of Paris and the Revolution of 1848 in the streets of Paris, Vienna, Berlin, Prague and Budapest. In 1870 too, the mood of the people of Paris and Berlin played an important part in deciding between war and peace. The extension of the franchise to all taxpayers towards the end of the nineteenth century assigned greater political weight to the small towns. A typical consequence was the phenomenon of the *Radau-Kleinbürgertum* (petty bourgeois radicalism).

In central Europe, then mainly agricultural, the post-war period initiated an involvement of the rural areas in political life. The religioconservative scale of values of these people, whose lives were still rooted in a state of semi-feudalism, differed markedly from the urban scale of values. Thus a revolutionary movement like the nationalsocialist one was ready to exploit the latent tension existing between town and country.[1] The country folk migrating to the towns of growing industrialization helped to produce a dynamic interplay of reaction within the urban proletariat. On the one hand the country people came immediately under the influence of the more urban ideologies such as Socialism, on the other hand they passed on to the urban population a subservient attitude towards authority which was widespread in the country, amounting to a naïve religiosity, an intolerant outlook and a distrust of intellectualism. At the same time the rural class went through the well-known sociological process of change with the usual phenomena accompanying them – the eradication and disappearance of social controls.

In central Europe this socio-psychological process was complicated by a twofold change of the class structure. To social metamorphosis there was often added national transformation. In particular the population of the city of Vienna came originally from Czech, Croatian and Polish as well as Italian regions of the Habsburg monarchy. Nationalism there now received a powerful stimulus from the sociopsychological process of over-compensation. The more dubious the purity of their national origin, the greater the determination people

[1] In his discussion of Tönnies's community theory and the German 'Youth Movement', von Krockow links them with the sudden shift from the agrarian to the industrial state in Germany. He points out that the 'Youth Movement' first started in the large German cities among the middle and lower middle classes badly hit by the economic crisis. He is right in describing the 'Youth Movement' as 'the manifestation of a crisis of adaptation', op. cit., p. 33.

showed in defending the cause of the national group of their choice. This applied to Czechoslovakia in the case of the Sudeten-Germans, who were often of Czech origin, and in the case of many nationalistic Czechs of Austrian and Sudeten-German origin. In the eastern parts of Germany, too, the unconscious over-compensation of the largely Polish population contributed to the greater emphasis which was laid on the anti-Polish movement.

Further problems resulted from the first contact of new strata of population with politics. With the help of the new means of mass communication politics now invaded the lives of people whom the authoritarian state had for long brought up to scorn politics, or who had not given politics any thought and had abstained from voting.[1]

A natural consequence of the rise of the new democracy was the unaccustomed interplay between government and parliament on the one hand, and the people on the other. The latter however were accustomed to respect the *arcana imperii*. In the dynastic state the ruler's private life had been idealized and carefully shielded from the curiosity of the public. But now a section of the press over-emphasized the weakness of the ruling elements. The paradoxical result of this use of the freedom of the press was that the prestige of democratic leadership suffered most from such depreciation of the charismatic aura of sovereignty. The fact that ministers now came from the middle and lower classes all too easily gave rise to public contempt. Moreover the press now revelled in reporting skirmishes in parliament or any scandals of corruption and patronage which, as we also know today from the developing Afro-Asian countries, are not a rare occurrence in young democracies. That the Anglo-Saxon powers had once more withdrawn from the continent of Europe meant in the first place that their proven democratic institutions remained largely unknown to the people of central Europe. What these people, whose standard of living was much lower than that of the West, saw of Western civilization was one-sided and too ostentatious to make them want to copy it. To the masses in central Europe the stereotypes of the travelling English lord or the American multimillionaire, jazz and the fantastic world of the Hollywood film industry seemed the embodiment of the West. The levelling process came up against resistance from the very first.[2]

---

[1] On the subject of national socialism's success among those middle-class circles who had not taken part in the elections until 1930, cf. Theodor Geiger, *Arbeiten zur Soziologie*, Neuwied/Rh., Berlin-Spandau 1962, pp. 335 f.

[2] Thus Jaspers observed before Hitler seized power: 'The levelling process began with the unifying of the planet, which is horrifying to see. What is common to everyone today is the superficial, the silly and the mediocre. . . The films shown in the world's cities are also seen in tropical plantations and in nordic fishing villages. Everywhere people wear the same clothes. The same manners and behaviour, the

The network of communication also developed more rapidly and intensively inside states than between states, since *international* rail and road systems were not actively planned and developed. The tendency of national states to isolate themselves also revealed itself in the most important means for forming political opinion, i.e. the press. The consequences for the development of relationships inside Europe were extremely serious: isolation led to a certain time lag in the formation of political opinion in the various countries. German–French relations between the two wars provide a typical example. It became evident that between the impact of a certain political event on a given country, A, in this case Germany, and its impact on another given country, B, in this case France, there occurred a definite time lag. In the meantime, however, the basic attitudes of public opinion in country A had changed and this would have required another, perhaps opposite re-action in B. Up to 1929 public opinion in Germany was predominantly democratic and in no way inclined to a war of revenge against France. This was the very time, however, when the French identified the Weimar Republic with the German militarism which had long since ceased to exist and thus continued with Clemenceau and Poincaré in those alliances that aimed at keeping Germany in a state of helpless-ness.[1] When finally everyone in France realized how mistaken this policy had been and when an attempt was made to reach agreement with Germany, public opinion there had turned against Stresemann's Locarno policy and Germany increasingly reverted to the very militar-istic outlook which France had feared. Once again French public opinion was slow to grasp the change and insisted that the French government should pursue a peaceful policy – a policy which was to be-come disastrous not only to France, but also to the whole of free Europe.

## Revolution and Arms

Developments in the fields of military technique and strategy were of far-reaching importance. In France, during the Revolution, arms had been almost equally divided between the ruling class and the people; hence the Paris street was able to defeat the King's regiments. This was also true of the Russian Revolution. Since the decisive tank battles

same dances, the same sport, the same slogans—a mixed linguistic mush derived from the Enlightenment, Anglo-Saxon positivism and the theological tradition—are con-quering the globe . . .' Karl Jaspers, op. cit., p. 67.

[1] Cf. J. M. Keynes, *The Economic Consequences of the Peace*, London 1919; Harold Nicolson, *Peacemaking 1919*.

on the Western Front in the First World War, the balance of military power between government and people had shifted in favour of any state power which was in command of a motorized army. The failure of the attempted coups by the extreme Left and Right in Germany after the First World War had shown this trend. If, in 1932, when the social democratic government in Prussia was dismissed, the supporters of the Weimar Republic had come out against the Papen government, their arms would probably have been ineffective against the armed forces of the state, the *Reichswehr*.[1, 2] The abortive rebellion of the Austrian Social Democrats against the Dollfuss regime in 1934 is a further example. The workers of Vienna, Linz, Wiener Neustadt and Bruck an der Mur defended their homes and trade union buildings, with rifles and a few machine-guns, against concentrated attacks by the Austrian army employing its artillery.[3]

It was also symptomatic that during the Second World War no uprising against national socialism and the occupation regimes it imposed could be successful so long as motorized armies and the *Luftwaffe* were on the spot. The only exceptions occurred in mountainous regions difficult of access, as for example in Yugoslavia and Greece. In those countries the resistance fighters could employ guerilla tactics.

These facts clearly prove that nowadays revolutions can be successful only when they take the form of military coups or when revolutionaries succeeded in winning over at least part of the army.

## The Special Case of Central Europe

In central Europe a whole series of decisive factors were responsible for the belated development of constitutional democracy. The political and social structure there had not remained wholly free of the influence of eastern despotism. The influence of the Turkish Empire must be recalled, which up to the time of the Congress of Berlin embraced large parts of south-east Europe. On the other hand the autocracy of Russian Tsarism had pervading influence in Poland, the Baltic border states and Prussia.[4]

[1] Cf. Otto Braun, *Von Weimar zu Hitler*, New York 1940, p. 305. Braun defended his passivity, pointing out that there had been six million unemployed. Therefore a general strike had been impossible.

[2] Cf. also O. E. Schüddekopf, *Das Heer und die Republik*, Hanover, Frankfurt am Main 1955, pp. 202 and 347.

[3] Julius Deutsch, *Der Bürgerkrieg in Österreich*, Karlsbad 1934; cf. Ch. VI, Part I of the present book.

[4] Cf., for example, Hermann Münch, *Böhmische Tragödie*, Brunswick, Berlin, Hamburg 1949, pp. 80 ff.

In Germany and Austria the ravages of the Thirty Years War had obliterated the highly promising beginnings of constitutionalism during the days of the Emperors Maximilian II and Charles V. The peace of Münster and Osnabrück, with its *cuius regio, eius religio,* perpetuated the fateful intolerance of the Thirty Years War; for the religious persecutions and expulsions which were the consequences of this principle proved to be an evil precedent. Later nationality replaced religion as a pretext for mass murder and mass expulsion; but the reason – human intolerance – remained the same.

A further reason for the difference between political development in central and western Europe lies in the different forms of land tenure. Compared with eastern Europe, serfdom was never enforced with the same severity in western Europe. Serfdom prevented the development of free personality, self-respect and a sense of civic responsibility. Thus territorial sovereignty was reinforced by the power of the latifundia: both were part of the essential foundations of the authoritarian state. The sovereignty of the absolutist state changed the once free and proud citizens of the imperial cities, subject only to the Holy Roman Emperor, into subservient and obedient servants of petty princes,[1] who in the end believed they needed the patronage of the sovereign. The instrument of this patronage, however, was a caste-conscious bureaucracy. Because of the difference which developed between nobles and sovereign and the advance of enlightened despotism, the community of interest between landowners and state bureaucracy grew weaker. This finally replaced the lord-of-the-manor system but, compared with the previous feudal rule, brought an ever stronger pressure to bear on the people.

A centralistic, hierarchically organized system of local government existed throughout central Europe until the Second World War, composed of well-trained professional officials and really allowing no democratically organized local and district administration to come into being. This bureaucracy regarded itself as the embodiment of authority and not responsible to the people. In origin and structure it was unpolitical. A latent opposition grew up between it and the political representatives of the people who sought to control it. A community which has lived for several generations under the influence of autocratic pressures is apt to lose its self-respect and obey imposed orders from an instinct of self-preservation. It is then merely a matter of time before

[1] Cf., for example, the privileges of the Bohemian cities and the introduction of supervision by officials of the king after their unsuccessful revolt in 1546–47, in F. Kavka, *An Outline of Czechoslovak History,* Prague 1960, p. 62. From then on a royal judge held office in the cities of Bohemia. These lost their financial autonomy. Cf. also S. A. Schmidtmayer, *Geschichte der Sudetendeutschen,* Karlsruhe, Leipzig 1936, pp. 183–4.

this community loses its last vestige of civic sense and finally submits to bureaucratic tutelage.[1] The heirs of these subjects find it hard to turn themselves overnight into citizens, even if fired with such a desire by the oratory of inspired prophets.[2]

The counterpart to excessive belief in authority is an exaggerated individualism. Max Scheler recognized this when he observed that in Germany an urge to submit easily to authority was matched by individualistic factionalism bordering on anarchy.[3] One cares little what the state does to one's neighbour since this involves the risk of interfering with the authorities. The compulsion to absolute obedience (both on the part of subalterns in giving orders and of subordinates in executing them) is bound to breed intolerance. In a true democracy the result of continuous practice in self-government and self-administration, on the other hand, is that those actively participating in it perceive that rational decisions about public affairs presuppose self-control, a willingness to compromise and respect for the convictions and interests of others. For the pride which successful team-work creates is nothing but the expression of men's preference for constructive co-operation. That is the basic truth contained in Aristotle's thesis of man as a political animal. Diametrically opposed to this idea is Thomas Hobbes' thesis that absolute despotism and man's anarchical nature are complementary. Men who have been born and have grown up in a social order of this kind can imagine democracy only as a regime based on force, since they form a community of anarchists all of whom are potential despots. This explained the tyrannous nature of the politics of forced national assimilation mentioned by Böhm. The national groups of Austria-Hungary had fought for their rights in the name of John Stuart Mill's principles. But they refused their own minorities the right of self-determination for which they themselves had clamoured.

The preponderance of ideological parties, with their rigid programmes and doctrinaire intolerance, was the natural outcome of this authoritarian heritage. Such a state of affairs did not encourage any

[1] Cf., for example, Max Weber, 'Government by Officials and Political Leadership', in *Gesammelte Politische Schriften*, op. cit., pp. 309 ff. According to Max Weber the belief in authority which the *subjects* (my italics) acquired under the authoritarian state was directed increasingly to the bureaucracy. Cf. also Max Weber, 'Politics as a Profession', op. cit., pp. 493 ff. Max Weber sought in vain to explain to the German public, which was still accustomed to the state where government was the prerogative of people of rank, that the professional politician in mass democracy is an essential counter-balance to the state bureaucracy. On the other hand it must be said that the ethical standard which Weber takes for granted in the professional politician (in the sense of a person who has a vocation for politics) seems to correspond less to the facts of the world in which we live than to the world of Plato's philosopher king.

[2] Cf., for example, Karl Mannheim, op. cit., p. 109.

[3] Max Scheler, *Krieg und Aufbau*, Leipzig 1946, p. 161, quoted by Eschenburg in *Die improvisierte Demokratie der Weimarer Republik*, op. cit., p. 32.

real political compromises based on the law of 'live and let live'. Moderation was hard to come by, as it was generally regarded as weakness, and political agreement was despised as 'horse-trading'. In as far as the parliaments of the young democracies represented people whose political horizon was circumscribed by quasi-religious ideologies, this was bound to lead to extremism and the polarization of political spectrum and public life.[1] This sort of radicalization and polarization acts like a millstone, crushing all moderate thought and action. Radicalism on the right was matched by radicalism on the left, as developments in the Weimar Republic and elsewhere did prove. The collaboration of Right and Left came to fruition in the Nazi–Communist collaboration in the Reichstag and was formally expressed in the Hitler–Stalin Pact of 1939. The ease with which, after 1945, Stalinist Communism adopted the ideology, social-psychological attitudes and methods of Nazism in east Germany, Hungary and Czechsolovakia clearly proved that both were simply different facets of the same central European revolution against which various groups reacted differently.

The First World War had led to a *levée en masse* in central Europe. Up to 1914 the upper classes could base claims to an economically and socially superior position on their relatively greater participation in the nation's armed forces. Now the masses had become aware of their own greater importance to the state and, linked with that, of their greater economic claims. In the industrial regions of Germany, Austria, Poland, Czechoslovakia and Italy the trade unions and the social democratic movement were able, at least partly, to satisfy the industrial workers by their social reforms and developments. The social democratic parties, however, were not completely successful in absorbing the lasting effects of the Russian Revolution, as their influence was above all confined to the industrial workers organized in the trade unions. As the economic crisis, mechanization and rationalization of methods of work led to the unemployment of millions, so the social democrats lost their influence over sections of the industrial workers. On the other hand their outlook, at that time still based on the doctrines of the class war, was not suitable for winning the middle and white-collar classes over to the cause of democracy.

The class support given to the bourgeois parties must not, however, blind us to the revolutionary infection which had also permeated the middle classes. It is in these classes that in democratic developing countries the best-trained and best-informed talent can be found. Since

[1] That becomes especially clear with Schuschnigg. On the one hand he complains of frequent attempts at obstruction, op. cit., p. 104; on the other he declares: 'The favourite battle-cry against the parties was the charge of "jobbery" ', p. 107.

post-war inflation and the subsequent economic crisis resulted in the impoverishment of the middle classes and their present descent in the social scale, their participation in revolutionary action had become feasible.[1]

The fact that in central Europe Jews were often members of these middle classes introduced the further factor of commercial rivalry. Since the Middle Ages the Jews had appeared in the role of traders and middlemen. That the sons of these Jewish traders often turned to the Marxist parties was doubly infuriating to the impoverished middle classes who were competing with the Jews. Thus, using the argument that un-German influences were at work, the nationalist elements (especially the national socialists) tried to weaken the position of the constructive democratic parties. The fight against an actual, or apparently at least partly, *foreign* ruling class was irresistibly attractive even then – as it is today in the Afro-Asian countries. Moreover, to large sections of the population, republican democracy appeared to be a form of state associated with the Western Powers, therefore with yesterday's enemies, and lost its attraction according to the degree of indifference, or even hostility, with which their own democratic governments were treated by the Western Powers.

As we have already mentioned, the dependence of the country population in central and south-east Europe on the traditional authority of the feudal landowner was deeply rooted. It was from these groups of the population that the strongest anti-revolutionary forces were recruited. To them the democratic parties and the ideas and culture to which they appealed were mainly portrayed as urban and unnatural. Post-war democracy could, therefore, depend on the peasants only if it succeeded in gaining their support by the implementation of successful agrarian reforms. Except for land reforms with a purely nationalistic complexion which, as in Czechoslovakia, Yugoslavia and Romania, were directed against the German and Hungarian-speaking nobles, agricultural reform never advanced beyond the initial stage.[2] In this way the new democracies threw away their greatest opportunity of stabilization as they neglected the task of creating the class of contented farmers who constitute one of the essential pillars of democracy in a society of this type.

As first the example of Russia and later that of China, Indochina and other countries of the Far East have shown, an enslaved and exploited peasant class, with the habit of blind obedience, can be equally depended on as docile subjects by a monarchical absolutism or

[1] Cf. Bracher, op. cit., Chap. VI, pp. 165–74 and Theodor Geiger, *Die soziale Schichtung des deutschen Volkes*, Stuttgart 1932. Cf. also Rudolf Schlesinger, *Central European Democracy and its Background*, London 1953, pp. 289 ff.

[2] H. Seton-Watson, op. cit., pp. 77 ff.

a revolutionary dictatorship ready to resort to terrorism. Whoever impresses them as a forceful personality invested with authority and does not turn too obviously against them wins their approval. Paradoxically their traditional conservatism does not safeguard them against their integration into the totalitarian state; hence the tactics, first used in Russia, of distributing land to the peasants, with collectivization following later. Nor did the revolutionary influence of bolshevism pass by the country people of central Europe without leaving some trace. In the first place, fascism and national socialism seemed to them to be the more attractive forms of revolution since these movements apparently paid heed to the peasants' love of the land and also opposed westernization and foreign modes of life, and also spoke to them in their own simple language.

Yet there was not a total absence of attempts on the part of strong democratic peasant movements to give democracy resolute support. The Slovak Hodža, the Bulgarian Stambolisky, the Croats Radič and Maček, together with Yovanovič's progressive Serbian peasant group, Maniu's Romanian National Peasant Party and Wito's Polish peasant movement, tried to build up a democratic agrarian bloc of small peasants.[1]

[1] Hodža, op. cit., pp. 108 ff.

# CHAPTER II

# The Conflict of Ideologies and Ties

## PART ONE

### Liberal Democratic and National Movements in Central Europe

### Origins of National Liberalism

'Italy wills to be a Nation both for her own sake and the sake of others, by right and from duty; by right of collective life, of collective education, from duty towards universal humanity, in which she has a mission to fulfil, a truth to promulgate, an idea to diffuse ... not in Napoleonic unity, in exaggerated administrative centralization ... but in the unity of international relations, armies, codes and education, all harmonized with the existence of local divisions, indicated by the history of the country, and with the life of large and powerful communities, participating as much as possible in the supreme power by election, and endowed with all the necessary power to fulfil the aims of their association. . . . '[1]

These words are both a legacy of the French Revolution, and a product of nineteenth-century national liberal thinking. The renunciation of 'Napoleonic unity' which they contain sounds, however, more like an honest, pious wish of their author's than a practical programme. To the twentieth century such dexterous interweaving of nationalism and democracy seems unreal. History has shown that men like Cavour and Mussolini rather than men like Mazzini, men like Bismarck and Hitler rather than Kerensky, have been able to complete the process of national unification in the nineteenth and twentieth centuries.

It is commonly alleged of the French Revolutionary and Napoleonic Wars that they diffused throughout Europe liberal-democratic ideas

[1] G. Mazzini, *Royalty and Republicanism in Italy*, London 1850, p. 103.

which had come from Britain to France and had there been diluted by radical patriotism. A general impression prevails among students of politics that the Napoleonic Wars effectively stimulated this process of diffusion by arousing the national consciousness of peoples conquered by the Napoleonic armies. Thereby the process of democratization was greatly advanced.

Such a view, however – as far as central Europe is concerned – disregards a large number of factors. It is true that the French Revolution and the ensuing wars did help the liberal system of society and law to be realized outside France. But the complementary role which the heritage of enlightened despotism played is insufficiently appreciated. Until a short time ago the requisite comparative experience had not been available. It was only the observation of the impact of democratic ideas and forms on Asian and African countries in their very different stages of development after the Second World War which made it possible, by the method of comparative studies, to acquire a better understanding of the political developments and complications of Europe in the nineteenth and twentieth centuries.[1]

In the eighteenth century central Europe had not reached western Europe's stage of development. Industry was technically in its infancy, the middle class was either quantitatively small, or, qualitatively, greatly limited in its opportunities of exerting any real influence; the nobility still set the standards in a largely feudal economic order. Therefore absolute monarchy in central Europe could absorb the shocks which it had received in the Age of Enlightenment from democratic ideas, and channel them into the path of 'enlightened despotism' and thus neutralize them. The result was a decrease in the power of the nobility, but, on the other hand, an extension of the life span of absolute monarchy.

Bureaucracy favoured the growth of absolutism.[2] The decline in the power of the estates was also matched by a complementary extension of bureaucratic organization and authority. First the concept of enlightened despotism must be defined more precisely if the complexity of these processes is to be grasped and their exact place in history recognized. This specifically central European phenomenon cannot be entirely attached to certain progressive personalities, as Frederick II

[1] Cf. Rupert Emerson, op. cit., especially Chapter X.
[2] This was a long process extending over several centuries. In spite of the rise of the Prussian administration under the Great Elector it cannot be maintained that the bureaucracy owes its existence to him alone. On this point see Fritz Hartung, 'Studien zur Geschichte der Preussischen Verwaltung' in *Staatsbildende Kräfte der Neuzeit* Berlin 1961, pp. 178 ff. On bureaucracy in France cf. de Tocqueville's descriptions in his book 'L'Ancien Régime et la Révolution' in *Œuvres Complètes*, Vol. IV, Paris 1877.

or Joseph II, and still less did it come to an end with their death. The form of internal policy and administration which is characteristic of this type of rule did not really reach its full maturity until the end of the Napoleonic Wars. Although the later monocratic organization of territorial administration had already been anticipated in Josephinism, it needed the confirmation of the Bonapartist experience to be completely realized. The same is true of the areas under Hohenzollern rule. Thus the Prussian institution of *Oberpräsident* (Divisional Commissioner) dates only from the post-1815 period.[1] In Austria enlightened despotism was made possible by a state bureaucracy of middle-class origin and lived on through it until the end of the nineteenth century.[2]

Since, however, the liberal bourgeoisie of central Europe – unlike England and France and also northern Italy – could only make its influence felt by becoming absorbed in the bureaucracy, centralist bureaucratic ideas also largely determined the development of central European liberalism. This partly explains the strong etatist tradition of central and eastern Europe.

There is a further factor which was of no less importance in connection with the difference between development in western and central Europe. With the etatist tradition there went a concept of the Nation whose beginnings can be traced back even further than to the beginning of the previous century. To understand it we need to revise the very concept of *Völkerwanderung*, the migration of peoples. While this migration in the West came to an end with the normal settlements in Italy, France and England, it continued right into modern times in central and eastern Europe. The frontiers of the Germanic, Slav and Turkish-Mongolian tribes remained fluid for a great length of time. This ebb and flow led to a fundamental mixing of races. This process, as well as later efforts at colonization, produced the peculiar linguistic geography of central Europe, where German, Polish, Czech, Hungarian, Yugoslav, Romanian and Turkish villages were often neighbours. Therefore in central and eastern Europe – unlike in the West – the concept of nationality was expressed basically in terms of blood relationship and not in territorial unity.[3]

Moreover in western Europe the Renaissance and the Reformation

---

[1] Hartung, op. cit., pp. 275 ff.

[2] Adam Wandruszka, 'Die Männer von 1948', in *Wort und Wahrheit*, Vienna 1947, Vol. 10, pp. 586 ff.

[3] Cf. also C. A. Macartney, *National States and National Minorities*, Oxford 1934, p. 52. Hugo Hassinger makes a very acute observation when he speaks of central Europe as 'Mediating Europe'. He calls it a compromise area for the conflict between the oceanic and continental or 'Western' and 'Eastern' cultures. Hence the demand for a 'special political style of architecture'. Cf. Hassinger, 'Österreichs Wesen und Schicksal', in *Wiener Geographische Studien* No. 20, Vienna 1959.

had a lasting influence on the social and political structure and promoted the formation of national sovereignty in the fields of politics
and economics – a decisive factor in the rise of capitalism. But this was
not the case in central Europe. There the Reformation and Counter-
Reformation resulted in the destruction of initial capitalism which in
the sixteenth century had been linked with endeavours of Maximilian
II and Charles V and, symbolically, with names like Fugger and
Welser. While in England under the Tudors and in France under
Richelieu national monarchy prevailed over territorial particularism,
in central Europe the wars of religion resulted in the victory of
particularism.

While the people of the West thus grew into states which provided
a ready-made framework for the emerging nations, events followed a
very different course in central Europe. On the one hand the sovereign
and despotic principality was able to dominate the population groups
more effectively because of its relatively small size. When, however,
on the other hand, the national state began to evolve in central Europe
it came up against a mosaic of multifarious, mutually contradictory
'loyalties' from the very outset.

Rousseau and Herder, perhaps the most important representatives
of nationalist thinking, illustrate this fundamental difference most
clearly. While for Rousseau the national community was above all
political and based on man's free decision,[1] Herder's concept was of a
nation which was natural, organic and arising out of the culture
created by the community of blood and language.[2]

This much quoted difference does not, however, adequately explain
the different courses of development. For it began not only with
Herder's thought, but also with the spread of the Western concept of
nationality to central Europe. Here, from the first, political was bound
up with cultural nationalism. Furthermore in central Europe political
nationalism appeared in its French, not its Anglo-Saxon form. In
England national feeling stems from the actual effect of the conventions and traditions of the community on the individual.

What is more, the nation came into existence in England in the seventeenth century in opposition to the king and not, as in France, through
the king. In England the Tudor monarchy had, indeed, taken over the
leadership of the nation and, in league with the middle class, had overcome the old feudal nobility. But this middle class, which had itself
founded a new nobility from its own ranks, felt strong enough in the

[1] Rousseau, *Considérations sur le gouvernement de Pologne*, 1772, in *Œuvres
Complètes*, Vol. 3, Paris 1817.
[2] Johann Gottfried Herder, *Ideen zur Philosophie der Geschichte der Menschheit,
1784–5*, Vol. IV, Karlsruhe 1790–4.

seventeenth century to challenge first the absolute monarchy of Charles I and similar aspirations on the part of the later Stuarts; whereas in France absolute monarchy had had two hundred and fifty years in which to consolidate its position of supremacy. There, as long as it was the standard-bearer of the national idea, the monarchy maintained its position until it became discredited through its own degeneration and because of military defeat in the eighteenth century. It was then felt by the middle classes to be a hindrance to their ambition and was removed. As Ranke saw, the basically stronger Bonapartist monarchy – and Robespierre's dictatorship even before that – clearly showed that the French Revolution was directed less against the absolutist form of government than against the inefficiency and weakness of Louis XV and Louis XVI. The French monarchy fell as it was unable to continue the popular programme of national enrichment and territorial aggrandizement begun under Louis XIV.[1]

In central and east Europe in the eighteenth century we are dealing with a time lag. Enlightened despots like Frederick the Great, Joseph II and Catherine II of Russia copied the French monarchy's pursuit of power and its mercantilist economic policy with the help of mercenary armies and centralized bureaucracies. These endeavours were felt to be progressive and enlightened because of the state of the social and economic structure in central Europe at the time.[2]

By confirming and strengthening absolute monarchy with the help of the new bureaucracy, enlightened despotism in fact eradicated the very traditions and institutions which could have ensured the organic evolution of freedom and self-government. It also bequeathed to the coming generations a fatal heritage, since it impressed on them the notion that progressive reforms can be effectively carried out only by a strong centralized government. That was a basic attitude which, up to the very end of the Second World War, that is for a period of almost two hundred years, was to continue to exert a dominating influence even on those who at least were liberals and democrats.

Thus the Emperor Joseph II – an 'enlightened' monarch – tried to impose the German language and even German names on the subjects of those parts of the Habsburg monarchy which spoke other languages. His motives for doing this were not nationalist but

[1] Lord Acton was also acutely aware of the peculiarly dynamic quality of Rousseau's doctrine, which was at the root of the French Revolution. In France, said Lord Acton, national consciousness was based on the idea of race and national unity overrides all rights and liberties and is based on the perpetual supremacy of the general will. Cf., for example, *Essays on Freedom and Power*, Boston (Mass.) 1949, pp. 173 ff.

[2] On the development of nationalism in the seventeenth and eighteenth centuries, cf. Hans Kohn, *Die Idee des Nationalismus*, Frankfurt am Main 1962, and Eugen Lemberg, *Geschichte des Nationalismus in Europa*, Stuttgart 1950.

technical and administrative. In point of fact he failed, but he did succeed in awakening the dormant national aspirations of the various peoples which made up his empire. The typical central European system of monocratic regional rule by officers in the form of provincial governors or captains, and district magistrates, was adopted at that time.[1]

The revolutionary effect of Josephinism appeared most clearly in the Austrian Netherlands and in Hungary. While Joseph's reforms led to open rebellion in the Netherlands, the organic development of nationalism in the eighteenth century appears at its clearest in Hungary.

The Hungarian nation then contained only about 5 per cent of the total Hungarian population, namely the magnates, the landed nobility and the clergy, including the Croatian, German and Slovakian nobles living there.[2] In the course of the eighteenth century the familiar conflict between royal absolutism and the Hungarian feudal nobility insisting on its privileges continued, like the well-known struggle that had taken place centuries before in countries like England and France. To justify further exploiting the rural serfs, national pride was invoked. The case of David Cvittinger, a Hungarian of German descent, clearly shows the way nationalism was propagated.[3]

In their struggle against the Hungarian nobility the Habsburgs, as absolute sovereigns everywhere, sought to strengthen the self-consciousness of the middle classes and the peasants. When, at the beginning of the French Revolution, the Hungarian estates adopted the revolutionary language of the Jacobins, the Emperor Leopold II, a typical 'revolutionary from above', tried using pamphlets – probably written by himself – to play Jacobinism off against the nobility.[4]

In this historical period we must differentiate between two kinds of nation: the so-called historical nations and the emergent nations. Historical nations were those whose historical and cultural development has not been interrupted at any earlier juncture, such as the Germans, the Poles, the Hungarians. New nations were those which had either lost their previous independence and fallen under the dominant

---

[1] 'The division of German-speaking Austria into thirteen administrative districts regardless of provincial and historical considerations already anticipated the French Revolutionary system of dividing France into départements', W. Hubatsch, *Das Zeitalter des Absolutismus*, Brunswick 1962, p. 185.

[2] Denis Silagi, *Ungarn und der geheime Mitarbeiterkreis Kaiser Leopolds II*, Munich 1960.

[3] Ibid., p. 4: 'As a student in Altdorf Cvittinger felt insulted by the lack of respect shown to the man from distant Hungary and to protect his own and his father's honour he compiled the first history of Hungarian literature (in Latin) in 1711. In it he listed 269 members of every nationality in the kingdom who had written literary works.'

[4] Op. cit., p. 71.

influence of another nation, as for example the Czechs, or the peoples and races which had not hitherto appeared as independent nations, like the Slovaks, the Ruthenes, the Slovenes, etc. Their languages remained dialects and were spoken mainly by illiterate peasants, while the upper classes and the intelligentsia spoke the language of the ruling peoples.

As in eighteenth-century France, nationalism in Germany remained in the first place subordinate to cosmopolitanism. The patriotism of a Klopstock, a Justus Möser, a Humboldt and a Herder was certainly intended for the whole of humanity, which was to benefit from it. Nevertheless Herder, that well-meaning philosopher and historian, can probably be considered as one of the most important pioneers of the theory of nationalism. The nature of his doctrines was such that they exactly met the cultural and emotional needs of the very nations which had been submerged. They appeared at a favourable period in history when national resurgence was being kindled by the example of Poland, which was fighting to avoid partition by Russia, Prussia and Austria. Even before the French Revolution, therefore, many factors contributed to the awakening of nationalism in central Europe.

Today, in the Afro-Asian countries, we find this process illustrated more clearly. Just as in Herder's days the European national groups who had been deprived of their rights based political claims on the humanitarian ideas, so the former colonial peoples now demand independence in the name of national self-determination. Just as the European nations in the past became increasingly uncompromising and intolerant, so the emancipation of the colonial peoples today leads to intensified racial hatred and chauvinism.

The evolution of the central European middle class in the eighteenth century shows a further analogy with the Afro-Asian situation in the middle of the twentieth century. Now, as then, a temporary concurrence of middle-class emancipation and national sentiment is clearly evident. Thus in Germany the rise of a wealthy merchant class was reflected in patriotic writings – for instance in men like Friedrich Karl von Moser, Thomas Abbt, and Justus Möser.[1] The middle class, which provided a growing section of the professional civil service, became to an increasing extent the bearer of the national idea.

Until now, however, the difference in social development of the various regions made very difficult a correct appreciation of the role of the middle class. The lively industrial and merchant class, characteristic of west and south Germany, by which the social structure of these parts of Germany were integrated into the economic complex of western Europe, was almost completely non-existent in Austria and

[1] Cf. Paul Kluckhohn, *Die Idee des Volkes im Schrifttum der deutschen Bewegung von Möser und Herder bis Grimm*, Berlin 1934, pp. 1–20.

Prussia, the military powers in central Europe at that time. In Prussia, which had, at an earlier stage, already attracted enterprising Protestant groups such as the Huguenots, an attempt was made to persuade foreign professional people to come into the country.[1] In Austria, too, business-men had often been called in from Switzerland, from the Rhine, from France, Belgium and England, and given special privileges. Con-sequently they adopted a different, more loyal attitude towards the state and the royal house than the industrial middle class in the countries from which they had come.[2] The result was that the industrial middle class in central Europe did not – as it did in France – establish a new privileged order after a middle-class revolution, but merged with the old privileged classes. Even before the First World War, Hermann Bahr recognized this aspect of the problem in Hungary: 'September 16th. These Hungarian matters make me very angry. Especially the rapid emergence of the middle class, a process which takes a few generations elsewhere . . . It is the tragedy of the middle class, usually, that having emerged it must immediately disavow and betray itself; here [i.e. in Hungary] this happens even before it has got there . . . And so, having got into the habit of lying, it dare not speak its own language but must instead resort to the ridiculous tirades of political bravado.'[3] Does this not remind us of the German middle class's drive to raise itself to the ranks of the nobility?

We find similar conditions today in the developing countries of Asia and Africa. In the Levant, in Ghana, even in India and Pakistan, the middle class is often a class of middlemen of foreign origin or else an industrial class, which is artificially subsidized and educated by the state and already associated with the authorities, and not yet in a position to develop independent, liberal tendencies.[4] This partly ex-plains the frequency of nationalist military dictatorships in Asia and Africa, which govern with the aid of the bureaucracy and are backed by this class. There the army and the bureaucracy provide much

---

[1] On this point cf. Bussenius-Hubatsch, *Urkunden und Akten zur Geschichte der preussischen Verwaltung in Südpreussen und Neuostpreussen*, Frankfurt and Bonn 1961, p. 72.

[2] Cf. Adam Wandruszka, 'Die historische Schwäche des Bürgertums' in *Wort und Wahrheit*, Vol. 10, Freiburg im Bresgau 1956, pp. 756 f. Cf. also Karl Eder, *Der Liberalismus in Altösterreich*, Vienna and Munich 1955, and Georg Franz, *Liberalismus, Die deutschliberale Bewegung in der habsburgischen Monarchie*, Munich 1955.

[3] Hermann Bahr, *Tagebuch*, Berlin 1909, p. 13.

[4] In the Levant the merchant class was made up of Greeks, Jews or Armenians. In parts of India, for instance in East Bengal, the employer class was at first often European, the wholesalers Greek or Armenian. On the other hand there are indigen-ous castes and groups of middlemen such as the Marwaris, the Parsees and the Kojas, who have a neutral relationship with the state and whose only loyalty is to their own class. They are, therefore, ill-suited for the role of self-confident citizens.

cherished careers for sons of the middle class unable to find sufficient scope in industry and trade.

In this respect there prevails, *mutatis mutandis*, a situation which is analogous to the former phenomenon in central Europe. As Wandruszka explains, 'There is a close correlation between the importance of the bureaucracy and the army in Austria and the weakness of an indigenous industrial middle class. The energies of the third estate found a wide outlet in the army. The sons of immigrant manufacturers often went straight into careers in the army or the civil service.[1] It is therefore understandable if those very citizens who might be expected to be liberal find it extremely difficult to stand up for their ideals, simply because of their economic dependence on the state.

This conflict of loyalties was further complicated by the rise of nationalism. The sons of the *Hofratsliberalen* (Privy Council Liberals) then had to decide whether their first loyalty was to the semi-absolutist state, to their own nationality or to liberalism. In this conflict liberalism was often sacrificed to nationalism – particularly in the German and Czech part of the empire. Later the national-socialist leader class (in Austria more so than in Germany) was composed of members of families who came from the German liberal, middle-class milieu.

The link between social and economic interests and the national idea was not new. We find it in earlier periods among the feudal landowner classes defending their privileges. But while patriotism among the nobility and clergy could be counterbalanced by cosmopolitan ties, by Christian and Western traditions, the middle classes were on the whole far less conscious of these values. When, however, the close relationship between monarchy and the middle class, which in sixteenth-century England already determined the political face of the country, was also repeated in central Europe, the result, under different geographical and historical conditions, however, was bound to be different.

The same is true today of the developing countries, where the military dictatorships hold similar views.[2] The army, which in these countries occupies the place formerly held by monarchy – there being no feudal interests represented in the legislatures and no intellectuals – tries to establish a direct relationship with the illiterate masses of agricultural workers living below the minimum level of subsistence. The ideology which results from this situation confirms this relationship: just as the absolute rulers of the eighteenth century felt themselves to be fathers of their subjects, so today Nasser feels he is the guardian of the

[1] A. Wandruszka, 'Die historische Schwäche des Bürgertums', op. cit., p. 766.
[2] For the Near East cf. K. J. Newman, 'The New Monarchies of the Middle East', in *Journal of International Affairs*, No. 2, New York 1959.

Egyptian people, still immature and under age, and the Syrian General Hussain Zain declared: 'The people are the spiritual force behind the coup but the army is its secular arm.'[1]

# PART TWO

## The Spread of Nationalism

The social effect of the French Revolution is organically related to the reforms of enlightened despotism. By the Revolution a concrete form was given to embryonic elements already in existence and under its influence stored-up energies were released. The Napoleonic soldier, spreading its gospel all over Europe, offered the people of central Europe a twofold gift. With one hand he gave democracy, but with the other hand nationalism, from which in due course many Bastilles were to be built throughout Europe. He was also the living embodiment of the idea that nationalism can fuse not only with democracy but also with monarchic forms of government.

The influence of the French Revolution on central Europe was not uniform. Germany, with its memories of the Holy Roman Empire, experienced a revival of the imperial idea on a nationalistic basis. But Romanticism quite clearly contains the synthesis of cosmopolitanism and ardent nationalism. But this sudden lapse from internationalism to nationalism is nowhere so clearly expressed as in Fichte for whom they both meant the same thing.[2] Although strictly rational he is no humanitarian nationalist in Humboldt's sense. According to him the Nation has the duty to assert its individuality however much ruthless force it may have to use. Only thus can it serve humanity. Between Rousseau and Humboldt on the one hand and Fichte on the other is in fact that world of difference which in our days has separated the ideas underlying the League of Nations from that underlying the Nazi 'New Order'.

Herder's and Fichte's use of 'national individualities' and 'individualism' makes it necessary to outline briefly the meaning of this term for the development of nationalism and democracy. The fact which long remained unnoticed is that as long as individualism was a concept covering the rights of individuals in terms of the law of nature it

---

[1] Joan Vigneau, 'The Ideology of the Egyptian Revolution', in Walter Z. Laqueur (Ed.), *The Middle East in Transition*, New York 1958, p. 130.
[2] Johann Gottlieb Fichte, *Reden an die deutsche Nation*, Hamburg 1955.

remained a democratic term; when it was broadened so as to include the rights of nationalities to full emancipation, it acquired aristocratic characteristics. It is impossible to ignore the close relationship between aristocracy and nationality. In both nationality and aristocracy there is the creed that it is a privilege to belong to a certain group which offers to all members certain privileges. In both cases the regular way of entry into the group is heredity, and in both cases the purpose of the group is domination.[1]

It appears, therefore, that the opposition between nationalism and democracy which was fated to play such a considerable role can be traced back to the different meanings of the concept of individualism. In states with mixed nationalities the result may be as follows.

The principles of liberty and equality demand that any minority within the state should be content to submit to the decision of a majority. Individualism derived from the law of nature demands that certain inalienable rights should be respected. But how can these rights be respected if the national individuality of the majority can only be asserted at the expense of that of the minority?

While in ethnically homogeneous nations the inclusion of nationality in the postulate of individuality led, in the field of external relations, to the moral justification of the idea of national power, the concept of national individuality had even more important consequences in those states which were made up of various linguistic, racial and religious elements. The ideas of liberty and equality require minorities within the state to submit to majority decisions. Individualism springing from national right, on the other hand, demands the preservation of certain inalienable rights.[2] A synthesis is conceivable if majority and minority are dynamic and are transformed and reconstructed in the political process. But how can these rights be preserved so long as the (static) national majority groups ruthlessly assert their individuality at the expense of minority groups, equally adamant?

This attitude was bound to lead to endeavours to suppress and assimilate the minorities, whose response would be the *irredenta*. Centrifugal tendencies in the form of territorial division and subdivision *ad infinitum* would be the inevitable outcome. Consequently the definition of what constitutes proof of national identity remains obscure even today. Why have the Czechs, the Poles and the Italians a right to national statehood and why cannot the Sudeten Germans, the South Tyroleans or the Ukrainians invoke the same right? In contemporary Asia and Africa, where there are thousands of different languages and

[1] Cf. in particular Baron Josef Eötvös, *Der Einfluss der herrschenden Ideen des 19. Jahrhunderts auf den Staat*, Vol. II. Leipzig 1854.
[2] Cf. Friedrich Meinecke, *Weltbürgertum und Nationalstaat*, Munich 1962.

dialects abound and where national states have never before existed even in rudimentary form, the problem assumes immense proportions. Why have India and Pakistan a right to their own national status but not Kashmir and Goa? If national states in Europe can be founded without regard to economic factors, why could not Tshombe in Katanga or the Ashantahene[1] in Ghana claim or appeal to national individuality? In the final analysis, after the national right to liberty has been achieved, the postulate leads back even more intensively to what is purely and simply a decision of power politics, the handling of which by the dynastic state in its time gave rise to the demand for the creation of nation states.

Let us now turn back to the repercussions of the French Revolution. In the first place it gave rise to attempts to achieve national unity in Germany and Italy. The Italian development went, as is well known, its own particular way, partly determined by the fact that, in their fight for liberty, broad groups of the Italian middle class openly came out for Napoleon. In Germany it was different. The German pre-March liberals did in fact take over the revolutionary ideology. While, however, the principles of liberty and equality demanded the emancipation of the middle class from the rule of the princes, the principle of nationalism, on the other hand, called for union with the princes, to make common cause against Napoleon's policy of expansion. They preferred the latter road and allowed themselves to be satisfied with empty promises of 'constitutional rights after victory'.

In multinational states – like the Habsburg monarchy, the Turkish or the Russian empires – the impact of the French Revolution was bound to have still further repercussions. Patriotism hardened into nationalism, first in the so-called historical nations. That came about in two ways: first directly by the support and sympathy given by new adherents to national democratic ideas; secondly by the rise of a counter-nationalism actually inside those nations which had been attacked by France. The nationalism of the historical nations then aroused the so-called submerged nationalities, due to the fact that the Czechs, Slovaks, Romanians, etc., encountered a growing aggressiveness on the part of the historical nations. If, previously, the nationalism of the French Revolution had made German, Italian, Polish and Hungarian national aspirations possible, now German nationalism in Austria provoked identical aspirations among the Czechs, Slovenes and the Italians. In the same way the attempted Magyarization of nationalities in Hungary awakened the Slovaks, the Croats and the Slovenes.[2] Polish nationalism in its turn stimulated German nationalism

---

[1] The tribal chief of the Ashantis.
[2] In connection with Hungary, cf. Denis Silagi, op. cit., p. 48.

and also the nationalism of the Ruthenes in the same way that German nationalism automatically engendered Polish nationalism.

The case of Hungary illustrates the course of this development. From 1790 onwards various political societies were formed. In the diet of 1825 nationalism began to take shape. In 1844 Latin was abolished as the official language and the Magyar language was given preference over German.[1] List's *System of Political Economy* was translated into Magyar. But in Hungary nationalism and liberalism did not mean the same as it meant in western Europe.

In the years following the Congress of Vienna nationalism spread out in wider circles, to take in new social groups. Although it still represented no threat to monarchical absolutism, it did, however, mean the end of willing submission to alien rule. If, before then, the Bohemian peasant had considered the landowner only as an oppressive feudal lord, he now saw him also as another German-speaking foreign exploiter.

From the end of the Napoleonic Wars liberal democratic and nationalist ideas spread throughout central Europe. But it did not become evident until 1848 that these two trends were incompatible. The reason lay in the peculiar socio-political structure of this part of Europe. As long as the Emperor of Austria and the King of Prussia fought for the hegemony of Germany, the German liberals were not yet forced to choose between nationalism and democracy. Nor had the monarchs yet agreed to identify themselves with the middle-class nationalist slogans. They were still too firmly rooted in the exclusiveness of old-style dynastic absolutism.

The period between the Congress of Vienna and the 1848 Revolution is usually considered to be a period of ruthless repression and political and intellectual stagnation. In actual fact, however, it was a time of intensive preparation for the popular forces of *nationalism* and *democracy*. Prince Clemens Metternich, the most important European statesman of the age, saw the two problems as different sides of the same coin. In Austria he sought to neutralize their influence and in so doing he exacerbated the national problem of his country. He proposed to restore or even to recreate the territorial unity of the Austrian Crown *Länder*.[2] The *Länder* diets were dominated by the local aristocrats, whose loyalty to the crown was beyond question. But very few of these historical lands were linguistically homogeneous. By restoring the *Länder* and their significance Metternich created in the large national

[1] Otto Bauer, *Die Nationalitätenfrage und die Sozialdemokratie*, Vienna 1924, pp. 401–9.

[2] This refers to the historical countries which the Habsburgs had acquired in the course of history.

groups – the Hungarians, the Czechs and the Poles – the impression that the diets served the monopolistic rule of a single nationality. If they desired to promote their own national culture and welfare, they had therefore to proselytize the national minorities within the historical *Länder*.

But the court and the aristocracy did not even support Metternich's feeble attempts at federalism because the tradition of a centralized and bureaucratic government had been firmly established since the age of Josephinism. Nevertheless, without really realizing it himself, Metternich cultivated in nationalism an ally against democracy which was to thwart the promising signs of a true federal and constitutional development during and after 1848. Metternich did not, in fact, understand the close connection between the consciousness of the estates in the historical *Länder* and the national consciousness of the ever-growing middle class. Hantsch has pointed out that the 'Greater Austrian national movement which was started by the Austrian government as an essential factor of moral armament in the struggle against Napoleon after 1805 . . . had intentionally promoted the awakening of "provincial patriotism".'[1]

The change from humanitarian to traditional nationalism was due mainly to the work of the Romantic School of Novalis, Friedrich Schlegel and Adam Müller, who revelled in the glorification of medieval life and society and who succeeded in linking their modern nationalism with their disposition towards a mystical concept of monarchy. The inner contradiction of Romanticism consisted in being nationalistic and universalist at the same time. Herder is the exception to this rule. Although he was one of the pioneers of Romanticism in Germany, he developed ideas which were opposed to Joseph II's efforts to Germanize everything. His defence for the principle of nationality greatly appealed to the Slav nations to whom it offered self-respect.

Fichte and Arndt, on the other hand, believed the progress of their own German nation was more important than the revival of small, oppressed nationalities. In this they were backed up by the Philological School of Adelung, Schlozer and Grimm, who traced the common origin of the Aryan language. Their followers confused the idea of language with that of race and thus sought to construct an Aryan race. Finally, mention must be made of the school of historians called 'Historismus'

---

[1] Hugo Hantsch, *Die Nationalitätenfrage im alten Österreich*, Vienna 1953, p. 37. The same author also points out that Czech national consciousness was also to base itself in the first instance on the institutions of provincial estates like the Prague *Ständetheater*, the Conservatory and the National Museum. In 1830, and directly connected with the National Museum, there was set up a 'committee for the scientific cultivation of Bohemian language and literature', the outcome being a concept of history which laid stress on its linguistic basis.

which gave nationalism its decisive stimulus. In England this school was represented by Carlyle, Freeman, Froude and Macaulay, in Germany by Böhmer, Luden, Dunker, Dahlmann, Sybel, Droysen, Treitschke and perhaps in the fairly recent past by Spengler. In Bohemia Palacký and Jirásek belong to this school; though Palacký was probably aware of the inherent limits to nationalism. Although they made an undeniable contribution to scholarship, they nevertheless created an atmosphere in which it was possible for lesser scholars to use historical research as a decoy to promote an intensive nationalism.

These historians discovered that certain events represented prototypes in the history of a people. Jászi had described how the Hungarians were reminded of their ancestors' glorious past. A picture was painted of a handful of Magyars suddenly rising to defend the whole civilized world against the Turkish hordes.

Under the influence of such deliberate suggestions the Poles regarded themselves as exponents of Western culture against Russian Tsarist barbarism. The Croats rediscovered their 'god-given' mission was to defend the West and its civilization against the Greek Orthodox religion. One section of the Czechs was so eager to have a 'mission' that a good and otherwise honest archivist named Hanka forged a manuscript which was concerned with what were ostensibly the Czechs' ancient heroic ages and deeds. He hid this in the church tower in the small Bohemian provincial town of Königinhof. Only later was it exposed as a forgery by T. G. Masaryk.[1] The lengths of absurdity to which these theories could lead was clearly shown by Bluntschli. In the course of his argument to prove that not every nation could found a national state – a statement which might be true for other reasons – he put forward the theory of 'masculine' and 'feminine' nations. The Polish national democratic politician Dmowski pointed out that Bismarck had called the Germans a nation of men and the Poles a nation of women and proposed that the Poles should go to school under the Prussians. This shows that, although he hated the Germans, Dmowski was nevertheless in many respects a disciple of aggressive Prussianism.[2]

In short there are three factors about 'Historismus' which are worth mentioning. Firstly, it is politically important because it not only describes and analyses the past but it also endeavours to determine the future through the past. Secondly, the movements which benefited from this kind of historical writing were national liberalism in the

---

[1] Cf. also Wenzel Jaksch, *Europas Weg nach Potsdam*, Stuttgart 1958, p. 87.
[2] W. J. Rose, 'Russian Poland in the later Nineteenth Century', in *The Cambridge History of Poland. From Augustus II to Pilsudski (1697–1935)*, Cambridge 1951, p. 403, with reference to Roman Dmowski, *Myśli nowoczesnego Polaka* (Thoughts of a modern Pole), London 1903.

nineteenth and the authoritarian movements of the twentieth century. Thirdly, modern 'Historismus' ignores social causation and inclines to be metaphysical and deterministic. In addition it provides pseudo-religious ideas for people who have no genuine religious beliefs.

It would be dangerous to ridicule the theory of the so-called 'mission' and to dismiss it as a mere collection of slogans serving the petty squabbles of nationalities. For this self-styled mission clothes its characters in garments which often come straight from the charismatic wardrobe. Also, the idea underlying the so-called national mission is always teleological in character;[1] which means that pseudo-historical arguments aim at justifying a specific political and military action which is envisaged as taking place in the near or distant future: or at least to provide a metaphysical basis for the ideology used for advocating a specific *status quo*.

If nationalism had been content with awakening national pride without at the same time encouraging contempt of neighbours, the national issue would have been less complicated. But the integral national state demands of its members belief in its superiority over every other nation. Thus before the First World War the Magyar gentry always spoke deprecatingly about the people who were members of their minorities in order to justify their deprivation of the latter's rights.[2] Viennese comedies created character types such as the Czech provincial uncle who arrives unexpectedly in Vienna and speaks German with a harsh Czech accent, while the Croat or Slovak is portrayed as an old rag-and-bone man who is himself dressed in rags. Again, in Germany people were taught to despise the Poles – which was easy to do, since the Poles were in fact the worst-paid and the poorest agricultural workers.

Thus, by its aggressiveness, one nationalism exacerbated the other. How prophetic the words of Lord Acton sound: 'The greatest adversary of the rights of nationality is the modern theory of nationality. By making the state and the nation commensurate with each other in theory, it reduces practically to a subject condition all other nationalities that may be within the boundary. It cannot admit them to an equality with the ruling nation, which would be a contradiction of the principle of its existence. According, therefore, to the degree of humanity and civilization in that dominant body which claims all the rights of the community, the inferior races are exterminated, or reduced to servitude, or outlawed, or put in a condition of dependence.'[3]

[1] Cf. Robert Michels, *Der Patriotismus*, Munich, Leipzig 1929.
[2] Cf. Oscar Jászi, *The Dissolution of the Habsburg Monarchy*, Chicago 1961, p. 309.
[3] Acton-Dalberg, op. cit., pp. 192 f.

# PART THREE

*Liberalism versus Nationalism*

The latest contradiction which had existed between the basic principles of the French Revolution – democracy and nationalism – still lay below the surface a few years before the Revolution of 1848. In 1844 the Polish democrat Lelewel sent a message of greeting to the Hambach Festival where the German liberals met in defiance of reactionary rule.[1] In 1848 this contradiction between democratic liberalism and nationalism wrecked the central European revolution. This revolution had an economic background. In 1840 the industrial proletariat of central Europe became, for the first time, a factor which had to be taken into account. In 1844 a serious economic crisis developed in Austria, bringing unemployment in its train. The peasants, who still had not shaken off all the indignities of the feudal system, revolted.[2] But both in Germany and in Austria, the most vociferous groups were the middle classes, who clamoured for a share in political power, one which would have corresponded to their actual economic importance. They were, on the other hand, frightened of their own democratic and plebeian allies, whose numbers were increasing rapidly, and who, far from being satisfied with passing liberal resolutions, preferred to man the barricades for their rights.

Karl Marx has pointed out these contradictions and sought to trace the collapse of the Revolution back to innate social contradictions. His economic interpretation of the 1848 Revolution explains some things: thus, for instance, why the middle classes, after securing some initial military and political successes, were so disconcerted that they sought to make peace with the defeated despotic regime, to the cry of 'law and order'. Friedrich Engels' analyses in the *New York Daily Tribune* of 1851–52[3] cannot, however, satisfactorily explain the national and constitutional aspects of this revolution.

Apart from the Turkish threat and the resistance to Napoleon rarely had various nationalities of the Habsburg empire shown any previous sign of solidarity. Now there was solidarity in revolution. From Vienna its spark leaped to Italy. But the Sardinian dynasty, which was regarded by a large section of the Italian population as the champion of Italian

[1] Cf. Joachim Lelewel, *Betrachtungen über den polnischen Zustand des ehemaligen Polens*, Leipzig 1845.
[2] In Germany at any rate Georg Büchner's attempt to incite the peasants to revolution in 1834 with the *Hessischer Landbote* was a failure.
[3] Marx-Engels, *Werke*, Vol. 8, Berlin 1960, pp. 105–8.

unity, mistrusted the democratic forces. It was not so wholeheartedly dedicated to the ideal of Italian unity as the romantic freedom fighters were. Its ideals were still rooted in the dynastic concept of the seventeenth and eighteenth centuries. Its members thought more about their own increase in dynastic power than the national unification of Italy.

The programme of democratic unification was championed by the republican Giuseppe Mazzini. His party was perhaps the most advanced and nationalist liberal movement in existence at the time. But even with Mazzini the idea of democracy differs from the traditional west-European concept. According to Ruggiero his party was a pure action party: its centre the piazza dominated by political agitators; a party, in fact, unfit to rule.[1]

The Hungarian parliament was under the dominant influence of the radical Ludwig Kossuth, who professed uncompromisingly liberal and nationalist ideals. He was a man exactly to the taste of the Viennese revolutionaries, who were less interested in the fate of the Hungarian section of the Habsburg empire than in the union of the German-speaking part of Austria with a reformed and liberal German Empire. For Kossuth, the nationalist ideal towered high above the liberal one. That became evident when he abolished the autonomous status of Transylvania and Croatia. In doing this Kossuth aroused the stormy opposition of the new Hungarian minorities who had, at first, supported the Revolution. The Croats rallied round Banus Jellachich, who was a vigorous defender of the Habsburgs and a born military autocrat into the bargain.

Throughout the whole of Germany revolutionary guards and mass demonstrations challenged the traditional power of royalty, aristocracy and bureaucracy. The Prussian king himself saw his glorious army defeated in the streets of Berlin by groups of workers, burghers and students.[2] As soon as the German Constituent Assembly had convened in the Paulskirche in Frankfurt, the German princes discovered their fears to be unfounded. The main interest of this Assembly, in which so many eminent men took part, was national unity not democratic revolution. The Assembly voluntarily renounced military power and relied mainly on the German principalities, that is on Austria and Prussia, to carry out its decisions and orders. The importance of the Schleswig Holstein question made the support of the Prussian monarchy appear even more urgent.[3] The genuine democrats remained a hopeless

---

[1] Guido de Ruggiero, *Geschichte des Liberalismus in Europa*, Munich 1930, p. 303.

[2] In his Memoirs, Bismarck tells how the revolutionary guards occupied the small country town bordering on his estate, tore down the Prussian flag and raised the black, red and gold colours of liberal Germany. Cf. also Veit Valentin, *Geschichte der deutschen Revolution von 1848–1849*, Vol. II, Berlin 1930–31.

[3] Veit Valentin, *Geschichte der Deutschen Revolution*, Berlin 1947, pp. 458 ff.

minority. It soon became clear that the liberal industrialists, merchants, professors and civil servants feared the revolution even more than the conservative groups. That – as Theodor Schieder shows – also emerged clearly in the discussion about the franchise:

'The theory that the right to vote is an innate right of the individual was not confined just to the supporters of radical democracy. But it can be said that the belief in a historical mission, held by the middle class, who claimed the franchise as a political right, as a prerogative of the propertied and cultured élite, became a reality. Added to this there was, however, the same fear of the uncontrolled and incalculable forces of society, which might destroy the social and political order with the help of universal suffrage . . . The Frankfurt Assembly's great debate on the franchise between February 15 and 20, 1849 puts the problems arising from basic principles into unusually sharp relief. The same is true of the discussions on the nationality question. At no time were the social questions which formed the background to the questions of the political constitution made so clear as in Frankfurt . . . The liberalism of 1848 was that of a cultured circle which counted itself to be part of the middle class and based its position on that.'[1]

Only a small group of radical democrats, grouped round the delegates Hecker, Struve, Fröbel, Robert Blum, Marx's friend Wilhelm Wolff, the poets Herwegh and Freiligrath, remained loyal to the ideals of the Revolution. They demanded the proclamation of a German republic.[2] The Assembly could not seriously hope to organize revolutionary guards in a national people's army and supplicate for dynastic support as well. Here it had to take a decision: either the radical solution of democratic revolution or the remote possibility of national unification, which might be organized from above. But all the time in many, widely scattered parts of Germany the social conditions necessary for the first solution simply did not exist.

While there was no lack of idealism and talent among the democrat leaders, they had no clear programmes or organizing ability. No true revolutionary situation existed in Prussia, Bavaria or north Germany. The exception was the allemanic parts of Germany, the states of Baden and Württemberg, in which liberalism had long secured a footing – perhaps in the Rotteck School. It is probably no mere coincidence that

[1] Theodor Schieder, *Staat und Gesellschaft im Wandel unserer Zeit*, Munich 1958, pp. 67 f.
[2] 'Deutsche Republik': the refrain of the so-called Hecker song of the South German People's Corps (*Volkswehren*) went:

> Hecker, Struvo, Zitz and Blum,
> Spell the German princes' doom.

Cf. W. Liebknecht, *Robert Blum und seine Zeit*, Nuremberg 1888.

it was the armies of Prussia, Bavaria and Hesse which defeated the revolutionaries, led characteristically by the Pole Mieroslawski, near Rastatt in 1849.[1]

In 1848 the Czechs had dealt the Frankfurt National Assembly a severe blow. Since the Middle Ages the kings of Bohemia had been electors of the Holy Roman Empire, usually the decisive ones. For that very reason Bohemia had always enjoyed a great measure of independence. Now, however, the Czechs refused to attend the Frankfurt parliament and, instead, called together a pan-Slav congress in Prague. Under Bohemia's influence an appeal was made to all Slav nations to found a confederacy of states. But Franz Palacký, the historian and statesman, and his pupil, Dr Ladislaus Rieger, like the vast majority of the Czech people, could not accept this proposal. At this congress Palacký undoubtedly played the role of Bohemian patriot, but did not shut the door to union with the other nations of the Danube basin. He advocated, rather, the transformation of the Habsburg monarchy into a democratic federation of the small nations of central Europe.[2]

The Austrian troops were a noteworthy factor in bringing about the collapse of the revolution. Most of the soldiers were Slav peasants who remained loyal to their generals Radetzky, Windischgrätz and Jellachich. Although the revolution had abolished serfdom, these peasants supported the dynastic state against their own economic and social interests. The alliance between monarchy and the peasantry, which began in the seventeenth century, still lived on.

In their account of the insurrection of the liberal-minded middle classes in active opposition from 1840, Engels and Marx proved their great sociological insight. But when they condemned the Slav peoples for their 'reactionary attitude' they overlooked the tyrannical nationalism which was inherent in the 'liberal' revolutions of the historical nations of Austria.[3] The Czechs felt threatened by the attempt to transform Austria into a German state, while the Croats, Romanians and Slovaks feared they might lose their nationality because of the threatened Magyarization. On the other hand, the German-Austrians, Hungarians, Poles and Italians did not live under the threat of losing their nationality. Consequently they were more open to liberal aspira-

[1] Veit Valentin, *Geschichte der Deutschen Revolution*, op. cit., Vol. 2, pp. 526 ff.
[2] Münch, op. cit., p. 193.
[3] Cf. the series of articles in the *New York Daily Tribune* already referred to. The negative appreciation of the Czech independence movement probably goes back to Engels and Marx's view of it as a device of pan-Slavism directed by the Tsar. But they passed a very different verdict on the Polish Revolution. Opposing the view prevailing in the Frankfurt National Assembly to regard Poland as a part of the Empire, Engels wrote that the 'establishment of a democratic Poland . . . is the first condition for the creation of a democratic Germany.' *Neue Rheinische Zeitung*, August 20, 1848, in Marx-Engels, op. cit., Vol. 5, p. 33.

tions and reforms. They were completely unaware that their nationalism appeared reactionary to the other nationalities.

Meinecke has shown that the only meeting point for liberalism and nationalism is to be found where the liberal endeavour to weaken the centralistic state coincides with the national claim to emancipation.[1] This means that federalism is the true solution to the problem of nationalism and democracy. Looked at from the politico-sociological point of view, even more important than the Frankfurt negotiations were the negotiations of the Austrian Constituent Assembly at Vienna and later at Kremsier. A unique opportunity occurred never to return. For once in the history of Austria it happened that the reasonable and moderate representatives of all nationalities (except Hungary) met, and seriously endeavoured to find a solution to the nationality problem.

Even then, however, a deep contradiction between the German-Austrian and Czech views appeared. Sudeten Germans like Ludwig von Löhner demanded the division of the monarchy into autonomous districts. Czechs like Palacký and Rieger, on the other hand, stressed the historical right of statehood, i.e. the indivisibility of Bohemia and Moravia.[2] On January 23, 1849, Palacký proposed the division of Austria into eight groups of *Länder* (states) – namely German-Austria, including German-Bohemia, German-Moravia and Silesia; Czech-Bohemia, including Moravia, Silesia and Slovakia as Czech-Austrian; then Hungarian, Polish, Italian, Illyrian, South-Slav, Austria (consisting of Croatia, Dalmatia and the Woiwodina). Similar but not so far-reaching was the proposal of the Slovene Kancič to create fourteen states on the basis of the language spoken in them but without their being given the status of a *Land*. It is interesting that he proposed the division of Bohemia but not of Moravia.[3] The difficulties were obvious: there had to be a decision either for a solution which would have rent the historical unity of the historic crown lands and allowed a reorganization on a purely ethnic basis, or for the maintenance of these lands, which would have destroyed the unity of the national groups. For in most areas the nationalities were so mixed and dispersed that it would have been impossible to establish homogeneous ethnic units on the Swiss model.

It was characteristic of the liberal spirit of the German-Austrian delegation, which eventually also found expression in the Kremsier

[1] Friederich Meinecke, 'Liberalism and Nationality in Germany and Austria', *Cambridge Modern History*, Vol. IX, Cambridge 1909.

[2] Anton Springer, *Protokolle des Verfassungsausschusses im österreichischen Reichstage 1848–1849*, Leipzig 1885, pp. 26 ff. Cf. also Hermann Münch, op. cit., pp. 207 ff.

[3] Cf. also Hantsch, op. cit., pp. 44 f., and Springer, op. cit., p. 23.

draft constitution, that the Slav point of view was nevertheless largely accepted. For the fourteen provinces of Austria division into national districts was envisaged. All the nationalities were to have equal rights and the inviolable right to nurse and to cultivate their nationality. The equality of all local languages normally spoken was guaranteed for schools, offices and in public.[1] Doubtless all this amounted to a serious effort to set up a successful federal structure. However, the Schwarzenberg government, which felt very strong after the suppression of the revolution by military intervention and was still fighting the revolution in Hungary and Italy, could not reconcile itself to such a progressive programme. Not even the enlightened Minister of the Interior, Count Stadion, who had formerly been an adherent of the intellectual traditions of Josephinism, could muster any enthusiasm for it. Just as in the fifties and sixties of this century in modern Asia, so it was argued then in Austria that a democracy could not possibly evolve from the democratic atmosphere of the diets. Before thinking of parliamentary rule the people must first learn local self-government, Schwarzenberg's Minister of the Interior oracled. A charter of local self-government was granted as a mere consolation:[2] 'The foundation of any free state is the free commune', declared Count Stadion, his Minister of the Interior, conscious of the importance of public relations.

The rabidly emotional, illogical and unprincipled nature of nationalism became even more evident when the industrial revolution struck central Europe. Economic and ethnic motives dovetailed, but often also overlapped. Most German-speaking industrialists supported the idea of a centralized Habsburg empire. At the same time they would have been happy to see federalism in Bohemia because of the high taxation imposed by the Bohemian diet, in which the Czechs formed a majority. On the other hand, most of the Czechs living by agriculture supplied the industrial Sudeten region and were very interested in the tax revenue from industry. Therefore the Czechs supported centralization in the state and federalism in the empire. At that time the Germans were still the most powerful factor in the Habsburg empire and the nationalities among them wanted to Germanize the other nationalities. In Bohemia, however, they were a minority and therefore demanded autonomy. The Czechs worked for a federal empire, but as they were a majority in Bohemia their aim was centralized in the *Land*.

[1] Robert A. Kann, *The Multinational Empire*, Vol. II, New York 1950, pp. 26 ff. Also Josef Redlich, *Das Österreichische Staats- und Reichsproblem*, Vol. I, Leipzig 1920, pp. 273 ff.
[2] 'The foundation of the free state is the free community': this sentence introduced the Austrian communal law No. 170 of 1848 and, although connected with Sections 130 and 131 of the Kremsier Draft Constitution, nevertheless revealed the spirit of the Minister of the Interior, Count Stadion.

The situation in Hungary was similar. The Magyars had long been demanding an autonomy which they refused to give to their own minorities. Since the eighteenth century they had not hesitated to ally themselves with powers outside Austria such as France, Prussia and Turkey in order to obtain autonomy and independence. After the defeat of Austria in 1866, Hungary won a new, independent status within the Habsburg empire. This meant in practice that, henceforth, Austria could no longer contest Prussia's hegemony in Germany. The so-called Hungarian compromise of 1867 gave Hungary absolute equality with Austria.[1] This dualism later proved to be a suspended death-sentence for the Habsburg empire. At that time the German-speaking inhabitants got a free hand in respect of Austria's other nationalities, while the Hungarians subsequently felt free to suppress their national minorities.

At least these far-reaching concessions should have pacified Hungary. Yet such is not the mechanics of a nationalist revolution. After the compromise of 1867 Hungary did, in fact, at first pursue a liberal and moderate policy towards her nationalities. But like the Czechs in Austria, the Croats in Hungary, themselves a majority belonging to a historic crown land,[2] wanted to know why equal rights were not granted to them as well. Hungary gradually gave up her moderate policy practised under Deak and reverted to ruthless denationalization.

Understandably, Hungary's success set a fashion. The other nationalities of Austria – the Czechs, Poles, Romanians, Slovenes, and Italians – asked themselves why the privileges granted to the Hungarians should not also be theirs. The Bohemians, whose country had suffered most in the war of 1866, felt this injustice most keenly.[3] It was a period requiring courageous and incisive reforms. For these, however, the conservative framework of the Austrian government system at the time was ill-suited. A few minor concessions in the matter of language as proposed by the Hohenwart government and later under Taaffe's leadership – that was all those in power were prepared to give the Czechs.[4] This unclarified position of the Czechs and the German-

[1] Louis Eisenmann, *Le Compromis Austro-Hongrois de 1867*, Paris 1904, and Richard Charmatz, *Österreichs innere Geschichte von 1848 bis 1907*, Part I, Leipzig 1909, pp. 75 ff.

[2] Cf. Jászi, op. cit., p. 315, also Kann, op. cit., Vol. I, pp. 133 f.

[3] The Austro-Hungarian compromise drove, so to speak, the Austrian Slavs into Prussia's arms. Nevertheless Palacký, who had visited Moscow with his friends, thought that a universal Russian monarchy would mean the violent subjugation and enslavement of the whole of cultured Europe, the suppression and stifling of all liberal and noble ideas and endeavours of the human race. Münch, op. cit., p. 328, Note 11.

[4] The Poles were Austria's only Slav nationality, able to achieve a position like that of the Hungarians. This was probably due to the not inconsiderable influence of the Polish aristocracy at the Viennese court.

Hungarian refusal to give them equal status was later to prove fatal.

All these difficulties resulted in another, contradictory aspect of the problem. In the Anglo-Saxon world it is considered self-evident that democracy goes hand in hand with a federal system of government, and autocracy with a centralized system. In central Europe, because of local traditions, a very different situation arose. There the idea of federalism was always associated with feudalism, while liberalism supported a centralized administration. In Austria this specific connection originated with Josephinism.

The conservative federalist Metternich was succeeded by the progressive centralist Kolowrat. The federalist constitution of the Polish Count Golukowski, the so-called October diploma, was followed by the centralist February patent of the German liberal Schmerling. The Hohenwart system, Catholic-aristocratic and federalist, was replaced by another German liberal minority. It is indeed noteworthy that the most important bureaucrats of the Bach era, Schmerling, Plener and Lasser, were originally liberals and had even been inspired by Jacobinism.[1] At the same time they were the very men who sought to suppress the nationalities: and Bach did perhaps more than anyone else to estrange the Czechs. On the other hand the aristocracy favoured the so-called 'Historical Political Individualities', this concept being adopted first by the Hungarians and then by the Czechs.[2] A similar situation developed in Italy. There conservative feudal circles supported federation, while Mazzini and Garibaldi were more in favour of national union in a centralized state.

In Germany too the federalist idea seemed to be the interests of the dynasties, except perhaps of Prussia, and the minority of liberals favoured centralism. It is true that in the past the Holy Roman Empire had resembled a federal structure. To cherish the ideal of the Holy Roman Empire meant in the first half of the nineteenth century siding with Austria. To be partial to Austria meant defending this *ancien régime*. And so the very poets and writers who, during the Napoleonic Wars, had supported the cause of German patriotism and liberalism, now hoped for a strong and centralistic Germany under Prussian leadership. King Frederick William IV however, himself a romantic who was advised by aristocratic conservatives such as Radowitz and Gerlach, continued to believe in a union of the Germans princes and saw himself in a self-sacrificing, idealistic role as the sword-bearer of a Habsburg German emperor. At the time it occurred to only a few

[1] Cf. A. J. P. Taylor, *The Habsburg Monarchy 1915–1918*, London 1941, pp. 102 f.
[2] A. Popovici, *Die Vereinigten Staaten von Gross-Österreich*, Leipzig 1906, pp. 120–142.

revolutionaries that Prussia was as ill-suited as Austria to be the leading power in a democratic Germany.

Bismarck, whose aim was to found the Prusso-German empire, looked for a class and a party to support his nationalist and autocratic policies. He hoped to find this support in the middle class and the National Liberal Party. Bismarck fulfilled their programme of national unification, supported industry and trade, protected them from competition by his tariff policy and accepted the sons of the middle classes into the Prussian officer corps. Yet his federalism was hardly more than a façade. It is true that, after the founding of the empire, Bismarck bestowed on the German princes the Constitution of 1871; which bought over the princes by guarding their income, but compared with Prussia the inequality of the remaining states was so crushing that it was hardly possible to speak of real federalism. Talk of genuine centralization was equally unjustified. The 'imperial unity' was in reality a Prussian hegemony. It in no way fulfilled the hopes of those who in 1848 had offered the Prussian king the crown of a free Germany.

At the time of the feudal, conservative Hohenwart regime in Austria and the Catholic renaissance in France there existed the possibility of a Franco-German alliance, which would probably have been supported by the more radical federalist elements in Germany.[1] Bismarck found himself up against a powerful opposition. Large sections of the population in the south German states were opposed to Prussian centralism; the Catholic miners of the Rhineland, the German and Polish Catholics of Upper Silesia, the population of Hesse-Nassau, Hanover, Saxony and Frankfurt – all of them would have preferred Austrian leadership. Then the *Kulturkampf* – the struggle between the State and the Roman Catholic Church stirred up by Bismarck – roused the enmity of the Junkers and the Protestant circles of Prussia – something which he had never expected. Among the reasons for this surprising phenomenon was the traditional inter-relationship between federalism and state particularism on the one hand and between aristocracy and conservatism on the other which were characteristic of central Europe.

[1] On this point cf. Arthur Rosenberg, *Entstehung und Geschichte der Weimarer Republik*, published by Kurt Kersten, Frankfurt 1961, pp. 18 ff.

PART FOUR

*Socialism and the Constitutional State*

## The Industrial Revolution

Karl Marx's observation that the Germany of 1848 was an industrially backward country applies to an even greater extent to the other regions of central Europe. The Industrial Revolution came to central Europe during the period of national emancipation and unification.

In Great Britain, the Industrial Revolution had taken place earlier, in the golden age of Enlightenment. England's *laissez-faire* economy had made her the centre of world trade. The Industrial Revolution failed, however, to penetrate into the centre of the Continent, remote from the Atlantic coast. There, mercantilist ideas gradually gave way to physiocratic ideas without the character of industrial and trade policy undergoing any fundamental change. The part in the industrialization of central Europe played by the immigrant businessmen favoured by the state, not only in Prussia but also in Austria, has been given its proper due only in the last few years.[1] These were bound to support the rigorous tariff policy taken over from mercantilism, by which the growing wealth inside the country's frontiers was to be maintained. International trade grew, but the internal trade of the new industrial nations grew faster, due to state support. However cosmopolitan the thinking of these early capitalists may have been, it was weakened by their dependence on the absolutist state and its trade legislation which made the businessman dependent on local business. In this way the new industrial middle class endeavoured to adapt itself to the nobles' national ideology.[2] Despite its basic internationalism, even the steadily growing working-class movement did not remain unaffected by nationalism, since its sphere of operation was limited to the state concerned. The First Socialist International association pledge to eliminate the frontiers of individual states was more a propaganda instrument than an effective working organization.

In any case an important feature of this belated industrialization is that it was not accompanied by social or political revolutions. In Germany the newly founded empire continued on the one hand the Prussian tradition of the east Elbe junkers and on the other supported heavy industry for political and military reasons.[3] In Austria-Hungary

[1] Adam Wandruszka, Die historische Schwäche des Bürgertums, op. cit., p. 768.
[2] Cf. Otto Bauer, op. cit., pp. 405 ff.
[3] Thorstein Veblen, op. cit., pp. 165 ff.

there was an industrial nucleus which had been inherited from the mercantile-physiocratic period. In northern Bohemia and northern Moravia the textile industry had been supported by the state since the eighteenth century.[1]

In Poland industrialization began after the 1863 revolt, which Prussia had helped to suppress by closing her frontiers. Industrialization came in, therefore, after the thwarting of an attempted political revolution. The Polish writer Boleslav Prus wrote: 'The nation stopped fighting and plotting and began to work.' For Poland, therefore, industrialization replaced the traditional policy of 'freedom or death'. The defeat of Napoleon III, on whom the Poles had set the highest hopes, proved that this was the right course. When Polish friends of Thiers sought his advice, his reply was: *Enrichissez-vous.*[2]

As elsewhere, industrial development in central Europe began on a patriarchal basis which retained many vestiges of the relationship obtaining between the feudal lord and his peasants. The worker lived very close to the factory, often in the 'back premises'. In spite of early industrial legislation passed during the Age of Enlightenment there was little evidence of social welfare.[3] Yet not infrequently a real community of feeling existed between employer and worker. The factory owner and his wife were frequently called in by the workers to settle their personal or domestic problems and they also often acted as arbitrators between employees. They were expected to help in an emergency. The impersonal relationship typical of capitalism did not develop until much later. Often the employer himself was an artisan or worker who had got on – a type which the workers feared most.

With the industrial revolution came socialism. It met with a peculiar situation in central Europe. For the reasons mentioned the middle classes – especially the industrial middle classes – were inclined to favour the *ancien régime* rather than the constitutional state. Thus to socialism fell the task of raising political demands which in the West had been the driving force behind the middle-class revolution. From the beginning the German socialists emerged as democracy's *avant-garde*. The first intellectual stirrings go back partly to the small radical

[1] In the Seven Years War Austria, by losing Silesia, had lost those very regions in which textile production had previously been centred. After the peace treaty substitute industries had been developed in areas which were strategically protected by the mountains and at the same time were not too far from the original production sites.

[2] From Professor W. J. Rose's lectures at the London School of Slavonic and East European Studies, which he left to me.

[3] 'I shall never forget the sight which could be seen at midday in the immediate vicinity of some of the largest factories [at Reichenberg 1873–4], where the workers camped outside with their lunch and spent their midday break in the gutters, so to speak.' From Joseph M. Bauernreither's *Fragmente cines politischen Tagebuches*, published by Joseph Redlich, Berlin 1928, p. 18.

democratic groups of 1848, to men like Herwegh, Freiligrath and the circle which gathered round the *Neue Rheinische Zeitung*. Socialism also owed something to the Wirth and Büchner group and the secret workers' associations which had already been founded in Switzerland by men such as Schuster, Vennedy and Weitling.

Two groups, the Lassallians and the Marxists, united to form the Social Democratic Party. The Lassallian group was more democratic and patriotic from the beginning.[1] In spite of their centralized type of organization the actual development of the Party was strongly influenced by Lassalle's thought and personality.

The compromise between Lassalle's followers and the Marxists did in fact lead to a certain disunity, since it was not until 1918 that the Social Democratic Party abandoned the practical present of their class-war programme; yet the Social Democrats were undisputably the most important democratic group in Germany to make dynamic efforts to make parliamentary democracy a reality. Over and above they had a great influence indeed on the development of democracy in central Europe as a whole. This tendency on the part of the Social Democratic Party increased after it had entered into an alliance with the left-wing liberals who styled themselves the Progressive Party.

Nor did the advance of socialist ideas fail to have a lasting influence on the Christian section of the working class and the lower middle class. For these produced a synthesis of socialism and moral egalitarian postulates which were rooted in Christianity. In Austria particularly this synthesis contributed to the development of a Christian-social movement and kept these classes from embracing extreme nationalism.[2] After the founding of the Hohenzollern empire, Germany's Catholic population still felt itself to be a minority which would always be denied full recognition in the semi-absolute state. Thus social and democratic aspirations also made the dissemination of nationalist ideas difficult within the 'Zentrum Party'.

The Paris Commune of 1871 was a great stimulus to socialism throughout Europe. As a result Bismarck thought it necessary to outline a plan for the international suppression of socialism. In 1872 Spain took the initiative and asked the British government to co-operate, as prominent socialists had been given political asylum in England. In connection with this Lord Grenville wrote to Bismarck: 'The law and

[1] Franz Mehring, *Geschichte der deutschen Sozialdemokratie*, Berlin 1960, Vol. II, pp. 371 ff.
[2] On the question of the Austrian Christian-social movement cf. Wiard Klopp (editor), *Die sozialen Lehren des Freiherrn Karl v. Vogelsang*, St Pölten 1894; and Richard Charmatz, 'Ein Konservativer Sozialpolitiker Karl Freiherr v. Vogelsang', in *Lebensbilder aus der Geschichte Österreichs*, Vienna 1947.

traditions of Britain favoured the unrestricted right of foreigners to reside as long as they were obedient to the Laws of the land.'

When, in 1878, two attempts were made on the Emperor's life, the social democrats were held responsible, in spite of no proof being available. The great anger among the German middle class over the men who were supposed to be behind the assassins gave Bismarck the excuse he had long wanted in order to pass his 'anti-socialist' laws. With the help of emergency laws a long period of persecution was ushered in. Socialist writings were banned and many convinced socialists emigrated to the United States, Switzerland and England.

Nevertheless, this persecution did not prevent the rise of the socialists. Their membership and voting strength grew continually until they became the largest party in Germany.[1]

In Austria socialism developed in the sixties. From the first, however, the nationality problem ran counter to the development of the supra-national Austrian Socialist Party.[2] In 1888 the wealthy physician Victor Adler, who left all his money to the Party, finally succeeded in founding the (supra-national) Socialist Party of Austria. From the very outset the Austrian Social Democratic Party was more international and revolutionary than its German sister party. This was partly due to the multinational structure of the Habsburg empire, which so to speak multiplied social tensions, partly due to the worse living conditions which the workers had to put up with in Austria.[3] During the first decade of the twentieth century, however, the difference between the workers' movements of the nationalities of Austria-Hungary grew more marked. Separate socialist parties, which had not remained unaffected by the conflict between the nationalities, exerted a stronger attraction over the workers; as members of smaller communities they took a full share in the cultural life in these communities. Typical examples are the Czech and Hungarian splinter parties. Yet Adler's central party supported the claims of the nationalities against the government in Vienna. Thus the Brünn Party Congress demanded universal suffrage as a precondition for the free, unrestricted development of the various nations of Austria and called for transformation of the empire into a federation of nationalities on a democratic basis.[3] Co-operation continued between

[1] Herwegh's poem *E pur si mueve* was apposite to this situation: 'Revolution's on, the world is spinning like a ball, Bavarian beer nor Prussian Christianity will give you any help at all.'

[2] Hans Mommsen, *Dis Sozialdemokratie und die Nationalitätenfrage im Habsburger Vielvölkerstaat*, Vienna 1963, pp. 99–120.

[3] Cf. G. D. H. Cole, *The Second International 1889–1914*, Part II, London 1956, pp. 523 ff.

[4] Rudolf Springer (*nom de plume* of Karl Renner), *Der Kampf der österreichischen Nationen um den Staat*, Vienna and Leipzig 1902. Cf. also the same author's *Grund-*

the various national social-democratic groups, which mutually supported each other against the middle-class nationalist movements.

In the nineties and during the first decade of this century, however, an ever-growing gulf opened between socialism and nationalism. This increasingly apparent development became particularly noticeable in Poland. Attempts to bridge the gulf resulted in the subordination of socialism to nationalism. At first, however, Pilsudski's synthesis appeared reasonable enough, 'The whole nation suffers, but to whom shall I turn if not to you, peasants and workers, who suffer most of all.' The Polish socialist paper *Proletariat* at the time carried articles about national liberation besides those on international solidarity. But there was a radical wing, which was led by Rosa Luxemburg and condemned the 'social patriotism' of party members such as Limanowski and Pilsudski. Rosa Luxemburg called for a unified Polish-Russian state and a common revolutionary policy on the part of the Polish and Russian proletariat. Meanwhile Limanowski, who represented a point of view in Poland similar to that of T. G. Masaryk in Bohemia, tried to establish a connection between nationalism, socialism and democracy.[1] In the final analysis national independence seemed to him to be infinitely more important than socialism. And Pilsudski's later political development demonstrated the alternative character of nationalism and socialism.

Proof that central European socialism made the first effective attack on the authoritarian political structure of society is afforded by the fact that until the outbreak of the Second World War democracy and social democracy were almost synonymous in central Europe.[2] The basis for this lay in the facts that have been mentioned – that the workers' movement had also adopted the programme of middle-class democracy. Thus the central European social democratic parties put forward, on the one hand, views which in England, for example, could have been found in the Conservative or Liberal programme, on the other also Marxist principles which the English Labour movement rejected. The explanation of this paradox is that in central Europe the struggle against an authoritarian tradition and a semi-authoritarian state apparatus seemed to social democracy to be its urgent task.

As the democratic shock troops in central Europe the social democrats were compelled to organize themselves as militant alliances. The old rule that in war the enemy always influences the methods and the

*lagen und Entwicklungsziele der Österreich-Ungarischen Monarchie*, Vienna and Leipzig 1906.

[1] Boleslaw Limanowski, *Socialism, Democracy, Patriotism*, published by the Polish Socialist Party, London 1902, pp. 167–90.

[2] In this sense the persecution of social democracy represents a continuation of the old persecution of demagogues.

nature of the troops fighting against him was also true in this case. For many of the alleged undemocratic traits in social democracy were due to their having, to some extent, to adopt the tactics and methods of the autocratic systems they were combating. Both the Russian and the French Revolutions show that even the most radical revolutionaries out to overthrow a hated social order still remained its children. Overcoming the political indifference shown by the people because of their age-long acceptance of the autocratic state was a difficult and protracted process. A further factor peculiar to the German Empire was that Bismarck's ruthless policy of unification pushed the political interest and sense of responsibility awakened during the Revolution of 1848 into the background. It is not, therefore, surprising that social democracy was compelled to give its leaders extensive powers and introduce strict party discipline. That is also the reason for the creation of the party bureaucracy, which was economically dependent on the leadership and therefore conservative in its behaviour towards it.

These are historical factors which are not taken sufficiently into consideration by Robert Michels in his analysis of the 'oligarchical tendencies' in the Social Democratic Party.[1] As Michels noted, these factors bore some relation to the habit of both the German and the Italian socialists to phrase their programmes in military language. The English and French socialists did not need to do so as they were already part of a democratic society. The central-European party programmes stressed the class war, misled not only the middle classes and the government of the Western democracies but – what was worse – also the social democrats themselves. They did not deceive the minions of the authoritarian power, against whom the social-democratic struggle was really waged.

After liberalism had abdicated in central Europe it was the social democrats who had to step into the breach as defenders of liberal ideas. After 1918 it fell to the socialists to defend the constitutional state based on the rule of law, a task which in England, France and America as well was usually the duty of the moderate right wing. Ruggiero holds the same view regarding Italy. In his essay on the Risorgimento he says:[2]

'A democracy, as an independent and lasting popular organization, was to arise in Italy only with the rise of socialism, the first political movement to have a strictly social content and to come into permanent touch with the masses so as to arouse them from their apathy.

[1] Cf. Robert Michels, *Zur Soziologie des Parteiwesens in der modernen Demokratie*, Leipzig 1925.
[2] Ruggiero, op. cit., p. 304.

The most obvious proof that Mazzini's democracy lacked this genuinely popular character was his own profound dislike of socialism.'

Even the socialists themselves were not always successful in rousing the masses from apathy. Even where they succeeded in doing so the loyalty of the masses to the old ruling classes was strong enough to expose the populace to authoritarian propaganda. As events were later to prove, the socialists made things easier for their opponents by their inability to find an answer to the use by fascism of contemporary methods and techniques based on mass communication media. A further difficulty was that of gaining a foothold in the countryside. The socialist parties were purely urban organizations; the people in the countryside distrusted their noisy demonstrations, parades and radical speeches. In so far as they had gained support in country districts the work of their members was limited to paying their subscriptions, voting at elections and buying the party newspaper. To people in the country, party policy appeared to be directed by the town. And so social-democratic efforts to enrol the peasantry were doomed to failure. In Austria-Hungary the peasants had not won their freedom from compulsory labour until 1848. Now they had to deal with their own economic difficulties without the help of the feudal lords and they looked back with a certain longing to their former patriarchal relationship with the landowners, who had guaranteed them a certain material security.

The spirit of the peasant class in eighteenth-century Germany is admirably caught in Moser's *Patriotisches Archiv* in a conversation between an official, a courtier and a peasant. After the difference between official and peasant has been discussed, the peasant says to the courtier: 'I am glad my son is in the army because he's learning to submit to discipline and in that way he's getting used to serve under officials later.'

The peasants' attitude changed only slowly in the second half of the nineteenth century. As far as it did so, credit goes to the spread of co-operatives and associations. Yet the peasant used to look back on his military service with pleasure. After all, submission to authority helped the emperor and the prince, whose pictures hung in the peasant's bedroom. In the peasant's world of ideas the ruler played the part of a strict but benevolent father who had to look after the well-being of his sometimes unruly children.

To the peasants and many of the middle classes the socialists at first were no more than ragged beggars who, prompted by Jewish or foreign demagogues, claimed to understand political problems better than the prince or the emperor and his ministers, who were well-informed, educated and cultured people. The peasants' understanding of politics was often limited to the information contained in the priest's Sunday sermon, 'public opinion' as heard in the village inn and the wisdom of a few proverbs or sayings such as : 'Don't eat cherries with the nobs or they'll spit the stones in your face.'

Even after the First World War this attitude was by no means uncommon in rural districts of Hungary, where the simple folk might agree with a socialist speaker from the city. The arrival of the estate manager with his smart uniform and impressive moustache was, however, enough to make them forget immediately everything the party secretary had wanted them to grasp. Even in 1905 and 1906 the Hungarian people were not ready to stand up for the ultranationalist slogans of the gentry intent on their privileges when the Emperor Francis Joseph, in his role of Hungarian king, forcibly introduced universal suffrage for elections to the Hungarian parliament.[1] Nor did the system change under the Horthy regime, as the peasants were still at the mercy of the economic pressure which the large landowners could bring to bear. Really free and secret elections were quite impossible in such circumstances.

There was a further fact which made it difficult for the socialists to win over the peasants. In the central European working-class movement positivist influences which had their origin in John Stuart Mill and Herbert Spencer merged with the Marxist challenge to Christianity.[2] These two influences resulted in an anti-religious attitude which became an integral part of progressive and socialist thinking. Such an attitude, striking to the very root of conservative tradition, was likely to alienate the peasant classes, not only from socialism but from democracy in general. This was not the case where the peasants were still too primitive to realize the contradiction which existed between religion and socialism – or else so revolutionary that they themselves ignored the differences. Thus the peasants in southern Italy often went to socialist meetings with their church banners. The same thing happened frequently in Slovakia or in Carpatho-Ukraine where, after 1918, the communist peasants transformed demonstrations into processions, carrying images of the saints along with portraits of Lenin and Stalin.

The peasants' hostility to socialism and democracy on grounds of religion was also the reason for Austria's later split into a Christian-social peasantry and a socialist urban class, which was to prove fatal to the republic.

The reactionary attitude of the middle classes did not spring solely

[1] Jászi, op. cit., p. 372.
[2] 'Christianity and Socialism are as opposed to one another as fire and water'—Bebel, February 1874.

from economic causes. It was no less conditioned by resentment at socialist demands for universal suffrage.[1] Putting this point in their programme into practice was bound to have an unfavourable effect on the prestige and power of the 'taxpayers'. The middle-class fight against the social democrats was waged on a broad front. Slander proved to be an effective weapon. When the socialist attitude towards the authoritarian state grew sharper it was not difficult to convince the people that the socialist movement existed solely for the benefit of a few agitators who were able to live in luxury on subscriptions extorted from the earnings of poor workmen. That was the time which saw the birth of the idea of the 'big-wig'. The already class-conscious middle classes drew a sharp dividing line between themselves and the proletariat.[2] The middle classes with their belief in 'order' were furious about the demonstrations, which showed what scant respect the proletarian agitators had for the recognized authorities, and this in a society in which the merchant addressed his customers according to their social rank, observing appropriate and carefully graded forms: 'Sir', 'Honoured Sir', 'Very Honoured Sir', 'Highly Well Born' or even 'High Born',[3] and in which bureaucratic rule sought to ensure that no intellectual or agitator should disturb middle-class peace and contentment.

The idea of a police state which this practice embodied was taken over from Prussian state law by the Austro-Hungarian government in 1853. The *Prügel-Patent* imposed on the district authorities the duty of maintaining public order and morality and preventing disturbances and restoring law and order if these were disturbed. For generations this principle had been described in German, Austrian and Hungarian universities as the basic principle of public administration. Later it was also adopted by the post-war democrats, who regarded it as a respectable tradition.

---

[1] On this point cf. especially: Theodor Eschenburg, 'Tocqueville's Wirkung in Deutschland', in *Alexis de Tocqueville, Werke und Briefe*, Stuttgart 1959, Vol. I, p. XLVII.
[2] The left-liberal middle class, which was organized in the Progressive Party, was an exception.
[3] W. H. Dawson, *Germany and the Germans*, Vol. I, London 1896, p. 85.

PART FIVE

*The Result – Multilateral Conflicts*
*between Ideologies and Ties*

Differences of language and race were not the only important elements of the drama of central Europe. They were complicated by rival loyalties towards the landowners, the ruling princes and the emperor. In the Middle Ages, when church and society were almost synonymous, loyalty to the church had been by far the most important. Both church and state were universal in scope and ideal and favoured the intermixture of peoples and races of central Europe.[1] But the Middle Ages also knew a threefold conflict of loyalties between Pope, Emperor and Prince.

Since the Reformation the situation had been complicated by religious disputes and wars of religion reaching a climax in the Thirty Years War. Princes, generals, officers, even mercenaries frequently changed sides and the people changed their religion. This created dangerous precedents for the future, for the principle of *cuius regio*, *eius religio* also meant, among other things, that it was a virtue to change one's faith if that should prove useful. These currents and counter-currents occurred to a very marked degree in Austria-Hungary, as Hermann Bahr says.

'In other countries the heir inherits a single steady development from his forefathers. But we have a hundred voices from the past, the mutual struggle of our forefathers is still not settled and each must decide it anew, each must choose his side, each must pass through the entire past himself. The past is never over and done with, the father is divided from his son but reunited with his grandson. In other countries a man can follow confidently in the footsteps of all his forefathers. But our ancestors were never united and make appeal to our judgement.'[2]

Towards the end of the eighteenth and the beginning of the nineteenth century, religion was ousted from its leading position in the scale of values of the bourgeoisie and the intelligentsia of continental Europe. But no uniform set of values evolved to take its place. That loyalties remained divided is shown by the events of 1848. Thus Ludwig Kossuth, who had liberated the peasants from serfdom, had to take the field against peasant armies fighting for the Habsburgs.

---

[1] Jászi, op. cit., p. 49.
[2] Hermann Bahr, *Dalmatinische Reise*, Berlin 1909, p. 95.

This situation gave rise to peculiar contradictions and complications which were not always absolutely clear to the actors at the time. In the first half of the nineteenth century the pioneers of nationalism believed they were campaigning for national unification, while the princes, with the help of the peasants, still went on fighting their dynastic wars. Men like Radetzky were not essentially different from the generals of the Thirty Years War, or the Wars of the Spanish and Austrian Succession. The war fought in 1866 for the hegemony of Germany was still to some extent dynastic.[1] This shows that the era of dynastic wars in central Europe had still not come to an end with the industrial revolution. Even the decisive defeat of Austria and her exclusion from Germany and Italy did not settle this rivalry. Thus in 1871 the Austro-Hungarian Foreign Minister, Count Beust, wanted Austria to take part in the war against Prussia on the side of France. Later, too, Austrian foreign policy, in spite of the alliance with the German Empire, was extremely sensitive about questions affecting the independence of the monarchy, and during the period of Anglo-German naval rivalry was indifferent to the maintenance of good German–Russian relations.

Instead, to old dynastic conflicts were added new ones arising from the consequences of the industrial revolution. The earlier linguistic antagonism was intensified by the antagonism between urban and rural areas. The Czech worker was attracted to the German industrial town, where he could earn more. This meant that he undercut the German worker, as a lower wage was enough to raise the Czechs' low standard of living. This was bound to excite the enmity of German-speaking workers who looked on the new arrivals as dangerous rivals in the wage struggle. At the same time the Czech worker envied the German for his relatively higher standard of living.

It is clear that the German-Bohemian industrialists tried to exploit this national rivalry to get cheap labour. The workers of both nationalities, however, came to see that it was not in their interest to exacerbate the existing wage competition still further by national rivalry. Besides, the Austro-German socialists' programmes before the First World War had a cosmopolitan and humanitarian complexion. The Czech worker was more nationalist if only because German was regarded as the language of the feudal and absolutist oppressors. This tendency was, however, firmly contained, at least among those who were politically organized. Membership of trade unions, party and workers' cultural organizations gave the Czech working men both a more tolerant attitude and a profounder insight into the inter-relationship

[1] Cf. Heinrich Friedjung, *Der Kampf um die Vorherrschaft in Deutschland 1859 bis 1866*, Vol. II, Stuttgart 1900; Count Beust, *Aus Drei Viertel-Jahrhunderten*, Vol. II, Stuttgart 1887.

which exists between social and political matters. A common international outlook developed on both the German and the Czech side and was the basis of the party political co-operation already mentioned.

From the end of the nineteenth century it seemed much more necessary for the nationalist forces to check socialism as an effective democratic force developing a new type of loyalty.[1] The socialists were accused of treason. An attempt was, therefore, made to stir in them the feeling of an older loyalty, one rooted in tradition. On the whole, however, it can be said that the nationalists' attempt failed to suppress socialism from within in the way they had undermined liberalism.

It was impossible for a supra-national class solidarity to develop among the middle classes. It must be borne in mind that the predominant feature of central Europe at that time was the small town community, usually dominated by a small clique consisting of the doctor, the priest, the schoolmaster, the chemist, the postmaster and possibly a rich farmer. But for the small shopkeeper or second-hand dealer, whose life was confined to his own narrow circle and had no trade union, economic rivalry from German competition easily turned into national rivalry as well. It was so much easier for him to be content with the attitude that went with it as it made no claims on his intelligence, and nationalism gave him an excuse to extend his circle of customers.

In other words the individual middle-class national groups felt not only politically threatened but also found themselves faced with economic competition. This was partly the reason why the maintenance of either the Czech or German linguistic character of a town was a matter of life or death – and therefore a cause of the most violent feelings. When in addition the new working class was politically active these cliques, who wielded power in the small towns, tended towards a rabid jingoism.

Thus the most uncompromising chauvinistic parties originated in the middle classes. Just when the way was being prepared for a reconciliation between the moderate Old Czechs under the leadership of men like Dr Rieger and the German-Austrians led by genuine liberals like Dr Fischlrof, the vociferous and coarse boulevard patriotism of the pan-German groups dominated by Georg von Schönerer, Karl Hermann Wolf and others on the one hand[2] and the Young Czech Party on the

[1] Cf. Paul Molisch (editor), *Geschichte der deutschnationalen Bewegung in Österreich*, Jena 1926; Rudolf Sieghart, *Die letzten Jahrzehnte einer Grossmacht*, Berlin 1932, p. 53; cf. also Henry Wickham Steed, *The Habsburg Monarchy*, London, Edinburgh 1914.

[2] Cf., for instance, Otto Hornung, *Neu-Österreich*, Zürich 1890; Herweg (E. Diehl), *Georg Schönerer und die Entwicklung des Alldeutschtums der Ostmark*, Vol. I, Vienna 1921–35.

other destroyed all chance of any genuine compromise.[1] In particular it was the Nationalist Party with its pan-German outlook, its extremism and its aggressive demeanour towards other Austrian nationalities, its vulgar anti-Semitism and its anti-Christian, neo-pagan sympathies, which became both the grave-digger of Austria and the forerunner of national socialism.

One of the gravest mistakes of the Vienna government was that, although not in principle approving of the nationalist extremists, it was never able to act energetically against them. Thus German-Czech relations in Austria remained permanently poisoned. It was only after the spirit of hatred and an irresponsible propaganda had infected large numbers of people that Austria decided to introduce universal suffrage. The immediate result was the defeat of the nationalist elements, brought about by the moderate workers and peasants who limited the power of the middle class. But it was already too late.

Even more complicated was the problem of overlapping loyalties because of religious differences. On the Czech side the urban middle classes were partly Protestant or, because of their special Hussite tradition, positively favoured Protestantism, while the Czech peasants, especially in Moravia, were strict Catholics. In Hungary the issue was the opposition between the peasants' Catholicism and the Calvinism of sections of the lesser nobility. Finally, in the case of the Southern Slavs, Romanians and Italians, the whole complex was overlaid by loyalties to a national monarchy outside the sphere of the Habsburg empire.

It was well known that even Germany, although linguistically almost homogeneous, was not spared these conflicts of loyalty. The agricultural east and north was opposed to the industrial west, the Catholic south to the Protestant north, the liberal west and south to the autocratic east. Prussian centralism was to oppose the federalism of other states; and the socialists, though they wished for a united empire, opposed the monarchy. The memory of dynastic and religious wars, like the struggle between reaction and liberalism, continued to exert an influence. Even within the Socialist Party a latent conflict between patriotism and internationalism became evident. The Emperor William II refused to recognize Social Democracy as a German party and advised their members quite bluntly to get out of Germany. Yet he was far from being right. Their spirit was indeed alien to his system but not to other German traditions. Social democrats were then, as they are today, fond of citing the proverb that the country's poorest son eventually proved to be its most faithful one.

[1] R. W. Seton-Watson, *A History of the Czechs and Slovaks*, London 1943, pp. 186 ff.; Joseph Redlich, *Kaiser Franz-Josef von Österreich*, A biography, Berlin 1928.

Immediately after the outbreak of the First World War patriotism did in fact gain the upper hand for a while, but in the course of the war a split developed in the party over the question of war credits.[1]

The conflict of loyalties assumed an unusual form in Poland. The partition of Poland between Prussia, Russia and Austria in the eighteenth century caused Polish patriots to turn to France in the first instance. When France failed to help the Poles recover their freedom, many people pinned their hopes on Germany, others on Austria and yet others on Russia. This was to some extent a reaction to the fact that, at the time of the so-called triple loyalty, demands were made on the Poles to accept the situation and remain loyal to their lords and masters. Religious loyalties were a factor in Bismarck's *Kulturkampf*, which was directed against Catholicism and in particular against the Roman Catholic Polish peasants. Further cause for conflict finally came from the clash between the political orientation to Russia and religious faith in Roman Catholicism. In Poland this always proved to be a counter attraction and a counterweight to pan-Slavism.

## PART SIX
*Attempt at a Synthesis*

To find a reasonable solution to these complicated and involved conflicts was an utterly impossible task. Various attempts to find a compromise were made, especially by circles under the influence of Western thinkers such as John Stuart Mill, Herbert Spencer and Auguste Comte. Masaryk in particular in Czechoslovakia and Limanowski in Poland were in the forefront of this movement. Their efforts to work out a compromise are important in as much as these were adopted as an official peace programme by the Allies in the First World War. These efforts found expression in the peace treaties; they were also to some extent part of the basic concept of the League of Nations, as expressed by President Woodrow Wilson.[2] Masaryk and Limanowski held views which were almost identical. Limanowski considered it impossible to carry out the social revolution without first winning political freedom. He therefore gave first priority to the fight for independence. He regarded patriotism as the most important bond linking human

[1] Cf. Joseph Berlau, *The German Social Democratic Party 1914–1921*, New York 1949; Ossip K. Flechtheim, *Die KPD in der Weimaren Republik*, Offenbach 1948; cf. also Herman Heidegger, *Die deutsche Sozialdemokratic und der nationale Staat, 1870–1920*, Göttingen 1956.

[2] But the idea of a League of Nations is the child of more renowned ancestors, in particular Kant.

communities; to kill this sentiment is to destroy the independence of the national organism, which is then swallowed up by neighbouring nations. Other Polish socialists also incorporated this theory into their own programmes; every nation should belong to a fellowship of nations, each respecting in others what it wished to secure for itself.

In this Limanowski was clearly going back to the ideas of John Stuart Mill, as can be seen from the following quotation from the English philosopher: 'It is in general a necessary condition of free institutions that the boundlessness of free government should coincide in the main with those of nationalities', and further: 'One hardly knows what any division of the human race should be free to do – if not to decide with which of the various bodies of human beings they should associate themselves.'

Masaryk – undoubtedly superior to Limanowski as a thinker – reached similar conclusions. In 1915, in his inaugural lecture at King's College, London, he pointed out that in Europe there were twenty-eight states but sixty-two different nationalities. But while recognizing the many and different nationalities he did not think nationalism must necessarily conflict with internationalism if the main principles of the French Revolution – *Liberté* and *Egalité* – were also recognized as applying to nations. That amounted basically to acceptance of the transformation of Austria-Hungary into a federation. But towards the end of the war Masaryk changed his opinion. In his book, *The New Europe and the Slav Viewpoint*, published in Washington in 1918, he again spoke out against the continued existence of the Habsburg monarchy. The policy of the Central Powers, he argued, amounted simply to a German advance into the territory of the small nations. In the sixteenth century the threat from Turkey had led to the voluntary unification of Austria, Bohemia and Hungary, but the Habsburgs had subsequently misused this union.

However it was often said in Allied circles at the time that the abolition of the Habsburg monarchy and the subsequent unification of the Empire with German-Austria would mean a strengthening of Prussian militarism, which the democrats certainly wanted to crush. Masaryk's argument against this was a simple arithmetical calculation: is Germany more dangerous with an addition of seven million German-Austrians or while it disposes of the fifty million inhabitants of the Austro-Hungarian monarchy? In this view the dismemberment of the Habsburg monarchy would be the greatest blow to Prussian Germany.

How had Masaryk, who in the pre-war years had stood out not only as a fearless protagonist of democracy but also of the federalization of Austria-Hungary, come to adopt this extreme nationalist point of view? Kann has proved definitely that no trace of reservations about the continued existence of the Habsburg monarchy is to be found in either Masaryk's or Beneš' pre-war writings.[1]

Masaryk's Realist Party approved, on the whole, of the federalist programme of Austrian social democracy. On the other hand the Realists complained that the German origin of social democracy made it impossible for this party to imagine the proposed democratic federation of the Austrian nation as anything but a convenient pretext for perpetuating the long-standing dominance of German-speaking nations in central Europe.[2]

The Czech *irredenta* in the First World War had some historical roots that sprang from the delays and frustrations which the cumbersome structure of the Danubian monarchy imposed on the aspiring and expansive nationalism of the West Slav peoples. The unsuccessful attempts of the Hohenwart-Schläffle and the Badeni governments to give the Czechs legal and linguistic equality with the Germans of Austria – attempts which were invariably thwarted by the opposition of the Germans (not only of the extreme nationalist but also of the liberal nationalist elements) – reinforced and intensified Czech nationalism, which was not averse to separatism. The Emperor Francis Joseph had twice entrusted this crucial problem to the ultra-conservative nobles, the only group which, in view of his own basic ideas about monarchy, he considered to have any sense of responsibility. He had twice shied off trying to find a solution to the problem out of consideration for the resistance which these measures provoked through reasons of foreign and domestic policy.

Later the extremely efficient and fair-minded Premier, H. Körber, with his compromise solution of dividing up the empire into lingually homogeneous districts, also came to nought because of the intransigence of nationalists on both sides. All this could certainly not inspire optimism in the Czech Realist Party which Masaryk had founded with Beneš and which, in the years before the First World War, was notable for its determined belief in the power and influence of democratic principles and the blessings of universal suffrage.[3]

Attempts at a synthesis between nationalism and democracy were, however, also made in circles among the Central Powers, who regarded the war as the starting point for a better, liberal Europe – in fact for a Europe which was, as usual, to be culturally and economically

[1] Kann, op. cit., Vol. I, p. 215; Kann refers to E. Beneš, *Der Aufstand der Nationen*, Berlin 1928, p. 5 onwards.

[2] T. G. Masaryk, *Das neue Europa*, Berlin 1922, pp. 65 ff. Masaryk complained that, in this respect, there was no difference between Social Democrats like Renner, Bauer and the pan-Germans.

[3] E. Beneš, *Der Aufstand der Nationen*, op. cit., p. 5; see, too, his thesis *Le problème autrichien et la question tchèque*, Paris 1908.

dominated by Germany.[1] According to Naumann's conception of a large Central Europe the German-Austrian-Hungarian economic region was to become the nucleus of a great power which would rank as the equal of other great powers such as America, the British Empire and Russia. All the same Naumann realized that there was a difference between the need for a large economic region and the desire to Germanize the Slav peoples. And so he expressly demanded the gradual separation of the national state from the economic and the military state.[2] He dreamed of a Central European Union limited to only three constitutional authorities – a common economic authority with a common customs frontier, a common defence system and a common foreign policy. The peoples' support for this plan was to be won by far-reaching liberal concessions and a large measure of national autonomy.

If Masaryk's position corresponded to what is seen to be a general tendency in favour of liberalism and democracy, his abandonment of the earlier, more comprehensive concept to embrace the idea of pure nationalism was due to the distrust which he felt towards the ruling circles in the Central Powers. This distrust was confirmed by his conversation with the Austrian reform politician, Körber, shortly before he, Masaryk, left the country. To Masaryk's question whether a victorious Austria would carry out national and democratic reforms, Körber replied: 'No, victory would strengthen the *ancien régime* . . . the military would get the upper hand and they would centralize and Germanize. It would be absolutism with parliamentary trimmings.' – 'And' asked Masaryk, 'will Berlin be wise enough to force its allies to accept reforms?' Körber's answer was: 'Hardly.'[3]

Masaryk's political programme also sprang from a view which was typical at the time. He himself had adopted Herbert Spencer's optimistic belief in the evolution of humanity. This belief was further strengthened in him by the metaphysical assumption that the majority nations had a divine mission which would solve the racial problems. In multilingual regions, Masaryk thought nations had a claim to independence and, at the same time, a duty to protect the minorities, who should be content with a status of national autonomy. In addition there was the optimistic hope that the increasing fragmentation of Europe was conducive to economic and technological co-operation. Since then history has taught us better. New European nations were created which strove to achieve cultural and economic autarchy, to the detriment of their peoples and of Europe. Autarchy rarely promotes harmony.

---

[1] Friedrich Naumann, *Mitteleuropa*, Berlin 1915, especially Chaps. VI and XII.
[2] Ibid., p. 249.
[3] T. G. Masaryk, *The Making of a State*, London 1927, pp. 43 ff. Cf. also Kann, op. cit., Vol. I, p. 140.

Similar hopes also inspired the idea of the League of Nations, which undoubtedly achieved a certain amount of good. But it was clear that the whole edifice would collapse if the ideological foundation ever proved fragile. Above all, the principle of self-determination clashed with the theory of the free national state. The nationalities which formed these democratic national states were so intermingled one with another that no clear frontiers could be drawn. If every nationality had been granted the right of self-determination complete anarchy would have reigned in central Europe. If, however, they were denied this right they could complain, not without reason, that the national state was merely another form of tyranny, even if it enjoyed the free institutions that go with democracy.

The concepts underlying both the peace treaties and the League of Nations are an attempt to strike a synthesis between nationalism and democracy, therefore between nationalism and internationalism. The League of Nations was built up on the premise that only anyone who, in the first place, is still aware of his national heritage can properly champion international ideas.[1] But this synthesis sprang from an incorrect assessment of nationalism, the radical nature of which was nothing new. It simply amounted to an organic continuation of stirrings which had already existed in the nineteenth century, that is to say the transformation of liberal nationalism into integral nationalism, which regarded nations as battle groups. Even in nations where the humanitarian idea of the League of Nations had taken root there was a profound difference between theory and practice.

Thus we came increasingly to be spectators of an ever-deepening tragedy, in which the League of Nations changed, turning into an institution in which the delegates wore a sanctimonious expression on their faces and paid lip-service to international co-operation, while acting purely in their own national interests.

This does not mean that the League of Nations contained no people inspired by high ideals or seriously interested in the development of reconciliation between peoples; but they were engaged in a hopeless struggle against the solid front of adherents of the unadulterated idea of the national sovereign state. The League of Nations suffered the whole time from the radical application of the principle on which it was based. All too often it had to set limits to the national egoism of its member states in their inter-state relations. Furthermore, it had to cope with the fight which the national minorities had to wage for their own self-preservation inside and against these member states.

[1] Cf. Alfred E. Zimmermann, *Nationality and Government*, London 1919, especially his two articles 'True and False Nationalism' and 'The Passing of Nationality'.

The complaints of the minorities may often have been somewhat exaggerated. But to focus attention on these exaggerations would be to misunderstand the real problem. The real reason for the difficulties was not that the minorities were badly treated but that they remained, as before, minorities – only this time within a pure national state. The national state, accepted in principle by the League of Nations, insisted on assimilation of other lingual groups and unification of its territory and it therefore denied the small national minorities the right of self-determination. At the same time the other principle, to which the League of Nations owed its existence, demanded that minorities should have the right themselves to determine whether they wanted to leave a union of states unacceptable to them and to found their own national states. The deeper cause for the collapse of the League of Nations is the inherent contradiction existing between the League's own principles.

It is often assumed that the end of the First World War marks a turning point in the treatment of nationalities. History, however, has proved this view to be wrong; the problems remained the same. The Austro-Hungarian monarchy perished because it neither wanted to become a federal state composed of nationalities; nor could it grow into a centralized state. For many centuries the Habsburgs tried to compromise, only to see, on the death-bed of the monarchy, that there was no *via media*.

After 1918 new dramatis personae appeared on the scene but the plot was unchanged. The new states felt obliged to fulfil the role of national states but they could not form the desired united front as, in every case, they contained more than one national community. Here, too, the way out was held to be a *via media*, a compromise between a federal state which, like Switzerland, is made up of several nationalities and a national state like France. In those Succession states the main lines of policy did not differ substantially from those which had proved so futile in Austria-Hungary. The only progress towards democracy was, perhaps, that now majorities ruled minorities instead of *vice versa*. But these minorities, which were now condemned to live in other national states, could not adapt themselves to the new conditions.

Now the destructive force of this principle revealed itself in its full strength. It was bound to have a particularly devastating effect in central Europe, with its intermixture of races and languages, where multilateral conflicts of loyalty persisted. The central European dilemma was that the principle – partly applied – was inevitably bound to be oppressive and tyrannical; while its absolute realization was bound to result in the utter disintegration of the communities, and therefore in international anarchy. When, therefore, authoritarian regimes appeared on the scene it was this very situation which provided them with a source of propaganda material and their greatest strategic advantages.

More than anyone else, T. G. Masaryk symbolized this gradual evolution from liberal to integral nationalism. As a politician in the Austrian parliament he had done much to promote the cause of mutual understanding between the nationalities of the Habsburg monarchy. When it came to the point, however, he came out in favour of national sovereignty for the peoples of the Habsburg state. His attitude towards the new Russia is a further ground for the assumption that he lacked historical foresight. It does not apply to him as it did to Beneš, that he championed the West when he had to and helped Russia when he could. However, the alliance made by the democratic West and Russia from the momentary need to conduct the war was accepted by Masaryk as an unalterable fact. The existence of Czechoslovakia as an independent state was nevertheless inconceivable without this permanent alliance between the West and Russia.

During the negotiations in St Paul's Church in Frankfurt and in the Kremsier Parliament, the Russian-Polish Count Valerian Krasinski, clearly under the influence of the Pan-Slav Congress in Prague, had written his book *Pan-Slav and Germanism*,[1] in which he advocated the formation of a West Slav confederation, including Poland, under a Habsburg. He considered this plan to be the only alternative to a pan-Slav Russian Empire.[2] According to Krasinski's plan, German-Austria was at the same time to be part of the German Empire and become the link between Germany and a predominantly West-Slav Habsburg monarchy. These two empires might well remain linked by close political and economic ties but not by any relationship based on individual independence.[3] At the same time, however, he warned Germany's politicians that any attempt to subjugate the West Slavs would drive these into the arms of Russian pan-Slavism. For central Europe this involved a concept which probably did not go as far as Naumann's but had a similar plan.

The span of time now separating us from that epoch enables us to see with more detachment the forces which were then at play. The attempt to find a synthesis between nationalism and democracy and internationalism, which was to be realized in practice by means of federalism, was doomed to failure from the outset because of

[1] Edinburgh 1849, see Kann, op. cit., Vol. II, pp. 18 ff.
[2] Krasinski, op. cit., pp. 309 ff.
[3] Ibid., pp. 327 f.

the emergence of a clear alternative programme in keeping with the national passions of pan-Germanism and pan-Slavism. As far as pan-Germanism is concerned this would have presupposed, by official imperial policy on the part of Germany, an expansion eastward based on the German minorities in the Russian Empire. There is little evidence that anyone in the Hohenzollern empire, whose relationship with Tsarist Russia was cordial to the very last, ever seriously contemplated such a possibility. Even Germany's support for Austria's Balkan policy before the First World War was given reluctantly and with considerable hesitation. There was definitely a pan-German group in both Germany and Austria. But its influence was never great and its aim was certainly not to extend German influence and expand into Slav areas. It strove rather for national consolidation in those regions where it had been predominant for a very long time. Partly for these reasons the Austrian pan-Germans did try to bring about the abandonment of Galicia and Dalmatia by Austria. By very reason of their racial policy the pan-Germans could not possibly have been considered expansionist, but much rather aristocratic and exclusive.

Austria's opposition to pan-Slavism had nothing to do with pan-Germanism. It was just the opposite. The efforts to preserve the Danube monarchy as a supranational empire was, however, bound to lead to a clash with a new form of pan-Slavism which had diverged greatly from the aims set by Palacký and Krasinski and allowed itself to become the instrument of the nationalist Russian 'drive to the west'.

Brandenburg has pertinently observed that this is one of the main causes of the First World War: 'Equally dangerous [as German–French tension as a basic cause of the First World War] was the antagonism between Russia and Austria, which had its roots largely in the efforts of the Slav great power Russia to obtain control of the Bosphorus and the Dardanelles and achieve supremacy in the Balkan peninsula.' The imperial state on the Danube did not want to sever completely its access to the Aegean Sea, nor allow itself to be encircled by Russia and her satellites.[1] There were, however, important internal reasons for these external ambitions on the part of Austria:

'In any case Austrian statesmen always lived in a state of great anxiety because they felt the growing strength of the centrifugal tendencies inside Austria-Hungary. They saw the moment approaching when they would no longer be able to control them. They believed that any loss of prestige in foreign policy, or any sign of softness

[1] Erich Brandenburg, *Die Ursachen des Weltkrieges*, Leipzig 1925, p. 12.

and weakness towards the small Slav states on their southern frontier would embolden these powers to act, and would therefore be fatal to the continuation of the monarchy. In Vienna the government was at a complete loss to know how to deal with the national problem. In spite of its preference for peace, Austria was extremely nervous and uneasy because it clearly felt the ferment of the volcanic, subterranean forces which were at work. It was well aware of the *close links which existed between its internal irredenta on the one hand and Serbia and Russia on the other*. Thus when the effect of these subterranean forces was brought home to them with terrible clarity by the assassination of the heir to the throne in Sarajevo . . . it was possible that Count Berchthold and his colleagues panicked and took unwise and desperate steps which were not, however, inspired by the desire to start a war so much as by fear of being completely annihilated through failure to take steps for their self-defence in good time.'[1]

Was Russia now really becoming the exponent of an aggressive pan-Slavism which encouraged the West Slav peoples to strike the decisive blow against the Danube monarchy? In the case of Serbia that is probably so. Pan-Serbian efforts designed to effect a union of all South Slavs were bound seriously to undermine the loyalty of the great Croatian-Sloventian – Dalmatian-Serbian racial groups inside Austria-Hungary. Yet Austria-Hungary was also especially vulnerable because the ambitious plans of its enlightened reformers were unable to overcome the conservatism of the Emperor Francis Joseph. The reformers included the heir to the throne, Francis Ferdinand, and the political writers closely connected with his plans, Karl Renner and Aurel Popovici, who wanted to give the South Slavs living in the Danube monarchy equality with the Germans and the Magyars. It was not only the Court which rejected their plans; they also encountered the most violent opposition from the pan-German elements and the Magyar nationalists. But the pan-Slav elements also hated the reforms, since they feared that a reasonable solution of the nationality problems would mean the end of their own plans. Thus the heir to the throne, Francis Ferdinand, had to die at Sarajevo not because he was an enemy but because he was a friend of the Slavs. His projected Danube federation would have made Colonel Apis's pan-Serbian conspiracy impossible.

Joseph Redlich, who must be credited with having a particularly penetrating foresight, wrote in 1912: 'I see the Balkan situation as being very serious for Austria, as always. We either yield to the

[1] Ibid., pp. 46 f.

pressure of events and allow Greater Serbia to be formed, in which case we lose Bosnia and perhaps Croatia too, as soon as Russia thinks the time is ripe and has armed sufficiently. Or we impose a customs union on Serbia, in which case she will reject it and force us into war with the Balkan states and Russia . . . In Parliament it is also openly said of the Czechs and South Slavs that these people cannot be relied upon in a war against the Slav states. The Archduke Francis Ferdinand, as always, wants peace. Now it might be thought that if we came to meet the Serbs half way the monarchy would be able to appear as a strong centre of attraction . . . But, to my mind, that is impossible because Magyar rule in Hungary will resist any pro-South-Slav policy on the part of the monarchy as it has always done.'[1]

Was the attempt to find a synthesis between nationalism on the one hand and democracy and internationalism on the other a genuine one, or does it, in the light of the source material, appear to be a mere means to an end in the hands of a large state animated by nationalism based on race? At the beginning of the First World War, when T. G. Masaryk in his English exile directed the activities which were to culminate in the destruction of the Danube monarchy, he was ready to accept Kramář's idea of putting a Russian Grand Duke on the Bohemian throne: 'The Bohemian people, that must be emphasized once more, are thoroughly Russophile. A Russian dynasty, in whatever form, would be most popular. At any rate the Bohemian politicians wish the establishment of the kingdom of Bohemia in full accordance with Russia. Russia's wishes and plans will be of determinating influence.'[2]

While Masaryk energetically represented his people's right of self-determination he was perfectly willing to make concessions at the expense of other people. Thus even the Sudeten Germans, who included the most rabidly nationalistic Germans in Austria, were to remain under the rule of a Czech majority.[3] Constantinople, which was certainly not populated by Russians, was to go to Russia. Turkey was to be wiped off the map.[4] Masaryk had little sympathy for the people languishing under Tsarist Russia: the majority of these nations, so his argument went, were uneducated and their national consciousness hardly developed.[5]

[1] Joseph Redlich, *Tagebuch, Österreichs Schicksalsjahre 1908–1910*, Graz, Cologne 1953, Vol. I, p. 165.
[2] R. W. Seton-Watson, *Masaryk in England*, Cambridge 1943, p. 133, quoted by Wenzel Jaksch, op. cit., p. 131.
[3] T. G. Masaryk, *Die Weltrevolution*, Berlin 1927, p. 7.
[4] Seton-Watson, op. cit., p. 192.
[5] T. G. Masaryk, *Das neue Europa*, op. cit., p. 31.

This already revealed the inner contradictions in the national-democratic solution, contradictions which were destined to ruin the Paris peace negotiations *ab initio* and deprive the League of Nations of any equitable basis.

# CHAPTER III

# The Constitutional State and Society

## PART ONE

### *Legislature and Proportional Representation*

Like many other democratic institutions the representative system originated in the idea of local self-government. The representative to the estates of the Middle Ages stood primarily for the city or estate which had chosen him to act on its behalf. But Burke in his address to the electors of Bristol voiced quite another theory of representation. His view was that a deputy, although elected by his constituency, represented the people as a whole. Whether he does his job properly is entirely a matter for his own conscience.

A third concept goes back to the English and American caucus system, according to which the deputy represents, in the first instance, his party, to which he owes allegiance. No doubt this struck Joseph Chamberlain and the liberals of Birmingham as a novel and convenient means of improving their party organization; for it tightened up party discipline and thus, the two-party system. On the other hand it also ran the danger of over-emphasizing narrow party interests. A deputy's one-sided attachment to party interests might easily lead to the closed curia system of the Middle Ages. Delegates would no longer be representatives in the true sense of the word but ambassadors at a conference of hostile powers. Instead of the three kinds of political representation usually accepted by political theory we shall find there are only two, namely community representation as Burke understood it and representation of local or vocational groups within the community.

In England proportional representation was first advocated by Thomas Hare. John Stuart Mill[1] – the representative of radical liberalism – also favoured this system. The idea behind these proposals for reforming the franchise was that the majority voting system

---

[1] J. S. Mill, *On Liberty and Considerations of Representative Government*, Oxford 1948, pp. 189 ff.

in single-member constituencies gives the majority an unfair advantage over minorities and that the distribution of seats in parliament will not reflect the real will of the people. In Belgium proportional representation was recommended by Victor d'Hondt and eventually introduced there. From Belgium it spread over the whole continent of Europe with grave consequences. In Britain, however, it was not adopted, as men of political foresight and imagination were alive to its defects. Thus Bagehot came to the conclusion that while this system does ensure fairer representation for all groups in the country, the price – rule by an unrestricted number of parties – is too high. Sidgewick[1] realized that proportional representation would turn parliament into a confused congress of the most diverse interests and associations. He forecast a parliament consisting of 'Total abstainers, Anti-Vivisectionists, Anti-Vaccinationists' and so on. In France Esmein[2] prophesied that proportional representation would lead to chaos and anarchy.

Closely linked with the problem of proportional representation is the question of the real character of parliamentary parties. In Anglo-Saxon countries a 'party' is taken to mean an organization of voters supporting certain sets of policies arising out of particular issues of public interest. In *Modern Democracies* Bryce noted that the idea underlying the word 'party' had a different meaning in France, where no political parties existed before the French Revolution. Here theory came before practice. When the monarchy fell there were only abstract doctrines and no practical basis for the party system.

According to Lowell[3] 'parties are based chiefly on political, philosophical, religious, racial or social traditions, not as in Anglo-Saxon countries on a difference of opinion on current public questions . . . The fact that an Englishman voted for Conservatives in 1895 from a dislike to Home Rule, is no reason why he should not vote for the Liberals in 1905 because he dreads preferential tariffs.'

Lowell saw that on the Continent the question whether a voter changed his party allegiance from one election to the next depended very little on the performance of the ruling party. In his view ideological questions play a far greater role. In the Weimar Republic, for example, it was unlikely that an industrial worker who was a member of the Free Trade Unions would vote for the German Nationalists or the German People's Party or that a retired general would opt for the Social Democrats. Where such a case had become

[1] H. Sidgewick, *The Elements of Politics*, London, New York 1897, p. 396.

[2] A. Esmein, *Eléments du Droit Constitutionnel Français et Comparé*, Paris 1927.

[3] A. Lawrence Lowell, *Public Opinion and Popular Government*, New York. London, Bombay, Calcutta, Madras 1919, p. 80.

public knowledge, it was thought of in terms of political 'treachery' or 'trimming'. It would mean a loss of self-respect. In central Europe the notion of a political party originated from that of the Church, to 'betray' an ideological party was thus tantamount to apostasy. The religious differences of the past still shaped the concept of parties as 'ideological camps'. Aretin has pointed out that, in the dying days of the old Empire, voting in parliament was along denominational lines, making a change of party on the part of the voter difficult to imagine.[1] The voter's ideology had to collapse before he was willing to opt for another party, quite apart from such matters as morality, efficiency, skill and the success of the government and opposition parties.[2]

Party structure was also affected by the absolute majority system with a second ballot of the Hohenzollern empire. It prevented the formation of large parties and led to the multi-party system in Germany. From the time of Bismarck this voting system allowed the semi-authoritarian state to conduct a 'policy of changing majorities' and later gave rise to the demand for proportional representation.

A typical example of German traditional distrust of parliamentary rule as a device for forming the national will is Thoma, who though a staunch friend of democracy, still expressed grave doubts whether the parliamentary majority would tolerate the minority. He was convinced that a socialist Reichstag majority would change into a proletarian, a middle-class majority into a fascist dictatorship. Proportional representation seemed, therefore, to be a safety device for the benefit of democracy[3] – to keep majorities weak.

Proportional representation rarely produces a stable one-party majority in parliament and thus leads either to government instability or to a continuous succession of coalition governments. But since the duration of a coalition government – and it is not only the history of France and Italy which shows this – depends on a precarious balance of the many and diversified interests and wishes of the coalition partners, frequent cabinet changes are the normal result of proportional representation. The voter, however, is powerless to influence these cabinet changes; for when a coalition government is being formed party bosses slip in between electors and deputies, robbing them of their influence on the formation of a government.[4]

[1] Karl Othmar, Freiherr von Aretin, *Die Konfessionen als politische Kräfte im Ausgang des alten Reiches*, Baden-Baden 1957.

[2] F. Glenn, op. cit., pp. 52 ff.

[3] Richard Thoma, 'Das Reich als Demokratie', *Handbuch des deutschen Staatsrechts*, edited by Anschütz and Thoma, Tübingen 1930, Vol. I, pp. 186 ff.

[4] Back in 1918 Max Weber spoke of the voluntary character of the party system of politics,' *Gesammelte politische Schriften*, op. cit., p. 389.

As Hermens[1] rightly remarks, proportional representation destroys the effects of the mutual interaction of majority and opposition. The minority (opposition) voices constructive criticism in the hope of convincing marginal voters of its greater integrity and ability and of its chances of winning the next elections. Lowell pointed out that, under proportional representation, changes in public opinion are rarer for the reasons stated above. Nevertheless they do occur. If, however, these amount to a 'landslide' – which commonly happens under the majority voting system – they take on a revolutionary or quasi-revolutionary character. In Germany the economic crisis between 1928 and 1930 led to a shift of this sort; the number of seats won by the extreme right- and left-wing parties increased considerably.[2] Under a majority voting system the electors would as usual have reacted to the government's inefficient handling of economic difficulties by turning to the parliamentary opposition and the government would have had to take this into account. Therefore the 1930 election results and the 'landslide' which these caused would scarcely have been felt to be revolutionary in England.

Hermens made an important contribution to our understanding of the fall of the Weimar Republic when, with the help of calculations based on the official statistics for the Reichstag elections of September 1930,[3] he proved conclusively that the dynamics of proportional representation produced a revolutionary landslide caused by the economic depression. According to the statistics the number of seats of the parties listed below totalled:

| | |
|---|---|
| National Socialists | 107 |
| German National Party | 41 |
| Country People's Party | 19 |
| German People's Party | 30 |
| Bavarian People's Party | 23 |
| Centre Party | 68 |
| State Party | 20 |
| Social Democrats | 143 |
| Communists | 77 |

In a franchise system based on the relative majority principle the number of votes would have been the equivalent of about 400 delegates, the Social Democrats would have remained the largest party, with a relative majority in 186 constituencies followed by the Centre

---

[1] F. A. Hermens, *Demokratie oder Anarchie*, Frankfurt 1951, pp. 61 ff.

[2] Ibid, p. 191. The National Socialists' seats jumped from 12 in 1928 to 107 in 1930, the Communists' from 54 to 77.

[3] *Stastistik des Deutschen Reiches*, Vol. 232, quoted by Hermens, op. cit., p. 201.

Party and the Bavarian People's Party, which would then have had a relative majority in 110 constituencies. The National Socialists on the other hand could have pointed to a relative majority in only 48 constituencies and the Communists in only 41. The number of seats of Hugenberg's National Party would have dropped to 8, while the German Liberal Party would have disappeared from the Reichstag.

Before this proportional representation had already helped to ensure the victory of fascism in Italy. Just as it had in other countries, proportional representation led to party disintegration and government instability which ultimately weakened the cabinet system and enabled the Fascists to seize power.[1]

On the pretext of preventing a 'tyranny of the majority' and protecting the political minority the advocates of proportional representation are really thinking more of the narrower interests of their own group.[2] Once, however, such a minority becomes a majority it is no longer interested in proportional representation. The Social Democratic Party was an exception which proves the rule. This party had, of course, been handicapped by the absolute majority system, which had weakened its representation in the Reichstag in proportion to its electoral strength. If, after 1918, it had succeeded in introducing the majority system, it would have been sure of a stable majority by itself[3] or with some other single partner anxious to protect the democratic republic, such as the Centre Party or the Democratic Party. In the hope of making a greater impact in bigger constituencies and spurred on by a sense of orthodoxy,[4] this party – the most influential one in the Weimar Republic – nevertheless clung doggedly to proportional representation.

It is probably true to say that in the Weimar Republic, even under the majority vote system, there would have been more than two parties because of the peculiar German territorial, social, religious, racial and ideological structure.[5] For the sake of fairness it should not be forgotten that under the majority system of Bismarck's Reich there had been only three influential groups – the Conservatives, who were allied to the National Liberals, the Centre Party and the Social Democrats, who frequently made agreements with the Progressive Party. By wanting to protect the political minorities against the

[1] F. A. Hermens, op. cit., pp. 141 ff., especially p. 155.
[2] George Horwill, *Proportional Representation*, London 1925, p. 11.
[3] F. A. Hermens, op. cit., p. 167.
[4] Cf. G. Leibholz, *Strukturprobleme der modernen Demokratie*, Karlsruhe 1958, pp. 9 f. He expresses the opinion that the introduction of proportional representation was a consequence of the mass democratic demand for equality of franchise.
[5] Hugo Preuss, quoted in Friedrich Glum, *Das parlamentarische Regierungssystem in Deutschland und Frankreich*, Berlin 1950, p. 71.

majorities by the device of proportional representation the authors of
the Weimar Constitution converted the Reichstag into a chaotic debating society, one in which not only the political parties but also
economic pressure groups and other combinations made their voices
heard. Thus all kinds of concealed economic interests were represented in the Reichstag. Friedrich Naumann had warned[1] that proportional representation would exclude stable parliamentary majorities.
His forebodings of evil were surpassed by actual facts. Not only
were there disputes between the political parties, but the individual
groups also carried on internal fights of their own. The result was
the sort of chaos which is always fertile soil for authoritarian intrigues.
Max Weber foresaw these consequences when he observed that
bureaucracy – and he knew a great deal about German bureaucracy –
would exploit this chaos and these conflicts and by a skilful use of
patronage play one material interest off against another. Sidgewick's
prophecy also proved true. An anti-drink party, a war-invalids' and
survivors' party, a landlords', peasants' and winegrowers' league, a
Saxon country people's party etc. contested the Reichstag elections.[2]
It was hardly surprising that this anarchy in party political life
discredited parliamentary democracy in Germany.

A parliament with this sort of structure makes political moderation
almost impossible. As we have already said, under a majority voting
system it is a democratic party's job to win over the marginal voters,
whom Disraeli described with the flattering phrase 'conscientious
and deeply meditative men'. The voter, for his part, is not likely to
elect a small splinter group which he knows can never become a
ruling party. In central Europe there were even fewer marginal
voters for the simple reason that profound ideological gulfs – increased
by proportional representation – separated the parties. Because ties
of party loyalty bound them to even the smallest groups, a strict
convention had grown up which forbade them from changing party
'like a shirt' from one election to another. Therefore the very people
who represented the moderate element in countries where the majority
voting system was the rule made political moderation quite impossible
under proportional representation.

Under the majority voting system it is not only the marginal voters
who enable a political will to be formed: the various interest groups
which, under the conditions of proportional representation, frequently
bring discredit to democracy also make this possible. The lobby is a
natural result of economic pluralism within constitutional democracy.
The bigger the party the more diverse the people and economic

[1] Theodor Heuss, *Friedrich Naumann*, Stuttgart 1937, pp. 608–10.
[2] Herbert Kraus, *Crisis of German Democracy*, Princeton 1932, p. 146.

interests it embraces; therefore it is far easier to establish the fundamental consensus between the two alternative parties. The two-party
system based on majority voting means that groups with the same outlook and interests are represented in *both* parties. Proportional representation, on the other hand, makes it easier for groups to be
represented in parliament by parties standing for specific interests and
this forces these to take up irreconcilable positions.

In the atmosphere of this kind of particularism deputies desiring
re-election must show themselves to be inflexible in order to acquire
a reputation for strength of character. If intransigent groups of men
meet in parliament they are unlikely to be as polite to one another as
in the British Parliament and not so objective as in the United States
Congress. Personal attacks, insults and even acts of violence and uproar were by no means a rarity in post-war parliaments. Exaggerated
reports in the boulevard press helped to discredit democracy. All
these factors were of grave consequence if only for the simple reason
that democracy was an innovation in central Europe. In Anglo-
Saxon countries or in Switzerland such behaviour by deputies would
reflect upon their party; but in young democracies it tends to discredit the form of government.

From what has been said it follows that proportional representation,
in conjunction with strict party discipline, led to the growth of splinter
parties. Even in 1933 Zürcher noted that while it is very rare for
such parties to grow at the expense of the radical movements they do
attract many moderate electors who would otherwise vote for the
bigger parties.[1] These splinter parties became very important in
Germany after 1930 because Brüning tried to find a majority against
the extremists, the National Socialists and the Communists, and therefore, in tacit agreement with the Social Democrats, formed a cabinet
with the help of the middle-class splinter parties.[2]

When Michels[3] wrote his well-known book he could have had no
inkling that future events would bear out his criticism of political
parties as they did. This criticism was true not only of the socialist but
also of the middle-class parties. Their strong party discipline was
strengthened by proportional representation with its large constituencies and the voting list system. It is true that at least two well-
organized and well-functioning mass democratic parties are the
*conditio sine qua non* for the constitutional state. The question is,

[1] Cf. A. Zürcher, *The Experiment with Democracy in Central Europe*, New York
1933, p. 89.
[2] F. A. Hermens, *Demokratie oder Anarchie*, op. cit., p. 216.
[3] Robert Michels, *Zur Soziologie des Parteiwesens in der modernen Demokratie*,
op. cit.

therefore, whether proportional representation helps to consolidate the large parties.

As we have already explained, mass parties have, significantly, proved to be more stable under the majority voting system, for instance in England and the United States, and in India too. This is due partly to the reasons stated above, partly to the Caesarist element in the British parliament already mentioned by Max Weber and Leibholz which became decisive after the people were enabled to elect the Prime Minister.[1] On the other hand, majority suffrage has a restraining effect on the parties. In the selection of candidates they can give less weight to a candidate's services and work for the party and concentrate more on other factors – for instance his political stature and merits as a citizen – a procedure which is an automatic safeguard against the danger of bureaucratization and ossification of the party machine.

Against this it must be admitted that majority representation as such is no guarantee that the multi-party system will not continue, although it does not favour this. This is shown by political evolution, e.g. in the Third French Republic, or in Pakistan. Even liberal parties (where the choice of candidates can be based on well-known public figures unhampered by large groups with special interests such as trade unions and peasant associations) could under the majority vote system obtain a number of seats which did not correspond to the actual size of the party membership.

## Proportional Representation in the Nationality States of Central Europe

If proportional representation contributed significantly to the downfall of constitutionalism in nationally homogeneous states like Germany, Italy and Austria, it was bound to make constitutional and political development in the linguistically and religiously heterogeneous states of central Europe even more complicated.[2] These states, in fact, inherited not only the parties but also the racial problems of the pre-war

---

[1] Cf. also F. A. Hermens, *Parteien, Volk und Staat*, Karlsruhe 1960, p. 10; Lowell, *The Government of England*, New York 1919, Vol. II, pp. 74 ff. and Karl Löwenstein, 'Soziologie der parlamentarischen Repräsentation in England nach der ersten Reform', *Archiv für Sozialwissenschaft und Politik*, 1924.

[2] In his Essays, Hume distinguishes between three different types of party – based respectively on a common interest, on various principles or on emotion. Parties which are based on religion and nationality belong, by their very nature, to the last group. The so-called Succession States (of Austria-Hungary) had inherited their parties from the pre-war period, when the countries in which they had evolved still belonged to different states. David Hume, *Essays and Treatises on Several Subjects*, Edinburgh 1793, Essay VIII, p. 69.

period. Thus in Czechoslovakia, for example, there was a Czech, a German, a Slovak and a Magyar Catholic Party, just as there was also a Czechoslovak, a German and a Magyar Social Democratic Party, two Agrarian Parties, etc.

A similar problem of stratification existed in Poland and Yugoslavia. It was possible to foresee that national and religious groups of this sort would make the work of the parliaments – already fragmented by the existence of political and economic groups – even more difficult. If democracy had had time to evolve in these states it might have reduced the number of parties. The introduction of proportional representation and the electoral list system was not calculated to produce such a result. In 1920, for example, the Yugoslav parliament consisted of 9 Slovene Liberals, 20 Slovene Clericals, 113 Democrats (most of them Serbians), 69 Radicals (most of them Serbs), 6 Independent Radicals, 10 Montenegrins and 27 Independents.[1] In the 1922 Polish elections the National Christian Union (the clerical party) had won 163 seats. The moderate Peasants' Party won 70, the Radical Peasant Party 55, the Polish Party 6, the Liberation Party 49, the national minorities 66, the Socialists 41, the Jews 18, the Ruthenes 5, the Communists 2, Independents 24, the Peasants' Party 4, National and Workers' Party 18, the left-wing Polish Populists 1.[2]

Horwill had hoped that nations composed of different races which retained a separate outlook and were unlikely to merge into the larger community, and races attached to differing religious beliefs, might find proportional representation useful as a precaution against their divergencies. The exact opposite happened. Linguistically heterogeneous communities also succumb to the dynamics of the electoral system; consequently the fundamental consensus within a community can be established most easily by the two-party system. On the other hand, under a multi-party system, anarchy leading to dictatorship or a coalition system is the only alternative. The formation of coalition will always be more difficult in multi-lingual communities since parties based on differences of race do not usually conform to ordinary party principles; they often remain irreconcilable.

If the majority system were to be adopted in such a state, linguistically heterogeneous parties which were homogeneous in ideology and

---

[1] Malbone W. Graham, *New Governments of Eastern Europe*, London 1928, p. 499; G. Horwill, op. cit., pp. 86 ff.

[2] In the 1920 Czechoslovak elections the Czecho-Slovak Social Democrats in conjunction with the National Social Party won 82 seats, the Agrarians 41, the Catholic Parties 32, the German Social Democrats 34, the Czech National Democrats 19, the German Agrarians 13, the German Catholic Party 9, the Czech Middle Class Party 6, the German Liberals 2, the Hungarian and Slovak Germans 10, the Communists 24 and the Independents 2.

religion would have to form a single party, and racial disputes would have to be thrashed out within the party and so would lose the acrimony which is continuously enhanced by the appeal to the electorate.

Polish and Yugoslav democracy broke down because of the irreconcilability of their national, religious, ideological and regional groups. In Poland it was these very disputes which made Pilsudski's coup possible in 1926. In Yugoslavia the stormy and violent scenes in the Skupština (the National Assembly), where regional questions were of major importance, afforded King Alexander a pretext for instituting his royal dictatorship.

In Czechoslovakia democracy was able to hold its own despite these differences. But it must be remembered that for geographical reasons Czechoslovakia was in an extraordinarily exposed position from the outset and the parties therefore had to do their utmost not to aggravate this critical situation by indulging in squabbles among themselves. The Czech and Slovak parties in particular had every reason to hold together. This constrained them to form coalition governments – with all the attendant advantages and disadvantages. In quest of partners for coalitions the Czech parties were often also obliged to try and include some of the moderate minority groups. In this way, in spite of proportional representation, Czechoslovakia came nearest to the two-party system found in the Anglo-Saxon countries. Three groups of parties evolved, only two of them of any appreciable strength. On the one hand there was the conservative bloc, consisting of the Czech and German Agrarian parties, the party of craftsmen and small shopkeepers and the National Democrats, while the left was made up, once again, of the Czech, German and Hungarian Social Democrats and the National Social Party. Between these two groups stood the Catholic bloc. In addition there were other small radical groups who, however, were unable to threaten the constitutional structure of the state, though the Communists could muster 10 per cent of the electorate. But had the majority voting system been introduced these radical groups would have disappeared altogether.

As soon as the political situation crystallized in the central European states after the war, it became apparent that divergent and heterogeneous elements lay concealed under cover of national and religious parties. *The national label was often merely a cloak for antidemocratic aims.* It was not always easy to deduce from these names the real interests which they served. By no means was it only fascist groups which were involved: it was often groups animated by regional and local interests. Under a majority voting system these particularist parties would never have got into parliament. They could have done really useful work in the sphere of local self-government. In central Europe (and to a significant extent this is true of developing countries even today) the parties had no principles or programmes but were simply a forum for ambitious politicians. Under the majority system they might perhaps have been elected because of their personal merits; their parties would have had hardly any chance of becoming strong enough to form a parliamentary faction.

The religious character of the denominational parties was often a cloak for a conservative group, as for instance in the case of the Austrian Christian Social Party and Czechoslovak People's Party. Or the name of denominational party concealed a strong autonomous movement, as for example with the Bavarian People's Party or Pater Hlinka's Catholic People's Party in Slovakia.

Although Austria was nationally homogeneous, except for the Slovene minority on the Carinthian frontier, this is an appropriate place to say something about the influence of proportional representation on the collapse of democracy in Austria.

In Austria during the period between 1919 and 1930, two largish parties, the Christian Social People's Party and the Socialist Party were the main contenders in the five successive elections. These were, however, prevented from achieving a majority by small parties – the Pan-German Party and the *Heimwehr* – kept alive by proportional representation.[1] Nevertheless in 1930, under proportional representation, the Christian Social Party still won 66 seats, the Socialists 72, the Pan-Germans, who were already strongly undermined by National Socialist influences, won 19 and the *Heimwehr* 8. Thus the right-wing radical Pan-Germans and the *Heimwehr* were able to impose their will on both the big democratic parties. Because the Austrian Chancellor, Dr Dollfuss, needed the 8 *Heimwehr* seats to form a cabinet, the *Heimwehr*, a small fascist group which was inspired and financed by Mussolini, became the most influential party. By exploiting its key position it compelled the conservative Christian Socialists to suppress social democracy. Here, therefore, is proof that while proportional representation can, indeed, prevent the tyranny of the majority it can also promote the tyranny of a minority.

## Parliamentary Committees and Proportional Representation

Proportional representation destroys the direct relationship between a deputy and the electors of his constituency since its size makes personal

---

[1] F. A. Hermens, *Demokratie und Anarchie*, op. cit., p. 236.

contact almost impossible. The voters have no influence on the choice of candidates, their sense of responsibility for the political consequences of their voting only develops slowly and the subject cannot grow up to become a real citizen.[1] And the deputies, who rarely make a personal appearance in their constituency – and then usually only a short time before the elections – have very little influence on the voters. The trust or distrust expressed by the latter remains impersonal and linked with the party list and associated symbols and the 'image' which goes with it.

Bryce had complained that the American public did not give Congress the attention and trust which was its due as the central organ of constitutional life.[2] The reason for this he felt was that the debates of the two chambers were unenlightening. While the legislative bodies of France, England and Canada rarely lacked a certain dramatic tension, the American legislative process, which takes place in the twilight of the committee room, was of little interest to the educated and still less to the broad masses of the general public. Therefore the people's attention turns to the President of the United States, who is elected by direct vote. For he is a *personality*, who is exposed to the full, harsh glare of publicity.[3]

This eminent political theorist was even more critical of the parliamentary committees of the Third Republic in France whose cabinet system was the model for all post-war central-European democracies. The French committee system, Bryce maintains,[4] robs the legislative procedure of coherence, makes fiscal policy unstable, encourages the unjustified expenditure of money and undermines the authority of the executive. In this way much of the activity which goes into forming the political will is transferred to bodies which function secretly and whose members cannot be made in any way responsible as they hold no official post.[5]

Even in England, parliamentary committees cannot be dispensed with altogether, but there the danger which this spells to the position and prestige of Parliament has been realized in time.[6] Therefore England never had the powerful committees which, in the United States and France, are responsible for an entire branch of government

[1] Cf. also Erich Eyck, *A History of the Weimar Republic*, Cambridge (Mass.) 1962, pp. 70 f.

[2] James Bryce, *Modern Democracies*, London 1923, Vol. II, p. 67.

[3] Ibid., p. 68 f.

[4] Ibid., Vol. I, pp. 276 f.

[5] Cf., for example, André Mathiot, *The British Political System*, London 1958, pp. 223 ff.

[6] On France cf. also François Goguel, *France under the Fourth Republic*, Ithaca 1951.

business and which, in the final analysis, strip the plenum of important functions. The British House of Commons has always been conscious of its exclusive monopoly in the field of legislation. In order to avoid having a number of separate committees it preferred to form itself into a 'committee of the whole House' where this is necessary.[1] Under Tudor absolutism in the sixteenth century the country had learned by bitter experience that the king could bring considerable pressure to bear on small committees. Proposals to introduce the committee system in England, as put forward by the socialist F. W. Jowett and also by Lloyd George,[2] fell on deaf ears.

The non-public negotiations of these committees can lead all too easily to opportunist compromises in which general principles are sometimes sacrificed to personal motives and selfish interests. There is a further drawback. If, after consideration in committee, an important legislative proposal comes before the full chamber, expert knowledge is often not available (in the United States and France committees frequently consist of experts) and there is not enough time to weigh up the pros and cons.

If the committee system has serious disadvantages even in states where the majority vote operates, the situation becomes much more critical under proportional representation. For under the majority vote system the deputy has two masters whom he must always be careful to try and satisfy. He must keep one eye on his party but the other on the voter or the people as a whole. Under proportional representation, however, his only concern is the party leadership, which alone decides whether he is to be a candidate or not, and the interest groups which are closely connected with his party and frequently finance them.

At this point it could be objected, perhaps not altogether unreasonably, that interest groups using the lobby represent a powerful force even under the majority vote system. But since majority voting is linked to the two-party system its dynamics automatically relieve this sort of pressure.

Under the two-party system, as we have already said, the two big parties embrace the most diverse interest groups. (Thus the Republican Party in the United States of America, for example, represents most of the industrialists and wholesalers and also many lower-middle-class people and workers. Again, the Democratic Party represents the majority of employees and also – especially in the South – landowners and industrialists.) In this way the danger is avoided that the committee recommendations to the plenum will take account only

[1] Cf. also Herbert Morrison, *Government and Parliament*, London 1954, pp. 154 ff.
[2] Ibid., pp. 156 f.

of the wishes of some interest groups at the expense of others. But under proportional representation and the multi-party system to which it leads the parties are obliged to concentrate on representing definite, often strictly limited groups.[1]

In central Europe the strong ideological basis of the parties was an additional factor. It had been the same in England and France in the past but in both these countries ideological party ties had grown blunt and weak during the nineteenth century. These ties were one of the reasons why in central Europe any kind of compromise which was otherwise essential for forming the political will was thought to be reprehensible. As the most important matters were considered in committee and because agreements between the coalition parties were previously decided, the assembly as a whole became a mere debating society in which the deputies, with their endless and pointless discussions, spoke only to get publicity in the press. Thus a contradiction arose between a deputy's real, personal opinion, which he only dared to express in committee, and his official opinion – often designed merely to catch votes – which he trotted out in the full assembly for party purposes.[2] With the electorate's hostility to compromise in mind, therefore, the deputies often indulged in endless debate in the assembly, stressing their ideological and party principles over and over again, while the serious work was done in committees and in inter-party discussions.

Among the central European peoples who were not yet accustomed to democracy this was bound to make them feel that parliamentary activity was barren and never produced definite decisions. It might also be argued that young democracies, where the people had been previously used to state symbols, the pomp and circumstance of court ceremonial and the apparently clear-cut decisions of despotic monarchs, themselves needed some sort of democratic symbolism. But a parliament in which the procedures are dignified and patriotic is the natural focus for this need. The parliaments of the post-war democracies did not understand this, unused as they were to political responsibility; consequently the arguments of critics hostile to the constitutional state gained in point.

Thus the secrecy surrounding the work of the committees roused suspicions – often well founded – that 'big capitalist combines' were able to enforce their demands behind the public's back. Carl Schmitt

[1] Thus in the Weimar Republic, for example, large-scale industry was represented almost exclusively by the DVP (German People's Party), the landowners by the DNVP (German National People's Party) and the trade unions by the Social Democratic Party. Cf. also Part Four of the present chapter.

[2] Cf. Chap. I, Part One.

made this claim in his attack on the parliamentary system. He went on to draw the premature conclusion that parliament had lost its *raison d'être* because the plenum had become a mere façade.[1] But Schmitt could not have greatly disturbed the young democracies of central Europe with his warning that a political theology[2] based on prophets like Cortés and Sorel who proclaimed myths and preached violence, and first appearing in the guise of Italian fascism, must be taken seriously.

Perhaps parliamentary optimism also hopes to minimize this movement; to let things drift as in fascist Italy; perhaps politicians think they can wait until discussion begins again. Perhaps too, they hope to make discussion itself a topic for discussion as long as there *is* nothing but discussion. But if discussion were resumed, these politicians would not be allowed to repeat their counter questions, 'If not the parliamentary system, what else', and assert there is so far no satisfactory substitute. That would be a futile argument and not calculated to revive the golden age of discussion.[3]

If Schmitt had taken a look at American aircraft factories during the Second World War, he would probably have learned that democracy, itself the most powerful political 'theology' of the twentieth century, is capable of taking more momentous decisions than a fascist or communist dictatorship. This is true above all else because it can rely on the voluntary and spontaneous co-operation of the people as a whole. Schmitt had overlooked the fact that the parliaments of the 1920s were debating societies for the simple reason that they were functioning in infant democracies and had not understood the true process involved in forming the political will. They still contained too many deputies who had grown up in the atmosphere of the semi-absolute state. Nobody was more aware of this than Hugo Preuss, the author of the Weimar Constitution. In his opinion one of its main defects was its political timidity and its servility towards the authoritarian state.[4] With this went an opposition which was habitually obstructive and propagandistic.

Since the Second World War this phenomenon has been reappearing, this time in the developing countries of Asia and Africa. In many of these countries an opposition which is often radical and irresponsible and almost anarchical makes any objective conduct of business

[1] Carl Schmitt, *Die geistesgeschichtliche Lage des heutigen Parlamentarismus*, op. cit., pp. 62 f.

[2] Carl Schmitt, *Politische Theologie*, Munich 1922.

[3] Carl Schmitt, *Die geistesgeschichtliche Lage des heutigen Parlamentarismus*, op. cit., pp. 89 f.

[4] *Bericht und Protokolle des 8. Ausschusses über den Entwurf einer Verfassung des Deutschen Reiches*, Berlin, No. 21 of the reports of the National Assembly, p. 275.

by parliamentary governments impossible. This encourages the seizure of power by elements in the army and bureaucracy, whose roots still go back to colonial tutelage or are influenced by communism.[1] British colonial policy had, in its scheme to get the peoples gradually used to responsible government, in fact used what is known as the dyarchic system. This envisaged the provisional retention of executive power in the hands of the British colonial bureaucracy and at the same time the partial participation of indigenous politicians in legislation at definite and agreed stages. The result was that emphasis was laid on the critical and propagandistic function of parliament at the expense of responsible, governmental action.

In the same way the exclusion of the Reichstag from governmental responsibility, engineered by Bismarck, led to a distorted idea of the functions of parliament and in particular of the opposition. Added to this was the decay and the fragmentation of the parliamentary process caused by proportional representation, leading to the undermining of the main functions of the parliamentary system, which resides in parliament acting as a plenum. Friedrich Naumann gave a timely warning about the consequences of proportional representation when he told the Weimar Constitutional Committee in no uncertain terms that the parliamentary system and proportional representation were mutually exclusive.[2]

Anyone anxious to lay responsibility for the collapse of parliamentary democracy in central Europe exclusively at the door of proportional representation lays himself open to not unjustified criticism. Various phenomena, which are characteristic of proportional representation, such as the fragmentation of parties, difficulty in forming a government, and cabinet instability, also appear from time to time under the majority vote system.[3] The best-known example in Europe is the French Third Republic. But they often occur also in the developing countries of Asia and Africa which adopted England's majority vote system and the same is true of other young democracies.[4] However, as these phenomena regularly appear in countries with proportional representation, in future where they

[1] Cf., for example, K. J. Newman, 'The Constitutional Evolution of Pakistan', in *International Affairs*, London, Vol. 38, No. 3, July 1962.

[2] *Bericht und Protokolle des 8. Ausschusses,* op. cit., p. 242.

[3] Thus Rudolf Schlesinger, for instance, points out the fact that the multi-party system in Germany and Czechoslovakia was inherited from the pre-1940 period, whereas in Austria a two-party system developed in Austria under proportional representation, op. cit., p. 258.

[4] K. J. Newman, *Die Entwicklungsdiktatur und der Verfassungsstaat*, Frankfurt 1963.

occur under the majority voting system they will be called quasi-proportional representation phenomena.

In the French Third Republic these symptoms, according to Beer and Ulam,[1] were due to a number of *concomitant* factors. The regional opposition between radical Paris and the conservative provinces mentioned by these authors had already been noted by Bryce.[2] Secondly, the impassioned rhetoric of parliamentary orators played a role originating in democracy's fight, against the remaining vestiges of the authoritarian state, which lasted until the Dreyfus affair. This atmosphere often helped to bring cabinets down.[3] In the third place – again according to Beer and Ulam – these para-proportional representation phenomena in France can be attributed to the pronounced individualism of French politicians. In this case the idea of 'individualism' probably includes ambitious egotism, political indiscipline – including lack of party discipline – and intellectual inconsistency. These symptoms are, however, the very ones which appear in a young democracy like Pakistan.[4] In France the weakness was a lack of any sense of political responsibility; these authors saw the reasons for it in France's bureaucratic authoritarian administrative system and the traditional distinction made between 'state' and 'politics'. Since the state, represented by the powerful and influential bureaucracy, always won in the end, French deputies thought they could afford the luxury of a less responsible attitude. This also tallies with analyses about the developing countries.[5] In France, as in other countries, parties were at first grouped around sets of notables (*Honoratiorenparteien*); a mass party only came into existence with the Socialist Party – a further feature which France has in common with the developing countries. Hermens has already drawn attention to the absence of the right of dissolution of parliament, mentioned by Bagehot,[6] the government's most important defence measure against an arbitrary and too self-willed parliament. And so, although she was not an infant democracy, because of the symptoms of quasi-proportional representation France also retained to some extent the basic traits of an infant democracy. It would not be altogether wrong to call her a quasi-infant democracy, if one

[1] Beer and Ulam, *The Major Political Systems of Europe*, New York 1958, pp. 225 f.

[2] Bryce, op. cit., Vol. I, p. 297.

[3] For a detailed analysis cf. A. Soulier, *L'instabilité ministérielle sous la Troisième République* (1871–1938), Paris 1939.

[4] For a comparative analysis of these phenomena in France and Pakistan, cf. K. J. Newman, 'Pakistan's Preventive Autocracy and its Causes', *Pacific Affairs*, Vol. XXXI, No. 1, March, 1959, p. 28.

[5] K. J. Newman, *Die Entwicklungsdiktatur und der Verfassungsstaat*, op. cit.

[6] F. A. Hermens, *Verfassungslehre*, op. cit., p. 326.

believes that a basic attitude which is anarchical, irresponsible and still autocratic enough to make difficult the formation of the popular will is characteristic of such a democracy.

It should be remembered, however, that in the Third Republic there was not a relative but an absolute majority voting system with a second ballot.[1] After the First World War, members of the French Lower Chamber were also partly elected by proportional representation. This fact and the growing extremism of the Right and Left led to mounting instability. While the average length of life of a cabinet between 1870 and 1914 had been ten months, between 1914 and 1932 it sank to eight and between 1932 and 1940 to a mere four months.[2] Under the proportional representation system introduced in the Fourth Republic the situation became completely untenable and, as in other countries, this led to an ever-growing call for a system of government which was able and willing to take executive decisions.

## PART TWO

*The Executive and the Post-war Democracies*

As the post-war democracies in central Europe had adopted the electoral system of proportional representation which rarely produces parliamentary majorities, minority governments or coalitions become the rule. Furthermore, states like Hungary, Poland, Yugoslavia and Romania can be considered as actual incipient democracies, whereas the Weimar Republic, because of the constitutional structure of the Second Empire accompanied by the continuing influence of the bureaucracy, may be described as a quasi-incipient democracy. Austria and Czechoslovakia, where general elections were first held in 1919, occupied an intermediate position. The difficulties which beset the parliamentary system in central Europe in the period between the two World Wars sprang therefore from processes which are characteristic of infant democracies and from the typical consequences of proportional representation described earlier in this chapter.

On the other hand coalition governments do not always

---

[1] *Protokolle der 25 Sitzungen des Weimarer Verfassungsausschusses,* p. 243. Naumann speaks of the harmful influence of the second ballot in France, by which 'the many undecided, shilly-shallying candidates' got into parliament.

[2] Beer and Ulam, *Patterns of Government,* op. cit., p. 229.

necessarily lead to instability. We have already mentioned that the Czech-Slovak coalition cabinets resulted in the formation of blocs which exhibited a remarkable degree of stability and therefore to some extent also brought the advantages of a two-party system. The same was true of the Austrian Republic, where a coalition system worked tolerably well, in the beginning.

The difficulties experienced in Austria after the National Socialists had seized power in Germany were due partly to a faulty notion of the role of the opposition. To mistake opposition for hostile obstruction is also characteristic of infant democracies. To some extent Austria's troubles were due to vexations from outside – from fascist Italy and the Third Reich. On the other hand the Polish parliament, because of the disintegration of the Peasants' parties, the Socialists' lack of backbone and the National Democrats' irresponsible demagogy, was so unstable that the coalition governments inevitably associated with proportional representation were always short-lived, so that by 1926 General Pilsudski had already led the march on Warsaw.[1] In Poland and Yugoslavia the phenomenon of incipient democracy went hand in hand with political and national intolerance, making effective parliamentary government impossible.

In spite of the relative stability of the coalition governments in Austria and Czechoslovakia it remains true that even stable coalitions leave the coalition partners unsatisfied. This has been well illustrated by Lowell. When three people come to a cross-roads they can vote where to go. But if four or five people are involved there might be no prevailing opinion. An indefinite number of tracks would make voting impossible. What can they do? They could draw all the roads on a piece of paper and then agree on an average course. But no collective opinion would emerge. Each one of them could say: 'I didn't really want to go this way.'[2]

Lowell wanted to make clear that *none* of the partners in a coalition government can carry out their programme to their satisfaction.[3] Experience in central Europe, including experience in the Weimar Republic, confirms the truth of Lowell's example. The elector was denied any clear alternative in the way of political programmes and leadership – the very choice he was offered by the two-party system. Instead he was confused and excited by a host of rival ideologies. If, before the election, Party A solicits and wins an elector's vote by

[1] Ahlers, op. cit., pp. 106 ff.

[2] A. Lawrence Lowell, *Public Opinion in War and Peace*, Cambridge (Mass.) 1926, p. 127.

[3] Cf. also Schuschnigg's objection to the Austrian coalition system in *Dreimal Österreich*, op. cit., p. 107.

making attacks on Party B, and subsequently is able to form a coalition with that particular party after the election, the whole parliamentary system must be discredited by such gross opportunism, especially if ideological parties are involved.

On the other hand the parties which joined coalitions regarded them as a pragmatic solution, with reservations in the background. Thus, when they joined the 1929 coalition, the Czechoslovak Socialists wrote in their party journal: 'The class war will be continued *inside the coalition.*' Inside the coalition, therefore, one partner sought to gain an advantage for itself at the expense of the other. In the Czechoslovak coalition formed by the Agrarians and the Socialists at the time of the economic crisis, each Socialist demand for a rise in unemployment benefit was capped by an Agrarian demand for an increase in the price of agricultural products.

This sort of 'horse-trading' obviously discredits parliamentary democracy in the eyes of the people. A coalition in which the partners represent economic interests is, especially because of its political compromises, unlikely to be inhibited by ethical principles. Although there was hardly any personal corruption worth mentioning in the young democracies of central Europe, the coalition system produced phenomena which in Austria for example were described by Schuschnigg, not without reason, as 'objective corruption'.[1] And the bartering over ministerial posts so typical of coalitions disgusts the electorate.[2] Another point to remember is that the coalition system alters the function of the prime minister as known in England: he is no longer the leader of the majority and cabinet spokesman to the people and parliament; instead he becomes an intermediary between the coalition parties which he tries to hold together with vague formulae. It is thus easy to understand that this kind of government fell as a rule not so much because of a vote of no confidence as from the chronic instability of the coalitions. In Poland and Yugoslavia cabinets came and went in ever quickening succession. In the Weimar Republic the average life of a cabinet was eight months, in Austria it was seven.

When Hugo Preuss put forward his proposals about the position of the President of the Reich in the Constituent Assembly, he had in mind the role played by the English crown in forming a cabinet.[3] He hoped that a two-party system would develop in Germany, despite proportional representation. Naumann had pointed out that the

---

[1] Schuschnigg, op. cit., p. 116, quoted public opinion on this point: 'What did those deputies groups get for giving in?'

[2] Zürcher, op. cit., p. 180.

[3] Hugo Preuss, *Um die Reichsverfassung von Weimar*, Berlin 1924, p. 63.

English or American two-party system is the product of the relative majority voting system,[1] which was rejected by Preuss at the twenty-third session of the Constitutional Committee on the grounds that in Germany the multi-party system would have developed in spite of the majority system used in pre-war Reichstag elections. Naumann's reply exposed this error by pointing out that the final ballot with its transferable vote, which was part of the former French absolute majority vote system, had led to multi-party government in France just as it had in imperial Germany. The French majority system was fundamentally different from the simple majority practised in Anglo-Saxon countries. The anticipated features of proportional representation would seem to have induced the Constitutional Committee to forestall the predictable fragmentation of the party system by strengthening the position of the President.

By 1924 Preuss was already deploring the fact that the incoherence of the German party system with the inevitable coalition governments it produced gave the President considerable influence in the solution of government crises. The impossibility of 'forming two parties or coalitions of equal stature which could alternate in the roles of government and opposition' he described as basically harmful to the political structure.[2]

According to Preuss the President ought to have had a free hand in choosing the Chancellor. But since proportional representation made a stable, one-party government impossible and rendered coalitions necessary, protracted negotiations by the party executive committees took place before the Chancellor and the ministers were appointed. In practice the list of cabinet members and the guide-lines for future policy were increasingly given to the President and the Chancellor by the party executive committees on the formation of a government.

With coalition governments there is always the danger that a government crisis will break out as soon as one of the coalition partners loses interest in participating in the government. Governmental stability was further eroded by the practice of forming *minority governments*. As in other developing countries, party politicians in the Weimar Republic also overestimated their actual power and underestimated their responsibility for the well-being of the nation. Their loyalty was to the party first and to the nation second. The notion that parliamentary government was a device for settling the differences between the various interest groups did irreparable harm to democracy in the Weimar Republic. Sir Ernest Barker speaks of the 'eruption of the group' as a disturbing feature

---

[1] Glum, op. cit., pp. 170 f.  [2] Preuss, op. cit., pp. 64 f.

of our times; the group strengthens its influence by unlawfully claiming the rights and privileges which rightly belong to both the individual and the community.[1] This is what Barker says about the post-war democracies:

'The supremacy of the legislature was thus combined with rival supremacies . . . it was actually doomed to work with allies who were rivals and adversaries'.[2]

The failure of the third Müller coalition government, which commanded a large majority in the Reichstag, meant the end of Weimar democracy. Glum is justified in stressing this failure as being symptomatic of Weimar's weakness.[3] This particular coalition collapsed because the German People's Party, representing industry, and Social Democracy, representing the trade unions, could not agree about a sum of seventy million marks for increasing unemployment benefit. This disunity led to the appointment of Brüning as Chancellor and later to the new elections of 1930, from which the National Socialists emerged as the second strongest party in Germany.

The parties in the Weimar Republic thus displayed a complete misunderstanding of the role of a democratic political party, a misunderstanding which was caused by the class-war outlook on the part of both capitalist and Marxist circles. To that extent Spann's criticism of the party state is justified. It did not differ fundamentally from the views of sociologists such as R. M. Maciver, among others, who stressed the integrating function performed by the community. Plato and Aristotle had taught that any disturbance of the economic equilibrium between the classes tends to political revolution. This is not, however, true of all democracies; it applies only to those governed by politicians who have not grasped that democracy is not only a form of government but also a pattern of thought, a way of life. Without tolerance it cannot survive.

As in all infant democracies, political intolerance was in this instance supplemented by an anarchical concept of freedom. For both the capitalist and the proletarian claim for exclusive power culminate in aristocratic claims which contradict the democratic principle and must prove fatal to the constitutional state because it questions the principle of sophrosyne.

[1] E. Barker, *Reflections on Government*, Oxford 1942, pp. 142 f.
[2] Ibid., pp. 97 f.
[3] Glum, op. cit., p. 233.

## Democratic Legislature and Autocratic Administration

One of Spann's complaints was that neither German nor Austrian democracy wholly fulfilled the democratic ideal, 'since', as he put it, 'after 1918 we ourselves still have a large and powerful civil service which is firmly in the saddle' and was appointed 'on the basis of professional expertise, not on the basis of election and party affiliation.'[1] As long ago as 1918 Max Weber had made the point: 'Modern parliaments are, in the first place, bodies representing *people who are governed* by the bureaucracy.[2] He had highlighted the importance of the bureaucracy in Germany in his famous sentence: 'Since Prince Bismarck's resignation Germany was ruled by "officials".' She had the 'best military and civilian bureaucracy in the world, outstanding in integrity, education, conscientiousness and intelligence'.[3]

The Prussian tradition meant that the civil servants were usually conservative in outlook and regarded the Hegelian tradition as embodying the 'supra-party' nature of the State. Hence the civil servant represented the opposite of the politician and the parliamentary deputy. But the bureaucrat's creed, which requires submission to one's superiors, presupposes a mentality different from that of the politician, who makes his own decisions.

Bracher has called the bureaucracy of the Weimar Republic 'a third organ of the State' on a par with parliament and the government.[4] With its stability and exclusiveness it remained, so to speak, a fixed star – in contrast to the fluctuations in parliamentary majorities and governments. He thinks it was natural for the republican parties to try to influence the bureaucracy and put convinced democrats into the most important posts, and for the anti-democratic parties to do the same with their own kind. This growing impact of politicians on the civil service was countered by the growing demand for the 'neutralization and independence of the bureaucracy which was still not fully integrated politically'[5] and which all too easily becomes the tool of a crypto-political power policy – until under Papen the bureaucracy threw off its cloak of neutrality[6] finally to become all-powerful in party and state under National Socialism. Apart from

[1] Spann, op. cit., p. 104.
[2] Max Weber, 'Beamtenherrschaft und politisches Führertum', in *Gesammelte politische Schriften*, op. cit., p. 327.
[3] Ibid., p. 323.
[4] K. D. Bracher, op. cit., p. 187.
[5] Ibid., p. 189.
[6] Ibid.

certain isolated cases, like those in Bavaria during Hitler's 1923 *putsch*, there is no real evidence of any general anti-democratic attitude on the part of German officials during the Weimar Republic. As for the armed forces, it was obviously not a simple matter for the officers who had been reared in the *esprit de corps* of the imperial army to adapt themselves to the reality of the Republic.[1] On the other hand, however, the majority of the civil service and the police in the largest province, Prussia, behaved in exemplary fashion.[2]

The administrative system inherited from the Hohenzollern empire was continued in the Weimar Republic. As in France and other West European countries the civil servants in the provinces and districts were appointed to monocratic posts in a pyramid-like hierarchy. Thus this type of civil servant assumes decisive power over his fellow citizens. As Friedrich explains, the system was developed by absolute monarchy and devised to serve its needs.[3] Because he is expected to carry out promptly the orders of higher authority on the one hand yet also having to make independent, responsible decisions of his own on the other, the civil servant acquires a basic outlook that is both authoritarian and inimical to the parliamentary system which functions through cumbersome collegiate committees. That may be one of the reasons why the civil service prefers monarchical and authoritarian types of government. Hannah Arendt is right when she describes the bureaucracy as 'the heritage of despotism' and rule by decree,[4] the very opposite of the rule of law. According to Arendt the Law seems powerless to the bureaucrat because 'as such . . . it remains divorced from its execution',[5] while decrees are carried out without the need to provide reasons, justification or advance notice. The bureaucrat feels he is a specialist who translates the decree into reality. Arendt expresses the opinion that the pseudo-mystical aura which lent a halo to the ruling dynasty in Austria-Hungary was the typical product of a fully developed and firmly established bureaucracy.

In the nineteenth century the Stein-Hardenberg reforms in Prussia and the self-government law introduced by Count Stadion in Austria-Hungary after 1848 had established a sound tradition of local self-government. Although the institution of district officers, who

---

[1] C. Otto Gessler, *Reichswehrpolitik in der Weimarer Zeit*, Stuttgart 1958.

[2] Karl Severing, *Mein Lebensweg*, Cologne 1950.

[3] Carl J. Friedrich, *Constitutional Government and Democracy*, Boston, New York, Chicago, London 1950, pp. 137 ff.; originally published under the title of *Constitutional Government and Politics*, New York and London 1937.

[4] Hannah Arendt, *Elemente und Ursprünge totaler Herrschaft*, Frankfurt 1955, pp. 394 f.

[5] Ibid., p. 396.

were ultimately responsible to the Ministry of the Interior, continued to function in both these states, alongside this system there developed a type of self-government which gradually prepared an ever-increasing number of citizens for their role in a future democratic state. This practical experience and familiarity with the administrative tasks which fell to small bodies went on for decades and contributed substantially to the development of civic consciousness and to a sense of political responsibility, especially in those parts of Germany where it could be associated with existing traditions of the medieval Free Imperial Cities.

After the First World War the Succession States which followed the break-up of Austria-Hungary decided to adopt the French version of parliamentary democracy. At the same time, however, certain features of the French administrative system were also introduced, especially in Poland, Yugoslavia and Czechoslovakia. But the resulting changes made little difference. In many cases the old system of district officials was simply dressed in the garb of the French prefect. The former imperial official had merely taken off his uniform. The French system had been in force at an earlier period in the Serbian part of Yugoslavia. Representative bodies at district level were now formed in the Succession States but their authority was very restricted.

In Poland people had been able to gain experience only in areas which had previously belonged to Austria-Hungary. The new constitution created elected representative bodies in the provinces, districts and parishes. But these were still headed by representatives of the central government. The parishes were less dependent but the central government made sure that it kept considerable control, by appointing the district chairmen (starosta) and the provincial governors (voivod). The governors were above the chairmen in the hierarchy, and final decisions lay with the Minister of the Interior.

In Czechoslovakia the officials appointed centrally were the provincial presidents and the district military governors. Only two-thirds of a provincial assembly consisted of elected members, the rest were appointed by the central government which took into account their nominees' economic, social, cultural and linguistic connections with the province. Where the work of provincial assemblies was concerned, the president was the person who counted. The district assemblies had even less influence and their authority was equally limited. As in the provincial assemblies, two-thirds of its members were elected and one-third nominated. The provincial assembly's job was to issue decrees in pursuance of the laws passed by parliament, but only at the request of the cabinet. In practice, this meant that these self-governing bodies were deprived of nearly all responsibility since the executive decided whether, when and how they should be given any actual business to undertake themselves. Apart from that the provincial assembly only had the right to draw up regulations for the various provincial institutions, to issue instructions about the administration of the parish, district and provincial budgets and to supervise the expenditure of this money within the limits set down by national laws and decrees. But these local bodies' modest powers were also illusory, because they needed to obtain the Ministry's agreement. The old Austria had allowed local governments more scope. The provincial diets had been able to make their own laws and their executive committees had exercised a certain measure of administrative jurisdiction. The laws and decrees issued by the provincial diets had not generally needed the approval of the central government, although in many cases imperial assent had to be obtained. But that did not prejudice the provinces' autonomy in any way since even the laws passed by the Austrian parliament were subject to the Emperor's approval.

In Czechoslovakia a law passed in 1920 transferred the executive power of the former provincial diets to the central government. That meant a clear limitation of provincial autonomy, but even this was to the benefit of the executive rather than parliament. Under the constitution of the Republic the new provincial diets, whose functions and authority were mere shadows of those enjoyed by previous diets, could convene only at the invitation of the provincial president, who also laid down their agenda. The provincial committee, which was to simulate an executive, could discuss political matters but was not entitled to make proposals. That was obviously a set-back to the cause of education for democracy and bound to make people indifferent to taking responsibility.

In this context it should be recalled that the Austrian Constituent Assembly of 1848 entertained very different intentions, proposing a local self-government system of urban, borough and district councils. The Austrian Local Government Law of 1862, enacted in pursuance of the February patent of 1861, was also a piece of progressive and enlightened legislation which had a permanent effect on the general public's education in democratic responsibility. Had this Austrian local government decree been taken seriously and adopted, the development of local self-government in the countries of Austria-Hungary might have developed analogously to local government in North America. According to this law the basis of the state structure was to be the local community, with the state at the top and the provinces, districts and towns coming below, in that order. Therefore, when the post-war states made it more difficult for their parliaments to influence the local self-government bodies, the effect was bound to be retrograde. By assigning to the Ministry of the Interior and the police an intermediate position between parliament and local authorities an extreme policy of centralization was ushered in.

Czechoslovakia was not alone in providing a haven for monocratism after abolishing the monarchic figurehead. Germany, Poland and Yugoslavia did the same. The reason for this was not perhaps a liking for centralization as such, but paradoxically an enthusiastic but uncritical adoption of Western parliamentary forms by unconstitutional lawyers who did not always bear in mind the sociological effects which follow from constitutional changes. The Weimar Republic rejected the French system because it led to chronic government instability, and instead wanted to adopt the English system; but this proved impossible because of the clamour for proportional representation. The resulting instability was to be off-set by strengthening the powers of the President of the Reich. Although it was not then realized, by the time the Weimar Constitutional Commission had finished its work it had actually returned to its starting point – the semi-constitutionalism of imperial Germany, without, alas, the former prestige of monarchy.

Again, when the authors of the constitutions in the Succession States introduced the French parliamentary system with its president, council of ministers and parliament, they felt it imperative also to adopt the prefect system which went with it. That, as we have already said, was not difficult in central Europe, where the office of district commissioner was in any case modelled on the Napoleonic prefect. One of the consequences of this rash and wholesale adoption of the French system was the abolition of the self-governing bodies in the provinces and *Länder*. These had embodied the solid traditions of central European constitutional development.

Nevertheless these countries also contained clear-sighted people who were aware of the anomalous situation in which a democratic legislature had to work with an autocratic executive. But Dr Beneš' statement is unsatisfactory that other problems were more urgent and that there had therefore been no time or opportunity to experiment with new institutions,[1] the more so when we consider that Dr Beneš' government found time to abolish the provincial assemblies, whose supervision took up much of the Ministry of the Interior's precious time and was a task which, if it really needed to be done, could have been performed much better by a parliamentary committee. The usual excuse advanced was that these assemblies were

[1] E. Beneš, *Democracy Today and Tomorrow*, London 1939, pp. 51 f.

financially neither strong nor experienced enough to grapple with vital problems and therefore needed the advice of the central authorities.

A similar problem had arisen in England in the nineteenth century. The solution there was to give the supervision of local government not to the Home Office, by its nature mainly concerned with police matters, but to a new ministry – the Local Government Board. Relations with mayors and councils at district and borough level are best fostered by people who themselves have had extensive and practical experience in bodies of this kind. In the case of Czechoslovakia, Poland and Yugoslavia, however, there was a well-founded suspicion that supervision by the Ministry of the Interior would amount primarily to a security operation to keep an eye on the aspirations for autonomy of Slovaks, Romanians, Germans, Hungarians and Croats. Here, again, the police state was an unsuitable means of effecting integration.

In Poland, as elsewhere in central Europe, the central government found it quite impossible to integrate the heterogeneous communities into the state. The country, divided into sixteen voivode (provinces), had, in accordance with the constitution of 1921, introduced the French parliamentary system. The cabinet, which was responsible to the *Sejm* (parliament), appointed the provincial governors (*voivode*) who held the rank of Under-Secretary of State and were in effect petty kings with almost unlimited powers.[1]

In much the same way the executive in Yugoslavia was subordinated to the Council of Ministers, which, itself subordinate to the king, was responsible to both him and the *Narodna Skupština* (National Parliament). Administratively the kingdom was divided up in a purely mechanical way into regions, districts and boroughs, in complete disregard for the historical provinces from which the state originally sprang. These were ruled by a governor, the Grand Župan, who was appointed by the king and conducted the state's administrative business in his region with the assistance of the bureaucracy.[2]

Spann's remark that the democratic revolution was only partly successful because the absolutist bureaucracy was still in the saddle after 1918 was therefore true of the whole of central Europe and not only of Germany and Austria. Officials imbued with the proud administrative traditions of imperial Germany and the principalities could hardly be expected to serve meekly under democratic lower-class politicians whom, only the day before, they could have penalized,

[1] Cf. Art. 95 of the Constitution of the Kingdom of the Serbs, Croats and Slovenes.
[2] Johannes Ahlers, *Polen, Volk, Staat, Kultur, Politik und Wissenschaft*, Berlin 1935, p. 99.

imprisoned or banished and who, as they were well aware, knew nothing about administration. The monarchical type of bureaucrat *per se* hated the laws which he saw as a trap in which 'the administrator became needlessly entangled.[1] Experience in the developing countries, with the bureaucracy[2] trained by the former colonial powers, fully confirms Arendt's view that the bureaucrat feels infinitely superior to the 'unpractical' people who have to spend their time puzzling over legislative details and yet remain outside the sphere of real power which for the bureaucrat generally means politics.[3]

Furthermore, in infant democracies, bureaucracy is bound to clash more with the parliamentary system than the administrative official who in the past was used to exercising a monocratic authority within his own district and who now must consider the wishes of the local deputies sitting in the central and provincial parliaments. For the wishes of the electorate must be a paramount concern of the member of parliament, because his re-election depends on them. His local reputation is often determined by the pressure which he can bring to bear on their behalf. But these wishes can best be met by the district civil servants or the departmental head of the appropriate ministry. It is not always possible for the deputy to distinguish clearly between public interest of some section of the electorate (e.g. tenants, metalworkers, craftsmen, etc.) and personal interest (e.g. government appointments for the sons of party friends, award of business contracts, etc.). In the smaller central-European states deputies were often over-burdened with such matters, which fell little short of corruption – a practice which the party leaders did not always oppose as resolutely as they should have. This type of intervention, however, puts unfair and unjustified pressure on the government officer. In the first place frequent requests for favours make his administrative work more difficult and in the second place he is well aware that the deputy can always complain directly to the minister responsible for his department; and if the latter is a member of the same party as the deputy the two form a community of interest because all of them have to respect the wishes of the electors.

The district official sometimes tried to make his job easier by taking the deputies into his confidence before making an important political decision – another practice which led to political pressure being brought to bear on the administrator.

---

[1] Popjedonostser, *Reflections of a Russian Statesman*, London 1898, p. 88: 'If, however, the executant of a law perpetually comes up against restricting clauses in that law . . . then all authority becomes a prey to doubt and is finally destroyed by the fear of responsibility.' (Quoted by H. Arendt, op. cit., p. 396).

[2] K. J. Newman, *Die Entwicklungsdiktatur und der Verfassungsstaat*, op. cit., p. 38.

[3] H. Arendt, op. cit., p. 396.

Writing about Germany, Eschenburg says that the new ministers of the Weimar Republic who 'lacked their predecessors' expert knowledge and administrative experience began to appoint reliable members of their own party so as to avoid becoming dependent on the superior administrative ability of their bureaucracy.'[1] Eschenburg points out that the law which was passed after the murder of Rathenau and laid down the civil servant's obligations on the subject of protecting the Republic, undermined still further the principle that officials could not be dismissed and helped to counter the politicalization of the civil service. In Germany, too, appointments, promotions and dismissals began to be made according to relative party strength. In the coalition governments which were unavoidable under proportional representation, however, this meant that when posts were distributed according to the composition of the coalition, the various protégés of the government parties also had to be considered.

Even if deputies and other politicians enjoyed party protection in their dealings with the authorities, the average citizen of central Europe enjoyed very little protection indeed. In the Weimar Republic the sense of duty which the civil servants had inherited from the time of the Prussian monarchy, their relative dedication to the rule of law, and the administrative courts which did much to produce a higher standard of administration all that afforded the ordinary citizen a certain degree of legal protection. But none of this applied to other parts of central Europe.

Even before the War, Austria-Hungary had had a civil service which was cosmopolitan, liberal and open to talent. The distinguished standards of its members and their administrative experience came from their being regularly posted to different parts of the Danube monarchy. The more varied the people and the administrative problems which the civil servant encounters, the more efficient will he become and the more tolerant and broad-minded will his general outlook be. For example an official who spent several years of his career in Prague, then went to Istria, later to Galicia and ended up in a ministry in Vienna was less likely to be narrowly chauvinistic than to be condescending towards the ordinary citizen, trying to impress him with his intellectual and social superiority. This arrogance was even shown to those members of the legislative bodies who came from a lower middle-class, peasant or proletarian background. In their outlook, manner and general disposition the senior Austro-Hungarian bureaucrats bear a certain resemblance to British colonial officials, especially in India. When groups of people of different communities

[1] Theodor Eschenburg, *Der Beamte in Partei und Parlament*, Frankfurt 1952, p. 45.

but identical organization spend many years dealing with the same sort of problems they tend to develop similar characteristics.

Hannah Arendt has described the typical British Empire administrator in her short but striking sketch of Lord Cromer. According to Cromer's *Government of Subject Races*, the qualities required of the administrator are personal influence, effective supervision of the public affairs of subject countries, lack of vanity and personal ambition, anonymity and the ability to exercise power behind the scenes.[1] Cromer said, 'the imperial administrative machine must be . . . a government of experts', the 'experienced minority', which 'shuns or opposes the inexperienced majority'.[2] But important matters like politics could not be entrusted to the inexperienced majority. The colonial official must remain completely aloof from politics and must not be carried away by patriotic feelings even to the extent of recommending his own country's institutions to the foreigner. As dictatorship in developing countries today represents a return to the ideas of the colonial era, the dictators in the developing countries have automatically adopted the colonial officials' way of thinking. Hence the argument is constantly heard that democracy is not a suitable article for export to underdeveloped countries. It is understandable that this type of official felt that the legislative bodies of his own country were inhibiting and interfered with his useful and philanthropic activity.

The same writer reminds us that contempt for laws and legality is common to all imperialist officials but was much more evident in continental imperialism in Europe because it was ideologically justified there. The great geographical distances which, in the overseas empires, lay between colonial methods of rule and the institutions and law of the mother country were absent from imperialism in Europe.[3] She points out that movements such as pan-Germanism and pan-Slavism started in the multi-social states themselves. The leaders of these movements would have countered rule and power only by taking arbitrary decisions, incomprehensible to the governed. She is quite right when she says that under the Austro-Hungarian monarchy the important status enjoyed by the bureaucracy was due to its having participated directly in governing, and because right up to the end rule had been exercised bureaucratically.

In spite of the emergence of ministries which were directly responsible to the legislative bodies, the Emperor Francis Joseph still scrutinized every detail of the administration himself. He was, so to speak, his own first Assistant Secretary of State, and quite apart from persistent interference by the court *camarilla*, the position of

[1] H. Arendt, op. cit., p. 345.    [2] Ibid., p. 346.    [3] Ibid., p. 394.

his ministers was always made more difficult by the Emperor himself, who considered every problem primarily from an administrative point of view. It is easy to see that the fragmentation of the Danube monarchy resulting from the Revolution of 1918 uprooted the Austrian bureaucracy for it made it superfluous at a single stroke and was bound to have a lasting effect on its members. In so far as they were absorbed into the civil service of the Austrian Republic or perhaps of the Succession States such as Czechoslovakia (in 1918 many Austrian government officials were of Czech origin) they were a beneficial influence in the evolution of the constitutional state. The same was true of the senior military officers of Austria-Hungary. As soon however, as the existence of the post-war democracies was seriously threatened, it became clear that both the civil service and the senior military officers were the enemies of democracy. In Hungary that had already become apparent in the case of personages such as Admiral Horthy and Gömbös, in Pilsudski with his officers and the Galician bureaucracy in Poland, and in the Frankists in Croatia. In Czechoslovakia a former senior Austrian administrator, Dr Hácha, became head of state just when democracy was suppressed.

This phenomenon was particularly striking in Austria and, because of Austria, in Germany. The names of men such as Major Fey and Starhemberg should be recalled. The number of Austrians among the top Nazi ranks, especially in the SS, was out of all proportion to the size of Austria's population – a fact which has been largely overlooked. It must also be emphasized that these men, who included notorious extermination experts like Seyss-Inquart, Kaltenbrunner and Eichmann, came from relatively higher social strata than their north-German counterparts. That is understandable, however, when one considers that the catastrophe which befell Austria-Hungary in 1918 was much more far-reaching and cataclysmic than what happened to Germany after Versailles. While it was possible for a section of the German officer corps to be absorbed into the *Reichswehr* the officers of the Austro-Hungarian Empire found their professional future blocked. While the German civil service could continue to function undisturbed in the Weimar Republic, the Austro-Hungarian civil servants, who had considered themselves to be rulers of an empire, might at best expect a third-rate post without influence in one of the dwarfed republics of the post-war world. They were likely to descend in the social scale, particularly as their savings were wiped out by inflation. The old-style Austrian civil servant who had lost his *raison d'être* in 1918 now gradually lost his prestige and influence as well. But the emergence of a new generation of civil servants from other social strata in the post-war states brought a clash between the old and new type of official, in which the old type proved to be the weaker.

During the twenties a noticeable change of attitude developed among the bureaucracies of the small central European states. Austrian generosity and tolerance gave way to a trivial, often narrow-minded local patriotism. The cosmopolitan outlook of the privy counsellor developed into a provincial and philistine attitude, the self-respect due to tradition and *esprit de corps* was succeeded by a timid subaltern demeanour hiding behind petty regulations and fear of superiors. The socio-psychological consequences of the spacial shrinkage which followed the division of the immense territory of Austria-Hungary into many small states and the narrower basis of their economies and fewer trading outlets caused by protective tariffs was a narrowing of intellectual horizons with the inevitable disappearance of humane sentiments. All this was made worse by the mutual hatreds of the national, religious and racial majorities and minorities inside the states.

As we saw, democratic executives in post-war Europe suffered from a number of congenital weaknesses resulting in a growing paralysis in the democratic states themselves. One of these weaknesses was a completely mistaken and paradoxical attitude towards all military and defence questions. Because the Russian and central-European revolutionaries owed their victory in 1917–1918 to the war-weariness of the troops, there was a tendency to confuse socialism and democracy with pacifism[1] – a fallacy which Trotsky realized before it was too late. It was only in Germany and Austria that the pacifist attitude adopted by the social-democratic parties survived. But because the persistent danger of civil war made it essential to have a military force, social-democratic government had to rely on the old officer corps.[2] When the German Army offered the Republic its support in the autumn of 1918, the Republic should have offered the army a political aim, as Rosenberg rightly observed. But it could not do that since it was itself without one.

The attitude of the post-war democracies towards military matters will be discussed elsewhere in this book (Chapter VI, Part One). This lack of understanding about military matters is quoted only as an illustration, since it arose from the mistake of over-stressing the principle of freedom at the expense of law and order. The outcome was socialist pacifism, which resulted in the rival dualism of government and army and, in Germany, led to the *Reichswehr* becoming a state

[1] Cf., for example, Konrad Heiden, *Hitler*, Vol. II, Zurich 1937, p. 155.
[2] Cf., for example, O. E. Schüddekopf, *Das Heer und die Republik*, op. cit.; Gordon A. Craig, *The Politics of the Prussian Army*, Oxford 1955, pp. 342 ff.

within the state. In Austria the Army Minister, Vaugoin, also used social democracy's advocacy of the class war as an excuse to purge the small Federal Army of social-democratic influences.[1] This is further proof of the truth of Plato's dictum that radical attacks on the notables drive them to rebellion.

The reason why a power vacuum continued to exist in Germany was, however, not only the Weimar Republic's inability to set up a national army but also its attitude to the security police. Scheidemann had, for example, reported that while taking a cure in Bad Kissingen in 1921 he had been so molested and abused that in the end he had stopped going to take the waters. When, at the same period, Erzberger was murdered, the only person who came to protect Scheidemann was his own daughter.[2] And when in the following year – the year of Rathenau's assassination – an attempt was made to poison Scheidemann, it was several months before those responsible were caught. His only reaction to the murder of Erzberger and Rathenau was his proposal to hold new elections.[3] All this showed the feebleness of the Social Democrat leadership to the problem of authority in the state.

Post-war democracy can, therefore, be justly charged with an exaggerated and perverted conception of freedom. In Germany the pre-war, traditional concept of the state as an entity rising above party and embodied in a conservative army and bureaucracy lived on. By stressing the impartiality of the *Reichswehr*, men like General von Seeckt and General von Schleicher could invoke this tradition, and it was widely believed that their attitude was objective and correct. The combination of Hegel's idea of the state and Mill's idea of liberty paralysed democracy's freedom of action. These spiritual Siamese twins – antagonistic and yet necessary to each other – were a feature of all post-war central-European democracies because they expressed the connection existing between the legacy of absolutism and the new anarchical idea of freedom. Because of Seeckt's concept of the impartiality of the *Reichswehr* the identity of state and government was lost. As the *Reichswehr* refused to lend its full support to republican government, the Social Democrats had to raise their own private force, the *Reichsbanner*. But if the government party maintained a private army was it not fair that other parties should do the same? And why should Erzberger, Rathenau or Scheidemann expect more police protection than anyone else? What the Weimar democrats did not realize was that by allowing excessive civic freedom to their

[1] Karl Renner, *Österreich von der Ersten zur Zweiten Republik*, Vienna 1953, p. 84.
[2] Philip Scheidemann, *Memoiren eines Sozialdemokraten*, Dresden 1928, Vol. II, p. 414.
[3] Ibid., p. 420.

opponents they promoted anarchy and encouraged the assassins of democracy – they really committed suicide.

## The Call for Stronger Executives

Clearly, many factors contributed to the growing paralysis which struck the post-war democracies. Proportional representation, which made strong effective parliamentary government impossible, and the perversion of the party system, which made for ambivalent, friend–foe relationships between the parties, were matched by the democratic leaders' aversion to power, springing from long years in the role of opposition. Experience had taught their executive members a great deal about the art of public oratory and debate but very little about the art of government and administration. Quite apart from their pacifism, their lack of expert knowledge compelled them to rely on a bureaucracy and a military class who by birth, education and ideology could hardly be expected to welcome democracy. As long as the democratic parties had a majority in parliament and as long as they could still call on the dreaded weapon of a general strike those groups nurtured in the absolutist tradition were forced to do as they were told. They were perfectly willing to do so because the democrats' ignorance about the realities of power gave them every chance to prepare positions from which to launch an anti-democratic offensive.

The democrats served too short an apprenticeship. Forced from the outset to crush coups attempted by both left- and right-wing extremists, they also had to wrestle with the daunting economic problems of the immediate post-war years. Germany and Austria received little help from Western democracies in building up their parliamentary systems. A move to establish an army of conscripts in the Weimar Republic was forbidden by the Allies, who favoured the professional *Reichswehr* instead. In the Succession States the economic situation was complicated by the splitting up of the vast economic areas of Austria-Hungary.

The world economic crises had disastrous effects in central Europe because they shattered political and social structures already on the verge of collapse. Every test which the democratic executives had to meet exposed further their inherent weakness and stimulated the call for a strong executive, the strong man at the helm of affairs.

Were the executives in the post-war democracies really weak? In so far as there was genuine weakness it was due to special circumstances rather than the fault of the constitutions. One of these was proportional representation and the coalition governments it produced. Also there was the fact that democracy in Germany and Austria had to bear the odium for the lost war. The post-war democracies also suffered from the innate defects of infant democracies. Their weakness was therefore partly absolute, partly relative compared with the semi-absolute states of the pre-war years.

Max Scheler had long expressed the view that the Germans wanted an authoritarian type of state, longed to be dominated, showed a tendency to political subservience and that though in Germany a political song would not always remain an ugly one yet it would always be an unimportant one.[1] It appears to be a reasonable hypothesis that something more than the weakness of the democratic executive prompted the call for the 'strong man'. Democracy, as Eschenburg observes, was not *persona grata* in Germany.[2] Those who fostered the legend that Germany had been stabbed in the back maintained it had been imposed on the Germans by the West.[3] The cry for a 'superman' was therefore not a call for a strong democratic executive but for a new system, which at once proceeded to crush democracy.

In 1930 Deutsch[4] wrote a most illuminating article on the background to this demand, which became increasingly insistent in Austria too. Deutsch believed that the propertied classes in post-war Austria had been alarmed by the taxes imposed on them by local governments dominated by the socialists. After weathering the inflation of 1923 the middle classes had joined forces and once the army and the police had been purged of socialists, the fascist *Heimwehr* had been organized. Retired imperial army officers rushed to join it and Major Pabst, one of the principal conspirators in the Kapp *putsch*, helped to build it up. Deutsch did not, however, mention the mistrust which the middle classes, already disillusioned by the socialists' advocacy of the class-war and their revolutionary slogans, felt towards their democratic aims. Nor did Deutsch say anything about the profound shock caused by the Russian Revolution and the revolutionary acts which occurred in Germany and Austria. Like national socialism in Germany, Austrian fascism appeared in the small towns. Deutsch vividly described their character:

'Narrow-minded philistines still dominate in the small town, living in a world of their own and out of touch with Europe. The petty officials determine public opinion. Magistrate, bailiff, forestry expert, public

[1] Max Scheler, op. cit., pp. 161 f. This refers to Goethe's *Faust*, Part I.
[2] Theodor Eschenburg, *Die improvisierte Demokratie*, op. cit., p. 45.
[3] Ibid., p. 46.
[4] Julius Deutsch, 'Zwischen Faschismus und Demokratie', *Neue Blätter für den Sozialismus*, First Year, Vol. 5, Potsdam, May 1930, pp. 193 ff.

notary, head clerk, etc. . . . were content to sigh for the good old days.
. . . Then, when times changed and there was a reasonable chance to
take cover behind the authority of the police sergeant and the
gendarmerie they dared again to show their anti-republican feelings.
In all the pubs screams in favour of the strong-armed ruler could be
heard. The example of Mussolini fascinated them. . . .'[1]

In Germany the Weimar Constitution had made the President
stronger than the cabinet. The change from constitutional monarchy
to quasi-parliamentary republic was not nearly as abrupt as one
might have imagined, to judge by previous revolutionary events.

The President of the Reich was elected directly by the people.
Hence he was equal, if not superior, to the members of the Reichstag.
His term of office was for seven years; he could be re-elected any
number of times. From the outset, therefore, there was the danger
that the office might revert to some form of monarchism or a
Bonapartist-style Caesarism under cover of pseudo-legality. It is
scarcely credible that men like Preuss and Naumann did not realize
this, and not even Friedrich Ebert, the first President, made this seem
unlikely. Articles 45 and 46 of the Constitution had transferred the
Emperor's prerogatives to the President. Anschütz has pointed out
that the President's right to appoint officers and ministers was no mere
formality.[2] As the Emperor's successor he was Supreme Commander of
the armed forces. Under Article 55 the President appointed the
Chancellor and, on the latter's recommendation, the ministers. He
could also dismiss these. The President could use his discretion in
appointing the Chancellor though the government remained in office
as long as it commanded the confidence of the Reichstag. What was
disturbing, however, was that the Constitution gave the government
two masters, the President and the Reichstag, both of whom it had to
serve simultaneously.[3] For the President could dismiss the Chancellor
while the latter still enjoyed the confidence of the Reichstag. Anschütz
thought this set the President above the members of the cabinet.[4]

---

[1] Ibid., p. 197.
[2] Anschütz, *Die Verfassung des Deutschen Reiches vom 11 August 1919*, Berlin
1933, p. 226.
[3] According to Article 54, Herrfahrdt held the view that *President* and *Reichstag*
were co-ordinated and he rightly feared that this would lead to anarchy and civil war.
Glum remarked that this proved that Herrfahrdt had not understood the parliamentary system. Glum, op. cit., p. 252. Herrfahrdt's interpretation was however justified,
as Weimar had deliberately given the President such power that his position lay
somewhere between the English King and the American President. Cf. Heinrich
Herrfahrdt, 'Die Kabinettsbildung nach der Weimarer Verfassung unter dem
Einfluss der politischen Praxis', in: *Öffentlich-rechtliche Abhandlungen*, edited by
Triepel, Kaufmann, Smend, Berlin 1927.
[4] Anschütz, op. cit., p. 318.

The dissolution of the Reichstag, which was the prerogative of the President, certainly required ministerial agreement. However, this restriction on the President's powers was illusory: for a President who wanted to dissolve the Reichstag could have dismissed an obstructive Chancellor and appointed someone more amenable to himself. The President had, therefore, greater powers *vis-à-vis* the Reichstag than the Emperor, who had to get the approval of the Bundesrat (Upper House) before the Reichstag could be dissolved. The President's power, allowing him to dismiss both the cabinet and the Reichstag, was clearly a legacy from the days of monarchy. The fathers of the Weimar Constitution undoubtedly believed that they had modelled the Presidency on the English Crown. But they overlooked the fact that in England the King had not brought his personal influence to bear on government affairs since the reign of George III (though the last time a Prime Minister was dismissed was during the reign of William IV, at the beginning of the nineteenth century). The system of cabinet responsibility had been born of a long struggle between Parliament and the royal executive, the Establishment. The events which took place in Germany between 1929 and 1933, the arbitrary appointment and dismissal of the Brüning, Papen and Schleicher cabinets, like the frequent dissolution of the legislature, were in many ways reminiscent of the struggle between legislature and executive in England.

Under the first paragraph of Article 48 the President was also empowered to take action against states which violated the Constitution and the laws of the Republic. The second paragraph of the same article also enabled him to exercise dictatorial powers 'if public security and order are seriously disturbed or threatened' in the Reich. In that event he could take any necessary measures to restore public security and order, including the use of armed force.[1] For this purpose the President could suppress the most important basic civic rights. According to Anschütz typical dictatorial measures were 'the abrogation of basic rights, the transference of absolute power to individual organs of the state, the appointment of special commissars and setting up of special courts'.[2]

The stormy events which troubled the post-war years meant that, even under President Ebert, Paragraph 2 of Article 48 was constantly invoked. Between 1919 and 1925 President Ebert issued no less than 136 emergency decrees. Thus people became accustomed to an expedient which became regular practice under Brüning, Papen and Schleicher. Hence the people regarded the Hitler cabinet formed on

[1] Anschütz, op. cit., 10th Edition, Berlin 1929, p. 239.
[2] Anschütz, ibid., p. 251.

January 30 simply as another Presidential cabinet. The change to dictatorship did not come suddenly enough to provoke any active resistance in the nation as a whole. Article 48 therefore gave the Weimar Republic a dual character. The Constitution envisaged a parliamentary, federal system for normal times and an authoritarian, centralized government for abnormal times. The term 'quasi-federalism', in K. C. Wheare's sense, also applies therefore to the Weimar Republic. Where there is frequent interference with the autonomous legal status of the units, that system is to be considered centralistic which allows the states to have certain delegated powers until such time as they are revoked. Yet the Länder have no legally protected sphere of autonomy.

Other countries provide precedents for a dual government. In India, as in other British colonies, during the long process of emancipation it was British policy gradually to make the people of the country familiar with the business of government without immediately handing over the entire administration.[1] That meant there was one type of rule for normal and another for abnormal conditions, i.e. emergencies. When the movement for Indian independence gathered momentum after the First World War, the so-called Montague-Chelmsford Reforms introduced the so-called dyarchic system. This gave practical expression to Britain's policy of gradually accustoming the people to responsible government.[2]

But as experience in different parts of the Commonwealth shows, the system allowing for two alternative types of government, however well-intentioned, has its disadvantages. To limit the politicians' actual responsibility is also to limit their sense of responsibility. Emergency powers are all too easily misused and applied to people whose politics are disliked. These regulations are invoked far too readily, instead of citizens being given an opportunity to exercise political responsibility, which is the *sine qua non* of successful democracy. In the tutorial dictatorship envisaged by this system the pupils are far too pampered and spoilt. As guardian, the state insists that its citizens place absolute trust in its conduct of affairs. The more obscure this is, the greater the trust which is expected from the citizen.

Similar considerations seem to have moved the fathers of the Weimar Constitution when they introduced this Article relating to a state emergency. Like India, Germany was a nation accustomed to a semi-authoritarian but well-meaning executive. As in India, neither the democratic politicians nor the people were trusted – not because

[1] K. J. Newman, 'The Dyarchic Pattern of Government and Pakistan's Problems', in *Political Science Quarterly*, op. cit., p. 98.
[2] K. J. Newman, 'Pakistan's Preventive Autocracy and its Causes', op. cit., p. 23.

the Germans were uneducated like the Indians but because they were unpolitical or even apolitical. Men like Ebert, Preuss, Max Weber and Naumann thought of the President not only as a 'substitute Emperor' or 'Emperor's shadow' but also as a teacher of democracy who had all the means of discipline at his disposal and who could do his job as long as he remained a democrat, that is, as long as the office of President was held by a man who believed in the basic democratic values.

If a section of the German people remained cool towards the parliamentary system, also the frequent cabinet changes, the inability of the coalition cabinets and minority governments to get laws through the Reichstag along with other features typical of a young democracy did much to undermine the prestige of the Reichstag and democracy.

The host of emergency decrees and enabling laws which were passed was evidence of the Reichstag's indecisiveness. The immediate result was that people in authority invoked the strong constitutional powers of the President. When he took office Hindenburg declared that Reichstag and President were one. The Reichstag was said to be the embodiment of the party conflicts whereas the President represented in his person the impartial body of eager and constructive forces in the nation. This was a clear reference to the former position of the Emperor *vis-à-vis* the Reichstag. It was also a clear rejection of the class-war advocated by the left and a confession of faith in the old Prussian executive state. This yearning for the return of the imperial, semi-constitutional system appeared clearly between 1930 and 1933. Yet these conservative, semi-authoritarian forces, which even in 1918 were not strong enough to overthrow the republic, proved equally incapable of withstanding national socialism, then looming large.[1] Events had proved time and time again that, in the twentieth century, an authoritarian state which is based only on the armed forces, the police and the bureaucracy can no longer check the progress of a popular mass movement.

It was to be expected that spokesmen to voice the growing discontent with existing conditions would also appear among the constitutional lawyers, who were ready to provide the politicians seeking greater power for the executive with the arguments and procedures necessary to achieve this. Herrfahrdt, and also to some extent Kaufmann and Triepel, must be reckoned among the political theorists supporting the Presidential system which had existed since Brüning. Herrfahrdt made a virtue of the necessity for minority governments, describing them as supra-party governments borne by the President's

[1] As national socialism is one of the consequences of the Russian Revolution the present writer will not call it right-radical.

will[1] and ascribing the role of umpire to the President – showing that Herrfahrdt's concept of the 'community' was political and ideological. In these circumstances, he thought, not even a majority government would reflect the people's will if it did not include important sections of the community, and the President would then be fully justified in intervening against such a government – in his role as 'protector of the constitution' (in Schmidtt's sense) – in order to prevent 'stasis'. Therefore Herrfahrdt saw the President as a philosopher-king who must allow himself to be intimidated by a vote of no confidence against his cabinet.[2] The President was to have stood out as the sole and supreme guarantor of the public good who, in the full Platonic sense, has a duty in the interests of the body politic to prevent economic conflict between parties and classes. Carl Schmitt considered the 'pluralistic party state' as the typical product of liberalism and its clash of interests. The 'protector of the constitution' is not (according to Schmitt) 'the sovereign lord of the state' but (in the Hegelian sense) completely represents the monarchical power. And nothing is altered by Schmitt's seeing this power as the *pouvoir neutre et intermédiaire*' (in Benjamin Constant's sense) – as a neutral, mediatory, regulating and preserving force.

Ebert believed that the German masses and leaders must first learn to run a constitutional democracy in order to become mature enough for socialism. He had therefore, to carry on the struggle against both 'right' and 'left'. But when the crucial moment came he realized where the greater danger lay.

But Ebert did not himself risk taking the decision which would have meant mobilizing all available forces against the threat of a right-wing revolution. He was motivated by the inherent pacifism and legalism of the SPD. But his restraint and mildness earned him no thanks. They were, rather, held to be a sign of the weakness and inefficiency of democracy.

## PART THREE

*The Judiciary and the New Constitutions*

The post-war democracies inherited from their predecessors judical systems with considerable traditional prestige. This was true of both the German Empire and the Austro-Hungarian monarchy. Both

[1] Herrfahrdt, op. cit., pp. 41, 43; see also Glum, op. cit., pp. 255 f.
[2] Herrfahrdt, op. cit., pp. 53 f.

possessed a conscientious professional judiciary which had for long been irremovable. The judges could look back to the traditions of the independent judiciary of the Holy Roman Empire. But as the dynastic principalities grew more powerful it became difficult for the judges to maintain their independence *vis-à-vis* the executive.[1] As elsewhere on the Continent the traditional method of appointing judges and public prosecutors is very different from the procedure in Anglo-Saxon countries, where these offices are an integral part of the liberal professions. On the Continent these careers can be entered upon by a young man after he has taken his university degree and continued until his retirement.

The civil population was accustomed to a criminal and civil law largely codified and based mainly on Roman Law. While constitutions in central Europe frequently changed, civil and criminal law had remained unaltered for generations. This continuity was undoubtedly one of the main reasons why the general public showed far greater respect for the courts than for parliament. The judiciary was proud of its independence, objectivity and impartiality. As in other parts of the world the judges in central Europe were conservative. It is open to conjecture whether the reasons advanced by Dahrendorf[2] (in agreement with W. Richter) to explain the conservatism of the judges in the Federal Republic are convincing or not. They certainly apply to a section of the judiciary in the Weimar Republic.

The judges who had grown up in imperial Germany saw themselves as the pillars of the Prusso-German state, which they regarded as non-party, sacrosanct and worth keeping. Furthermore, judges are conservative by nature of their profession and are expected to uphold the legal ruler. The law itself, which changes only very gradually, moulds their character much more than an individual judge can mould the law. The German judge considered himself as a servant of the state and in pre-war Germany the image of the state had always been ultra-conservative and semi-authoritarian. As a judge entered public service direct from university with its student corps

[1] For example, in the case of the miller Arnold, who successfully defied the Prussian King, Frederick the Great.

[2] Ralf Dahrendorf, *Gesellschaft und Freiheit*, Munich 1961, pp. 180 ff. Dahrendorf gives the following reasons:

1. Their regional immobility. Two out of three Federal Republic judges have been born in the district in which they sit. This is linked with the phenomenon of professional inheritance.
2. Their social immobility. 'Nearly two out of every three judges come from families who because of the father's profession constitute only one twentieth of the total population, namely the upper 5 per cent (op. cit., p. 182).
3. Dahrendorf notes that half the judges come from a civil service background (ibid., p. 185).

and fraternities he was to some extent ignorant of social conditions in an industrialized society. On this point Dahrendorf has remarked that everything to do with the working class with which a judge does not come into contact is enveloped in 'mysterious twilight'.[1] Yet, most of the offences which came before the courts involved defendants from these very classes. Hence allegations of class justice might easily be controlled. We are reminded of Laski's statement that an offence which was called theft in the east of London was described as 'kleptomania' in the West End.

Bracher speaks of 'political' justice in the Weimar Republic. He suggests that, together with the right of judicial review which we shall discuss, this became evident above all in the inconsistency of the verdicts pronounced on political offences, due to the judges exceeding their authority.[2] It is undoubtedly true that the crimes committed by the Right and by the Left were judged by different standards; that whereas the sentences on National Socialists were never longer than a few months or weeks, those on left-wing offenders often ran into years.[3] It is also true that the judges did not afford the Weimar Republic and its elected representatives the legal protection to which they were entitled.[4]

The justiciary's attitude was particularly striking in the cases of the 795 monarchists involved in the Kapp *putsch*. 412 were pardoned; 109 escaped conviction because of death or for other reasons; proceedings against 176 were stopped; only one was sentenced.[5] In such circumstances it may well be asked whether there was not a *partial dissolution* of legal order in the Weimar Republic. A partial collapse of law and order with the ensuing power vacuum and the inability or unwillingness of the courts to protect the law finally compels citizens to take the law into their own hands because they can no longer rely on the protection of the state. That must happen, especi-

---

[1] Ibid., p. 194.
[2] K. D. Bracher, *Die Auflösung der Weimarer Republik*, op. cit., pp. 191 ff.
[3] E. J. Gumbel, 'Treason Statistics', in *Menschenrechte* (1928).
[4] In *Vom Fememord zur Reichskanzlei*, Heidelberg 1962 (p. 46), Gumbel gives the following figures for political murder between 1919 and 1922:

| Political murders, committed by: | Rightists | Leftists |
|---|---|---|
| Not convicted | 326 | 4 |
| Partly convicted | 27 | 1 |
| Convicted | 1 | 17 |
| Total number of murders | 354 | 22 |
| Number of sentences | 24 | 38 |
| Self-confessed murderers acquitted | 23 | – |
| Length of imprisonment per murder | 4 months | 15 years |
| Number of executions | – | 10 |
| Fine per murder | 2 Marks | – |

[5] Ibid., p. 4.

ally when the organs of state themselves no longer consider the state to be worth protecting. This partly accounts for the large number of political para-military bodies. The very fact that the state was forced to make use of them proves that it was in retreat. By allowing millions of citizens to set up organizations which waged what was in effect civil war, the state proved that it was too weak to exercise its rightful monopoly of power. That the state was unable even to defend itself against the direct attack of these organizations is proof that it had disintegrated even before this was formally demonstrated by Papen, Schleicher and Hitler.

On the other hand, if sections of society take matters into their own hands the courts are clearly unable to carry out their functions, since there is no certainty about the identity of the state and the social and legal institutions to be protected.

What were the reasons for the predominantly negative attitude of the judiciary to the Weimar Republic? How is it that in the Anglo-Saxon countries and the British Commonwealth, which are influenced by their legal systems, lawyers have tended to be a bulwark of the constitution? Where democracy can no longer defend itself against authoritarian and totalitarian attacks, as in many developing countries today, judges and other lawyers frequently turn against authoritarianism and, as in Ghana, risk their jobs and their livelihood to defend constitutionalism. How is it that in central European countries, as in Czechoslovakia, Poland or Yugoslavia, the judges were neutral or, as in Germany and Austria, hostile to democracy?

In both cases the reason is the conservatism of the judges. In the Anglo-Saxon countries lawyers are brought up in the tradition of British constitutional history which still bears witness to the constitutional struggle of the common-law lawyers against the royal prerogatives and the executive. To be conservative in those countries means, therefore, to defend the firm traditions of the constitutional state based on the rule of law.

In the United States even judges of the highest integrity, like Chief Justice Marshall, are not always free of social and political prejudices. In the Bollman case, the legal sequel to the abortive attempt of an American to rescue the revolutionary hero Lafayette from prison in the Austrian town of Olmütz, Marshall remarked:

'It is not the intention of the Court to say that no individual can be guilty of this crime [high treason] who has not appeared in arms against this country [the United States]; on the contrary, if war be actually levied, that is if a body of men be actually assembled for the purpose of effecting by force a treasonable purpose, all those who perform any part, however remote from the same conspiracy, are to be considered traitors.[1]

A few months later, in the Aaron Burr case, Marshall expressed a far more liberal opinion:

'If in the one case the presence of the individual makes the guilt of the treasonable assembly his guilt, and in the other case the procurement by the individual makes the guilt of treasonable assemblage his guilt then presence and procurement are equally component parts of the overt act and equally require two witnesses which the Constitution requires for condemnation.'[2]

This judgement must be understood in the light of Marshall's hostility to President Jefferson's system, which had been greatly embarrassed by Burr.

The Supreme Court, which claims for itself the most extensive right of judicial scrutiny in the world, undoubtedly makes political decisions. Thus it may be seen that the horror expressed in this contest over the 'politicalization of justice' by liberals in the Weimar Republic is not shared universally. In America the 'political jurisdiction' of the Supreme Court was sometimes in harmony, sometimes in conflict with the executive and legislative powers. There the following rule holds good: the longer an executive can stay in the office, the greater the influence which it can exert by its appointments to any vacancies in the Supreme Court. But the important fact is that because the majority of the appointments were made not by the present but by the earlier governments, the Supreme Court acts as a check on any excessive government bias. It acts therefore like a counterbalance and is a guarantee of constitutional continuity.

Even in the Weimar Republic the administration of justice was not always anti-republican. Where a specific case challenged the monarchist and conservative traditions – for example the expropriation of the princes – jurisdiction was plainly conservative. In this respect the German judiciary was no exception to the rule that judicial verdicts tend to safeguard the sanctity of property. Thus, in India after 1947, attempts by a number of state governments to carry out a programme of land reforms were declared unconstitutional when challenged in the courts by the big landowners. In the end the Central Parliament had to amend the constitution. Even in Germany judgements did not always favour the National Socialists. Thus Dimitrov and other communists were acquited in the Reichstag arson trial. As this trial took place under the National Socialist regime it proved that the judges were by no means spineless, especially as their verdict seemed

[1] Corwin, *Twilight of the Supreme Court*, New Haven 1934.      [2] Ibid.

to confirm the then widely held suspicion that the National Socialists had themselves started the fire.

It is therefore a reasonable assumption that the conservative judges in the Weimar Republic believed implicitly that they were defending the constitutional state. The state they sought to shield was not the Weimar Republic but its predecessors, the Kaiserreich. In their favour it must be recalled that the judges were still unable to see any real signs of stability in the Weimar regime; that they were still suffering from the shock of the Russian Revolution and the subsequent attempts to make Germany communist; and that they completely misunderstood the revolutionary character of National Socialism, which they regarded as a vigorous conservative counterbalance to left-wing extremists. To the end their ideal remained the order of Prussian semi-constitutionalism.

Nor should it be forgotten that the tradition of Roman Law and the close connection between legal profession and bureaucracy made the judges part of a politically neutral element. However, such a vital component of state power as the law cannot exist in a vacuum, isolated from political events. Therefore the judges' 'unpolitical' attitudes proved merely to be a form of camouflage for their support of the conservative, authoritarian trend. The accusation which can rightly be levelled against the Weimar judges is, therefore, not that they were forced to act under political pressure but that, on the contrary, they did not bother to find out enough about the contemporary social and political situation. Not even the judges are an exception to the rule that the vitality of democracy depends on education in citizenship.

## The Right of Judicial Review

Although the post-war constitutions were based on the principle of the supremacy of constitutional over ordinary law, they contained no clear and general provisions for a system of judicial review. In Austria the most important power possessed by the Constitutional Court was its competence to decide what was constitutional law and what was ordinary parliamentary legislation.[1] Common citizens had no right to apply for a judicial review of legislation. 'The Constitutional Court was to weld the federal, dualistic structure of the Austrian Republic into a single unit but not give direct protection to the private individual.'[2]

[1] H. Kelsen's article in the *Jahrbuch des Österreichischen Rechts*, Vienna 1922, p. 266.
[2] F. Ermacora, *Verfassungsgerichtshof*, Graz, Vienna, Cologne 1956, p. 8.

Only the government possessed this right, *ex officio*. The highest courts had also had this right since 1929. The semi-authoritarian constitution promulgated by the Dollfuss regime abolished the Constitutional Court and transferred to the Federal Court[1] its competence to review decrees issued by the Federation if a *Land* made a similar request. The Federal Court was also empowered to review decrees of the *Länder* at the Government's request.

The Czechoslovak Constitution envisaged a seven-member Constitutional Court to consider whether laws were constitutionally valid, the members being appointed partly by parliament and partly by the Supreme Court and the Supreme Administrative Court.

A law passed in 1920 neutralized the Constitutional Court as the agreement of five Senate members was required for the Court's decision to be valid. It was highly unlikely that these would vote to invalidate the laws passed by their own parliament.

Nor could the Constitutional Court declare a law invalid *ex post facto*, which complicated the work of the judges who were members of the Senate.[2] If, therefore, the Court declared a law to be invalid, this could have been operative only from the moment the decision came into effect *pro futuro*. Even a genuine breach of the constitution could not be allayed unless brought to notice within three years of the law coming into force. As in Austria, the power to bring constitutional complaints was limited and not available to private persons. Consequently no use was ever made of this right. Section 102 of the Constitution, however, gave the common courts the right to review executive orders having legal nature. Considering the far-reaching practice, to pass such orders in the former Austria-Hungary meant that this competence was still a sign of progress.

The so-called Electoral Court was also entitled to review decrees. This court was a political organ comprising twelve members chosen from the House of Deputies, its President being the President of the Supreme Administrative Court. One of its most important functions was the hearing of electoral complaints which might lead to an annulment of an election. Originally, a criminal conviction was the only valid ground for such action. In practice, however, this system strengthened the parties; for every breach of party discipline by a deputy was declared 'dishonourable' by his party and gave it the opportunity to deprive him of his mandate. This must be seen as the logical extension of the Czechoslovak coalition system based on

[1] Ibid., p. 83.
[2] Opinions differ as to the nullity of a law *ex tunc* or *ex nunc*. Cf. *Verfassungsgerichtsbarkeit in der Gegenwart*, edited by H. Moser, Cologne, Berlin 1962, pp. 785 ff.

proportional representation. The constant danger with coalitions is that they will lose their stability because deputies from other parties are promised ministerial posts etc. as an inducement to desert their own party. However, this regulation strengthened the dominance of the party secretariats. Therefore the parties had a common interest to uphold it.

The Weimar Constitution, which acknowledged the federal character of Germany by introducing constitutional jurisdiction and investing this in the Constitutional Court, gave no positive directives on the judicial review of the constitutional validity of laws. In pre-revolutionary Germany the prevailing theory had been against any such right, and after the revolution this view was upheld by constitutional lawyers such as Thoma,[1] Anschütz[2] and Radbruch.[3] On the other hand men like Triepel and C. Schmitt were among those who supported the right. 'If it [judicial review] had frequently acted as a control in the democratic sense under the monarchy, in the new political circumstances its effect was the opposite, reinforcing a tendency to conflict with democratic organs and processes.'[4] Bracher concluded: 'The growth of the power of the judges amounted to a "dangerous attempt to give political character to justice".'

Against Bracher it might be argued that the advocates of the right of the judicial scrutiny also included constitutional lawyers like Kelsen, Merkl, Morstein-Marx, Leibholz and Smend, whose positive attitude to the Weimar Republic was unquestioned. Nor should the judges' conservatism during the life of the Republic blind us to the fact that the judiciary, as the third power, ought to be coequal with the legislature and the executive. For it is a corrective indispensable for the maintenance of constitutional balance. By adopting a critical position *vis-à-vis* the government and the legislature in both imperial and republican Germany the judiciary proved its independence.

Under Article 19 of the Weimar Constitution, the *Staatsgerichtshof* (court of state) was envisaged as the Constitutional Court of the Republic. As Carl Schmitt realized at the time, constitutional jurisdiction had developed in the nineteenth century as a corrective to encroachments on the part of the executive, but later turned against parliament as being the centre of power.[5]

Article 108 foresaw the setting up of the *Staatsgerichtshof*. This was effected by the Law of July 9, 1921.

[1] Thoma, *Archiv des öffentlichen Rechts*, op. cit., pp. 43, 272 ff.
[2] Anschütz, *Verfassung des Deutschen Reiches vom 11 August 1919*, op. cit.
[3] Radbruch, *Archiv Soziale Wissenschaften*, N.F. 4 (1906).
[4] S. Bracher, *Auflösung der Weimarer Republik*, op. cit., p. 193.
[5] Carl Schmitt, 'Das Reichsgericht als Hüter der Verfassung', in *Verfassungsrechtliche Aufsätze*, Berlin 1958, p. 67.

The Court sat –

1. Under Article 19 of the Constitution: as Constitutional Court, to settle 'constitutional disputes within the state where no court existed to settle those', i.e. in *Länder* which did not have their own constitutional courts.

2. Also under Article 19: to settle disputes of a non-private nature between the Central Government and a *Land*, provided there was no other competent court.

3. Under Article 15 of the Constitution: to settle differences of opinion between the Central Government and *Land* in order to redress shortcomings pointed out by the Central Government.

4. Also under Article 19: to settle disputes of a non-private legal nature between *Länder* where no other court of the Republic was competent. The following could be parties to and bring actions; the *Länder*, the constitutional organs of the Central Government and *Länder*, parliamentary minorities, parliamentary committees, individual deputies[2] and political parties. The individual citizen, on the other hand, could not bring an action.

In the sphere of control of the constitutional legislative enactment the Supreme Court of Germany (*Reichsgericht*) or the Federal Finance Court could, at the instance of a competent Central Government or *Land* authority, make a legally binding decision as to whether a *Land* law regulation contravened federal law.[3]

Another question was whether the courts deciding in the ordinary process of law were entitled to exercise the right of judicial scrutiny and decide whether the laws before them were unconstitutional or not. As we have already mentioned, there were differences of opinion on this question. But the right of judicial review was gradually acknowledged by a number of German courts and finally the Fifth Civil Senate of the Supreme Court (*Reichsgericht*) decided in its favour in connection with its own review of the Revaluation Law of July 16, 1925.[4] The Supreme Court based its decision primarily on the observation that the Constitution itself contained no directive divesting the courts of this right and transferring it elsewhere and therefore it must be recognized that it was the right and duty of judges to examine the constitutional validity of laws. That argument was also the basis of

---

[1] Cf. Anschütz, op. cit., pp. 165 ff.

[2] Ernst Friesenhahn, 'Die Staatsgerichtsbarkeit des Deutschen Reiches' in Anschütz-Thoma, *Handbuch des Deutschen Staatsrechts*, Vol. II, op. cit., denies that states and individual deputies can be parties.

[3] E. Friesenhahn, 'Die Verfassungsgerichtsbarkeit in der Bundesrepublik Deutschlands', in *Verfassungsgerichtsbarkeit*, op. cit., pp. 97 f.

[4] *Reichegericht*, III, 320.

the conclusion that the Supreme Court claimed the right to declare invalid any law which violated the Constitution.

Carl Schmitt thought that this 'gave expression to the principle of circumstantial subsumption': 'There are constitutional provisions under which that part waiting to be decided can be subsumed.'[1]

Schmitt believed, therefore, that a law can be declared invalid by the Supreme Court 'if a law contradicts a legal maxim embodied in the Constitution' and 'the requirements necessary prescribed for amending the Constitution have not been fulfilled'.

Then, however, the Supreme Court would have set definite limits to the right of judicial review. Schmitt expressed the opinion that, according to that argument, there was no 'judicial review for a simple Federal law as to whether it conforms to the general principles of the Constitution as distinct from the question if a definite constitutional provision has been violated'. There was no general review, i.e. no review with regard to the spirit of the Constitution, apart from the question whether a legal provision was contrary to a concrete Article of the Constitution; also no right of review in respect of the maintenance of principles which make up the principles of the rule of law in the Constitution.[2] Thus there would be 'no judicial review of a simple Federal law in respect of its conformity with *general principles of law*', loyalty and faith, morality, reasonableness and similar concepts, which it has been the practice of the Supreme Court of the United States to use in reviews of trust and social legislation.[3]

Ernst von Hippel[4] held the opposite view. According to him 'right of review exists in respect of laws which were formally and legally passed' for 'the competence of the constitutional legislator is free only within the limits of the concept of law. Arbitrary measures are therefore illegal and basically non-binding.[5]

Hippel, who bases much of his argument on the tradition of natural law, rejected the positivist view that a legitimate body of law can be built up on the arbitrary exercise of power. He refers to the modern ideas of organic society which set limits to the legislator's omnipotence and sovereignty and 'whose historical roots go back via Roman Law to the Caesarism of late antiquity and to modern absolutism'.[6] The present author has traced this omnipotence back to the theological legislative competence of Byzantine Caesaropapism and, even further,

---

[1] C. Schmitt, *Verfassungsrechtliche Aufsätze*, op. cit., p. 90.
[2] Ibid., p. 91.
[3] Ibid., p. 92.
[4] 'Das richterliche Prüfungsrecht', in *Handbuch des Deutschen Staatsrechts*, Vol. II, op. cit., p. 549.
[5] Ibid.
[6] Von Hippel, op. cit., p. 550.

to the oriental temple state.[1] Hippel regrets that the Supreme Court expressed this positivist view of the 'autocracy' of the legislator who 'is restricted only to those limits which he himself has drawn in the Constitution or in other laws'.[2]

The real reason for the limitation of the right of judicial review is to be found in views which can be described simply as fear that justice will be used for political ends. In point of fact, judges hearing constitutional complaints are frequently forced to decide political questions. In the work quoted above, C. Schmitt expressed the opinion that in a judicial clarification as to whether the Constitution has been violated, the point involved is 'a decision reached by an autocratic removal of doubt'.[3] That would mean that the judges make political decisions instead of the executive and the legislature, which is undoubtedly the case in the United States.

This means that because the United States Constitution is based on John Locke's view of the social contract the courts claim the right to review laws according to the general principles of natural justice. The American Constitution, one of the shortest such documents in the world, confines itself to enunciating the basic principles of the democratic state based on the rule of law. As this Constitution stems from the eighteenth century it must be reinterpreted from time to time to take account of the changed social, economic and political conditions. But the very brevity of the Constitution allows a great deal of room for judicial action, which Chief Justice Marshall called 'constitutional construction'. Even in the United States this judicial, constitutionally constructive activity has not gone unchallenged since it is the judges of the Supreme Court who extend and alter the Constitution. The opposite views have been clearly expounded by Corwin in his discussion of the right of judicial review. According to Corwin there are two conceptions on which the interpretation of constitutions can be based:

1. *The juristic conception.* This works a miracle. It supposes a kind of transubstantiation. As a result of this the court's interpretation of the Constitution expressed in a judicial decision on a case conducted according to due process of law becomes the life blood of the Constitution.

2. *The political conception,* which regards the Constitution as an instrument of democracy. This conception ascribes the primary role

[1] K. J. Newman, 'Papst, Kaiser, Kalif und der Basileus', *Politische Vierteljahresschrift*, Cologne, Opladen, 4th Year 1963, pp. 32 ff.

[2] Von Hippel, op. cit., p. 551.

[3] C. Schmitt, *Verfassungsrechtliche Aufsätze*, p. 81.

in the interpretation of the Constitution to the people or its representatives. While national leadership based on the office of President
of the United States is the driving force behind the political conception, professional judicial opinion is the force behind the juristic
conception. The same writer maintains that the main political problems which engaged the Supreme Court and by which it changed the
Constitution were nationalism versus federalism, property versus
democracy and law versus individuals.[1]

The position of the present Federal German Constitutional Court
is in many respects similar to that of the Supreme Court of the USA.
According to Leibholz, the judiciary is not superior to but coequal
with the legislature, the government and the executive.[2] Leibholz's
answer to the question of who is the guardian of the Constitution is,
therefore, the Federal Constitutional Court, because it 'makes final,
legally binding decisions for people and state on the legal questions
submitted to it for judgement'.[3] Leibholz answers the charge that the
powerful position of constitutional jurisdiction leads to the 'politicalization' of justice by pointing out that 'the separation of powers has
never been carried out absolutely' and that 'there has always been
some overlapping in the system'. Consequently because for example
the British Parliament exercises judicial functions through the House
of Lords it has not thereby ceased to be legislature. In the same way
the Federal Constitutional Court's decisions, which have the force of
law in the control of legislative enactment and therefore go beyond
pure jurisdiction, could not throw doubt on its basic character as a
true court.

The controversy about the 'politicalization of justice' also continues
in the Federal Republic. As the two fronts which expressed the
different opinions in the Weimar Republic are vague and confused
for the constitutional historian, the further development under today's
conditions in the Federal Republic is of the greatest importance because it clearly shows us which views then upheld the democratic
state based on the rule of law, which views consistently undermined
it and which endeavoured to save it with the best of intentions but
with unsuitable methods.

Even in 1950 Erich Kaufmann, for instance, expressed the opinion
that if the Constitutional Court 'wishes to remain a genuine court it
will have to draw a clear distinction between political and legal

[1] Corwin, *Twilight of the Supreme Court*, op. cit., Chaps. I–III, cf. also Warren,
*The Supreme Court in United States History*, Boston Hill 1922.
[2] Gerhard Leibholz, *Strukturprobleme der Demokratie*, op. cit., p. 172.
[3] Ibid., pp. 173 f.

questions'.[1] For example he sees the government's request for a ban on a totalitarian party as a political question and wishes to confine the court to a review of the legal question as to 'whether the decision implied in the suit is well-founded in itself, reasonable and not arbitrary in respect of the facts submitted.'[2]

This attitude reminds one of Corwin's thesis of the political conception regarding the interpretation of the constitution. This conception stresses the role of public opinion in the constitutional interpretation. Corwin thought that in the United States the driving power behind the political conception is presidential leadership, whereas the driving power behind the juristic conception is the professional opinion of the judges.

It is significant that Carl Schmitt in his book also referred to a 'danger' which he saw in an 'inadmissible broadening of some factual contents of specific constitutional provisions'. It is uncertain what Schmitt actually intended by his volte-face towards legal positivism and by his sudden wish to restrict the powers of the judiciary which, as we have said, was then highly conservative in Germany. His motive becomes clearer when we realize that it was the national socialist regime which reaped the fruits of this quasi-positivistic attitude. For since national socialism came to power in a pseudo-legal manner and took over the legislative power in 1933 by means of the Enabling Law, the courts were no longer in a position to review the validity of illegal laws and decrees issued on the basis of this law. The judges were restricted to considering a subsumption under the facts of the case. In this way, one might well say, the state based on the rule of law was dissolved in a perfectly 'legal' manner and the judges had to act as loyal servants of the state based on injustice.

If Schmitt's adherence to positivism is understandable because of his complete dependence on Hobbes's totalitarian concept of the state, the ideas of Weimar's defenders such as Thoma and Anschütz appear traditional and incredibly naïve. Thus Anschütz cites Thoma approvingly: 'German jurisprudence can henceforth retain the valuable asset of non-scrutiny of laws formally perfect as far as, in the new constitutional law, sufficiently strong and reliable guarantees are established, so that the more hallowed clauses of the constitutional documents cannot be overthrown either in roundabout ways or directly by parliamentary majorities.'[3]

But what did Thoma and Anschütz consider to be the guarantees? The independent right of review of the German President and the Government, the upper chamber's right of veto and the right of a

[1] Erich Kaufmann, *Autorität und Freiheit*, Göttingen 1960, p. 509.
[2] Ibid.                     [3] Anschütz, op. cit., p. 324.

third of the parliamentary deputies to demand a referendum – an almost irresponsible optimism when one remembers that Anschütz wrote the preface[1] to this commentary on the Constitution in February 1933, that is after Hitler had seized the reins of power.

The meaning of the right of judicial review was not properly clarified until after the war. Thus Leibholz, for example, starts from the fact that the Federal Constitutional Court is not only a court but also a constitutional organ.[2] In agreement with his opinion[3] the Federal Constitutional Court[4] regards itself as the 'supreme guardian of the Constitution'. Leibholz does not deny that 'constitutional jurisdiction impinges on the political sphere',[5] but observes: 'Constitutional law – like international law – differs from all other forms of law in content by making political questions the subject of legal standardization and therefore political law is involved'. Like his teacher Triepel, Leibholz also admits that an innate antagonism exists between the nature of politics and the nature of law. The political, Leibholz continues, is 'always something dynamic-irrational . . . which seeks to adapt itself to the constantly changing conditions of life'.[6] It is concerned with questions which in some way concern the foundation and preservation of the community. Therefore the politician is always trying to make pragmatic decisions, according to the demand of the situation, to restrain the incalculable political forces, therefore attempting to make what wants to be free 'calculable by rational standards'.[7] But this *desire* (to be free) does not bind the constitutional judge for whom the existence of judicial norm is a mere assumption.[8]

Moreover, it is impossible to see why the constitutional judge cannot apply the principles of natural justice to the interpretation of the constitution, like the Supreme Court, especially where there is a lacuna in the constitution.

We must therefore once more point out that in the Weimar period there was a fundamental misunderstanding about the meaning of the right of judicial review and an ignorance of what was 'political', an artificial distinction being made between the politics and state. This misunderstanding stemmed from the absolutist tradition of the monarchy, which had succeeded in turning the judiciary into a part of the executive, expected to apply the sovereign's edicts and decrees without question. Just as in Acton's sense the general will sat down on the throne of the Bourbons via the French Revolution, so the positivists

---

[1] Anschütz, op. cit., p. VI.     [2] Leibholz, op. cit., p. 174.
[3] Ibid., p. 175.
[4] Cf. report on status, *Jahrbuch des öffentlichen Rechts*, N.F. (1957), Vol. 6, p. 127.
[5] Ibid., p. 175.     [6] Ibid., p. 122.
[7] Leibholz, op. cit., p. 176.     [8] Ibid., p. 177.

of the Weimar period thought the law-based state had sat down on the throne of Frederick the Great. Whoever sat on this throne was therefore justified in issuing party-political laws in his sense and in favour of his course. According to Lenin the state is a club and exists for the benefits of its members. The fight against the 'politicalization of justice' in the Weimar Republic was therefore a party-political fight which was directed against the politicalization only in so far as this could benefit an opposition party. It is not true that justice saw itself as a *pouvoir neutre* (neutral power); it regarded itself as maintaining the constitution, only the judges were not unanimous about *which* state was to be maintained. According to Bracher[1] the court also ought to have examined the President's discretion when it reviewed emergency regulations under Article 48 of the Weimar Constitution and Papen's deposition of the social-democratic Prussian Government in 1932. But where can the court be found which would venture to pass judgement on the discretion of the executive?

In conclusion it should be said that for the constitutional state constitutional jurisdiction must, by its nature, have a controlling and compromising function. Since the constitutional state must be basically a mixed state, in Plato's and Aristotle's sense, the legislature represents the democratic, and the executive the monarchical, but justice represents the aristocratic element (in the sense of an intellectual aristocracy). The democratic element in the legislature can easily be influenced by the fluctuations of public opinion. Because of its dependence on the voters the legislature is continuously exposed to the temptation to yield to these. The executive also, even if it is only a committee of the legislature, as in parliamentary democracy, has nevertheless the basically different function of making quick and effective decisions. In this it relies on the civil service, which often enough considers expediency and rationality as the highest administrative values. Both legislature and executive can easily make decisions by which the individual or a group of individuals are dangerously prejudiced in their rights or the future good of state and people is threatened. In these circumstances the function of the constitutional judge is to balance and protect and in doing so he circumscribes the real significance of the political body.

[1] Bracher, op. cit., p. 197.

## PART FOUR

*The Experience of Direct Democracy*

'*The greatest, most permanent, and most fundamental of all the difficulties of Democracy lies deep in the constitution of human nature. Democracy is a form of government, and in all governments acts of state are determined by an assertion of will. But in what sense can a multitude exercise volition? The student of politics can put to himself no more pertinent question than this.*'[1]

Here is a problem which is particularly acute and urgent where members of an assembly vote directly on legislative measures – as was formerly the custom in the New England townships or in Swiss Landesgemeinden – or where they participate in legislation by the referendum. The referendum has undoubtedly proved its value in Switzerland. Lord Bryce believed it also had its disadvantages,[2] but acknowledged that the Swiss had shown judgement, cool-headedness, intelligence and balance in their use of it. On the other hand he thought that a body such as the Landesgemeinden cannot reach decisions as quickly as a legislature. Bryce agreed that the patriotism and sense of responsibility of the Swiss are directly correlated to their awareness of their actual involvement in legislation. In Switzerland the people's parsimony and slow grasp of the requirements of an urgent situation arose out of the comparison (necessarily inexpert) made by the voter between his own personal needs and national expenditure. Expenditure is low in the peasant households in the Swiss mountains.[3]

The American type of referendum was born of the Puritan communities of the New England townships. The Swiss type, however, is much older, going back to the Germanic Thing. In both cases the system is based on stable traditions which enjoyed an uninterrupted period of development. Thus they became traditional and in these two countries stood on an equal footing with the representative system and local self-government. Almost the entire history of the referendum in Switzerland shows that for the sober Swiss it was never much more than an extension of local self-government to cantonal and national affairs.

In other parts of Europe the traditions were different. The revolutionary government of the National Convention during the French

[1] Sir Henry Maine, *Popular Government*, London 1909, p. 88.
[2] Bryce, *Modern Democracies*, Vol. I, London 1921, pp. 442 ff.
[3] Ibid., p. 435.

Revolution adopted radical democracy in Rousseau's sense. This tradition was continued by Napoleon Bonaparte, who abolished the Republic by a referendum which gave him 372,329 votes against a mere 2,569. Napoleon III also governed with the help of a referendum.

This type of referendum has the following features:

1. The electorate is given no genuine alternative choice or else the alternative is not clear.
2. Voting takes place unsupervised by representatives of other parties and it is impossible to check whether the voting figures are correct.
3. These referenda are frequently held under the impact of military victory or the threat of violence.
4. In every case the elector is under the impression that whichever way he casts his vote he could not possibly influence the final result.

As we have already seen, the democratic system, which was introduced into central Europe after the First World War, was influenced to a considerable extent by the national democratic teachings of Comte, Spencer and John Stuart Mill. It was this doctrine which led to the adoption of the plebiscite as a regular means of asserting the will of the inhabitants of certain territories about whose disposal the peacemakers of 1918–19 were uncertain. These referenda enormously enhanced nationalism by suggesting to the voters that language was their most urgent allegiance. Self-determination and language were quite wrongly identified. Suddenly, many whose parents would not have dared to criticize the regime of the princes were called upon to handle the most radical of all the devices of democratic government; and this under conditions which might have meant selling up their homes at once, forsaking all that was near and dear to them, for a future whose very outlines they were scarcely able to imagine.

As constitutional changes require normally a higher majority than a mere simple one, it is incredible that anyone should think that any way of life which evolved from centuries of communal living could be changed basically or permanently by a simple plebiscite. This type of plebiscite must be rejected for the same reasons that a totalitarian party is denied the same rights as a democratic party. After coming to power in apparently legal manner by winning a majority over other parties, it denies these parties the chance of regaining power by a future plebiscite. Likewise, the nationalist minority which has lost in a plebiscite are branded as traitors if they try to join another state.

No account is taken of the fact that something more than the right to use one's own language is needed to create a harmonious community. The peoples were led into the tragic mistake of breaking up the old communities without putting new ones in their place. Consequently the plebiscite which, used in conjunction with political agitation, suddenly forces people into taking a decision which possibly jeopardizes their whole future is hardly rational. For this decision, which bears a superficial resemblance to election, is irrevocable and final. These plebiscites often took place under duress; in the post-war period under Allied pressure; in the Saar under international pressure. They are a form of referendum and thus much more akin to the Napoleonic than to the Swiss type.

Some post-war constitutions, including those of Germany and Austria, introduced the referendum as a regular procedure. The Czechoslovak Constitution also promised a special law on the referendum. Some of the Baltic states also employed the referendum. The Weimar Constitution, however, opted for three forms of 'direct democracy': the national petition, the referendum and the plebiscite for electing a President.

Since, however, a referendum was difficult to carry out in practice, the electors, especially the moderates, preferred the regular methods of parliamentary legislation. In Germany the referendum had even more fateful consequences: the people who were accustomed to parliamentary elections distrusted the referendum and remained apathetic; its rarity made it a revolutionary measure.

In Germany people knew very little about the Swiss and American type of referendum. On the other hand they had often read in their newspapers about post-war plebiscites to decide whether particular areas should remain part of certain states or be detached from them. This was enough to give the referendum a quasi-revolutionary character.

After getting used to parliamentary elections, this unexpected and direct participation in the legislative process seemed to the Germans to be a gift of revolutionary significance. The history of the first referendum is typical. In 1926 the Communist Party organized a public petition in support of the expropriation of the German princes. Since the Social Democrats were unable to carry out one of their own they gave the communist proposal hesitant support. Although only four million signatures were necessary for a national petition demanding a national referendum, the petition bore no less than 12,523,939 signatures. That was impressive; but the move was revolutionary not only because of its content and the attitude of its instigators but also because of the reaction of the right-wing and the centre parties. The Right threatened that everyone who voted would be branded as a communist, thus using the most effective weapon against a referendum – *abstention*. The result proved the success of their tactics. 14,455,184 Germans voted for expropriation, but that was only 36·4 per cent of the total electorate of 39,736,509. But of these only 584,710 voted against the proposal. Therefore the 24,136,712 people who abstained were the real winners.[1]

In the next referendum the initiative was taken by Hugenberg's German National People's Party and the *Stahlhelm*, supported by the National Socialist Party. This so-called 'petition against the enslavement of the German people' demanded what was called a freedom law which would refute once and for all the 'war guilt lie'. The government was to be compelled to tell the Allies that the war guilt clauses of the Peace Treaty were based on lies and therefore Germany was not under any kind of obligation.

The authors of the petition also called for the immediate withdrawal of all Allied troops from the Rhineland. In its intention to make the signature of all international documents based on the 'war guilt lie' a punishable offence, the petition was directed against Stresemann's foreign policy. Even fewer people took part in the plebiscite of December 22 – namely 6,308,758 (14·9 per cent of the electorate), of whom 5,838,890 voted for the law.[2]

In both cases, therefore, the plebiscite was won by the largest party – the non-voters. Despite its failure, the last referendum had, however, important political consequences. The circumstances at the time, which were greatly affected by the economic depression, produced an emotional upheaval among the German middle class, which had previously been politically apathetic. The traumatic experience they had gone through as a result of losing the war and the subsequent threat of communist revolution and inflation found its outlet in an increasing extremism on their part. Politically inexperienced and ill-informed, it suffered severely from the economic crisis which brought a steep rise in unemployment not confined just to the working class. The depression, with the sudden restriction on credit, meant financial ruin for a number of medium and small employers and businessmen. The situation was made worse by deflationary factors which – like the collapse of prices – added to the pressures on business and also affected agriculture.

The power vacuum which has been referred to and the continued instability of the Weimar government destroyed middle-class confidence in the possibility of any sound, purposeful leadership from the Weimar coalition. Where could it turn? Socialists and communists were internationalists and, in any case, the structure of the ideological parties made middle-class support out of the question. The German National People's Party was weakened by the internal disunity be-

[1] *Statistisches Jahrbuch für das Deutsche Reich*, Berlin 1926, pp. 452 f.
[2] Ibid., Berlin 1930, p. 566.

tween its Hugenberg and Westarp wings; it was also disqualified because it was a capitalist, arch-reactionary party and had failed to carry the plebiscite attacking the concept of German war guilt.

This is why the National Socialists who, in the 1928 general election a few months before the plebiscite, were able to get only 179,000 votes, but then in the 1930 general election, i.e. after the plebiscite, were able to command some $6\frac{1}{2}$ million votes (18·3 per cent).[1] The increase in the National Socialist vote between 1930 and 1932 came, therefore, from the liberal and other middle-class parties (except the Zentrum Party), 'in so far as it was not due to the mobilization of the hitherto politically indifferent'.[2] Consequently it is, first, proof of the organic development (already referred to in Chap. 2) within national-liberalism, in which nationalism ousted liberalism from 1848 onwards to culminate in National Socialism. Secondly, by rousing electors who normally abstained from voting as well as other politically in-different or non-political people whom Chancellor Brüning had re-peatedly urged to vote, the national petition and the plebiscite of 1929 were also partly responsible for the National Socialist success. Ger-many's tragedy was that the nadir of the Weimar cabinet system with its centrifugal tendencies (due to proportional representation) coin-cided, after the dismissal of the Müller government, with the great economic depression, which could only have been tackled adequately by a strong democratic government. Furthermore, the German National People's Party (DNVP) wrongly assumed that it could exploit this weakness and restore the monarchy.

Before the 1930 elections Chancellor Brüning had appealed to the non-voters to use their vote. The landslide which followed in favour of the National Socialists, i.e. of an extremist party, was their answer. But this showed that in infant democracies it is useful to introduce *compulsory voting* along with universal suffrage. Had Weimar, like Belgium or Czechoslovakia, done this in 1918, all the electors would have been used to carrying out their duties as responsible citizens. Compulsory voting provides not only an excellent training in self-government but is also an antidote to extremism in public affairs be-cause it compels moderate sections of the public to help decide the nation's fate. Without compulsory voting the development of infant democracy into politeia in the Aristotelian sense is delayed, i.e. it cannot educate the middle class conscientiously to carry out its mediat-ing role in the community.

Here national-socialist technique, which clearly seeks to discredit the parliamentary system, must be mentioned. Part of this technique

[1] Ibid., Berlin 1931, pp. 546 f.
[2] Theodor Geiger, *Arbeiten zur Soziologie*, Neuwied, Berlin 1962, p. 338.

was to frustrate parliamentary activity by exploiting to the full the rights of parliamentary opposition to the point of sheer obstruction. These methods, which will be described in detail later, also included the constant demand for the dissolution of the Reichstag and the Diets of the *Länder* after new elections and plebiscites. National Socialists were strongly urged by their leaders to work the whole time for the dissolution of the Reichstag and for new elections.[1] Any occasion seemed to them an adequate reason to call for the premature dissolution of the Reichstag.[2] Thus Goebbels confessed: 'The Führer wants the Reichstag to be dissolved at all costs. We can only stand to win.'[3] In May 1932 the National Socialists promised to support the Papen government if they were given a pledge that the Reichstag would be dissolved.

With the two Presidential elections and the 1932 Prussian Diet election, altogether six elections were held in the Weimar Republic in one year: on March 30th, April 10th, April 24th, July 31st and November 6th, 1932 and on March 5th, 1933, as well. Thus the National Socialists succeeded, in a perfectly 'legal' manner, in whipping up a feeling of revolutionary crisis. *All* elections took on the character of a referendum and as the plebiscite gave the National Socialists endless opportunity for anti-democratic propaganda this technique was perfect for carrying out their aims. The National Socialists appeared to be able to prove that this form of democracy cannot give the state a stable government. They made it look as though the democratic system was responsible for the threat of civil war in Germany; further, that the democratic system lacked all dignity and sang-froid and that its collapse was imminent. Furthermore, in this way it was possible to create a mass psychosis which made the majority of inexperienced voters disregard all rational considerations. By their terrorism during the election campaigns, the National Socialists so intimidated the non-political voters and those people who had so far supported the middle-class parties for economic reasons that they thought it personally dangerous to oppose national socialism in any way. The higher the fever of this electoral revolution rose the more doubtful the secrecy of the ballot became.

The coincidence of these factors made the referendum of 1929 a critical turning-point in the conflict between democracy and fascism in Germany. Henceforward, in the wake of the referendum an ever-

[1] Hans Fabricius, *Geschichte der nationalsozialistischen Bewegung*, Berlin 1956, p. 31.

[2] German Archives, p. 135/6266; cf. also *Völkischer Beobachter*, April 16, 1930, Berlin.

[3] J. Goebbels, *Vom Kaiserhof zur Reichskanzlei, Eine historische Darstellung in Tagebuchblättern*, Munich 1937, p. 23.

spreading hysterical psychosis increasingly absorbed elections to all the other institutions. Parliaments and the *Land* Diets were dissolved at an ever-increasing rate. The result was that the plebiscitary character, which Carl Schmitt rightly observed to be latent in the Weimar Constitution, became much more pronounced and began to effect elections in states, towns and even trade unions as soon as the propagandist and terrorist methods of the extremist parties, i.e. the National Socialists and the Communists, were added to the general climate.

Furthermore the system of electing the President was from the first in the nature of a plebiscite. The third Presidential election, in which Hindenburg was re-elected, and the election of Hitler could only just be prevented, was the climax of the plebiscitary-revolutionary flood. It is not all that unreasonable to assume that it was this experience which finally drove the old President to swallow his aversion to Hitler and appoint him Chancellor.

The Weimar Republic's conduct of public affairs shows, therefore, that the 'national petition' and the 'national plebiscite' became propaganda weapons by which the aggressiveness of the supporters of radical groups was increased. On the other hand the relatively small percentage of the electorate who actually voted proves that the referenda by themselves could not be used to rescue the system. The relatively high proportion of electors who voted in the parliamentary elections means that the parties were considered to be more likely to solve specific practical problems. It was also due to the increasing scale and complexity of politics. In this sense the referenda were devices for intensifying political emotion. In critical situations such as these the bewildered electors are more willing than usual to put their trust in dubious programmes and personalities who seemed able to command success and the future. At this point in Germany's history national socialism was able to give the people 'rising' symbols in Lasswell's sense of the word and to stamp the symbols of the Weimar Republic as 'sinking' ones. 'Violence' was all that was needed to be added to the new symbols to ensure the victory of national socialism. That happened because from 1930 onwards all elections held in Germany were overshadowed by the menace of semi-military formations who waged war on one another, that is under conditions of both latent and virtual civil war.

The revolutionary situation consequently assumed the character of a permanent and escalating plebiscite which progressed implacably, gradually absorbing, in addition to the referendum, all democratic forms of the expression of the general will such as parliamentary and *Land* elections, presidential and even local and factory elections. A tremendous emotional pressure was set up by the use of new and unfamiliar methods of technical propaganda and this brought on something like a national nervous breakdown. Electors increasingly lost their sense of responsibility. Another important factor was the sense of personal commitment which people felt: they gave up any attempt at objective judgement and succumbed to the appeal to make personal decisions.

Both forms of direct democracy in Germany, the Presidential elections and the referendum, were intended to produce emotional decisions on which the representative system finally foundered. They fulfilled Rousseau's demand that the general will should issue from a direct, spontaneous expression of the popular will. But just as Rousseau's idea came to be embodied in Napoleonic Caesarism, under the conditions of a modern industrial state it assumed its ultimate form and true expression in the crisis natural to Hitlerism and in Hitler's plebiscites, which only allowed a simple Yes or No answer. These plebiscites are, therefore, the logical extension of Caesaristic democracy by plebiscite which, by destroying the voter's sense of responsibility, is bound to lead to dictatorship.

# CHAPTER IV

# Consequences of Nationalism's Triumph in the Paris Peace Settlement

## PART ONE

*National Minorities and National Self-Determination*

At the Paris peace negotiations President Wilson and the British delegation failed to achieve acceptance of their more conciliatory attitude towards the democratic governments of Germany and Austria. Clemenceau's more shrewd handling of the negotiations seemed at the time to assure the triumph of extreme nationalism.

Acting in the spirit of Wilson's proposals the new states appealed to the principle of national self-determination.[1] This principle was one of the postulates of the French Revolution. Every nation's absolute right to statehood had already been recognized as an elementary right in the nineteenth century and one which fair-minded Woodrow Wilson hoped would be easy to put into effect.[2] The Western rationalist theory of nationality had stressed the politically subjective and voluntaristic aspect of nationhood. Later, however, the equally characteristic exclusiveness of nationalism came increasingly to the fore. Now the objective element in the concept of nationality became more pronounced. In accordance with the Eastern organic concept mentioned above, which went back to Herder, a man is born into a national community. Membership of a definite nationality was now regarded as an exclusive privilege of those whom destiny had called to belong to it.

Once, however, it became possible to determine nationality objectively there grew up a potential incongruity between nationality and self-determination.[3] If nationality was decided by birth and every element of free choice excluded, there was no longer any room for self-determination.[4] National self-determination then became national

---

[1] Cf. G. Decker, *Das Selbstbestimmungsrecht der Nationen*, Göttingen 1953, pp. 47 f.

[2] Lloyd George, *The Truth about the Peace Treaties*, London 1938, pp. 237 ff.

[3] E. H. Carr, *The Future of Nations*, London 1941, p. 19.

[4] Alfred Cobban, *National Self-Determination*, Chicago 1944, p. 53.

determinism, as the national socialist racial policy was to show most clearly. Cobban very rightly sees that this determinism – in a weaker form – was already enshrined in the terms of the Paris Peace Settlement. What Cobban overlooks, however, in his criticism of the national-socialist nationality policy – which he describes as a pretext for imperialism – is that it was only a further development of the unilateral practice of the peacemakers of Versailles and St Germain. They did not understand this incongruity. They assumed that nationality and self-determination are identical and that a man who had the objectively characteristic features of a Pole or a Croat, for instance, also wanted to be a citizen of a Polish or a South Slav state.[1] Carr is right when he observes that this hypothesis is proof of western Europe's complete ignorance of east-European relationships. Had an east-Polish peasant been asked his views on self-determination he would have said he simply wanted to keep his local dialect and customs, go to his own church and have a better landlord.[2]

The plebiscites which were held in central and eastern Europe in connection with the Peace Conferences were in general defensive measures on the part of the defeated nations.[3] They proved that men's civic loyalty is not determined by their mother tongue. Thus in Allenstein, where, according to the census of 1910, 46 per cent of the population spoke Polish, only 2 per cent voted for Poland. In Upper Silesia, of the 65 per cent who were Poles only 40 per cent voted to join the Polish state; and in Carinthia, where 68 per cent of the population were Slovenes, less than 40 per cent voted for secession from Austria.[4]

Furthermore, the principle of self-determination was applied in the sole interest of the victors or of those who had joined them at the right moment. Self-determination, like every ideal whose meaning and interpretation are not clear, is liable to abuse. In connection with the Paris Peace Settlement the peoples claimed it only in so far as their national interests required it but passionately rejected it, by appealing to geographical, strategic, national grounds, where it would have entailed sacrifice on their part. No state ever claimed this right for minorities living in its midst. T. G. Masaryk, for example, clearly pointed out that it was only after the Bolshevist revolution in 1917 that the Western Powers were ready to encourage the small nations of Austria-Hungary to secede by claiming the right of national self-determination. Previously such a policy would have had repercussions in imperial Russia with which the Western Powers were allied.

[1] E. H. Carr, op. cit., p. 14.
[2] Ibid., p. 17.                                    [3] Carr, op. cit.
[4] T. G. Masaryk, *The Making of a State*, London 1927, p. 17.

Lloyd George was not far wrong when he said:

'The resurrected nations rose from their graves hungry and ravening from their long fast in the vaults of oppression. They were like Athelstane, in "Ivanhoe", who rose from his bier with the insatiable cravings of famine raging in his whole body. Like him they clutched at anything that lay within reach of their hands.'[1]

Furthermore the victorious powers were divided amongst themselves about the importance of national self-determination. While President Wilson regarded this principle as a panacea for all the world's ill, Italy rejected it out of hand because it obstructed her claims to the South Tyrol and a part of Turkish Asia-Minor. And France made it an excuse for dismembering her enemies. For France and England self-determination was the price which they had to pay, with due caution and reserve, for the advantages to be gained from supporting *irredenta* among the minorities of the Central Powers.[2] When these minorities presented their bills the Western Powers redeemed them but never for one moment believed that peace had been secured.

The liberation of the peoples of Asia and Africa has produced similar situations, as Kashmir, Dutch New Guinea, Tibet and Egypt and the Indonesian–Malaysian conflict show. As long as the peoples sought independence from colonial rulers they appealed to the world's sense of responsibility and conscience; but once they had achieved national independence they appear in the role of imperialists towards their own minorities.

After the First World War the Habsburg monarchy fell victim to the right of self-determination. David Lloyd George, the British Prime Minister at the time, maintained that the dismemberment of Austria-Hungary had not been the intention of France, Russia, England, America and Italy; but after the collapse of the Austro-Hungarian army the centrifugal forces in the Habsburg empire had taken over and, even before the peace treaty with Austria came up at the Conference of Paris, the Western Powers were faced with an irrevocable situation:[3] Lloyd George's view is disputed by a fellow countryman, Harold Nicolson, the honest, self-critical historian in him getting the better of the diplomat.[4] 'We arrived [in Paris]', says Nicolson, 'as fervent apprentices in the school of President Wilson: we left as renegades . . .

---

[1] Lloyd George, op. cit., p. 307.
[2] G. M. Gathorne-Hardy, *A Short History of International Affairs, 1920 to 1939*, London, New York, Toronto 1960, p. 22.
[3] D. Lloyd George, op. cit., pp. 90 f.
[4] G. M. Gathorne-Hardy, op. cit.

We arrived determined that a peace of justice and wisdom should be negotiated; we left it, conscious that the Treaties imposed upon our enemies were neither just nor wise . . . The fact that, as the Conference progressed, we were scarcely conscious of our own falsity may indicate that some deterioration of moral awareness had taken place.'[1]

This is, however, contradicted by Dr Beneš' disclosure that on September 3, 1918 he had already informed T. G. Masaryk by telegram that France and Britain had recognized the Czechoslovak government abroad. This information had already been sent on September 15th, via Switzerland, to the leading members of the Czech National Committee headed by the Peasant leader Švehla. When the Czech delegates met on September 29th to discuss the constitutional revision which the Austrian Prime Minister Hussarek had proposed and which would transform the Danube monarchy into a federation of states, they were faced with Masaryk's and Beneš' letter refusing to allow negotiations with Austria. The grounds for this prohibition was an indication that the United States had recognized the Czechoslovak government abroad, that the Allies were on the brink of final victory and that they would not negotiate with Austria. To induce them to undertake active negotiations against Austria, Beneš promised the Prague politicians that they would be included in the future Czechoslovak government. This shows that the *faits accomplis* which, according to Lloyd George, the Allies could not alter had been engineered by the Allies themselves.[2] It is also interesting to note that the elected representatives of the Czech people, in order to preserve their political position, were prepared to take the steps which led to the dissolution of Austria only after they had learned through Beneš and Masaryk of the Allies' intention to destroy Austria-Hungary.

The manner in which Austria-Hungary was dismembered meant that the Succession States still contained considerable German and Hungarian-speaking minorities who did not join these states voluntarily but were compelled to do so, in some cases by force of arms.

After the Second World War the British, French and Dutch colonial empires also became the victims of the principle of self-determination. Today the difficulties experienced in forming states in Africa bring out very clearly the contradictions which hinder realization of the idea of the national state. The nature of nationhood has, in any case, never been scientifically clarified. Historians, geographers, scientists, anthropologists, sociologists and philologists are still arguing about its essential characteristics. The question being asked in Africa today is why must temporary rule by the Colonial Powers, over areas

[1] Harold Nicolson, *Peacemaking 1919*, London 1933, p. 187.
[2] E. Beneš, *Der Aufstand der Nationen*, Berlin 1928, pp. 564 ff.

which have been thrown together by chance, form the criterion for national statehood, rather than tribal membership. On this point Emerson asks a few embarrassing but highly pertinent questions:

1. How is it possible to decide on the peoples to whom the principle is to be applied?
2. If a national majority and a minority live in one specific territory, does the right of self-determination apply to the majority only, or does it apply to the minority as well?
3. If the majority decides on one particular solution today, can it decide on another tomorrow?
4. Who is authorized to speak for the people claiming self-determination and what means are permissible in order to realize the claim?[1]

The victory of nationalism in association with national self-determination is therefore an attempt, partly absurd but also partly hypocritical, to put into practice the most extreme demands of John Stuart Mill.

The practice is to demand that state and nation be territorially co-extensive. But because the idea of nationalism is relatively new, because human settlement of the world occurred according to other principles in the many centuries before nationalism appeared, the practical application of this principle means permanent suffering for millions of innocent people. It is still more tragic and stupid when we are dealing with the right to self-determination on the basis of an appeal to superior right and a moral demand which is to serve as a corrective to the positivist legal basis of the state. Emerson observes quite rightly that this involves an innate contradiction. On the one hand the state is allowed the right to defend its legal and legitimate existence, on the other nationality is allowed the right to overthrow this legality.

The situation became very different where the nation concerned was a pluralistic structure – as in central Europe. That pluralistic structures like Austria-Hungary had made outstanding contributions to culture and civilization is an undoubted fact. Yet it was in these very states that the principle had a destructive effect. In states which are a mosaic of nationalities the question which then arises is: Who shall dominate whom? and this is where the democratic majority principle breaks down. Was it, for example, tolerable that five and a half million Czechs should permanently dominate three million Germans, two million Slovaks and one million Hungarians, and can those who were dominated be accused of disloyalty? If the answer is in the

[1] Rupert Emerson, *From Empire to Nation*, Cambridge (Mass.) 1960, especially pp. 89–169 and pp. 296–359.

affirmative why then could not the Czechs be expected to show loyalty to Austria?[1]

No one has described better than Macartney the lot of the nationalities who by reason of the mistaken or opportunist application of the principle of self-determination have come under the yoke of national states:

'It is the worst which is the corruption of the best. For democracy seeks to govern the affairs which are Common to the community in the best interests of that community, and the wishes of the few must in justice be overridden by those of the many. But the majority in a state which seeks to impose its own national culture upon a national minority is misusing the machinery set up for the regulation of their common affairs to those affairs which, by definition, are not common.'[2]

The consequence of any compulsory integration of reluctant minorities in a state dominated by another nation is the creation of a state in which any hope of a 'fundamental consensus'[3] in the democratic sense of the word is doomed from the outset.

In the case of the Sudeten Germans it was a considerable section of the population of Bohemia, Moravia and Silesia together with their territory which were forcibly allotted to Czechoslovakia. Their interest in the continuation and the welfare of the state was therefore bound to be doubtful from the first. When the Sudeten Germans insisted on sending their representatives to the Austrian parliament, serious disturbances broke out, to be bloodily suppressed by Czech troops.[4] Although two representatives of the Sudeten Germans, the Social Democratic Seliger and the middle-class nationalist Lodgman, stayed in St Germain during the peace negotiations they were 'confined to their hotel where they sat like prisoners behind barbed wire'.[5] They were not allowed to address the Peace Conference. Their replies to the peace terms of the Allied and Associated Powers could only be submitted in a memorandum which was attached as an appendix to the statements of the leader of the Austrian delegation, Karl Renner.

---

[1] Cf. also S. Rabl, *Staatsbürgerliche Loyalität in Nationalitätenstaaten*, Munich 1959.

[2] C. A. Macartney, *National States and National Minorities*, London 1934.

[3] Fundamental consensus in the sense of James Bryce's classical theory of the state means that the groups which make up the state clearly realize the need to rule the state together and that the inter-play of government and opposition turns only on the question of what are the best measures for achieving the common constitutional aim.

[4] When Seliger wanted to negotiate with the Czechoslovak government he was sent packing and told 'We don't negotiate with rebels': R. W. Seton-Watson, *A History of the Czechs and Slovaks*, London, New York, Melbourne 1943, p. 325.

[5] Wenzel Jaksch, op. cit., p. 209.

Either their memorandum did not reach the leaders of the Allied delegation or else it was not taken seriously. On the basis of Hunter-Miller's diary, Cobban reported that the Conference was informed that the German Bohemians favoured union with the Czechs provided they were granted economic equality in accordance with the rights of minorities.[1] As Jaksch remarked, the justice of the Sudeten German cause could not counterbalance the good relations which Masaryk and Beneš had established during the war years with men like Pichon and Clemenceau in order to promote Czech interests. In the meantime, however, the Sudeten Germans were suppressed in their own homeland by terrorist methods.

The fact that the German-speaking population of Yugoslavia (for example in Marburg) clung to their Austrian citizenship clearly showed that the minorities would hardly be satisfied with mere promises on the part of the new national states. Once the community and unity of the Danubian peoples had been rejected by the Treaty of St Germain, the claim that national self-determination should be generally valid was well founded. The new national states were, however, so intoxicated by their unexpected success as to overlook the fact that the continued economic and cultural association of the peoples of these regions was vital.

Here the mistake was made of considering the purely arithmetical principle of democratic majority and forgetting the need for the fundamental consensus. The Treaties of St Germaine and Trianon therefore created permanent minorities which rejected the state on principle. Here Rousseau's totalitarian demand for an intolerant plebiscitary democracy has a pernicious after-effect which considers every minority objectionable. Even if, because of a lost plebiscite, a minority is allotted to a state in which it does not wish to live, its future government by the majority group is still undemocratic. Even if we agree that the demand for self-determination to decide topical issues is ethically permissible, it is extremely doubtful whether it is acceptable in law that people should be compelled to give up their cultural heritage as a result of simple majority plebiscites.

The pressure on the linguistic minorities to opt for this or that state destroyed the spirit of moderation and tolerance. The suppression of national and racial minorities brought not only inordinate suffering to the oppressed but also resulted in the moral perversion of the oppressors. For example it is no accident that the cruel suppression of the Jewish minorities in Romania, Poland and Hungary served as a model for national socialism. H. Seton-Watson refers to a particularly unpleasant aspect of this kind of terrorism. In Poland

[1] Cf. H. Raschhofer, *Die Sudetenfrage*, Munich 1953, p. 114.

and Romania, he wrote, the impatience, dissatisfaction and idealism of the young and the intellectuals were exploited by governments and politicians to start riots and acts of violence against the Jews. In Poland the National Democratic Party demanded an anti-Semitic policy in order to embarrass the government and the government in turn terrorized the socialists, the democrats and the national minorities. In Romania in 1925 students were hired by the police to smash Jewish shop windows in Oradea Mare. The notorious fascist terrorist group, the Iron Guard, started as a student organization in Jassy University. In the 1920s the students there spent almost their whole time organizing anti-Semitic demonstrations, carrying out pogroms, breaking strikes and beating up left-wing intellectuals. The leader of the Iron Guard, Codreanu, won his reputation as a national leader by murdering the Jassy police chief and then being acquitted.

The feature of the universities of east Europe, continues Seton-Watson, was their atmosphere of unhealthy romanticism, nationalist arrogance and intellectual and moral dishonesty, which also extended to the press, literature, the theatre and official propaganda.[1] The ruling classes had no sense of responsibility towards the rest of the nation, no understanding of personal freedom and no knowledge of the real problems facing their own country, to say nothing of those facing their neighbours. The younger generation had been brought up to despise other nations, to fear their own people and to look on every proposal for co-operation with other states as a diabolical plot on the part of the 'Reds', the Jews and the Freemasons. These young people had been taken in by a kind of demagogic, anti-Semitic or anti-democratic agitation and had therefore easily succumbed to national-socialist propaganda. Seton-Watson concludes his melancholy account with the remark that it is not surprising that Hitler and his henchmen found people of their own kidney in east Europe but it is surprising that they were unable to win an even larger following than they did.[2]

The stipulations on the minority issue which resulted from the Paris peace negotiations were imbued with the spirit of national liberalism. Treaties guaranteeing protection for minorities were concluded between the Allies on the one hand and Poland, Czechoslovakia, Yugoslavia, Romania, Greece and Turkey on the other. Although the Treaty of Paris guaranteed the minorities a nominal protection of life and liberty, accorded them a formal equality before the law and political and civil rights irrespective of race, language and religion, the minorities were really branded second-class citizens by

[1] Hugh Seton-Watson, *Eastern Europe Between the Wars*, op. cit., p. 143.
[2] Ibid., p. 144.

these treaties.[1] The principle of national sovereignty had triumphed all along the line in the Paris peace negotiations.[2] The states concerned accepted only with the greatest reluctance the guarantees of protection which were imposed on them and as they ran counter to their own denationalizing tendencies they honoured them only where they had to and ignored them whenever they could. The League of Nations, which was to see that these guarantees were observed, was as powerless when it came to enforcing observance as it was in other vital issues.

The form which these minority guarantees took had been developed during the nineteenth century in the course of the dismemberment of the Turkish Empire. Their application to central Europe was made as a result of generalizations based on inadequate knowledge of the social, economic and intellectual structure of the countries involved. In addition, the small states on which these conditions had been imposed asked, not unreasonably, why they in particular were expected to display such a measure of magnanimity if bigger states with minorities of their own, for instance, France, England and Italy, were not placed under a similar obligation.

The nationalism which drove the small states to oppress minorities was a form of emotional compensation for their own plight under their former rulers. Yet the unfortunate result was a policy of repression and denationalization towards minorities, and in the case of Czechoslovakia Czech language and culture was forced on the areas inhabited by the German and Hungarian minorities. In Czechoslovakia this was carried out by making Czech the official language and requiring German and Hungarian officials to pass an examination in the Czech language; the land reform laws and a narrow-minded personnel policy designed to exclude the minorities from government service were all part of the same pattern. Thus Jaksch quotes the case of the social-democratic delegate Taub who in 1924 stated in Parliament that 7,000 German railway workers who passed the language tests had nevertheless been dismissed. And the right-wing extremist Minister Stříbrný boasted that 40,000 German railway workers and postal officials had been sacked through his efforts and replaced by Czechs.[3]

If this mean and bigoted policy affected even petty officials and workers it is not surprising that very few Germans held senior positions in the bureaucracy. This was a complete reversal of the former Austrian policy under which many Czechs were given leading appointments in

[1] W. Jaksch, op. cit., pp. 250 f.        [2] Cobban, op. cit., pp. 31 ff.
[3] Jaksch, op. cit., p. 228.

the Vienna ministries. In pursuit of this policy Austria had helped to train qualified Czech officials. In particular much ill feeling was aroused by the so-called *hraničáři* (frontiersmen), Czech officials and employees who knew no German but were posted to purely German-speaking areas and rudely repulsed all attempts by the German population to conduct official business with them in their own language. On top of this there was an economic policy which intentionally discriminated against the Germans.

President T. G. Masaryk's personal attitude made but little difference to this policy. Masaryk, who still embodied the old Austrian tradition of tolerance and conciliation towards minorities, had from the outset envisaged the participation of the Germans as citizens with equal rights. Having himself grown up on the Redlich family estate in Göding, he tried to persuade the historian and former Austrian minister, Professor Josef Redlich, to leave Vienna and to settle in Prague and join the Czechoslovak government. The actual situation which made it impossible for Masaryk to carry out his liberal and well-meant plans against the tide of chauvinistic nationalism is strikingly illustrated by an article which appeared in the Legionaries' organ, *Národní Osvobození*, and by Masaryk's reply. The paper claimed that the Czechs had received their freedom in return for a promise to the Allies that they would form a dam against German imperialism – i.e., not therefore on account of their glorious past, their culture and economic development, not therefore because they are the people who produced Hus, Komenius and Palacký but because their representatives abroad helped to strengthen the Allies against the danger of German imperialism. The Czechs must honour that agreement and therefore their state must be nationalist in character and its government Czechoslovak in spirit. In a personal reply Masaryk declared that if nationalism was understood as love of one's own people no possible objection could be raised. The ideal of nationalism in this sense was a lofty and noble political force which welded the nation into a unified body willing to sacrifice itself. The only things to discuss were the quality of this love, its aims and the methods by which it was to be realized. Jaksch gives a vivid description of a conversation which Alfred Weber had with Masaryk in 1921: 'Few foreign visitors to Prague Castle had the same ability as Alfred Weber to distinguish between the façade of Masaryk's philosophy and the reality of the nationalist state egoism which was released.'[1]

Poland's attitudes to minorities is well known. Even a writer like Roucek, with his profound understanding of Poland's national policy,

[1] Ibid.

refers to her hostility towards her minorities.[1] In connection with the German minority this writer, by no means sympathetically disposed to Germanism, admitted that the Poles used their superiority mainly to suppress German influence in Upper Silesia and other former German provinces and that immediately after the non-aggression pact between Germany and Poland in 1934 the government pursued its policy of imposing the Polish way of life with greater fervour, especially on her western frontier. [2, 3]

The fate of the Hungarians, the Szekler and Transylvania Germans who were assigned to the Greater Romanian state under the Trianon Peace Treaty, was even less enviable.[4] The familiar picture of repression, denationalization, penalties on the use of other languages, economic oppression, was made worse by the rabid violence of the Romanian police.

Macartney vividly describes the hard lot suffered by the national minorities. It was hard because they were denied the right of self-determination which most other nations sought and they were in no position to found their own national state. But if the national minority is compelled to join another nation state against its will its lot is doubly hard. Then members of that minority are legally excluded from all the hopes and ambitions which have gone into creating the community in which they must live. This community was established to safeguard freedom and to sustain certain ideals which are alien to them. The more completely the majority expressed their joy in their own nationality, continues Macartney, the more bitterly the minority felt its inferior status.[5]

Hannah Arendt is right when she says that the misfortune of minorities – 'the first-cousins of the stateless' – was that they were not officially represented or protected by any state and therefore had to live under laws which the states concerned had been very reluctant to adopt:[6]

'The realization of the national state principle throughout Europe meant that the national state was further discredited; it could give sovereignty to only a fraction of the people concerned and, as their sovereignty was achieved everywhere against the disappointed aspira-

[1] Joseph S. Roucek, 'Minorities', in *Poland*, edited by Bernadotte E. Schmitt, op. cit., p. 158.

[2] Ibid., p. 163.

[3] Cf. also Theodor Bierschenk, *Die Deutsche Volksgruppe in Polen*, Kitzingen am Main 1954, pubd. as Supplement X to the Albertus University Yearbook.

[4] Cf. Zsombor De Szász, *The Minorities in Roumanian Transylvania*, London 1927.

[5] Macartney, op. cit., p. 17.

[6] Hannah Arendt, op. cit., p. 433.

tions of other national groups, they were forced into the role of oppressor from the outset.'[1]

When the minorities appealed to the League of Nations, Arendt says, 'it became clear that the treaties were regarded only as a method of painless and humanitarian assimilation . . . Complete respect for minorities . . . would have meant severe restriction on national sovereignty . . .'[2] But that would have undermined the principle of sovereignty on which the League of Nations was based. This had been the first step in the development of integral nationalism. When the peacemakers of 1919–20 made it possible for whole population groups to be compelled against their will to join hostile national states, the principle of integral nationalism was recognized. The total state, however, is based on precisely this sort of compulsory integration. If states were allowed to violate those subjects who belonged to a minority (they cannot be described as citizens in the true sense of the word) without the latter being able to claim effective help, why should national states shrink from doing violence to their own nationals who were not protected by treaties?

It is therefore clear that because it did not know how to give effective protection to 'minorities' the League of Nations set a bad example. Was not, for instance, the National Socialist government bound to come to the conclusion, with justification, that if the Western Powers and the League of Nations displayed indifference to the fate of minorities this would apply to an even greater extent to the Hitler government's attitude to the German Jews and still more so to the German democrats who had been suppressed? This conclusion proved to be correct up to the time when the national socialist policy of expansion appeared as a threat to the Western states.

Even from the point of view of their own interests, however, the governments of the central European nationality states were guilty of serious mistakes. Although they refused to recognize their minorities as equals under their constitutions and made no attempt to awaken in them any civic sense and despite their policies of suppression and assimilation, they allowed the extreme nationalist elements in these minorities to have a great deal of freedom to challenge the state. That meant that within the minorities the very elements who had been authoritarian and jingoist before 1918 remained in key positions. This gave the militant groups in the minorities the chance to defeat the efforts of people who were conciliatory and co-operative.

Thus, under the leadership of the Agrarian Party, the Czechoslovak government had dissolved the Sudeten German National

[1] Ibid., p. 439.                    [2] Ibid., p. 440.

Socialist Party as being a fascist, anti-democratic party, but tolerated the formation of a party to replace it. This was the Sudeten German Party led by the *Turnlehrer* (physical training instructor) Konrad Henlein which, until 1938, was to all outward appearances a national democratic party but whose leadership was working to the orders of the Hitler government.[1] The right-wing, radical Czech nationalists were also ready to collaborate with Henlein and a number of attempts were made to replace the German Social Democrats in the government by Henlein followers.[2]

The Czech Right was also ready to co-operate with the Third Reich and there was active collaboration after the Sudeten crisis in 1938. Kramář's Czech National Democratic Party, which had previously refused to co-operate with the German democrats, put forward a candidate of their own (against Beneš) in the 1935 presidential election and with the help of the Agrarians and the Henlein party, hoped to win a majority for their candidate. Had the right-wing candidate been elected, it would have undoubtedly resulted in a foreign policy dictated by Hitlerite Germany and an internal policy allowing the nationalists a free hand to deal with the German democrats even before 1938.

Even Dr Beneš made friendly approaches to German nationalism. When, for example, two emissaries sent by Hitler, Count Trautmannsdorf and Dr Haushofer, proposed a non-aggression pact. Dr Beneš suggested that he himself should draft the terms and send them to Berlin.[3]

It is understandable that in his memoirs, which appeared at a time when his pan-Slav foreign policy had made him the prisoner of the protecting Russian power in Prague, Dr Beneš tried to make out that his relations with Hitler were innocent. No less a person than Winston Churchill testified that Beneš had previously tried to prove himself useful to Hitlerite Germany when he sent Stalin the documents, handed to him by the National Socialist government, about the alleged collaboration of the Soviet Marshal Tukhachevsky with German military circles.[4]

[1] These instructions were at first conveyed secretly through liaison organizations such as the League for Germanism Abroad. It was not until March 1938 that Hitler received Henlein and K. H. Frank and advised them always to demand so much of the Czechs that the Germans could not be satisfied. Cf. *Akten zur deutschen auswärtigen Politik*, Series D, Vol. II, Germany and Czechoslovakia, Baden-Baden 1950, p. 158.

[2] The President of the Agrarian Party, Beran, later Prime Minister of the second Czechoslovak Republic, made this suggestion to the German Ambassador, Eisenlohr. Cf. Jaksch, op. cit., p. 303.

[3] Beneš, op. cit., pp. 17 ff.

[4] Winston Churchill, *The Second World War*, Vol. I, London, Toronto, Melbourne, Sydney, Wellington 1948, pp. 258 f.; also Walter Hagen, *Die geheime Front*, Stuttgart, pp. 64 ff.

As the head of the German Secret Service in the Third Reich, Walter Schellenberg, reported in his memoirs, the archives of the German *Wehrmacht* and the headquarters of Military Counter-Intelligence were burgled in 1937 by the Chief of the Criminal Police, Nebe, on Hitler's personal orders. Material about collaboration between the Red Army and the *Wehrmacht* was discovered. On Heydrich's instructions this material was supplemented by the addition of forgeries. Heydrich immediately despatched a trusted SS-Standartenführer to Prague to contact Dr Beneš. Hitler wrote and told Stalin that Tukhachevsky had conspired with German generals and was planning his (Stalin's) overthrow.[1] Hitler's intention was, at first, to weaken the Red Army, secondly – as becomes evident from Heydrich's plot against General Fritsch, resulting soon afterwards in Fritsch's dismissal[2] – he wanted to strike a blow against the German generals. That Beneš, who knew the source of the material, consciously intended to render Hitler and Stalin a service is clear from his whole attitude. As a pan-Slavist Beneš hoped to prevent a future reconciliation between Germany and Russia.

The strengthening of the *Wehrmacht* at the time might also have resulted in the collapse of national socialism and the restoration of the German monarchy. But that, in conjunction with Schuschnigg's policy in Austria, could have meant the immediate recall of the Habsburgs. The considerable sympathy which the Habsburgs had enjoyed among the Czech, Hungarian, Slovak and Croat populations and the (already completed) dissolution of the Little Entente conjured up the spectre of a resurrected Austria-Hungary.

The episode of Beneš' betrayal of Tukhachevsky proves, therefore, that on the very eve of the Second World War the possibility of collaboration between Hitler, Stalin and Beneš was not out of the question, any more than Italian oppression of the German minority in South Tyrol affected Hitler's alliance with Mussolini. But it is in the nature of nationalism to develop into imperialism, that is, to become supra-national. This is also shown by Hitler's repeated expression of admiration for British imperialism, with which he wanted to share the world. Hitler started from the assumption that England would not make a stand on a matter of principle against a militarily strong European power as long as its foreign policy ambitions were confined to the Continent.[3]

That Dr Beneš, a sworn enemy of a Danubian federation, thought co-operation with Hitler was possible, is fully consistent with his

[1] Walter Schellenberg, *Memoirs*, London 1956, Cologne 1959, p. 49.
[2] Ibid., p. 39.　　　　　　　　　　[3] Ibid.

foreign policy ideas. Only Hitler appeared at the time to provide a guarantee that integral nationalism would prevent the resurgence of the Danube monarchy.

The consequences of the Czechs' sudden liberal attitude to Henlein's camouflaged national socialism were catastrophic. The Sudeten German Party was not deceived by the apparent benevolence. In the first place it was obvious that it was due not to a sudden change of heart but to a new European balance of power, and in the second place we now know from documents which have since been published that the Sudeten German Party already had its policy laid down by Berlin, and that it served Hitler's programme of imperial expansion. Yet National Socialism enjoyed the support of the Czech fascists, of Gajdas's group as well as of Stříbrný's. Thus their agitation prevented the construction of a democratic German-language radio station to combat propaganda among the Sudeten Germans. The upshot was that the Sudeten Germans never got into the habit of listening to the Czech-language radio stations of Bohemia and Moravia but to the National Socialist propaganda station at Breslau.

It now became evident that the nationality states could not become integral national states. One solution, for instance, would have been to grant the minorities regional autonomy. But the jingoists would not hear of it. Even the cultural autonomy which had been proposed by Karl Renner before the First World War and had been conceded in the Soviet Union's Chamber of Nationalities, seemed to them unthinkable.

# PART TWO

*The New States and their Integration Problems*

'*The principal and general cause of an attitude of mind which disposes men towards change is the cause of which we have just spoken. There are some who stir up sedition because their minds are filled by a passion for equality, which arises from their thinking they have the worst of the bargain in spite of being equals to those who have got the advantage. There are others who do it because their minds are filled with a passion for inequality (i.e. superiority), which arises from their conceiving that they get no advantage over others (but only an equal amount, or even a smaller amount) although they are really more than equal to others . . . Thus inferiors become revolutionaries in order to be equals and equals in order to be superiors.*[1]

The truth of Aristotle's observation is constantly being confirmed. So far we have traced the course of the conflict between nationalism and liberalism and the failure of the attempt to achieve a synthesis. The outcome of the war, the peace and the establishment of the League of Nations made little difference. The basic theme in the tragedy of central Europe remained the same; only the actors changed their roles.

Aristotle's analysis explains why the attempt at a compromise in President Wilson's Fourteen Points was bound to fail. All nations professed to the ideal of international equality but openly or with mental reservations clung to the idea of national superiority. This egotistic interpretation of the nationalist-liberal compromise also dominated the Paris peace negotiations where, according to Nicolson, the mood was characterized not only by dishonesty and a desire for revenge but also and above all by a sense of weariness.[2] The principle of national self-determination, in whose name the dissolution of the Danube monarchy had been demanded and achieved, now proved to be a right which was granted exclusively to the victors and their protégés.[3] It is therefore hardly surprising that the same attitude was also reflected in the constitutions of those countries which owed their very existence and their rise to the Paris Peace Settlement.

Although this applies primarily to the Succession States of the Austro-Hungarian Empire, the Weimar Constitution itself is no exception. It, too, contained the compromise between nationalism and democracy. The author of this Constitution, Hugo Preuss, had advocated the introduction of democracy even during the war.[4] At the same time, however, he also stoutly championed the unitary and centralized national state.

He argued that the disaster in Germany had been due to the belated development of national sovereignty. He believed that the difference between Germany and other nations was due to the collapse of the medieval system and the ensuing application of the idea of the

---

[1] Aristotle, *Politics*, Book V, Chap. 2: translated by Ernest Barker, *The Politics of Aristotle*, Oxford 1946, p. 207.

[2] Harold Nicolson, *Peacemaking 1919*, op. cit., p. 187.

[3] Cf. also Christian Höltge, *Die Weimarer Republik und das Ostlocarno-Problem, 1919–39*, Würzburg 1958.

[4] *Bericht und Protokolle des 8. Ausschusses über einen Entwurf einer Verfassung des Deutschen Reiches*, Berlin 1920, pp. 1–171: Cf. also Erich Eyck, *A History of the Weimar Republic*, London 1962, p. 73; Hugo Preuss, *Das Deutsche Volk und die Politik*, Jena 1915.

absolutist, centralized state to the German principalities. Study of the *Berichte und Protokolle des Achten Ausschusses* (Report and Protocols of the Eighth Committee of the Constituent Assembly of the German Republic) proves beyond all doubt that Preuss was a convinced believer in the Hegel-Mill synthesis of a strong centralized power based on the principle of nationality and anchored in a central parliament.[1] His profound knowledge and his position as Minister of the Interior explain the great influence which he had on the negotiations of the Weimar Constituent Assembly.

Pulling against these tendencies to centralization, however, there were the traditional feelings of independence and the religious, political and historical differences within the German people. Once again the association (so typical of central Europe) between centralism and progressive thought on the one hand and between federalism and conservative movements on the other were factors of major importance. Those favouring a federal structure belonged mostly to the Right, out of fear of social democracy.

The pan-Germanic idea – the union of Germany with German-Austria and the Sudeten territories – also found an eloquent spokesman in Naumann, who also took a leading part in framing the Constitution.[2] Under the impact of the dissolution of the Danube monarchy Naumann had abandoned his original plan. Did he, who had the best knowledge of the problems of central Europe, realize what that meant? Did it not mean abandoning the rest of central and eastern Europe to Russia?[3] Might not Naumann of all people have been expected to make constructive and cosmopolitan proposals which would have taken the post-war situation into account? But his nationalist-liberal outlook was the stumbling block. This is another example of the common views held by the 'progressives' of that period who based their thinking on the compromise between nationalism and democracy.

As this basic nationalist-liberal outlook had been adopted by the progressive intellectuals of all central European peoples it was bound

[1] 'The (Prussian) House of Deputies and the Reichstag became increasingly two powers which were different in spirit and set on different courses, so that the government had to bargain now with one, now with the other...Much can be done in this way but one thing is extremely difficult, a thing which must however be the aim of a truly internal policy: uniformity in all spheres of public life; Friedrich Meinecke, *Weltbürgertum und Nationalstaat*, p. 487, quoted by Hugo Preuss, op. cit., p. 179. Cf. Preuss, *Um die Reichsverfassung von Weimar*, Berlin 1924, p. 31, Chap. III: Provincial sovereignty – national impotence: 'National democracy had to be pan-German and act.'

[2] *Bericht und Protokolle*, op. cit., p. 115.

[3] Although the events taking place in Russia at the time had removed this problem from day-to-day policy.

to be embodied in the constitutions. Because language was regarded as the main characteristic of an integrated community the authors of the Weimar Constitution had every reason to hope for success in view of Germany's linguistic homogeneity. With the exception of the Austrian Republic, however, the other post-war democracies lacked this advantage. Czechoslovakia consisted exclusively of territories of the former Austria-Hungary. This was also largely true of Yugoslavia, while Poland included not only parts of Austria but also of Germany and Russia.

Neither the Austro-Hungarian monarchy nor Russia had been linguistically homogeneous and this was equally true of their succession states. Yet in their constitutions and the preambles to these they claimed to be unified national states, whereas they were in reality states made up of several different nationalities. Thus the preamble to the first post-war Polish Constitution declares:

'We, the Polish people, thank Providence for our liberation from a century and a half of servitude . . . and at the same time guarantee the development of all its moral and material forces for the well-being of the whole resurgent population.'[1]

In the Czechoslovak Constitution much greater use was made of the expressions 'Czechoslovak Republic' and 'Czechoslovak People', even in the section dealing with the rights of minorities.[2] In this respect the semi-authoritarian Polish Constitution of 1935 was far more carefully worded. It emphasized that the Polish state was the common possession of all its citizens. Although these constitutions did not expressly refer to the concept of the 'unified national state', it emerged clearly in the names of these states. The words 'Poland' and 'Czechoslovakia', for example, concealed the fact that they contained many large national and linguistic minorities.

The previous national history of these countries was bound to give the minorities who did not take part in the parliamentary voting on the constitution the impression that they were not considered as having equal rights with the rest of the nation. It was beside the point whether this impression corresponded to the facts or not. The collective self-consciousness, the image of these racial minorities was damaged beyond repair and they lost interest in the fate of these states with the result that once again the minorities could not become identified with the new states.

[1] Quoted by Walter Schätzel, 'Entstehung und Verfassung der Polnischen Republik', *Jahrbuch des Öffentlichen Rechts der Gegenwart*, Vol. XII, 1923/4, p. 300.
[2] Quoted by Franz Weyr, 'Der tschechoslowakische Staat', *Jahrbuch des Öffentlichen Rechts der Gegenwart*, Vol. XI, 1922, p. 363.

The 'fundamental consensus' (as understood in Anglo-Saxon democracy in the sense of: "We have agreed that we shall agree") is, however, the *conditio sine qua non* of any successful form of democratic state. Thus the central European nationality states voluntarily gave up the integrating power of constitutional symbolism, and when it comes to winning mass loyalties a symbol is often more effective than facts. In the case of Czechoslovakia the Sudeten Germans felt the omission of their name to be a highly discriminatory act as they were more numerous than the Slovaks, who had now achieved the status of first-grade citizens.

At the same time the continental brand of radical liberalism forced the governments to give full freedom of action to the jingoist parties who pretended to be the standard-bearers of the national interest. Dr Kramář's National Democratic Party in Czechoslovakia is an example. Kramář, who came from the Young Czech Movement, had been one of the main defenders of the Austrian Empire before the war. But now he advocated an extreme form of nationalism with the professed aim of the forcible denationalization of minorities.[1] Even moderate Czech politicians like Beneš, Klofáč and certain circles among the Agrarian and Social Democratic Parties were weak and gave in to the inordinate demands made by this small group[2] – apparently to gain popularity but really because integral nationalism had taken on the role of a super-ego or political conscience in state leaders' scale of values – a judicial authority against which there was no appeal. The Sudeten German counterpart to Czech national democracy was the German-National Party which, under Dr Lodgman's leadership, frustrated all attempts at a rapprochement between Czech and German activists.

The failure to integrate into the state the national minorities and also racially related groups which had long belonged to other states and cultural groups – such as the Slovaks and the Carpatho-Ukrainians in Czechoslovakia, the Croats and the Dalmatians in Yugoslovia or the Ukrainians in Poland – left one possibility open, however, in the view of the new national states: the ruthless suppression of these minorities by an uncompromising policy of centralization. The attempt of men like Švehla, Hodža and Czech to effect a national compromise between Czechs, Germans, Slovaks and Hungarians and even the limited participation of these minorities in the coalition governments made very little difference.[3] Events simply swept over these men who had retained their tolerant outlook from the pre-war period.

[1] Cf., for example, Malbone Graham, 'Parties and Politics', in *Czechoslovakia*, ed. by R. J. Kerner, Berkeley and Los Angeles 1949, pp. 140 ff.

[2] Cf. J. W. Brügel, *Ludwig Czech, Arbeiterführer und Staatsmann*, Vienna 1960, p. 70.

[3] M. Hodža, op. cit., pp. 92 ff.

This policy of centralization led, once again, to autocracy and dictatorship in some states. Jaksch mentions the Romanian state police's ill-treatment of Pistiner, the Socialist leader in the Bukovina, who wanted to retain the democratic gains won under the Habsburg empire. He also mentions the murder of the Croat peasant leader, Stefan Radič, during a public session of the Yugoslav parliament on June 20, 1928, and the banishment of Pribičevič.[1] In 1938 Lloyd George accused Yugoslavia of ill-treating her Macedonian minorities and Poland of doing the same to her Ukrainians and Jews.[2] He complained that the German National Socialists were following the evil example of Romania and Poland.[3] All these facts suggest there is a close correlation between an intolerant and autocratic attitude towards minorities and the gradual spread of the idea of state authoritarianism after the First World War. The fact that it failed to integrate the national and other minorities by means of the post-war constitutions was a major reason for the development towards autocracy and why incipient democracy's weak defences were breached by nationalism.

The most important example of the prevalence of the radical *laissez-faire* of democratic constitutional practice at the time was the situation resulting from proportional representation, which discredited the parliamentary system in public opinion.[4] The government instability to which it gave rise undermined the republican system and prevented it from functioning properly. Once again this particular weakness helped to engender excessive intolerance. In multilingual states the national majorities, as Hegel understood the term, refused to treat national minorities as equals among equals. But Mill believed they ought to give them complete freedom of action. By being stamped as second-class citizens they were able to use such rights as they enjoyed to destroy the state. But this happened only where these minorities had no hope of attaining equality. In countries like Poland and Yugoslavia the fear of *irredenta* by the heterogeneous communities precipitated the appearance of authoritarian regimes and, later, the destruction of these states. The Germans and the Hungarians living in these countries had been among the privileged before 1918. They were therefore not inclined to accept minority status, however good their treatment might be.

Perhaps the authors of the Polish Constitution had the most difficult task of all. They had to weld into a single unit regions which had previously belonged to Russia, Prussia and Austria. There were more linguistic and religious minorities there than anywhere else. According to Polish statistics the Ukrainians formed a solid group of almost 5

[1] W. Jaksch, op. cit., pp. 247 ff.  [2] Ibid., p. 225.
[3] Ibid.  [4] Cf. Chap. III, Part One on this point.

million out of a total population of nearly 32 million; the Ukrainians themselves estimated their numbers at 7 million.[1] In addition there were 1 million White Russians, almost 1 million Germans, about 3 million Jews and some 900,000 people of other nationalities. Nor was there a common religion. Besides the 20·6 million Catholics there were 3·3 million Greek Uniates. 3·8 million Greek Orthodox, 3 million Jews and 835,000 Protestants. Furthermore, these various groups had belonged to states which, over the centuries, had evolved different traditions and cultures.

Congressional Poland had been governed according to the Napoleonic Code, Russia by Russian law, Silesia by German law and Galicia by Austrian law. Caution and tact would have been the best policy. But Poland which, like Czechoslovakia, Yugoslavia, Romania and Greece, had adopted the institutions of the French Third Republic, had also taken over the French system of centralized administration or adapted her existing institutions to it.[2] Although many members of the Polish National Assembly favoured a federal state, the nationalist ideas and tendencies as expressed by Pilsudski, Limanowski and Dmowski made it unlikely from the outset that federalism would carry the day. This was bound to make integration impossible.[3]

The case of Yugoslavia was not unlike that of Poland. There, too, heterogeneous communities had to be forged into one bloc. The major part of the state territory had formerly belonged to the Austro-Hungarian monarchy. Slovenia (which was composed of the predominantly Slovene-speaking areas of Krain, Carinthia and Styria), Dalmatia and a few Istrian islands were detached from Austria. From Hungary Yugoslavia received Croatia, Slavonia, the Upper and Middle Mur area and the Slav-speaking regions of southern Hungary.

Serbia, which was probably the predominating but not the largest or the most populous part of the state, had always had a centralized government. It was modelled on France and divided up into departments, arrondissements and municipalities. The peoples however, who had long belonged to the Habsburg monarchy, were accustomed to a system of local self-government. Serbia had been, culturally, part of the Ottoman Empire for centuries, a community which differed fundamentally in traditions, conventions and outlook from that which had formed the common life of the Habsburg monarchy. Furthermore the Serbians were members of the Greek Orthodox Church, while the

[1] Joseph Roucek, 'Minorities', op. cit., p. 157.
[2] Walter Schätzel, op. cit., pp. 289 ff.
[3] Ahlers observed as late as 1935: 'Throughout those regions of Poland which had once been partitioned the administration, especially in its lower levels, still retains many features and distinctive differences characteristic of the administration of the old Germany, Austria and Russia.' Johannes Ahlers, *Polen*, Berlin 1935, p. 99.

overwhelming majority in the areas ceded from Austria-Hungary were Roman Catholics.[1] Even the Slav language which was common to the Serbs and Croats was written in a different script, the Serbs using the Cyrillic and the Croats the Latin alphabet, so that it was impossible for the two peoples to read one another's literature. Here was a country in which the most favourable conditions for federation existed. But the constitution of the Kingdom of the Serbs, Croats and Slovenes adopted on June 28, 1921, was purely unitary and centralized in character.[2]

Compared with Poland and Yugoslavia, the authors of the Czechoslovak Constitution were faced with an easier task. Only two communities had to be amalgamated into one state, the so-called historical *Länder* of Bohemia, Moravia and Silesia on the one hand and, on the other Slovakia and Carpatho-Ukraine which had been acquired from Hungary and Czechoslovakia. Czechoslovakia also had only two fair-sized minorities which spoke different languages, namely the German-speaking Sudeten territories and the Hungarians. Differences of religion presented few problems.[3]

It is nevertheless important to remember that in October 1918 the German-Bohemian representatives in the Reichsrat in Vienna constituted themselves into a Provincial Assembly, and the representatives of Moravia and Silesia as a Sudetenland Assembly, and elected a governor, Dr Lodgmann and his deputy (Seliger). On October 29 and 30, 1918, the Germans in these areas declared their adherence to the German-Austrian Republic and were given the legal status of citizens by the provisional National Assembly in Vienna on November 25, 1918.[4]

The Austrian Chancellor at the time, Dr Renner, observed that these associations of the German-speaking areas in the Austrian Republic – which were envisaged in the law relating to the extent, frontiers and relationships of the state territory – were 'in complete accordance with the ideas expressed in President Wilson's Fourteen Points'[5] and actually contained a proposal for the voluntary division of the empire. It was, as Renner said, a proposal 'which naïvely pro-

[1] According to the 1921 census 46·7 per cent belonged to the Greek Orthodox and 39·3 per cent to the Roman Catholic Church, while 11·3 per cent were Muslims. *Osteuropa-Handbuch Jugoslawien*, op. cit., p. 147.

[2] Iwan Zogler, 'Die Verfassung Jugoslawiens', *Jahrbuch des Öffentlichen Rechts der Gegenwart*, Vol. XI, Tübingen 1922, pp. 182 ff.

[3] Out of the total population of 13,712,172 in 1921, 10,381,833 were Roman Catholics, 535,593 were Greek Uniates, 525,333 members of the Czechoslovak Church, 75,097 Greek Orthodox.

[4] Walter Goldinger, 'Der geschichtliche Ablauf der Ereignisse in Österreich 1918–1945', in *Geschichte der Republik Österreich*, Munich 1954, p. 63.

[5] Karl Renner, *Österreich von der Ersten zur Zweiten Republik*, op. cit., p. 23.

ceeds from the assumption that Wilson's principles were to be realized in the peace treaties, a proposal which does not overlook the fact that we are defeated and have to bear the burden of defeat, but which disregards the fact that not only the states belonging to the Entente . . . but also the former associates and presumptive coheirs of this empire might face the vanquished nations as victorious powers.'[1] Renner acknowledged that it was unthinkable that there should be a permanent territorial association between the German-speaking areas of the Sudetenland and Austria, from which they were spatially separated. Renner had hoped that negotiations with the Czechs in consultation with the Sudeten German representatives might give the Sudetenland a considerable measure of autonomy, in order to 'avoid' their incorporation as a people without rights, defeated, subject and thus permanently alienated from the state of which they were part through the fortunes of war.'[2]

This law is also a notable document from another angle. Although it appealed to the right of self-determination and thus went to swell the then fashionable national-liberal chorus, it nevertheless symbolized the idea of the continued existence of the community of the small central European peoples. The fact that the Germans of Bohemia and Moravia inhabited areas which were not always territorially cohesive and were sometimes scattered in linguistic islands demonstrated much more clearly the impracticability of the national idea. Meanwhile Czechoslovakia, in flagrant defiance of the right to national determination, occupied the German areas of Bohemia, Moravia and Silesia by force. But an attempt was made to settle the Austrian claim by holding out to the Sudeten Germans the propect of representation in the Czechoslovak parliament proportionate to their numbers. Yet this did not help the Germans; for, *ab initio*, they saw themselves exposed to the danger of being outvoted by the large Czechosiovak population.

From the first it seemed to be clear that should a bill about national and linguistic relations come before parliament, the Sudeten Germans could not hope to defend their interests with any success. This fear did not always prove to be justified. As the party system evolved decisions in which ideological and economic interests were more important than national political ones became more frequent. Thus for example Sudeten-German social democracy often had much more affinity with Czech social democracy than with the German National Party and, vice versa, the Czech Social Democratic Party enjoyed better relations with its German sister party than with Dr Kramář's National Democratic Party. Likewise the relations between the German and Czech

---

[1] Ibid., p. 24.     [2] Ibid., pp. 23 f.

Catholic Parties were excellent. Nevertheless the attraction and impact of the nationalist idea was so strong that these parties, *per se* tolerant on the national question, carefully avoided giving the impression of being over-friendly towards the minorities.

The old regime had disappeared but its policy of domination of national minorities continued. The pledge given in St Germain by Dr Beneš, in connection with the Sudeten German and Hungarian minorities, that a racially mixed state would be set up on the Swiss model was not carried out. That would have meant making a clear and unmistakable reference to the German-speaking population of Czechoslovakia in the very title of the state and in the text of the Constitution. Czech insistence that their state should have a nationalist structure reminded the German-speaking population in the country of the Austrian declaration of 1918. On the other hand the Sudeten German leadership was not equal to the needs of the crisis.

At this period, when the Germans were offered full participation in the rights and duties of the Czechoslovak Republic, their leaders, Dr Lodgman and Seliger, flew to Dresden, where they failed to win support for their revisionist policy. But it was also very significant that national-socialist propaganda had only limited success among the Sudeten Germans until the occupation of Austria, but that subsequently the great majority of Sudeten Germans succumbed to it. As the events of March 1939 showed, Czechoslovakia would undoubtedly have been occupied by the National Socialists even if none of its inhabitants had been German-speaking, but the unsettled claims of the linguistic minorities, which went back to 1919, had done great moral harm to the cause of the one Succession State which could claim to be something like an authentic democracy.

Beside this constitutional weakness, Czechoslovak democracy had a further structural flaw. This had to do with the Slovak problem. The Slovak Catholic People's Party was originally an autonomous party, not unlike the former Bavarian People's Party. Having grown in the traditional political and social structure of Hungary, it looked very coldly on the spread of democracy in Slovakia and made a point of stressing the specific Slovak tradition. Yet it was consistent with the facts that the majority of Slovaks voted enthusiastically in favour of the new Czechoslovak state in 1918.[1]

During the First World War, T. G. Masaryk and the Slovak General Štefánik succeeded in winning the support of the Slovak language communities in the United States for the new state. As a result of these agreements, embodied in the Cleveland Agreement and the Pittsburgh

[1] Joseph M. Kirschbaum, *Slovakia: Nation at the Crossroads of Central Europe*, New York 1960.

Convention, the financially strong Slovak language communities living in America championed the cause of Slovakia's integration into a democratic Czechoslovak republic. The Slovaks, including those serving in the Czechoslovak legions in Russia, imagined, however, the new state as a union of the Czech and Slovak nations and not as a monistic synthesis of a single Czechoslovak nation. When Dr Beneš seemed to be getting this thesis accepted at the Versailles Peace Conference, the Slovak leader, Monsignor Andreas Hlinka, went to Paris. But the French authorities were told he was a Habsburg spy; he was expelled from France and arrested and imprisoned on his return to Czechoslovakia. This was the beginning of a political struggle between the Czechs and the Slovaks which lasted twenty-five years.[1] A large number of Slovaks believed that the Czechs had broken their promise to give them autonomy.

Once again the narrow concept of the national state proved to be neither capable of uniting the peoples forcibly nor of giving the country internal peace. The situation was made worse by an unsuccessful administrative policy. If Czechoslovakia had not continued the policy of centralization begun in 1920,[2] the Hlinka Party would have lost much of its influence. In 1925 this party did join the newly formed middle-class coalition government. But as the former Czechoslovak Prime Minister Hodža admitted, there were increasing tendencies to centralism[3] and 1928 saw a further swing in this direction when the functions of the Minister for Slovakia were split between the provincial authority in Pressburg and other ministries.[4]

The central government's attempts to put Czech officials into key positions in Slovakia and the deliberate neglect of the Slovak language which, together with the Czech language, was forced into the Procrustes' bed of a common Czechoslovak language, did much to stimulate the growth of Slovak separatism. Even in 1937 the Czech centralists refused to allow any concessions in the way of autonomy.

This autonomous party, with its religious associations, which continued a particularist tradition within the national community, was by no means an isolated phenomenon in the post-war states. The Croation Peasant Party was a parallel case in Yugoslavia. In Germany, apart from the Bavarian People's Party, we think of the Welfen Party in Hanover. But the fact that these parties were partly responsible for the collapse of post-war democracy can be explained not only by their preference for conservative and reactionary movements but also, and

[1] Ibid., p. 97.
[2] R. W. Seton-Watson, *Slovakia Then and Now*, London 1931, pp. 42 ff.
[3] M. Hodža, op. cit., p. 92.
[1] J. Hoetzel, *Československé Správní Právo*, Prague 1934, p. 130.

in particular, by the obstinacy with which the new post-war states clung to centralist policies. These new national democratic states had in many cases adopted the orthodox, unitary and centralistic constitutional institutions of the French administrative system. But they had not thought about the possible social effects which these institutions might have on peoples and communities whose structure was very different.[1] The forms of social and community life which had evolved over the centuries in central and south-eastern Europe had, therefore, to give way to new and artificial forms introduced in the wake of the centralized constitutions. No great thought had been given to the question whether they were suitable in a different social milieu. On the other hand many laws and decrees were taken over from the old regimes, including a number which were incompatible with democracy.

The development in Yugoslavia was similar to that in Czechoslovakia, in so far as the two most important Croat parties, the Peasants' Party and the Constitutional Party, worked for an independent Croat state. The Croatian separatists boycotted the Constitutional Committee and the Skupština. Therefore the constitution which was agreed on reflected the wishes of the deputies, who came almost exclusively from Serbia, for a unitary, centralistic, pan-Serbian solution. The strength of the federalist opposition within the Constitutional Committee is evident from the fact that the name of 'Yugoslavia' for the new state was rejected and, unlike Poland and Czechoslovakia, it was called the 'Kingdom of the Serbs, Croats and Slovenes'. Nevertheless the unsatisfied claim of the Croatian Federalists, led by Stephan Radič, did not allow the state a peaceful birth.

That the Croat Peasants' Party was a federalist and democratic movement is clear from Dr Maček's oration at the funeral of the party leader, Stephan Radič, who was assassinated in the Skupština:

'Stephan Radič fought for a free Croatian state, where neither individual people nor, even less, any social groups would be oppressed. Stephan Radič became the champion of . . . equality between Serbs and Croats. The concept of a free Croatia excludes any form of state limiting Croatia's freedom to the advantage of other national groups, except the State itself. Croatia will never give up the right to autonomy pertaining to a partner in a common state, not even for the sake of that common state; for the state came into being to guarantee, not to reduce this freedom.[2]

---

[1] In his book *Demokratie heute und morgen*, Zürich, New York 1944, p. 85, Beneš sought to justify himself. He declared that the architects of the central European constitutions and the politicians had had to grapple with the stormy post-war political and economic crises and had no chance to change fundamentally the existing conditions.          [2] Quoted by Maček, op. cit., p. 117.

In this connection the conversation is instructive which Maček had with King Alexander of Yugoslavia shortly before Alexander abolished the democratic system in Yugoslavia and instigated his royal dictatorship. The king, who despaired of forging a unified nation under pan-Serbian leadership by parliamentary methods, asked Maček how he would solve the constitutional crisis. Maček quoted the liberal Hungarian statesman Deak, who had said to the Emperor Francis Joseph: 'Your Majesty, when a waistcoat is wrongly buttoned up, it must be undone and buttoned up again.'[1] Maček's proposal was for a federation to consist of seven units each with its own provincial assembly but with a central government and a central parliament. But the king had already informed the pro-Croat Serbian leader Pribičevič of Maček's attitude. Tearing the sleeve of his uniform he remarked that he could not deny his own blood,[2] he wanted to emphasize once again that he had decided to adopt a pan-Serbian solution.

The *coup d'état* which took place on January 6, 1929 and made General Živkovič Prime Minister led to the dissolution of the independent parties and trade unions. Yugoslavia's administrative system was now organized in administrative units called banates. The Serbs, who formed 45 per cent of the population, were assigned 6 banates, but the Croats received only 3. It was only then that the state of the Serbs, Croats and Slovenes was re-christened Yugoslavia, the state of the South Slavs.[3]

The pan-Serbian course taken by the dictatorship, which was intent on weakening the Croats, led to measures against the Catholic Church reminiscent of Bismarck's *Kulturkampf*. The Opposition leaders Maček, Korošec, Trumbič and Spaho were arrested in 1933. As a result the struggle between the Serbs and the Croats took the form of terrorist action. The Croatian conservative and right-wing circles, round Pavelič for instance, were supported partly by Mussolini, partly by former Croat officers of the Austro-Hungarian monarchy living in Austria. Under Pavelič, who had allied himself with the Macedonian terrorists, the Croatian terrorists embarked on the gruesome career of the Ustaša, culminating in the assassination of King Alexander in Marseilles on October 9, 1934. Just before the War Dr Maček succeeded in persuading the Regent, Prince Paul, to grant Croatia autonomy, but during the War the antagonism between Croats and Serbs erupted again. It was not resolved until the victory of the communist partisans under the Croat Tito.

[1] Ibid., p. 127.    [2] Rudolf Kiszling, *Die Kroaten*, Graz, Cologne 1956, p. 142.
[3] Ibid., p. 151.

## PART THREE

### The Squandered Inheritance of the Danubian Countries

The dismembering of the Austro-Hungarian monarchy split the Danubian region into a number of small states left without any new economic links to replace those which had disappeared. Even if the intentions that lay behind this partitioning – the prevention of any German expansion of power – are clearly recognized, the solution which was decided on in the treaties of St Germain and Trianon was hardly calculated to fulfil them. For in that case the small new states would have had every reason to co-operate as closely as possible in the strategic and economic fields. Perhaps the Little Entente and the attempts to establish a Balkan union were moves in this direction. But as the small states concerned had set their hearts on a severe and unadulterated form of nationalism these steps were bound to remain half-hearted and ineffectual and their only success was to keep the Habsburg King Charles I off the Hungarian throne.

All attempts to bring Austria and Hungary into the Little Entente were also bound to fail because of their distrust of its aims. Thus it was ludicrous to form the Little Entente as a military safeguard against Hungary and at the same time declare that the other Danubian countries including Hungary could join the alliance between Czechoslovakia, Yugoslavia and Romania. How could Hungary and Austria join the Little Entente and not feel anxious about their independence? Finally Beneš, the principal advocate of the Little Entente, must also have been doubtful of its value. When, after 1935, the authoritarian governments of Yugoslavia and Romania turned increasingly to the totalitarian powers, they withdrew their support for Czechoslovakia as soon as she stood in mortal danger from Nazi Germany.[1]

The short-sightedness of the nationalist solution became clear first in the limitations placed on people's freedom of movement and the steady deterioration in the economic situation. A journey across central Europe meant battling through a tangle of passport and customs barriers. Hertz pointed out that the revenue of the Austro-Hungarian monarchy had risen by 86 per cent between 1910 and 1912[2] and that the profits were distributed equally to all races of the Empire. In the German-speaking Alpine lands (with the exception of Lower Austria) revenue during this period went up by 95 per cent and wages by 87 per cent, while in the three Bohemian crown lands, where the Czechs were in the majority, there was a rise of 97 and 94 per

---

[1] Cf. Edward Beneš, *Memoirs*, London 1954, pp. 29 ff.
[2] F. Hertz, *The Economic Problem of the Danubian States*, London 1947, p. 38.

cent. In the predominantly south Slav regions of the Adriatic coast the figures were 94 and 92 per cent, while in Galicia and the Bukovina, in which the languages spoken were mainly Polish, Ukrainian and Romanian, the increase amounted to 91 and 148 per cent.[1]

These and other figures quoted by Hertz show not only that Vienna was impartial and uniformly benevolent towards the races of the empire but also that it pursued a positive economic and financial policy in the underdeveloped eastern regions. The aid given to these peoples was part of a carefully considered industrial and agrarian policy which included provision for the free passage of goods between the countries of the Danube monarchy. While wages rose by 34 per cent in the period immediately preceding the First World War, the rise in the cost of living was only 20 per cent. Even emigration is no evidence to the contrary. While 1,034,813 people emigrated overseas between 1908 and 1912, 401,802 returned from the United States alone in the same period.[2] Unemployment was minimal.

After the war the irrationality of the principle of nationalism became immediately evident. All the Succession States isolated themselves by erecting customs barriers and aiming at autarchy. At first an attempt was made to ruin Vienna – which was hated by the nationalist leaders of Austria's new neighbours as the seat of their former rulers – by severing all economic links. 'Vienna shall die' was the theme underlying the policy pursued by the Czechoslovak Finance Minister Rašin. Despite Allied attempts to bolster it up, the Austrian currency was devalued, the middle classes, as in Germany, being impoverished and driven into the arms of fascism. The economic nationalism of these states, which artificially raised the price of essential foods like grain and sugar in their own countries so that their exports might remain competitive in the world markets, created a short-lived prosperity which could not withstand economic crises. External trade between the Danubian states sank to a sixth of its pre-war volume.[3]

Before 1914 Hungary was the most important agricultural country in the monarchy. Now, protected by tariffs, new industries were started up. In 1921, 152,000 people in Hungary were engaged in industry, but by 1936 the number had risen to 264,000. Expansion in the textile industry, formerly concentrated in the Sudeten regions, was particularly striking.[4] But the increase in Hungarian industrialization was

[1] Ibid., p. 41.

[2] Ibid., p. 47. On the other hand the Czech economist, Antonin Baseh maintains in *The Danube Basin and the German Economic Sphere*, London 1944, that the economic and social advance of the Danube monarchy was slow and that Austria's national income measured in international units, was only 425 compared with Great Britain's, which was 966, and Germany's which was 764 (p. 6). [3] Ibid., pp. 82 f.

[4] Cf. Royal Institute of International Affairs, Chatham House, *Report on South Eastern Europe*, Oxford 1939, p. 116.

offset by her sharp agricultural losses. While the population of post-war Hungary increased by 18·7 per cent between 1910 and 1937, grain production rose by only 9·3 per cent.[1] Discrimination by the other Danubian states against Hungarian agricultural products led to the collapse of agricultural prices inside Hungary and a definite deterioration of living conditions on the land. The customs policy of the Czechoslovak government, dominated by the Agrarian Party, must also bear much of the blame and further strained the bad relations existing between Hungary and Czechoslovakia.

Before the war Czechoslovakia and Hungary were the principal industrial regions of the Danube monarchy. But now the fragmentation of the whole economic area, following the erection of customs barriers, led to the decline of Austria's most important industry, which was only minimally offset by the emergence of the minor industries. Before the war the Alpine countries' main industrial products had been pig-iron, steel and machinery. Taking the 1913 index as 100, steel production dropped to 25 during the economic crisis but then recovered and rose to 63, while the output of machinery still stood at 36 as late as 1937.

Before the war Bohemia, Moravia and Silesia had been the largest industrial region in Austria-Hungary but it was also one of the most efficient agricultural areas in Europe.[2] This relative equilibrium between industry and agriculture, with industry predominating slightly, should have made Czechoslovakia the most prosperous state in central Europe. Among the most important branches of this industry were milling, brewing and malting, sugar production, the leather, paper and textile industries, glass-making, ceramics, the chemical, iron and machine industries. The mines were able to provide these with cheap coal.[3] Most of these, in particular the mills, the paper, textile, glass and ceramic industries, were in the German-speaking Sudeten region. According to the figures of the Czechoslovak Statistics Office, it was some time before the loss of the former markets in the Danube area became apparent. The drop in production which corresponded to this loss began with the economic crisis but persisted even after this had ended. The industries of Bohemia were geared to supplying a large economic area. Drop in production and chronic unemployment were therefore the natural consequences of its disappearance. But they affected the Sudeten region much more severely than the rest of the country as it still contained most of the textile industry.

According to 1938 Czechoslovak statistics cotton imports in 1933 declined from the pre-war figure of 192,000 tons to 71,000 tons, but

[1] Hertz, op. cit., p. 129.
[2] Cf. Forst de Nattaglia, *Zwischeneuropa*, op. cit., p. 207.
[3] H. Hassinger, *Die Tschechoslowakei*, Vienna, Leipzig, Munich 1925, pp. 404 ff.

after the economic crisis rose to only 95,000 tons by 1936. In 1937 there was one-third fewer cotton spindles and almost half the number of looms than there were in 1920, and the glass industry's output went down by two-thirds.[1] These sober figures express the harsh fact that the German-speaking textile towns of north-eastern Bohemia, northern Moravia and Silesia became industrial graveyards. On the other hand the output in the coal mines and the iron and steel industries in the Czech areas rapidly equalled the best achievements in the boom year of 1929. The disproportion in the employment of German and Czech workers was made worse by the government establishing new industries in the Czech areas and also by the dismantling of industry in the *German* region and its transfer to the Czech part of the country. These factors hastened the growth of national socialism among the Sudeten population.

However, the Czech population did not benefit from their economic supremacy. Statistics show that the consumption of meat, wheat, sugar, beer and tobacco declined slowly but steadily.[2] The annual purchase of cotton goods in Czechoslovakia was only 4·2 kilogrammes *per capita* compared with 8 kilos in western Europe and 5·1 kilos in Austria.[3] While there were 120 wireless sets per 1000 people in western Europe and 92 per 1000 in Austria, there were only 69 sets among the same number of Czechoslovaks.

The reason is that all the Succession States built up their own industry and cut themselves off from Czechoslovakia by protective customs. Thus Austria also made efforts to start a sugar industry of her own so as to be independent of Czechoslovakia. On the other hand the Agrarian Party, always represented in the Czechoslovak government, opposed the import of agricultural products from the other countries, which again pushed up the cost of living inside Czechoslovakia itself.

Before 1914 the living standard of the industrial workers in the Sudetenland was relatively high; now they were unemployed. Although the democratic spirit, together with a positive attitude to the Czechoslovak state after the Treaty of Locarno, survived longest, due to the influence of Sudeten German social democracy, the unemployed textile workers in towns like Reichenberg, Trautenau, Hohenelbe, Jägerndorf, Mährisch-Schönberg and Troppau turned increasingly to first, the Communist Party but later in ever-growing numbers to the

[1] Hertz, op. cit., p. 173.

[2] *Statistisches Jahrbuch der Čechoslowakischen Republik*, published by the State Office of Statistics, Prague 1938.

[3] *Economic Development in South-Eastern Europe*, published by the Organization for Political and Economic Planning, 1945, p. 40; quoted by Hertz, op. cit., p. 182.

National Socialist Party – while the middle-class parties (the Christian Social Party, the Farmers' Union and the Liberals) were to a large extent absorbed by the extreme right-wing parties.

The policy of the Henlein party, devised by the German National Socialists, was to accuse the Czechoslovak Republic of responsibility for the Sudeten Germans' economic distress. The German democratic parties, which in 1929 still had over 51 deputies in the Czechoslovak National Assembly (compared with 8 National Socialists and 7 German Nationalists), were weakened by the government's anti-German financial and economic policy. The three German members of the government had to fight hard to get the slightest concession, such as the appointment of individual German civil servants and teachers. Thus at the height of the economic crisis the social democratic welfare Minister, Dr Ludwig Czech, was allowed to introduce the unemployment cards – contemptuously described as 'Czech cards' – which gave an unemployed married man with two children the totally inadequate sum of 20 crowns (about 2·5 marks) and an unemployed single man 10 crowns a week. 'During the economic crisis,' says Jaksch, 'events in Germany, Austria and Czechoslovakia exerted a mutual effect on one another.'[1] In 1932, out of a total Austrian population of $6\frac{1}{2}$ millions, 400,000 were unemployed and of the 1 million unemployed in Czechoslovakia 500,000 lived in the Sudeten region. Hunger and unemployment weakened the powers of resistance of the democratic working class. It became increasingly difficult for agricultural countries like Hungary, Yugoslavia and Romania to market their products.

The splitting up of central Europe was now revealed as a policy of catastrophic stupidity. During the pre-war years of 1911–13 the Austrian, Czechoslovak and Polish parts of the Danube monarchy imported from those areas which later were to form Hungary, Yugoslavia and Romania goods to the value of 508 million dollars and exported goods to the value of 574 million dollars. In 1935 these figures had dropped to 88 and 79 million dollars. Total trade in the Danubian region shrank from 1,082 to 167 million dollars, i.e. to 15·5 per cent of its former volume.[2] Even the pan-Slavist and anti-German Karl Kramář confessed: '*Now we are feeling the full gravity of the loss of the Austro-Hungarian customs area.*'[3]

The increasing aggression of the Third Reich's foreign policy since 1935 appreciably strengthened national socialism in Austria. In the Sudeten region the difficulties of the German democrats were increased by Czech distrust. They continued their denationalizing policy and

[1] Jaksch, op. cit., p. 262.     [2] Hertz, op. cit., p. 84.     [3] Jaksch, op. cit., p. 263.

their internal economic nationalism, thereby compromising the German democratic parties in the eyes of their supporters. Proof of this was the increase in the growth of the National Socialist Party, which organized its SA (Storm Troops) units as 'People's Sport'.

The plight of the Hungarian peasants and agricultural workers, and unemployment without adequate unemployment benefit enabled Hungarian reactionaries to shift the responsibility on to the other Succession States. Thus the situation became more explosive everywhere. The possibility of federal solutions of the Danubian problem appeared increasingly unrealistic because industries kept artificially alive by the state in the agricultural countries developed and thus influential economic interests added their voice to the general national bitterness.

It is evident that there was much distress in the Danube region which was not due to the economic crisis. But the depression on top of all the other factors did make the people's lot intolerable. The Nazi seizure of power in Germany boosted the pan-German movements in Austria and the Sudetenland. In 1935 the National Socialist rearmament programme had put an end to unemployment. The inhabitants of the Sudeten region could thus compare prosperity in the Reich with their own misery. Moreover, while the Czech regions began to boom with government help the economic distress in the Sudetenland and Austria persisted. In 1934 Austrian social democracy had already become the victim of Mussolini's intervention with the Austrian government and the West had done nothing to help democracy in Austria. Now the Sudeten Social Democratic Party, the only surviving democratic German party, had to carry on a battle that was already lost. Even when, after Hitler's occupation of Austria, the tide of national enthusiasm seemed to sweep away all doubts about national socialism, 10 per cent of the Sudeten Germans still declared their allegiance to social democracy.[1]

Although the new national states were encouraged to indulge in an excessive nationalism by the Peace Treaties, they did not get the strategic frontiers consonant with their selfish ambitions. Perhaps the most astonishing decision was to create an Austrian state with a population of six and a half million, of whom two million lived in the capital, Vienna. Austria's economic structure was such that she could neither live nor die. Her neighbours' chauvinism prevented the foundations of a Danubian union. On the other hand the alliance of the Little Entente with the Western Powers led the latter to oppose a union between a democratic Austria and the Weimar Republic. Such

[1] Ibid., p. 300.

a union would have been a notable success for the foreign policies of the two countries which might well have been reflected in their domestic affairs, in favour of democracy.

As the Curtius-Schober plan failed and the West was allied with the Little Entente, Austria was compelled, for economic and security reasons, to seek protection from Fascist Italy, at that time considered to be an effective safeguard against encirclement by Nazi Germany. Austria's pro-Italian foreign policy which, after the assassination of Dolfuss in 1934, seemed to his successor, Schuschnigg, not only logical but also consistent with her internal policies, was soon to prove a failure.[1] The common declaration by England, France and Italy at Stresa made no difference. After the Italian attack on Ethiopia, which antagonized England and France, and Mussolini's rapprochment with Hitler, which paved the way for the Rome–Berlin Axis, Schuschnigg's policy led to the isolation of Austria. All his attempts to effect a reconciliation with the socialists were extremely tentative because of the continuing influence of the *Heimwehr* and the mounting strength of the Rome–Berlin Axis.[2]

It was only now that the grotesque nature of the territorial solution of the Treaty of St Germain was revealed for all the world to see. Geographically Czechoslovakia was a country extending over a great distance. From Eger to Marmoros on the Theiss it was 600 miles, that is, further than from Eger to London.[3] It took two days to travel by train from one end of the country to the other. But in places, for example where Silesia bit into Moravia, it was only 100 miles wide and in parts of Carpatho-Russia only 44 miles. The total length of the Czechoslovak frontier was 2,360 miles, a large part of it being common with Germany even before Hitler's occupation of Austria. But after March 11, 1938, Czechoslovakia's strategic situation became hopeless. For then the tanks of an aggressive Germany could overrun the 100 miles between Mährisch-Ostrau and the Austrian-south-Moravian frontier in a matter of a few hours. But as soon as Czechoslovakia was occupied the position of Hungary and Poland was bound to become precarious from the military point of view, and as soon as Hungary succumbed Yugoslavia and Romania were also bound to be exposed.

The rape of Europe which began with the occupation of Austria proved that Austria was the key to the strategic domination of Europe. This made it all the more difficult to understand why this vital position had been kept as defenceless and as weak as possible by the peace makers in Paris – a mistake which was to be repeated after the

[1] *Geschichte der Republik Österreich*, op. cit., pp. 231 ff.
[2] Ibid., p. 243.     [3] Hassinger, op. cit., p. 341.

Second World War. An alternative solution would have been to incorporate Austria in a federation of the small and medium-sized Danubian nations. A number of attempts were made but they failed, partly because of the opposition of the Little Entente, partly because of Italy.

In Czechoslovakia the Danubian federation had found a convinced advocate in Dr Hodža. It would have been necessary to base such a federation on the principle of national equality and a sense of common tradition and a common way of life. But the jingoist elements in these states would have had to have shown an understanding of which they were incapable. For it would have meant abandoning the basic idea of integral nationalism and its *raison d'être* – the interplay of 'dominant and dominated nationalities'. Such a federation could not have come about without constructive ideas and symbols which the peoples of central Europe were not yet mature enough to produce.

On the other hand the existence of important factors which would have cemented such a union was an undoubted fact. The common democratic traditions of central Europe, as they were embodied in the supra-national social democracy of the old Austria, would have provided a starting-point. The common basis of Catholicism and a common movement of small farmers in Czechoslovakia, Austria, Hungary, Yugoslavia and Romania could also have made a national contribution. The common civilization, the existence of a community with a similar way of life and moral code, which had been formed as a result of these peoples living together for more than seven hundred years, could have found expression in a federation based on a parliamentary form of government under a republican president or a parliamentary monarch.

# PART FOUR

*Central Europe and Western Democracy*

Nationalism, which had triumphed in the Treaties of St Germain and Trianon with such dire results for the Danubian peoples, had also set its mark on the Treaty of Versailles and the structure of the League of Nations. The clash between the liberal and nationalistic elements in liberal nationalism that had occurred in central Europe in 1848 was repeated at the Paris peace negotiations on a global scale. President Wilson was the exponent of the liberal school of thought and the French Premier, M. Clemenceau, of the nationalistic school. In his speech in Oakland, California, on September 18, 1919, President

Wilson had explained his plan for making the world safe for democracy when he announced that no autocratic government could join the future League of Nations.[1]

Keynes held Clemenceau responsible for the mistakes of the Versailles Peace. Lloyd George in his memoirs pointed out that Clemenceau's extreme anti-German stand was due not so much to his own sentiments as to those of the French President, M. Poincaré.[2] Yet it is true that for Clemenceau, as for many other statesmen of his generation, the First World War was simply a repetition of the Franco-German War of 1870–71, with a happier outcome for France. It was a profound disappointment for him that the Germans sitting opposite him during the peace negotiations were the representatives of the Weimar Republic and not Bismarck or the German Emperor. He would have found it easier to speak to Hindenburg and Ludendorff, who were nearer to his idea of Prussia, than to Weimar's representatives. In spite of his liberal and tolerant attitude in the Dreyfus affair, he was a genuine representative of nineteenth-century liberalism. This explains why, despite his dislike of Poincaré's chauvinism, Clemenceau was unable to escape his influence.

In the light of the distinction we have made between French and Anglo-Saxon ideas of nationhood, this situation is fully in keeping with our thesis. What Clemenceau thought in Versailles was less important than what he stood for – Rousseau's national general will against whose explosive dynamism the liberal American professor of political philisophy was as impotent as the German liberal professors were against the Prussian monarchy in St Paul's Church at Frankfurt am Main in 1848–49. The defeat of liberalism by nationalism in the Paris Peace Treaties was to have disastrous consequences. These became apparent even during the negotiations, grew, in the next few years, to dimensions never thought possible, and finally, in 1939, led to the Second World War.

While the ruling classes which had borne considerable responsibility for the First World War lived comfortably on their pensions and were able to work undisturbed for the future attack on democracy, and while other classes which had precipitated the outbreak of war by their pan-Slavist and ultra-nationalist intrigues (as in Serbia) also had their reward, the Paris peace makers dealt harshly with the victims both of autocracy and of war, namely the *peoples* of central Europe and the leaders of their *democratic* parties. The humiliations to which

[1] G. M. Gathorne-Hardy, op. cit., p. 148.

[2] Lloyd George tells how Clemenceau was repeatedly called out of the conference hall during the peace conference. Poincare attempted to urge the aging and over-burdened Prime Minister to press for higher reparations and for the occupation of the Ruhr. D. H. Lloyd George, *The Truth About the Peace Treaties*, op. cit., p. 250.

the Weimar statesmen were subjected in Paris did a lot towards destroying the political authority which they had built up by a lifetime's work. The United States, whose President had been the moving spirit behind the movement to form the League of Nations, withdrew into isolation. The League of Nations did not become the guardian of democracy as originally intended, but the biased supporter of national sovereignties. The member states made use of it so long as it seemed to further their national interests. But as the League of Nations went on pretending to carry out its original democratic purpose while actually serving only the selfish national interests of the leading member states, the liberated peoples of central Europe saw it as undermining both democratic ideas *and* respect for the Western Powers dominating it, namely France and England.

The occupation of the Ruhr was one of the events particularly detrimental to the cause of democracy. Carlo Sforza reported that a few days before this actually took place (in January 1923) Bonar Law had submitted to France and Italy a British Government plan for settling the war debts they had incurred from Britain.[1] Had France and Italy approved this plan the occupation and exploitation of the Ruhr would have been unnecessary. While he was the leader of the Italian delegation he had warned the French against such a move. In 1922, however, two important and fateful events happened simultaneously, destroying the prospect of peace in Europe. Poincaré became Premier in France and Fascism triumphed in Italy. Poincaré came to power in a constitutional manner, Mussolini by a *coup d'état*. But they were united by the common tie of extreme nationalism. Mussolini and Poincaré rejected Bonar Law's proposal and insisted on the occupation of the Ruhr. As the Flick case in Nuremberg in 1947 proved, Poincaré was pressed into this policy by the Comité des Forges which wanted to annex the Ruhr and ensure the supply of coal needed for the former German steel industry in Lorraine.[2] And so even at that early date Mussolini had dealt a major blow at German democracy.

Inside Germany the occupation of the Ruhr gave a tremendous stimulus to national socialist and national communist tendencies. The abortive *coups d'état* of Major Buchrucker in north Germany[3] and Adolf Hitler in Munich in 1933 can be viewed as an expression of these tendencies. Nor was it illogical that Laval, who after Poincaré's death most faithfully embodied his ideas, should become Hitler's ally in the Second World War.

On the other hand an urgent warning against occupation was given

---

[1] Carlo Sforza, *Europe and the Europeans*, London, Bombay, Sydney 1936, pp. 55 f.
[2] Case No. 5 Military Tribunal, United States of America, Friedrich Flick, p. 4,005.

by Sir John Bradbury, the British representative at the session of the Reparations Commission which on December 26, 1922, had decided to occupy the Ruhr. He alluded sarcastically to the pretext that Germany had failed to fulfil her deliveries of timber and expressed the opinion that this irrelevant accusation had been made to the Commission as an excuse for a move in another direction. History, said Sir John, had known of no similar use of wood since the capture of Troy by the stratagem of the Trojan Horse.[1]

It is known that the Poincaré–Mussolini axis and French heavy industry which backed them were ready, even a short time before that, to come to an agreement with the German Nationalist Hugo Stinnes. He was a profiteer from the days of the war and inflation, who had built up his empire on the decline of the German middle classes.[2] Stinnes' plan for the reconstruction of France amounted to restoring the social conditions of pre-1914 Germany. For Germany he envisaged the introduction of a 10-hour working day for about fifteen years, together with a five-year ban on strikes in all major industries. It was Stinnes' influence in Cuno's cabinet which led to the rejection of small deliveries of timber, thus precipitating the long-planned occupation of the Ruhr. His aim, clearly, was to stifle socialism in the Ruhr and at the same time to fan the flames of German nationalism.[3]

Gathorne-Hardy attributed the agreement of the British delegates to the occupation of the Ruhr to the withdrawal of the American representatives. The United States' refusal to join the League of Nations was, in every way, a disaster for the fate of the central European democracies as it greatly weakened British efforts to effect a reasonable settlement of post-war relationships. But even the British government had to consider public opinion at home, which was affected by the anti-German views in the press. While, therefore, the hostility of French and Belgian democracy to the Weimar Republic is perfectly understandable, American democracy's crime was indifference and isolationism, while Britain could not always translate good will into appropriate action.

Lloyd George wrote that Poincaré, as a Lorrainer born and bred, had also been obsessed by the familiar 'frontier complex'. Therefore he was a mortal enemy of Germany and all Germans. This had won him great popularity in France which had been devastated by the German armies. Poincaré had refused to allow any French premier to behave courteously and tolerantly to the beaten Germans. It was

[1] G. M. Gathorne-Hardy, op. cit., p. 49.
[2] G. F. W. Hallgarten, *Hitler, Reichswehr und Industrie*, Frankfurt am Main 1958, pp. 13 ff.
[3] Ibid., p. 18.

Poincaré in particular who was responsible for France's refusal to disarm: he would have subsidized rearmament in Poland and Czechoslovakia, encouraged revolt against the German Reich in the Rhineland, conspired with the anti-German circles in England in order to wreck any chance of an understanding between men of goodwill in Europe – in other words he was the real creator of the new (National Socialist) Germany.[1] What Lloyd George overlooked was that Poincaré could achieve his aims only by co-operating with fascism, already emerging in Italy, and the influential nationalist circles centred round Stinnes, Cuno and von Seckt in Germany.

The Versailles peace terms struck a Germany which was struggling to cope with an economic and social situation already near to breaking-point. Until the first boom, German economy was obviously conditioned to needs imposed by the war, especially rationing. As in other combatant countries, agriculture had been bled of its best workers. There was a dearth of tools and essential fertilizers: yields dropped. In addition, the currency had lost much of its purchasing power.[2]

The first weak signs of a boom, 'the revolutionary boom', were suddenly interrupted by the conclusion of the Peace Treaty on June 8, 1919. Reparations in effect ruined Germany's economy partly because of extensive demands on her for massive deliveries in kind and – what was far more decisive – because of the 5-year preferences given to the Allies and associated states, which meant that Germany was excluded from world markets.[3] The pure deliveries of goods in kind and the reparations to be paid in foreign exchange bills did much to bring about the collapse of currency. Both these things had the same effect. The export of goods from current production with no counterbalance in the way of imports produced an increasing surplus in purchasing power, just like the compulsory reduction of foreign exchange which had to be purchased with the internal currency which flowed back into the German market to buy real values. Lloyd George said:

'There seems no doubt that immediately after the war Germany was so exhausted and impoverished that its government was really unable to collect enough in taxation to meet internal expenses and at the same time satisfy the demands of the Allies. In its despair it had recourse to the printing press, and manufactured paper money which did not represent any real increase in the sum total of its national wealth but only wrecked its currency and ruined its investing classes.'[4]

[1] Lloyd George, op. cit., p. 252.
[2] Julius Hirsch, *Die Deutsche Währungsfrage*, Jena 1924; *re* England cf. J. M. Keynes, *Ein Traktat über Währungsreform*, Munich 1924, p. 14.
[3] Hjalmar Schacht, *Das Ende der Reparationen*, Oldenburg, 1931, pp. 25 ff.
[4] Lloyd George, *The Truth about Reparations and War Debts*, London 1932, p. 81.

This development was bound to destroy the German middle class. Julius Hirsch's figures indicated the decline: 'In terms of gold marks, the German population had about 90 gold marks per capita in peace time, 51 at the end of 1919, 14 in October 1922 and about 1 gold mark at the beginning of November 1923.'[1]

At the end of November 1923 inflation was checked by the introduction of the Rentenmark. The currency was finally stabilized by the Dawes Plan and its economic consequences. It placed German reparation deliveries on a different basis and no longer fixed a definite total sum for payment. German industry was to be given the chance to produce the goods requested abroad. The resultant exports surplus was to count as reparation payments. To finance the first instalment of over 1,000 million gold marks, the United States granted Germany a loan of 800 million gold marks.

The stabilization of the currency and Germany's readmission to world trade produced a short-lived economic boom. However, since German export prices – measured in terms of the value of foreign trade – rose compared with what they were during the inflation, her export trade stagnated. But the boom could last only as long as exports continued. The foreign exchange fund created by the restoration of the country's finances and the 800 million gold mark loan from the United States at first concealed the fact that in 1925 there was a trade gap of 3,000 million marks. This imbalance was bound to become evident in the end; for the profits made during inflation were used to build more industrial plant; sometimes capacity was increased, making for heavy indebtedness with subsequent bankruptcy. The immediate effect of the drop in exports was an increase in unemployment which, by February 1926, had already topped two million.[2] But, in view of this new burden, the Entente was not prepared to relax the financial pressure. Germany could make reparation payments only if she raised further foreign loans. Yet continued borrowing meant an increase in her foreign debt which, according to the German Office of Statistics, amounted to over 2,000 million marks at the end of September 1930. However, the loans flowed not into the German economy as a whole, but back abroad – except for a relatively small sum to settle the chronic trade deficit – to make cash reparation payments and to meet the growing capital charge for credits and loans.

The result was that when foreign loans were not forthcoming or were called in, the *Reichsbank* had to impose credit restrictions which slowly paralysed the economy. Von Beckerath had given a warning

---

[1] Julius Hirsch, op. cit., pp. 17 ff.
[2] Bruno Asch, 'Der Kamp gegen die Arbeitslosigkeit', in *Die Gesellschaft*, Vol. II, Berlin 1926, p. 206.

of the dangers in the situation: 'The whole system can collapse over-night because of some political strain and then we shall be limited to our own resources if we are to solve the current problems of raising and transferring money . . . The question is whether it is possible to deal with the whole situation . . . by a sudden export drive. It is ob-vious that it is not possible by suddenly expanding the export industry. I consider it highly probable that an acute deflationary mechanism and an extremely effective deflationary policy will come into play.'[1]

Although the post-inflation crisis, evident in the higher unemploy-ment figures and growing number of business crashes – there were 2,092 cases of bankruptcy in January 1926[2] – slowly eased off from March 1926, the seed of the great economic crisis was sown.[3] That is clear from the currency and financial position, since the supplies of gold and foreign exchange went to pay the war and reparation debts, thus inducing an uncontrollable collapse in prices;[4] as for merchan-dise, since Germany used large sums to rationalize and mechanize her industry, the creditor states were not willing to take the mounting stocks of manufacturers. Keynes observed that 'the seed of the latest collapse was sown about 1925',[5] especially by settling reparations and war debts. Consequently the balance between capital import and capital expenditure was of decisive importance.

The higher the deficit grew in the country as a whole, in the provinces and the towns, the more rapidly foreign money was withdrawn. Keynes explained how in 1927–28 the United States lent, at high interest rates, a sum of money which was many times larger than its active balance. Most of this money went to Europe because by far the largest part of it which was lent there on long-term rates was for short-term credits. In this way, within two or three years, some 500 million pounds had been borrowed on a long-term basis but then transferred back to repay short-term credits. The resultant collapse was on a far greater scale than the depression in the inflation period; it was not to be compared with the immediate post-war crisis or that of 1926, as in both the occasions official programmes of public works were undertaken.

The events of 1918, the inflation and the thousands of business failures in 1925–26 had already resulted in a social upheaval which

---

[1] Herbert von Beckerath, in *Das Reparationsproblem*, Friedrich-List-Gesellschaft, Berlin 1921, Vol. I, p. 35.     [2] Ibid., p. 250.
[3] *Deutschland und der Dawes-Plan*, Report of the General Agent, Berlin 1926.
[4] Cf. also J. M. Keynes, *Vom Gelde*, Berlin 1955, p. 602.
[5] Ibid.

involved between $4\frac{1}{2}$ and 5 million *déclassés*, that is some 7 or 8 per cent of the German population. The economic crisis at the end of the 1920s with its 6 or 7 million unemployed, of whom up to $2\frac{1}{2}$ million had lost their right to unemployment benefit and were therefore destitute, created the conditions which brought on the final collapse of the crisis-ridden Weimar Republic. The cause of this was, therefore, selfish nationalism on the part of both the Allies and the big German industrialists, plus an inadequate understanding of the fact that the economy was one and indivisible. That rightist, conservative circles were generally antagonistic to the new democracy in central Europe is apparent not only from the skilful way in which French chauvinism and Italian fascism co-operated with the German conservatives and nationalists, wanting to restore the Hollenzollerns, but also from the circumstances which accompanied the Treaty of Rapallo.

The occupation of the Ruhr also gave communism a fillip. A report by the Soviet Embassy in Reval entitled 'Communism and Nationalism' indicates that the Soviet Union used every available means of propaganda and persuasion to encourage the nationalist revolutionaries in the Ruhr and to urge the German communists to co-operate with them. Schüddekopf reports that at a meeting in Moscow, attended by Stalin, Radek was given control of operations in Germany and Czechoslovakia. 'As far as Germany was concerned, the socialist points in the National Socialist programme were described as the expression of the "healthy urge to make a final break with the old regime".'[1]

It was, moreover, clearly stated in this report that the authority of the middle-class democratic government must be undermined by all possible means. General von Seckt was all for military co-operation between Germany and the Soviet Union and a comprehensive alliance, but this was rejected by President Ebert and the Social Democrats.

The Locarno Treaties and Germany's subsequent membership of the League of Nations created a more favourable climate for democracy. This positive turn of events was a matter of chance; in both France and Germany foreign policy was conducted by two statesmen, Briand and Stresemann, who were both liberal rather than nationalist in outlook. Yet both came up against insoluble difficulties in trying to carry out their domestic policies. The leader of the German National People's Party, Hugenberg, conducted a campaign against Stresemann. It was not without effect on Stresemann's own German People's Party and it finally wore him down. On the other hand, in France, Briand was unable to ensure the early evacuation of the Rhineland and the effective disarmament of the French army. German and French nationalism now

---

[1] Otto-Ernest Schüddekopf, *Link Leute von rechts*, op. cit., p. 141.

acted like two interconnected pipes. The delay in the evacuation of the Ruhr and the disarmament of the Western Powers gave a boost to German nationalism and the rising fortunes of national socialism. If the Western Powers were not ready to disarm, Stresemann's policy of fulfilment and unilateral German arms limitation seemed of questionable value and Hugenberg was able to convince many Germans of the truth of his accusation that Stresemann was a 'traitor' and a 'national disgrace'.[1] And the vicious campaign against Locarno and the German Nationalists' call for rearmament undermined the position of Briand and other French representatives, who favoured an arrangement between Weimar and French democracy. French public opinion was therefore in no mood to agree to the speedy evacuation of the Ruhr and disarmament. This, however, meant that in Germany not the nationalist and authoritarian forces but the democratic patries became the target of the National Socialist attack.

The masses of central Europe became increasingly aware that there was no real bond of friendship or solidarity between western and central European democracies. During the war and in the post-war years they had also placed their trust in the central European democratic parties because of the military prestige which victory had brought the West. But they now found out not only that the official representatives of the West held the democrats of central Europe directly responsible for the war, but also that the Allied governments seemed to prefer fascist and reactionary parties to the representatives of democratic organizations in central Europe.

The development of international relations in post-war Europe reinforced this impression. After the wars in Manchuria and Abyssinia the League of Nations seemed to be a mere debating society which even its main representatives, France and England, scarcely took seriously. The German and Italian peoples could not overlook the fact that the Western Powers were prepared to tolerate Germany's unilateral abrogation of the limitations placed on her arms, the re-militarization of the Rhineland and the invasion of Abyssinia.

The Spanish Civil War,[2] in particular, diminished the self-confidence of Europe's democratic forces. While the German and Italian fascists supplied General Franco's rebels with volunteers and arms, volunteers streamed from England, America, France, Austria and Czechoslovakia to help the cause of the republican government in Madrid. The German democratic *émigré* organization also sent a large contingent to support the Republicans. But these volunteers were very different from Hitler's and Mussolini's. The Republicans' comrades in arms were

---

[1] Theodor Eschenburg, *Die improvisierte Demokratie*, op. cit., p. 201.
[2] Cf., *inter alia*, Hugh Thomas, *The Spanish Civil War*, London 1961.

idealistic young democrats fired with enthusiasm who, to get to Spain at all, had not only to elude their own police authorities, but also to slip across the frontier of democratic France, which pursued an extreme policy of non-intervention. The 'volunteers' ordered to Spain by Hitler and Mussolini were, on the contrary, regular army units. 20,000 German troops were already fighting in Spain by the end of 1936; the number of Italians was much greater. Characteristically France and England were neutral, i.e. advocated the removal of *all* troops from Spain, while the Soviet Union was the only power to support republican Spain.

The democratic freedom fighters in Spain were thus placed in a hopeless position. Those of them who escaped the combined forces of Franco, Mussolini and Hitler ended up in the International Brigade. The very fact that only the Soviet Union supported Franco's opponents meant that the democratic wing in the International Brigade was overborne by the better-organized communist cadres. The democrats were therefore engaged in a war on two fronts – one against Franco and the German and Italian troops, the other against the commissars from the Soviet Union who attacked them from behind. One of the most depressing features of the situation was that France, at the time, had the largest social democratic party in existence and a premier who belonged to its left wing and yet rendered very little help to the cause of democracy. Finally, Great Britain forced the Republicans to decide on capitulation, thus ensuring Franco's neutrality in the Second World War. After the Spanish Civil War ended, the valiant democrats who had fought in the International Brigade met each other once more, this time in French internment camps, bullied both by the French police and by communist camp leaders, rejected by every country and denied by their own.

The outcome of the Spanish Civil War and Hitler's invasion of Austria and the Sudetenland were bound to make the central-European democracies feel that their world had collapsed. In every case the Western Powers had shown themselves profoundly unconcerned about what happened, so long as their immediate interests were not directly affected. This and the Hitler–Stalin pact marked the high points of the totalitarian advance. It seemed as though all decisions about the future would be the prerogative of the totalitarian powers. The democrats of central Europe partly withdrew from the political struggle, since it was pointless for them to imperil their very lives and existence for a cause which had been generally abandoned, and partly turned to the Soviet Union and communism as their only hope of finding active and vigorous allies in the fight against fascism.

Yet, as is usual with most contemporary observers of great historic events, their judgement was at fault, for two reasons. In the first place, the Soviet Union quickly dashed these hopes by its increasingly totalitarian structure, by the liquidation in the great purges of all those who deviated from the party line, and by the pact with Hitler. In the second place, it was not democracy which was dead but democracy's national framework, which had proved to be shaky and unreliable. The Godesberg talks between Chamberlain and Hitler and the Munich meeting of Chamberlain, Daladier, Hitler and Mussolini showed that the statesmen of the Western democracies were duped by a skilful compound of deceit and violence *no less than* the leaders of the Social Democratic and Zentrum parties of the Weimar Republic had been. The Republic's representatives could be excused for their ignorance of the national-socialist technique, but by this time the statesmen of Western democracy could hardly plead the same excuse. The reason for their failure was not perhaps – as was claimed later – their wish to gain time to rearm but ignorance about the way the National Socialists had engineered the downfall of the Weimar Republic. They were unable to fill this gap in their knowledge because they still adhered to the thought patterns of World War I, thinking which made any solidarity with central European democracy impossible. In terms of nationalism and power politics, they did not perceive the ideological character of events leading to World War II.

Nationalism had routed liberalism in the West as well. It needed a Winston Churchill, who had a far profounder understanding of the Machiavellian roots of the technique of totalitarianism than men like Baldwin, Chamberlain and Halifax. After the self-satisfied British Prime Minister's return from Munich, Churchill shouted out in the House of Commons: "Chamberlain had to choose war or shame. He has chosen shame and will reap war!' The Weimar democrats had been faced with the same choice in 1932 and 1933, taken the same decision and reaped the same bitter harvest. If, however, one remembers that the effective power at their disposal under Hindenburg, Papen and Hitler was far less than that possessed by the British Empire and France at the time of Munich, when Germany was only semi-armed,[1] the Weimar Republic's failure is far more excusable than that of the Western democracies.

Shirer's thesis that national socialism was a manifestation of the

[1] The author saw the German motorized columns when they entered Prague on March 15, 1939. They consisted of hastily requisitioned private cars and lorries. Even the campaign in the West in 1940 was fought by the *Wehrmacht* partly with Skoda tanks taken over from the Czechoslovak army in 1939. Resistance by the Western Powers and Czechoslovakia at the time of the occupation of Austria would in all probability have resulted in opposition to national socialism by a part of the German people. The invasion of Austria was unpopular with the German conservatives.

German national character seems, therefore, hardly tenable.[1] Shirer's view was the one which prevailed at Teheran and Yalta during the Second World War and which once again delivered central Europe into the clutches of totalitarianism, this time in the form of Stalinist communism. Alas – the mistakes made in Munich were repeated at Yalta! Even Berlin and Prussia, which had resisted national socialism to the last, were handed over to the new form of totalitarianism and the democrats of Czechoslovakia, Poland, Hungary, Yugoslavia and Romania, in so far as they did not emigrate, were once more abandoned to their fate. After the Second World War the democrats of East Germany revolted against their bitter fate in 1953, those of Hungary in 1956 and last but not least, those of Czechoslovakia in 1968. Even then, the answer which Western democracy gave was not substantially different from the one given in the thirties.

[1] William L. Shirer, *The Rise and Fall of the Third Reich,* London 1960.

# CHAPTER V

# The Concept of Democracy in the Caricature of the Authoritarian Tradition

## PART ONE

### *Liberty and Equality*

Liberty, Equality and Fraternity have not symbolized democracy merely since the year 1789. Plato and Aristotle also speak of liberty and equality as the main foundations of democracy, but they were probably not aware that such precious commodities need to be taken in moderate doses if the constitutional state is not to come to an untimely end. They knew that different interpretations could be placed on the concepts of liberty and equality and that the relationship and balance between the two could affect the manner in which the state evolved. Plato and Aristotle were aware of the polarity of these two principles. Both held that it is the specific relationship existing between the monarchical, aristocratic, plutocratic and democratic factors which determines whether freedom or tyranny prevails.

Rather like Kant, they conceive of the partial liberty and equality of the constitutional state as a restraint which we voluntarily impose on ourselves by accepting laws. On the other hand they often speak of liberty in the sense of arbitrariness and licence. Even the generally accepted idea of liberty – which Plato, in *The Republic*, says is the main characteristic of democracy – has changed in the course of two thousand years. Acton-Dalberg saw that a detailed description and analysis of this development was an almost insuperable task because of its vast scope. For man's freedom *vis-à-vis* the state and state power is bound up with the philosophical problem of free will and this, in its turn, is bound up with human reason.[1] From the very beginning freedom appears as a synonym for self-determination. It develops first

---

[1] Cf. Carl J. Friedrich, *Der Verfassungsstaat der Neuzeit*, Berlin, Göttingen, Heidelberg 1953, pp. 5 f.

not as the right of the individual but, as for instance in the Greek city-state, as the citizen's freedom from oppression by tyrants or oligarchs. In Athens, therefore, liberty means 'isonomia', that is, equality before the law – or, in the modern sense, recognition of civic freedoms and rights which afforded the citizen protection against the arbitrary exercise of state power.[1] In Athens, however, freedom itself at first contained an aristocratic element. It was a privilege enjoyed by a limited class – at first by patricians, then by property owners and finally by citizens. Freedom was the feature which distinguished the citizen from the slave and the resident foreigner. The right to engage in political life, which spread steadily to ever-wider circles, sprang from the demand for equality. Hence equality appeared from the beginning as liberty's twin.

As soon as such a philosophy was incorporated in Roman civil law and in the *ius gentium* it was bound to create a fundamental ethical claim to freedom for the slaves and a claim for equal rights for all inhabitants of the Roman Empire, although the principate was able to undermine the political rights. A claim to equality helped, therefore, to extend the claim to freedom.

As soon, however, as Christianity became the official religion of the Roman Empire, the doctrine which held that the dignity and integrity of the individual must be respected by the ruling power became an article of faith.

The natural law, as embodied in Justinian's *corpus civilis*, now became associated with the specifically Germanic juristic idea of the traditional law for the protection of the freedom of the individual against the ruler's despotic power. Patristic literature, especially the writings of St Augustine, had taken these ideas further. According to St Augustine, God made man, with his gift of reason, lord of the animal creation but not of his fellow men. That was the natural order of things but worldly dominion over men was the result of sin.[2] The view that temporal power is basically evil was stated with increasing frequency by the church during the Middle Ages. But the church's ability to maintain her independence from temporal power meant that eastern despotism was unable to extend its sphere of influence westwards across the frontiers of the Byzantine Empire. Thus natural law, whose rational basis was strengthened by the rediscovery of Aristotle's teachings, became associated with the respect for the Germanic *Volksrecht* (people's law) to which even the king was subject, protecting the personal dignity and freedom of the individual. This connection

---

[1] James Bryce, *Modern Democracies*, Vol. I, op. cit., p. 58.
[2] St Augustine, *De Civitate Dei*, Book XIX, Chap. XV (Kempten and Munich 1911–16).

was embodied in the medieval recognition of the people's right to resist the unjust ruler.[1]

As, however, in the Middle Ages the common people were culturally and economically backward, the classes which were militarily and economically influential came forward as the representatives of the people's rights, as in the case of the Magna Charta. There now began in western Europe a process which is reminiscent of developments in classical Athens; the extension of freedom and its associated rights from a privileged class first to the burghers, then to the middle classes and finally to the whole population. As Bertrand Russell explains, the state grew more powerful from the fifteenth century, especially as a result of the discovery of gunpowder[2] but also as a result of the increased revenue from taxes and the rise of a professional civil service which strengthened the middle class. The increase in the power of the state, which was expressed in absolute monarchy's claim to sovereignty and in the emergence of state churches, was matched by a growing desire for freedom. The political philosophy of the social contract now acquired an individualistic complexion because of writings of the epoch of the Wars of Religion and the new rationalistic form of the natural law.[3] In addition to the demand for personal freedom and for freedom of legitimate possession religious persecution also inspired the call for freedom of belief.

From the end of the seventeenth century England's great contribution to the idea of liberty and to the modern world was the recognition that civic and religious freedom are impossible as long as the state constitution leaves political power in the hands of a monarch or one class.[4] The movement which stood for freedom against the claims of absolutism was liberalism, and it found its first embodiment in the Whig Party. Although liberalism appeared to be negative in its attitude towards the state, it was nevertheless, Barker says, a positive doctrine of the free man who maintains his position within the community, not in opposition to the state but with the assistance and the guarantee of the state, which assured him his rights, especially the rights of free speech and discussion.[5]

Like Barker we deny that liberalism can ever be divorced from democracy. For just as the idea of the majority represents the quantitative aspect of democracy, liberalism represents its qualitative aspect, which is concerned with the dignity and the rights of the individual.

[1] For example, Thomas Aquinas, *Summa Theologica*, 2a, 2ae, q., civ. cv, Salzburg 1933–9.
[2] Bertrand Russell, *Authority and the Individual*, London 1949, p. 35.
[3] A. P. d'Entrèves, *Natural Law*, London 1951, pp. 48 ff.
[4] James Bryce, op. cit., Vol. I, p. 8.
[5] Ernest Barker, *Reflections on Government*, Oxford 1945.

Therefore freedom in the traditional sense means above all else man's right to develop and perfect his noblest and truly human qualities. To achieve this, however, he needs personal, civic, religious and political freedom, the only restriction being his fellow men's equal claim to freedom. But as soon as freedom is divorced from democracy both must inevitably perish.

The evolution of representative democracy is closely connected with the idea of freedom. This is borne out by the ancient Germanic *Thing* and the *legem emendare* already mentioned in the Carolingian Capitularies, in which the king or emperor, together with the assembled representatives of the people, absolves the traditional law of its mistakes and proclaims the law – therefore in effect creating the law, which is the living conviction of the general community.

It is therefore clear that, in the first instance, the origins of parliamentarism go back to Germanic law and its principles that the law makes the king and that the king is subject to the law but does not make it. Parliament's legislative function also grew out of its judicial function.[1]

The development of a legal method of dethroning an unjust or tyrannical king is doubtless one of the West's most important and original contributions to the evolution of the constitutional state.[2] The exercise of this right by the members of the Assembly of Estates arose naturally out of the medieval conception of law. It is often forgotten that the development of the British parliamentary system – which represented the estates and the people against the king but at the same time also integrated the king and people – was merely the application of a principle which had been generally valid in the West since Charlemagne.

The dualism of Church and State undoubtedly contributed to this development. The theory of this dualism was first expounded in St Augustine's[3] *Civitas Dei*, but then became firmly established institutionally because of the changing relations between Church and State.[4] The idea of individual freedom from the absolute and arbitrary power of the state as it developed in the West was, therefore, greatly advanced by this dualism. So Carl Schmitt believed when, in his defence of *Leviathan*,[5] he deplored the fact that Christianity destroyed the unity of state and religion which both pagan antiquity and Judaism possessed. But he overlooked the fact that even in the time of classical paganism,

[1] F. Kern, *Gottesgnadentum und Widerstandsrecht im früheren Mittelalter*, Münster, Cologne 1954, p. 127.

[2] Ibid., p. 104.

[3] Cf. Etienne Gicson, *Introduction à l'Etude de St Augustine*, Paris 1929.

[4] Cf. K. J. Newman, 'Papst, Kaiser, Kalif und Basileus', op. cit., pp. 22 ff.

[5] Carl Schmitt, *Der Leviathan in der Staatslehre des Thomas Hobbes*, Hamburg 1938, p. 21.

as in the Athenian 'Council of the Five Hundred' or in the Roman constitutional system, there existed institutional guarantees to ensure that there should be freedom and that state should be based on the rule of law.

The great antagonist of Western constitutionalism, however, was always the oriental despotism, the temple state, which was imported to the West by the Hellenistic kings and the Roman *princeps*. This despotism became firmly established in the Byzantine Empire and then, through the Byzantine state tradition, also influenced Islam.[1] Islam's conquests in Asia, Africa, Spain and Sicily on the one hand and the continuation of this political tradition by Russian Tsarism on the other led to the deification of the Leviathan. Moreover, eastern despotism continued in unchanged form in areas where Christianity was never able to gain a foothold, as in Persia, India and China.

As the centuries passed there were frequent opportunities for the two rival principles – the Western principle of gradualism, dualism and natural law and the Eastern autocratic, Caesaropapist but more egalitarian principle – to influence one another. During the first thousand years of our era the invasions by barbarian Turkish tribes with their military and despotic organization, the conquests of the militarily and culturally superior Arabs and also the central influence of the power of Byzantium, whose culture and civilization were pre-eminent at the time, brought the idea of kingship to the West. The Crusades led to the further interpenetration of these two systems. Thus it was no accident that the first experiment in absolute monarchy – by the Emperor Frederick II, who was greatly influenced by the political practice of Arab despotism – was made in Sicily, which was accustomed to the Muslim tradition, and that after the Moorish conquest, the Spanish monarchy became a permanent centre of authoritarianism.[2]

If, in the Middle Ages, the feudal nobility often appears in the role of representative of the people's rights against the monarchy, so a traditional association arose between the parliaments of the estates – in which the burgher class was represented at an early stage – and the idea of democracy. The theories about the social and constitutional contract from John of Salisbury and Thomas Aquinas to the monarchomachs, Althusius and Locke, gave repeated expression to the democratic idea.

In Europe, however, since the sixteenth century an ever-mounting antagonism has been developing between the Anglo-Saxon and the continental conceptions of the state. This raises the question as to the

[1] Cf. Claude Cahen, 'The Body Politic', in *Unity and Variety in Muslim Civilization*, ed. by G. E. von Grunebaum, Chicago 1955, pp. 134 f.

[2] K. J. Newman, op. cit., p. 42.

origin and cause of this difference. Otto von Gierke pointed out that medieval man was always striving for unity; he believed that unity is the constructive principle of the universe. Therefore the dualism of Church and State was always the result of unsuccessful attempts by one to achieve hegemony over the other.[1] Or, as Lotte Knabe so pertinently wrote when describing the relations between the Papacy and the Empire: 'There is no solution. One will always dominate the other and all attempts to co-ordinate the two powers are only possible in theory.'[2]

Nevertheless the idea of papal sovereignty developed from the time of Gregory VII onwards, by way of Innocent III, Innocent IV and Boniface VIII, and this idea was adopted by the French monarchy after the Babylonian captivity of the Popes. The opposition of medieval constitutionalism to the absolute power of the Papacy was then embodied in the Crusader movement. Its failure was one reason why absolutism was adopted by the territorial princes. This was reinforced by the disunity of the Holy Roman Empire, by the religious split caused by the Reformation, and by the weakening of the feudal estates, which were incapable of resisting a policy based on increased revenue, effective bureaucracy and mercenary armies. It was natural that the territorial sovereign state should combat the many systems of local government which had been developed in the Holy Roman Empire.

The essential difference between constitutional development in England and on the Continent, is that in England the development of the constitutional state based on the Assembly of Estates, never suffered any serious interruption. Although absolutism had also made ground in England under the Tudors, the alliance of king and parliament was enough to ensure the survival of Parliament. This co-operation was based on a compromise, as a result of which the Crown championed the cause of patriotism, the Protestant efforts for reform which were popular with the people and the struggle for emancipation by the lesser nobility and the middle class. In return absolute monarchical rule was allowed much room for manoeuvre.

The conflict between the executive on the one hand and the legislature and the judiciary on the other led, in the seventeenth century, to the overthrow of kings claiming to rule by Divine Right, and to Cromwell's dictatorship. This is why, on the Continent, the constitutional doctrine of the social contract, as expressed in the *Vindiciae contra tyrannos*, by Althusius or by Jesuits such as Bellarmin and

[1] Otto von Gierke, *Das Genossenschaftsrecht*, Berlin 1863–1913, Vol. 3; 'Theory of the State and Corporation in Antiquity and the Middle Ages and their adoption in Germany'.

[2] Lotte Knabe, 'Die Gelsianische Zweigestaltentheorie bis zum Ende des Investiturstreites', in *Historische Studien*, Berlin 1935, p. 6.

Mariana, withered away or, as in Germany, was sublimated into a legal formalism; whereas in England this concept (whose main elements went back to Thomas Aquinas, Marsilius and Occam) underwent further development through the writings of Thomas Moore, Hooker and the Puritan independents.[1]

## Hobbes' Idea of Liberty

The other concept of liberty, which is akin to anarchy, appears in the Epicureans and the Sceptics but was first clearly expounded by Thomas Hobbes. His mechanistic-materialistic view of man, deriving from Cartesian philosophy, stresses the volitional aspect of liberty. Hobbes applies this concept of freedom to the human psyche. According to him the desire for freedom springs from our anarchical and covetous impulses. They inspire us with the desire to do what we want, regardless of the social order. One of these desires is to get on in life, to become powerful, rich and influential, to go one better than others, to be superior to them.[2] The effect of Hobbes' premises are more convincing than the conclusions which are drawn from them. The check restraining these impulses is, according to Hobbes, the constitutional order created by men from their fear of this urge for liberty. Because of its strength and because of the satanic side of man's nature he considers it essential to have a system of government which is uniform and, as far as possible, one which puts all men on the same level, preferably an absolute monarchy or a dictatorship. Opposed to this unlimited state power which, Hobbes argues, can be embodied in a tyrannical majority just as much as in a personal tyrant, is man's natural right to self-determination. The traditional liberties of an hierarchical – Tönnies' gradualistic – order were threatened in Hobbes' days first by the absolute monarchy of Charles I and then by the dictatorship of Oliver Cromwell.

It follows therefore that the hierarchical system – as the social embodiment of a completely aristocratic type of claim to freedom – limits the claims of both tyranny and egalitarian democracy. The more extensive a hierarchy is, the greater the distance between the top and bottom of the ladder and the greater the freedom; freedom for those on the intermediate rungs to move upward or downwards.[3]

[1] Cf., for example, A. D. Lindsay, *The Modern Democratic State*, New York 1962, pp. 115 ff.

[2] Thomas Hobbes, *Leviathan*, Oxford 1958, pp. 66 ff.

[3] This was clearly realized by Simmel: 'The striving for and the attainment of freedom immediately produces the striving for and attainment of domination.' Cf. *Soziologie*, op. cit., p. 169.

The fact that the demand for liberty often conceals a new claim to dominate is perfectly consistent with Hobbes' idea of liberty. This is true not only of individuals but also of groups. Thus the demand for more freedom is often merely the prelude to a policy of conquest. This became clear in connection with the problem of national self-determination. The peoples who clamour most for national freedom become the most ruthless oppressors of their own national minorities. The same is true of colonial peoples.

The believers in natural law with their concept of the social and constitutional contract also, in general, defended the basic, civic liberties, only Hobbes' and Spinoza's materialist-rationalist view of natural law forming a striking and – by its justification of absolutism – easily understandable exception. Hobbes' distinctive feature compared to other exponents of the natural law is his fundamental rejection of the traditional conception of man as a political animal and his original goodness and sociability. If we were all as murderous, savage, ambitious, envious and wild as Hobbes declared, we should indeed need a tyrant who can restrain us, only because he is an intensified embodiment of our evil qualities and therefore inspires our respect.

Once again the difference between constitutional development in Anglo-Saxon countries and on the Continent becomes clear for, as Carl Schmitt remarked, the theory of the Englishman Hobbes was carried into effect not in England but on the Continent, in France and Prussia.[1] The English constitutional state, which changed into the two-party system during the eighteenth century and into the democratic state in the nineteenth century, was based not on Hobbes' doctrines but on those of his opponent John Locke, the philosopher of the Glorious Revolution. But Locke's ideas came into their own in the United States

---

[1] Carl Schmitt, *Der Leviathan in der Staatslehre des Thomas Hobbes*, op cit., p. 119. Although one can agree with Carl Schmitt that Hobbes' concept of the state was more influential in continental Europe than in England, it is untrue that it had no effect in England. Evidence of this today is the fact that there is no separation of powers in the British governmental system, which is expressed in the subordination of the executive and judicial powers to the legislature. But since the executive power, which resides in the strongly centralized ministries, and the Prime Minister are in possession of all necessary information, the legislature can exert a decisive influence only in exceptional circumstances, for instance in a government crisis. But both of these are more powerful than the judiciary; for, in spite of the excellence of the judges, because Parliament is sovereign, the judiciary has no constitutional means of asserting itself against an executive which is protected by the legislature. Above all, the fact that the House of Lords is recognized as the supreme judicial authority can, as the case of the extradition of the Nigerian politician, Chief Enahoro in 1963 clearly showed, lead to a dangerous confusion about questions of basic human rights and political opportunism. According to Hobbes' constitutional theory the absolute sovereign power can also reside in a legislative assembly. That is why Bentham thought the Leviathan sat in the British Parliament.

of America[1] and in the overseas dominions of the British Empire. Even the constitutional jurisdiction which has also become more common in continental Europe since the Second World War can, in the final analysis, be traced back to this source.[2]

This shows that the true concept of liberty made an important contribution to the development of the constitutional state and the parliamentary system and that the latter, although originally serving the aristocracy in particular, nevertheless gradually adapted itself to the needs of democracy as further social strata became emancipated. Since, however, Hobbes' ideas were carried on in Rousseau's theories on the one hand and in the Utilitarian doctrine, Adam Smith's and Ricardo's classical economic theory and Marxism on the other, the idea of freedom was still open to many different interpretations even in our time. As will be shown later, it was transformed into the opposite by Rousseau[3] and Hegel, just as in Hobbes' social contract. The radical freedom of the individual becomes the freedom of the state *vis-à-vis* the individual. With the Utilitarians, especially John Stuart Mill, and later with anarchists like Bakunin and Sorel as well as with Marx, it means the anarchical freedom or caprice of the individual person or the individual class *vis-à-vis* the community. With Marx, Engels and Lenin the claim of class becomes the claim of the state.

## Equality and Authority

According to Aristotle there is both an absolute and relative equality: the only thing they have in common is the word 'equality'. Absolute equality is the democratic equality which demands that the simple, unskilled worker shall have the same power and income as the best-educated and most eminent man in the state. On the other hand relative equality demands that a group of people with the same qualifications and the same education shall have equality of status and income. Therefore the demand for relative equality is really the aristocratic desire for government by the best. These two basic forms of equality were therefore always contradictory. Materialism, however, as depicted by Hobbes and systematized by Marx, cannot recognize the principle of relative equality in the aristocratic sense. Consequently an almost insuperable antithesis has arisen in our time between liberty

[1] A. D. Lindsay, op. cit., pp. 115 ff.

[2] Cf., for example, J. W. Gough, *John Locke's Political Philosophy*, Oxford 1956, p. 103.

[3] The most exhaustive study of Rousseau's political doctrines is still that made by C. E. Vaughan, *The Political Writings of J. J. Rousseau*, Cambridge 1915.

and equality in the *general* sense. We envy others who, by exercising their freedom, get more out of life than we do. We consider that to be unjust, since we assume in our hearts that we are just as good as those who are more successful, better educated and wealthier, and who have better connections and qualifications than us. The source of this impulse, as Hobbes observed, lies in our pride and imagination, because we assume either that we are equal or – if we are not – that we ought by right to be equal. Therefore freedom in its materialistic aspect and equality in its general aspect represent the two sides of human nature concerned with *taking*.

Unlike liberty and equality, however, fraternity is the child of man's nobler, altruistic impulses. Classical political philosophy knew fraternity as *sophrosyne*, the principle of friendship, which reconciles and unites man's hostile tendencies. That means, therefore, that liberty and equality are only compatible with one another if they are associated with fraternity as a third principle.

Othmar Spann saw democracy simply as a more intensive form of liberalism. Both, Spann rightly recognized, had their roots in natural individualism.[1] As, however, Spann rejects the idea of natural freedom in favour of an irrational-romantic 'Universalism', he can offer us no solution to the problem of liberty and equality. For Spann regards equality as a sub-species of liberty and depicts both as atomistic – disruptive as opposed to the concept of 'social'. The principal characteristic of society, he thought, is its absolute inequality, its polarity of values, its law of stratification – order according to various levels of value. By conceiving the state as a structure based on different castes, where the best[2] shall rule, Spann revealed himself as the champion of the aristocratic class as it appears in Plato's *Republic*. Like Plato, Spann, too, conceives of democracy as ochlocracy, the rule of the masses, the common people. Like Nietzsche, Ortega y Gasset and Orwell, he feared the onset of the technocratic mass age in which mechanization and equality reign supreme[3] and the noble is trodden underfoot. He dreamed of a world based on an idealized version of the medieval corporation and was opposed to centralization because in central Europe the Enlightenment happened to be associated with centralization – although the principle of centralization is incompatible with the idea. Spann, the Austrian, however, in common with contemporary German constitutional lawyers, regarded political parties as springing from Manchesterism, that is from the competitiveness natural to liberal capitalism. He did not see that liberalism represents a new form of

---

[1] Othmar Spann, *Der wahre Staat*, op. cit., pp. 80 ff.: 'Kritik des Liberalismus und der Demokratie'.

[2] Ibid.                    [3] Ibid.

the aristocratic claim glorified by him and that the concept of natural freedom was already familiar to the state based on the estate system.

Fraternity is not possible in the corporate state, as Spann understands it, since his Platonic concept assumes a rigid system of caste which is alien to the actual conditions of Western industrial society because it presupposes that the great uneducated masses will be ruled by a small body of government and administrative experts. The state based on the estate system extolled by Spann was possible in medieval Europe as long as the educational privilege of the clergy had its counterpart in the illiteracy of the masses. In India, where it was able to guarantee a harmonious society for nearly four thousand years, the caste state which, as Spann conceives it, is forcibly maintained by social inequality collapses when as a result of education and the advance of technology and mass communication media, the small community – such as the village and the small town – disintegrates.

However, the failure of the corporate experiment in fascist Italy proves that the corporate state had become impossible in the years between the two World Wars. Fascist reality was state syndicalism plus dictatorship.[1] The fascist and later the national socialist economic system is, in effect, a 'capitalist' economy with unlimited opportunities for state intervention.

When the French Revolution and other liberal movements attacked the principle of authoritarianism they were unaware that democracy cannot function successfully unless it has authority. In the absence of authority, fraternity is rarely found keeping company with liberty and equality. Fraternity perishes when liberty is locked in conflict with equality. The word 'authority' comes from the Latin *auctoritas*, an 'addition or furthering' according to Friedrich, that is, it is 'more than a counsel and less than an order, a counsel which cannot reasonably not be observed'.[2] The *auctor* is also the creator of a relationship who, by virtue of being the creator, possesses authority. Those who follow or join him wield a derivative authority.[3] Without authority, therefore, fraternity cannot fulfil its conciliatory role.

The principle of liberty and equality is, of course, not limited to democracy; for equality is also the underlying assumption of absolute monarchy. Despots have constantly proclaimed themselves to be the friends of the common people. Their struggle was primarily against the aristocracy, as this class limits or not infrequently threatens the power

[1] Erwin von Beckerath, *Wesen und Werden des faschistischen Staates*, op. cit., p. 138.

[2] Carl J. Friedrich, *Die Philosophie des Rechts in historischer Perspektive*, Berlin, Göttingen, Heidelberg 1955, p. 125.

[3] Hannah Arendt, *Fragwürdige Tradionsbestände im politischen Denken der Gegenwart*, Frankfurt 1957, pp. 117 ff.

and influence of the monarchy. Again, the members of an oligarchy demand for themselves a freedom and equality which they never allow the common people. They must therefore have recourse to authority to maintain their privileged position. Nor is a democracy which is concerned only with liberty and equality a stable form of government. Weimar democracy's inability to acquire for itself any real authority was one of the main reasons for its collapse.

The gravest threat to democracy was always that its principles might be carried to extremes. Excessive liberty leads to anarchy and this in turn leads to tyranny, Plato noted in his *Republic*; excessive equality follows from the alienation of the most valuable elements in society and eventually leads to oligarchy. One of the greatest dangers in the age of mass civilization and the mechanization of life, as Ortega y Gasset realized and as we see in Orwell's *1984*, is that radical equality can lead to an inhuman and technological form of government.

Spann maintains that the sociological concept of society as such excludes equality because of the functional differences inherent in society. This view has been generally voiced by sociologists since Simmel. 'For even where democratic or socialist movements plan or partly achieve "equality", the point at issue is always only the *equal value* of people, achievements and positions, whereas an equality between human beings in accordance with their talents, their aims and their fate cannot possibly be involved.'[1] And social systems or political institutions are equally unable to fulfil their claim that they can radically change human forms of life.

The phenomena incident to the industrial revolution whetted the desire for equality and freedom. On the one hand society's general standard of prosperity had risen, the chances of luxury living had increased. Modern transport brought food to wherever it was needed. Modern machines put an end to long hours and hard work by the masses, giving them leisure and the opportunity of further education. The difference in the standards of feeding and dress, among the various social classes, was already far less than it had been eighty years earlier, when it was appreciable. The development of towns at the expense of agricultural areas meant that larger numbers of people lived the impersonal and uniform life of the city.

And so the development which had already begun at the end of the Middle Ages with the gradual destruction of the corporations, especially, and guilds and estates in the towns, and the patriarchal protection given to the countryfolk by the feudal nobility, was approaching its climax. It was no accident that the forerunners of social unrest – the peasant risings and the anabaptist movement in Germany and the

[1] G. Simmel, *Soziologie*, op. cit., pp. 28 f.

Netherlands and the Digger movement in England – coincided with the advent of early capitalism, which Thomas Moore had already lamented in his *Utopia*. With the artisan losing his independence, his pride and his social security and sinking steadily to the degrading status of the wage-earner employed by the business or industrial concern, the Middle Ages seemed more and more to be a lost paradise of social security.[1]

Socialism was therefore, from the first, a constructive movement with a conservative purpose, based on Christianity and natural law and, in view of capitalism's indifference to revolutionary, utilitarian and human values, stood for values such as social justice, honest work and social welfare. From mercantilism the new economic system had already acquired the features of state capitalism. It was immaterial whether the basis of capitalism was the *laissez-faire* principle or state capitalism, it was hostile to the old basis of Christianity and natural morality. But the utilitarian philosophy was so clearly vindicated by the visible success of the industrial revolution that the counter-movements representing the human values were themselves inevitably forced to take materialism as their starting-point and even the powers considered to be the counterpoise to capitalism, namely church and state, had themselves been influenced by materialistic-utilitarian ideas.

In the Middle Ages the economic system of the corporations had been indissolubly bound up with the constitutional basis of society. With the help of dynastic absolutism early capitalism succeeded in destroying what security and protection the corporations and guilds had been able to provide. On the other hand absolutism had used the money raised by taxation of the wealthy merchant and entrepreneur classes to build up its military strength, which enabled it to abolish the old constitutional system.

It was no accident that the rebirth of constitutional theories in the eighteenth and nineteenth centuries led to demands for a renewal of economic constitutionalism.[2] This first appeared as workers' associations and trade unions and only later took the form of political socialism. The advance made by science and technology, with their direct bearing on industry and business, meant that economic power became concentrated in the hands of a new oligarchy. Working conditions in the middle of the nineteenth century[3] could, therefore, not unreasonably be considered a new form of slavery – in Aristotle's definition of the slave as a living tool; for absence of a sense of

[1] Eduard Bernstein, *Sozialismus und Demokratie in der grossen englischen Revolution*, Stuttgart 1919.

[2] This was realized by Hans Kelsen, *Vom Wesen und Wert der Demokratie*, Tübingen 1920, pp. 47 ff.

[3] Cf. Friedrich Engels, *Die Lage der arbeitenden Klassen im England*, Stuttgart 1921.

responsibility and disinterest in work is characteristic of slavery. The dangers of the emergence of a modern slave state were alleviated partly by the feudal residues which still survived and partly by the efficacy of humanitarian, practical religious ideologies. The existence of parliaments based on the aristocratic principle of rule by the socially respectable who did not always take the saying of *noblesse oblige* lightly, also provided a safeguard against materialistic exploitation. This aristocratic element provided a relative guarantee of liberty because it rested on the hierarchical principle. The social system existing before the First World War therefore afforded a significant measure of freedom to the various sections of the middle class standing on the intermediate rungs of the hierarchical ladder. The franchise and the guarantees of basic rights gave them protection from those above them, and in the other direction the system afforded them a great deal of leisure and social distance from the lower classes.

The collapse of the ideal of the semi-aristocratic constitutional state governed by the socially respectable did not first collapse in front of the Tsar's Winter Palace: it had already perished on the battlefields of Verdun, and on the Marne and the Somme. In all countries the war was won by the armed workers, who formed the bulk of all the armies. When the war ended a new class was ready to seize power. This class formally adopted the parliamentary institutions of the upper-class state – with the exception of Russia – but had to give them a new content. Since, however, the economic system remained unchanged, there was a disparity between this and the political power of the new ruling class and it vented itself in revolutionary upheavals.

Between the wars the workers in the big industrial countries faced the following alternatives: either their material and moral existence was threatened by unemployment or else they found work and, due to the great demand for labour, came under their employers' control. There was little room for personal initiative. They noticed that their wages were not commensurate with the work they did. The young among the unemployed had never worked and therefore could not be politically educated and trained by the trade unions. Marxist theory had declared that economic equality can be secured by socializing the means of production and that real political freedom is possible only in socialist society. The classless society, which was to follow the dictatorship of the proletariat, would also mean political equality. But power considerations are still part of the labour relationship even where profit is not the main concern.[1] One of the main merits of Marxist doctrine was its appreciation of the fact that for the worker

[1] A. D. Lindsay, *Christianity and Economics*, London 1933—Appendix: 'The Organization of Labour in France during the War and its Lessons.'

respect for his humanity is just as important as his wage. He must feel that he is recognized by society and has the opportunity to use his initiative and stand on his own feet.

But political freedom is not possible without economic freedom. The worker who is employed by an industrialist not only sells his labour; he also surrenders part of his personal freedom. His independence is not only restricted by his formal contractual obligations. Generally he cannot afford to wait for a favourable opportunity. Where a man's whole concern is concentrated on the need to assure a bare existence for himself and his family, he has no time or energy left for free self-development. The majority of people in central and south-east Europe lived under this pressure. They had neither the time nor the means for individual self-development.

A country in which this kind of economic inequality exists cannot, therefore, be described as free. On the other hand complete equality in the exercise of power is impossible to realize in practice; for in this case inequality is a consequence of the functions and tasks which have to be performed in society.

Is any sort of compromise between liberty and equality possible? The believers in the social-democratic theory which has been realized in our time hold the view that this compromise is effected when economic equality is not only acknowledged but also put into practice by democracy. That then leads to the demand for a form of state planning which takes cognizance of individual freedom and allows for it.[1] But Mannheim did not answer the question of whether a psychological compromise is possible between the unavoidable differences still persisting where there is a division of power. Simmel was the first to draw attention to this important fact.[2]

As we have already stated, all forms of government are doomed which carry their inherent principles to extremes. Thus monarchy in the form of one-man rule perished when authority degenerated into despotism. Again, aristocracy perishes as soon as its basis narrows and it degenerates into an economy run by an oligarchical clique. The constitutional state and its politics are in the greatest danger when they lose their solid middle-class basis or when the harmony of the principles on which the constitution is based is disturbed. And democracy is doomed as soon as it grants an excess of liberty and equality, since then there is always the danger that it will degenerate into anarchy, which will justify tyranny.[3]

[1] Karl Mannheim, *Mensch und Gesellschaft*, Darmstadt 1958, pp. 279 ff.
[2] G. Simmel, *Soziologie*, op. cit., p. 173.
[3] On this point cf. also Gerhard Leibholz, *Strukturprobleme der modernen Demokratie*, op. cit., p. 67.

It is doubtful whether this hypothesis, advanced ever since the days of Plato and Aristotle, explains why radical democracy tends to develop into tyranny. A more satisfying and more complete answer can perhaps be deduced from Montesquieu's explanation of the stability of absolute monarchies. Montesquieu holds the view that monarchies differ from despotisms not only by their being based on the rule of law but also by their having a privileged class[1] – the aristocracy whose status is fixed by law and tradition and is independent of the monarch, and from whose ranks the monarch fills the country's senior official and military posts. Their privileged role gives them a vested interest in the continuation of the monarchical system as such, and they come forward to act as its protectors. But the greater the equality and the more thorough-going the process of levelling among the various social strata, the more indifferent everybody becomes. For where all are equal, interest in the maintenance of the form of the state must be evenly distributed and no one can see why he and not someone else should play the role of protector of the state. Therefore any increase in social levelling only leads to an increasing sense of anonymity and decreasing sense of civic responsibility.

The history of the Athenian city-state is an outstanding example of this process. There, in the fifth century B.C., the institution of ostracism, originally intended to safeguard democracy, was used by the masses as a weapon for attacking everything intellectually and ethically superior.[2] The citizens became apathetic about their public duties, for which they demanded payment. Tradition and responsibility lost their power. The increasingly dependent and cossetted masses, only interested in material advantages, succumbed more and more readily to demagogic appeals and felt an ever-growing need for a strong leader.

A similar phenomenon was one of the causes of the downfall of the Roman Republic. While Rome's conquests brought great wealth to the country, it also meant that hordes of people flocked to live in Rome itself and their demands for equality of status grew more and more insistent. The demand for *panem et circenses* was the call of these masses, who lacked any civic sense whatsoever, for leaders who could provide them with material goods – their only real concern – without their having to make any personal effort.

Tyranny can give the levelled masses the most far-reaching equality. The expulsion or liquidation of the groups or people in the middle ranges of the hierarchy satisfies the innermost need of both the tyrant

---

[1] Montesquieu, *De l'Esprit des Lois*, 1748, II, Chap. 4.
[2] David Riesman, N. Glazer, R. Denney, *Die einsame Masse*, Darmstadt, Berlin, Neuwied 1956, p. 44.

and the masses. The tyrant is interested because this provides his surest safeguard against the threat of rivalry. The masses are interested because their desire for equality can be satisfied most quickly by the removal of intellectually, culturally and economically superior individuals without their having personally to take decisions likely to endanger the benefits which material equality brought them. If the tyrant can project an image of himself as the leader of the masses and these identify themselves with him, the ideal of 'absolute equality' has in fact become for them subjective reality. Freedom is temporarily eclipsed – temporarily because the greater material prosperity made possible by equality produces once again increasing intellectual, cultural and social differences and therefore, in due course new demands for freedom.

Thus, according to Hans Buchheim, fascism was primarily a rebellion against liberty.[1] That is also true of all other totalitarian and authoritarian dictatorships between the two World Wars. It is impossible, however, to agree with Buchheim and other writers who draw a qualitative distinction between totalitarianism and authoritarianism. On the contrary, the difference is quantitatively determined by the degree of restriction placed on freedom, the amount of positive terrorism and the efficiency of the propaganda machine. Only where the state seeks to govern and direct *all* aspects of public and private life, only where, as Hitler said, it dominates the *whole* man and where, thanks to modern techniques, it is really in a position to do this, can one speak of totalitarianism in its true sense.

Qualitatively, this form of tyranny does not differ essentially from its predecessors in antiquity, in the Orient and under absolutism; it merely represents the latest stage in its evolution, after adapting itself to the facts of the present mass age and the general acceptance of democratic ideas. Even the apparent difference, that authoritarianism rules with the help of the state while totalitarianism rests in the hands of an ideological movement and undermines and misuses the state for the benefit of this movement, is not a qualitative difference but is simply due to tyranny's more effective powers of ideological penetration in winning over certain sections of the demagogically led masses. This secret – that the tyrant is the radical democrat's twin[2] – was already known to Pisistratus and Julius Caesar. On this point Nolte made the following pertinent observation:

'The poles of authoritarianism and totalitarianism are spanned by an arch extending from Pilsudski's regime over the political totalitarianism

[1] Hans Buchheim, *Totalitäre Herrschaft*, Munich 1962, pp. 17 ff.
[2] Cf. also Hans Frank, *Im Angesicht des Galgens*, Munich 1963, p. 49.

of Falangist Spain to the calculated, all-embracing totalitarianism of Mussolini and Hitler.'[1]

The crux of the matter is, therefore, the amount of personal and social freedom, individual and national self-determination which the state leaves to the individual and the autonomous groups within the community. Every slave economy is, substantially, totalitarian. The idea of totalitarianism is also compatible with the external forms of democracy, as the Athenian city-state and the southern states of the United States proved up to the time of the American Civil War. Totalitarian dictatorship is also compatible with oligarchical elements supporting it. That is proved by the importance ascribed in fascist ideology to the concept of an élite, in particular the role given to the SS as an élite which became a state within the state. Totalitarianism, therefore, introduced no new categories but with the aid of modern techniques, sought to introduce archaic forms of slave rule into the present era, an undertaking which, in the event of a military victory, it could have performed successfully because modern techniques of compulsion and communication are eminently suited to such a task.

That fascism was a reaction against the extremes to which freedom was taken is evident from the effects which proportional representation had on the legislatures and executives of post-war democracies in central Europe, and from the toleration which was shown to the intolerant, which will be described later.[2] The situation was undoubtedly similar to that described by Plato and Aristotle where excessive democratic freedom was bound to lead to anarchy and tyranny.[3] That is true as regards the German as well as the Italian, Austrian and Hungarian propertied classes. Revolutionary conservatism, determined to spur deposed or threatened oligarchies to resistance, is an integral part of the ideology which made fascism possible, whether we think of Frenchmen like de Maistre, de Bonald, Gobineau, Barrès and Maurras, or of Italians like Pareto and Mosca, an Englishman like Houston Stewart Chamberlain, or Germans like Nietzsche, Spengler and Moeller van den Bruck. The radical political changes which came in 1918, suddenly bringing unemployment to the militant elements in society – which were also the conservative and upper-class elements – proved to be the last straw.

It was only when Hitler had sufficiently consolidated his position that he could dispense with the conservative elements by acquiescing to the wishes of a smaller section and then eliminating the larger one.

[1] Ernst Nolte, *Der Faschismus in seiner Epoche*, Munich 1963, p. 49.
[2] Cf. Chap. VI.
[3] Aristotle, *Politics*, Book V, op. cit., Chap. 6.

The evolution of the Hitler system into full totalitarian tyranny was a gradual process. After the suppression of the National Socialists' conservative colleagues in the cabinet the position of the *Reichspräsident* was undermined and the *Wehrmacht* subjugated.

But all Hitler's possible rivals inside the national-socialist movement itself were also eliminated. After the liquidation of the SA (Storm Troops) and the assassination of Gregor Strasser, both the Reichstag and the cabinet (which were dominated by the National Socialists) were stripped of their powers, and the influence cut down of the intellectuals and academics within the movement and finally of the Reichsstatthalter and Gauleiter. During the course of the war the power of Göring himself suffered a decisive set-back. Finally Hitler's private secretary, Bormann, became the most powerful man in the Third Reich after Hitler, a position which he shared only with Heinrich Himmler, the head of the Gestapo, and Joseph Goebbels, the propaganda chief.

As, in the course of time, particularly after the outbreak of war, party and state merged into a unified and indissoluble entity, Bormann's position as head of the party chancery became of the first importance. Terror and deception are essential elements of totalitarianism. In a despotic system, however, the despot's private secretary is in fact the man who wields the greatest influence of all because he is the despot's effective will, and is just as powerful, if not more powerful than the despot himself. He is the king's shadow who makes the king a shadow. 'The more direct power is concentrated in his individual person', the greater grows the ruler's isolation.[1] The isolated ruler – the tyrant – is, therefore, finally himself enslaved. Tyranny has begun to carry the principle of arbitrariness to excess. It has initiated its own downfall – since the tyrant, because of his growing isolation from the totally dominated masses, is progressively less able to dominate them.

# PART TWO

*Caricature of the Constitutional State*

Because of the polarity between liberty and equality, the more fully the democratic ideal of equality became realized in practice towards the end of the nineteenth century and at the beginning of the twentieth century, the more the constitutional principle of individual liberty was

[1] C. Schmitt, *Gespräch über die Macht und den Zugang zum Machthaber,* Pfullingen 1954.

relegated to the background. This is what Carl Schmitt meant by his statement that, in the nineteenth century, 'Parliamentarians advanced in the closest association with the advance of democracy without either being clearly differentiated'.[1] In the twenties and thirties of the present century this idea prompted the belief that there was a real difference between democracy and parliamentarism or, as was often said, between democracy and the 'party state'. According to this view, parliamentarism, whose aim was to overcome differences by means of discussion, was a system which was part of the ideology of middle-class liberalism whereas the basis of democracy was the equality of the members of the homogeneous community.[2] That writers who rejected Weimar democracy, like Spann, Schmitt and Herrfahrdt, used the polarity between freedom and authority to attack democracy is less strange than the fact that these distinctions were accepted and discussed even by democracy's supporters.

This attitude is understandable. The social revolution of 1917–20 experienced by German constitutional lawyers of this period made working-class integration seem an urgent problem. Before 1918 the German parties which had supported the government had, in the main, been upper-class parties. Now the Social Democratic Party, which was both a mass party and one representing specific interests, came forward as the principal supporting arch of the parliamentary state; and yet the Spartacist rising, like other revolutionary movements throughout central Europe, had shown that the working class was certainly not wholly an integral part of the parliamentary system. Even the Social Democratic Party's Marxist programme, with its emphasis on the class war, was diametrically opposed to the strictly constitutional attitude of the Majority Socialists, and seemed to throw doubt on the value of the young Weimar Republic.

These things, like the fact that people were not used to parliamentary responsibility and that German liberalism had sprung from a semi-authoritarian regime based on the monarchy and bureaucracy, led to the widely held theory that there was a structural difference between mass democracy on the one hand and liberalism, parliamentarism and the party state on the other.[3] It was thought that mass democracy corresponded to a Caesarist tendency, which Max Weber believed was exemplified in the election of the British Prime Minister and which is undoubtedly much more evident in the American Presidential election.

---

[1] C. Schmitt, *Die geistesgeschichtliche Lage des heutigen Parlamentarismus*, op. cit., p. 6.

[2] Ibid., pp. 13 f. Smend agrees but stresses parliament's integrating role. See, for example, Friedrich Glum, *Das parlamentarische Regierungssystem in Deutschland, Grossbritannien und Frankreich*, op. cit., pp. 197 f.

[3] Cf., for example, Walter Jellinek, *Verwaltungsrecht*, Berlin 1928, p. 60.

Thus Thoma, for instance, rejected Great Britain's majority franchise (which produces the two-party system) primarily because he feared that class distinctions might be intensified.

The Weimar Constitution expressed the spirit of the intellectual power of Max Weber, Preuss and Naumann in particular, all of whom were associated with the (liberal) Democratic Party. Before the war, however, this party, as a progressive party, had acted as a link between the middle-class parties and social democracy. Thoma in particular saw very clearly that the new Constitution meant an attempt at democratization – democratization in a quite specific sense, one which resulted from the revolutionary events of the years 1917–19 and forced itself on his attention and that of the more thoughtful of his contemporaries. Thoma considered this to be only one aspect of the process going on in the West since the end of the eighteenth century, to supplement the ideas of civil liberty already represented in the 'upper-class' parliaments with the ideas of equality represented by the socialists.[1] A similar view was later expressed by Leibholz, who considers the change-over from the representative system to mass democracy to be the crucial problem of the modern constitutional state.[2]

A demand for equality means, however, that all strata and groups are represented equally. This school of thought, to which Radbruch[3] also subscribed, would have the political parties to look after those interests. The result of this attitude was that each party and each interest group was regarded as being equally good, irrespective of the interests they represented or whether they supported or opposed the Weimar Republic. Each party wanted its parliamentary representation to be on a strict arithmetical basis, with the number of seats exactly proportionate to the number of people voting for it. Proportional representation embodied this principle. Radbruch's ideas can be seen in the political philosophy underlying the conception of the Weimar Republic, which, in his opinion, had its roots in Rousseau's Social Contract.

The fallacy in this idea was that it linked Rousseau, the sworn enemy of the representative system, with parliamentarism.[4] His theory that the general will was created by demagogues was bound to lead to the dictatorship of Robespierre as it did to the Caesarism of Napoleon and Hitler. The electoral system on which the Weimar Constitution was based and which reflected the ideas of Preuss, Thoma and Radbruch, had much in common with John Stuart Mill's radical liberal ideas.

[1] R. Thoma, *Handbuch des Deutschen Staatsrechts*, op. cit.

[2] Gerhard Leibholz, op. cit., p. 21.

[3] G. Radbruch, 'Die politischen Parteien im System des deutschen Verfassungsrechts', in *Handbuch des Deutschen Staatsrechts*, Vol. I, op. cit., p. 287.

[4] Cf., for example, B. W. T. Jones, op. cit., Vol. 2, pp. 318–26.

This system, therefore, embraces in the first place Rousseau's and Hegel's tyrannical majority will which, as Thoma feared, can at any moment turn into a dictatorship, and in the second place its opposite, the anarchical right which Mill advocated and which would allow even a small minority to push its interests through against the majority. This synthesis was bound to prove impracticable because the absolute dictatorship of the majority on one hand and anarchy on the other contain polarizing elements.

Carl Schmitt's main criticism of the Weimar Constitution was directed against this incongruity and also the system advocated by Smend, based on the premise that parliament's primary function is one of integration, which approached the Anglo-Saxon concept. Schmitt employed the time-honoured method used by theologians in inter-denominational controversies. It consists in pointing out the disparities between doctrine and practice in an opponent's religion and comparing this with one's own doctrine while saying nothing about one's own practice. Carl Schmitt[1] agrees with the above authors that parliament as a place of discussion was a feature of the middle-class liberal state. According to Schmitt the ideal principles of parliamentarism are:

1. Parliament represents the whole nation and, in this capacity, after public discussion and resolution, issues laws, i.e. reasonable, just, general norms. . . .
2. The individual deputy also has a representative role.

Schmitt then holds the mirror up to Weimar democracy and proclaims that proportional representation, factional pressure and the committee system have destroyed the representative character of parliament. The coalition system, he argues, has reduced the chancellor within the coalition to the role of a mere party official.

In his attack on parliamentarism, which he wrongly described as a product of the seventeenth century, Schmitt equated liberalism, in the materialistic sense, with the economic theories of the Utilitarians and the school of Adam Smith by applying their theories to politics:

'It is necessary to see liberalism as a consistent, comprehensive, metaphysical system. Usually only the economic inference is discussed – that private individuals are the natural outcome of free economic competition and social harmony of free contract and free trade. All this, however, is only a case of the application of the general liberal principle. It is like saying that truth is born of the free clash of opinions. . . .'[2]

[1] Cf. Chap. III.
[2] C. Schmitt, *Die geistesgeschichtliche Lage des heutigen Parlamentarismus*, op. cit., pp. 45 f.

These theories, which ascribe the representative parliamentary system to liberalism and therefore want to damn it as a hollow institution serving material interests and detrimental to the nation, contain a germ of truth in so far as the political tendency of liberalism, as Tönnies observed, is aristocratic and, therefore, was not, at first, of use to the concept of mass democracy.

From these alleged distinctions between parliamentarism and democracy, however, the theorists of the totalitarian state deduce the idea that Caesarist dictatorship is perfectly compatible with democracy. This theory of democracy harks back to Rousseau's general will. Rousseau, who makes the formation of the general will in democracy feasible by fondly believing the fiction that those who have been outvoted in a plebiscite have approved the proposal which they had in fact rejected, proceeded from assumptions akin to those underlying Hobbes' *Leviathan*. In both cases the ruler is absolute. The fact that, with Rousseau, the people is sovereign makes very little difference since it needs men to carry out its will and the power which they wield is just as absolute as that of Hobbes' totalitarian ruler. In both cases the installation of the ruler and the surrender of natural rights is irrevocable. In both cases the minority is declared evil in itself and therefore proscribed.

Carl Schmitt had realized this at an early stage[1] and examined the problem in great detail in his book *Die Diktatur*.[2] 'The general will (like Hobbes' *Leviathan*) is raised to the status of a god and destroys every separate will and separate interest since it considers these to be nothing less than robbery . . .[3] every particular force and concern is in itself irrelevant in view of the unity and sovereignty of the general.'[4] Schmitt then referred to Rousseau's importance in the evolution of the idea of dictatorship.[5] In conjunction with his theory about the origin of dictatorship and the possibility of a presidential dictatorship, he gave the most extreme interpretation of Article 49 of the Weimar Constitution in the appendix to his book. During the Weimar Republic he had already turned against the liberal parliamentary state on the grounds that it was incapable of taking decisive action; but his motives were not yet clear. People wondered whether his attitude was just a part of the general reaction, partly conservative, partly revolutionary, against democracy, which was widespread at the time. Under national socialism, however, it became evident that his political theory was unequivocally based on

[1] Ibid., p. 41.
[2] C. Schmitt, *Die Diktatur*, Munich and Leipzig 1928, pp. 119 ff.
[3] Ibid., p. 120.
[4] Ibid.
[5] Especially by the concept of the 'legislator', who follows his 'inspiration' (like Hitler later) and then puts it to the vote in a Caesarist plebiscite.

Thomas Hobbes' doctrine. Such a doctrine could never accept the
Weimar Republic as a state.

As Strauss observes,[1] Hobbes, who as a student had openly expressed
his antipathy to the basic tenets of Aristotelian philosophy, was strongly
influenced by science, which was then becoming a force to be reckoned
with. Even his scientific individualism saw men only as atoms of
society. Like atoms, they are all completely equal to one another and
can therefore kill one another. As they are all proud, vain and grasping
and all want to have the same things they would not fight shy of
murder. But as we are all endowed with such 'lovable' qualities we
need the firm hand of an absolute monarch or a dictator to make us
reasonable.

Schmitt speaks of the mystic origin of the Leviathan: but we are,
in fact, dealing with a god, whose 'identity' can easily be established
historically. It is the god of the Eastern temple state, the source of
Eastern despotism. In it the unity of state and religion finds concrete
expression;[2] nor are the Jews at first an exception to this rule. It is
not true that the Church was alone responsible for the dualism of
state and religion. For almost a thousand years, in pursuance of St
Augustine's teachings, it strove to absorb the State, just as the State
always strove to absorb the Church. But the Leviathan found a habita-
tion in the Byzantine Empire and from there extended its absolute
dominion over the whole Islamic world on the one hand and over the
whole Greek Orthodox world as far as Moscow on the other. It can
probably be argued that state authoritarianism can always, in the final
analysis, be traced back to this source. Schmitt in particular had, in
his writings, shown the way to Germany's future development. In the
first chapter of his book *Der Leviathan in der Staatslehre des Thomas
Hobbes*, Schmitt, writing in the very spirit of the Nazi attitude to the
state, emphasized that Hobbes' main aim was to fight against the
'typical Jewish–Christian splitting of the original political unity'.[3]
Schmitt remarked, quite rightly, that Hobbes held the divorce of the
temporal and spiritual powers to be alien to the Gentile world because
it considered religion to be a part of politics, while the Jews established
unity in the religious sphere. Only the Roman papal church and the
power-loving Presbyterian churches or sects would have thriven on
the destructive effect which the separation of the spiritual and temporal
powers had on the state. Schmitt also makes Hobbes out to be a
thinker of the political act, as he had previously done in the case of
Donoso Cortés and Sorel. By, finally, at the end of *Leviathan*,

[1] Leo Strauss, *The Political Philosophy of Hobbes*, Oxford 1936, pp. 30 f.
[2] K. J. Newman, 'Papst, Kaiser, Kalif und Basileus', op. cit., pp. 18–42.
[3] C. Schmitt, *Der Leviathan in der Staatslehre des Thomas Hobbes*, op. cit.

showing in great detail how Hobbes' monistic-total concept of the state was opposed to the concept of the state based on the rule of law as advocated by Stahl in Germany, Schmitt acknowledged Hobbes as his ideological mentor, whose influence thus helped to destroy the weak foundations of Weimar parliamentarism.

Schmitt's theory looks extremely dated because he considers the middle class from the point of view of the class war. Yet even for Aristotle it is the sound middle class which represents the main support of the constitutional state. Schmitt had not, of course, yet discovered that the working class becomes integrated into the constitutional state because, being itself a majority, it becomes the middle class. What, however, defenders of Weimar democracy such as Preuss, Thoma and Radbruch overlooked was that this integration, as the United States showed, is best effected through the two-party system and the relative majority franchise. American democracy is not based on Rousseau's and Mill's theories, but on John Locke's. According to Locke, man retains his inalienable rights. Parliament is only a trustee with sole authority to protect and clarify basic human rights.[1] Therefore a law passed by the legislature is no law if it contravenes these rights. Should parliament itself abolish them by majority vote, men are entitled to have recourse to revolution (the Appeal to Heaven). Locke's concept of parliament, therefore, is fulfilled by an executive which, whether one thinks of the British Prime Minister or the President of the United States, is subordinate to the legislature. But the legislature cannot exercise this control if it is prevented by an anarchical electoral system from regularly and effectively forming and exercising volition. On the other hand Locke's concept leads to the control of a legislature which oversteps the limits set by the basic rights, as defined by Locke, by a constitutional jurisdiction equal[2] to the other powers.

# PART THREE

## Liberty and State Power

The relationship of individual liberty and state power in the constitutional state and the related problem of the place of the minority in the state (meaning not only the political but also the religious and national minority) is even today the subject of continual and never-ending discussion. In England, during the stormy course of the seventeenth

[1] *Second Treatise of Civil Government*, Chap. XIII, § 149.
[2] G. Leibholz, op. cit., pp. 172 ff.

century, a successful compromise between liberty and state power was established. This balance gradually adjusted itself to changed social conditions. The Puritan settlers took this conception to America and the French Encyclopedists endeavoured to introduce it in France (although Rousseau's theory of the general will clearly shows the difficulties which lay in the way of this attempt to transplant the Anglo-Saxon concept into continental Europe). As we have said, west-European democracy (French style) destroyed the monarchy but recognized and strengthened state absolutism.[1] This was also the basis for suppressing national and political minorities.[2]

In the nineteenth and early twentieth century the slogans of democracy were used by the liberal pioneers of the constitutional state as weapons against the strongly entrenched authoritarian state. These early pioneers were, however, children of their own milieu, whose absolutist traditions they naturally could not shake off. To fight, even to die, for the ideals of liberty and to realize these in the state are two very different things. Cromwell's Model Army, which marched forth to eliminate the arbitrary rule of the Stuarts but then put a military dictatorship in its place, had already shown this. The same happened with the Jacobins. The totalitarian stamp which Rousseau gave to the general will with which he wanted to inaugurate the democratic millennium, and the belief of Marx, Engels and Lenin that they could make human rights a practical reality with the help of the dictatorship of the proletariat can be traced back to the indebtedness to authoritarian thinking. A community which has been living in the shadow of autocratic compulsion for several generations loses its self-respect and obeys orders dictated to it. It is only a matter of time before this community loses all civic spontaneity and comes to rely on completely bureaucratic tutelage.[3] The heirs of these subjects, however, find it difficult suddenly to become responsible democratic citizens, even if from time to time they are fired to do so by inspired prophets.

The counterpart to inordinate belief in authority is an exaggerated individualism. Max Scheler had noted this in connection with Germany when he said that there the spirit of individual freedom which was very near to anarchy was to be found alongside the urge to knuckle under to the state.[4] People concerned themselves less with their neigh-

[1] Cf. Chap. II.  [2] Cf. Chap. IV.

[3] Cf., for example, Max Weber, 'Beamtenherrschaft und politisches Führertum', Chap. 2; 'Von Parlament und Regierung im neugeordneten Deutschland', in *Gesammelte Politische Schriften*, op. cit., pp. 309 f. According to Max Weber, in Germany the 'subjects' (my quotation marks) belief in authority, acquired under authoritarianism, was transferred increasingly to the bureaucracy.

[4] Max Scheler, *Krieg und Aufbau*, Leipzig 1916, p. 161; quoted by Eschenburg, *Die improvisierte Demokratie der Weimarer Republik*, Schloss Laupheim, Württemberg 1951, p. 32.

bour's affairs since this involved the risk of interference in the power of the authorities. The compulsion to absolute obedience (both of the subaltern in giving orders and of his subordinate in carrying them out) inevitably breeds intolerance. Continual practical experience in self-government and local administration means that those who take part learn how much is called for in the way of self-control, restraint, readiness to compromise and understanding of other people's convictions and interests when making rational decisions about public affairs. For the pride which comes from successful team work is nothing less than the expression of human preference for constructive co-operation. That is the basis of Aristotle's thesis that man is a political animal.

Against this is Thomas Hobbes' theory, according to which absolute despotism and man's anarchical nature afford one another mutual support. But men who have been born and have grown up in a social order of this kind can only conceive of democracy as a coercive measure imposed by the majority; for they see society as a collection of anarchists, all of whom are potential despots. That is the reasoning behind every intolerant racial policy. The nationalities of Austria-Hungary had fought for their rights in the name of John Stuart Mill's principles. But they denied their own nationalities the right of self-determination for which they themselves had clamoured. They sought to justify this inconsistency by etatist ideas about territorial integrity. But this misconception of democracy produces the same two-edged effect as Rousseau's general will which, logically, leads to Bonapartism[1] and Caesarism. Spengler's prophecy of the coming of Caesarism was fulfilled only because the Weimar Republic was based on Rousseau.[2]

In spite of his critical attitude to liberty Simmel had understood the value of parliamentary democracy. Looked at from the sociological point of view, parliamentary democracy makes possible a simultaneous and reciprocal relationship of domination and subordination between rulers and ruled. 'This double relationship is one of the most powerful forms of reciprocity and can, if properly distributed over many different fields, form a very strong bond between individuals.'[3] Therefore the importance of parliament lies in its power of co-ordination; it represents an ideal constitution when 'A is B's superior in some respect or at one time but B is A's superior in some other respect or at other times'.[4]

Stirner defines the essence of constitutionalism in this way: 'The ministers dominate their master, the Sovereign, the deputies their

---

[1] H. A. L. Fisher, *Bonapartism*, London 1957.
[2] O. Spengler, *Untergang des Abendlandes*, op. cit., p. 183.
[3] G. Simmel, *Soziologie*, op. cit., p. 172.
[4] Ibid.

master, the People.'[1] And in an even profounder sense parliament provides this form of correlation. The equality of two citizens can consist in neither being more privileged than the other. But the fact that everyone elects a deputy who then has to participate in legislation which applies to his elector creates a reciprocal relationship of domination and subordination which is essentially an expression of co-ordination. For where constitutional issues are involved this form is of vital importance.

It is clear, therefore, that in the period in question in central Europe, we are dealing with a concentric attack on democracy which comes from several directions and springs from various causes. This attack is based mainly on the theories of Plato and Hobbes. Central European representatives of democracy involuntarily gave it support especially because, as far as they were concerned, democracy had been realized only in accordance with Rousseau's concept. The representatives of the Platonic school (especially Spann, Mosca, Scheler) insisted that there is an antithesis between the democratic state and the community, in the sense that they assume a difference as between an artificially mechanical structure and organic growth. They emphasized the difference between democracy, which they understood as levelling, and the natural, functionally determined scale of values, which they saw as being represented by the élite.

As we have already explained Carl Schmitt and Triepel, among others, fabricated an antithesis between parliamentarism and democracy. Parliament was seen as deriving from middle-class liberalism and was identified with it, while democracy was conceived as the spontaneous expression of the people's will which is best expressed by means of plebiscites. But the use of plebiscites inevitably leads to Caesarism which, according to these writers, represents the people better and which alone can produce effective government to take the place of the fruitless debates of liberal parliamentarism. Schmitt accuses liberalism of the murder of the mighty Leviathan. But a new Leviathan can arise if bold decisions are taken, backed up by the Leviathan's natural violence, as understood by Cortés and Sorel.

Consequently, there was a certain contradiction, within the theory of fascism, between the Spann and Schmitt schools of thought. Schmitt's ideas prevailed. Spann's corporate state was realized in fascist Italy, in Austria at the time of the *Heimwehr* and on a small scale in the national-socialist economy, but soon proved quite unsuited to the modern industrial age. Spann's concept of the élite produced the SS state and its *Ordensburgen*. National socialism was 'socialism' only in the sense that it wanted to create, under a nordic leader, complete

[1] Ibid.

equality among its weak and underprivileged citizens and acknowledged the principle of Caesarism. Hence Schmitt's ideas seem more
suitable and more effective than Spann's.

It is clear that there was no effective opposition put up against
anti-democratic, authoritarian ideas in central Europe. The only people
in Germany who understood the crux of the problem (namely Georg
Simmel, Max Weber and Friedrich Naumann) had died some time
before and their influence dwindled. The almost insular separation of
continental political theory from the rest of the world meant the
exclusion of any influence which Anglo-Saxon ideas might have had.
Consequently the passivity of the democratic institutions in the Weimar
Republic matched the failure of the constitutional lawyers and the
political theorists to defend democracy. In political practise this passivity was reflected by a fading vitality on the part of the democratic
movement.

It is necessary, however, to make a point which will help to clarify
the situation between the wars. The source of an intensified faith in
authority was not the compulsion to blind obedience but primarily
traditional patterns of thinking such as, for example, respect for the
authority of the monarchy or for those movements which kept its
memory alive. Another source was people's feeling of their utter inability to overcome their desperate plight by the use of their own
initiative. The trauma experienced by the feudal as well as the middle
classes under the shock of the Russian Revolution and those revolutions
which subsequently broke out in central Europe, with their talk of class
war, resulted in a synthesis of ideas taken from the authoritarian state
and the Russian Revolution. Ideologies, as they were peculiar to the
conservative revolutionaries or to national socialism, are symptomatic
of this. As a result people left their own decisions to a 'leader' who was
to relieve middle-class society of its anxiety about its decline. Liberty,
which had once been these people's most precious possession, was surrendered almost absolutely. The voluntary surrender of all liberty
meant, however, absolute submission to the will of the leader who
claimed to act in the name of 'people, state and nation'.

An uncritical attitude to state power was accepted as 'normal' and
valid and was felt to be right. So too was the unlimited power which
the Führer took to give his decisions the force of law and which, ultimately, was turned against society itself.

It is essential – as the evolution of political thinking and its accompanying actions shows – to distinguish between the various concepts of
authority, that is, to investigate its origins. Only then is any basis of
understanding of the dialectic of liberty and authority possible.

Hannah Arendt's researches into the question of authority in Plato provides us with important clues: '. . . the essential characteristic of specifically authoritarian forms of government – that the source of their authority which legitimates the exercise of power, must be beyond the sphere of power and, like the law of nature or the commands of God, must not be man-made – goes back to this applicability of the ideas in Plato's political philosophy.'[1]

According to Aristotle, on the other hand, natural reason is the basis of authority. Aristotle believed that reason in itself was innocent of tyrannical ambitions and could therefore dispense with a philosopher king who would organize human affairs totally. Arendt says: 'His [Aristotle's] reason for maintaining that "each body politic is composed of those who rule and those who are ruled", does not derive from the superiority of the expert over the layman, and he is too conscious of the difference between acting and making to draw his examples from the sphere of fabrication. Aristotle . . . was the first to appeal, for the purpose of establishing rule in the handling of human affairs, to nature, which "established the difference . . . between the younger and the older ones, destined the ones to be ruled and the others to rule".'[2]

These different conceptions of authority had – and still have – political repercussions. If the source of authority is not human reason, which is the underlying assumption of genuine legality and legitimacy,[3] but must instead be sought in a higher sphere, and therefore is not embodied in and conveyed through men, the exercise of might and power, which in contrast is and always will be man-made, can be legitimated only by a destiny standing above men and history. National socialism logically created 'Providence' in this sense and the Führer claimed to act as its instrument. His authority was consequently represented as a god-given and inviolable authority demanding a confession of faith, which must take the form of blind obedience.

But the considerable social, religious, cultural, economic and political differences of modern pluralist industrial society are very real obstacles to the achievement of a unanimous faith of this kind, even if the worst terrorist methods of state compulsion are employed. Since the prestige attaching to legality and legitimacy – partly from constitutional monarchy, partly from democratic republicanism – still hung about post-war central Europe, totalitarian movements whose aim was dictatorship were compelled to 'borrow' democratic legality, legitimacy and authority. This was done by using techniques which concealed their intentions and confused the public. On the one hand the totalitarian party programmes rejected monarchy and democracy,

[1] Hannah Arendt, 'What Was Authority?' in *Authority*, op. cit., p. 91.
[2] Ibid., p. 94.
[3] Carl J. Friedrich, *Die Philosophie des Rechts*, op. cit., pp. 142 ff.

but on the other they made use of their external forms. By this means they sought to convince the masses conditioned to legality and legitimacy that the leaders of totalitarian movements were 'more genuine monarchists' than the monarchists and 'truer democrats' than the democrats. The communists did not have the same success with this technique; but the fascists were able to borrow from both monarchy and democracy, hence their pseudo-legality and pseudo-legitimacy. Their techniques of concealment were aided by the monarchical-aristocratic reaction to democracy, which greatly weakened the feeling of legitimacy and authority in respect of the Republic.

An illuminating example of this is the National Socialist *putsch* in Munich in 1923. Hitler proved himself a shrewd tactician who knew how to exploit for his own purposes the legitimacy that still invested both the Prussian military monarchy (Ludendorff) and the Bavarian kingship (von Kahr). In much the same way the Austrian *Heimwehr* exploited the legitimacy associated with the Austrian monarchy. In both cases fascism was helped by the fact that it could use monarchist-conservative groups like the German National People's Party and the Bavarian People's Party in Germany as temporary allies of the Fatherland Front in Austria. But after Hitler had realized that the legitimacy and drawing-power of the monarchy were inadequate he turned to democratic legality and legitimacy. This proves the truth of Friedrich's thesis that tyranny, as such, can have no authority since legality depends on laws and legitimacy on law and authority, as a rational basis, strengthens legality and legitimacy. But in the industrial age tyranny never appears naked and in the form it assumed in antiquity or the Renaissance; it always appears with an authority borrowed from legitimate forms of state.

But totalitarianism bases itself on this 'borrowed' authority only in respect of the masses; in respect of its followers it derives its authority from metaphysics in the Platonic sense. Thus, in its relations with the masses, communism uses authority 'borrowed' from democracy, but in its dealing with party members it uses the Marxist-Leninist dialectic as a pseudo-rational but really quasi-divine law. Where there was no 'Holy Writ', as in the case of national socialism, the opportunistic manipulation of the power of the party and the SS was justified by the belief in Hitler as the 'saviour' of the Nordic race.[1]

This dualism of totalitarian authority is, however, only transient and is conditioned by the piecemeal seizure of power. The real aim in respect of the masses is also to replace the authority 'borrowed' from monarchy or democracy by its own metaphysical authority. Propaganda

[1] Cf. also Hermann Rauschning, *Die Revolution des Nihilismus*, Zurich, New York 1938, p. 59: 'Das Charisma der Führergestalt'.

and terror serve this intention. Totalitarianism is intellectually and spiritually a retrograde movement. As, since the fall of the Byzantine Empire and the overthrow of the Divine Right of Kings, reason in the Aristotelian sense replaced faith as the basis of state authority, totalitarianism in the Platonic sense endeavours to establish its authority by means of a new creed. Under this system all 'objectivist' thinking about state and society must, therefore, appear to be either damnable heresy deserving death, or witchcraft.

# CHAPTER VI

# Democracy's Political Mistakes

## PART ONE

*The Pseudo-Revolutions of 1918*

At the end of the First World War democracy seemed to have won its greatest victory so far. Throughout central and eastern Europe, monarchical and autocratic systems collapsed and were replaced by democratic republics. Even the communist regimes which, within a short time, ousted liberal democracy in Russia and Hungary, appeared at first only to be extreme forms of the democratic state. The fate of the Tsar's family had shocked and terrified the dynasties of central Europe and induced them to capitulate to middle-class and moderate social-democratic republics which at least guaranteed their personal safety.

The peoples, however, were neither agreed nor clear as to the aims of the revolutions. While the revolutionary movements in the linguistically heterogeneous nationality states were predominantly national-democratic in character, in the linguistically homogeneous states like Germany, Austria and Hungary they were chiefly social-democratic. Although the officers had been stripped of their imperial insignia and the memorials and street signs recalling the past were smashed or removed, the people of these nations found it much more difficult to discard the spiritual values and the cultural ties which they had inherited, their pattern of life, their respect for traditional authority, or the delicate and fine-spun texture of emotional and intellectual relationships which constitute a sense of community.

Much of what subsequently happened in central Europe reminds one of the effects which the French Revolution had on the structure of French society. As in France, the central European Revolution, apart from the modest liberal achievements of the German constitutional systems of the pre-war period, had not come as the natural climax of a gradual evolutionary process. As in France, prior to 1918, apart from the working-class movement, democracy had been represented only as an abstract ideology by a small group of social scientists, theoreticians and politicians. Their idealism and self-sacrifice were great enough to fire the masses with enthusiasm for democracy; but whole peoples are not turned into democrats by enthusiasm and faith alone.

For the central European masses democracy had so far been nothing more than a programme propagated by a few parties and all too often bearing the marks of a Messianic belief when expounded in public statements, in the press and in parliament. But that did not mean that these people were yet ready to adopt democracy as a way of life or that they had the civic education and the experience in self-government which would have fitted them for such a way of life. On the contrary, democratic republics came into existence overnight in states with social structures which had preserved from their monarchical, authoritarian past a spirit of subservience, romantic reverence for power and bigoted intolerance.

Parties and groups which had previously been no more than militant political units with liberal, democratic and socialist ideologies suddenly had to assume much real political responsibility, far beyond their wildest expectations. The revolutionary events which followed one another thick and fast found the middle and lower officials in the democratic parties completely unprepared for the tasks now facing them. For these people the magic word 'democracy' had, in the past, frequently meant the hope of a modest measure of material betterment for the masses. They had always been good popular orators, trusty members of their parties and movements, but had never nursed hopes of rising to positions on the fringe of government or even in government itself. Nor were the small number of reliable and self-confident democrats enough to fill the essential posts in the legislature and the administration.

Consequently the young democracies could not afford to dispense with the civil servants who had served the monarchical regimes and who now made no attempt to conceal their anti-republican sentiment; nor could they prevent large numbers of time-servers, who at heart still longed for a return to the old ways, from securing key positions. Many of the democratic officials had been used to doing hard physical work and others had spent years in prison or in exile. Their experiences had taught them to steer clear of the police and to brave press censorship to spread their ideas among the people. But such experiences were not calculated to make them good ministers, parliamentary deputies or senior civil servants. Nor had they any academic or professional training to compare with that of the judges and statesmen appointed by the *ancien régime*. As a result the ministers often had to rely on executive organs which felt little devotion to democracy.

The pioneers of democracy now had to immerse themselves in the business of government and had little time to continue the struggle for their ideals. The easy victory which they had gained in 1918 was a big factor in the feeling of security which made them believe that their political recruiting days were over. Their new and unfamiliar tasks blinded them all too easily to the fact that many of the people who had voted for them had done so because, for the time being, they could see no alternative and not because of any real belief in the truth of democratic principles or in the ability and efficiency of the democratic parties' leaders.

As was to be expected, the converts at first acted in an extremely radical fashion. On the mistaken assumption that their radicalism was helping democracy, they behaved even more intolerantly than their autocratic predecessors.

## PART TWO

*The New Democracies and the Question of Defence*

Every state has the right to a monopoly of armed force. No state can surrender this right without seriously jeopardizing its existence and the survival of its social and legal order.

Dispassionate study of the events which took place in Germany in 1918 raises doubts as to whether these can be described as a German revolution in the true sense of the word. The events which were the immediate cause of the upheaval were set in motion by the German Supreme Command's request for an armistice. The various uprisings and mutinies which broke out with the collapse of the Western Front, and which remained localized and on a surprisingly small scale, were born of general war-weariness and disillusionment over the victory which had never materialized and which people believed in for far too long. In point of fact, social democracy succeeded in coming into power in Germany because of support from the Army Supreme Command. As Obermann rightly says: 'The First German Republic was the child of the Ebert-Groener alliance.'[1]

Social democracy in the person of Scheidemann had proclaimed the Democratic Republic against strong opposition from Ebert and soon found itself in an extremely difficult situation. It needed reliable troops immediately to be able to take strong action against communist and other left-wing revolutionary risings in Berlin, Munich and many other parts of Germany. But where were the troops to come

[1] Emil Obermann, *Soldaten, Bürger, Militaristen*, Stuttgart 1958, p. 237.

from? The corps of guards was no longer on a proper combat footing. In its Eisenach (1869) and Erfurt (1891) programmes the Social Democratic Party had indeed called for a *Volkswehr* (People's Army) in place of the regular army; but during the war radical pacifist ideas had gained ground among the socialist working classes, becoming especially articulate in the Independent Social Democratic Party (USPD). Thus at the Party's Congress in Berlin in 1919 the deputy Künstler declared that national defence was now an irrelevance as far as true socialists were concerned because wars were caused by imperialist and capitalist policies, and the Congress adopted a resolution on these lines.[1]

But generally speaking pacifist ideas of this kind were not confined to the Independent Social Democratic Party; they were also echoed by members of the Majority Social Democrats.[2] Although the Social Democrats then pressed for a shorter conscription period and a *Volkswehr*, they ran into difficulties because many members of the party were pacifists. Moreover, the Weimar Republic was forbidden by the Allies from setting up an army of conscripts. Yet the Republic found itself compelled to take immediate and decisive action against the left-wing socialist revolutionaries in order to forestall an Allied occupation of Germany. Government circles were aware that the Allies would not have been prepared to tolerate a communist regime in Germany.

The former officer corps was, therefore, social democracy's only possible saviour in the crisis. It was quite impossible at the time for Ebert, Noske and their cabinet colleagues to ask too many questions about the motives and ultimate aims of their rescuers. The necessary help came to President Ebert and his government by way of the *Freikorps* (Free Corps) which was raised and commanded by former officers. Certain officer circles hoped to win substantial Social Democratic support for a national military policy.

They would even have been prepared to support a dictatorship under Ebert and Noske if this had been ready to push through a policy of national regeneration and introduce a socialist economy. Familiarity with war-time economic ideas and methods had made ideas of state socialism acceptable to the general public. However, this attempt at co-operation between the militarists and the Social Democratic leaders broke down because of the workers' pacifism, which made it impossible for the Social Democrats to raise burgher' and

[1] Quoted by Gustav Caspar, 'Die sozialdemokratische Partei und das deutsche Wehrproblem in den Jahren der Weimarer Republik', Supplementary Volume XI of the *Wehrwissenschaftliche Rundschau*, Frankfurt am Main 1959, p. 5.

[2] G. A. Caspar, 'Die deutsche Sozialdemokratie und die Entstehung der Reichswehr (1918–1921)', *Wehrwissenschaftliche Rundschau*, Frankfurt am Main 1958.

workers' units because of the Social Democratic Party's hatred of any form of dictatorship and also because of the officers' aversion to democracy and the Republic.

The ideas of the Russian Revolution made an impact *not only* on extreme left-wing circles in the working class but also on the German middle classes, as is shown by the well-known memorandum 'Germany's immediate political tasks', which General von Seekt sent to the President, the Chancellor, the Foreign Minister and the Defence Minister on June 26, 1920. In this the then Chief of the Army Command declared *inter alia*:

'The ideas of the Russian Revolution exert a powerful attraction for our people. Such developments in the midst of great crises in world history cannot in the long run be held down by armed force. It is therefore essential to take the initiative and harness them to the service of the people's future. Wide sectors of the German people would regard any fight against Russia as a fight against their own ideals . . . It would swing the broad masses sharply against us and in the end probably bring bolshevism in its worst form to Germany . . . The Entente fears the pan-Russian movement . . . because, in the sphere of foreign policy, it is directed against the system which won this war, against Anglo-Saxon capitalism and imperialism . . . A Russian defeat by the Entente seems out of the question because that vast land mass and its peoples is unconquerable . . . The future belongs to Russia . . . This must be done publicly and with the greatest frankness – for in this period of extraordinary difficulty for German internal politics we must win over the broad masses for our policy and lead the German people to ideas of unity . . . at the same time we ought to to give assurances that we wish to live in friendship with Russia . . . and we ought to set our hopes on Russia, fully respecting the 1914 frontiers . . . In this way we should have found a few words to draw everyone together, including German nationalist circles, thereby laying the foundation for ways of overcoming disunity. State power . . . needs . . . a politically intact, well-disciplined army with leaders who understand the modern age and the people's plight. But it is even more important for the government to deal with the present troubles by internal reforms.'[1]

Von Seekt's proposals about internal policy, which, like his foreign-policy proposals, were strongly opposed by the Social Democratic President Ebert, represented an attempt to shape Germany on the lines of the Soviet Union by introducing a nationalist-communist

[1] Cf. Otto Gessler, *Reichswehrpolitik in der Weimarer Zeit*, Stuttgart 1958, pp. 186 ff.

system. He recommended a further advance 'along the road of agreed co-operation (*Arbeitsgemeinschaften*) suggested by the Industrial Councils Act and the Reich Economic Council leading to corporate co-operation of the people by an organic system of workers' councils', to the 'socialization of large-scale coal and iron production', and 'land reform'. 'The purpose of the measures', Seekt declared, 'was to take the wind out of the sails of the bolshevist agitators, to become politically a subject and no longer an object of foreign influence.' Seekt seemed prepared to adopt much of the Marxist-Leninist programme, only, of course, as long as this was done under German leadership. But the Social Democratic Party, and in particular President Ebert, who saw the events of November 9, 1918, only as the final triumph of the abortive liberal-democratic revolution of 1848, were not ready for such a rapprochement with the Soviet Union.

The Treaty of Versailles allowed Germany to maintain an army of 100,000 regular soldiers. The upshot of the Weimar Republic's positive dependence on the *Reichswehr*, which began as an emergency solution only to develop into a permanent source of reactionary pressure, was that the *Reichswehr* finally came to constitute a state within the state. It considered itself – and was considered – as standing above the parties.[1] That meant, however, that the main supporters of the Weimar coalition, namely the Social Democratic Party, the Liberal Democratic Party and the Zentrum Party, were, as far as the *Rechswehr* was concerned, no better and no worse than any other party rejecting the Republic with the exception of the communists. Because of its whole social structure in the circumstances of the time, the *Reichswehr*'s impartiality could never be more than temporary and unquestioned as long as there was no active political movement which promised to carry out its ideals. That was demonstrated in the Kapp *putsch*, when von Seeckt flatly refused to support Ebert against the rebellious General von Lüttwitz and his followers.

It was demonstrated again in the vacillation shown by sections of the officer corps over the Hitler-Ludendorff *putsch* in Munich in 1923, and also in the part played by General Schleicher and General Hammerstein-Equord in Brüning's dismissal, and in Hindenburg's consultations about Hitler's fitness to rule. Gumbel believes that the following factors had determined development in the *Reichswehr*:

[1] O. E. Schüddekopf, *Das Heer und die Republik*, Chapter on 'Der Staat im Staate: Reichswehr und Demokratie', Frankfurt, Hanover 1955, pp. 194 ff. Cf. also Obermann, op. cit., pp. 248 ff. Gumbel believes that the *Reichswehr* regarded itself as the continuation of the Imperial Army, as the only remaining part of a legal government and quotes Schüddekopf: 'As the government has fallen into the hands of traitors the officer must put the Fatherland above the Constitution'. Emil J. Gumbel, *Vom Fememord zur Reichskanzlei*, Heidelberg 1962, p. 21.

1. The terms of the Versailles Treaty and the technique of circumventing them.
2. The open and latent civil war situation, revolutionary in 1919, counter-revolutionary in 1920–23.

Gumbel goes to the heart of the matter when he observes that the absence of political leadership was decisive. 'The *Reichswehr* Minister was not the executive organ of a political will (which the Social Democrats in particular lacked) . . . but, vice versa, the army's executive organ against a political will which showed little power of resistance.'[1]

One of the main reasons for the estrangement that grew up between the Weimar Republic and the *Reichswehr* was the gradual exclusion of democratic elements from the lower ranks of the *Reichswehr*, especially when recruitment was taken out of the hands of the Defence Minister and transferred to company commanders. The bad relations between Weimar and *Reichswehr* were also due to the Social Democratic Party's hostility towards the military circles. Noske believed the reason for this lay in the reunion of the Independent Social Democratic Party and the Social Democratic Party, when the more uncompromising Independent officials had come to hold many key positions. One of the Social Democrats' main objections to the *Reichswehr* was the latter's unauthorized collaboration with the Soviet Union which was carried on behind the government's back and solely on the *Reichswehr*'s own initiative.[2] Other reasons were the anti-republicanism of the officer corps[3] and the system of part-time volunteers, a device for evading the limitation placed on the *Reichswehr*'s numbers.

The gradual ebb of monarchical sympathies within the *Reichswehr* did not, however, make it more pro-republican but, as the Leipzig *Reichswehr* trial in 1930 revealed, led to a growing enthusiasm for National Socialism on the part of the young officers. The Social Democratic deputy Julius Leber was the first man to point out that the Republic had failed to inspire the young officers with ideals or provide them with symbols. The question of the replacement of officers and other ranks came to be an increasingly important factor in determining the Social Democratic attitude; this shows that the Social Democratic Party was aware that it was losing its influence on the *Reichswehr* to an increasing extent.

As we have already mentioned, the Weimar Republic was com-

---

[1] Gumbel, op. cit., p. 22.

[2] *Protokolle des Görlitzer Parteitages der SPD*, p. 263.

[3] G. A. Caspar, *Die Sozialdemokratische Partei und das Wehrproblem*, op. cit., p. 32.

pelled to call on the help of *Freikorps* such as the Ehrhard, Rossbach, Oberland and Werwolf Brigades in order to be able to make any sort of stand against the powerful left-wing revolutionary currents which came to the surface in Germany in the wake of the Russian Revolution and military defeat. These active fighters against left-wing radicalism received, understandably, not only moral but also financial support from German industrialists.[1] The spirit of these *Freikorps* was altogether different from that of the former Prussian army. It reflected the class equality, based on war-time comradeship, which had sprung up in the trenches in the First World War at Verdun and on the Somme. Although the majority of the men who fought in the front line tried, as they did in other countries, to get back to civilian life as quickly as possible, there was a small minority who had been so morally and physically uprooted by the war that for them the end of the war meant literally 'the outbreak of peace'. War had taught this *condottiere*-type of trooper that the patriot's supreme virtue lay in his use of force. They had learned about strategy and tactics and had also seen that even in seemingly hopeless circumstances the counter-offensive can carry the day. The ideas of liberal democracy were bound to fill them with horror. 'The spirit of shaping parliamentary majorities by way of compromise, government by discussion should give way to the feeling for authority, voluntary submission to leaders who know how to lead . . . A Republic of front-line soldiers was the aim, a true people's community.'[2] They believed that if the front-line techniques can prove their worth in war against mighty armies they could also be used successfully in the political fight against undisciplined hordes of workers and parliamentary wind-bags.

These *Freikorps* revealed a new nationalist or conservative-revolutionary spirit – a spirit which spread increasingly to the German Youth Movement. Typical of the *Freikorps* were scorn of middle-class comfort, a sense of comradeship which looked down on social distinctions, and an absolute devotion to the leaders of the corps which bore their names. Many regarded themselves as the nucleus of a future national German army; the *Reichswehr* leaders seemed to confirm this view by giving the *Freikorps* occasional support. Others looked on themselves as defenders of the traditional social order against revolutionary socialism.

Another important point is that the *Reichswehr* was unable to re-engage all former officers. The *Freikorps* provided unemployed officers and N.C.O.s with a field of activity which satisfied their wishes and

[1] Ibid., p. 37.
[2] J. Neurohr, *Der Mythos vom Dritten Reich – Zur Geistesgeschichte des Nationalsozialismus*, Stuttgart 1957, p. 77.

their taste and the compulsory disbanding of these formations, throwing their members out of employment once again, only hardened their anti-republicanism and their national-revolutionary sentiments.[1] The collapse of the Weimar Republic therefore promised these 'renegade officers' not only the fulfilment of ideological ideals but also their social rehabilitation. It was therefore clear that they would agree with National Socialist propaganda, which made democratic parliamentarians and officials out to be useless and harmful drones.

These men constituted the real *avant-garde* of the national-revolutionary movement; they were hostile to the Democratic Republic and unsympathetic towards the officers in the *Reichswehr*, who endeavoured to carry on the traditions of the Prussian state of Frederick the Great. On the other hand, however, this *avant-garde* abjured the spirit of the National Socialist Storm Troops (SA). Adolf Hitler's Caesarism, which was based on mob democracy and partly sustained by the riff-raff of the nation, had little in common with these conservative-revolutionaries' ideals. But it was this *avant-garde* which, after Hitler had seized power, filled key positions in the SS and later in the *Wehrmacht*. When, in 1934, there was real danger of a conflict between the *Wehrmacht*, which was still conservative at the time, and the proletarian Storm Troops, Hitler was able to turn to the men of the *Freikorps* and with their assistance he finally stripped both the Storm Troops and the *Wehrmacht* of political power. He weakened the *Wehrmacht* by making *Freikorps* personnel Nazi Party officers and thus providing a counterbalance to offset the old professional officers of the *Reichswehr*. 'The rootless "renegades", however, the secret assassins, the strategists of the fighting in the meeting halls, the marches and demonstrations became willing tools of a new will, a totalitarian state and community will, which promised to realize most of their hopes and ideals.'[2]

The ideology and the methods of communism had undoubtedly had their effect on these national revolutionaries. The violence and terror of the Russian Revolution also had their origin in the experience of war. The national revolutionaries had not been able to establish friendly relations with international socialism of the Marxist-Leninist brand, but after Stalin's nationalist change of front their own attitude also changed. The German nationalists were fascinated by what they regarded as Stalin's unpretending and fanatical personality as a leader, his implacable campaign against Jewish international Marxism which they thought was proved by his hounding of Trotsky, Kamenev, and Zinoviev among others, and his readiness to put national interests before world revolution. In Russia was to be seen at last a realization

[1] Obermann, op. cit., p. 268.　　　　　　　　　　　　[2] Ibid., p. 270.

of Fichte's self-contained commercial state, a realization of 'the corporate medieval state organism applied to a large, unified state structure'— a favourite idea of German nationalists since the Romantic period in Germany.[1] Hitler therefore, as he said himself, 'put Marxism into effect'.[2] According to Hitler, national socialism was 'a potential socialism that is never consumated because it is in a state of constant change'.[3] Also according to Hitler, if the Social Democratic Party had rejected the mistaken ideas of a democracy in the framework of which the revolution would be fulfilled, it would have been successful in Germany.

In order that the Versailles peace proposals might be carried out, victors and vanquished alike promised to carry out comprehensive disarmament measures. This obligation did not apply equally to all the parties involved; for the vanquished it took the form of a strict verdict, while the victors were allowed to interpret this solemn commitment in their own interests. Germany was presented with a categorical demand to abolish her armed forces, reduce her army to 100,000 men and her armaments to a minimum. This bore no relationship to measures to be undertaken by the victorious powers.

The new German state could only survive if it based itself on the army. At the same time, however, it was compelled to abide by the restrictions imposed on it and that meant cutting down on the army. On the other hand it was faced with the threat of revolutionary upheaval. If the state wanted to be assured of the army's loyalty in this situation it was forced to come to an understanding with the army leaders and permit the organization of corps from the ranks of the demobilized units; but their existence had to be kept secret. And secret rearmament was necessary in order to maintain these units. Furthermore, a use had to be found for these organizations and this took the form of their employment by the government against the enemies of the new regime. The connections which grew up between the illegal aims of the *Reichswehr*, secret rearmament and the toleration of the illegal military *Freikorps*, including the *Schwarze* (Black) *Reichswehr*, became unbreakable.[4] If the new leaders of the state did not want to deprive themselves of their only source of power they had to 'legalize' this inherently illegal relationship – a relationship which

---

[1] O. E. Schüddekopf, *Linke Leute von rechts*, Stuttgart 1960, p. 180.
[2] H. Rauschning, *Gespräche mit Hitler*, Zurich 1940, p. 174.
[3] Ibid., p. 177.
[4] Emil J. Gumbel, *Vom Fememord zur Reichskanzlei*, op. cit., p. 70. 'The attitude of the *Reichswehr* to its shadow was stereotyped. Three Defence Ministers, the Social Democrat Noske, the Democrat Gessler and General Groener, evolved the following syllogism: 1. A *Schwarze Reichswehr* has never existed. 2. It has long been dissolved. 3. Whoever mentions it is a traitor!'

was incompatible with the constitutional principles of Weimar. In order not to let the army, as the potentially legal and official executive of the new state, disintegrate because of an unavoidable conflict with the working class, the leaders of the state snatched at the chance of using the strictly organized defence units and *Freikorps* to stifle the latent but open threat of communist revolution. For these units, however, their task was clear: to combat all socialist movements whose aim was to set up a system of soviet-style councils.

The members of these units did not, however, possess the necessary political knowledge to distinguish between communists, socialists, democrats and republicans.[1] Furthermore, this struggle seemed to them an opportune means of raising their lowered social status, which they considered to be due to the November revolution resulting from the 'treachery of Versailles'. Consequently their ideas about their original 'mission' underwent a transformation and became 'the patriotic mission to cancel out the November revolution'. This attitude, in its extreme form, led to political murder.[2] The political leaders' attitude meant that the state had to recognize, by jurisdiction, the existence and employment of the armed units and the *Freikorps*, secret rearmament and the *Schwarze Reichswehr*. If it had abandoned this syllogism it would have openly opposed the *Reichswehr*. But Weimar could not afford to do that. It would have needed a concrete political symbol in order to carry on the conflict in the name of democracy. Such a symbol was not, however, to be had. Instead, the state allowed its major power factor to stand aloof from the Democratic Republic and thereby contributed to its own devaluation.

On account of the services which these semi-official military units had performed for the Republic, they became a permanent institution whose development was bound, in the end, to lead to the collapse of state power. Their very existence appeared as a provocation to the working class. Because their violent and anti-working-class actions in the years of civil war were notorious, the police had to take extensive measures to ensure the safety of a *Freikorps* when, for example, it marched through an industrial town. Although the *Freikorps* were eventually disbanded, the Weimar Republic's hesitant and vacillating attitude towards them had created a most dangerous precedent. For through the existence of the *Freikorps* the ordinary citizen became so

[1] Emil J. Gumbel, *Verschwörer*, Vienna 1924, p. 209. 'In this fight against what they consider to be socialism . . . all the secret associations are united.'

[2] Because of the permanent civil war situation it was part of the day's 'job' for these mercenaries and, at first, in line with the mission they had been given. The later 'national mission' carried on by them in the fight against the 'November criminals' turned it in the end against their former bosses, as the murders of Rathenau and Erzberger and the attempt on Scheidemann's life proved.

accustomed to the possibility of private armed formations that it finally became normal for all major ideological and political groups in Germany to set up their own, sometimes well-armed, private armies. The spirit of thuggery and assassination was a decisive factor in generating the spirit of terrorism which marked the murderous security squads (SD) of the SS and the Gestapo.

A state which surrenders its monopoly in the use of power commits suicide. Considered from this angle it might seem today that by permitting the creation of private armies the Weimar Republic fully deserved the fate which later befell it. It must, however, be said in its defence that it was forced to do so partly by the urgent requirements of the post-war period, partly by the short-sighted policy of the Allies – although in the years of stabilization between about 1924 and 1929 there was a period of grace in which German democracy could probably have strengthened its influence in the *Reichswehr* and eliminated the influence of the *Freikorps* and the private armies.

Against this, however, must be remembered what has already been said about the democratic executive being crippled by proportional representation and the coalition and minority governments which that made inevitable. The Weimar parties were not always completely united among themselves and often had to accept in the coalition a party such as, for example, the German National People's Party, which thoroughly approved of the *Reichswehr*'s indifference towards the Republic and the *Freikorps*' anti-republicanism. Even the German People's Party agreed with the *Reichswehr*'s special policy, as became apparent from Stresemann's agreement with the Defence Minister, Gessler.[1] Although the German People's Party supported Locarno in the sphere of foreign politics, its internal policy aims were to defend capitalist interests against the working class and win backing on the right, that is among the German Nationalist Party (DNVP). For the Weimar parties could not take any really vigorous action against the *Reichswehr* and the political associations. They could only set up their own private army, the red-black-gold *Reichsbanner*, thus clearly exposing their weakness.

On the other hand the Weimar Republic added to its difficulties from the very outset by adopting a mistaken policy towards the veteran and front-line soldier associations.[2] These have always created special

---

[1] Ludwig Bergsträsser, *Geschichte der politischen Parteien in Deutschland*, Munich 1960, p. 260; cf. also Gustav Stresemann, *Vermächtnis*, edited by H. Bernhard, Vols. I–III, Berlin 1932–3.

[2] Cf., for example, O. E. Schüddekopf, *Das Heer und die Republik*, op. cit., p. 100, who says the political demands of the volunteers who had fought in the Baltic provinces were for a speed-up in plans for housing and accommodation and land for settlement, 'so that the troops can see that the Government has their interests at heart

problems, in other countries as well. In Germany, however, they were particularly dangerous because of the specific structure of German society. They took – not only in Germany – the form of pressure groups and presented the post-war democracies with a difficult problem. It is indisputable that men who were ready to sacrifice their health and their lives for their country in war, and who went through all its horrors, have an especial claim on the understanding and help of the community.

Therefore the way in which the problems of war veterans is handled is one of the major tests of a government's ability. Demobilized soldiers undoubtedly have a claim to a proper share in political responsibility. But it must be borne in mind that the qualities which make a soldier do not necessarily make a good politician and even more rarely do they make an ideal cabinet minister in a democratic government. The soldier's virtues – primarily obeying and giving orders – are not enough. On the other hand there is no disputing that much more in the way of team-work was required of officers in the Second World War than ever before and that is a quality which is also essential to the democratic system. But in central European armies during and after the First World War strength of character, a sense of honour and a spirit of patriotism were still held to be the highest qualities in an officer.

The concept of a 'sense of honour' implied, among other things, that a responsible officer was obliged to carry through his decision or the orders he had received to the death, whatever the difficulties or the sacrifices called for. These officers had learned and taught others that the enemy must be fought with every possible means. This, however, is out of the question for the democratic statesman who must always try to understand and bring about a compromise of the views and wishes of others – both in his own party and among the nation as a whole. This is the only possible way of arriving at the fundamental consensus which is the *conditio sine qua non* of any and every democratic community. But in war there can never be a basic consensus between the two hostile sides. This is the fundamental difference between war and politics. The ordinary people in the post-war democracies realized the difference much too late – to their great disadvantage.

The material, moral and economic ravages of war were to be repaired in peace-time by the parliamentary systems, whose structure has been described above.[1] As we have already explained, proportional

in grateful recognition . . .', otherwise, threatened General von der Göltz, the Baltic contingents' spokesman, 'a body of reliable Government troops might become a crowd of dissatisfied men who would defect and join the Government's enemies.

[1] Cf. Chap. III.

representation led increasingly to a multiplicity of parties, including small, irreconcilable parties with uncompromising programmes. Such a development was fatal to the formation of a genuine political spirit based on the fundamental consensus, and to the formation of a genuine democratic will. If a large number of men, who have learned in war to regard compromise as dishonourable, take this attitude into parliamentary life with them, these democracies are burdened from the start with a mortgage which makes their survival improbable. And we must remind readers that contempt, on principle, for tolerant and generous compromise was not confined merely to the right-wing parties in the Weimar Republic. Because of their strict adherence to Marxist class-war slogans the socialist parties were obliged to adopt the same attitude.

Mussolini's fascists had also begun as pressure groups of war veterans who insisted on making their influence felt on the government – a fact which in itself made their suppression almost impossible. Were they not good patriots who had fought for Italy? It seemed impossible, therefore, to repay their sacrifices by political persecution. In Poland, too, it was veteran groups who in 1926 made possible Pilsudski's *coup d'état* against Polish democracy.

If the Weimar Republic can be accused of letting the *Reichswehr* become a 'state within the state', it is not possible to level the same charge against the Austrian Republic. The Socialist leader, Julius Deutsch, appointed Minister for Army Affairs immediately after the revolution, was well aware of the danger which the retention of the old officer corps signified for democracy. 'When I took up my post,' he wrote, 'I found there were several tens of thousands of regular officers and N.C.O.s, and a few hundred generals as well.' Deutsch made certain that at least some of them were pensioned off; for he believed that, if the officer corps of the Habsburg monarchy were left intact it was bound 'sooner or later to become an instrument for all kinds of adventures'.[1]

It was not until much later that the Socialists lost influence in the Austrian Army, due to the Christian Social Army Minister Vaugoin. The unfavourable economic conditions of the post-war period narrowed the essential basis of the former officer corps until it became a *déclassé* group from which National Socialism was able to recruit willing helpers. The reader will recall such figures as General Glaise von Horstenau[2] or Carl von Bardolff,[3] the former Major Fey for the services he rendered to *Heimwehr* fascism and probably to National

[1] Julius Deutsch, *Ein weiter Weg*, Zurich, Leipzig, Vienna 1960, p. 121.
[2] Edmund von Glaise-Horstenau, *Die Katastrophe*, Zurich, Leipzig, Vienna 1928.
[3] Carl von Bardolff, *Soldat im alten Österreich*, Jena 1938.

Socialism as well, and Dr Wächter, the son of an Austrian War Minister, who led the National Socialist *putsch* in July 1934. The disillusionment and despair of the former imperial officers over the dismemberment of the Danube monarchy was without doubt partly responsible for the feebleness of Austrian resistance to National Socialism and also for the success of the *Heimwehr* movement.

The democratic leadership in Czechoslovakia was the only one to show a high degree of statesmanlike insight. The front-line fighters' organization became the nucleus of the new republican army. The veterans received generous treatment in the way of posts, pensions and medals. Common soldiers were granted quick promotion in the public services such as the post office, railways and police force. The officers were given remunerative if not very responsible positions in the higher ranks of the civil service and in industry. In this way the great majority identified their ideological and material interests with those of the democratic republic and their veteran organizations became trusty protectors of democracy. Their energies and experiences were as passionately pro-democratic as in other countries they were anti-democratic.

On the other hand, by its reprimand and dismissal of the extreme nationalist General Gajda, the Czechoslovak government showed that it was unwilling to allow the army a dominant role in politics. The influence of the Czechoslovak President, T. G. Masaryk, was a decisive factor in this development. In spite of the weak points in his policy[1] his general approach and outlook were wise, being a fusion of the best traditions of central European idealistic liberalism and the practical democratic experience which he had received in the West.

## PART THREE

*Post-War Democracy in Theory and Practice*

Social Democracy in the Post-War World

The contradiction engendered by the compromise between social democracy's Marxist theory and its liberal democratic practice (which was far less concerned with socialization as such than with purely social policy) began to have damaging effects in the post-war period. For the ambivalent attitude bred by this compromise persuaded the masses that the socialists, strongly represented in government, were

[1] Cf. Chap. II, Part Six.

doing relatively little to improve social conditions. Their main and primary concern seemed to be the establishment of sound relations with their middle-class coalition partners.

In point of fact, however, the mounting distrust of the socialist parties was hardly justified. Proportional representation made it impossible for the socialists to form majority governments without middle-class help. They were, therefore, compelled to heed the wishes of their bourgeois coalition partners. But the result, especially in times of economic crisis, was that the Social Democratic Party in Germany appeared to share responsibility for the catastrophic economic situation. Karl Marx had prophesied that capitalism's periodically recurring crises would create a revolutionary situation favourable to the collapse of the capitalist system; now, every economic crisis was a blow to socialism. Thus the first economic crisis after the World War, that of 1922–23, helped to bring Italian fascism to power, while the great depression which began in 1929 destroyed German democracy and greatly damaged socialism's prestige in almost every country in Europe.

Mussolini had always expressed the opinion that fascism owed its triumph to the urgent need for vigorous action. There is a grain of truth in this claim. The social democrats, whom Marxism had conditioned to the idea of deterministic fatalism, wrote and spoke of their future victory over capitalism but were obliged to tolerate its existence. The materialistic philosophy of history meant that socialists thought in terms of economic categories in the first instance, so that questions such as the winning and holding of positions of power in the state were bound to seem of secondary importance.

In central Europe this period saw a consolidation of social-democratic party bureaucracy. Robert Michels[1] described the origin of party discipline and the history of the development of party officialdom. Because of its social structure and its immanent evolutionary laws, every bureaucracy is suspicious of dynamic initiative. On the other hand a radical party which renounces dynamism is bound to develop conservative characteristics. This process strengthened the authority of the experienced party members who had grown old in the service of the movement, but discouraged the talented and more vital younger men. After the decline of revolutionary enthusiasm in the years of upheaval this conservatism became the prevailing attitude among the party leaders and forced the vital elements to conform.

But as conformity and party discipline became one and the same,

[1] Robert Michels, *Zur Soziologie des Parteiwesens in der modernen Demokratie*, op. cit.; cf. especially: 'Die konservative Basis der Organisation', pp. 464 ff., and 'Die Demokratie und das eherne Gesetz der Oligarchie', pp. 479 ff.

dynamic forces were faced with the alternative of either submitting to party discipline or being expelled from the party. Consequently many of the ablest members of the social democratic parties were either driven into the political wilderness or joined other parties. As a result the socialist movement lost its attraction for the younger generation, who now looked on social democracy as a party of the old and the effete, and a movement which wasted its time in pointless debate, unrealistic theory and in making dishonest speeches to the masses. This disillusionment greatly enhanced the attractions of the radical parties whose programmes and actions seemed to offer everything that social democracy lacked, i.e. the fascists and the communists.

Two basic tendencies in social democracy which had set in long before the war were now definitely crystallized. The first was the tendency to bureaucratic centralism, further strengthened by the dovetailing of the party with state institutions. The party became a miniature state as far as was concerned the structure of its own bureaucracy and the obstinate, almost conservative, 'never-take-a-risk' mentality of its official stratum. This tendency took the form often described as the 'institutionalism' of the party, and the related oligarchical structure which is the inevitable consequence of thinking in terms of hierarchy.[1] The second tendency was expressed in the loyalty of members. For them the party had become their political homeland and represented what Matthias calls an 'emotional value' and was the single manifestation of their political outlook. The party had become incapable of manoeuvre, so to speak, its ideology rejecting both the 'bourgeois-capitalist' order and also any revolutionary action, as it equated 'revolution' with the Leninist experiment.

It is true not only of social democracy but also of the democratic parties in general that they lost their spirit of enterprise as soon as they felt themselves *beati possidentes*. Bryce had observed in the case of France that every deputy's main wish was to remain a deputy.[2] As we have already explained, under the conditions of proportional representation and strict party discipline, this had particularly unfortunate consequences. Politicians who had gone much further than they could

---

[1] In *Das Ende der Parteien 1933*, Düsseldorf 1960, edited by Erich Matthias and Rudolf Morsey, particular reference is made to the process of institutionalization, in which the Social Democratic Party (SPD) leaders tended to think only 'in the categories of the tradional party apparatus', p. 196. In *Wirtschaftsdemokratie*, the publication sponsored by the Free Trade Unions, Fritz Naphtali urges the social democratic trade unions to extend their activities to include the establishment of 'public enterprises', 'consumer co-operative societies' and 'concerns owned by the trade unions'. This publication, which appeared in Berlin in April 1928, ignored the real possibilities which existed for achieving these institutional aims and abandoned a detailed analysis of trends in political development.

[2] James Bryce, *Modern Democracies*, op. cit., Vol. I, p. 280.

ever have hoped, and who had lost their independence and initiative because of their continued subordination to the party executive, came to regard the younger generation's spirit of enterprise and idealism as an unqualified and unpleasant disturbance to their work, long become a matter of routine, and also a latent danger to their own position. On the other hand socialist anti-intellectualism had a negative effect, in that it restricted the field of choice for party leaders. The 'horny hand' slogan, which originally had only meant the demand for the recognition and participation of manual workers in government and administrative business, now became a device used by the party bureaucracy to protect itself from new ideas and intellectual influences.

It is clear, therefore, that social democracy lost its influence on the masses in central Europe the moment it changed from a radical party with social reform inscribed on its banner to a party supporting left-middle-class political trends. In addition, the war had destroyed many of the traditional behaviour patterns. People were no longer as willing as formerly to comply with laws and administrative decrees issued by the state institutions. The great social and economic problems created by the war and post-war conditions were in urgent need of a solution. The European working classes, hitherto supporters of the socialist parties, had hoped that social democratic participation in coalition governments would bring nearer the long-promised relief from their most pressing material worries. They had expected from social democracy not only a democratic constitution but also a speedy improvement in their social conditions. The situation in central Europe after the First World War called for a radical and energetic assault on these pressing social problems. But the masses were fobbed off with radical slogans and promises. That the socialists who were actually members of coalition governments had to fight for every concession not only earned them little prestige but, because of their readiness to compromise, even lost them the trust of broad strata of the lower-middle and working classes. On the other hand however, in spite of extensive support for the progressive middle-class groups, social democracy was not in a position to win the trust of the bourgeoisie, which sensed a constant threat in the Marxist programme.

The loss of prestige suffered by social democracy had devastating consequences for democracy as a form of government in central Europe. As we have mentioned, in many parts of central Europe the concepts of 'democracy' and 'social democracy' were almost identical. Social democracy used the language and phraseology of revolution, which meant that its supporters complacently swallowed the promises made by their leaders, and this enabled the communists and national socialists to argue that words unsupported by deeds were characteristic of democracy. On the other hand the property-owning classes and the middle class, still shaken by the Russian Revolution and the left-wing revolutionary uprisings in Germany, Austria and Hungary, believed that social democracy intended to put its Marxist programme into effect.

The conservatism of the socialist official strata, who refused to use modern propaganda methods and technical aids in electoral campaigns against fascists and communists, gave the non-political masses the impression that the socialists were old-fashioned, timid and mediocre men only concerned about their positions. It was a common experience to come across people who held the view – undoubtedly mistaken – that socialism had already been in operation in central Europe for some years and had proved that the best it could do was to provide the masses not with work but at most with a small amount of unemployment benefit. In such circumstances to point out that the present transitional stage was nevertheless a road leading to the future socialist state was not much help. This kind of argument was easily countered by a question such as: 'But aren't there socialist ministers in the government?'

The effects of social democratic policy on the democratic form of state in central Europe might therefore be summed up as follows:

1. The workers and small peasants abandoned their democratic idealism and loyalty to political democracy as their civic education was still in its infancy. The trade unions became increasingly big unemployment insurance institutions.
2. Among the masses this loss of idealism resulted in a further consolidation of middle-class ideals, including their traditional respect for authoritarian government.
3. Because of the uncertainty overshadowing foreign as well as internal and social policy, people came to feel more confidence in conservative and reactionary groups. This uncertainty weakened the traditional patterns of behaviour and aroused emotions which favoured violence and which, for that very reason, could find no outlet within the socialism movement because the bureaucratization of the party and its continued participation in coalition governments had altered the very structure of the movement. On the other hand the communists wanted to launch a revolutionary social programme at a time when the military were regaining political influence and the army was being strengthened, so that any thought of a revolution seemed unrealistic. The communist parties lacked any constructive and realistic policy. Instead of rallying to the defence of democracy against fascism they

joined forces with fascism against democracy. At the time of national socialism's triumphant advance the communists always regarded social democracy's 'social fascism' as its main enemy, to be undermined by a 'united front' policy. Yet at this time the Social Democratic Party made repeated attempts to form at least a limited defensive alliance with the German Communist Party against the menace of fascism. In the autumn of 1932, the Social Democratic leaders Breitscheid and Stampfer – with the full knowledge of the party executive – contacted the Soviet Embassy in Berlin on behalf of the Social Democratic Party, since they did not consider the German Communist Party to be a free agent but directly dependent on the Third International.[1] Yet, 'one day in January' (1933) they were informed by the First Secretary at the Soviet Embassy, Vinigradov, that Moscow was convinced that German fascism would seize power.[2]

Even after Hitler had in fact seized power, the German Communist Party continued to attack the Social Democrats. Fascism was seen as a necessary intermediate stage, preparing the way for the seizure of power by the proletariat. That is why Ulbricht described the Social Democratic Party's call for democracy as a 'reactionary Utopia' . . . 'The "democracy" demanded by the Social Democratic Party is a fascist form in the sense of "authoritarian democracy", as represented by Masaryk in Prague and Tardieu in Paris. . . . In the present circumstances the call for "democracy" is a reactionary Utopia. There is no road from fascism to democracy.'[3]

The Social Democratic Party and Fascism

The Social Democratic Party had accepted the idea that the conquest of the state could be achieved only by parliamentary methods, through the ballot box. In its struggle against Bismarck and William II the Social Democrats had come to think in a conservative-historical way and, with the help of historical materialism, to interpret all given political situations according to historical precedent. They had also adopted a formally legalistic attitude so that the party felt bound by the rules of parliamentary democracy whatever the the circumstances and regardless of their opponent's programme.[4] The fact that the Social Democratic Party and the Free Trade Unions had educated

[1] Cf. Erich Matthias, *Das Ende der Parteien 1933*, op. cit., p. 156.
[2] Friedrich Stampfer, *Erfahrungen und Erkenntnisse*, Cologne 1957, p. 264.
[3] Quoted by Carola Stern, *Ulbricht – Eine politische Biographie*, Cologne, Berlin 1963, p. 81.
[4] Cf. Part II, p. 234, note 3.

the workers to accept strict party discipline was a further factor strengthening the feeling of most people that they must abide by the constitution and the law.[1] Finally, because of the predominantly materialistic attitude on the part of the trade unions, members of the Social Democratic Party were rather vague about constitutional problems and questions of political power. Millions of workers believed that if they paid their membership subscriptions regularly, took the party paper and did as the party officials told them they had done everything that was necessary to bring about a better future and the 'inevitable victory of democratic socialism'. In connection with problems of political power many who believed firmly in democratic symbolism nevertheless rejected the constitutional state. This particular attitude was due to Marxist determinism, which holds that the liberal constitutional state is a middle-class creation which will be abolished by the irresistible rise of the working class. These two theses contained an inherent contradiction: consequently, when fascism arrived on the scene it found the drawbridge into the democratic fortress already down.

The Social Democrats looked on Hitlerism as an anti-humanist movement and, because it was directed against the Weimar Republic's achievements, also as a reactionary movement. But their mechanistic view of history prevented them from grasping that national-socialist fascism, in association with upper-middle-class military circles, represented a new and revolutionary political force which was able to break off historical 'progress' and which, in accordance with its ideology and structure, was far more removed from the politics of imperial Germany that it was itself. Thus until the end of the Weimar Republic social democracy believed that the historical size of the working-class movement and the ballot box, its old and trusty weapon, could undermine the Nazi position. Even the Social Democratic head of police, Grzezinski, one of the leading men who actively opposed Papen's *coup d'état* of July 20, 1932, honestly thought that the National Socialists' main aim was to influence the coming general election.[2]

The majority of workers and members of the Social Democratic Party accepted the course being followed by the party leadership as they could see no alternative. Furthermore, the tactic designed to effect the 'conquest of Parliament as a pre-condition for social reorganization' was only logical if the state was conceived of as an entity standing above the classes and as a juristic category. In order to make their parliamentary tactics credible, the Social Democratic

[1] Cf. Chap. II, Part Four.
[2] *Berliner Montagspost*, June 27, 1932, quoted by Matthias, *Das Ende der Parteien 1933*, op. cit., p. 136.

leaders had to accept and advocate this theory. Hegelian étatism had also made progress in the Social Democratic Party.

This positivist definition of the state was such that the organs of state were also included, with the result that the executive in particular was excluded from every sociological angle. Formal juristic, positivist thinking increasingly determined political practice, so that the question of the origins and forms of power was logically reduced to the problem of managing catalogues of legal formulae. This positivism stemmed from the social democratic philosophy of history. It is due to the fact that the proletarian revolution postulated by Marx, on the grounds of the increasing stabilization of capitalism, disappeared as a concrete aim. The retention of this goal meant that there grew up an ever-increasing discrepancy between ideological claim and ordinary political practice. This discrepancy became a permanent fact under the influence of a mechanistic philosophy of history which says that the imperial, feudal state is succeeded by the middle-class parliamentary state, from which the socialist state will automatically evolve. Thus political action as such became superfluous.

Legalism, together with the habit of automatic compliance with party directives, led to a growing passivity on the part of most party members. But the active members of the Social Democratic Party – who, seeing the rising tide of national socialism, formed the *Reichsbanner*, the *Eiserne Front* (Iron Front) and the *Hammerschaften* (groups of working-class activists) as well as the Socialist Youth Movement – found this attitude intolerable. The less active members and the Free Trade Unions succumbed increasingly to a paralysing fatalism. In the critical years of 1930–33 the difference of outlook between the activists and legalists in the party leadership proved extremely dangerous. Thus, for example, the editor of *Vorwärts*, Friedrich Stampfer, expressed the opinion that any resistance in Prussia to the coup on July 20, 1932, would have been crushed by the *Reichswehr*. But Julius Leber retorted that the decision of the Social Democratic government in Prussia to give in without offering any resistance was fatal since it had publicly exposed 'the whole inner weakness and indecisiveness of the Weimar Front'.[1] We now know that Goebbels, with his peculiarly devastating perspicacity, also clearly realized this. A note in his diary about July 20 says: 'You've only got to bare your teeth to the Reds and they lie down. The Social Democrats and the trade unions don't lift a finger . . . The Reds have missed their big chance. There won't be another.'[2]

[1] Cf. Julius Leber, *Ein Mann geht seinen Weg, Schriften, Reden, Briefe,* edited by his friends, Berlin, Frankfurt am Main 1952, p. 243.
[2] Joseph Goebbels, *Vom Kaiserhof zur Reichskanzlei,* Munich 1934, pp. 131 f.

One of the people largely responsible for this abject surrender was the Prussian Prime Minister, Otto Braun, who, as he himself said in his memoirs, had already departed from the scene before July 20.[1] Braun was of the opinion that the National Socialist victory in the earlier Prussian election had seriously shaken his position. Believing that the people's will must always be respected, even if it has been misled, Braun concluded that any sort of resistance by the Social Democratic Party would have amounted to usurpation of power in defiance of the arithmetical majority. Thus in the crucial situation of July 20 when the very meaning of democracy and the constitution were at stake, formal legalistic and democratic thinking could provide no valid guide for a responsible decision which would meet the extraordinary circumstances.[2] Even the undoubtedly capable and experienced Minister of the Interior, Severing, considered himself to be in no position to oppose the appointment of a *Reichskommissar* (commissioner imposed by the central government) in Prussia[3] – an attitude which can be explained by his earlier career as a Prussian civil servant. Acting strictly according to the law, the deposed Prussian government decided to lay a complaint before the *Staatsgerichtshof* (Supreme Court),[4] which, though it sided with the complaint, did not help the Social Democratic Party to obtain its rights.

Furthermore, the trade unions decided against calling a general strike. Only the enthusiastic but ill-equipped *Reichsbanner* units, which would have been able to use the arms at the disposal of the Prussian police in the event of resistance, urged the party leaders to take vigorous action. When the latter gave orders that all resistance was to cease, the militant elements in the *Reichsbanner* and the *Eiserne Front* still refused to give the cause up as lost. The idealism of the activists, however, was channelled into the mere organizing of mass meetings which confined themselves to making purely defensive and abstract speeches about the defence of the Republic.[5]

[1] Otto Braun, *Von Weimar zu Hitler*, New York 1940, p. 410.

[2] Matthias, op. cit., p. 130.

[3] Albert Grezezinski, *Im Kampf um die Deutsche Republik*, Federal Archives (typewritten manuscript in German of 'La Tragi-Comédie de la République', Paris 1934), p. 291, quoted by Matthias, op. cit., pp. 134 f. For Severing's own account, in which he defends his inaction, cf. Carl Severing, *Mein Lebensweg*, Vol. 2, Cologne 1950, pp. 341 f.

[4] The *Staatsgerichtshof* gave the following judgement: Under the powers conferred on him by Article 48 of the Constitution the President of the Republic 'could not dismiss provincial ministers, nor alter nor prejudice their relations with their provincial parliaments, nor exclude them or their representatives from the *Reichsrat* [Senate], nor forbid them the use of their constitutional right to speak in their capacity as representatives of their province in the *Reichstag*'. Cf. Arnold Brecht, *Vorspiel zum Schweigen*, Vienna 1948, pp. 97–8.

[5] Matthias, op. cit., pp. 145 f.

But the feverish military training carried on by the *Reichsbanner* and all attempts to raise arms were useless as the Social Democratic Party had now lost what had previously been its main support – the Prussian administration and the police. The party's lack of political vision was demonstrated by the fact that its energies were directed less against the Nazis than against the reactionary Papen regime. This failure on the part of the Social Democrats was, however, in keeping with their view of history. During their long years of political activity the party had acquired the habit of using mass rallies and the ballot as their chief weapons. They saw Papen as their main enemy because he came nearer to their stereotype for 'reaction' than the proletarian Hitler. Even after Hitler's seizure of power on January 30, 1933, the Social Democratic Party still did nothing more positive than to hold mass rallies.

The Reichstag elections of November 1932 had, meanwhile, shown that the people were looking for decisive action and were not satisfied with election meetings. While the number of National Social seats fell from 230 to 196, the German National People's Party seats rose from 39 to 54, since von Papen's coup of July 20 benefited this right-wing party; on the left, the workers reacted to the inaction of the Social Democratic Party, whose seats dropped from 133 to 121, by going over to the Communists, whose seats went up from 89 to 100. The drop in the electoral turn-out is an indication that people were tired of meetings and elections.

It is significant that even after Hitler's seizure of power the number of Social Democratic seats fell by one only in the 1933 March elections. This shows that henceforth, because of its passive policy, the party leadership was forced to rely solely on those workers who were organized in trade unions and its own party members, since even in November, despite the set-back suffered by the National Socialists, the rest of the electorate had transferred its allegiance. The wave of terror which broke over the German democrats after the Reichstag fire drove the party to take illegal action. German democracy began its *via dolorosa*.

Humanitarian considerations, which motivated the actions of men like Stampfer and Severing, had not been sufficient to maintain the life and the health of the party as a whole. Yet in the parliamentary vote on the Enabling Law, the party recovered its spirit, rejecting Hitler's dictatorship in an impressive and dignified denunciation fully in keeping with its great democratic traditions and its view of history. It was, in fact, a manifestation of the whole tragedy of the party's role as a champion of democracy in central Europe. The party leaders had proved that they were always prepared to defend their high principles and ideals and to die a martyr's death for them. The Social Democratic Party's humanitarian principles had prevented it from taking the road of civil war, had not allowed it to engage or sacrifice its members in other than traditional forms of political conflict. When the party chairman, Otto Wels, read out the formal rejection of the Enabling Law in the building, surrounded by SS men and Storm Troops, his hands were shaking. The Social Democratic leaders had been unable to spare the German people the great catastrophe but they had saved the honour of German democracy.

One cannot fully agree with the widely held opinion that the party leaders' passivity disheartened the democratic workers who had placed their confidence in the military attitude of the *Reichsbanner* and the Social Democratic Youth Movement. It is doubtful whether armed resistance would have made any difference. Even if the hypothesis of Hindenburg's strict belief in legality were true, it must be borne in mind that police action against the militant Social Democratic Party and militant trade unions after July 20, 1932, would have been a measure which was legal in the terms of the Weimar Constitution and would have had the support of a majority of the Reichstag. If such an action had been supported by the *Reichswehr*, the latter would undoubtedly also have been able to count on support from the *Stahlhelm*, and even more from the Storm Troops and SS terrorist organizations. On the other hand, however, there was always the chance that General Schleicher and the *Reichswehr* might have set up a military dictatorship, which had long been in the minds of conservative circles. This assumption, however, is disproved by the fact that at this period important groups of conservatives were already allied with the National Socialists through the Harzburg Front. In the opinion of the former Chancellor, Brüning, it seemed doubtful whether the *Reichswehr* would in fact intervene against the Prussian cabinet, as it all depended on whether or not General von Schleicher would withhold control of the Prussian police from the national socialists after their victory in the Prussian elections.[1]

---

[1] Heinrich Brüning, 'A Letter', in *Deutsche Rundschau*, edited by Rudolf Perchel, Berlin, 70th Year, Vol. 7, July 1947, pp. 13 ff. In connection with this remark Brüning points out an interesting fact which in all probability played a decisive part in the Nazi seizure of power. Brüning writes: 'I learned from Gregor Strasser that immediately after the Reichstag elections of July 1932 the National Socialists intended to introduce a motion under Article 59 of the Constitution to bring an accusation against the President before the *Staatsgerichtshof* and asking for Hindenburg's dismissal in accordance with Article 43.' Brüning believes they would have received the necessary two-thirds majority in the Reichstag with the help of the Communists and the Social Democrats (pp. 13 f.). It was – according to Brüning – fear of this which had eventually decided the elderly President to appoint Hitler Chancellor (p. 15).

## The Decline of Liberalism

As readers will remember, in the nineteenth century the liberal parties had stressed nationalism at the expense of liberalism. In the last decades of the century there came a split within the liberal movement. One section identified itself with the rising capitalist industrial development; another opted for a policy of social improvement among the working classes. Thus in Bohemia and Moravia one small section of the liberals joined the party of the so-called Realists, led by T. G. Masaryk, who later became President. These left-middle-class circles, who even before the war favoured co-operation with social democracy, came to power as a result of the 1918 revolution. As social democracy did not have enough outstanding leaders to fill all the posts in the government and administration the members of the left-middle-class groups, who were better trained and educated, gradually received many more posts than they would normally have been allotted on the basis of their actual strength. As a result capitalist industrial interest groups frequently tried to establish links with this left-middle-class section of the new social stratum which was slowly finding its way into positions in the government.

In other central European countries, too, these progressive middle-class groups belonged to the governing element which was now emerging as second most powerful after social democracy and, because of proportional representation, frequently formed coalitions with it. These liberal groups (such as Beneš' National Social Party in Czechoslovakia) were strengthened by the addition of progressive small farmer parties, for example, Wito's Polish Peasants' Party, the left wing of the Czechoslovak Agrarian Party which was under the influence of Hodža, and Maček's Croatian Peasant Party.

Liberal democracy was no more in a position to provide a long-term basis for the democratic state than social democracy was. The Weimar Constitution, which owed its existence mainly to liberals such as Preuss, Max Weber and Naumann, collapsed because the process of decay which had been attacking liberalism for some time finally came to a climax in the post-war period.

This development looks like a paradox, for the classic ideas of liberalism's democratic left wing – the free play of forces in all spheres of social, economic and political life – was only realized fully for the first time in the Weimar Republic. According to these ideas the state should remain restricted to its compromising function, in which – as this then also corresponded to the juristic norms – it had to renounce any executive intervention of its own in the social and economic issues. In accordance with the ideas about the functioning of the market mechanism, disturbances would have been righted by this itself.[1]

Yet political liberalism had lost its unity both in the sphere of ideas and of organization even in Bismarck's days, since the contradictions which had been emerging within liberalism since 1848 had reached the point where two parties became necessary one (the National Liberals) in which nationalism and a second (the Progressive Party) in which liberalism was the predominant element. The collapse of 1918 did not bring about the hoped-for unification of the liberal middle class into one united camp embracing all the trends. On the contrary the rift among liberals grew wider and three more or less sharply differentiated parties appeared to compete for 'middle-class votes' and seats. The emphasis which the National Liberal Party laid on nationalism and its readiness to compromise with monarchist and conservative circles, which made it one of Bismarck's strongest supporters, was continued after 1918 in the German People's Party (DVP).

The fact that William II's *Reich* had favoured a fusion of the aristocracy and the upper middle class eventually resulted in the assimilation of the political ideas of the big East Elbian landowners and those of the leaders of heavy industry, the political outcome being that heavy industry inclined to conservatism. This symbiosis found expression in 1918 in the German Nationalist Party (D.N.V.P.).

However, the liberal People's Party remained primarily the class-conscious champion of the economic interests of heavy industry, while the Nationalist Party represented predominantly agricultural interests and – before the rise of national socialism – the interests of the extreme right-wing groups among the populace as a whole.

On the other hand the German Democratic Party – later the nucleus and organizational framework of the State Party – kept alive the progressive element in German liberalism. In 1848 this wing of the liberals at first favoured revolution, later social reform and finally close co-operation with social democracy. The ways in which the various parties came to be founded were already a clear indication of a serious crisis in the structure of German liberalism which became more and more obvious in the course of the next fourteen years.[2]

Thus the central core of middle-class liberalism was stricken with

---

[1] Cf. in this connection in particular Kelsen's concept of the state *vis-à-vis* its opponents, who were inclined to authoritarianism.

[2] An account of how the middle-class parties came to be founded after Germany's collapse is given by Werner Liebe ('Die Deutschnationale Volkspartei 1918–1920') and Wolfgang Hartenstein ('Die Anfänge der Deutschen Volkspartie 1918–1924') in *Beiträge zur Geschichte des Parlamentarismus und der politischen Parteien*, Düsseldorf 1956 and 1962, Vols. 8 and 22.

paralysis at each successive election. No longer in a position to govern the state alone, the middle-class parties were constantly compelled to take part in a series of coalitions with the Social Democrats. This merely served to discredit them. They found it increasingly difficult to harmonize their ideological programme with their governmental practice. Their problem was, in fact, insoluble; for not to have joined in coalition governments would only have made their decline more rapid. Yet for the members of these parties – especially the People's Party[1] – partnership with the Social Democrats was tantamount to heresy. After Stresemann's death the German People's Party came to be completely dominated by its heavy industry wing. It lost its independence and was constrained tacitly to accept the anti-liberal and total dictatorship. Stresemann had probably been aware that he was an isolated figure in his own party.[2]

The development of the Democratic Party showed most clearly the inner logic about the decline of the liberal and democratic middle class. It fought to the end for the Weimar idea. Its political integrity was never in doubt – names such as Theodor Heuss, Reinhold Maier, Friedrich Meinecke, Ernst Lemmer and Theodor Wolff are sufficient evidence. But the middle class, always sceptical of the Weimar state, had been driven into radical, anti-democratic nationalism by inflation and economic crisis. Feelings of resentment against the Treaty of Versailles and reparations had a telling effect. Even parliamentarism no longer gave any feeling of security and the widespread anxiety psychosis brought on by social insecurity destroyed its basis. The free play of forces increasingly devoured its substance. The economically independent middle class, as a factor helping to carry the state, succumbed to the rival pressure of large capital. When the party was nearing its end a few leading personalities from the ranks of the German Democratic Party and the German People's Party endeavoured to form a united middle-class central group. Yet even in 1925 a similar idea had proved an illusion. The Liberal Union founded at the time – a union of the left wing of the People's Party and the 'right' wing of the Democratic Party – was a failure.

Five years later the German State Party[3] was to represent the *fait accompli* which was once again to halt the disintegration of middle-

---

[1] Unlike the German Democratic Party, Stresemann's German People's Party was founded as a direct challenge to the Social Democratic Party.

[2] Cf. Theodor Eschenburg, *Die improvisierte Demokratie*, Munich 1963, pp. 214 f.

[3] The German State Party originated in an association of leading figures in the Democratic Party, the *Volksnationale Reichsvereinigung* set up by the Young German Order, individual members of the People's Party and Christian Trade Unionists. The Democratic Party put its party organization at the disposal of the new body and was absorbed in it.

class liberalism already worn down by fascism. The party embodied the old idea of putting an equal 'middle' party between the Social Democrats and the 'Zentrum', but was unable to do so as it represented a social vacuum. Ernst Lemmer[1] accurately summed up the situation when he declared, in June 1932: 'Unless it has "an equivocal social basis",[2] no party can possibly win seats.' This went to the very heart of the reason why political liberalism failed: its 'social basis' had disappeared. The 'classical' concept of a 'pre-established harmony' was crushed between the advancing fronts of a rampant monopolistic capitalism and a class-conscious proletariat. The completely amorphous bourgeois-liberal class had long given its ideological allegiance to the cause of 'the unity of state and people'. It thereby hoped to save itself from the proletarianization which was threatening.

Thus the Reichstag which was elected in September 1930 remained incapable of functioning, not because of Communist, National Socialist and German Nationalist obstruction, but primarily because of the 'disintegration of the middle-class central core'.[3] Parliamentarism, which had at one time developed out of liberalism and had then been modelled in Weimar, had reached a state of open and irremediable crisis.

## The Role of the Zentrum Party

The great range of ideas which political Catholicism embraced in Germany was clearly shown by the fortunes of the Zentrum Party in the Weimar Republic. Names like Erzberger, Wirth, Marx, Brüning or Kaas are impressive examples of this. They represented a development which was in no way conditioned by any politico-sociological pattern of theological observance but by the hard social and political facts of the Weimar Republic. Nevertheless it would be wrong to speak of opportunism. Through the medium of the Zentrum Party and the Catholic trade unions, political Catholicism endeavoured to give effect to the ethical basis of its ideology by using the available constitutional institutions. For this reason no change of principle was involved when the Zentrum, against its originally declared intentions, started concrete negotiations with the National Socialists, on the one hand to escape the threat of political tutelage but also, on the other, to 'parliamentarize' or canalize the Hitler movement. The profounder ideology underlying Zentrum policy was expressed in the words used by a prominent politician: 'The Zentrum has a dual nature. Its unique-

---

[1] Ernst Lemmer was a member of Erhard's cabinet.
[2] Matthias, *Das Ende der Parteien 1933*, op. cit., p. 61.  [3] Ibid., p. 31.

ness is the expression of ideological thinking. The Zentrum Party's roots lie in the unchangeable principles of a religious-ethical philosophy of life in all its aspects. Yet, in a certain sense, it is free in the way it applies these principles to life's changeableness.'[1]

The first middle-class government in the Weimar Republic was led by the Zentrum politician Fehrenbach. He resigned because of a grave foreign policy crisis (caused by the Entente's unlimited demands for reparations) to be replaced by his party colleague Wirth. The 'right' saw to it that Wirth's government bore the odium associated with the policy of fulfilment, although he and Rathenau, together with their Social Democratic partners in the coalition, acted from national and democratic motives when they accepted the Entente's demand. In this way they hoped to demonstrate Germany's good will to the world and thus eventually to mitigate the burden of reparations. This assumption was a fallacy. The reparation claims became heavier, internal distress increased. In conjunction with the socialists, the Zentrum was determined to save democracy from *putsches*, foreign pressure and internal crisis, but it had to pay not only blood money – Erzberger and Wirth's Foreign Minister, Rathenau, were assassinated – but, in common with the Social Democratic Party, was saddled with the 'stab in the back' legend, so that the party's democratic wing was paralysed.

In 1923, when the conservative and reactionary forces had recovered their firm hold on their old positions of power in the army and the civil service, when heavy industry, freed from the latent threat of expropriation, again began to play the leading role in society, when the working class failed to develop any vital democratic counter-impulses, the Zentrum Party's conservative wing also gained the upper hand. The Christian trade unions broke off the alliance with Social Democracy and, under Stegerwald, tended to favour ideas of a corporate society. This became clear later in the theoretical concept and government practice of M. Brüning and reflected perfectly the actual situation, which was characterized by the decay of parliamentarism. Thus even at the end of August 1928 the Zentrum leader, Kaas, was speaking of the 'longing for leaders to lead us along the thorny path ahead'.[2] In November 1932 he said: 'We do not want to relapse into parliamentarism; we want to give the President moral and political support for an authoritarian government inspired and instructed by him.'[3]

Shortly afterwards came the first negotiations with the National Socialist Party. They had no effect on parliament but nevertheless

---

[1] Joos, Chairman of the Catholic Workers' Unions, 1928 (quoted by Rudolf Morsey in *Das Ende der Parteien 1933*, Düsseldorf 1960, p. 283).
[2] Quoted by Morsey, op. cit., p. 290.　　　　　　　　　　　　　　　[3] Ibid., p. 330.

showed that the Zentrum alone among the Weimar parties possessed enough inner force to act.

The fact that a year later the Zentrum, as a political party, had to accept the same fate as the other political parties is due to its misjudgement of the Nazi movement. The end of political Catholicism in Germany is, however, essentially different from that of liberalism, (Social Democratic) socialism or even communism. The Zentrum broke up as a party when Hitler concluded a concordat with the Papal Curia. Had the Curia as well as the Zentrum allowed themselves to be taken in by Hitler? The concordat meant the peaceful integration of the Catholic section of the nation in the new state. If it had not been concluded – or at least not concluded so soon after Hitler's seizure of power – the Zentrum, in certain circumstances, would have become a significant element of resistance. For had it not been for the readiness of the Catholic section of the nation to submit to Hitler, the latter would have had to precipitate an open conflict, the outcome of which he could not possibly have predicted.

The Weimar Republic to a very considerable extent owed its vitality to the existence of the Zentrum Party. Its name reflected its position within the general party structure. For ten years it was impossible to form a government without the Zentrum. This unique position was due not so much to the party's outstanding personalities – these were also to be found in other parties – but rather to a constant and ever-faithful electorate which embraced *all* social strata, but whose votes were not swayed by emotions coloured by day-to-day events or ideologies and slogans geared to economics and political theories.

Consequently the Zentrum displayed a considerable amount of political flexibility. Erzberger must be given the credit for the Zentrum becoming a 'constitutional' party; and the change which lay at the basis of the Zentrum's policy became apparent in Kaas. In contrast to the constitutional trend represented by people like Brüning and Adenauer, Kaas, and Papen too, embodied the older, conservative church tendency.

The Zentrum's flexibility and adaptability – the expression of an extraordinary ability to sense the political climate – came to grief, however, on the rocks of the Nazi movement. Like social democracy, the Zentrum had evolved as a party in the nineteenth century; the ethical and Christian basis of its faith in constitutionalism was, however, unable to cope with national socialism's Machiavellian revolutionary tactics and camouflage manoeuvring. That is why it took Hitler's pseudo-legality seriously, whereas it mistrusted Papen. This trust in Hitler's promises, as well as fear of the future on the part of a large number of civil servants who owed their jobs to the Zentrum, are reasons why the Zentrum faction in the Reichstag agreed unanimously to the Enabling Law. Finally, Hitler's conclusion of a concordat with the Holy See was a masterpiece of Machiavellian tactics. In spite of Brüning's warning, Kaas, Stegerwald and the other influential Zentrum leaders believed the interests of Catholicism in Germany would be guaranteed. The concordat made the Zentrum Party superfluous and in fact it dissolved itself soon afterwards. Its self-sacrifice, however, could not save it and its members from the mounting Nazi terror.

Although Brüning is known to have been one of those who, in the Zentrum's inner councils, opposed Kaas' policy of political self-denial, even in 1947 he attempted to justify the party's approval of the Enabling Law:

'To sum up: rejection of the Enabling Law would in itself have achieved nothing, since the decree of February 28, after the Communists had already been banned, would have remained in force and would have been used to dissolve the anti-Nazi parties. These parties had to choose between two definite and unalterable alternatives: either to vote for the Enabling Law and rely on a subsequent change in President Hindenburg's attitude, or to reject the Law and to live under the direct threat of personal arrest and the dissolution of the party, together with the charge pending against President Hindenburg and Hitler's election to the office of President.'[1]

## The End of Austria's Infant Democracy

If there was one state outside Germany in 1918 with real parliamentary and constitutional traditions and by nature suited to parliamentary democracy, that state was Austria. Austria had far greater right than Czechoslovakia to look back to her parliamentary tradition, which went back to the pre-war period. The classical architecture of the Parliament buildings in Vienna symbolized the spirit of ancient

[1] Brüning, op. cit., p. 20. K. G. Repgen has tried to deny that the voluntary dissolution of the Zentrum Party, after it had voted for the Enabling Law, and the conclusion of the concordat were in any way connected. The arguments which he put forward do not, however, help his case; on the contrary, they tend to confirm the suspicion that the Vatican, acting at the time on the advice of Cardinal Pacelli, hoped to negotiate cultural and political concessions from Hitler in return for the dissolution of the Zentrum. That a man of Pacelli's intellectual stature, who knew Germany's political spectrum far better than most men, was ready to take this step poses something of a riddle: for, according to Repgen's testimony, there are good sources for believing 'that in the summer of 1933 Pacelli entertained far fewer false hopes or illusions about the dangers of Hitler's rule and its probable duration than most contemporary politicians in the East or West'. (K. G. Repgen, address at the main session of the 'Community of the Catholic Men of Germany', on April 21, 1964, in Fulda.)

Athens, to which multilingual, open-minded, frank, tolerant and art-loving Vienna was spiritually akin. In the Christian Social Party and social democracy the Republic possessed a ready-made capital of democratic traditions rich in promise for the future. Austria now had no dissatisfied linguistic minorities and was a country of one religion. She had more land than her six and a half million inhabitants needed, possessed judges and civil servants who had acquired solid experience and traditions in a great empire, and also had an industrious working and peasant class accustomed to a modest style of life.

On the other hand the country's former ruling circles were clearly suffering from the psychological shock caused by the collapse of the Habsburg empire and the destructive Treaty of St Germain. The sudden transformation of a major empire into a minor state, the painful *capitis diminutio* of Vienna as the foremost cultural centre in central and eastern Europe was bound to shatter self-confidence and lead to a general collapse of values. The Austrian Republic felt the need of some form of association because it was cut off from its former economic hinterland and immediately exposed to conditions of severe privation and hardship, so that its economic survival at first seemed doubtful. But, as later became evident, these doubts were not justified and were merely the consequence of upheaval and emotional shock. However, Austria found herself barred from entering into any form of association. In a period which saw the triumph of the idea of self-determination, Austria was forbidden to form a union with Germany. On the other hand the country became a target of the resentment of her Slav neighbours, Czechoslovakia and Yugoslavia.

After the upheaval Vienna became the depository of pensioned aristocrats, penniless officers and unemployed civil servants from the days of the Empire, whose resentment of the new order boded ill for the future. Added to this was the general impoverishment of the middle class as a result of the inflation. Although the inflation in Austria was not as extreme as in Germany, it nevertheless came harder on the Austrian middle class – harder because jobs were much more difficult to come by. After the restoration of the currency the number of unemployed civil servants and officers rose to hundreds of thousands. Of decisive importance in these circumstances was the fact that the Austrian civil service had for a great many years been largely pan-German, that is German nationalist, at heart, although the traditions of Josephinism had been conducive to a centralistic yet liberal spirit.[1]

[1] A. Wandruszka, 'Österreichs politische Struktur – Die Entwicklung der Parteien und politischen Bewegegungen', in *Geschichte der Republik Österreich*, edited by H. Benedikt, Munich 1954, pp. 382 ff.

In accordance with this spirit the Pan-German People's Party, whose main representative in the government was Schober, sacrificed the interests of its members, who were civil servants, and of its own programme, in which union with Germany was a fundamental issue, to the general good of the state. 'The ideas of the "conservative revolution" flooding in from Germany, the ideas of Spengler, Moeller van der Bruck, the myths and traditions of Langemarck, the *Freikorps*, and the Upper Silesian and Ruhr fighting were associated in Austria with the neo-romantic, corporative, anti-democratic and anti-liberal ideas of the Othmar Spann school as well as with the traditions of the Carinthian and Burgenland fighting.'[1]

As a result Austrian pan-German circles became extremists, to the eventual benefit of first the *Heimwehr* and then the National Socialists. Yet Austrian patriotism, which stemmed from the old rivalry with Prussia, was compatible with such sentiments. Apart from the small group of extreme pro-Prussians, of the Schönerer and K. H. Wolff school, the people particularly concerned were those in whom the old idea of a large Austrian empire lived on, who refused to accept the 'Balkanization' of Austria, and therefore turned to the idea of union with Germany – with a Germany in which Austria, strengthened by the South German elements, could have become an equal partner with Prussia.

In Austria even more than Germany, moral standards degenerated in many spheres of life, especially in trade and banking. The Austrian currency had hardly been stabilized before the French franc crashed: speculation on the Vienna exchange[2] led to financial scandals and bank failures. Many Jews were engaged in banking. Non-emancipated Galician Jews who had emigrated to Austria were prominent in many other fields. And so, in the eyes of many middle-class people and peasants, Jews were held responsible for obvious post-war phenomena, especially profiteering and speculation. Anti-Semitism was further increased by the fundamental changes which had taken place in the nation's social structure, resulting in the impoverishment of the intelligentsia.[3] The middle class could not forgive the Socialists for having advocated and to some extent raised the living standards of the manual workers. The fact that not only some of the millionaires but also some of the Socialist leaders were Jews inspired an inordinate anti-Semitism in the lower middle class.

[1] Ibid., p. 391.

[2] Charmatz, *Vom Kaiserreich zur Republik*, Vienna 1947, p. 161.

[3] According to Siegfried Strakosch's statistics, a coachman in Vienna earned one thousand three hundred times as much, while a university professor had to be satisfied with two hundred and fourteen, a Hofrat one hundred and twenty-four, an assistant doctor a hundred times as much.' Charmatz, op. cit., p. 163.

The Austrian Socialists have been held responsible for many of the things which contributed to the failure of Austrian democracy. The Socialists undoubtedly bear some of the responsibility, but it is very doubtful whether they can be said to bear it all. The Austrian Republic was the common creation of the Socialists and the Christian Socialists. In view of the communist threat – the Bavarian and Hungarian Soviet Republics were set up in 1919 – the Socialists proved to be true champions of democratic constitutionalism. But in their case the gap between Marxist revolutionary practice was even greater than it was in German social democracy. On the one hand the Social Democratic Party of old Austria had been a democratic centre of orthodox Marxism; their post-war leader, Otto Bauer, saw himself as the trustee of the heritage of Viktor Adler and Friedrich Engels. On the other hand, in Austria, unlike neighbouring Germany, there were no serious communist uprisings to be put down by force.

In 1918 the Socialists could easily have carried through a social revolution, but deliberately refrained from doing so. Consequently the apologetic of conservative, reactionary circles, who used the doctrinaire revolutionary programme of the Socialists' left wing as a pretext for taking violent measures against the Socialist Party and to abolish democracy, was based on inadequate evidence. Yet whenever the Socialists' militant wing took up arms – as in 1927 and 1934 – it was to defend democracy and not to attack in order to extend socialist influence at the expense of other parties. This purely defensive attitude, which was also due to the socialist view of history, was, however, as in Germany, not calculated to inspire the masses to rise in defence of democracy. The Austrian socialists, who left the government coalition as early as 1920 and thus lost their influence on the army and the police, must be charged with showing even less understanding than the German socialists of the basic conditions governing the exercise of power in the state.

The republican constitution drafted by Kelsen was accepted in Vienna in 1920. The strong position which Parliament acquired because of the parties' lack of preparation was seen by Gordon Shepherd as one of the main reasons for Austria's later relapse into authoritarianism. Shepherd thinks the makers of the constitution should have given the office of President greater powers.[1]

This is a very doubtful hypothesis, as events in the Weimar Republic showed. Shepherd takes as his starting point the experience of the British Commonwealth, in which the peoples were gradually educated to take political responsibility. He overlooks the fact that in Austria this policy had been initiated before 1914. If Austria had not

[1] Gordon Shepherd, *Die Österreichische Odysee*, Vienna 1958, p. 93.

adopted proportional representation, if under a relative majority voting system there had been stable Socialist and Christian Socialist governments based on solid majorities in the Austrian parliament, then the German nationalist pan-Germans, the fascist *Heimwehr* and the National Socialists would never have acquired an importance incommensurate with their character as splinter parties.

But having adopted proportional representation, Austria could not escape the inevitable coalition governments. In addition, both the big parties, the Christian Socialists and the Social Democrats, must be criticized for failing to understand the basic principles of democracy. They lacked mutual trust, the fundamental consensus which is expressed in the Anglo-Saxon phrase "We have agreed that we shall agree", as well as an understanding of the constructive role of the opposition which – and this is typical of an evolving democracy – was confused with implacable hostility. Renner believes the unbridgeable gap which separated the two big parties at the time to be the reason why democracy failed in Austria and that their mutual antagonism was largely due to the mentality of the two party leaders, Monsignor Seipel and Otto Bauer.[1]

Dr Seipel considered the Social Democrats to be enemies of the state on principle, and he therefore steered a sharply anti-socialist course. The Socialists' anti-Church propaganda made a lasting impression on him as a Catholic priest. His mistake was that he always judged the Socialists by their most radical statements.[2] In the opposite camp was Otto Bauer, an equally doctrinaire and dogmatic Marxist theologian.[3] He rejected bolshevist dictatorship; but he also considered the parliamentary system to be merely a transitional stage.

The mutual respect which these two priests of diametrically opposed religions showed for one another's ascetic and uncompromising nature typifies the country's authoritarian tradition and the resultant misunderstanding of the true nature of democracy. Seipel's contempt for moderate and liberal-minded men like Renner was a logical outcome of this fundamental and tragic mistake.

It would, however, be incorrect to ascribe the antagonism between Austria's two major parties to their leaders' rigidity alone. The very marked social difference between town and country was also a fundamental factor in the Austrian situation. The deeply religious peasants in the conservative, nationalist-minded Alpine provinces were strongly opposed to the red workers in free-thinking, internationalist Vienna.

---

[1] Karl Renner, *Österreich von der Ersten zur Zweiten Republik*, Vol. 2, Vienna 1953.

[2] A. Wandruszka, op. cit., pp. 324 ff.

[3] Cf. Karl Renner, op. cit., p. 42: cf. A. Wandruszka, op. cit., pp. 443 ff.

These farmers were also annoyed that socialist legislation – for instance decrees issued in 1921 and 1922 and affecting agricultural labourers – extended the application of social policy and social insurance to the countryside, thus raising agricultural labourers' wages. Townspeople and countryfolk rarely met and consequently they both judged one another in accordance with deeply ingrained prejudices.

Another major factor affecting Austrian internal and foreign policy was the existence of armed units, the Republican *Schutzbund* associated with the Social Democrats and the right-wing *Heimwehr*. The *Heimwehr* had been formed as a result of the frontier fighting with Yugoslavia and Hungary, and also in connection with the Escherich organization active in Bavaria at the time of the political murders and Hitler's Munich *putsch*.[1] Chancellor Seipel, who inclined more and more to authoritarian ideas as he grew older, gave it his support. But the *Heimwehr* was not an old-style Austrian movement and it soon began to think along the lines of Italian fascism and national socialism. The *Heimwehr* was under particularly strong Nazi influence in Styria and Carinthia. It acquired a very able chief of staff with the appointment of Major Pabst, well known from the German Kapp *putsch*. It soon became a haven for adventurers and soldiers of fortune like Starhemberg, Fey, Steidtle and the Styrian lawyer Pfriemer.

The *Heimwehr*, which was split up into various groups, did not become a decisive political factor until after 1927. The main feature about the movement was its militant 'anti-Marxism', which made its inner contradictions largely irrelevant. It was first financed by aristocratic circles and by industry, later mainly by Mussolini. Its recruits came from almost every sector of the population except the socialist working class. In 1930, with the Korneuburg Oath, it publicly professed fascism. Yet although it won only eight seats in the elections that year it was able to play a decisive role as the Christian Socialists needed these eight seats to form a government. The middle-class coalition government never identified itself with the *Heimwehr*'s aims and ideas but it always sought to co-operate with it. It could never bring itself to disarm it, although the Ministry of Justice fire in 1927 had clearly demonstrated the dangers which attached to its existence.

In post-war Austria it soon became clear that the socialists' opponents were banking on their defensive attitude. At the Austrian Socialist Party Congress in Linz (1926) Otto Bauer had defeated the radical demands of the Max Adler wing. The 'dictatorship of the proletariat' was only envisaged as a defensive measure against fascism,

---

[1] Cf. Franz Winkler, *Die Diktatur in Österreich*, Zurich, Leipzig 1935, p. 24.

which the socialists wrongly regarded as a radical form of capitalism.[1]

Neither Bauer nor the other leaders of the Austrian Socialist Party reckoned that the masses' political dynamism might be influenced not only by the Viennese workers but also by the Viennese mob. Since 1848 – when the Austrian Minister of War, Count Latour, had been hanged from a lamp post – the Viennese mob had been notorious for a Jacobinism which quickly flared up into violence. Until February 1934 their passions inclined to socialism: after Hitler's entry into Vienna the mob went along with the Nazi terror. In 1927 there had been a clash between the *Heimwehr* and the socialists, in which a number of socialists had been killed. The jury in the 'Schattendorf trial' acquitted the *Heimwehr* members accused of murder, whereupon the enraged mob set fire to the Ministry of Justice. It was clear that in spite of making honest efforts the socialist leaders were unable to make their followers observe the law. This gave Seipel an opportunity to use the armed forces of the state to suppress the workers' demonstrations, regardless of casualties.

The socialists' failure in 1928 became the leitmotive for Austria's future development. But the decisive crisis of Austrian democracy did not come until 1932. By then the whole European climate was conducive to an authoritarian solution. Totalitarian and authoritarian states on Austria's frontiers were exerting a growing influence on her. To the constant influence of fascist Italy and authoritarian Hungary was added the powerful attraction of the National Socialist Party in neighbouring Bavaria and Sudeten German nationalism in Czechoslovakia, which had common roots with Austrian pan-Germanism. The rising tide of German nationalism in particular meant that the liberals among the pan-Germans succumbed increasingly to national socialist influences. For understandable reasons, the Czechoslovak model was rejected by the majority of the Austrians and Hungarians, even though it was democratic.

Seipel's intervention in favour of the *Heimwehr* movement made this an important factor after the fire at the Ministry of Justice. The movement acted as a pressure group for the Christian Socialists against social democracy. Among middle-class circles everywhere the cry went up for a 'Big Brother' who, like Mussolini, would 'bring order' and 'teach the workers to work again'.

Othmar Spann and his doctrine of the 'Ständestaat' (corporative state) which was directed primarily against social democracy, was a live influence in the universities. With Christian Socialists his ideas were associated with class and corporative concept which grew up

[1] A. Wandruszka, op. cit., p. 448.

in the nineteenth century and which became even more popular after the publication of the papal encyclical *Quadragesimo anno*.[1]

In 1932, when the differences between the two big parties became increasingly marked, Dr Engelbert Dollfuss became head of the Austrian government. He was the illegitimate son of a wealthy peasant's daughter and at first wanted to go into the Church. Dollfuss was a scholar of only moderate ability who distinguished himself as a lieutenant in the Tyrolese Kaiserschützen in the war and afterwards went to Vienna University. There he joined the German Catholic Student Club, Franco-Bavaria, and was elected its chairman. At the Catholic Students' Congress in Regensburg in 1920 he joined the Cistercian father Professor Schlögel in calling for the introduction of the Aryan paragraph and supporting the German nationalist movement. Another student who later became a Christian Socialist, Ernst Karl Winter, advocated, however, racial tolerance and the old, traditional monarchist idea.[2]

Monarchism, tolerance and democracy had never been incompatible in Austria. Even in 1926 the Christian Socialists had professed their faith in the parliamentary system, but the banking scandals at the outbreak of the economic crisis had done much to discredit the democratic wing. This was one reason why Seipel was successful in the authoritarian course on which he had embarked. Renner points out that this was the period when, in all parties, including the Socialists, the members of the younger generation – 'who had received their all-important youthful impressions in the trenches and were more familiar with the rules of war than the complex rules of parliamentary procedure'[3] – were coming to the fore. Dollfuss was one of them. It has not been proved that he took up office already determined in his mind to solve the question of the Socialists by authoritarian means. Nevertheless he was just the type of man to impose such a solution from ideological and personal reasons – a short man's need to compensate for his lack of height.

Deutsch describes how, on May 8, 1932, he had travelled with Dollfuss from Klagenfurt to Vienna and how Dollfuss had told him he had just been offered the Austrian Chancellorship. Dollfuss asked his companion whether the Social Democrats would vote for his government. Deutsch replied that he thought this would be impossible as parliamentary rules precluded the Austrian Socialist Party from voting for a government immediately.[4] (Bauer had refused to form

[1] K. Renner, op. cit., p. 121.
[2] Gordon Shepherd, *Engelbert Dollfus*, Vienna, Graz, Cologne 1961, pp. 47 f.
[3] Ibid., p. 118.
[4] Julius Deutsch, op. cit., p. 185.

a coalition with Seipel the year before.) Dollfuss replied that he did not want a shaky government of "muddlers" but a *strong* one. If the Socialists were not prepared to respond to his government declaration by at least abstaining in the vote he would form a government with the *Heimwehr*.[1]

Yet Dollfuss made efforts to win the co-operation not only of the Socialists but also of the pan-Germans. After his attempt to form a presidential cabinet on the Papen pattern had come to naught because of the President's objection, the pan-Germans' rigid attitude forced him to call on the *Heimwehr* to form a parliamentary majority.[2] But when he put the adventurer Major Fey in charge of the entire security service Dollfuss made a move of disastrous consequences. It brought the Trojan horse of fascism into the cabinet. Dollfuss was in a difficult position. His coalition government had a majority of only one vote in parliament. The new Chancellor was personally inclined to authoritarianism, but could see no way of putting this into practice. Chance gave him an opportunity. The coalition parliamentary majority of one was threatened by Renner's resignation as president of the National Assembly – which gave the Social Democratic Party an extra vote. The Christian Socialist vice-president refused to take Renner's place. When the third president, the pan-German Dr Straffner, convened the Assembly for March 15, Dollfuss declared this inadmissible and tried to keep the deputies out of parliament by calling in the police.

The result of the election of March 5 in Germany, by which Hitler's dictatorship had been confirmed, had undoubtedly encouraged him. Until the promulgation of his new corporate type of constitution Dollfuss governed exclusively by emergency decree, on the pretext of the war-time Enabling Law which went back to the imperial period. Once again social democracy's defensive attitude proved crippling. Like the German Social Democratic Party at the time when the Braun-Severing government in Prussia was dismissed, the Austrian Socialist Party allowed itself to be beaten by refusing to call a general strike in view of the virtual dismissal of the National Assembly by Dollfuss. Dollfuss and the *Heimwehr* not incorrectly interpreted the Socialist Party's restraint as *weakness* and now had the *Schutzbund* dissolved and its leaders arrested.[3] On the other hand, Dollfuss was compelled to act because of Austria's weak position abroad. To counter the possibility of intervention in Austria's internal affairs by

[1] Ibid., p. 118.
[2] Walter Goldinger, 'Der geschichtliche Ablauf der Ereignisse in Österreich 1918–1945' in *Geschichte der Republik Österreich*, op. cit., p. 196.
[3] Walter Goldinger, *Geschichte der Republik Österreich*, Vienna 1962, p. 189.

the Third Reich he sought and obtained the support of fascist Italy. Mussolini used the Hirtenberg incident – in which socialist workers had held up a shipment of arms destined for Hungary – to demand from Dollfuss the dissolution of all political parties.

Events were now to show that Dollfuss's political stature had not risen above that of the former student leader. His attitude to national socialism had been determined by his experience in German student clubs. If it had been possible to co-operate with the nationalists in those clubs, why could not the nationalist forces be incorporated in the Austrian state? It would be possible to retain the leadership and the initiative, Dollfuss concluded, if, secured by the support of fascist Italy, links were forged with the German national socialists and at the same time the ties with the democratic groups, such as Social Democracy and the *Landbund*, were not broken off. State affairs were, in fact, conducted in his cabinet as they would have been in a student club in the years between the wars. Dollfuss negotiated with the national socialists (*inter alia* to secure for himself a certain freedom of manoeuvre *vis-à-vis* Mussolini); Fey and Starhemberg negotiated with others. Altogether, between September 1933 and February 1934, Goldinger reports, half a dozen attempts were made to reach an agreement with the national socialists.[1] These efforts were, however, foredoomed to failure; for Hitler, as was soon to be demonstrated, had a clear idea about Austria's future; and it excluded any kind of agreement.

Nor was Dollfuss a match for Mussolini's dynamic and unscrupulous policy. We now know that Mussolini demanded the destruction of the Social Democratic Party and its auxiliary organizations in return for a further guarantee of Austrian independence *vis-à-vis* Germany. His demands were put forcibly when the Italian Under-Secretary of State, Suvich, visited Vienna in January 1934. What Mussolini finally demanded was the dissolution of all parties and the establishment of a fascist state on a corporative basis like Italy.

The socialists' response to this challenge was again purely defensive. Bauer's 'declaration of war' on the Dollfuss government at the Austrian Socialist Party Congress in October 1933 did not threaten violent socialist resistance because of the dissolution of their defence organization, the *Schutzbund*, but only in the event of the 'imposition of a constitution, the appointment of a government commissioner for Vienna', the main socialist stronghold, 'dissolution of the Social Democratic Party, abolition of the free trade unions'.[2]

---

[1] Goldinger, der geschichtliche Ablauf der Ereignisse in Österreich 1918–1945, op. cit., p. 210.
[2] Ibid., p. 212.

The socialists' right wing adopted an even more defensive position and tried to ally itself with the Dollfuss government to combat national socialism. Even the orthodox Marxist Otto Bauer was ready to agree to corporative regulations in the constitutional changes which Dollfuss was contemplating.[1] In view of the government's negative attitude, hardened by the pressure from Mussolini, it was not surprising that a certain radical tendency now made its appearance in the socialist camp. Dollfuss behaved just as stubbornly to his own party's democratic wing, which urged him to reach an agreement. The socialists now knew that Dollfuss was determined to eliminate them in the immediate future.

Open conflict finally broke out when a leader of the Linz *Schutzbund* refused to allow the party headquarters to be searched. There were armed clashes in Vienna and other towns between the *Heimwehr* and members of the *Republikanische Schutzbund*. The general strike now called by the Socialist Party was only partially observed. The members of the *Schutzbund* heroically defended the blocks of workers' flats in the suburbs of Vienna, which came under artillery fire from the army. The Social Democratic Party was dissolved. Catholic circles now admit that socialist resistance was morally justified; thus Alexander Spitzmüller, a leading figure from the Habsburg period, says that as Social Democracy's rebellion was against an illegal government it was fully in accord with the teachings of Thomas Aquinas.[2]

Austrian democracy was decisively beaten. The cause of that defeat was the poor support which was given to the call for a general strike and inadequate organization on the part of the *Schutzbund*. In spite of the valiant resistance put up by the militant wing of the Austrian Social Democratic Party it soon became clear that the attitude of the leadership was too defensive and quite unable to rouse the freedom-loving supporters of the Social Democrats to embark on the popular rising which was needed in the circumstances. Otto Bauer regarded resistance as hopeless from the start. Even a short-lived victory for Social Democracy in Vienna, he thought, would be illusory as it would soon be reversed by Hitler and Mussolini. Bauer fled to Czechoslovakia. Too late, he realized that his refusal to go along with the Christian Socialists was a mistake. Nor did the democratic wing of the Christian Socialist Party any longer have a part to play in the *Vaterländische Front* (Patriotic Front) now founded by Dollfuss. The struggle for power now starting in Austria was fought out between fascist authoritarian groups. Only a few months later

[1] Ibid., p. 212.
[2] Alexander Spitzmüller, '*Und hat auch Ursach' es zu lieben.*' Vienna 1955, p. 387.

(after the assassination of Dollfuss by the National Socialist SS Standarte) the ambitious Major Fey of the Vienna *Heimwehr*, who had played a major role in crushing Austrian social democracy, played a more than doubtful role in the no-man's-land between Nazism and *Heimwehr*.

Finally, it must be acknowledged that soon after the birth of the Austrian Republic it became obvious that, in spite of the outwardly favourable conditions, democratic ideas and the democratic way of life in Austria lacked the broad basis necessary for the undisturbed growth of parliamentary democracy. This is all the more surprising since in Austria, unlike the Weimar Republic, the radical parties were not all that strong. Nevertheless the social and ideological basis of democracy in Austria proved to be even narrower than in Germany. Democratic traditions and patterns of thought were confined to relatively small intellectual and party circles. As the parliament of imperial days had been made up of a host of linguistically hetero-geneous parties – the embodiment of the tensions between the aggres-sive and intolerant nationalism of the many races comprising Austria-Hungary – an attitude inimical to the spirit of parliamentarism and scornful of compromise had become part and parcel of the climate of the representative assembly. In the Republic, in spite of the linguistic homogeneity which now characterized the country, this attitude survived in the notion of parties as hostile camps. That is proved by the terms used – 'Christian social', 'socialist' and 'nationalist' camp. Austria also lacked a Catholic party of marked constitutional tradi-tions such as the Zentrum in Germany.

From the start the Christian social movement also included cur-rents which supported the rights of the worker as conceived by pre-reformation Catholicism, but sought to realize these rights in the anti-democratic sense by neo-romantic ideas of the corporative state,[1] whereas in German Catholicism, thanks to the work of the *Volksverein*, the corporative idea was absorbed into modern democratic theory. Mayor Lueger, who before the First World War had supported the democratic trend within the Christian Socialist Party, was aware at the end of his life that the interests of the owning classes had gradu-ally come to the fore in this party. In as much as broad, hitherto unpolitical groups took part in politics after the war – groups which under the monarchy had left the country's leadership to the royal house – a politically intolerant, because untrained, spirit came to prevail in all the parties. This spirit was transformed into one of bitterness by the traumatic experience of the loss of the empire, the

[1] August M. Knoll, 'Karl von Vogelsang und der Ständegedanke', in *Die soziale Frage und der Katholizismus*', pbd. By Görres-Gesellschaft, Paderborn 1931.

social decline of the upper and middle classes and the general economic distress.

In these circumstances no genuine feeling of confidence or trust could develop between the two major parties in Austria. Introduction of the relative majority franchise would probably have given one or the other an absolute majority and therefore created the basis for stable government. But even then it is doubtful whether the parliamentary majority would have tolerated the minority. The minority would never have felt certain that the majority government would not have prevented them from winning control of parliament in a legal and legitimate manner. Consequently Austria's evolution was also bedevilled by factors typical of infant democracies. Her chances of survival were bound to appear slim because of her hopeless geopolitical position, wedged in as she was between the two strongholds of fascism. In the context of the inter-state relationships prevailing in Europe during the inter-war years the Christian socialists and the socialists would need to have given evidence of a very different relationship and sense of mutual trust for the Western Powers to feel morally obliged to defend the country against fascism and national socialism. As, however, Fascism was not only on Austria's frontiers but had its supporters inside Austria herself, in the army, the police forces and the civil service, even in two of the three government parties, quite apart from the *Heimwehr* and the National Socialists, and as these supporters accused the third party, the Socialists, of communist intentions, the 'appeasers' in the West were easily able to convince their peoples that it was not worth taking action against the fascist powers on behalf of Austria.

That was later to prove one of the great miscalculations. The end of Austrian democracy turned out to be not only the end of central-European democracy but also a mortal threat to continental democracy. Austria's cultural heritage was an integral part of Europe as a whole: its destruction was therefore bound to affect the whole of Europe. Czechoslovakia realized too late that the death of Austrian democracy meant that her own fate was sealed and that those Western Powers which had not been ready to back Austria would not defend Czechoslovakia, despite all the existing agreements. What happened in Austria between 1934 and 1938 appeared like a judgement on the peacemakers of St Germain. Had these realized in 1918 the need for a strong, democratic Danubian federation, had Austria never been allowed to become a catspaw of the fascist powers, national socialism would never have been able to obtain from Austria the inspiration and support which was to allow it to challenge the world.

## PART FOUR

### Democracy and Totalitarian Pseudo-Legality

Is the democratic state legally and morally obliged to grant totalitarian movements the same rights and liberties as democratic parties? Is the democratic executive obliged to wait until totalitarian parties or their members break the law, or is ideological support for a totalitarian party programme sufficient grounds for action? In the event of a deliberate attempt by totalitarian groups to stage a coup, must there be an overt act before proceedings can be started or is it enough for the government to have received reliable reports about the plan?

The new young democracies of central Europe were faced time and time again with questions such as these. In principle, the right of free expression of opinion and free assembly is sacred to democracy. Can a democratic state refuse to allow its citizens to hold posts in the law or other state services because they hold totalitarian views? A democracy in which there is no freedom to teach or to learn is inconceivable. In the truly constitutional state no film producer, no newspaper proprietor or theatre owner may be prevented from carrying on his work or be arrested for his political opinions. At the root of these questions – whose full implications were not understood by the post-war democracies and which therefore could not be correctly answered – lay a misconception about the rights of self-defence on which the constitutional state itself must insist if it is to survive attack by its enemies. Again, the means which it is entitled to use, at the appropriate juncture, for its own preservation without forfeiting its right to exist depend on a proper understanding of the idea of tolerance.

### Origin and Evolution of Political Tolerance

Political tolerance has developed from religious tolerance.[1] This was first demanded in England by the Puritans, for example John Milton. One of the pioneers of this idea was John Locke. Eventually, due to the impact of the American and French Revolutions, this principle was incorporated in most liberal-democratic constitutions. The radical application of the principle in the constitutions of the democratic states after the First World War, however, was due to the

[1] Johannes Kühn, *Toleranz und Offenbarung*, Leipzig 1923.

influence of John Stuart Mill. The absolute freedom, bordering on anarchy,[1, 2] which was demanded by an absolute tolerance failed to be victorious in the United States or Britain, but it was accepted as part of the constitutions of the states on the European continent. This unqualified principle of liberty had become part and parcel of European thought during the nineteenth century, but in the end it was responsible for striking the weapons of self-defence out of the hands of democratic governments.

Another of Mill's views was embodied in the central European constitutions after the First World War. This is that the preparation of treasonable action is not criminal as long as no overt attempt to overthrow the government takes place. This principle was accepted by almost all the codes of criminal law and procedure. It gave totalitarian movements and parties the opportunity openly to prepare insurrection under the very eyes of the government and the law. Many enemies of democracy in the judiciary and the civil service could, under the aegis of Mill's principles, pretend to act democratically and yet, by applying these principles, make their own contribution to the overthrow of democracy. These principles compelled the democratic executive organs to tolerate totalitarian assemblies and rallies. The fascists, therefore, exploiting the concept of legality, were able to prepare their *coup d'état* under the eyes of democratic governments, since these believed they could act only if open revolt broke out.

Thus groups of uniformed fascists could march through the streets shouting their slogans and challenging the majority of democratic citizens. The police of the democratic state found itself compelled to protect these disturbers of the public peace. This gave the impression that the totalitarian parties enjoyed the especial favour of the government. Thus the totalitarian groups forced the authorities to protect them against the majority of the people.

Infringement of liberty need not necessarily come from government. The national socialists, like the communists, organized their

[1] J. S. Mill, *On Liberty*, Oxford 1946, pp. 12 ff.

[2] 'If all mankind were of one opinion, and only one person were of the contrary opinion, mankind would be no more justified in silencing that one person, than he, if he had the power, would be justified in silencing mankind.' (Ibid., p. 14) 'Firstly, if any opinion is compelled to silence, that opinion may, for aught we can certainly know, be true. To deny this is to assume our own infallibility. Secondly, though the silenced opinion be an error, it may, and very commonly does, contain a portion of the truth; and since the general or prevailing opinion on any subject is rarely or never the whole truth, it is only by the collision of adverse opinions that the remainder of the truth has any chance of being supplied. Thirdly, even if the received opinion be not only true, but the whole truth; unless it suffered to be, and actually is, vigorously and earnestly contested, it will, by most of those who receive it, be held in the manner of a prejudice, with little comprehension or feeling of its rational grounds.' (Ibid., p. 46.)

meetings in such a way that it was physically dangerous, if not impossible, to express adverse viewpoints in them, since Storm Troops, SS men and members of the *Rotfront* regularly assaulted people holding differing opinions. Yet many convinced liberal civil servants and police officers held the view that, in spite of their intolerant and subversive methods, the followers of totalitarian parties must themselves be protected from demonstrations of disapproval by their democratic opponents. Thinking confined to strict observance of the letter of the law which was traditional in the constitutional and party state was responsible for this attitude of mind.

Furthermore, the idea of tolerance was given a new turn by developments in the United States after the First World War. After the Russian Revolution of 1917 communist agitators also appeared on the scene in the United States; people began to fear a communist revolution on the Russian model. Yet the Supreme Court, under the direction of Judge Brandeis, insisted on drawing a sharp distinction between justified protection of democracy from intolerant movements on the one hand and unjustified violations of freedom of opinion, speech and thought on the other. In his view democracy should curtail freedom of speech and assembly only if democratic government is in actual danger.

In one of his judgements, Whatney *v.* California, Brandeis expressed the following opinions:

'Fear of serious injury alone cannot justify the suppression of free speech and assembly. At one time men feared witches and burned women as the result, and it is the function of speech to free men from the bondages of these and other irrational fears. To justify suppression of free speech there must be reasonable ground to fear that serious evil will result, if and whilst it continues to be permitted. There must be reasonable ground to believe that the danger apprehended is imminent. There must be serious grounds for believing that the evil to be prevented is a serious one.

'Every denunciation of existing laws tends in some measure to increase the probability that there will be a violation of it. Condonation of a breach enhances the probability. Expression of approval adds to it. Propagation of the criminal state of mind by teaching syndicalism increases it. Advocacy of law-breaking heightens it still further. Even advocacy of violation, however reprehensible morally, is not a justification for denying free speech where the advocacy falls short of incitement, as there is nothing to indicate that the advocacy would be immediately acted on.

'The extent of the difference between advocacy and incitement, between preparation and attempt, between assembling and conspiracy, must be borne in mind. In order to support a finding of clear and present danger, it must be shown either that immediate serious violence was to be expected or was advocated, or that the past conduct furnished reason to believe that such advocacy was then contemplated. Those who won our independence by revolution were not cowards. They had no fear of political change. They did not exact order at the cost of liberty. To courageous, self-reliant men, with confidence in the power of free and fearless reasoning, applied through the processes of popular government, no danger flowing from speech can be deemed clear and present unless the incidence of the evil apprehended is so imminent, that it may fall before there is opportunity for full discussion. If there be time to expose the menace by open discussion and to avert it by a process of education, the remedy to be applied is greater freedom of speech and not enforced silence. Only an emergency can justify repression. Such must be the rule if authority is to be reconciled with freedom. Such in my opinion is the order of the constitution. It is, therefore, always open to Americans to challenge a law, abrogating free speech and assembly by showing that there was no emergency justifying it.'[1]

Brandeis' judgement was undoubtedly proper in American conditions. Modern propaganda methods, however, make it impossible for a democratic government today to warn the public in time. The danger either occurs too quickly or the cumbersome machinery of the constitutional state based on law can be worn down by the well-organized groups familiar with subversive techniques. Therefore when the central European democracies took steps to defend themselves against the techniques of totalitarianism they should not have drawn any dividing line between preparation and attempt. Conspiracy and assembly were often one and the same. The democracies lacked the premises on which to base the struggle against the fascist method of gradual erosion of the constitution. To draw a dividing line between propaganda and incitement proved to be difficult.

The views which Walter Lippmann formulated in the *New York Herald Tribune* on February 2, 1935, did not go as far as those of Judge Brandeis:

'A free nation can tolerate much and ordinarily toleration is the best defence. It can tolerate feeble communist and feeble fascist parties as long as it is certain they have no hope of success. But once they

[1] Louis D. Brandeis, *Essays*, edited by F. Frankfurter, New Haven, Yale 1932, p. 109.

cease to be debating societies they become formidable organizations for action, they present a challenge which it is suicidal to ignore.'

But a totalitarian party is not a debating society, not even if it temporarily assumes this form in circumstances where any open profession of its political doctrines would do it harm. Likewise, totalitarian movements at first always make use of the outward form of a political party. In the first place this form makes it easier to recruit converts from democratic parties and groups. Highly emotional speeches and processions flaunting banners designed to produce a mass psychological effect serve the same purpose. Thus totalitarian movements in central Europe were able to develop as long as they did not patently violate the law. Not only individual adherents of fascism, but also the parties themselves and their militant formations were allowed freedom of conscience, toleration and equality before the law. As long as these were not guilty of treason or committed specific actions of violence as defined by the criminal law of the countries concerned, as, for example, a breach of the peace, the democrats believed they had no defence against them. To ban a totalitarian party demonstration and to allow one by a democratic party was held to be undemocratic.

By virtue of modern techniques of influencing the masses and modern organization this practice was to prove suicidal for the central European democracies. The concentration of modern weapons in the hands of a few and the means of influencing the masses had transformed the situation fundamentally. Thus by tolerating national socialism Weimar democracy endangered not only its own existence but also world peace. The inadequate defence of the democratic state allowed fascism to achieve its aim 'legally'. A democracy which waits until high treason had been committed before attacking condemns itself to death by suicide since a totalitarian movement usually has a three-fold structure. On the one hand the official party claims for itself all the democratic liberties – freedom of speech, assembly and freedom of the press. Alongside this is a second organization which prepares the party élite for future government tasks. This organization, however, begins its activity under a cloak of secrecy and infiltrates its members into the key positions in the state. Finally, there is also a third, para-military organization. In Germany this had evolved out of the *Freikorps*, in the Sudetenland out of harmless gymnastic clubs, in Austria out of the *Bürgerwehren* (home guard). The democratic executive organs remained blind to this danger and justified their position by apologetic references to legal technicalities – for example, if a party's 'private army' behaves 'in a disciplined manner' when marching in the street the police have no grounds for intervention.

## Hitler's Technique of 'Legal' Rise to Power

It is clear from *Mein Kampf* that Hitler had repudiated the parliamentary system even in his youth. Although he admired the British parliament as an institution, he was disgusted by the typical features of an initial democracy which came to mark the Austrian parliament, which he considered to be 'unworthy of the great model'.[1] In a democracy, Hitler notes, the standard is always set by a majority of ignorant and incompetent people, of 'cowardly' and 'irresponsible' parliamentarians. The majority principle must be rejected because it sins '*against* the aristocratic fundamentals of nature' and ruins a man's character, compelling him to take up a position on 'questions which do not concern him.' Hitler was not only an implacable enemy of the parliamentary system but of democracy as such. But being a son of the proletariat himself he was well aware that he was living in a mass age. Mussolini's success in Italy had shown that a small minority of resolute, well-armed and unscrupulous fighters could seize power in the state. The Russian Revolution was a further proof of this truth.

The Munich *putsch* in November 1923 indicated Hitler's 'contempt for legal order and state authority.'[2] But its failure also convinced Hitler that he must change his methods. Even before 1923 some of his followers had urged him to contest parliamentary elections;[3] but it was only when the armed might of the state, in the form of the *Reichswehr*, was turned against him that Hitler came to realize that he could achieve his goal only by pretending to be loyal to the constitution. 'It was only the legality attaching to his Chancellorship which could spare him, before any constructive work was started, from first having to combat all other political forces as opposition and experience the ordeal of constant troubles with the *Reichswehr*.'[4] Therefore, when the party was refounded in 1925, Hitler decided that 'instead of working to achieve power by an armed coup we shall enter the Reichstag, for the greater annoyance of Catholic and

[1] Cf. also, for the rest of this account, Adolf Hitler, *Mein Kampf*, Munich 1936, Vol. I, pp. 82, 84, 92, 94, 96 and 99.

[2] Hans Frank, *Im Angesicht des Galgens*, Munich-Gräfelfing 1953, p. 44.

[3] Berlin Documents Centre, Hauptarchiv der NSDAP, Munich, Ordner 106.

[4] Henry Picker, *Hitlers Tischgespräche im Führerhauptquartier 1941/42*, Bonn 1951, p. 428.

Marxist deputies. If out-voting them takes longer than out-shooting them, at least the result will be guaranteed by their own Constitution.'[1]

Between the years 1925 and 1933 Hitler brought the technique of pseudo-legality to a fine art. His collaborator, Hans Frank, himself a lawyer, gave evidence that during those years Hitler developed an anti-state sentiment, in the sense of a resentment of the rule of law, without letting slip the slightest hint of his real feelings except by his 'refusal [a refusal which was carried to the point of idiosyncrasy] to make use of legal language in any formal order and his repudiation of its exponents, the lawyers'. Yet, Frank observed, during the years of struggle, Hitler made great use of 'the independent jurisdiction which was guaranteed and also really practised in the Republic'. Here we see already an aspect of pseudo-legality which was later to become even more pronounced. He attempted, successfully, to deceive his opponents; he always stressed the legality of his movement and in the Leipzig trial of the *Reichswehr* officers accused of Nazi activities, he swore a formal oath attesting its legality. It was only later that Hitler told Rauschning where he had learned his deceitful tactics. It was primarily from the Jesuits.[2] From the 'Protocols of the Elders of Zion' – which Hitler knew to be a forgery – he had learned 'political intrigue, the technique of conspiracy, revolutionary subversion, prevarication, deception, organization';[3] from the freemasons 'the principle of an order with its inviolable oath of obedience and secrecy and its esoteric doctrine revealed in stages through symbols'.[4] He admitted on many occasions that he was familiar with Lenin's theory of revolution. He considered Machiavelli's *The Prince* to be a book worth study by every statesman.

Yet Hitler cannot be accused of having concealed his ultimate aim. He left no doubts about his intention to impose a dictatorship. In the court which examined him as a witness in the trial of the Nazi *Reichswehr* officers in 1930 Hitler declared: 'I can assure you, if the National Socialist movement and its spirit triumphs, we shall set up a National Socialist court, the revolution of 1918 will be revenged and heads will roll.'[5]

Hitler's experiences in 1923 had convinced him that he must deceive the circles near President von Hindenburg and the *Reichswehr* about his aims. The honour which the court showed to him when he appeared as a witness was a sure sign that he was on the right road. How can a mass parliamentary party abolish parliamentarism? asked

---

[1] Quoted by Alan Bullock, *Hitler, A Study in Tyranny*, Penguin Books, 1962, p. 130.
[2] Rauschning, *Gespräche mit Hitler*, op. cit., p. 225.
[3] Ibid., p. 227.          [4] Ibid.
[5] *Frankfurter Zeitung*, September 26, 1930.

a leading conservative.[1] Even a constitutional lawyer like Koellreuther believed 'the temperamental utterances of public speakers and political writers' were no proof of the 'revolutionary aims declared in the programme of the German National Socialist Party . . .'[2] The Party historian, Fabricius, declared outright: 'It was a question of seizing positions of power within democracy and that meant first winning parliamentary seats, particularly in the Reichstag . . .'[3] Hitler hoped the crisis would become more severe and that there would be more elections. 'Along with repeated protestations of legality the Nazi speakers always threatened that terror would be let loose should they assume power.'[4] Göring, for example, declared on December 5, 1931, in the Berlin Sportpalast that the abolition of democracy would be the first legal act. But after he had become President of the Reichstag he stressed the policy of legality 'to inspire confidence in the President'.

Goebbels' statements are particularly frank and unequivocal. He was the first to introduce the theme which has, ever since, become a stock argument for supporters of totalitarianism: 'If democracy allowed us to use democratic methods when we were the opposition, this was right and proper under a democratic system. We National Socialists, however, have never maintained that we are representing a democratic point of view. On the contrary, we have openly declared that we used democratic methods only to gain power and that once we had it we would ruthlessly deny our opponents all those chances we had been granted when we were in opposition.'[5] And again: 'if our opponents had been cleverer, considering that political weapons were so unevenly distributed, they could undoubtedly have found ways and opportunities to make our success impossible.'[6] As deputies, the leaders of the Nazi Party enjoyed all the benefits of immunity, expenses and free tickets.[7] Thus they could not be detained by the police, could say much more than the ordinary citizen and have the cost of their activities paid for by the enemy into the bargain.

After the National Socialists had entered the Reichstag as a strong faction in 1930, the aim of their legality policy immediately became obvious. Their prime object was to obstruct the Reichstag, discredit it by creating uproar, riot and violence, reduce government stability by

---

[1] Count Kuno Westarp, *Am Grabe der Parteienherrschaft*, Berlin 1932, p. 105.

[2] Otto Koellreuther, *Der Sinn der Reichstagswahlen vom 14. September 1930 und die Aufgaben der deutschen Staatslehre*, Tübingen 1930, p. 34.

[3] Hans Fabricius, *Geschichte der Nationalsozialistischen Bewegung*, op. cit., p. 30.

[4] Frick and Gregor Strasser, for example, spoke in this vein; quoted in Wilhelm Högner, *Die verratene Republik*, Munich 1958, pp. 240 and 317.

[5] Joseph Goebbels, *Der Angriff aus der Kampfzeit*, Munich 1935, p. 61.

[6] Joseph Goebbels, *Wesen und Gestalt des Nationalsozialismus*, Berlin 1934, p. 13.

[7] Ibid., pp. 13 f.

constant motions of no-confidence[1] and continually call for new elections. By such machinations they wanted to create a crisis and a revolutionary situation.

To a growing extent both the totalitarian parties, the Nazis and the Communists, worked hand in hand. This teamwork proved especially effective in votes of no-confidence in the Reichstag. The fact that the two parties together formed a majority seemed to justify the authoritarian policy pursued by Hindenburg and Papen.

Although a totalitarian movement is not a party in the democratic sense, both the National Socialists and the Communists retained the word 'party'. In totalitarian movements, unlike democratic parties, the recruiting of members[2] is regulated by strict directives and restrictions laid down by the party leadership. As we have already mentioned, the Social Democrats in Germany had built up their party as a militant organization of the working-class movement. But the National Socialists who wanted to seize power had an absolute need of at least the silent support of a section of the working class. Had Hitler called his party *Kampfbund* or 'Movement' – which is what he would have liked – the recruiting of workers would have been more difficult. By pretending that his 'party' was both national and socialist he was able to split the working class and attract a section of it to himself. Hitler openly confessed that he had largely adopted the organizational forms and methods of the Social Democratic Party. He said, to quote his own words: 'All I had to do was to take over these methods and adapt them to our purpose . . .'[3] Workers' gymnastic clubs, political cells in industrial concerns, mass marches, propaganda deliberately written for the mass mentality – all these new methods of political warfare derived basically from the Marxists.

Here Hitler put his finger on a weak point in Social Democratic policy. Those methods which Social Democracy had developed in the nineteenth and at the beginning of the twentieth century could be employed equally well against as for democracy. Hitler declared: "I had only to develop logically what Social Democracy repeatedly failed in because of its attempt to realize its revolution within the framework of democracy. National Socialism is what Marxism

---

[1] In 1930 a total of 27 motions of no-confidence were tabled; 11 by the Communist Party, 9 by the German National People's Party, 5 by the National Socialist Party, 2 by the Social Democratic Party. In 1932 there were 23 such motions; 8 by the German National People's Party, 7 by the National Socialist Party, 6 by the Communist Party, 1 by the German National People's Party and 1 by the Social Democratic Party. Cf. Bundesarchiv R 43/12682 and Joseph Goebbels, *Vom Kaiserhof zur Reichskanzlei*, op. cit., p. 101.

[2] Cf. also Max Weber, *Wirtschaft und Gesellschaft*, Tübingen 1925, p. 167.

[3] Rauschning, *Gespräche mit Hitler*, op. cit., p. 174.

might have been if it could have broken its absurd and artificial ties with a democratic order.'[1] This way of thinking, this technique and these tactics by the National Socialists makes the Weimar Republic's tolerance of fascism seem very difficult to understand.

Although the Weimar coalition parties' freedom of action was hampered in respect of the National Socialists, they cannot be absolved of the charge of having been extraordinarily gullible about National Socialism and of not having shown enough political vigour. One example is Hitler's premature release from arrest after the 1923 *putsch*; and the fact that neither the German nor the Bavarian government made use of their right to deport Hitler to his native Austria as an undesirable alien must be put down against Weimar.

The weapon of pseudo-legality was later developed *even further* by the communists. If Hitler was right in saying that National Socialism learned from Marxism, it is even truer to say that after the Second World War the Leninist technique, which was a *further development* of that employed by the Nazis, benefited the Stalinists. The National Socialists had once more provided drastic and striking proof of the vital importance of gaining control of the key positions in the Ministry of the Interior, the police and the army as well as the press for the seizure of power. This experience was extremely useful to the communists for carrying out their coup in Czechoslovakia.

After the Second World War, therefore, the communists were able to draw on the experience of two different but similar sources. They could resort either to the Leninist *coup d'état* technique or the Nazi technique which, in central Europe, had proved more successful than their own. What exactly was this? It was, for example, a question of how to transform a private army into an auxiliary police force, how to seize power in stages, how to cripple parliament by continually raising demands for new elections and so on. The amalgamation of organizational work, propaganda, secret police and intelligence, which first appeared in embryo under Lenin but was developed into a regular system under Stalin, had been perfected to meet the conditions of a modern industrial state. The communists took over this important weapon at this pitch of perfection.

These statements show that the degree of liberty which a democracy can safely allow totalitarian movements must suit the social and political structure of society. Liberties which can safely be granted to fascist groups in England or the United States were bound to prove extremely dangerous for democracy in central Europe. Yet the democracies always faced a dilemma. It would have been contrary to their very nature to persecute people for their opinions. On the

[1] Ibid., p. 175.

other hand, however, there was a clear threat to their own existence if they began criminal proceedings against totalitarian parties only after an open violation of the law. The right solution, the *via media*, was discovered, too late, by the British Home Office, for example, during the Second World War. In Britain, Sir Oswald Mosley and his followers were prosecuted the moment a situation arose in which they might become dangerous. Again, after the overthrow of fascism in Italy the Allies only authorized the existence of those parties which had no Nazi or fascist programme. Such a solution does, of course, mean that a definite limitation is set to a people's right to choose its own form of government.

It is therefore evident that the practical synthesis of Hegelian etatism and Mill's radical theory of liberty was partly responsible for the toleration of the intolerant fascists. On the one hand, Hegelian etatism contributed the centralist form of the nation-state, so that for broad groups of the population these concepts assumed the role of a normative-transcendental imperative, which isolated every sectional body or minority as being harmful. On the other hand Mill's liberalism demanded of the state the unconditional, unquestioned toleration of all movements and groups, even of those ideas which were a threat to the existing state. This produced a polarity of tyranny and anarchy in which the two elements supplemented one another and which, therefore, was bound to result in the disintegration of law and order.

That a tyranny can occur only in a monarchy, that is, under the rule of one man, is, says Locke, a common illusion. It is equally possible in an oligarchy or in a democracy. Tyranny consists in the unlawful suppression by an arbitrary, unlawful power.[1] That is to say: where law ends tyranny begins. Whoever misuses state power for issuing unlawful orders to the subjects of that state automatically ceases to be a lawful official or minister. Everyone may oppose such an unlawful use of power, which is directed against man's basic rights; for a government which abuses its powers should be dissolved. If, however, the legislators attempted to destroy the people's rights and degrade men by the arbitrary exercise of force, they put themselves in a state of war with the people which is thereby released from its obligation to obey. If the legislators violate this basic social law and either seize for themselves or hand over to a *third* party absolute power over life, liberty and property they are, says Locke, breaking trust with the people. The same is true of the executive. Whoever himself attempts to corrupt the electors by promises or threats in

[1] John Locke, *Second Treatise on Civil Government*, Oxford University Press (The World's Classics), p. 167.

order to establish his absolute power puts himself into a state of war with the people.

From this we may draw the following conclusions for our study:

1. In the terms of Locke's democratic theory of the state the Enabling Law whereby the Reichstag invested absolute power in the Hitler cabinet in 1933 was invalid. Those deputies who voted for it, in so far as they were aware of the consequences of their action, became guilty of robbing the people of their liberty.
2. A democratic state is under no obligation to tolerate authoritarian or totalitarian parties which either in their programmes or, in the sense of a *reservatio mentalis*, aim at absolute rule, nor to accord them equality with democratic parties before the law.
3. A democratic executive which tolerates such movements incurs part of the guilt of enslaving the people.
4. Tolerance of totalitarian movements therefore appears intolerable because, by stating their aims, these have placed themselves outside the law and therefore cannot claim its protection.
5. These totalitarian movements are in a state of war with society, which may therefore combat them with all the means permitted in war. According to Locke any man who seeks to overthrow constitutional and law-based states is guilty of the greatest crime of which a man is capable. He becomes the common enemy of all mankind and must therefore be treated as such.[1]

It is therefore an irrelevance whether totalitarian movements seek to attain their ends with illegal means, that is by the open exercise of force or by undermining the instruments of state power, or 'pseudo-legally', that is, by political parties and the use of methods of influencing opinion. What is and remains decisive is the purpose behind their activity, namely to seize power in the state for themselves in order to curtail and abolish basic human rights.

Looked at from this point of view the Weimar Republic must bear part of the guilt because it tolerated totalitarian and authoritarian movements. It must nevertheless be recognized that there were mitigating circumstances. Firstly, from the start the Republic disposed of inadequate means of enforcement. Secondly, it was insufficiently supported by its judges and its officials. Thirdly, it was falsely associated with the stigma of Germany's defeat; and finally economic difficulties robbed it of the prestige and strength it needed to meet the challenge of totalitarian and authoritarian movements.

[1] Ibid.

# CHAPTER VII

# Deception and Structural Destruction as Totalitarian Techniques

## PART ONE
### *Deliberate Manipulation of Conflicts*

Both Germany and Italy were finally unified in the second half of the nineteenth century when, in other parts of Europe, the extreme and virulent form of nationalism had abated. The overseas expansion of the older imperial powers was still incomplete but the morality of colonialism was already under fire. People's consciences had to be mollified by the idea of the 'white man's burden' of spreading civilization and Christianity among the savage heathen. In Europe itself was finally ended the era of territorial expansion by force of arms which was the common practice in the age of the cabinet wars of the seventeenth and eighteenth centuries. In France nationalism had been moulded ideologically by Rousseau's formula of the general will and had evolved into authoritarianism of the Jacobin and Bonapartist type; and those nations of Europe which subsequently proved susceptible to nationalist ideas were not spared this phase of development either.[1]

We have already pointed out that the national unification of Germany and Italy inspired similar aspirations in the smaller nationalities of central and south-east Europe. These aspirations coincided in time with industrialization and the development of modern

[1] Max Scheler, *Schriften zur Soziologie und Weltanschauungslehre*, Das Nationale im Denken Frankreichs, Bern and Munich 1963, pp. 131–57. Scheler reiterates Acton's analysis, mentioned in Chapter II, in these words: 'It is the particular tragedy of this people [the French] that its passionate urge for freedom time and time again throws up a supreme, centralized power which it puts into authority and which brings it a new form of slavery. . . . The Gallic concept of liberty is ignorant of both liberty of the intellectual individual and that liberty of a member in a community which has grown up naturally and historically, according to which the state is neither a contract providing the maximum guarantee for every act of selfishness nor an artificial will imposed from above, but only the highest organization of the separate units of the people's will flowing in it' (p. 44).

communications which made it essential to have larger territorial units than those provided by national and linguistic frontiers. From the outset, therefore, the national aspirations of the European peoples were confined within narrow limits. Nevertheless Germany and Italy endeavoured to expand by founding colonial empires and extending their influence in south-east Europe. In doing so they came up against sharp opposition from the older colonial powers.

Before the First World War political leadership in Germany and Italy was in the hands of those who had effected national unification. Now in Germany, no more than forty-eight years after her unification, the princely houses whose independence had made this unification possible were dispossessed of their thrones.

After the memory that these circles were responsible for the military defeat in the First World War had partly faded and partly been replaced by the 'stab in the back' legend, it became evident that the people were emotionally attached to their monarchist past. Furthermore, Weimar democracy was compelled to rely on an army and a bureaucracy whose roots still went back to the monarchy. In these circles the aristocracy still set the tone. And here we must distinguish between two structurally different forms of the nobility – a fact important for a proper analysis of post-war developments.

As we have explained, the older function of the aristocracy is that of an intermediate power, independent of the monarch, whose authority in relation to him is either co-ordinated with or, occasionally, even superior to him. It owes its power and position not to the individual ruler but to its role as a former pillar of the medieval feudal order. In this function the nobility acts as the representative of the nation *vis-à-vis* the ruler (like the Bohemian nobility in the seventeenth century and the Prussian in the eighteenth) or as the spokesman of regional interests, like the Fronde in France. The more recent function performed by the nobility arises out of the strengthening of the absolute and sovereign monarchy. The result was that the nobility lost something of its supremacy and became a state-servant class which supported the monarchy by providing the bulk of the diplomats, officers and civil servants, and jealously fought to protect its exclusive domain against competition from the middle-class intelligentsia.

As peasant emancipation in the eighteenth and nineteenth centuries reduced the aristocracy's economic basis, it became increasingly dependent on the monarchy and had to identify itself increasingly with the latter's interests. In the process the dividing line between the aristocracy's two functions was never clearly distinguished in central Europe. Thus in Hungary the nobility's older, anti-monarchist attitude

predominated. The more large estates there were and the less industrialization there was, the more influential the nobility remained.
After the 1918 Revolution, the nobility found its economic as well as
its professional and social position impaired. In countries where land
reform remained a dead letter (as in Germany), the nobility retained
its economic basis, as, for instance, in the Junker estates east of the
Elbe, from where the fight for the restoration of the monarchy seemed
possible. Large sections of the military nobility had been absorbed
into the *Reichswehr*'s officer corps. But although the German nobility
had been damaged and robbed of its pre-eminence in society, it remained basically sound and resilient. Thus the German military
nobility took a leading and active part in the only German resistance
movement, the one which culminated in the attempt to assassinate
Hitler on July 20, 1944.

The Austrian nobility played a very different role after 1918. Its
economic basis – large estates – lay principally in the Succession
States of the former Austro-Hungarian monarchy, especially in
Czechoslovakia and Yugoslavia, and it therefore disappeared. The
break-up of the Danube monarchy completely destroyed the position
and status of the Austrian military and official nobility. The importance of this process in the rise of national socialism in Austria has
been insufficiently appreciated. Thus in 1929 General Glaise-
Horstenau wrote bitterly: 'How Masaryk imagines what is left of
Austria can perform its mission as "Ostreich" and Palacký's ideas can
be continued is not explained in his proposals.'[1] 'And that', wrote this
future representative of the National Socialists in the Austrian
cabinet, 'is why Austrians look in particular to the west and north-west,
where the sources of their strength flowed . . . An overwhelming
majority always spoke in favour of "returning home" to the Reich.'
As a rule Austrian National Socialists came from a higher social
milieu than German Nazis. The fact that several of the most notorious
extermination experts were of Austrian origin is an indication of the
extent of the moral collapse engulfing an ancient community of
peoples as a result of the sudden catastrophe of 1918.

The growing interdependence of economic and social units after
the First World War called for greater integration between the national
administrations of the states of continental Europe. The outcome was
increasing international interrelationship, a development which the
former ruling classes and their supporters – who still regarded a
return to power as a real possibility – felt to be a threat to themselves.
Particularly in those states for which the war had ended in defeat,
many members of the former ruling classes who had managed

[1] Von Glaise-Horstenau, op. cit., pp. 489 f.

to hang on to important key positions looked on international co-operation as a pioneer act unmatched by any corresponding effort on the part of the Western Powers. They were therefore always inclined to represent the international forces active in society as a danger to national security.

The devaluation suffered by the old, positive symbols of the monarchy and the authoritarian state as result of the revolution also loosened family ties, with a reduction in parental, especially paternal authority. Traditional values were also affected by the fact that, in the eyes of youth, the older generation had shown themselves to be incompetent and unadaptable.[1] The deterioration in social conditions gave rise to a psychological projection, especially among the middle classes, with the result that the latter began to see their own fate as that of the nation.[2] Lasswell holds the view that nationalism and anti-Semitism met the emotional needs of the lower middle class in particular.[3] The period after the First World War, when the lower-middle-class masses were faced with economic and political events which they did not understand, is similar to the sixteenth and seventeenth centuries. Just as the helplessness and alarm felt then by members of a social order which had remained static in the face of social and economic changes found an outlet in the persecution of people for black magic and witchcraft, so now, after 1918, the Jews became a substitute for the failing attraction of the institutionalized religion of a secularized social order.[4]

The religious factor is also important. The Russian revolution and the subsequent communist risings had destroyed the firm hold of Christian beliefs and Christian ethics without providing new ethical principles to take their place. In point of fact the middle classes in the countries of central Europe did not really accept those aspects of the socialist programmes which were inspired by the freethinkers; nevertheless it made a decided impact on their basic religious outlook. This came out clearly later in the anti-Christian attitude of the SS. The anti-religious trend in socialism was, in any case, much more pronounced among the working class. That was to prove particularly dangerous because the experience of war had already destroyed many of the traditional elements of social and moral resistance.

The weakening of religious belief among the middle classes also showed up in other ways. A typical feature of the period between the wars was the spread of superstition, false prophets, astrologers,

---

[1] Erich Fromm, *Die Furcht vor der Freiheit*, op. cit., pp. 210 f.
[2] Ibid., p. 211.
[3] Harold D. Lasswell, *Politik und Moral*, Stuttgart and Düsseldorf 1957, p. 272.
[4] Ibid., pp. 272 f.

spiritualists, chain letters and other forms of charlatanism. Thus Adolf Hitler's teacher, the renegade Cistercian Lenz von Liebenfels, whose periodical *Ostara* was considered as belonging to the 'lunatic fringe' in Vienna before the First World War, enjoyed notable success in Austria and Germany after the war. Liebenfels, who had concocted a dualistic philosophy of history whose theme was the eternal struggle between noble and heroic, fair Aryans and the dark, avaricious and criminal 'chandalan' (outcasts), frankly admitted: 'But for Lenin and Trotsky I should never have got a hearing, this letter would never have been written and the Aryan Christian renaissance, which will now take hold of one Christian nation after another, would never have happened.'[1]

Hitler adopted these ideas although he never acknowledged his debt to Liebenfels.

The conflicting loyalties generated by central Europe's social and cultural heritage were of considerable help in making totalitarian methods effective. As religious, dynastic, linguistic and ideological conflicts had always been a feature of central Europe's history, totalitarian leaders found a rich source of substitute symbols ready to hand. Such symbols may be divided into positive and negative ones. The positive ones will be examined more closely in connection with their function as a means of integration. Of the negative symbols the so-called scapegoat[2] was of major importance. In Hitler's book *Mein Kampf* Jews and communists are the scapegoats, in Ludendorff's writings it is the Roman Catholic Church, the freemasons and international Jewry. Hitler admitted that from the point of view of their propaganda value the actual characteristics of these communities were less important than the traditional ideas which many people held about them.[3] Thus the freemasons were known to form a secret, international organization of influential figures who used mystic names and signs as well as a secret language.[4] In Roman Catholic countries memories of the Church's struggle against the freemasons, to whom diabolical powers were often attributed from the pulpit, were still fresh in people's minds. Those who are familiar with the

---

[1] Quoted by Wilfried Daim, *Der Mann, der Hitler die Ideen gab*, Munich 1958, p. 100.

[2] Gordon W. Allport has gone into this question. He gives the following reasons for the scapegoat practices: (a) privation difficulties; (b) escape from guilt; (c) fear and anxiety; (d) excessive self-consciousness; (e) herd instinct; (f) thinking in generalizations. Cf. his *Treibjagd auf Sündenböcke*, Berlin, Bad Nauheim 1951.

[3] Hermann Rauschning, *Gespräche mit Hitler*, op. cit., p. 223 – Hitler candidly admitted that anti-Semitic propaganda was useful not only for increasing his popularity but also for undermining the traditional political and economic order.

[4] Ibid., p. 226 – Hitler admitted that he had known his allegations about the freemasons were untrue.

history of the Jewish pogroms in the Middle Ages, which could often also be traced back to mystic accusations of ritual slaughter, will at once recognize the mystic elements in modern anti-Semitism.[1]

Hermann Rauschning has rightly pointed out that the fight against Judaism was only an indirect help to Hitler in realizing his real goal – the undermining of all the fundamental concepts and standards on which the nation and Christianity were built.[2] Hitler declared, 'The principle of race is good. It breaks up the old and provides opportunities for spreading the new ideas. But once the principle of race has been admitted by the exposure of the particular case of the Jews, the rest is simple. Then there is no option but to end the political and economic order step by step . . .'[3] Furthermore, historical records about the supremacy of the universal church before the Reformation and about the religious conflicts of the Reformation were still in existence.

The National Socialists, seeking socio-psychological devices to destroy the life of the community, first chose symbols and scapegoats to apply to certain classes and groups where they were bound to strike a favourable response because of long-standing tradition. Thus the battle-cry raised against the freemasons, especially in the Roman Catholic parts of south Germany and Austria, proved a highly effective weapon, while the myth of Rome's 'dark plots' was spread by means of a whispering propaganda campaign in the Protestant regions of north and central Germany, in the patent hope of impressing the peasants and the middle class. National Socialist propaganda believed the application of this symbolism could extract advantage from a past age when these slogans and associations of ideas had fulfilled very different functions.

Once a few such groups had accepted *one* of these scapegoat symbols which suited their particular regional outlook and tradition, they were clearly ready to accept *further* scapegoat symbols as well, provided these emanated from the same source (i.e., from the National Socialists). It did not matter whether these further symbols could be made compatible with the religious and social ideas of these groups or not; the vital thing was that they were propagated like the original symbol. Thus, after national socialism had gained an ideological foothold in Austria, it was common to hear both there and in the Sudetenland convinced Catholics talking about Rome's 'dark plots'. Again, in Protestant Prussia, the legend of the freemasons' secret

---

[1] Cf., for example, Franz L. Neumann, *Angst und Politik*, Tübingen 1954, p. 32. The author shows the basic cause of racial anti-Semitism, namely the catechetic description of the Crucifixion and the blood-guilt of the Jews.

[2] Rauschning, *Gespräche mit Hitler*, op. cit., p. 222.    [3] Ibid., p. 223.

intrigues was an everyday topic of conversation. These phenomena, coinciding and confirming each other, allow us to draw the following conclusion: once a sizeable section of the population is induced, by the persistent propaganda of some movement, to accept a number of identical symbols, this movement is able, by the use of these symbols, to unify and integrate these groups in the way it wants.[1]

Those people who repeated these slogans still formed part of their original social milieu. Although many of them voted for the National Socialists, they never joined the party. The average sympathizer was able to go on living as he always had. But it enabled Nazi propaganda to score important successes by being in a position to disseminate, first among the minority and then among the majority of the German people, a system of scapegoat symbols which were homogeneous even if superficial.

By artificially generating and reawakening the intense national self-consciousness characteristic of the period when Bismarck carried through his policy of national unification, national socialism's political strategists endeavoured to strengthen national unity. That Hitler's fanatical propagation of nationalism was only a move in the game of political chess is clear from his contempt for the nation which he described as a 'political tool of democracy and liberalism'.[2] Hitler deliberately exacerbated the virulent emotions of nationalism with the aim of replacing these eventually by the concept of race. He wanted to 'fuse the "nations" into a higher order.'[3] The new techniques amounted to a mixture of social democracy's political methods and the psychological mass strategy recommended by a few officers in the Supreme Army Command during the First World War. With the help of these techniques not only was the mass basis of the party in the people to be strengthened and secured but, internationalism being considered one of the main enemies, they were also to be the vaccine for immunizing the nation against 'harmful international influences'. As it happened, the scapegoat strategy only served to open breaches in the community in order to exploit these for further infiltration.

However, national socialism had little time in which to carry out the 'hardening' process which is wanted to apply to national unity. It tried to make up for this by using force. From the historical point of view the attempt to catch up on centuries of neglect in the way of national unification by six years of violent absolutism might be described, not inaptly, as quixotic. The National Socialists' task was made still more difficult by their simultaneous attack on the traditions

[1] Georg Simmel, *Soziologie*, op. cit., p. 115.
[2] Rauschning, *Gespräche mit Hitler*, op. cit., p. 218.       [3] Ibid., p. 219.

of the constitutional state and democracy whose beginnings, in Germany, went back in the first instance not to the period of Bismarck's bogus constitutionalism but to the old Reich. The Nazis sought to undermine these traditions by destroying the ties existing within social groups and by propagating substitute symbols for the monarchist symbolism still ingrained in the people's minds. Eschenberg and Sternberger drew attention to the role of the president as a substitute, shadow emperor; but that applied with far greater force to the Führer. The Nazis wanted to create symbolic links with the institutions of the Holy Roman Empire by introducing *Reichsstatthalter* (imperial governors). Power, however, always remained the *ultima ratio*, so that propaganda, symbolism and terror became mutually complementary.

H. D. Lasswell has tried to explain the connection between these phenomena. He suggests that in order to be successful a political group needs symbols which mark its own movement as being positive and in the ascendant and the symbols of the opposing group as negative and in decline. But behind the propaganda which is based on this symbolism there must be a credible threat that force will be employed.[1] It is a moot point, however, whether Lasswell does not give excessive credence to Thomas Hobbes' view of human nature. He assumes that all men are as dominated by fear and covetous of power and wealth as Hobbes makes out. It is also doubtful whether the same mechanistic social psychology can be assumed to hold in Europe, where the people are much more historically and traditionalist minded, as in the United States or in Britain's colonies and the Commonwealth countries, which are less burdened by such traditions.

According to Mannheim, substitute symbols are of great practical political importance because, in the second stage, the symbol becomes the driving power behind new forms of spontaneous group integration, while, in the third stage, it becomes the fixed emblem of the organized group. While people cling to symbols in the first stage in order to gain a breathing space in the stage where the traditional social order is dissolved, in the second stage people are integrated into spontaneously growing groups by means of symbols such as the swastika, the fascist salute, the clenched fist, etc., where the symbol acquires a 'utopian' significance and a new prestige. Pressure groups come into being; important changes take place in the individual person; traditional behaviour patterns break up. That is the prelude to the third stage – integration into the totalitarian state. Now the symbols are deliberately manipulated. As Max Weber realized,

[1] Harold D. Lasswell, 'Politics: Who Gets What, When, How', in: *The Political Writings*, Glencoe (Illinois) 1951, pp. 311 ff.

psycho-pathological types prove successful as leaders within this re-construction process. Hitler represents this type in Germany, a type not unlike the ecstatic Old Testament prophets who successfully inveighed against the power of convention and the organized priest-hood.[1]

Weimar democracy was slow to recognize the dangers posed by this new form of propaganda. Even after the first Hitler *putsch* in 1923 many leading democrats saw in Nazi anti-Semitism merely a sort of swaggering romanticism on the part of a lot of beer-hall swash-bucklers. Moreover, religious indifference prevented the Weimar coalition from taking sides either for or against religious or anti-religious propaganda. There were also opportunist politicians who feared unpopularity if they were to take any tough action against a movement which was obviously patriotic. By its poisoned attacks on democratic ministers or civil servants of the Jewish faith, for instance the vice-president of the Berlin police, Weiss, National Socialism also played skilfully on Jewish inferiority complexes (which were only too understandable in the circumstances) and in this way they weakened Jewish willingness to serve Germany democracy.

Nevertheless, Weimar must be censured for the following serious failure. The adoption of the democratic republican form of govern-ment was the direct outcome of the military defeat suffered by the Central Powers. The majority of those who at first backed the new regime had been swept to support democratic republicanism by a wave of protest against the economic distress and humiliation accruing from the pseudo-constitutionalism and the militarism of imperial Germany. But in the years which followed the signing of the peace treaties and brought further national humiliation, the occupation of the Ruhr and economic crises, it was difficult for Germany democracy to retain the sympathies of the masses. Yet between 1924 and 1929 there was a time when a lasting bond between the masses and the Weimar state could have been forged. In this relatively short period Weimar democ-racy could have created its own independent symbols, which would have lent the republican democratic form of government an attractive image. Although a few tentative attempts at something of the sort were made they always ended in failure because of the almost purely materialistic outlook on the part of Weimar's ruling circles. This was bound to give rise to a dangerous situation: the military defeat of the monarchy had left an emotional vacuum among large sections of the population and deprived the hero-worshipping masses of any object on which to focus their feelings.

However, between 1924 and 1929 the powerful intellectual and

[1] Mannheim, *Man and Society*, op. cit., pp. 13–137.

ethical ferment which became articulate in the *Jugendbünde* (youth organizations) came into its own in Germany. It soon became evident that the arid, rational, materialistic outlook of Weimar's leading circles could never appeal to the idealistic and adventurous spirit of the country's youth. National socialism had a far deeper understanding of this need.

Jews, freemasons and the Roman Catholic Church performed the function of scapegoat symbols for national socialism in another sense too; it adopted many of their true or supposed qualities, organizational forms, techniques and fighting methods. Thus Hitler, for example, declared that the methods and programmes described in the 'Protocols of the Elders of Zion' were akin to national socialism with its 'new belief in the eternal character of this movement.'[1] It was from this source that Hitler claimed he had learned his policy of political intrigue, revolutionary subversion and concealment.[2] The freemasons impressed Hitler because they were a 'sort of priestly nobility'.[3] The hierarchical structure and education by means of symbols and rites' had fascinated him. He had to fight the freemasons because they represented 'the hierarchical order of a secular priesthood'. But Hitler wanted to use an order of this nature for his own movement, in the way he believed the Catholic Church did. And so Hitler came to the conclusion that he must eliminate both the Church and the freemasons.

Hitler admired particularly the doctrinal orthodoxy and the discipline of the Catholic Church, while Himmler built up the SS in accordance with the principles and organization of the Jesuit Order. The German *Ritterorden* (Order of Teutonic Knights) also served as model.

The psychological reasons for Hitler's profound hatred of Jews, freemasons and the Church are therefore easy to understand. He utilized their techniques and organizational forms and felt much too like them to tolerate them. He had to try to destroy them.

Other scapegoat symbols used by Nazi propaganda were, for instance, the 'November criminals', the 'Red Peril', etc. Totalitarian and authoritarian movements in other countries also employed scapegoat symbols suitable for their specific regional needs. Thus the fascist movements in countries such as Czechoslovakia, Poland and Yugoslavia had to proffer 'Germanism' as a scapegoat symbol. The fact that, after 1933, the Nazis did not protest against the anti-German propaganda of these fascist groups bore testimony to the unscrupulousness and subtlety of the Nazi party's political methods. The National Socialists had agreed to the anti-German agitation in

---

[1] Rauschning, *Gespräche mit Hitler*, op. cit., p. 224.
[2] Ibid., p. 225.  [3] Ibid., pp. 226 f.

these countries as long as the latter also indulged in anti-Semitic propaganda.

The heterogeneous, territorial, political and religious elements within society were also forced into conformity. Internationalism was one of the leadership's major taboos. Yet national socialism, which dominated militarily almost the whole of Europe during the Second World War, was compelled to think of constructing a European system on an international basis. It is true that, in the framework of the New Order, an attempt was made to establish an international organization on a national basis – an attempt which was doomed to failure from the start. Nevertheless, this attempt represents a deviation from the principles of pure nationalism. Furthermore, the construction of a gigantic industrial and military apparatus brought about fundamental social changes. The upshot was a compromise with ideas originating from the field of international co-operation. A typical example was the widespread employment of foreign workers in German industry. This afforded opportunities for a great number of direct contacts between members of different races and nations – which again helped to undermine the national prejudices which were an important element in Nazi ideology. Contacts between the population of foreign countries and German soldiers, which the latter in their turn discussed with the Germans at home, and contacts with foreign workers, especially in times of military reverses, were just the kind of thing to destroy the emotional impact of Nazi propaganda. The sudden realization by people who had so far been fully integrated in the totalitarian state, that there was a great gulf between the theory and practice of national socialism, coupled with their feeling of social insecurity and fear of the future, did much towards destroying a uniformity which was purely superficial.

# PART TWO

## Exploitation of the Frontier Complex

Although democracy presupposes that people will be free to form their own opinions, more than any other type of government it needs a system of civic training to teach citizens to appreciate free, democratic institutions.[1] This training varies not only from country to

[1] In the United States the continuous influx of heterogeneous racial groups afforded a rich experimental field. See, for example, Charles Merriam, *The Making of Citizens, A Comparative Study of Methods of Civic Training*, Chicago 1931. Merriam's series

country but attains different levels of intensity in the various classes and groups of any single country. The frontier areas of states are regions in which the different training systems come into conflict. These might even be described as experimental fields in which loyalties crystallize only to clash in bitter conflict, in a conflict which overshadows and excludes all other material and ideological interests. These frontier areas, which thrust out into the territory of other states, are totalitarianism's outposts.

In central Europe outposts of this kind were often separated by language differences from the state to which they belonged under international law, while having a way of life, an economy and communications in common with that state. On the one hand language differences made it more difficult for the people to join in the cultural and intellectual life of the country and on the other a different socio-psychological structure, arising from different traditions, and different economic interests, excluded their co-operation with those speaking the same language beyond the state frontiers. Thus the *Reichsdeutsche* (German nationals) looked on the Sudeten Germans as members of a foreign community.

People living in frontier areas are in an unhappy intermediate position. On the one hand, in a period of expansive nationalism, they are regarded as a national minority by the own state, without however being recognized as equal by the state to which they ought, by virtue of language, to belong. To preserve their specific character, the 'frontiersmen' clung that much more obstinately to their language and customs, thus cutting themselves off from their fellow citizens who spoke a different language. The was bound to lead, in particular, to a certain backwardness as regards culture and civilization, when these 'frontiersmen' lived mainly by agriculture. In general, this kind of exaggerated 'frontier' nationalism is matter for amusement rather than anxiety. It is only when the *outposts* concerned are those of a people whose national unity is not yet completed that the situation can become dangerous.

As we have already mentioned, examples of this type of outpost were the Sudeten Germans in Czechoslovakia, the German minority in Poland, the Polish minority in Germany before 1918, the Italian minority in the Habsburg monarchy, the German minority in the Italian South Tyrol and the Yugoslav minority in Italy. In the case of the people of Alsace, however, their cultural ties with France proved to be stronger than their linguistic ties with Germany. To all appearances a German frontier post, they lived in a state which had

of studies contains a comparative study of civic training systems in the larger states of Europe and the United States.

been unified long before Germany and which had, therefore, been able to train its citizens in the spirit of national unity earlier than Germany. This also explains the result of the plebiscites in Allenstein and Marienwerder after the First World War, when large sections of the Polish-speaking population voted for Germany precisely because Poland's national unification lagged behind Germany's.

In their daily contacts and dealings national outposts[1] and peoples only now treading the road to national unity come up against nationalist emotions which in structure and expression are similar to their own but are antagonistic to them because they belong to the other nation. As these emotions are expressed in another language they are felt to be hostile.[2] Lasswell believes that 'negative identifications' of this kind, which result from direct contact with other racial groups, are an important factor in the generation of competing symbols. That means that the national or social symbols, with which the negatively identified group is commonly connected, inspire or strengthen rival symbols in the negatively identifying groups.[3] Lasswell quotes as an example the fact that many Italian immigrants who were greeted with 'wop' or 'dago' – derogatory terms coined in the United States to describe Italians – felt so deeply insulted that they joined the fascist movement.

As will be shown later, Lasswell's theory of the socio-psychological effectiveness of propaganda is of only limited application in Europe. It was substantiated in the national outposts of central and southeast Europe because there the rival symbols were especially powerful. Here the national group speaking the same language as the national outpost lived across the frontier, outside the sphere of the outpost's daily life and experience, and formed the population of a state which

[1] National outposts are national minorities which by language, culture or religion are part of a people who live outside the frontiers of the state containing those outposts, assuming that the area of such a minority and the area of the bulk of the people of which they are by language, culture or religion a part are geographical neighbours and that this people has the will to national expansion.

[2] Harold D. Lasswell, 'World Politics and Personal Insecurity', in *A Study of Political Power*, Glencoe, Illinois 1950. By 'negative identification' Lasswell understands the classification of people, groups or situations into certain unfavourable categories of ideas which the identifying person or group has acquired through membership of a certain social or community milieu in respect of definite groups, types or situations (p. 169). Lasswell divides up these identifications according to the attitude adopted by the identifying person or group. If this attitude is positive, he calls the identification 'positive'; if not he calls it 'negative'.

[3] The following may be quoted as an example. A Czech postman who does not speak German is posted to a German-speaking town in the Sudetenland. He cannot make himself understood to the German-speaking householders when he delivers their letters. He is negatively identified by them – as also is the Czechoslovak state which sent him to the town for aggressive, nationalist reasons. The rival symbols which are stimulated are those of the pan-German Reich.

was often larger and more powerful than the one in which the national outpost constituted a national minority. Consequently the symbols of the powerful state across the frontier became the rival symbols[1] in respect of those of the state speaking a different language. If this is complicated by the factor of social insecurity, the social and economic difficulties of the state of which this minority are citizens seem that much worse, while the difficulties of the state whose members across the frontier speak the same language are not clearly recognized because they are more remote. They therefore seem unimportant and are dwarfed even more by the emotional attitude creating the linguistic and cultural affinity.

In central Europe this gave rise to the following situation. The German minorities belonged by language to a major power which had become a united nation comparatively recently. The intense national feeling symptomatic of the period of national unification was still alive. The years after the peace treaties of 1919 and 1920 was a period of national and social uncertainty throughout the world and to an even more marked degree in central Europe. Those politicians who came either from German–Slav frontier regions or at least from, politically, relatively backward German-speaking regions, like Hitler,[2] Konrad Henlein (whose mother was a Czech), K. H. Frank, Seyss-Inquart with his Czech forbears, Globocznigg or Rosenberg, were peculiarly fitted to co-ordinate these factors and bring them to bear on the situation. It must be remembered that the National Socialist movement had evolved among the German national outposts long before it triumphed in the German Reich. The explanation is partly that this fanatical movement was first opposed in Germany – a fact which is to be attributed to constitutional traditions and also, above all, to a higher degree of civic training and national self-cofindence.

It would be possible to give many other examples of national outposts entertaining ultra-nationalist feelings. The South Tyrolese are an eloquent example for the years after the Second World War. Although German nationalism became more tempered in Germany and Austria, it retained much of its original virulence in the South Tyrol.

With the march of colonial emancipation the same problem has

---

[1] 'Rival symbols' here mean symbols of the states competing for the members of the frontier area. See also Robert E. Park, *The Immigrant Press and its Control*, New York 1922, and Robert E. Park and Herbert A. Miller, *Old World Traits Transplanted*, New York and London 1921.

[2] Meinecke has also stressed this fact. 'On the other hand the aggressive frontier-German form of the racialism which he [Hitler] represented is by no means specifically German; it is the common creation of all nationalities living in the indeterminate areas of eastern Europe and treading on one another's feet.' Friedrich Meinecke, *Die deutsche Katastrophe*, Wiesbaden 1946, p. 111.

come to affect other countries outside Europe. Although Turkey and Greece lived amicably together as allies in NATO after the Second World War, the same is not true of their national minorities – for example in Cyprus. The nationalism of the homeland is often aggravated by the nationalism of these outposts. It was also a threat to the relationship between the mainland Greeks and Turks. Vice versa, this kind of nationalism among minorities and outposts often ebbs when the homeland nationals pay less attention to it. A separate nationality then develops among the members of the national outpost. Once again, Cyprus is a case in point and with Greece waiving for the time being their demand for *enosis* (union with Greece and Cyprus) the Greek Cypriots look on themselves as a separate nationality. Likewise, in south-east Asian countries like Malaysia, Vietnam, Laos and Burma, the foreign Chinese today play a role typical of a national outpost.

Not all social strata among the national minorities are equally nationalistic. Thus in the Sudetenland there were groups which still clung to a tradition diametrically opposed to pan-Germanism, as for example the Social Democratic and Christian Social Parties. And regional traditions which respected the historical unity of Bohemia and Moravia lived on there. Among both Sudeten Germans and Czechs there also survived traditions which looked to a larger political community, namely that of the Danube basin. But, as we have mentioned, Czechoslovakia did not prove willing or capable of ultilizing these loyalties to form a common civic sense.

Existing or latent animosities, due to the existence of particularist political organizations and national outposts, enable totalitarian propaganda to engineer open conflicts. For many years the central European as well as the Western democracies failed to understand the social nature of these problems. Hence they were unable to draw the correct conclusions and provide the necessary remedies. While the democratic governments of central Europe often took the line of expediency and classified the political groups in the state according to whether they were ready to support the governments or not, the Western democracies were mostly the victims of tendentious newspaper reports and accordingly supported this or that party in the central or east European countries. When the need for a thorough analysis of these problems was finally realized it was too late to save the central European democracies because fascism had already become too powerful.

There were also similar but perhaps less urgent problems in the linguistically homogeneous parts of multi-lingual states. In central Europe these had more often to do with the the antogonism between town and countryside.[1] American sociological literature has devoted much attention to this relationship.[2] While the spread of urban ways to the countryside met with little resistance in America and western Europe, in central Europe there was a much wider gulf between urban civilization and thinking on the one hand and both moral conduct and hierarchical ideas in the agrarian regions of central Europe on the other. This gave rise to dangerous animosities. Common among countryfolk was the stereotyped view that townspeople were rootless, unreliable, superficial and politically unstable; against this the towns-people looked on countryfolk as simple, uncivilized, superstitious and hard-hearted. The democracies paid scant attention to these facts. This difference was later exploited by fascism and was a major factor in its success among the more backward and isolated agricultural populations, for example in the regions east of the Elbe, in the Palatinate, Austria, Slovakia, Hungary and especially in Romania. A scapegoat symbol which helped to win over the agricultural population was 'godless communism' which rural traditionalism and conservatism sharply repudiated. And anti-Semitic slogans were sure to make an impact in areas where the grain trade was largely in the hands of Jewish merchants.

## PART THREE

*Modern Communications and Totalitarian Techniques*

The dense network of modern roads and communications – such as railways, buses, cars, aeroplanes, the telephone, radio and television – which link the whole world is taken for granted today. Yet the creation and expansion of modern communication systems had important social and political repercussions. Looked at superficially, these seem to reinforce the trend towards interstate association. But this development does not proceed at a uniform pace, going ahead faster in some countries than in others and varying in intensity from area to area within a particular state. Although the development of traffic and transport has an integrating and unifying effect eventually, it can temporarily exacerbate existing antagonisms or provoke new conflicts.

[1] This was, for example, especially true of the Republic of Austria. See Chap. VI, Part Four.

[2] Cf., for example, B. R. M. Maciver and Charles H. Page, *Society*, London 1950, pp. 310 ff.

According to Willey and Rice, the extension of the road network in America was accompanied by an increase in local patriotism.[1] Contacts within local communities were multiplied considerably by modern communication links such as the telephone, cars and local bus services, the spirit of local patriotism was intensified by local newspapers. The standardization of life in areas remote from one another is also a slow process; what is more it is costly and therefore, at first, confined to the wealthy classes. These two writers therefore came to the conclusion that in a country as large as the United States of America the development of communications did not, in the first instance, strengthen national unity but local and regional prejudices and antagonisms. Nor did the development of a unified community go forward with the same intensity within its various classes.

In central Europe similar conditions produced different results. Here states were often so small that the growth of local patriotism induced by the improvement in local communications strengthened feelings of nationalism not regionalism. Thus the bus services in Czechoslovakia were extended and improved from the '20s onwards and were naturally centred in Prague. Papers published in the late evening were obviously available next morning in even the remotest parts of the country. In the larger cities newspaper boys were shouting out the headlines of the Prague boulevard press the same day. It was the same in Austria, Poland and Germany. In central Europe, where the centres of population are not more than ten or twelve hours' train journey from the capital cities, the increase in the number of main roads meant that those trends, which in America fostered local patriotism, here boosted nationalism—because of the attraction of the capitals and the relative smallness of the European states. This phenomenon encouraged nationalist tendencies.

In present-day Europe television has a similar integrating effect because the range of television transmitters is limited and therefore does not extend beyond a country's frontiers and because language is a barrier excluding most foreigners and providing a natural focus for the national cultural community. Television also enables a determined government to unify its citizens' thinking by providing a rigidly organized service.

The post-war democracies either showed little understanding of the possibilities opened up by modern communications or did not draw the necessary conclusions from them. In Germany these social trends were exploited with the utmost skill in the fight against democracy. In Bavaria, the intensification of feelings of local patriotism and regional

[1] Malcolm M. Willey and Stuart A. Rice, *Communication Agencies and Social Life*, New York and London 1953, p. 213.

sentiment greatly helped the National Socialist movement, which first developed on a regional basis after the war. In North Germany, however, Gregor Strasser and Goebbels built up the National Socialist movement by methods which were quite different from those used in Munich. Their success is also partly explained by the Weimar Republic's disregard of the importance of communications and propaganda. The Nazi Party, for example, achieved a dominating position in the sphere of civil air transport even before it seized power. It had tremendous influence in the *Lufthansa* (German Air Lines) which had suffered severely from the economic crisis. The Nazis were kept out of the radio service for a long time but their propaganda was put over with great success largely with the aid of convoys of loudspeaker cars and by the clever use of aircraft, which whisked party speakers like Hitler, Göring and Goebbels from city to city within a matter of hours and this at a time when air travel was still considered an extravagant luxury.[1] Thus Goebbels was able to coin the famous slogan 'The Leader over Germany', which was meant to suggest Hitler's omnipresence.

Hitler admitted that he adopted the techniques of the mass rally, marches and processions, press campaigns and his usual methods of political propaganda from the Social Democrats and simply applied and developed them to their logical conclusion. But why did the democratic parties not use these for their own self-defence in the post-war period, when they still controlled important means of communication? Thus the Weimar Republic had, in the very early days, developed all the possibilities of radio but was unwilling or unable to apply them for disseminating democratic ideas in Germany. As in other spheres of public life, behind the insistence on the 'non-political' character of radio there lurked a conservative attitude of mind which was particularly marked in Bredow, who was responsible for the radio.[2] The Social Democratic government in Prussia, especially the Minister of the Interior, Severing, was acutely aware of radio's political possibilities, but because of the multifarious character and the disunity and instability of the coalition and minority governments inevitable with proportional representation, he was unable to make his views prevail. Bausch makes this pertinent remark: 'The departmental ambition of ministerial bureaucracy, the rivals between *Reich* and *Länder*, the democrats' mutual mistrust of one another and the constant pressure of the anti-democratic elements prevented the radio from being a publicity integration factor in the first German republic.'[3]

[1] Sington and Weidenfeld, *The Goebbels Experiment*, London 1942, pp. 33–36.
[2] Hans Bausch, *Der Rundfunk im politischen Kräftespiel der Weimarer Republik*
[3] Ibid., p. 193.

But under Papen the politicalization of the radio became a fact.[1] Yet Bausch's apologetic conclusion – that the non-political bureaucratic control of the radio at least saved it from falling prematurely under the influence of anti-democratic forces – is dubious. The reason given by Pohle for this refusal – namely, the relatively late technical development of radio – is also dubious. According to Pohle the radio fell into the Nazi regime's lap 'like ripe fruit, and without their having anything to do with the planting and the growing'.[2] It is difficult to believe that the Social Democratic Party, which was well aware of the political possibilities of radio, could not have brought more pressure to bear through the Prussian government, just as it is hardly credible that the Weimar parties could not have agreed on a common, even if impartial, democratic radio service.

Immediately after the Nazi seizure of power, control of the radio was transferred from the Ministry of Posts and Telegraphs to the Ministry of Propaganda[3] and the organization of the radio service was linked directly with the Nazi Party.[4] The role it played in the Nazi seizure of power from the very outset is described by the former Director General of state radio services, Hadamovsky, who relates how from February 10 to March 4, 1933, German radio stations broadcast speeches by Hitler almost every evening. The radio was the vanguard of faith for the National Socialist State; 'out of forty million who have said "Yes" to a political action it had to make a nation which is national socialist in its profoundest thinking and behaviour. Its aim must be to create in the nation an inner attitude which says an unconditional "Yes!" to everything which emanates from the Führer and thus from national socialism.' These words clearly outlined the radio's future task and its totalitarian intention.[5]

As Hitler's technique as an orator was not particularly suitable for the studio, his speeches were broadcast direct from Nazi rallies, where 'the acclamation, the approval and the shouts of "Sieg Heil!" were addressed not to cool reason but to the emotions alone'.[6] The extent to which Goebbels exploited the radio for political propaganda is clearly demonstrated by the technical resources employed to cover Hitler's state visit to Hamburg on August 17, 1934:

4 broadcasting vans with built-in receiving apparatus
1 short-wave transmitter

[1] Ibid., p. 191.
[2] Heinz Pohle, *Der Rundfunk als Instrument der Politik, Die Geschichte des Deutschen Rundfunks von 1923–1938*, Hamburg 1955, p. 296.
[3] Ibid., p. 198.    [4] Ibid., pp. 215 ff.
[5] Eugen Hadamovsky, *Der Rundfunk im Dienst der Volksführung*, Leipzig 1934. pp. 19 f.    [6] Pohle, op. cit., p. 289.

1 van with radio engineers
4 loudspeaker vans
5 mobile short-wave transmitters
1 launch with built-in short-wave transmitter
42 microphones
9 portable radio receivers, etc.[1]

Goebbels also demonstrated his superior strategy by planning his propaganda campaigns like military operations in which the various communication devices boosted one another in a *crescendo* of effect. Teams of broadcasters accompanied Hitler on his air journeys all over Germany. The *Reichsautozug Deutschland*, a convoy of eighty vehicles, made it possible to carry out radio broadcasts, install batteries of loud speakers, erect platforms and so on without calling on local help.'[2]

The small states of central Europe offered Nazi propaganda technique an even richer field of experiment. The states did not have the financial resources to counter Nazi propaganda technically. The massed 'drum fire' which, according to Hadamowsky, was intended to bring 'the whole nation to heel', made due impact on Austrian and Sudeten Germans. As soon as terror was used to reinforce propaganda, the smaller states were completely defenceless. Their governments even failed to protect the non-Nazi broadcasting stations in their areas. This was exploited by the National Socialist regime when it sent a gang to assassinate Formis, a member of Otto Strasser's *Schwarze Front* (Black Front), which had set up and used an anti-Hitler transmitter in Czechoslovakia, and when the Austrian broadcasting station was invaded during the July *putsch* of 1934.

The circumstances surrounding the assassination of the Austrian Chancellor Dollfuss, the engineer Formis and Professor Theodor Lessing also proved that the police forces in these countries were behind the times in their technical resources. When the Nazi terrorists gathered in the gymnasium of Vienna barracks to attack the Austrian Chancellery in lorries, the police confined themselves to a telephone warning and wrote a report. When Formis was murdered the terrorists' cars were infinitely faster than those used for the police pursuit.

It is evident that the democrats were insufficiently aware of the vital importance of means of communication for combating fascism. In the case of the Social Democrats it was often also a question of a mistaken sense of responsibility to the workers. Thus in Czechoslovakia proposals that the Social Democrats should use aircraft to drop recruiting pamphlets were turned down. It was argued that the workers

[1] Ibid., p. 296.                         [2] Ibid., p. 297.

would misinterpret any outlay on luxuries of this kind during the economic crisis.

Before and after its seizure of power, national socialism attached the greatest importance to intensive mass propaganda. It evolved a technique which paid handsome dividends because it helped the movement to climb to power. When, after the elections in November 1932, the decline in the Nazi fortunes seemed absolute, the Party concentrated on the small state of Lippe where diet elections were being held in January 1933. Hitler and the other party bosses bombarded the villagers with rallies and propaganda day after day[1] – something which the other parties neglected to do – and so the Nazis won a cheap electoral victory and were able to enter the government. Hitler never uttered so much as a word of gratitude to the masses for their help. The fact that they were susceptible to pressure merely increased his contempt for them. It was precisely this knowledge which made him determined to put them in tutelage for ever.

# PART FOUR

## National Socialist Economic Policy

National socialism's realization of its role as a decisive counter-movement to liberalism was evident not only from Carl Schmitt's writings but also in the disputes over economic policy and its conduct.

As with political theory, national socialist criticism of economic liberalism had been voiced by earlier critics who, while not actually fascists, were inspired by both the *Kathedersozialisten* (academic socialists) and the Austrian school. Although both these currents were differently motivated and therefore pursued different and mutually excluding aims, they nevertheless found common ground in rejecting liberal economic theory. National socialist doctrine had some reason, therefore, for regarding this criticism as one of the sources of the ideological concept of 'national socialism', not only by referring expressly to it but also looking on itself as its logical heir.

There are many passages in the contemporary literature on the subject to substantiate this view. The following quotation from Vleugels is typical:

'The reference of our account of the evolution . . . to the criticism of economic liberalism can easily mislead one into exaggerating the part played by the social moralists of our economic science as the pioneers

[1] Arno Schröder, *Hitler geht auf die Dörfer*, Detmold 1938.

of national socialist ideas. . . . Basically, in my opinion, the strongest *unifying* link between them and the contemporary executor of the synthesis of nationalism and socialism is to be seen in the German concept of the state . . .'[1]

Throughout this book by a representative national socialist economist there is not a single mention of the corporative state. Just as the Hitler movement's 'socialism' had nothing in common with the 'academic socialists', so the national socialist economists' concept of a new order was nothing like Spann's. Although there were some ideologists who saw national socialism as the realization of corporative state ideas,[2] these features soon disappeared from the literature on the subject. In practice they were unable to make any practical impression because Hitler had seen that the corporative state was impossible and incompatible with his totalitarian ideas. Economic practice was dominated by a completely different concept, which did indeed contain basic elements of pre-Nazi criticism of liberalism but also contained a fair number of original features, such as the idea of the *Volksgemeinschaft* (racial community). Thus Vleugels also speaks of Hitler as having resuscitated the German concept of the state and realized the importance of 'the great idea of the *Volksgemeinschaft*'.[3]

The *Volksgemeinschaft* was therefore regarded as the organic link between state and society, organized in the industrial sphere in accordance with the 'leader' principle, after the fashion of a combine imposed from above in the field of general economic policy, and in accordance with the principles of the *Arbeitsfront* (Labour Front) in social life. That this practice was developed directly from the criticism levelled against liberalism is made clear by Vleugels, who says that national economic and financial policy are *political* disciplines and that it is essential to discard the liberal principle, which is based on the error that the maximum social product was the necessary premise for the maximum profit as welfare for the *Volksgemeinschaft*.

Now all questions of domestic and foreign policy came under the absolute control of the Nazi-organized and Nazi-run state. And it was also vital to try to keep Germany isolated from the 'liberalism' of the outside world. Germany was to be made independent of the conditions of free international trade and henceforward develop along the lines of 'autarchy'. The aim was the 'closed national economy' (described as a defence economy) which, it was believed, alone could ensure unin-

[1] Wilhelm Vleugels, *Die Kritik am wirtschaftlichen Liberalismus in der Entwicklung der deutschen Volkswirtschaftslehre*, Munich, Leipzig 1935, p. 36.
[2] See Max Frauendorfer on this point: *Der ständische Gedanke im National-sozialismus*, Munich 1933.
[3] Vleugels, op. cit., p. 36.

terrupted rearmament and the capacity to wage war. Thus the terminology and symbolism of Stalin's Russia could confidently be adopted. In this sense the Chief of the Economic Staff in the Supreme Command of the Armed Forces, Major General Thomas, declared, *inter alia*, in *Der Vierjahresplan* (The Four Year Plan): 'The German Four Year Plan has become an established idea for every German. It is seen not only as the means of liberating the German economy from its dependence on the outside world . . . The soldier also sees the Four Year Plan as the economic foundation of German rearmament . . .'[1]

But the transformation of the autarchic idea into economic reality was only possible if, instead of a multiplicity of individual and mutually competitive decisions by employers, the state took over sole direction of economic policy. Private property, however, was never threatened under Hitler as it was under communism. On the contrary, national socialism's tendency to monopoly capitalism is emphasized by Franz Neumann:[2]

'It is certainly true that the state could, if it wanted, utilize this situation for nationalizing at least the new industries. But national socialism has not done that. On the contrary, the financial help given for the establishment of the new enterprises redounded primarily to the benefit of the long-established monopolies.'

The economy was completely reorganized after 1933 to comply with the demands and the political objectives underlying national socialist economic policy. The first incisive measure was the 'Law for the preparation of the organic construction of the German economy', of February 27, 1934, which, in conjunction with the ensuing decrees, transformed the industrial units hitherto based on voluntary membership into an organization requiring compulsory membership. The foundation of the new economic organization comprised six national groups (industry, handcraft, commerce, banking, insurance, and electricity, coal and gas) subdivided into economic groups, specialized groups, specialized sub-groups and district groups. A unified geographical organization was guaranteed by the so-called *Reichswirtschaftkammern* (Chambers of Commerce). The decrees of July 7, 1936, assigned to them a further task of major importance – the transfer to their control of the district groups belonging to the national industrial group as industrial departments. It was a political edict with a war purpose; for during the war this regulation was made the basis of

[1] Quoted by Jürgen Kuczynski, *Studien zur Geschichte des staatsmonopolistischen Kapitalismus in Deutschland 1918–1945*, Berlin 1963, pp. 165 f.
[2] Franz Neumann, *Behemoth, The Structure and Practice of National Socialism*, London 1942, p. 230.

combines which in the so-called *Reichsvereinigungen* (National Units) created the links between organizations of industry with those of trade on a regional basis. Production, marketing and distribution was thereby unified.

In the socio-political sphere the creation of the *Reichsstand* (Corporation) of German Industry as an amalgamation of the *Reichsverband* (Association) of German Industry and the workers' organizations in June 1933 established the basis for the *Deutsche Arbeitsfront* (German Labour Front) which was founded on December 14, 1933. The Free Trade Unions had been dissolved on May 22, 1933, so that workers and employees were compelled to join the *Arbeitsfront*. Free negotiations about rates of pay and settlements were abolished and henceforth wages and salaries were fixed by the state.

By virtue of labour and industrial legislation a *Betriebsführer* (Industrial Leader) was appointed in every concern. As the owner he was a state official and a private capitalist in one person. The merging of state and employer organizations in a tightly knit central organization was clearly indicated, not least by the organization of the economy since August 2, 1942, when the country's entire production was put under the Minister for Armaments and War Production, actual direction coming, on a somewhat lower level, under the *Wehrwirtschaftsführer* (War Economy Leaders), who were recruited from the employer stratum.

The practical financial-political measures to carry out the primary economic purpose—rearmament—were: (1) control of the whole capital market, surveillance of money and credit transactions by law;[1] (2) the wages and prices freeze of 1936 in connection with the first rationing measures; and also (3) compulsory exchange economy.

All these measures were due to the initiative of Schacht, who introduced them with his 'New Plan' in the autumn of 1934. The necessity and 'inner logic' of this economic structure, dictated by the preparation for total war, led to an enormous expansion of heavy industry. While this was proceeding all other economic interests had to yield to the demands of the 'defence economy'. Franz Neumann rightly observes: 'The incorporation of the total economy into the monopolistic structure . . . means that the automatism of free capitalism . . . has been severely restricted.'[2] But that also meant that Hitler, who was striving to achieve the maximum possible efficiency of the economy for the sake of his war aims, could not allow a temporary disorganization, such as would have occurred if the economy had been socialized on the lines

[1] Fritz Morstein-Marx (Ed.), *Symposium on the Totalitarian State*, Philadelphia 1940.
[2] Neumann, *Behemoth*, op. cit., p. 295.

of Gottfried Feder's national-socialist economic programme. He therefore believed that a temporary compromise with the captains of
industry was advantageous for his purposes. In return for the big industrialists' support for his war plans he offered them the enslavement
of the workers.[1] Neumann's analysis must, however, be modified as
the employer's power over the worker was limited, in as much as any
blatant and stupid act of oppression, which, moreover, would be very
difficult to justify from the standpoint of the totalitarian state, could
easily earn the employer a spell in prison or in a concentration camp
on the evidence of a worker or an official.

The National Socialist authorities' policy of deception was handled
in such a way that an example was usually made of those employers
whose sympathies for Nazi ideology were dubious or whose firms were
of secondary importance for the planning of the war. Particularly
ruthless in this respect was Reinhold Heydrich, who as Protector of
Bohemia and Moravia wanted to win the support of the Czech industrial workers for the Nazi war economy by occasionally unleashing
terror also against employers of German origin.

An essential feature of the National Socialist economic system,
therefore, was that it was based not on trust but fear. It did not rest
on credit but was, according to Friedrich, a 'Timet System'.[2] He also
observes, very pertinently: 'When trust is replaced by fear the whole
form of the economy changes. It ceases to be a capitalist one.'[3]

National Socialism forcibly introduced capital taxes in a disguised
form. This was done by loans which were raised by bills of exchange
drawn on the state and redeemable at some date in the distant future.
This increased the country's internal debt from 14,000 million Reichsmarks in 1933 to almost 42,000 million in 1938. In contrast, tax
revenue for the same period rose from almost 7,000 million Reichsmarks to 18,000 million.[4] This vast indebtedness on the part of the
state was, however, only partly due to the Timet System, that is, to
indirect compulsion, as industry received an increasing number of
orders as a result of the booming war economy. Although industry
may well have regarded the forced loans as a 'creative sacrifice',[5] it
could nevertheless account for these loans as capital investment which
it could recover by the flood of orders which it received.

[1] Ibid., pp. 295 f.: 'National Socialism utilized the daring, the knowledge, the
aggressiveness of the industrial leadership, while the industrial leadership utilized the
anti-democracy, anti-liberalism and anti-unionism of the National Socialist Party.'

[2] Friedrich, *Totalitäre Diktatur*, op. cit., p. 187, which is here based on Gunther
Reimann, *The Vampire Economy*, New York 1939.

[3] Ibid.

[4] René Erbe, *Die nationalsozialistische Wirtschaftspolitik 1933–1939 im Lichte der
modernen Theorie*, Zurich 1958, pp. 36 and 54.

[5] Friedrich, *Totalitäre Diktatur*, op. cit., p. 188.

Friedrich argues quite rightly that in his dealings with the minor European states Hjalmar Schacht applied the Timet System in such a way that by making threats of a politico-economic nature he extorted concessions from them and obtained goods which were never paid for.[1]

The speedy build-up of the German armaments industry after 1933 required the centralization of all branches and man-power of the economy as well as centralized control over the distribution of income. In doing this National Socialism could not and dared not hope to reap the fruits of its propaganda, that is that centralization would be carried through voluntarily. German fascism knew that time was short. For the promises of propaganda to become part and parcel of the whole nation's thinking, however, a discipline was necessary which must be maintained to the point of self-sacrifice. Even before there was any military training or actual armed conflict it had to form the basis of all action and planning. The preliminary steps for this were the *Reichsarbeitsdienst* (Labour Service) and the *Arbeitsfront*, the shock troops on the road to victory in an imaginary 'labour battle'.

The reason for compulsory membership of the *Arbeitsfront* was to prevent employers and workers from themselves negotiating settlements on rates of pay and productivity, which would be a threat to the concentration of the whole nation on war. In point of fact this pressure was the first act in the creation of a modern slave society; for henceforth the National Socialist state ordained not only the manner, the extent and the duration of activity but also fixed a price which no longer bore any relation to output. The *Arbeitsfront* was the precondition for the subsequent practice of the use of decrees which, in December 1934, first restricted the freedom of movement of workers in the metal and building industries and in 1938 finally abolished it altogether. In this connection one of the National Socialist economic ideologists used the following formula:[2]

'The Führer's order sends the able-bodied Germans out on to the autobahns, into the motor factories, the barracks, the aircraft factories and the gun foundries...'

In February 1935 a law was passed instituting the personal Employment Book, whose 'terrorist significance'[3] was revealed by Seldte, the Labour Minister at the time, when he decreed 'a right to withhold the Employment Book in cases where employers or employees leave their place of work'.

[1] Ibid.
[2] B. Köhler, *Die zweite Arbeitsschlacht*, Munich 1936; quoted by Jürgen Kuczynski, op. cit., p. 148.
[3] Kuczynski, op. cit., p. 151.

Finally, on June 22, 1938, legislation was passed introducing general labour conscription. It enabled the state to direct every individual as service obligations required. Before this a decree had been issued placing young people of fourteen years of age upwards under the control of the labour exchanges.

It is not difficult to deduce the vital importance of the role of the *Arbeitsfront* in this development. Because membership was obligatory for both employers and workers the employers, who in accordance with the aims of the National Socialist state, were entrusted with this slave-owner mandate, henceforth functioned as the workers' task-masters.

Here the totalitarian state emerges in its absolute form. Every need and sense of individual self-determination was gradually extinguished. All social differences were eliminated, all values made relative by order of the state. The state acted through every individual. Behind the fire-curtain of war, which national socialism regarded as an indispensible stage in its world mission, the pattern of Plato's caste state began to be discernible. At the summit stands an élite master class which, in order to establish its power, disposes of a subordinate military caste which, in its turn, commands the broad masses of the workers. On the lowest level, on that of mere animal existence, would be an even larger helot class, made up of the peoples of the conquered empires, the racially inferior. They would have been driven to work by fear of mass liquidation – like the prisoners in the concentration camps – while the workers above them would have been spurred on by fear of being reduced to the helot caste.

# PART FIVE

*Deception as Totalitarianism's Main Weapon*

Terror is only an additional, supplementary weapon in totalitarianism's armoury. Because terror is so obviously inhuman and the human sufferings which it causes arouse the most powerful human emotions its secondary character is easily overlooked. The main weapon is deception. The two serve both the attainment and the maintenance of totalitarian power in such a way that terror makes its appearance on the scene as a complementary element when the technique of deception proves inadequate. This serves to paralyse the will of the individual and of society to resist totalitarian integration. Propaganda has often been regarded as an autonomous totalitarian technique; but it is in fact only the application of the general will to deceive in the sphere of public communications media. In this process the effectiveness of the policy of deception does not always depend on the full success of the corresponding manoeuvre. It is enough if it inspires uncertainty and indecision, which excludes any possibility of successful counter-action and helps natural opportunism to triumph. The fear of terror then increases the likelihood of an opportunist decision. This explains why it was possible to deceive, with such comparative ease, the majority of the German people about the existence of the annihilation camps and the concentration camps. The doubts which many people came to feel about the activities of the SS as the war went on were at first stilled by propaganda and various deception manoeuvres. In view of the risks which went with terror the number of people who continued to have their doubts was not, however, large enough to compel disclosure of the truth.

This weapon of deception is aimed particularly against totalitarianism's enemies, who are to be overcome and held down. Just as Hitler was proud of having taken his enemies' techniques and made them his own, he also admitted that he had learned the technique of concealment and intrigue from the 'Protocols of the Elders of Zion'. His cunning and vicious personality was almost the perfect embodiment of this aspect of totalitarianism. Stalin's own low cunning was only slightly inferior to Hitler's. In fact the whole Stalinist organization and recruitment system was based on cunning and deception. Examples which spring to mind are the policy of 'cells' and 'infiltration', the 'front organizations' or even the 'banishing' of opponents of communist organizational activity.[1] After the seizure of power, however, the weapon of deception is turned against the subjects of the state who still remain to be integrated and against other states. It is even directed, both before and after power has been seized, against its own allies, even against the members and the leadership of the totalitarian party itself! Deception is, in fact, totalitarianism's universal and omnipresent technique.

How National Socialism deceived the Weimar parties and especially the German National People's Party has already been described. Hitler had already revealed his unique talent for deception at the time of the 1933 Munich *putsch*. He deceived both Baron von Kahr and General Ludendorff. The technique of inventing scapegoat symbols is also part of the wider aspect of this strategy.

One of the Nazis' outstanding achievements was based on the

[1] Philip Selznick, *The Organizational Weapon, A Study of Bolshevik Strategy and Tactics*, New York, Toronto, London 1952, especially pp. 66 ff., 113–63, 207 ff., 215, 225–60.

successful deception of conservative circles, especially the Prussian and Austrian military and civil service aristocracy. In their case, splitting was the method which was first employed. The radicalization of a section of the conservatives made the National Socialists' programme and methods seem acceptable at the beginning. Thus Spengler's 'Prussian Socialism' was an important stimulus for National Socialist method[1] and a sociologist like Othmar Spann believed that National Socialism would realize his concept of the 'Christian corporative state'.[2] The very day that Hitler invaded Austria, Spann drank to the health of the Greater German Reich, only to be arrested by the Gestapo two hours later. The young generation of conservative revolutionaries[3] were especially bitter at having been duped by National Socialism and their disillusionment during the Second World War contributed towards the attempt by Count Stauffenberg and a whole band of misled idealists to overthrow Hitler on July 20, 1944.

When Hindenburg appointed Hitler as the German Chancellor the National Socialists were only a small minority in the government. Hitler's position *vis-à-vis* the President and the *Reichswehr* was extremely vulnerable. Shirer gives a very vivid account of how Hitler and Goebbels deceived the aged Hindenburg and the rest of Germany's Conservative and monarchist circles:

'Hitler would open the new Reichstag, which he was about to destroy, in the Garrison church at Potsdam, the great shrine of Prussianism, which aroused in so many Germans memories of imperial glories and grandeur, for here Hindenburg had first come in 1866 on a pilgrimage when he returned as a young Guards officer from the Austro-Prussian war . . . Hindenburg was visibly moved and at one point in the ceremony the old Field-Marshal had tears in his eyes.'[4]

Shirer points out that this performance was staged two days before the Reichstag session in the Kroll Opera House, where Hitler was given his Enabling Law. When, shortly afterwards, the President, aged, weak and ill, withdrew to his estate, Gut Neudeck, he became in effect the prisoner of the SS. Papen, to whom Hitler owed his appointment as Chancellor, only narrowly escaped the same fate as befell Schleicher on June 30, 1934, the night of the long knives. One after another the senior generals in the *Reichswehr* were slandered and rendered powerless.

[1] O. Spengler, *Preussentum und Sozialismus*, Munich 1924.
[2] Ernst von Salomon, *Der Fragebogen*, Hamburg 1951, p. 214.
[3] Cf. Moeller van der Bruck, *Das Dritte Reich*, Hamburg 1931; Armin Mohler, *Die Konservative Revolution in Deutschland 1918–1932, Grundriss ihrer Weltanschauungen*, Stuttgart 1950.
[4] William L. Shirer, *The Rise and Fall of the Third Reich*, London 1960, p. 197.

Hitler's real opinion of most of the guests who had been invited to Potsdam was very different: 'This paper aristocracy, these degenerate descendants of ancient noble families have one remaining task, "to die in beauty".'[1] The treatment which Mussolini experienced at the hands of the Italian royal house even spurred Hitler into making one of his rare acts of generosity. It made him want to raise the pensions of Social Democrats like Severing and Löbe because they had abolished the Hohenzollern monarchy in 1918. After the attempt on his life on July 20, 1944, Hitler wrongly thought that it had been inspired by the Hohenzollerns.

In 1933 Hitler had concluded his concordat with the Holy See. What had been his motives? He himself said: 'Fascism may make its peace with the Church in God's name. Why not? I will do the same. That won't prevent me from tearing Christianity up root and branch[2] for ... they can't make an Aryan of Jesus.'[3] The Führer spoke harshly about the Protestants and also about the 'German Christians'. He believed they were not even worth fighting against.[4] Hitler's aim was literally the founding of a neo-pagan religion.

It must, however, be pointed out that in the years between the wars the success of Hitler's deception tactics was also conditioned by the social structure at the time. In periods when the steady balance of social and national life is upset the most important social values are frequently undermined and must be re-established. If a social upheaval of this kind fundamentally changes the functions of whole groups and classes, conflicts can break out within the groups themselves and between the group and the community because of the change in the sense of values. If this phenomenon is looked at only in the light of the transformation of class society into mass society, that is taking too general a view, since this transformation is not confined simply to societies threatened by totalitarianism.[5] The fact that national socialism's success could be attributed not least to the economic consequences of the lost war and in particular to the repercussions of the world economic crisis makes it appear at least doubtful whether Hannah Arendt's thesis of the disinterested nature of the masses is valid. Today the mass age has reached a far more advanced stage than it had in the thirties; but the susceptibility of European states in respect of totalitarian solutions was diminished, not the least important reason being that the masses came to share in the general economic prosperity. It is not only totalitarianism which can give them *panem et circenses*, but it is only totalitarianism which can confine itself to giving *circenses* and nothing else.

[1] Rauschning, *Gespräche mit Hitler*, op. cit., p. 44.
[2] Ibid.    [3] Ibid., p. 50.    [4] Ibid., p. 51.    [5] Hannah Arendt, op. cit., pp. 489 ff.

Hitler's primary concern was to deceive the masses, for which he felt the profoundest contempt: "But it gives us a very special, secret pleasure to see how the people around us are unaware of what is really happening to them. They gawp at a few familiar superficialities."[1] Hitler strove to exclude the masses, which he called a 'drunken voting herd' from participating in the formation of the political will. He believed their days were past.[2]

Here we should remember the sociological law discovered by Karl Mannheim, according to which a partial dissolution of the social order reawakens a mentality which was predominant in an earlier stage in the evolution of society.[3]

According to Wangh, anxieties aroused by crisis situations cause men to adopt regressive defence mechanisms. 'Fear of the loss of the object of love, loss of self-respect, of individual identity and anxiety about the super-ego, which we experience as a feeling of guilt, can be held at bay in this way.'[4] Regression to earlier stages of psychical development then went still further if the individual identity was threatened and was no longer able to recognize the limits of the self with any certainty. Then one takes refuge in one's childhood mother and one exaggerates the slightest difference so that one can say to oneself: "That's not I".'[5]

This rule also applies to our problem – the relationship of important large groups in society to the government. Government symbols, which almost perform the function of mediators between the government machine and the public, make the effect of this rule more pronounced. In a social crisis not only do the antagonisms inherent in contemporary society come to the surface, becoming correspondingly more acute, but so do also the conflicts from earlier social epochs which seemed to have been finally overcome in the preceding stage of apparent stability. The latter are, however, usually not topical enough to emerge as independent ideological forces. They do not possess sufficient dynamism of their own to overcome the tendencies characteristic of the present stage. But they are important in so far as, in the conflict between contemporary ideologies, they are often decisive, especially where these are equally balanced.

As we shall show, Hitler's deception technique was by no means

---

[1] Rauschning, *Gespräche mit Hitler*, op. cit., p. 181.

[2] Ibid., p. 187.

[3] Martin Wangh, 'Psychoanalytische Betrachtungen zur Dynamik und Genese des Vorurteils, des Antisemitismus und des Nazismus', in *Psyche*, XVIth Year, No. 5, 1962, p. 274.

[4] Ibid., p. 275.

[5] With reference to the integration of the German conservatives, cf. Rauschning, *Make and Break with the Nazis*, London 1941, pp. 49–60.

applied only against his opponents; it was also employed on the vast majority of the Nazi leader strata and the ordinary party members. This technique was to be used later to conceal the formation of an ever-shrinking circle of dedicated élite. It appeared also, for example, in the relationship of the top leadership of the National Socialist Party to the 'markedly-national' and 'Catholic-national' elements within the German-national movement in Austria, which was increasingly pushed into the background after the German invasion.[1] It was equally conspicuous in the dissolution of the Sudeten German *Freikorps*. After it had done what Hitler wanted of it and had provoked an international crisis it was relegated to being the recruiting arsenal for the SS.[2]

Austrians and Sudenten Germans, who had hoped for a certain measure of autonomy within the Greater German Reich, soon had their hopes dashed; for the pan-German course of Hitler's policy was also to prove to be part of the general plan to deceive. Hitler exploited the pan-German sentiments in these countries in order to acquire a better base from which to launch into war and world conquest. As he looked on nationalism as a part of the liberal and middle-class programme he also used it to deceive the 'despicable mass'. There had already been evidence of this in his betrayal of the South Tyrolese in favour of Mussolini. And so Konrad Henlein, the leader of the ultra-nationalist Sudeten German Party, was also under constant surveillance by the Gestapo in 1938 because his relations with British circles seemed to suggest that he might be satisfied with autonomy for the Sudeten Germans within the Czechoslovak state.[3] Once the Sudetenland had become part of the Third Reich Henlein became a political nonentity.

## The Method of Pseudo-Legitimacy

National Socialism had come to power with the help of pseudo-legality. The retention of constitutional and democratic forms is a characteristic technique of Caesarism[4] and goes back to the time of the Emperor Augustus, who engineered his own election to the office of people's tribune. After his death his successors in the principate retained the outward forms of the Roman Republic.

[1] A. Wandruszka, *Österreichs politische Struktur*, op. cit., pp. 417 ff.
[2] Cf. Martin Broszat, 'Das Sudetendeutsche Freikorps', in *Vierteljahrshefte für Zeitgeschichte*, Year 9, 1961.
[3] Schellenberg, op. cit., pp. 56 f.
[4] Cf. Frank, op. cit., pp. 205 ff.

Hitler was proud that he was able to influence the mass; as far as possible he wished to avoid any sort of friction with it. That is why he preferred to retain the existing institutions and simply to give them a new meaning, to drain them of their original meaning and to transform them into expedients which could be of use to his movement.

Mussolini, too, never tried to abolish the monarchy during the twenty years that he ruled Italy. Both the Senate and the imperial army remained in existence and the civil service continued to function in its former form. The very survival of these institutions was, in the end, a contributory factor in the downfall of fascism, yet Mussolini did not discard them as he had to consider the public's sense of legitimacy and constitutionality.

In Germany, too, the Weimar Constitution remained in force after January 30, 1933. Hitler was careful not to forget that power was transferred to him by a quasi-constitutional Enabling Law – a measure which, however, was basically illegal because of the forcible expulsion of the Communist deputies from the Reichstag and their arrest and prosecution. Parliaments also continued to be 'elected'. Hitler's system of government after Hindenburg's death showed that he apparently heeded the German sense of constitutionality. Thus in the dispute between the *Wehrmacht* and his own Brown Shirts (Storm Troops) he came down on the side of the legitimate symbol of Prussian-German unity. In the administration, the *Landrat* (District Magistrate) of the old Prussian monarchy was always coupled with the Nazi *Kreisleiter* (District Leader). And in the sphere of law and justice the normal courts – except in the final stages of the war – were far more in evidence as far as the general public was concerned than the Special National Socialist Courts for legislation.

The post-war dictatorship in the small European states also endeavoured to retain the outward signs of legitimacy and constitutionality. In Hungary, for example, there was the constant emphasis on the importance of the 'thousand-year-old constitution', although the system chosen by the deputies had scarcely anything to do with a genuine choice. For the same reasons the Hungarian dictator, Admiral Horthy, called himself 'The Representative of the King' – a king whose return was forbidden. In Poland, Pilsudski for a long time resisted attempts to elect him as Head of State. However unimportant the role of the *Sejm* (Parliament) was during the Beck period the people were content so long as the *Sejm* was called the *Sejm* and met from time to time. Similarly in Yugoslavia, in spite of the undemocratic elections to the *Skupština*, there was never any outburst of public anger as long as the *Skupština* met and the government kept up the appearance of legitimacy with the help of the royal assent. Despite this patent misuse of democratic institutions, however, the obstinacy with which public opinion clung to them was a good augury for the future.

In comparison with the intuitive understanding and the skill of fascist technique, the dissolution of the Austrian Parliament and the suspension of the Austrian Constitution by Dollfuss is more reminiscent of the absolutist methods of the nineteenth century. In fact this semi-dictatorial regime meant to reawaken memories of the Habsburg state among important sections of the population by means of association. The republican Constitution was loathed among the upper and middle classes in Austria. This is proved by the fact that no real protests were made against the violation of the constitution in 1934 although these same classes condemned the violation of the criminal law by the socialists, who for that reason alone were in a position to defend the Constitution. It must be remembered, however, that the Criminal Law book was older than the Republican Constitution and had therefore become more generally accepted.

The illegal dissolution of Parliament and the suspension of a Constitution was not an unusual occurence in Austria. Dollfuss and Schuschnigg deliberately intended to create the impression of a return to the semi-absolutism of the Emperor Francis Joseph. Another indication of this was that the uniform of the army was again that worn by the imperial army. The uniforms of the *Vaterländische Front* and the *Heimwehr* were also eminently suitable to awaken these associations. Thus Dollfuss appeared in the officer's uniform of his former regiment when he made his famous speech in the Vienna Trabrennplatz on September 11, 1933, and announced that Austria was to have a corporative constitution.[1] And his recourse to the wartime economic enabling law was intended to undermine the still uncertain legality of the Republic by means of the more deeply rooted legitimacy of the Habsburg state.

## Pseudo-Democratic Forms and Institutions

Until now the question why the peoples consented to losing their rights has received insufficient attention. How is one to account for this process, this strange capitulation of the general will?

To transform a democratic community into a totalitarian dictatorship was a far more difficult and protracted undertaking than it might appear to the outside world. This is true of Italy, Germany, Poland, Austria and also Yugoslavia. There were several phases to this

[1] Cf. the illustration facing p. 145 in Gordon Shepherd's *Engelbert Dollfuss*, op. cit.

transformation process. With the exception of Germany no state came anywhere near to achieving full totalitarianism. This, however, is not due to any lack of will on the part of the governments concerned but to the inability of the dictatorships, which showed little understanding of the social requirements of a modern tyranny. They also often lacked the courage which is needed to carry the totalitarian system through to its logical conclusion.

Even in the total state the process which finally destroys and eradicates democracy is a slow one and its success depends on whether it is systematically pursued. At the start it was necessary to consider public opinion. Later, fascism was able to exploit both the new and the old conflicts between the ideologies and the loyalties we have already mentioned. This meant that the peoples were ready to accept measures which in normal times they would have repudiated as illegal and unjustified. Being clever tacticians the fascists never tried to do too much at once, preferring to realize their aims step by step. This was done in such a way that the outer shell of the law-based state was preserved until the total state had grown and matured under its protection.[1] Later the Hitler regime showed its true face – even to its own adherents. From 1937 cabinet meetings were abandoned and the *Gauleiter* (District Leaders) acted as a mouthpiece for pronouncements on matters which had never been the subject of objective criticism or discussion.[2]

One of the reasons why the people surrendered their liberties was also the great disparity which existed between the actual government technique and the masses' idea of what it should be. This allowed totalitarian propaganda to breach the democratic stronghold and destroy the people's ties with democratic institutions. The outward forms of the constitutional state were preserved in both Italy and Germany.[3] In neither state did the great majority of the people understand in the first instance that their elected members of parliament were no more responsible for the laws apparently passed by them than theatre-goers are for a play they are watching. Although the links with democratic institutions remained intact among a large part of the population it is true that, as a result of fascist policy, these institutions became increasingly to be justification symbols in Lasswell's sense.[4]

The newly-awakened memories of the 'iron age of national unity' which was associated with the memory of Bismarck's semi-absolutist

[1] This problem is dealt with in detail by Ernst Fraenkel in *The Dual State*, New York, Toronto 1941.　　　　[2] Cf. Frank, op. cit., p. 206.

[3] This was understood by Machiavelli who, however, only applied the government technique practised by the Roman Emperor Augustus during the changeover from the republic to the principate to the small tyrannies of the Italian cities of the Renaissance.

[4] Lasswell, *World Politics and Personal Insecurity*, op. cit., pp. 29 ff.

regime served to increase the popularity of the military parade into which the Reichstag meeting degenerated after Göring had become its president. The symbolism thus created was meant to persuade the man in the street that through the national revolution the Reichstag had, basically, acquired a new meaning and importance; it was to give the impression that it was no longer a futile debating society, a picture of inner disintegration but a model of military discipline, thoroughness and purposefulness. Consequently the Reichstag deputies were also addressed by the Nazi ministers in a tone of voice appropriate to the issuing of an order of the day. This idea was reinforced by intensive propaganda. People constantly heard that the Reichstag was actually a parliament which had been abolished because of the abuses inherent in the party system. The new system was certainly authoritarian, but united, and a regime could not be damned out of hand without proof that it had committed serious mistakes.

This view was expressed in particular in conservative circles, which wrongly associated National Socialism with the constitutionalism of the imperial era. People attempted to console themselves with the argument that dictatorship was merely a temporary remedy indispensible for the nation's development. There could be no clearer proof of the dangerous effect produced by totalitarianism. For these opinions already influenced by propaganda, were to allay the uneasiness of the nation as a whole and suggest to it the idea that dictatorship adheres to constitutional principles both in the actual process of seizing power and in its administrative policy.

## The Totalitarian State and the Concept of Party

Even after seizing power totalitarian movements always describe themselves as 'parties'. But by definition the one-party state excludes every rival party. The totalitarian party recognizes obligations towards itself alone. It represents the following of a Leader. Thus, according to Mussolini, the Italian Fascist Party represented 'neither heart nor head, but the blood vessels through which the blood of the party ideology, party policy and the feelings which move it flows out into the rest of the population'. It unites in itself the élite of the totalitarian society in the general sense. According to Friedrich, the totalitarian party is the embodiment of Hobbes' concept of the state, in which all members depend as individuals depend on the sovereign and are individuals in their relationship to him.[1] Against this should

[1] Friedrich, *Totalitäre Diktatur*, op. cit., pp. 65 f.

be pointed out the existence of a leader hierarchy within the National Socialist Party. Thus, for example, the relationship between Göring, Goebbels or Bormann and Hitler was not that of an ordinary individual, to say nothing of Himmler's SS and the Gestapo, whose relationship to the party as a whole was actually that of a state within the state. Yet the essential trend in National Socialism was to the absolute and boundless despotism of Hitler, so that Friedrich's analysis is justified.

But the totalitarian one-party system finds it expedient to retain the word 'party' wherever the democratic party is already well and truly rooted in a country's political theory. The rapidity with which the long-banned political parties in Italy, German and Austria reappeared after the collapse of fascism is further evidence of that. It shows that the links with the parties had survived the government systems under which they had come into existence.

In Germany, for example, the Social Democratic Party and the Free Trade Unions had, for many decades, educated the working class in a spirit of party discipline, which in its turn did much to strengthen the bonds between the people and the Constitution. If the National Socialists wanted to cling to power, they definitely needed at least the silent support of sections of the working class. Had Hitler called his party *Kampfbund* (militant alliance) or *Bewegung* (movement) he would have made it much more difficult to recruit workers. But by claiming that his 'party' was both national and socialist he was able to divide the loyalties of the workers and thus absorb at least sections of them into his movement.

Fascism needed only to adopt the constitutional framework and to replace democratic principles by such as were only pseudo-democratic. When the National Socialists dissolved the Free Trade Unions and replaced them by the *Arbeitsfront* (Labour Front), the material interests of the great majority of organized labour were at first unaffected, as they neither had to make extra financial payments nor to forfeit their rights to such payments. Certain psychological palliatives were to act as a further spur to the workers. By becoming members of a privileged 'Master Race', the proletariat suddenly felt it had been transformed into a sort of aristocracy; by getting the chance to travel through their 'Strength through Joy' organization they felt they had come nearer to being capitalists. The following arguments were suggested to the workers:

| POSITIVE | NEGATIVE |
|---|---|
| 1. I still have the vote. | It is dangerous to admit to being a member of the working-class parties. |
| 2. I haven't got to make the difficult decision whether to vote for Social Democrats, Communists, National Socialists or the Zentrum. | Not to vote for the Führer is risky. |
| 3. The *Arbeitsfront* gives me the same advantages as the trade unions. | I cannot strike against the employers. |
| 4. There is now plenty of work and no danger of unemployment. | Of course, I earn rather less, but... |
| 5. The material prospects for the future are very hopeful. My wife and children can sleep peacefully. My wages will go up again in the future. | |

The positive attitude has triumphed.

Typical of the way the German workers were deceived was the technique used when the Free Trade Unions were taken over by the Nazi Labour Front on May 2, 1933. First the Hitler government declared May 1st – the Socialist workers' traditional holiday and the day when they held their big annual demonstrations – to be the national holiday of 'German Labour'. Labour delegates from all parts of Germany were flown to Berlin where, at the Tempelhof airfield, Goebbels organized the greatest mass rally Germany had ever seen. At the opening ceremony Hitler received the workers' delegates and declared: 'You will see how untrue and unjust is the statement that our revolution is directed against the German workers.'[1] The same day Goebbels wrote in his diary: 'Tomorrow we shall occupy the trade union buildings. There will be little resistance.'[2] Some time before, on April 21st, Dr Ley had already signed a secret order for the SA and the SS to occupy the trade union buildings on May 2nd, take the trade union leaders into protective custody and confiscate the trade union funds.[3]

[1] Shirer, op. cit., p. 202.    [2] Ibid.    [3] Ibid., p. 202, footnote.

While the attention of the German people was focused on to the destruction of the chains of the Versailles Treaty, the workers were deprived of their personal and economic freedom. The catch-phrase 'The common good before personal good' was meant to conceal from the German people the corruption and the ill-gotten wealth of the Nazi leaders. In spite of the slogan 'Honour to German Labour', the workers were deprived of their freedom of movement by the laws of May 1934 and June 1935. The employment book and the ban on strikes made the worker completely dependent on the employer. The introduction of compulsory labour (by the law of June 22, 1938) now added bondage to the state to the already existing bondage to the employer. The 'Strength through Joy' activities and participation in the *Arbeitsfront* rallies, etc., which were made obligatory, also cut down the workers' leisure.

The small shopkeepers and manufacturers to whom Hitler owed his electoral successes were made the biggest dupes of all. A large part of these groups were impoverished by the enforced centralization. The businessmen, too, whose associations had put up the money which made the National Socialist Party's victory possible, were also deceived. They soon found themselves trapped in a labryinth of bureaucratic orders and controls. A worker who had been sacked often took revenge by making to the Gestapo and the party authorities a false accusation against his employer which could lead to his prosecution.

## Deception Manoeuvres and the Artificial Creation of Antagonisms

By adopting socialist class-war phraseology simply to apply it exclusively to Jewish capitalists, national socialism managed to convince sections of the German working class that Hitler was able to carry out socialist ideas more effectively than the 'pluto-democracies' in the West which Nazi propaganda maintained enslaved the workers. The distinction drawn by the Nazis between 'creative and rapacious' capital was used to bolster this claim.

With the help of the party programme worked out by Gottfried Feder, the National Socialists were able to convince the German peasant, who still but rarely left his village, that National Socialism protected him from becoming a 'slave of interest rates' which, again, made it easier for Hitler to appoint the banker Schacht as economic dictator; they could tell the peasants that National Socialism protected the Christian faith and at the same time persecute the Christian churches; they could conclude the concordat with the Holy See and at the same time destroy Catholic political organizations; they could say that the regime was at pains to preserve old ways and customs and at the same time erect ultra-modern but tasteless buildings for party purposes.

In Austria, Dollfuss succeeded in winning the support of the peasants by hinting at the freethinking outlook and behaviour of the Viennese socialists while at the same time trying to make a pact with the Nazis. In Poland, Colonel Beck's regime could persecute the socialist working class without arousing the opposition of the peasants whose economic plight was just as desperate. In Yugoslavia, the Stojadinovič government could, in one and the same breath, claim to be the representative of monarchical legitimacy, national unity and sovereignty and yet betray the country's independence without meeting any resistance from the people.

What had proved effective in the field of internal politics was also applied unscrupulously to foreign affairs. Thus even when he concluded the non-aggression pact with Poland, Hitler admitted that he wanted peace with Poland only so long as he felt there was no danger from the West.[1]

As regards Austria, Hitler pursued his policy of deception with the help of people, such as the ostensibly respectable and patriotic Seyss-Inquart, who were imposed on Schuschnigg at the appropriate moment with suicidal conditions.[2]

When Germany invaded Austria Göring deceived the Czechs by taking their ambassador Mastný aside at a reception and assuring him that the Third Reich was well disposed towards Czechoslovakia. At the time of the Sudeten crisis in October 1933 Hitler deceived the Western Powers: 'I don't want a single Czech', and: 'The Sudetenland was my last territorial demand.' One of his closest associates, Hans Frank, realized, too late, 'the monstrous transference of his [Hitler's] political experiences at home to world politics, even to the point of believing he could conquer the democracies of the world just as he had defeated democracy in Germany'.[3]

Hitler was proud of his deceitfulness and merely laughed at any thought of pursuing a straight and honest policy:

'If these out-of-date gentlemen imagine that they can conduct politics like an honest merchant runs his business, in accordance with precedent and convention, they can get on with it. But I am engaged in power

---

[1] Rauschning, *Gespräche mit Hitler*, op. cit., p. 113.
[2] Cf. Ulrich Eichstädt, *Von Dollfuss zu Hitler*, Wiesbaden 1955, pp. 292 ff.
[3] Frank, op. cit., p. 364.

politics, that is, I use any means which seems to help without feeling the slightest concern for what people say or for any code of honour. And if people come and complain, like that man Hugenberg and his tribe, that I break my word, that I violate treaties, that I go in for trickery and deception and misrepresentation, I simply reply: "So what? Go and do the same?" '[1]

One of the main objectives of totalitarian technique is the creation and exploitation of antagonisms and conflicts to inhibit the formation of the general will, the democratic consensus and then ensure that it never again becomes possible. The enemy's camp must be split, crippled, disrupted, confused and finally undermined.

Conflicts of this kind are the distantly visible roof of the unseen edifice of uncertainty, subversion and disintegration.[2] For, given the state of civic training and the widespread democratic conviction of our era, a tyranny which set to work with naked force and violated truth could hardly succeed. Indirect and subtler methods were necessary and were in fact evolved.[3] These consisted in giving a biased account of new antagonisms, creating new pseudo-loyalties and then engineering an artificial confrontation between these and the old antagonisms and loyalties.

If totalitarianism wishes to integrate individuals into its system it must first destroy society. Yet so long as men are under the influence of social groups like the family, the Church, trade unions, political parties, etc., they are removed from possible influence and integration by totalitarian movements. The premise for this integration is, therefore, the destruction of social groups. The pluralistic society and totalitarianism are mutually excluding. Only by successfully destroying the groups to which the individual members belong can totalitarianism, Mannheim believes, break the resistance of the individual psyche: 'A man without his group is like a snail without its shell'.[4] Once the destruction of the pluralistic group is accomplished there comes the new integration into the totalitarian organization. So long as this objective can be attained by deceit, confusion and the manufacture of antagonisms, terror remains in the background. As we have already said, terror is generally of only *secondary* importance

[1] Rauschning, op. cit., pp. 252 f.
[2] Cf. also Gerhard Schultz, 'Der Begriff des Totalitarismus und der National-sozialismus', in *Soziale Welt*, 12th Year, Göttingen 1961, p. 116.
[3] Thus Hitler declared: 'Mastery always means the imposition of a stronger will on a weaker one. How do I impose my will on my adversary? By first splitting and paralysing his own will, putting him at odds with himself, confusing him.' Rauschning, *Gespräche mit Hitler*, op. cit., p. 200.
[4] Cf. also Karl Mannheim, *Diagnose unserer Zeit*, Zurich, Vienna, Constance 1951, pp. 134 f.

and the increase in its use is directly proportional to the failure of other means of disruption and integration.

This explains the fact noted by several writers that after totalitarianism has overcome its adversary and seized power terror does not decrease but, on the contrary, increases.[1] Then, as Arendt observes, terror positively serves the realization of the totalitarian fiction about the classless society or the *Volksgemeinschaft* the racial society. But Arendt's assumption that terror has thus a positive function within the totalitarian system is not acceptable. As the total state is erected on a basis which contradicts every principle of natural human community life, the clearer the antisocial nature of the regime appears after the destruction of the pluralistic groups, the more necessary does terror become.

The fact that it is always easier to whip up the anger of the masses against concrete and visible foes is the reason why, once totalitarianism has liquidated its political and social enemies, men's comprehension of the need for compulsion grows increasingly weaker and the technique of deception becomes increasingly ineffective. Therefore the regime must artificially create an enemy out of some specific group in the state as Hitler did with the Jews and Stalin with the 'Trotskyites' and other 'deviationists'. The more the totalitarian party begins to turn into the one-man rule of a tyrant, as in the case of Hitler and Stalin, the more prevalent terror becomes. Totalitarian rule has a smoother passage in war because there is a generally recognizable enemy to hand. So long as the totalitarian regime continues to enjoy a run of victories, as was the case with National Socialism from 1939 to 1941, the totalitarianism can get by with its primary techniques of deception, paralysis, division and disruption. It is certainly no accident that the Nazi terror was unleased on a large scale only when the prospect of a swift and victorious end to the war became more and more remote. It assumed gigantic proportions when the military inferiority of the Axis became increasingly obvious and the deception techniques failed in Germany and other countries in Europe. The Stalinist terror increased again when the economic consolidation of Europe, the outcome of the Korean War and American resistance against the communist 'cold war', deception, infiltration and disruption from within caused the postponement of world revolution to some distant future. Terror always remained a negative and subsidiary means for totalitarianism.

Yet it must be admitted that the task which the fascists had set themselves was anything but simple, since the general rise in the

[1] Hannah Arendt, op. cit., pp. 666 f., and Friedrich, *Totalitäre Diktatur*, op. cit., pp. 128 ff.

educational level in central Europe and the strengthening of democratic traditions and ways of thinking made it seem inadvisable to ignore public opinion altogether. The fascist regimes in fact learned that criticism and opposition, which they believed to be safely under lock and key, in the end broke out in the immediate proximity of the centre of power itself. If that was not the case, so much the worse for the government. Morstein-Marx reports that Hitler told an Associated Press correspondent that he always showed the draft of a law to his advisers and experts and expected them to tell him frankly if anything was wrong with it. 'I don't want them to say "Yes" to everything. They're quite useless to me if they don't criticize things.'[1]

This method of tyranny's to keep in touch with the public is as old as tyranny itself. Today, however, its value lies in the contacts which the advisers of modern tyrants maintain with the public through officials. But it must be remembered that the information which officials gather and forward to their superiors are coloured and biased. The will to power, which dominates a totalitarian party machine from top to bottom, means usually that information is transmitted from below upwards, a fact which increases the sender's chances of promotion. He will therefore only report on the possible difficulties of the regime or the enemy's successes if he can assume that such reports will enable his superiors to take drastic action. In the course of the Second World War government and party officials close to the Führer finally became increasingly afraid to tell him bad news and the truth.

According to Friedrich, this drying up of all reliable information creates a vacuum round the rulers of a totalitarian state. Terror and propaganda bring about the collapse of the social structure. The real disaster is the atomization of the population, the suppression of all free expression of opinion, the way men are set against one another and learn to distrust one another, the alienation which grows up between employer and worker, university teacher and student, lawyer and client, even between parents and their children, and between brothers and sisters.[2]

This shows that, in the end, terror must work against its own inherent aim. Totalitarian leaders, past-masters in the art of deception, themselves fall victim to this deception. As Lasswell has rightly realized, totalitarian leaders live in an imaginary world[3] of self-

---

[1] Morstein-Marx, *Government in the Third Reich*, New York 1937, p. 92.

[2] Friedrich, *Totalitäre Diktatur*, op. cit., p. 159.

[3] Harold D. Lasswell, 'The World Revolutionary Situation', in *Totalitarianism*, edited by Carl J. Friedrich, Cambridge (Mass.) 1954, p. 367, quoted by Carl J. Friedrich, *Totalitäre Diktatur*, op. cit., p. 159.

deception and auto-suggestion. Hitler's last days in the Berlin bunker are eloquent testimony to this truth.

It should also be remembered that terror loses much of its effectiveness if it becomes too common. For if, in the total state, ever bigger groups of society are exposed to terror, the result is on the one hand a hardening, on the other the spontaneous and silent formation of a common front by these strata against the regime. The final outcome is a change of mood, which ultimately also grips the élite and undermines its unity and solidarity. It is a well-known fact that at the end of the war Hitler could no longer rely even on Himmler, one of his most faithful henchmen.

As artificial conflicts within the structure of society can only effectively be engineered if they are reinforced by terror, any easing immediately raises doubts about the existence of the totalitarian system as such. This truth was proved when the Stalinist terror was relaxed in Poland and Hungary in 1966. In Germany the collapse of the Nazi terror led directly to the collapse of the whole totalitarian system. It was the same once fascist terror had ended in Italy, Austria and in all the Nazi-occupied parts of Europe.

Inside Germany itself, the technique of creating scapegoats was above all designed to provoke antagonisms; for example between Catholics and Protestants, Aryans and Jews, town and country, conservatives, liberals and socialists, and between employers and workers. Abroad, the hostility between socialists and conservatives, legitimists and pan-Germans was exploited in Austria. In Czechoslovakia the animosity between Czechs and Slovaks as well as that between Czechs and Germans provided an opportunity for the employment of these methods. The hostility between Hungary and Romania, between Yugoslavia and Croatia, also proved invaluable.

Yet the success of all these techniques depended on the efficacy of Nazi terror and this in turn depended on Hitler's military success. The whole tissue of lies and terror was bound, therefore, to lose its power as final victory became a matter of doubt. This proves that a totalitarian system can seldom be got rid of without outside pressure. The exception to this rule is the demolition of Stalinism. As soon as terror threatens the inner circle of the oligarchy, so that even the more important leaders must fear for their lives, then the requisite basis for a successful revolution against totalitarianism, without the aid of outside pressure, is already in existence. This was also an important factor in the collapse of National Socialism in 1945.

CHAPTER VIII

# Dictatorship and Group Integration

The seizure of power by a fascist party did not lead to the immediate elimination of all democratic factors; for many of democracy's ideological and structural elements had had a decisive bearing on the mould of society in central Europe and in the nineteenth and at the beginning of the twentieth century.

Never before had there been a genuine tyranny in a highly industrialized country in which illiteracy was as good as non-existent. The principle of *laissez-faire* was widely recognized and the pluralistic structure of the state was bound to bring totalitarian aspirations up against difficult problems. Among fascist systems, only German National Socialism succeeded in systematically setting up a thoroughly systematic tyranny which was tailored to the structure of modern society. A few of the social techniques applied by Nazism will therefore be described to show how an all-pervading tyranny can be securely established in a pluralistic society.

The merest glance at the problem makes it clear that Nazi propaganda was based on a masterly knowledge of the social relationships between individual and group (such as political party, church, trade unions, etc.) and between group and community and that the Nazi utilized this knowledge for their own political purposes. As a member of a pluralistic society, the individual belongs to various groups. These groups, especially the larger ones, reflect the religious, political, linguistic and economic divisions of society. Loyalty to the state is mediated through such groups. In its efforts to integrate all individuals into its scheme of domination, national socialism had to manipulate the loyalties of the masses in such a way as to distintegrate these intermediary groups. The special social structure of central Europe with its vestiges of the Middle Ages went a long way towards facilitating its plans.[1] Thus, as a socializing form, the pseudo-medieval association became, under modern conditions, a suitable basis for the fight against democracy. Secret societies and similar groups often

[1] For example, military and nationalist secret societies, student fraternities with medieval features, vestiges of the old guild spirit in the cities and the feudal structure of the big estates.

acted as pressure and interest groups. These organizations were more often than not a cross between a medieval and a modern association.

## PART ONE

*Dictatorship and Group Ties*

In *Problems of Philosophy* William James speaks about the 'faith ladder'. He lists a whole range of positions which an individual can adopt towards a particular ideology. This ladder extends from the declaration: 'There is nothing absurd in a certain view of the world being true,' nothing self-contradictory to the statement: 'It must be true,' and finally to the declaration: 'It shall be true, at any rate for me.'

The last rung of this ladder leads to the unanimity of thought demanded by the Nazis;[1] and from 1933 until the present day this maxim was repeated by all adherents of totalitarian regimes where the *credenda* and *miranda*[2] of dictatorship was concerned. At that point, in many countries, all hope of social harmony disappeared and the only alternative left was unconditional submission to tyranny or the extermination squad.

This 'either – or' remains the *ultima ratio* only for the man who values a definite belief infinitely more than his capacity for rational thought. He is mostly aware that his belief runs counter to what his reason tells him. It is therefore essential to examine the various degrees of intensity which this subservience to a totalitarian movement and its ideology can attain; in other words, the point at issue is the relationship between totalitarianism and the loyalty or solidarity which it demands. Until 1914 sociology, under the influence of utilitarianism, was inclined to assume, with Marx and Razenhofer, that 'self-interest' was the mainspring of social behaviour. But after 1918, due to the nationality and the social problem, far greater factors of uncertainty appeared in central than in western Europe and therefore deeper layers of human nature also rose to the surface.

In settled times it is difficult to distinguish between self-interest and loyalty, because the relationships between individual, groups and various kinds of associations and between these associations and the state appear to be harmonious. If the various associations within the community are well co-ordinated, the loyalty of the individual to any particular one is not put to the test. Thus in a static society the behaviour of the individual seems to be in harmony with his interests

---

[1] C. J. Friedrich, *Totalitäre Diktatur*, op. cit., pp. 122–30.
[2] The expression comes from Charles E. Merriam, *Political Power*, Glencoe, Ill; 1950 pp. 107 ff.

and wishes. In such a society nothing prevents an individual from being a loyal citizen and, at the same time, a member of a religious community within the state. He is at liberty to join a trade union, the political party which appeals to him most, a sports club, a literary society or any club based on the voluntary principle. When this man applauds the chairman's speech at a local trade union meeting, repeats the Creed during divine service or votes for a candidate in parliamentary elections, we cannot say that a different mind actuates him on these particular occasions although they involve a somewhat dissimilar activity. The homage he pays during the national anthem seems at any rate to indicate a specialized function of the mind on that occasion, namely that function in terms of which his relation to his own state may be determined; and if this specialized function of his mind arises out of a complex of emotions and interests positively attached to the nation or state, we have an example of a loyalty.

In peaceful, settled times membership of a religious community, a political party or a trade union does not imply treason. A man who stands up and sings the national anthem can, if he wants, go off and sing the Internationale at a socialist party meeting. Although these behaviour patterns seem to have become set they are, nevertheless, subject to certain changes. Personal interests often get out of balance, that is to say, at one time greater weight is laid on religion, at another on politics. There are people who at one time in their life are drawn more to the orthodox or national church and at other times more to the various sects. It is possible for a man who feels attracted to politics in his youth to become a convinced nationalist when he joins the army, and then, in his old age, to devote himself mainly to religious matters.

It is obvious that even in normal times one of the various groups and associations is preferred to the others. An individual's relationship to the group is determined by his education, his social status, his profession, his cultural and social background. When he makes a decision it will be rational, that is, he is convinced of its reason and its logic. The man who, in time of war, gives up all his peacetime interests to serve his country will rightly argue that the common good is more important than his private pursuits.

However, a man sometimes leaves a political party to join a secret society or leaves a religious sect because a political leader makes a greater impression on him. This not only shows that people do not always set the same value on their various loyalties, but that a particular loyalty goes up or down in their scale of values according to the time and the circumstances. The units comprising this system of values are not watertight compartments, being integral parts of the individual's mind. If, therefore, a citizen – as in the above example – sings his national anthem the other values are not completely banished from his mind at that particular moment.

It can definitely be assumed that the scale of values is altogether or largely established in that part of the consciousness which determines behaviour towards the group – either in the form of adaptation or participation. According to Simmel these are the layers of the consciousness through which the individual contributes to the levelling process (*nivellement*) without which there is no group and mass behaviour.

The distinguishing feature of individual and group behaviour is that different value accents are assigned to various real and ideal spheres. The highest values in the scale by which men live are so lofty that in certain circumstances a man will sacrifice everything for them, even his own life. These supreme values, which we feel to be our bounden duty to observe, we shall term 'transcendental values'. Under present-day conditions the 'nation' or the 'just social order' are regarded as transcendental values, whereas in the past only God, the emperor, the king, the prince and the city occupied this exalted position.

C. G. Jung has made a valuable contribution to the elucidation of the pseudo-religious basis of totalitarianism. He has realized that ever since the Reformation and under the influence of mechanistic science we have underestimated the power of the unconscious:

'Before the First World War broke out, were were quite certain that the world could be righted by rational means. Now we behold the amazing spectacle of *States* taking over the age-old claim of theocracy, that is of *totality*, inevitably accompanied by suppression of free opinion. Again we see people cutting each others' throats to support childish theories of how to achieve paradise on earth.

'Modern man has lost the protection of ecclesiastical walls carefully sited and reinforced since the Roman days, and owing to that loss he has approached the edge of the world-destroying and world-creating fire. Life has been quickened and intensified.'[1]

Another of Jung's contributions to sociology is his theory of archetypes and the collective unconscious,[2] although he does not take sufficiently into consideration the practical uses to which these archetypes have been put by the powers of 'the world-destroying fire'.[3] The

[1] C. G. Jung, *Psychologie und Religion*, Zurich 1947, pp. 87 f.
[2] C. G. Jung, *Integration of the Personality*, London 1940, pp. 52 ff.
[3] Ibid.; cf. also Karl Mannheim, *Diagnose unserer Zeit*, Zurich 1951, pp. 134 ff.

Roman Catholic Church has utilized the father symbol with great success, for example when it modelled the Church hierarchy on a patriarchal basis. And the roots of nationalism can be traced back to the position of the king or prince as the 'Father of the Fatherland'. The great mythical figures of German history such as Charlemagne and Frederick Barbarossa are father figures, and Hitler endeavoured, not altogether unsuccessfully, to continue this tradition, although he came nearer to Jung's concept of the 'animus' and the 'id', that is to the irrational element which, according to Jung, dwells in every soul.

Fromm holds that the psychical projection of the German middle class which we have already mentioned became clearly visible in Hitler's personal evolution.[1] Hitler's authoritarian personality, his sadistic-masochistic temperament, which communicated itself to his movement, was a compensation for the loss of the father symbol resulting from defeat, revolution and economic impoverishment. He knew that the mass will not govern itself – its only need is the father who rules it. Thus Mitscherlich believes that 'the character of the idol, the pin-up, the leader is, therefore determined less by the primary, outstanding quality of an individual than by the inevitable tensions which a certain ruling type of association generates'. Therefore all forms of effective propaganda play 'first on people's expectations and invent symbols to reflect these hopes . . .'[2]

This raises the question of the importance of the symbol. It is a well-known fact that primitive peoples choose especially aggressive and powerful animals as symbols of the community. Thus among American Indians birds of prey such as eagles, falcons, hawks etc. play the part of the totem symbolizing the tribe. Medieval heraldry, in which lions, eagles, bears and leopards predominated, provides further confirmation of this fact. And in India's 'pantheon' animal emblems in the form of elephants, apes and snakes play an important role. The character of a nation is often determined by their emblem. Thus in India deadly cunning and lightning-swift rapine are not scorned by society as they are in Europe, reflecting as they do the positive emblems of snake and ape. Man's emblems are, on the one hand, always a projection of his aggressive instincts, which he is unable to indulge in the framework of society; on the other hand they serve as a pretext or spur for aggressive, antisocial acts. His emblems enable him to undergo a change of identity – he performs anti-human acts not as a man, but as a lion, an eagle or a bull. It is not he himself

[1] Fromm, op. cit., p. 212.
[2] Alexander Mitscherlich, *Auf dem Weg zur vaterlosen Gesellschaft*, Munich 1963. p. 441.

who has acted but the collective, the community, which is a lion or an eagle.

The 'Leader' played a similar role for the masses in National Socialism. By identifying themselves with the 'Leader' people were absolved from the necessity of making a free decision made with due regard to their conscience. The 'Leader' was allowed to perform anti-social and aggressive acts which the 'id' urges on man but which the 'super-ego' forbids. On the other hand, as the Nuremberg, Auschwitz and other war crimes trials showed, men believed that even the most monstrous acts were justified if they were committed in the name of the Führer. Refusal to comply with the Führer's orders was therefore followed by 'just' punishment from the symbolic 'father'.

The veneration of Joan of Arc in France is a demonstration not only of the reality of archetypal mother-symbol but also of the 'anima'. The Nazi ideal of the 'German woman' was modelled exactly on the mother-symbol. It would widen the scope of this book far too much if we were to examine the extent to which worship of the nation as godhead contains elements of the mother-symbol and the archetypal 'anima' symbol. Between 1924 and 1928, for instance, German nationalist youth, student and gymnastic associations issued a special coin depicting a Teutonic goddess wearing a helmet on her flowing hair and with dark clouds floating above her head. It bore the words: 'The storm breaks'.

Anti-Semitic propaganda represents the Jews as the modern incarnation of the devil. If we compare the *Stürmer*'s caricatures of the Jews with anti-Jewish prints and etchings made during the Reformation it is apparent that the Nazis portrayed the Jews as the opposing religions portrayed each other in the age of the wars of religion, that is as the 'power of evil'. In the Tyrol and the Sudetenland the miners, who had never set eyes on a Jew, attributed to them all the qualities which are popularly ascribed to the devil or to witches. Anti-Semitism is, of course, a specific form of the regression we have already mentioned and it was strengthened in particular by the social uncertainty felt by the middle classes.[1]

Jung is well aware that the collapse of the protective walls erected by the Church applies to Protestants as well as Catholics, but he does not see sufficiently clearly that the consequences of this collapse have, generally speaking, been as marked in Catholic as in Protestant countries. Apart from Lutheran Protestantism the people living in countries which were almost completely untouched by the Reformation proved to be the most susceptible to the autocratic claims of the sovereign

[1] Cf. also Béla Grunberg, 'Der Antisemit und der Ödipuskomplex', in *Psyche*, August 1962, pp. 275 ff.

nation-state; for example, in Bavaria, Italy, Austria, Poland, Slovakia, Croatia and Spain; and also in the Latin-American republics. In those states, in particular, where Calvinism had established itself, the masses continued to live under the quickening influence of Christianity, which formed a counterweight to the state's attempts to impose absolute and theocratic forms of rule; for example in the Anglo-Saxon countries or Holland. In spite of all this, however, the numerous instances of Catholic resistance, as in the Rhineland, Bavaria and France, cannot be ignored.

On the other hand, as soon as state power had fallen into authoritarian hands in Lutheran regions the doctrine of passive obedience was a considerable impediment to organizing resistance to tyranny, although the Protestant conscience is a guarantee of tenacity. In Catholic areas, the resistance theory of the Catholic Church, which went back to John of Salisbury and Thomas Aquinas and was taken further by the Jesuits in the sixteenth and seventeenth centuries, enabled the Catholic Church to remain an 'island of isolation' under totalitarianism. Active resistance to despotism is most difficult of all for societies which are associated with the Greek Orthodox or the Islamic tradition of the unity of Church and State.

H. D. Lasswell's school of social psychology tackles the problem from a completely different angle. Lasswell does not believe that modern psycho-analysis is needed to solve it. He is interested in propaganda methods from the phenomenological standpoint. He investigates the conditions of various psychological techniques designed to score immediate and clear-cut successes.[1]

Lasswell's arguments are extremely convincing and political parties willing to follow his advice would be well placed for winning elections, not only in America but also in Europe. Yet it is more than doubtful whether European fascism in general and national socialism in particular would have been so successful if they had relied on the methods which Lasswell considers to be the secret of political success. Totalitarian propaganda campaigns mounted on the basis of these principles would hardly succeed in disrupting European society as profoundly as Nazi propaganda in fact did. Lasswell's theory is true to a much greater extent of societies which have not gone through a long historical evolution, as for example the United States of America, Australia, New Zealand. Both Lasswell's and Jung's theories are useful for our

[1] Cf. in particular Lasswell's 'Strategy of Revolutionary and War Propaganda' in *Public Opinion and World Politics*, Quincy Wright, New York, London 1934. Cf. also Lasswell, *Psychopathology and Politics*, Chicago 1930; *World Politics and Personal Insecurity*, New York 1935 and *Politics, Who gets What, When, How*, New York 1950.

inquiry, although they only provide an adequate account of a part of reality.

By employing modern psychological techniques, totalitarianism was able to effect the disintegration of central European society. But it only achieved any real success when it penetrated into deeper layers of the European cultural heritage. We have already spoken about the Nazi propaganda methods of finding scapegoat symbols and we have quoted examples which clearly show that the symbols were consciously derived from archetypes. We may conclude, therefore, that national socialist propaganda, which profoundly affected the behaviour of groups and the masses with regard to certain values, only achieved this result – apart from the rational manipulation of such changes – when it succeeded in establishing a connection with the symbols deeply rooted in the cultural heritage of the peoples.

National socialism was, therefore, always compelled to resort to an element of mystical daemonism. It was determined to wage war against the Christian religion but was always striving to borrow from it symbols which were deeply embedded in the collective unconscious of the European peoples. What interested Hitler about the Catholic Church, which he was determined to destroy once he had won the war, was not only its clever 'tactics and its knowledge of human nature' but, and above all, its power to resist 'all attacks made on the basis of logical criticism against the original formulation of its Creed'.[1] From his mentor, Liebenfels, Hitler had adopted the mystical idea of the order of the Brotherhood of the *Tempeleisen*, which considered its task to be the preservation of pure nordic blood in a mockery of the Holy Grail,[2] while other National Socialists adopted the symbolic emblem of 'Luther'. They repeatedly tried to appropriate Christian symbols for their own purposes and to transform them into something daemonic. The Catholic Church, declared Hitler, was not content with the devil alone. It had to have visible foes as well, lest it should flag in the course of the fight. 'The Jew is always in us. But it is easier to fight him in the flesh than as an invisible daemon.'[3] Himmler, again, endeavoured to inject the SS with the mystique of the Holy Roman Empire,[4] the Jesuit Order and also the Germanic Teutonic Order. Kogon mentions the midnight dedication ceremonies of young SS officer cadets in Brunswick Cathedral.[5] In all these cases the links between the totalitarian integration techniques and transcendentalism are clear.

[1] Rauschning, *Gespräche mit Hitler*, op. cit., pp. 225 f.
[2] Wilfried Daim, *Der Mann, der Hitler die Ideen gab*, op. cit., p. 140.
[3] Rauschning, op. cit., p. 233.
[4] Cf. Felix Kersten, *Totenkopf und Treue*, Hamburg 1953, p. 314.
[5] Eugen Kogon, *Der SS-Staat*, Düsseldorf 1946, p. 2.

## Changes in the Hierarchy of Values[1]

Admittedly the word hierarchy implies *static* organization. But this is not the kind of hierarchy we envisage. Let us compare the complex problem with a complicated piece of machinery. The machine has two sides. The outward side which is clearly visible and which shows the various values to which the group and mass loyalties relate; the loyalties are hands of dials indicating the order and rank which these values hold in the human hierarchy at a definite time. Some of the hands move so slowly that we may assume them to be at a standstill, unless we can visualize what is continuously taking place on the other side of the machinery. Other indicators move slowly but steadily in normal and secure times, but swing rapidly in times of crisis and insecurity. But if we look behind the dial into the works we shall be able to understand why the same value changes in popularity at certain periods and under certain circumstances. For there are millions of diminutive wheels representing the individual minds, all connected by minute transmissions with larger wheels representing the influence of groups and associations in a community, and still larger wheels representing the social impact of community.

It is not difficult to imagine that the complexities of the various valuations are beyond the comprehension of the man in the street. It is often difficult to know the exact importance which the individual attaches to some particular value. If, however, one looks at a whole group or several groups representing constitutive elements in the state, one can discern a hierarchy of values which is subject to a constant process of change.

Before we review the process of change in detail let us return to William James' 'faith ladder'. In times of social security, life seems to flow along smoothly and men, generally, seldom have to decide between various loyalties. In times of upheaval and uncertainty, however, the situation is quite different. Then, groups which pursue the most varied and even opposite tendencies often approach the individual. If he decides in favour of one particular system of values he will have to suppress the others much more firmly. If someone says: 'It shall be true, at any rate for me,' he forcibly represses other ties lest they threaten the one which is now dominant.

Group loyalties are more relevant to our problem than individual loyalties. In normal times it is possible to deduce from the symbolism

[1] This problem was discussed by the author in an article published in 1943 – 'Tyranny and Group Loyalties, in the periodical *Philosophy*, Vol. 18, No. 70, London 1943, pp. 163–72.

334 / EUROPEAN DEMOCRACY BETWEEN THE WARS

characteristic of a group whether its members see it as embodying 'transcendental values'. Symbols which personify nations, like John Bull (England), Michel (Germany), Marianne (France), flags, emblems, party leaders' names, even book titles, often belong to the realm of the transcendental.

In settled times it is often difficult to predict how individual loyalties will be formed with regard to certain groups, although in circumstances such as these the individual's consciousness is generally unclouded by emotion and he is therefore in a position to make a rational judgement. But even in comparatively stable and settled times far-reaching changes take place in the economic and social spheres. The more of them that are associated with certain groups and communities, the easier it is to calculate the effect of these changes on the consciousness. For this reason it is easier to predict the trend of group than of individual loyalties. Our knowledge of social, political, economic and pedagogic developments can be utilized for making a prognosis of this kind. One could, for example, reckon that the French working class would continue to resist the Nazi regime even in the most difficult circumstances, whereas it was *a priori* unlikely that the peasants of Hungary and Romania would put up any lasting resistance.

Mass and group consciousness is compounded of fragments of individual psychology and thought, of those individual impulses, interests and energies which are suitable for integration[1] and are finally integrated in a definite group. We must bear in mind that the parts of the individual consciousness which help to make up group consciousness are more strongly influenced by historical, social and economic developments than are the spheres of personality, which remain 'private'.

Group loyalties come under the influence of the 'transcendental realm' in two ways:

1. On the one hand, the group loyalties are marked to a considerable extent by the scale of values belonging to the 'transcendental realm'. By group loyalties two things are to be understood:
 (a) The loyalty of the individual to the group.
 (b) The loyalties within the group which determine its relationship to the all-embracing total group of state or community.
2. On the other hand, the 'transcendental realm' is influenced and transformed in the consciousness of the individual by both types of group loyalties. What is involved here are processes which take place at the same time, and exert a reciprocal influence on each other.

It is clear, for example, that the relationship between individual

---

[1] Georg Simmel, *Soziologie*, op. cit., pp. 153 f.

members and the trade union or the political party to which they belong is variable. Should a person change his profession nobody will really make any serious effort to stop him from joining another trade union. In England and America a man who is no longer satisfied with the politics of his party will not scruple to change party. The relationship is quite different where 'transcendental' elements are involved. Generally speaking, it is not easy to embrace another religion; it is equally difficult to leave a totalitarian party. Until the seventeenth century the man who wanted to leave his church was subject to the same sanctions as the man who, between 1918 and 1933, wanted to leave the secret German military units or the Communist Party. The I.R.A. is a further example. The usual sanctions were social ostracism, psychological and economic pressure against the renegade and, in extreme cases, physical extermination.

All these examples only go to show even more clearly the sort of loyalty demanded by those bodies which lay claim to the whole person. They all stand high in the scale of values and their demands can neutralize the result of rational consideration. If certain groups claim the whole man they may give different reasons for doing so, but whatever their aims may be they are in a position to destroy the harmony of the total group, that is to say the state.

In a pluralist society the individual's relationship to the group is affected by shifts within the system of values. In such a society the individual can decide to give up his political activity and devote his time to the Salvation Army if he becomes convinced that this is his duty as a Christian. He can leave his party if he thinks its politics are detrimental to his personal interests or do too little for the common good. He can join another party if he believes that the government is not doing what needs to be done. In normal times people who regard religion and patriotism as integral elements of their personality are far more deeply affected by changes in their relationship to their religious community or their own nation than those with looser ties.

As we said before, in times of uncertainty not only contemporary but also traditional loyalties come into conflict and are involved in the process of establishing new personal ties. It must be remembered that the archetypal ideal of the family always plays a role in politics.[1] The result of progressive urbanization is that the intimate ties which townspeople used to enjoy with a few immediate neighbours are now replaced by contacts which are numerous but superficial.

The town-dweller must build up his social relationships on the principle of selection. He is, in the first instance, accepted by his

[1] Cf. what has been said about archetypal symbols and the comparison which is often made between the nation and the family.

acquaintances for his personal qualities. His social instincts are not fulfilled in a framework created by tradition and family but by his belonging – more or less voluntarily – to a number of groups.[1]

It is therefore not surprising that the town can neither create nor preserve constant emblems and loyalties but, instead, fosters a fluctuating collective unconscious[2] which becomes articulate through parades and demonstrations. Yet the townsman keeps, at least partly, his earlier emblems although his personal experience no longer tallies with these. If, however, a crisis arises, his original symbol is transformed into a distant ideal and appears to him as a future reality.

We can therefore see that the individual's relationship to a political party is unstable and liable to frequent fluctuations, especially as many personal considerations come into play. The atmosphere prevailing in many local and regional minority party organizations as well as the behaviour and the personal ambition of local officials are not unimportant factors.

It should be added that, under normal conditions, the relationship of the sub-group to the encompassing total group is more stable. The individual's relationship to the total group was determined by the progressive levelling process, which consisted in isolating that part of his psyche which is orientated to the group. That this process is now completed means that the group's relationship to society is no longer dependent on individual decisions which are influenced by private considerations and feelings but by the opinions of those who actively and regularly participate in the life of the group and whose votes, therefore, are not only counted but also carry weight. These people, whether they be delegates or officials, regard the relationship of their group to the state and the community from a particular angle, which removes the element of incalculability from their decisions. If, on a particular issue, they have to take into account their group's relationship to the community, personal experiences and respect for the tradition which moulds their whole mental outlook will form the criteria for their decisions.

The higher the official's position within the group and the community, the less he can be influenced by the symbols of rival groups. (Totalitarian forms of government are no exception to this rule.) In times of social stability this leads to the stabilization and consolidation of the ties between groups and community; it can even result in the hardening of these relationships. But it makes it easier to calculate in

[1] On the modern city and its relationship with the country, cf. P. Sorokin and C. C. Zimmermann, *Principles of Rural Urban Society*, New York 1929.

[2] Ortega y Gasset, *Aufstand der Massen*, op. cit. [*The Revolt of the Masses*, London, Allen & Unwin, 1951.]

advance the practical outcome of the co-operation of the various groups because the group leaders' lines of argument can be more or less predicted.

In periods when social and national life is seriously disturbed, however, the loyalties of the groups will take on very different forms. Far-reaching social developments are more or less guaranteed to effect fundamental changes in the functions of whole groups and classes in a community, a process which also embraces all standards of value and loyalties. A social upheaval like that which occurred in Germany and throughout central Europe between the two world wars was bound to affect the structure of the 'transcendental sphere' of a large number of people who in normal times had known no emotional ties with religion or the nation but were integrated in particular groups either from interest or the adoption of traditional ideals and beliefs. Their emotional stability was profoundly shaken and the archetypal symbols were subject to the impact of propaganda, which exploited them with the express aim of manipulating loyalties. Fluctuations, even the reversal of values occurred within this sphere.

Furthermore, many states contain a large number of people who have never adopted any definite point of view. The group ties of such people are weak and liable to change frequently.[1] In periods of social upheaval a considerable proportion of those among them who were previously integrated in groups relapse into a state of mind which is similar to that of the non-integrated person.

Such a development will also affect the leaders and officials who, in normal times, form the stabilizing element. They immediately become aware that the masses, hitherto indifferent to political processes, are now, in view of the new situation, ready to accept new symbols. They will therefore endeavour to adapt themselves to this new situation in order to preserve the existence of their group and their own position in society. Although their scale of values changes more slowly and often remains quite undisturbed, they are compelled to make certain adjustments. If a totalitarian regime then comes to power they often pay lip service to it. This was how a number of Church dignitaries and many of the workers' leaders reacted in Austria and Italy:[2] churches, bureaucratic machines, officer corps and industrialists must at least make a show of conformity. There is no reason to believe that, in a future crisis, the reactions would in any way differ from those

[1] That is the converse of the problem of the marginal voter, whom Disraeli described as 'conscientious and thoughtful'.

[2] However, the example of Italy has taught us that by using these tactics the democratic leaders there were able to keep the nucleus of their parties intact throughout the twenty years of fascist rule.

which were occasioned by the events in eastern Europe after the Second World War.

As, first, classical economic theory and then Marx and his disciples have shown, economic interests play a major if not an exclusive part in historical processes of this kind.

Moreover, in the consciousness of the individual the 'transcendental sphere' is influenced by both group loyalties – by the individual's loyalty to the sub-group and also by the predominant loyalties within the group to the total group or the state.

In times of slow social progress and in times of certainty the 'transcendental sphere' is relatively stable since it is under the constant influence of clearly defined loyalties.

In times of sudden upheaval an equally radical modification of values takes place. The masses see for themselves the sudden change in the social and economic structure of the state. Their own lives are deeply affected without their being able to explain the process. Life has ceased to be harmonious and the old ties have been dissolved. Their values are subject to far-reaching changes. Old loyalties are destroyed or weakened under the impact of the new situation occasioned by social and economic developments. This pressure is felt even in the 'transcendental sphere', inspiring a new set of values.

At the same time the communication path between individual and central power is shortened. For the groups which, under normal conditions, act as links between the individual and the state are weakened by totalitarian propaganda and later are either suppressed altogether or at least silenced. By eliminating these intermediary groups and with the aid of symbols like the scapegoat figure mentioned in the preceding chapter, national socialism was able to establish a direct relationship between the individual and the state. Thus, by exterminating or strictly controlling intermediary groups – such as the family, other political parties, churches, trade unions and universities – organizations which could form 'islands of isolation'[1] and co-ordination centres of competing loyalties, were eliminated. On the other hand, the human need to belong to intermediary groups is more than satisfied if old conflicts between different loyalties are revived and artificially whipped up.

## The Effect of Totalitarian Integration

People have often wondered why there was no serious resistance to dictatorship in Germany, for the National Socialist Party had always

[1] C. J. Friedrich, op. cit., pp. 219 ff.

been in a minority, even in the first of the 1933 elections. Our analysis so far suggests that in Nazi Germany the scale of human values, including those belonging to the 'transcendental sphere', had been changed by clever manipulation. The first step in any attempt to destroy Nazism from within would have had to be a well-thought-out plan to demolish the loyalty of the masses on which Nazism was based and which, nevertheless, it despised.

Its destruction of Nazism would have been easier before the beginning of the Second World War. In times of war the people of all nations tend to rally round their leaders even if they disagree with their political views. This was a decisive factor in the failure of the plot of July 20, 1944. On the other hand Allied propaganda became increasingly effective as the war went on; numerous observers have confirmed the tremendous impact it had on the loyalty to Nazism. At the beginning, however, Allied propaganda was ill-suited to the ideological character of the war. It was directed in the first instance against the strong ties linking the masses with Nazi ideology and its symbols. Yet the essential feature of 'transcendental' values is that they are associated with the image of certain people who embody these values and who are in a position to inspire the masses to sacrifice their lives, even if the last rational hope of victory has already vanished.

## PART TWO

*The Neo-Medieval Association as a Device*
*for Destroying a Modern Democratic Community*

One of the weaknesses of central-European society was that it had not outgrown its medieval structure and the concomitant attitudes of mind. The power of the state, the church and the guilds was never clearly defined. If, for example, we compare the medieval guild with a modern employers' association or a workers' union, the feature which strikes us at once is the hierarchical structure of the guild, which formed a closed society and often held a monopolistic position. Yet it represented not any one particular interest but a whole collection of different interests. Because its relationship to the state was ill-defined, its jurisdiction was arbitrary and its sphere of influence constantly changing.

It has not been sufficiently realized that the spirit of this medieval organization had long outlived its outward form. In those countries of central Europe which had formerly belonged to the Holy Roman

Empire the middle class nurtured the spirit of these medieval bodies which had helped it to win its early victories, secured its social status and created the conditions for a peaceful life. When the sons of the middle class went to the universities they naturally took something of the spirit of their class with them. Although the German student fraternities (*Burschenschaften*) in the first half of the nineteenth century fought to throw off the shackles of feudal society, they had nevertheless a very elaborate hierarchical system; to belong to them gradually became the privilege of certain classes. Even if they did not actually achieve their ambition of attaining a pre-eminent position in society as a whole, they were nevertheless firmly convinced that they held such a position in their own circle. Until 1948 they formed part of the national liberal movement and its failure meant defeat for them too. After that they gradually adopted the outlook of the aristocratic student corps.

These student bodies also played an important part in the formation of the ideology of the German, Austrian, Hungarian, and Romanian intelligentsia. It was to be expected that men whose ideas and loyalties had been moulded by associations of this kind would never really be in a position to cope with modern society and its more highly integrated system of organizations built up on a constitutional and voluntary basis. The result was a permanent state of tension which became a very marked feature in linguistically mixed states such as Czechoslovakia, where the German-speaking students were often still under the influence of these neo-medieval bodies, while the Czech youth was the product of modern organizations.[1] In two-language cities this dualism stimulated the activity of two racial groups in a situation where there had been no chance of co-operation and fusion.

### Modern Secret Societies and their Significance

The organization of medieval secret societies was no more sharply defined. Thus, for example, the Westphalian vehmic court, a secret society of peasants and burghers, was directed against the nobility and endeavoured to replace a corrupt and unreliable jurisdiction. It might be argued that the vehmic court was democratic in its day. But secret societies of its type automatically undergo a basic change in their structure when they appear in modern society. In the twentieth century they represented a serious threat to the democratic state. In a discussion on the nature of these secret societies Simmel writes:

[1] A few German-speaking student associations and youth organizations also called themselves 'guilds'.

'It is one of the characteristics of the secret society that it absorbs the entire individuality of the person even where it pretends to be an association claiming only one part of an individual's activities with a definite end.

'Every secret society claims the liberties which the community of which it is a part does not allow the general public. Secret societies sometimes endeavour to supplement the inadequate judicature exercised by the community, as for instance, "Fehme" did; or they may, like the ancient Hellenic "mysteries", claim a liberty that is beyond the moral bonds of the community. This exclusiveness – which is typical of the secret society – is meant to stress a liberty; it introduces its members to a sphere which is exempt from the codes and rules of the general environment. The essence of the secret society as such is autonomy. But it is an autonomy which approaches anarchy. For release from the bonds of the community is apt to deprive the members of the secret societies of the firm roots of their intellectual heritage and morality. The exact and detailed "ritual" is meant to compensate for the deficiencies. This proves man's need of a definite balance between the elements of freedom and law. Wherever one source (the community or the state) is incapable of establishing that balance, man seeks to supplement the lack of the one by an overdose of the other elsewhere.'[1]

Simmel's description of secret societies is fresh confirmation of the fact that centralization and strict discipline merely prove that a group needs a special cohesion, although this cohesion is not always achieved by these means. Blind, absolute obedience was not always a typical feature of secret societies, although this is, in fact, contrary to their anarchical character, which itself runs counter to many of the community's ethical principles and standards.

We would not quote Simmel in such detail if his views did not apply directly to national socialism. This connection is not just fortuitous. Many of the leading Nazis came from secret or semi-secret organizations. We need only remind readers of the Ehrhardt Brigade, the Consul Organization, officially registered under the trade name of *Bayrische Holzverwertungsygesellschaft*, the Rossbach Brigade and various smaller groups and youth organizations.[2]

Gumbel's account of the inner workings of the Consul Organization throws a very illuminating light on the structure of German secret societies. Every member could, at all times, rely on the support of the other members. They vowed to stick together through thick and thin and thus, as a group, form a power factor if 'the need and the honour

[1] Simmel, *Soziologie*, op. cit., pp. 292 f.     [2] Cf. Chap. VI, Part One.

of the Fatherland' should demand this. Each one owed the organization absolute obedience. Jews and other races were excluded. Membership ceased on death or if a member were expelled for dishonourable conduct, for disobedience to his superiors or if he left voluntarily; expulsion for dishonourable conduct or disobedience as well as cases of treachery were dismissed or punished by the vehmic court.[1]

Simmel's thesis that the moral principles of members of secret societies are very easily undermined is borne out by many cases of disloyalty as well as the fact that, despite their chauvinistic attitude, many members were ready to accept money from foreign agents.[2] The secret societies also attracted a large number of adventurers and many of the doubtful elements in society.

The rules of the Ehrhardt Brigade give us a very clear picture of the aims of the secret societies:

1. To cultivate nationalist ideas;
2. To fight anti-nationalism and internationalism;
3. To fight Judaism;
4. To fight social democracy and other left-wing movements.[3]

The Viking League can be regarded as a link between the Ehrhardt and Consul Organizations and the National Socialist Party. This particular body consisted mainly of members of these two secret societies and it officially adopted Hitler's National Socialist programme.[4] The huge number of youth organizations were also important.[5]

It was no accident that when Captain Ehrhardt was being hunted by the police he should be given asylum by the Horthy regime in Hungary. From the very first the secret societies had close links with this regime, from which they adopted various tortures.

The National Socialist student associations in Germany, Austria and the German-speaking part of Czechoslovakia had the same character as secret societies. The German ones were amalgamated into one formation, called *Waffenring*, which maintained close contacts with the Ehrhardt and Rossbach Brigades.

The *Ring der Nibelungen* secret society used the following secret signs: (—) law of the society, (¬) brother members, (=) non-member, (+) sub-group. The leader was called 'Hammer-wielding Master'.[6]

Many other organizations, as for example the *Turnerbünde* (Gymnast Leagues) in Austria and the Sudetenland forced their members to take secret political instruction. For their festivals and offices they chose names and titles from the Teutonic calendar and medieval history. They also gave expression to their neo-romantic aspirations

---

[1] F. Gumbel, *Verschwörer*, op. cit., p. 77.  [2] Ibid., pp. 185 ff.
[3] Ibid., p. 75.   [4] Ibid., p. 78.   [5] Ibid., pp. 63 ff.   [6] Ibid., p. 45.

by introducing transcendental elements which were used artificially to foster a sense of unity. They had a high opinion of their own exclusiveness. 'Reliability in national and racial matters', not social status, were the main considerations for membership.[1]

When the members of the former secret societies formed the nucleus of the Nazi movement they applied the secret societies' rules to the larger group without giving the matter a second thought, despite the fact that the National Socialist Party was run on the lines of a modern political organization. The old system of differentiating between initiates and non-initiates was the best way of determining the difference in status between the real élite and the mere agitator. After 1933 this form of differentiation was also applied to the total group, to distinguish between genuine party members and mere fellow-travellers.[2]

Although we have no definite proof that by cultivating pagan and mystical symbols the Nazis wanted to resuscitate the old Germanic faith in its pristine form, it is an undeniable fact that under modern social and economic conditions, and because of the gulf which exists between cultural and technical progress, the secret society practices which were adopted became a deadly weapon in the fight against democracy.

In his analysis of secret societies, therefore, Simmel anticipated some of the most important techniques and structural elements of total rule. The fact that many leading Nazis had been members of secret societies suggests that Nazism adopted a fair number of the methods used in them.

Like a secret society, national socialism, in its inner ring, combined a total claim on the person with the gift of a freedom which did not exist in the total group. Prior to 1933 the German state represented the total group for Nazism; after 1933 the states of the Western world fulfilled this role.

Prior to 1933 in Germany and prior to 1938 in Austria and Czechoslovakia the exclusiveness and the semi-secret status of the military units were effective weapons in the struggle conducted by the Nazis. Inveterate opponents were publicly defamed in order to reduce their political influence.

Like the secret societies, national socialism hedged its ideology round with a whole system of outward symbols and rites for the simple reason that they were intended for the total group of the Aryan race. The National Socialists had the army in their power and were set on

---

[1] In his *Soziologie*, Simmel distinguished *inter alia* between two principles. One is: 'He who is not excluded is included'; the other is: 'He who is not included is excluded'; this is the principle of the secret society.

[2] Sebastian Haffner, *Germany: Jekyll and Hyde*, London 1940, p. 109.

suppressing the religious groups, in which they were partly successful. Where they met with no success they introduced their own ritual style in an attempt to found a sort of independent religion of their own, which they called *Gottgläubigkeit* (Belief in God). Within this religion Hitler, as he himself stressed, wanted to assume the role of the Messiah.

Like the secret society, national socialism claimed the whole individual in all the various aspects of his life. Forsthoff recognized this peculiar trait at a very early stage; he spoke about the 'state of total responsibility', which would have represented the 'total obligation of each individual to the nation'. This obligation would have completely destroyed the private character of private existence.[1]

In common with the secret society, the total state sought to possess the total person, although one must agree with Schulz that the idea of this total possession amounted in effect to 'the general transference of military discipline to the whole of society'.[2] And the secret military units in Germany which have already been mentioned were, in fact, the point of contact between military discipline and the totality of the secret society.

Nazism likewise pitted itself against the total group and attempted to appropriate the forms of this group. The Brown Shirt (SA) formations were given, for example, the same regimental numbers as the regular army. In Germany this was taken to such lengths that after 1933 a state of dualism existed between state and party offices.

Any student of national socialism is struck by the fact that many party members knew neither social ties nor ethical principles. That was a necessary compensation for the strict discipline and blind obedience given to the leaders. Rauschning has given us a detailed account of the anarchical and nihilistic character of the movement.[3]

Nazism differed quantitatively from the classical forms of dictatorship by its totalitarian nature. This essential feature about the movement originated in the secret society, yet the techniques used in the Middle Ages could develop to the full only under the conditions of modern technology and with the help of modern communications media.

But the organization and workings of the SS provide the most complete confirmation of Simmel's secret society theory. The SS became the counter-state, the centre of the total state within the existing national-socialist state. But to achieve this Himmler had to resort to

---

[1] Ernst Forsthoff, *Der Totale Staat*, Hamburg 1933, p. 42. Cf. also Carlton J. H. Hayes, 'The Novelty of Totalitarianism in the History of Western Civilization' in *Symposium on the Totalitarian State*, Philadelphia 1939.

[2] Gerhard Schulz, 'Der Begriff des Totalitarismus und der Nationalsozialismus' in *Soziale Welt*, Vol. XII, Book 2, Göttingen 1961, p. 120.

[3] H. Rauschning, *Die Revolution des Nihilismus*, Zurich 1938.

neo-medieval forms. In his endeavour to organize the SS as a medieval crusader order – which marched forth with the swastika (the hooked cross) against the cross of the Saviour – Himmler often referred to Emperor Frederick II's state in Sicily and to the Order of the German Teutonic Knights.[1] Ostensibly in accordance with medieval models, the SS was to represent a despotic, knightly nobility and the SS state became the embodiment of this fanatical, amoral order. Since, however, the crusaders of the Middle Ages did not serve the ideal of despotism, the fanatical religious wars waged by the Islamic Caliphs provided Himmler with a more suitable model.[2]

'Only the SS counterstate existed. There was not a single state official whom the Order, on Hitler's instructions, could not have stripped of its office and brought up for this or, more simply, liquidated. The Order had taken possession . . . of all power.'[3]

Thus the Waffen SS saw itself as the rebirth of the warriors in the Germanic peoples' migrations.[4]

Kogon observes that Himmler himself came from the ranks of the *Artamenen*. This was an obscure branch of the German youth movement and its aim was the renewal of German peasantry and self-training for a peasant army[5] – another medieval idea. The training of the leaders went on in the SS *Ordensburgen* (special SS castles), many of them built in a pseudo-gothic style. Hitler and Himmler had intended to give the new SS nobility estates in the eastern marches after the war had been carried to a victorious conclusion. There they would have lived as overlords and would have been allowed to marry two wives in order to inject fresh blood into the nation.[6]

The idea of founding orders was one of Hitler's most cherished dreams. He saw it as combining all the neo-medieval ideas which have been mentioned together with the concept of the 'Leader' and his following into a dynamic force which would help him carry out his plans to destroy modern society first in Germany and then, after final victory, throughout the world. One difficulty was that the great majority of National Socialist Party members themselves still clung to the ideology of the pluralist society and the law-based state. The fact that most of the minor leaders looked on the National Socialist Party simply as the one party which had survived from the Weimar period

---

[1] H. Himmler, *Die Schutzstaffel*, Munich 1937, pp. 16 ff., 31.
[2] Cf. Kersten, op. cit., pp. 203 ff.
[3] Karl O. Paetel, 'The Reign of the Black Order' in *The Third Reich*, London, New York, Toronto 1955, p. 661. Cf. also Alfred Rosenberg, *Der Deutsche Ordensstaat*, Munich 1934.
[4] Ibid., p. 663.          [5] E. Kogon, *Der SS-Staat*, op. cit., p. 3.
[6] Felix Kersten, *Totenkopf und Treue*, op. cit., pp. 116, 216.

was something which Hitler found utterly unsatisfactory. He therefore became increasingly inclined to agree with Rosenberg's ideas that the deception technique should also be applied to party members and functionaries, while retaining all the old outward forms for their benefit. 'But for the circle of party members in the know it would be best to create an inner ring within the party itself. Thus not only would a clear form of the party gradually crystallize but it would also take on the character of an order, with the appropriate stages of initiation, responsibility and co-operation.' He therefore wished to have the *Ordensburgen* for the education of a 'violent, masterful, fearless, cruel youth'.[1] And so Hitler planned the rebirth of the medieval state of Burgundy which, together with Belgium and Luxemburg, was to form a sovereign SS state.[2] The counterpart of this wish was the anti-state of the order comprising an élite body bound to one another by oath.

Here was the most comprehensive and detailed verification of Simmel's analysis of the secret society, which reproduced within itself the form of the state, society and the family (through the oath-bound units) and also of the church, because its aim was to destroy all these.

The resuscitation of the neo-medieval bodies and the role which the latter played in totalitarian technique does not, however, mean that they could have produced the kind of social relationships established in the Middle Ages or that any of the totalitarian leadership stratum had any serious desire to recreate those social and political conditions. This is clear from the description of the intellectual and political structure of medieval Europe described in Chapter 5, which, in keeping with Germanic constitutional traditions, never questioned the supremacy of judicial values and therefore of human individuality.

Any such reversion was also unthinkable because the dualism of church and state, which was the real foundation underlying the world of the Middle Ages, was diametrically opposed to the idea of totalitarianism; a dualism served by the ecclesiastical orders and in particular by the orders of the Knights Crusaders. Moreover, National Socialism never acknowledged any revival of the idea at the basis of feudal society, namely the mutual obligations of lord and vassal. In any case there were historical models for the state form to which this totalitarianism aspired. These, however, are to be found not in the West but in the East. They are discernible in part in the Caesaropapism into which the Eastern Roman Empire evolved after Justinian, where all political and economic as well as all spiritual and intellectual power lay in the hands of the Basileus autocrat who was both elevated

---

[1] Rauschning, *Gespräche mit Hitler*, op. cit., pp. 234, 237.

to the throne and also deposed by the praetorian guards of the capital.[1]

An even closer analogy to National Socialism would have been the Islamic caliphate,[2] as it developed between the time of Muawijah and Haroun-al-Rashid, on account of the even more despotic rule exercised by the Caliph as the representative of the Prophet and the fanatical, uncritical obedience given to him by all believers. But Himmler's admiration for Islam was mistaken, for the Islamic state recognized the Koran as a God-given constitutional law. This was also why the Emperor Frederick II, whose system of government in Sicily was deliberately modelled as nearly as possible on the Caliphate, became one of the prototypes for the Nazi élite. But even more akin to National Socialism than Byzantium and Islam was the oriental temple state of the Babylonians and Assyrians which, erected on a racial basis, raised the king to the supreme status of god in whose name both in his lifetime and after his death the oath-bound élite of priests and warriors ruled by means of terror and whose mystique demanded human sacrifice.

## PART THREE

*Pressure Groups and Totalitarian Methods.*
*The Structure of Pressure Groups*

American literature is rich in studies of pressure groups.[3] These owe their existence to various interests who organize them to put pressure on the government of a state to promote certain aims. The interests represented are mostly materialistic, where trade, agriculture or the workers are involved. They can, however, be more idealistic, for example in the case of political parties or bodies with humanitarian aims, women's organizations and religious sects.

These groups have been formed within the democratic party system but tend to take the place of the political parties in as much as, in the minds of the masses, they are often identified with them. To the very heart of the problem goes the question which Edmund Burke addressed

[1] Cf. Wilhelm Ensslin, 'The Emperor and the Imperial Administration', in *Byzantium*, edited by H. Baynes and H. Moss, Oxford 1948; cf. also K. J. Newman, 'Papst, Kaiser, Kalif und der Basileus', op. cit., p. 33.

[2] Cf. Carl Brockelmann, *Geschichte der islamischen Völker und Staaten*, Berlin 1939, p. 393; and E. I. J. Rosenthal, *Political Thought in Mediaeval Islam*, Cambridge 1958, p. 30.

[3] Cf. in particular P. Odegard's classic study, *Pressure Politics, the Story of the Antisaloon League*, New York 1928.

to his contemporaries, whether parliament, in which the most important interests in the country meet, is a congress of ambassadors from different countries or the consultative assembly of the nation, representing the public interest only. The great advantage of democracy is that all vital interests of the different groups within the state become openly articulate and can be weighed one against the other from the standpoint of the common good until the best compromise has been found. However, this weighing in the balance is not a simple matter. It is not easy to see which group interests are identical with the public interest and which are pursuing only limited and selfish aims at the expense of the general public. The groups exerting the pressure and having the right kind of people and plenty of financial resources do not necessarily represent the most deserving interests. A danger, to which coalition governments are especially exposed by their very nature, is that a compromise on principles not only ignores the public interest but disregards the interests of all or some groups in favour of the interest of the group leadership at that particular moment. On the other hand there is a danger that interest groups will assume the form of political parties if by going in for hard-hitting political propaganda they destroy the mood of political moderation and themselves achieve relative stability.

Where interest groups and parties are one and the same democracy can no longer function. The leaders may perhaps reach a superficial agreement on their diverse interests but an ever-widening gulf can open up between the ordinary party members, a gulf which the leaders must, in the end, recognize and which is liable to destroy democracy. If a parliament consists almost entirely of interest groups this will affect the composition of the cabinet and the executive. In central Europe one of the greatest threats to democracy was that interest groups and party systems often became identified in the public's mind. Where proportional representation is in operation, interest groups will always try to become political parties, especially if debates take place in committees instead of plenary sessions of parliament. Modern parliaments tend, moreover, to become 'working parliaments', whose committees and their experts do most of the work, instead of 'debating parliaments', where the emphasis is on discussion.

The fact that there is no clearly defined demarcation line between interest group and political party was fatal for many young democracies. There was no lack of competing interests in the days of absolute monarchy but they did not come to the surface, being hidden by the brilliance of the royal authority. In a democracy, however, they come too much to the fore and certainly add nothing to the authority of this form of government.

The more parties there are the more the separate interests oust the general ones. This can be used as a strong argument against democracy. There is, however, another side to the problem. As there is no precise dividing line between political parties and pressure groups, sooner or later the political parties will adopt the radical pressure techniques used by the latter. It is, however, a very different matter whether interest groups or political parties apply pressure techniques, even if the actual techniques are exactly the same. In the individual scale of values political ideologies hold a far higher place than mere ties with groups whose aims are purely economic. These therefore endeavour to achieve the status of a political party with its appertaining ideology and symbolism.

## Disruptive and Preventive Pressure

The pressure exerted by interest groups and political parties is disruptive in the sense that these groups want to change the *status quo* to their own advantage by the application of pressure. In this way a totalitarian group can insinuate itself into the political system of a democratic society without being noticed. If it brings pressure to bear and conducts an aggressive propaganda campaign there is no ground for complaint as it is part and parcel of the general framework. If one particular group does the same as the rest, but does it more skilfully and more thoroughly, there is no reason for suppressing it. If a group of desperadoes forms a political party, it will not be the first time this has happened. The situation is so complex that totalitarianism is blindly tolerated: for the system of interest groups and pressure groups makes it difficult to detect the beginnings of a totalitarian movement. It is therefore the duty of every democratic government to keep a very watchful eye on the behaviour of all pressure groups and to set up proper machinery for combating their propaganda and provide a sound corrective to every one-sided group standpoint.

The difficulties of distinguishing between political parties and interest groups in the modern pluralistic state also worked to the Nazis' advantage. The democratic parties use pressure in order to put a political programme through; but as soon as they have gained a majority and become the government they are content to control the traditional power apparatus, which is the monopoly of the state. The totalitarian party wants to apply pressure in order to destroy society. This pressure is, however, merely the first step towards a far more extensive system of 'preventive pressure', with the help of which it sets up the dictatorship, its primary aim. In the last stages of the struggle for power this 'preventive pressure' is a pretext for 'organized in-security'.[1] It is therefore only logical that, once power has been seized, those bodies and organs which were originally given the task of apply-ing 'disruptive pressure' are employed to exert the 'preventive pres-sure'. For this purpose a unit is created which, in the first instance, is nothing less than a private army of thugs and which is finally legalized as the police force of the dictatorship.

It must, however, be remembered that the fascist movements were never able to carry out this scheme as it was originally conceived. The fascists, who on the whole had an outstanding intuitive under-standing of the mentality of their followers and of mob psychology, did not see at an early enough stage that disruptive and preventive pressure call for qualities which are quite different. Men who are trained to fight the government develop certain habits. After they had seized power the Italian fascists could not employ their gangs of thugs for police duties. The fact that the SA (Storm Troops) became an embarrassment to the Nazis led to the blood bath of June 30, 1934. Nor could Dollfuss use his secret *Heimwehr* units. Preventive pressure must be exerted by other means. After 1933 the state took over the functions of all the groups which had hitherto been active as pressure groups. But 'pressure' cannot be switched over from democ-racy to totalitarian dictatorship as simply as that. In a dictatorship the power relationships are quite different and the relationship be-tween individual and group and between group and state also changes. That is one of the reasons why, once a totalitarian party has seized power, those elements which gave help and support in the period when disruptive pressure was being applied are, in the end, always disappointed, like Röhm and his Storm Troopers before June 30, 1934. As soon as the fascist dictatorship has defeated democracy, it realizes that it must tolerate the supporters of democratic parties and to a certain extent also rely on them.

# PART FOUR

*Integration of Groups and Individuals by Totalitarianism*

Having examined the origins of national socialist totalitarianism we must go into the techniques by which total integration was achieved. We must refer back to Simmel's observation that in a dictatorship

---

[1] Karl Mannheim, Mensch und Gesellschaft im Zeitalter des Umbaus, Darmstadt 1958, pp. 157 ff.

each subject is bound to the dictator with only a fragment of his personality, whereas the dictator puts his whole personality into this relationship. Here we come up against the same distinction between total personality and that part of it which is integrated in the group and the community.

Simmel also maintains that the political art of both the church and the state normally consists in selecting those aspects of the personality which can be most easily absorbed by the group consciousness:

'The groupings differ characteristically from one another according to the ratio between the total personalities and that quantum of them with which they become part of the "mass". The extent to which they can be ruled depends on the relative amounts of this quantum, so that a group will be dominated more quickly and more completely by one individual the smaller the part of the single personality which the individual gives to the mass! Where the social unit (the group in our case) integrates so much of the personality that nearly the whole of the individuality is absorbed (as in the Greek City States), tyranny becomes untenable. There are two important limitations to tyranny: the size of the subject group; and the variety of the personalities in it. The wider the circle the smaller will be, *ceteris paribus*, the sphere of thoughts and interests, emotions and attributes which the individuals have in common and which make them into the mass (or group). In so far as domination is concerned with what the individuals have in common, it is clear that the individual will bear domination the more easily the larger the circle dominated. The following principle is hereby demonstrated: the larger the number of individuals ruled by the one (the tyrant), the smaller the part of the individual he dominates.'[1]

Simmel's thesis can be applied to most of the tyrannies of the ancient world. The following features were common to the despotisms of Egypt, Syria and Persia as well as the Roman Empire: however crushing the oppression in the capital, life at the periphery of the Empire was largely unaffected.[2] The inhabitants of the Roman provinces had to pay their taxes, worship a few Roman deities in addition to their own, but otherwise they were left alone. Under the tyrants of the Italian Renaissance and even during the absolute monarchies of the sixteenth and seventeenth centuries, the subject who did not come into contact with the court had nothing to fear provided he steered clear of politics. In the Russian Tsarist empire and under the absolutism of

[1] Simmel, *Soziologie*, op. cit., p. 116.
[2] K. J. Newman, 'Georg Simmel and Totalitarian Integration', in *The American Journal of Sociology*, Vol. LVI, No. 4, January 1951.

the Prussian kings, the state authority claimed only a relatively small part of the personality.

Even the modern totalitarian regimes observed this rule in their early days of power. Italian fascism did not bother overmuch about the behaviour of the non-political citizen and the same was true of Polish, Hungarian and Yugoslav authoritarianism. The Austrian dictatorship also followed this practice and it was partly thanks to this tactic that the Nazis, who did not interfere noticeably in the normal citizen's life in the years immediately following their seizure of power, were able to consolidate their rule and domination. The Nazis pursued this policy as a tactical means of attaining further objectives. The fact that in the early period of their rule they deliberately left loopholes open for possible critics took in most of the German opposition leaders who had gone into exile.

Nazism had camouflaged itself, so to speak, under the traditional trappings of autocracy. The final result of its efforts amounts to a striking refutation of Simmel's analysis. The National Socialists well understood the social mechanism described by Simmel; but as this would have run counter to all their intentions they decided to go one better. They therefore founded a complete system of organizations to take over all those spheres of individual life which threatened to elude their clutches. The professions were politicized, the children taken over by the Hitler Youth, the mothers had to attend the meetings of the 'National Socialist Womanhood' and the fathers had to do their para-military training several times a week. 'Strength through Joy' took care of their leisure time. In this and similar ways the National Socialist movement succeeded in getting such a firm grip on the life of the individual that it hardly seemed possible that it could become worse. Henceforth Hitler no longer needed to bother about keeping and carrying out the 'socialist' part of his programme.

Yet it is doubtful whether the totalitarian movement could overcome the difficulty which Simmel sums up in this sentence: 'The more people one man rules over, the less of each separate individual does he dominate.' Whether this law, to which dictatorship is subject, can, within certain limits, be nullified, depends on three main conditions: the proportion of external loyalties absorbed by the tyranny; the number and usefulness of the available controllers; and the efficacy of the methods used in the social sphere. In the last phase of the Second World War the second condition created ever-mounting difficulties for the Nazis.

The evolutionary tendencies of both national socialism and Stalinist communism indicate the existence of an automatic law which continually reduces the number of those dominating the total state. The oligarchical structure evolves progressively into the monarchical – in the sense of single rule. The result, however, is that the number and intensity of the loyalties which sustain totalitarianism become fewer and weaker all the time. Since the 'supervisor' stratum below the small group of top leaders contains an evergrowing number of disappointed and embittered members of the élite who can never hope to get into the top group, the feelings of hatred and resentment at this 'injustice' increase; and this applies even to the real élite immediately below Hitler. Thus one such disillusioned national socialist writes:

'As the succession apparatus functioned quite automatically and no concrete, permanently self-renewing inclusion in the Führer's confidential circle compelled or demanded any concrete planning or action at any time on his part, the boxing-in process of Hitler . . . began to develop into the total isolation of his person. Therefore once the Reichstag and the Cabinet were eliminated as autonomous, self-operating control centres, following the total militarization of the state; once the *Wehrmacht*, after the elimination of a real War Ministry and the creation of the Supreme Army Command under Keitel and directly responsible to the Führer, also became technically subordinate to him; and when, due to the increasing support which Hitler gave to Bormann, the National Socialist Party became technically a command apparatus made up of the Reichsleiters, Gauleiters and lower leaders, Hitler did not need to bother any more. He had become the sole, absolute ruler.'[1]

## Limiting the Number of Rulers

The totalitarian state's tendency to one-man rule springs from the laws to which, as Aristotle knew, oligarchies are subject:

'Oligarchies are disturbed from *inside* when their members themselves play the demagogue, for reasons of personal rivalry . . . Troubles also arise when some of its members try to make an oligarchy still more exclusive . . . Still another way in which oligarchies may be undermined from inside is when an inner oligarchy is created within the outer.'[2]

This tendency to limit the National Socialist leader stratum had became noticeable even before the Second World War. It showed itself in a continual reduction of the élite, the first instance being

---

[1] Frank, op. cit., p. 131.
[2] Aristotle, *The Politics of Aristotle*, Book V, Chap. 6, translated by Sir Ernest Barker, Oxford 1946, p. 218.

when the SA (Storm Troops) were deprived of power after July 30, 1934. In the SS, too, the élite structure was modified by the division of the organization into Special Units, Death's Head Units, General SS, Security Service, Gestapo (Secret State Police) and Armed SS. After the abortive revolt on July 20 Himmler was given supreme command over the *Wehrmacht*. The tendency to decrease the number of senior groups and to one-man rule was undoubtedly increased and speeded up by the war. Yet Hitler's assumption of the Presidency after Hindenburg's death and the merging of this office with the Chancellorship had, however, already been an indication of the monarchist tendency. Aristotle also recognized that, in its need for a supreme command, war furthers the development towards one-man rule.[1]

In making a distinction between 'normative state' and 'prerogative state' Fraenkel has drawn attention to this process, which cannot be fitted into formal juristic categories. This dualism was thought of only as a transitional solution, which was to allow the true objectives of totalitarianism to be achieved within the political system of deception. As an analogy he quotes the struggle between 'common law' and royal prerogative in England in the sixteenth century.[2] In England, too, there was a long period of dualism between the principle of law-based constitutionality and prerogative and a long struggle was fought between parliament and common-law jurists on the one side and the king and the establishment on the other before the latter was defeated. Under National Socialism, however, there was exactly the opposite development: for a time a dualism did exist – namely between the state and anti-state (the SS), in which the state was gradually to be dissolved and totally and utterly subordinated to the latter. Therefore the question of prerogative did not arise, because this concept described the residue of the absolute and authoritarian power which the crown wanted to retain outside the constitutional sphere, while in the Nazi period these were the last vestiges of constitutionality which, one after the other, were gradually devoured by the total anti-state.

The facts given here indicate that totalitarianism is *not* an exception to the old, general rules governing oligarchy and tyranny as systems of government and that it represents in principle only a modern variation corresponding to the changed social, technological and economic conditions.

The events which took place in Germany in 1944 and 1945 show that tyranny is bound to fail in modern total war, in which everything depends on the citizens' willingness to sacrifice themselves and on the mutual trust of those who operate the complicated machinery for conducting the war and the war economy. For modern war pre-

[1] Ibid.          [2] E. Fraenkel, *The Dual State*, op. cit., p. 153.

supposes an extremely high degree of rationality in planning and decision-making, and those irrational deception techniques which were so successful previously are bound to fail under war conditions. Thus Hitler was unwilling to follow the highly rational proposals of his military advisers and, regardless of catastrophic losses in men, stubbornly clung to positions which, strategically, had long been lost.[1]

Finally, disagreement erupted between the generals and the National Socialist élite. After July 20th the ablest generals fell victim to this élite and were executed. The 'leadership and responsibility chaos' grew worse in every sphere. Himmler, Bormann, Göring and Speer became 'competence giants' fighting out 'power battles' among themselves.[2] These disputes, however, were already a foretaste of the struggle for succession to Hitler's absolute rule. Bormann's influence finally brought about Göring's dismissal[3] and Himmler's 'treachery' cost him his inheritance. In his political testament Hitler once more separated the topmost positions. He nominated Dönitz as President, Goebbels as Chancellor, Bormann as Party Leader. But even before Hitler died the one-man rule had already come to an end.

## The Device of Pseudo-Tolerance

To achieve the necessary compromise between liberty and government the Nazis used the device of pseudo-tolerance. Journalists from western countries who visited Germany before the war wondered how far Germans could criticize the government. It was a shrewd political move to keep people who disagreed with the political developments in the party as long as possible. But as soon as the party became convinced that these people were undoubted opponents of the regime they were punished and penalized with the utmost severity.

## The 'Demise' of Democratic Parties in Fascist Systems

It has often been asked how it is possible for the old democratic parties to disappear completely after a modern totalitarian power has seized power. Their whole political vigour was broken and after the arrest of the democratic leaders their adherents were forced to be-

[1] Cf. Percy E. Schramm, *Hitler als militärischer Führer*, Frankfurt am Main, Bonn 1962.
[2] Frank, op. cit., p. 413.
[3] Alan Bullock, Hitler, *A Study in Tyranny*, London, Penguin Books, 1962, p. 787.

come part of the supine army of supporters of the totalitarian regime. This was what happened in Germany, Italy, Austria, Hungary and, although to a lesser extent, in Poland and Yugoslavia as well. On this point Simmel writes:

'There is a measure of antagonism between social elements which is cancelled out when both are subject to a common pressure making way to an outward, nay inner uniformity. If, however, the original aversion exceeds a certain limit the common suppression has the opposite effect. Not only because, in the case of a strong sense of bitterness in one direction every sense of bitterness arising from another source exacerbates the general annoyance and, against all reason, also flows into and widens the bed, which is already deep, but above all because the common suffering forces the elements closer together; but by very reason of this enforced proximity, only then does the whole inner divergence and irreconcilibility of these elements emerge in its full and striking force. Where a homogeneity which has been created in some way or other is unable to overcome an antagonism it does not let this exist in the *status quo ante* but exacerbates it, the disparity becoming sharper and more conscious in every sphere as the two sides move closer to one another. Another, more obvious revulsion is caused by jealousy among the subjects of the common oppression. It provides the negative antithesis to what has been mentioned above: that common hatred is a stronger bond if the common object of that hatred is also the common master . . .'[1]

From acquaintance with English history Simmel knew that the laws against the non-conformists had never really had any positive affect on the attitude of the Protestant sects to the Catholics. In Germany Nazi oppression did not at first bring about any sort of positive co-operation between Christian groups and parties on the one hand or socialists and democrats on the other; furthermore, the animosity between socialists and communists was heightened by oppression.[2] It was only after war had broken out that the opposition groups – Social Democrats and German Nationals – recognized that a common front against the Hitler regime was to their interest. Thus the common oppression eventually brought about the collaboration of former political enemies, namely conservative monarchical and social-democratic circles, in the movement which culminated in the attempted assassination of Hitler on July 20, 1944.

'. . . it often happens – and this is equally true of children at play as it is of religious groups and political parties – that common interests are

[1] Simmel, *Soziologie*, op. cit., p. 111.
[2] Cf. *Der Neue Vorwärts*, Prague 1934, 1937; and also Kogon, *Der SS-Staat*, op. cit.

established by the addition of some new aim to what have hitherto been divergent or indifferent intentions and certainties of the parties concerned; and this new objective can act as a focal point and proves what has hitherto been moving in different directions to be compatible.'[1]

After successfully absorbing the sectional groups in the community, national socialism, with great skill, supported now the peasants, then industry, at other times the working class, the small trades and the great business concerns.

To this policy of absorption let us add what we have said about creating a pseudo-unity by an appeal to nationalism, the creation of substitute symbols and the formation of new artificial loyalties. If we compare this whole policy with the hierarchy of values theory and the transcendental sphere within that scale, then the circle is completed of the techniques of exerting social influence by which national socialism was able to impose totalitarian dictatorship.

We have no wish to ignore the fact that the German people pressed into this iron mould was bound to constitute a foreign body among the nations of the world. When the structure and spirit of medieval associations were transplanted into modern society a new and highly-explosive mixture was created. The moment the Nazi methods were applied on the international plane they revolutionized law and politics and changed the very nature of many international institutions and rules. For the first time there loomed on the horizon of history a dictatorship which was all-embracing.

[3] Simmel, *Soziologie*, op. cit., p. 111.

# CHAPTER IX

# The Diffusion and Impact of Fascism

When, after conquering Italy, fascism also triumphed in Germany, it set about imposing its system on the world. It was able to base itself on authoritarian regimes, social structures and ideologies already existing in eastern and central Europe.

But first we must point out a fundamental difference between Italian fascism and German national socialism. The opportunities for the diffusion of fascism were more limited and operated rather in the framework of a programme of imperial expansion. And so its diffusion became noticeable in particular on Italy's frontier – in Austria, Yugoslavia and France, also in Spain and in areas outside Europe like Abyssinia, which Mussolini intended to incorporate into his colonial empire.

As we have already explained, national socialism was not a nationalist movement in the traditional sense; it was, rather, a totalitarian movement which aimed at the domination and enslavement of the world and took Germany as its starting point. While Mussolini was content with the role of successful politician, Hitler saw himself as a prophet and the appointed repository of a mission with which he meant to bless the peoples of the world, whether they wanted it or not. In this he counted on the support of individuals and groups from many different nations who were open to his ideas. Hitler's ideas were particularly acceptable in the countries which had either relatively strong authoritarian tendencies and traditions or which contained peoples, minorities or tribes which were linguistically or racially distinct from the national race, as, for example, in Austria, Hungary, Poland, Yugoslavia, Romania and Czechoslovakia. His ideas were less acceptable in France, Holland and Scandinavia as democratic traditions and a homogeneous structure were predominant features of these countries, with the result that influential authoritarian groups dared not openly support national socialism before a German invasion.

However, this does not explain why opposition to national socialism in western Europe was not stronger before the Second World War, nor the not inconsiderable support which it found during the occupation of the western and northern democracies on the continent of Europe.

It is probably true that after 1933 national socialism's immediate concern was to register, co-ordinate and organize all the authoritarian tendencies and factors, all the differences and antagonisms existing in the areas to be conquered. Thus the names of all leading or otherwise useful individuals who might prove of value in the near future were recorded, with or without their knowledge. This preparatory activity embraced political parties, members of the armed forces, the police forces, the bureaucracies and groups which were of cultural, economic and religious importance as well as nationalities. The work followed the lines of the police methods used by Fouché, Metternich, the Ochrana and the OGPU. This was based on the systematic work done by the central organs of the Nazi Party, Germany's diplomatic representatives and the organizations of *Reichsdeutsche* (German citizens of German blood) and *Volksdeutsche* (people of German blood but of non-German citizenship, living abroad) operating abroad but directed from Germany as well as with the assistance of tens of thousands of agents and spies.

The murder of the *émigré* German Professor Theodor Lessing[1] in August 1933 and of another *émigré*, Rudolf Formis, a close friend of Otto Strasser, on January 23, 1935, in Czechoslovakia, the assassination of the Austrian Chancellor, Dr Dollfuss, on July 20, 1934, as well as the kidnapping of many political opponents of national socialism from Switzerland, Austria, Czechoslovakia and Holland kept alive the fear of the fifth column in the years before the outbreak of the war. Yet the majority of people in western Europe were sceptical about the Brown Book or the Black-Red Book. It took a German military invasion to convince people of the reality of the fifth column. But this scepticism later swung to the opposite extreme. People got the impression that the fifth column was lurking everywhere. De Jong has given us a vivid picture of the terror which seized the Dutch at the German advance:

'People had the feeling that they were unable to cope with the menace of the fifth column. A fire in one place had hardly been extinguished before ten others started up. Again there was a flood of rumours: meat and drinking water were poisoned; fifth columnists were handing out poisoned chocolates and cigarettes; whole towns had been razed to the ground . . . On May 11, 1940, there was so much shooting going on in the streets that the troops thought they were fighting a general up-

[1] Lessing was Professor of Philosophy at the Technical University in Hanover and a well-known opponent of National Socialism. He emigrated to Czechoslovakia.

rising by the Dutch Nazis . . . No one knew exactly where the enemy was but he was suspected everywhere.'[1]

In Belgium and Holland, de Jong continues, the panic resulted in mass arrests and people were given a rough handling, and even anti-Nazis were not safe.

Above all, in these first days of war, the capital, Brussels, was buzzing like a beehive with rumours and fears. It was known that the Germans had taken three vitally important bridges across the Albert Canal north-west of Liège. How was that possible? For they were within the range of the guns in the forts round Liège! . . . It was a mystery. Was Hitler using secret weapons, gas or death rays? Or had there been treason.'[2]

France also became panic-stricken when Germany attacked her. Millions of refugees and their belongings blocked the roads and spread the most fantastic rumours about the efficiency of the German fifth column. In the French Senate on May 21, 1940, Reynaud declared that false messages, false evacuation orders, treachery and sabotage had done much damage to the French forces.[3] This was the only way he could explain to himself and his fellow citizens the breakthrough in the Maginot Line.

This account of the impression and effect of the Nazi attack on western Europe raises the question as to how far these phenomena were, in fact, due to national-socialist activity and organization outside Germany. De Jong explains these events partly by certain socio-psychological phenomena which started a mass panic. He speaks of an imaginary fifth column.[4] However, this fear would have contained a grain of truth in so far as national socialists would have thoroughly prepared and organized everything before the war.

But a sociological analysis cannot be satisfied with this sort of explanation. The starting point of our inquiry is this: what reasons can be discovered for, first, the possibility and efficiency of national socialist organizational work abroad; secondly, for the support given to Nazi organizations, aims and methods by influential circles in the Western countries; thirdly, for the Western democracies' unpreparedness against the aggressive expansion of national socialism before the war; and, fourthly, for the surprising collapse of the Western armies when Germany attacked in 1940. If this was the prevailing mood not only in the countries which Germany attacked, like Poland, France, Belgium and Holland, but also in Great Britain and South Africa as well as North

---

[1] Louis de Jong, *Die Deutsche Fünfte Kolonne im Zweiten Weltkrieg*, Stuttgart 1959, pp. 79 f.

[2] Ibid., p. 83.     [3] Ibid., p. 92.     [4] Ibid., pp. 235 f.

and South America, the element of chance can be excluded. A more detailed investigation will therefore have to examine the structural forces and the changes which produced this sort of phenomenon.

These social factors cannot, however, be studied without first discussing the interplay and exchange of forces which normally underlie the reciprocal effects among the various social groups in pluralistic states. Only then will it be possible to analyse the situation described here. The essential feature was that a totalitarian type of society and state invaded the structure of pluralistic society like a foreign body and infected it. Then, by manipulating conflicts, employing violence and deliberately disturbing the normal social processes it created a mass psychosis in which the main element was a sense of personal insecurity.

## PART ONE

*Europe in Transition*

*From National to International Forms of Organization*

A pluralistic social structure began to build up in western Europe and America from the earliest years of the modern period. Geographical discoveries, the development of transport and communications and the conquest of overseas territories by European states meant that this form of society spread throughout the greater part of the world. Communities moved closer to one another and began to intermingle.

A feature which is characteristic of most of the great religions, for example Roman Catholicism, Islam and Buddhism, is that they are not restricted to one particular country; but where the sphere of influence of a church or a religious community is coextensive with state frontiers, as in the case of the Anglican High Church, these mostly form sister churches of a similar organization abroad. The steel, mining and oil industries are connected with one another through various industrial cartels. Bodies like the freemasons or the Rotary Clubs have spread to country after country. And the various scientists' associations extend well beyond the national framework. It is the same with political ideologies. A German socialist often has more in common with his French counterpart than with the middle class or the conservatives in his own country. Hitler, although a German, had a far greater affinity with an Italian fascist than a German liberal.

This kind of overlapping is not a new historical phenomenon. It can be seen in medieval universities and guilds. The guilds extended beyond the boundaries of a town, a region or even a country, and within the guilds themselves there were separate organizations for apprentices and journeymen dividing the guilds vertically. The universities were international, the language used for teaching was Latin, and scholars who could speak it well moved from school to school. Universities often refused to take local-born students because they preferred to have foreigners.

There is often a certain harmony between spheres which overlap one another and it is considered quite natural for a man with some particular talent or qualifications to leave his own group and join another one. This is why the activity of modern specialist bodies frequently extends to two different spheres; for it goes on within one specific state and is bound up with the organization of that state at the same time also spreading out beyond the individual state. Although the representatives of a national group within an international organization are members of a particular state, collaboration with fellow specialists abroad may result in their having a decisive influence on the political life of their own state.

The fact that there are international organizations to deal with public and political problems suggests that the state itself is not always the best judge of its citizens' interests or the one most fitted to protect them. But the modern state has no reason to look on every such organization with unmitigated suspicion. Very often the aims of the state can be co-ordinated with those of an international organization. In general an organization's opposition endangers the state in two cases only:

1. When the aims of such an organization run directly counter to the state's official policy or its political aims, especially when an expansionist, aggressive international link-up is involved;
2. when the international organization has such a strong hold on the citizens' loyalty that their loyalty to their own nation and state threatens to take second place.

The time factor is also important. When England's Catholics turned to the Pope for help and support against the oppression they were suffering at the hands of some of the Tudor monarchs they needed this help at once. But their news took several days to reach Paris and then a further fortnight to get to Rome. Even if the Pope agreed to help, still more time would have passed before they could have persuaded any ally to raise an army to aid the Catholics of England.

As we have already explained, between the two World Wars the traditional ruling classes of central and eastern Europe feared the growing importance of international organizations which might divide the loyalty of the citizens in their countries.[1]

As their claims to ruling status were not in the first place based on ability and merit but on religious, family and dynastic traditions or national privilege, they felt their position threatened.

In central Europe the supporters of authoritarianism had learned from the First World War and its aftermath that military dictatorship and monarchical absolutism were no longer practical politics. Dictatorships had to seek new forms. Why should not modern technology, which had served the Western Powers so well in the First World War, do the same for them? International interdependence was a fact and a highly developed intelligence service was already in existence, offering every prospect of success. The working-class movement was split into social democrats and communists. The socialist parties could no longer ignore the fact that even for their electoral supporters the nation took first place and the party second. Liberalism's influence made increasingly less impact. The democratic states, which simply pursued their own interests, disavowed their solidarity with democrats in other countries.

It was soon to be proved that it was no accident that Mussolini's fascism developed within the imperial frontiers of a national state, which German national socialism appeared within a concept of world domination. Until 1806 Germany had been the centre of the Holy Roman Empire, which had never renounced its claim to universalism. It was characteristic that the enduring fame of its most important emperors, namely the Hohenstaufen Frederick II and the Habsburg Charles V, was based not on military conquest but on their cosmopolitan, universalistic policy, their world-wide connections and their objective mediatory role among the nations. This was how Dante's *De Monarchia* conceived the Emperor's role as world arbitrator.

The Reformation and the ideas of a sovereign nation-state then led to a rival concept, namely that of an international community of sovereign states which, by observing certain standards of international law, felt themselves to be bound to one another. In the age of dynastic hostility this etatist concept was carried into effect, in the German areas of Europe, under the Habsburgs in Austria and under the Hohenzollerns in Prussia. After the Peace of Westphalia in 1648 the

---

[1] In their *Systematic Sociology*, New York 1932, p. 323, von Weise and Becker have given an account of east-European peasant immigration to America's urban centres. In their former social environment they occupied an established status in the social scale; selection went according to traditions established by family and community, religious customs, etc. Cf. also William J. Thomas-Thomas Znaniecki, *The Polish Peasant in Europe and America, Monograph of an Immigrant Group*, Vol. 5, Boston 1918.

universalist idea of the Holy Roman Empire faded because of the rise of these two dynasties, which steadily grew in power, and to them it finally yielded its political efficiency.

This process was confined, however, to central Europe. When the Holy Roman Empire came to an end in 1806 the universalist idea did not die with it but survived, although it remained entirely latent. And so, when the Hohenzollern and Habsburg dynasties collapsed in 1918, it was evident that the medieval concept had assumed a new form, one which, while connected with the original idea, gave it an entirely new content, namely Hitler's idea of a national socialist European order. The old empire idea was now interpreted only in biological terms and adapted to the interplay of international forces – a further example of how totalitarianism wanting to breathe new life into medieval forms of society in its fight against modern pluralist society.

The gradual transformation of national socialism's élite force, the SS, from a German to a Nordic-Germanic and then to a European fighting order was also part of this trend. Both the attempt to conquer European Russia and the desire to gain a footing in South America and to convert the United States of America to national socialism are evidence of the universalist aspect of the Nazi claim to wield a power far wider than one which was merely national.

## PART TWO

*Social Evolution and the Tendency to Totalitarianism*

Biological, technological and cultural factors are all part of the evolutionary process.[1] Max Weber has stressed the importance of culture in this connection and has shown how religious and intellectual factors can influence the development of the economy.[2] Marx and Thorstein Veblen, on the other hand, lay more emphasis on the importance of technical and economic factors in the evolution of society.

Both schools of thought can be accused of bias, although Weber was not a philosopher of history and did not imagine his thesis, on the effect of the Protestant ethic on capitalism, would be taken as a general law. The influences, of course, operate in two opposite directions. Thus culture, morals and customs influence technological and economic progress which, in their turn, affect cultural development. Both are

[1] R. M. Maciver and Charles H. Page, *Society*, London 1950, Chaps. 23–6.
[2] Max Weber, *Die protestantische Ethik und der Geist des Kapitalismus*, Tübingen 1934.

THE DIFFUSION AND IMPACT OF FASCISM / 365

powerful factors of social change, the cultural factor generally having the greater impact on the personality of the individual. It is also slower in taking effect but in times of crisis the curve indicating its importance will rise much more quickly. The influence of technology on culture is a gradual and unobtrusive affair, as it always meets resistance from those groups and individuals whose interests and loyalties are affected by technological and economic developments. It also runs counter to the habits, behaviour and attitudes of a larger section of the population.

It is easier to track down these influences in the experimental field of a single society, A, than in the overlapping complexities of the modern interdependent world. In the diagram on page 366 counter-trends – the effect of culture on technology and vice versa – are represented by two horizontal arrows pointing in opposite directions. If we draw in another horizontal line to represent an analogous development in country B, which is adjoining or has a similar structure, it is still adequate as a graphic representation of the social development in the two countries. We complete it by

(1) closing the rectangle with vertical arrows pointing in opposite directions, which means:
   (a) cultural and ideological development in country A influences cultural and ideological development in country B and vice versa;
   (b) technological and economic development in country A influences technological and economic development in country B and vice versa.
(2) drawing in the diagonals in the rectangle, which means:
   (a) ideological and cultural development in country A directly stimulates technological and economic development in country B and vice versa;
   (b) technological and economic development in country A directly stimulates cultural development in country B and vice versa.
(3) noting that the elements which go to make up these trends themselves continually assume new forms during these processes and that, for example:
   (a) elements which are vertically (culture – culture) transmitted from A to B, and likewise in country B move horizontally (culture – technology); or
   (b) elements, which are transmitted horizontally (culture – technology) in A, also move vertically (technology – technology) from A to B; or
   (c) elements which move between two countries A and B along the diagonals (e.g. culture A – technology B) are transmitted both vertically and horizontally and react on technological development

in country A – after these elements have received new stimuli in B – and simultaneously influence cultural and ideological development in country B.

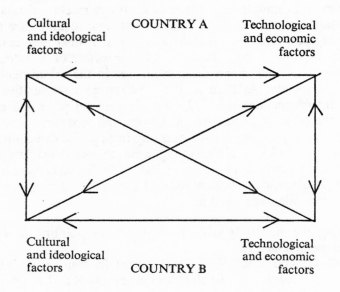

(4) we more or less grasp the complexity of the social processes if we realize that these complicated links between two countries represent only a tiny part of the world-wide network or social connections and that they are multiplied if still more countries are included in the investigation.

(5) remembering that every individual relationship is a compound of many different social processes. Let us, for example, take the vertical trend (culture – culture) between countries A and B. This trend includes a number of associative, dissociative and mixed processes.[1] Competition, domination, submission, imitation, adaptation and the stressing of individuality can be part-processes of this one trend.

All four processes go on independently of the state's claim to dominate its subjects. This has a number of far-reaching consequences. Let us take, for example, country A, which enjoyed an unbroken religious and intellectual development for centuries on end. Suddenly a new historical phenomenon appears, due to the activity of a more

---

[1] Leopold von Weise, *System der Allgemeinen Soziologie*, Munich and Leipzig 1933, pp. 240 f.

modern generation, prophets or politicians; a new consciousness is born and spills over into the neighbouring country B, perhaps in the wake of military conquest. This process can lead to technical inventions and discoveries as well as an economic boom either inside or outside the country where it originally began. Advances of this kind are possibly adopted by third countries for various reasons – self-interest, competition, imitation or because they believe in the same ideology. At the same time economic and technological developments in one particular country enforce a change of consciousness, a process which, as we know, is very slow and the actual way the adjustment is made will, in its turn, strongly influence the attitude of other countries. Both the French and Russian revolutions are examples of this. For instance, the ideas of the French Revolution were taken to central and southern Europe by the French armies. The liberal principles and ideas which it spread prepared the ground for the gradual industrialization of Germany; that, in turn, compelled the German lower and middle classes to make a mental adjustment to a new image of society. This found its way into neighbouring countries, especially Austria, as did technological and economic developments. Social processes still to be discussed were also responsible for the diffusion of fascism (in its wider sense) over the whole of Europe. Before giving a general picture of these processes, however, they must first be considered in isolation and their effect on the outside world examined.

## PART THREE

*Economic Factors*

The development of economic liberalism in Europe resulted in considerable industrial growth and a corresponding increase in competition. After 1918 the prevailing ideology of the nation-state favoured industrial expansion in the smaller states. Their industries would never have been competitive in world markets but for government support in the form of export subsidies and protective customs and if the industries themselves had not maintained wages below the minimum level of subsistence. The big industrialists knew that their supremacy would last so long as their state frontiers formed economic bulwarks against other states. At the same time the trend towards rationalization and nationalization was strengthened in most of these countries.

Not only in central Europe but everywhere both the big and the smaller industrialists were forced to rationalize. This led to chronic unemployment, which was unavoidable under the liberal economic system, and it also meant that the small industrialists were exposed to ever-growing competitive pressure. Daily contact with their workers brought them much more into touch with current socialist views than the big industrialist, who was shielded from any sort of direct contact with his workers by a whole hierarchy of directors, administrators and technicians. The small industrialist did not remain completely impervious to socialist ideas, but he was not prepared to surrender his position or his power. It was hardly strange, therefore, that he should see his salvation in the totalitarian state. This became abundantly clear during the economic crisis which came after 1929, when the liberal economic system collapsed in most European countries. This crisis proved how advanced the technical and economic trend towards interdependence and internationalism was already.

After 1933 Berlin became fascism's main citadel. The authoritarian elements in central and south-east Europe knew that they no longer stood alone.[1] When the National Socialists assumed power they set to work to eliminate the upper class – that is to say those classes in central Europe which favoured authoritarian, reactionary systems of government – and to replace them by the middle and lower classes. We have already shown how this happened in Austria.[2] In Hungary, too, the most ardent supporters of national socialism were to be found among the lesser landed nobility and the middle class. The Nazis had sound reasons for pursuing this policy. They knew that they were bound to disclose their real plans in so far as they affected these countries. But then they would no longer have been sure of the loyalty of the reactionary upper classes, since the social position which national socialism meant to allow those would not have been anything like the superior status they had enjoyed before 1918. National socialism hoped, however, to find support among the middle classes because democracy and socialism had long been hated by them. A totalitarian ideology could compensate them for their loss of social status. The *Kameradschaftsbund* (League of Comradeship) in the Sudetenland and the nationalists in Austria were groups where the sons of senior civil servants, university teachers and industrialists who could not reconcile themselves to the loss of their former positions of authority met. Now new careers beckoned to them. The idea that national socialism was anti-religious and appealed to the mob was not exactly pleasant, but people decided to support the 'lesser' against the 'greater' evil.

Rauschning confirms that many German conservatives joined the National Socialists because they believed that by doing so they could

[1] Cf. Chap. VI, Part Four.　　　　　[2] Cf. Chap. VI, Part Three.

arrest the dissolution of the traditional social order. He cites people like Ernst Jünger and other 'conservative revolutionaries' who, by putting their idealism and integrity at the service of a Utopian purpose, became valuable allies of totalitarianism, giving it a respectability which its own party members never could.

Various élites who were inclined to authoritarian forms of government, for instance those in Austria and Poland, would have nothing to do with national socialism. But they supported it indirectly, imitating a number of its most important techniques in the belief that they could turn its methods against its German authors. This national socialist penetration of the small nations of central and eastern Europe was something so deep and enduring that it survived the collapse of German national socialism in 1945. Thus the mass expulsions of the German-speaking minorities from Czechoslovakia, Poland, Yugoslavia and Romania, like the mass murders copied from SS practice, must be counted as the evil legacy of Nazi ideology to which the ruling strata of these countries had been converted and which proved such a powerful factor that the Soviet occupation power, primarily concerned with integrating these areas into the Soviet sphere of influence, deemed it wiser to reach an agreement with it. For it must be emphasized that, for example, the expulsion of the Sudeten Germans had been decided on by President Beneš and Dr Ripka when they were living in exile in London and unaware of what fate had in store for them. The Czech communists cannot, therefore, be held solely responsible for this expulsion. Even the specific forms taken by the Polish, Czech, Hungarian and Romanian national communist governments after the Second World War were influenced by National Socialism.

After the National Socialists had dissolved political parties in Germany Dollfuss did the same in Austria. At the same time he proscribed the Nazi Party. It was argued that the dictatorial measures were temporary and directed only against totalitarianism. In point of fact, however, these measures favoured national socialism. When Dollfuss smashed Austrian social democracy he destroyed the only group which could have held up the advance of national socialism. Also, by persecuting the Austrian Socialist Party, he severed his last links with the European democracies and at the same time concluded the alliance with Italian fascism. After only five months it became evident that he had succumbed to the dynamism of totalitarianism.

By destroying the constitutional system and favouring the rise of an authoritarian ideology, Dollfuss also sanctioned dictatorship and created the conditions needed for the victory of national socialism, namely that the believers in authoritarianism joined the stronger and not the weaker side. The sentencing of democrats to several years' imprisonment and of national socialists to no more than a few weeks, the Wöllensdorf concentration camp, the continuous negotiations with Germany, the vain appeal to non-existent feelings of consanguinity, due to the use of the same language, all clearly showed the Austrians that the triumph of national socialism was not to be baulked. The *Gleichschaltung* (forcing into line) and infiltration process had begun long before the first German soldier set foot on Austrian soil.

The big European industrialists did not fear socialism, especially the social democratic brand, as they were acquainted with the conservative trends within the movement. But their material interests were frequently antagonistic to those of the working class and they did little to correct the fear of socialism widespread among the property-owning class. This permanent threat damaged the interests of socialism; the latter had no intention of carrying out this threat in the immediate future and so the socialist parties merely incurred the hatred of influential circles. The firm hold which Marxist ideology had on the socialist parties on the Continent and the perpetual struggles of the trade unions against the employers led millions of social democrats to believe that the best way to smash fascism was to destroy capitalism. The lack of political training which still marked not only central Europe but also western Europe at this time and which was almost as pronounced among large sections of the more prosperous classes as among the lower middle classes meant that both were equally incapable of distinguishing between communist and socialist parties. In any case the socialist programmes not only in Germany but in France and Spain as well were partly to blame; the revolutionary principles proclaimed were not borne out in social democratic practice.

Even in Great Britain, where the Labour Party had evolved as a means of looking after the purely economic interests of the workers, who absolutely refused to countenance a revolutionary policy, the social gulf between the upper strata of society (aristocracy, big industry and upper middle class) which, allied to an aristocratic school and university system, filled all the posts of any consequence in the Foreign Office, the Army and in the Colonial Service, and the working class and employees on the other hand became increasingly evident.

National socialism and fascism used those means which, from the point of view of propaganda, were most effective in giving the impression that they were communism's main adversaries. This made recruitment among Western conservative circles much easier, for example, inducing the oil magnate Detering to give his support to the Dutch National Socialists and making inroads into the English, French and Belgian upper classes. Also, the fact that liberalism was castigated as something decadent, flabby, corrupt and a relic of the *ancien régime* was bound to mean that the reactionary wings of the conservative groups in western Europe felt even more strongly drawn to fascism. The outstanding example of this switch in conservative allegiance to fascism was the *Action Française*, which has made an outstanding contribution to national socialist ideology.[1]

Thus the French National Committee of the *Akademie für die Rechte dev Völker* (Academy for the Rights of Peoples), the 'National Internationale', included collaborators and people like Baron Robert Surcouf, Clement Serpeille de Gobineau, Comte H. de Manneville and General Paul Pouderoux.[2]

It is indicative that the Second Congress of the National Socialist International was held in London. The Rt. Hon. Lord Queensborough acted as chairman of the meeting. The English members had joined this movement partly out of concern about the future of the British Empire, partly out of hostility to the League of Nations and, in particular, out of hatred of the Soviet Union and France, which was regarded as the Western bastion of radical socialism.[3]

From the organization's connection with Lord Lothian,[4] it is not difficult to deduce that there was a spiritual affinity between the circle round Neville Chamberlain, Lord Halifax, Thomas Jones, Conwell-Evans, Lord Londonderry and Sir Nevile Henderson and the anti-socialist objectives of national socialist pre-war policy. We now know that the policy of appeasement, which favoured and stimulated Hitler's war policy, scored considerable success under Stanley Baldwin's government and found an influential exponent in Baldwin's secretary, Thomas Jones.[5] The important and decisive role which Lord Lothian played in the fatal policy of appeasement is now generally recognized.[6] Lord Lothian was one of those influential Britons who went to stay with Hitler for some considerable time at Hitler's personal invitation and who did everything possible to promote co-operation with Nazi Germany.

Less well known is the role which the historian Philip Toynbee played as an intellectual sympathizer with Adolf Hitler. Toynbee had a conversation with Hitler lasting one and three-quarter hours and informed Thomas Jones that he was convinced of Hitler's honest desire

[1] Cf. Nolte, op. cit., pp. 141 f.

[2] 'Akademie für die Rechte der Völker', *Der Kampf um die Völkerordnung*, Berlin 1939.

[3] Ibid., pp. 76–96.  [4] Ibid.

[5] Cf. A. L. Rowse, *All Souls and Appeasement*, London 1961, p. 35. Rowse, himself a member of All Souls College, Oxford, points out the vital part played by a few important members of this College at this period. but stresses that only a minority were involved, although it was a very influential one.

[6] Cf. J. R. M. Butler, *Lord Lothian (Philip Kerr), 1822–1940*, London, New York 1960.

for peace in Europe and for close friendship with Britain.[1] This was the report of a man who was a leading expert in foreign affairs (Toynbee was Director of the Royal Institute of International Affairs, even when it became the research department of the Foreign Office later in the war), for which Thomas Jones, the close friend and helper of Ribbentrop, had been waiting. Jones asked Toynbee for an immediate account in writing of his impressions of Hitler and took care to see that it was in the hands of Baldwin and Eden the very next morning. Hitler was well aware of the favourable impression which Toynbee had indirectly conveyed to Baldwin and went ahead with his plans, occupying the Rhineland a few days after Toynbee's return to England.

Jones allowed himself increasingly to be used as a benevolent interpreter of Ribbentrop, who was himself Hitler's mouthpiece. Baldwin and other members of the British cabinet were always being told that France was in Moscow's pocket as the Paris press and a hundred French deputies were being paid by the bolsheviks. It was Jones who returned to London from his talk with Hitler an enthusiastic and unquestioning supporter of German foreign policy and, as a result of his influence with the Prime Minister, Stanley Baldwin, succeeded in getting the Ambassador in Berlin, Phipps, replaced by Sir Nevile Henderson.[2] It must, however, be noted that Vansittart, who was notoriously anti-German, also had a hand in Henderson's appointment. Martin Gilbert and Richard Gott[3] believe that Vansittart preferred a professional diplomat rather than a politician as ambassador because he would work directly for him as Under Secretary of State instead of for the Prime Minister. He could never have suspected that Henderson would firmly pursue a policy of his own, ignoring the normal channels. Vansittart's mistake was in not recognizing the ideological and moral character of the struggle against national socialism, a struggle which was far bigger than any conflict with traditional nationalism. Henderson was in sympathy with authoritarian ideas. He therefore urged that England should tolerate the ideology of the Third Reich even if it meant the enslavement of central Europe.

Under its editor, Geoffrey Dawson, and his assistant, Barrington-Ward, the venerable *Times* came to be an important support to Hitler's foreign policy. Its help was not, of course, confined to acting as the mouthpiece of Baldwin's and Neville Chamberlain's appeasement policy; the great political influence wielded by Dawson, whose opinions even affected the composition of the British cabinet, was a decisive factor

[1] Rowse, op. cit., p. 38.
[2] Ibid., pp. 42 ff.
[3] Martin Gilbert and Richard Gott, *The Appeasers*, London 1963, p. 74.

in the formation of this policy.[1] Dawson undoubtedly had a substantial share in the efforts made to conceal the totalitarian nature of national socialism with its potentialities for blackmail and gangsterism. Thus in a report on the London Conference of the International Labour Movement (*Arbeitsgemeinschaft*) on July 11, 1935, *The Times* observed:

'The movement is a body for research for international affairs . . . the movement is not political but scientific and believes in the devotion to country.'[2]

It is difficult to credit that Dawson, one of the best-informed and most powerful men of his age, did not know from what sources the London Conference had been financed or that Helmut Nicolai of the German Intelligence Service and Lt.-Col. Fleischhauer, editor of the anti-Semitic *Weltdienst*, financed by Rosenberg and published in several languages, had taken part in the Berlin Conference in 1934.[3]

In any case, in the very year that the London Conference took place, *Das Braune Netz*, published in Paris, had clearly shown links between the International Arbeitsgemeinschaft and Alfred Rosenberg.[4]

The services which Dawson rendered to the Nazi system were far greater than giving this sort of idealized picture of its spy and Quisling organizations. Dawson, who was in constant contact with the official, leading appeasers like Baldwin, Chamberlain, Halifax and Lothian, felt entitled – because of their wish for an understanding with Hitler Germany – to lay down the law about the need to act, using the medium of editorials and other articles in *The Times*. Thus, before the German invasion of Austria, there was a leading article on February 16 which justified in advance the violation of Austria. The article was written by Barrington-Ward. If one considers Hitler's summoning of Schuschnigg to Berchtesgaden on February 13 and how the Austrian Chancellor was browbeaten and forced to take Hitler's agents into his cabinet, this editorial cannot but appear in an ominous light. The *History of the Times* explains:

'Barrington-Ward's views about Germany derived from the moral decision he felt forced to make as to the Versailles Treaty. In principle Barrington-Ward accepted the German thesis that the Treaty was unjust, and he had believed ever since Versailles that the *Anschluss* was inevitable and should have been conceded to Brüning. Having

[1] Cf. John Evelyn Wrench, *Geoffrey Dawson and our Times*, London 1955, especially pp. 365–82.
[2] 'Akademie für die Rechte der Völker', op. cit., p. 97.
[3] H. Keller, *Volksgemeinschaft und Völkerfriede*, Berlin 1935.
[4] *Das Braune Netz*, Paris 1935, p. 49.

come to this decision before Hitler was ever heard of, he could see no reason in conscience for refusing justice to Germany after Hitler was in power; especially as he thought that power was largely created by Germany's possession of a just grievance, and Goebbel's adroit exploitation of it. The leading article of February 17, 1938, is a characteristic expression of Barrington-Ward's attitude.'[1]

On March 10, 1938, Dawson and Barrington-Ward attended Ribbentrop's farewell reception at the German Embassy in London and the next day Hitler marched into Austria. Rowse is right in thinking that the invasion of Austria could scarcely be a matter of surprise since Hitler, via Dawson and Ribbentrop, had received assurances from the highest British authorities that strong British action was unlikely.

The procedure was exactly the same in the case of Czechoslovakia.[2] Barrington-Ward remained opposed to any British pledge to Czechoslovakia. 'In Barrington-Ward's times the paper inclined to support Germany rather than France.'[3] And 'at the beginning of the summer [of 1938] leading articles displayed a frankly pro-German tone'.[4] In a leading article on September 7, 1938, Dawson recommended the cession of the Sudeten regions to the Third Reich. Although the British Foreign Office officially denied that it wanted Czechoslovakia to cede territory to Germany, Dawson, after lunching twice with the Foreign Secretary, Lord Halifax, persisted in his view in a leader on September 9, and admitted to Barrington-Ward that Lord Halifax privately shared his opinion.[5] Chamberlain who, with the help of his adviser, Sir Horace Wilson, had taken personal charge of British foreign policy, at the same time prevented any independent military intervention by France by warning the French Foreign Minister, M. Bonnet, that in the event of any military involvement with Germany, England could make available only two non-motorized divisions and 150 aircraft. The immediate sequel was Hitler's diatribe against Beneš and Czechoslovakia, which precipitated the crisis leading to the Munich Agreement.

The attitude of the British Ambassador in Berlin, Sir Nevile Henderson, at the time of the National Socialist Party Congress in Nuremberg in September 1938, when Neville Chamberlain sacrificed Czechoslovakia to Adolf Hitler, is proof of the effectiveness of the Nazi tactics of claiming to be leading the fight against socialism and communism. At Göring's instigation, an SS officer, Unterstürmführer

---

[1] *History of The Times*, London 1952, Vol. 4, Part II, p. 913.
[2] Winston Churchill, *The Second World War*, Vol. I, p. 266.
[3] *History of The Times*, ibid., p. 919.      [4] Ibid., p. 920.
[5] Ibid., p. 934.

Baumann, was assigned as A.D.C. to Henderson while he was at the Congress.

At that time the fate of European democracy was indissolubly linked with the fate of the Czechoslovak republic. In the Sudetenland, where German social democracy was desperately resisting national socialism – a stand which was soon to bring its representatives either into the German concentration camps or to emigrate – Lord Runciman reviewed a march-past of the camouflaged SS and SA formations of the Sudeten German national socialists, his arm outstretched in the Hitler salute.

Assuming that Henderson, as a Conservative, would be interested in the fate of the landowners, Baumann tried to impress on him the danger threatening the German landowners in Czechoslovakia. He told him that radical workers with left-wing sympathies were being trained in arson and the use of explosives by Czech N.C.O.s;[1] civil war could be expected to erupt very soon and this would be the signal for a communist uprising. Baumann believed 'there would soon be a crisis and said the Czech Chief of the General Staff was also known to be a former Russian officer with pan-Slav views who intended to establish close links with Soviet Russia'. Sir Nevile Henderson said he thought much of what Baumann said was true and inquired about the SS leader, Himmler, 'whom he seemed to think highly of'. On Sunday, September 11, continues Baumann, Henderson could not attend the service in honour of the dead as he was expecting an important telephone call, but 'he later watched the march-past of the SS and SA with great interest'. He simply could not have enough of it. Even after lunch he was still keen to see the last part of the parade.

When Baumann was cross-examined in detail by Secretary of State Paul Körner about England's and Sir Nevile Henderson's attitude, Baumann's answer was to refer to his earlier report:

'In Sir Nevile Henderson's opinion England was to be regarded not as a democracy but as an aristocracy. This aristocratic upper class was at present violently opposed to the broad masses in the popular front. The settling of the British–Italian conflict had been a stiff and crucial test for the Conservative Party, as the broad masses of the British people condemned anything that smacked of surrender to Mussolini's claims. In the Czechoslovak question the British government, by sending Lord Runciman, had pledged itself to trying to find a friendly solution to the conflict. The British government could not accept any military intervention before the Runciman mission had finished its

[1] *Akten zur Deutschen Auswärtigen Politik 1918*, Serie D, Bd. 2, Baden-Baden 1950, No. 482. Published in England as *Documents on German Foreign Policy, 1918–1945*, Series D, Vol. 2, London 1950.

work; for its cowardice it ran the risk of being swept away by the Labour opposition in the next election. But then the fate of the old aristocratic class in England would probably be sealed. England's need to intervene was therefore also based on considerations of internal policy. If I had heard Field Marshal Göring's speech at the time I should have noticed that the English also, as a manly Germanic race, preferred to be led by the brave and fighting type and not by the cowardly and effeminate.'

Later, at the party in the Nassau Keller in Nuremberg, where every single seat was occupied by SA, SS and political leaders and the atmosphere was extremely convivial, Sir Nevile Henderson gave proof of his great diplomatic ability. He got up and said: 'When I was a young man in Bonn I was a drinking member of the Bonn confraternity (*Corps Borussia*) and still know the Duke of Coburg, Bodo, Count of Alvensleben-Neugattersleben and Herr von Grunelius.' When the party broke up after midnight, says Baumann, 'the first morning papers were out'. When Sir Nevile Henderson saw the headlines, which were again about the Czechs, he merely remarked: 'Oh, these blasted Czechs!'

The great efforts which the group of appeasers made to gain the favour of the Third Reich is clearly indicated by a remark of Henderson's, after Beneš had announced that he would make a speech on September 10: 'The unfortunate thing was that nobody believed Beneš.' On this occasion Henderson said he thought that freemason connections between him and French politicians had been decisive for the good relations which he enjoyed with them.[1] In the book he wrote in his self-defence, Henderson even admits to being responsible for the visit of the Czech Foreign Minister, Chvalkovsky, and indirectly also for President Hácha's visit to Berlin on March 14, 1939. The outcome of this particular visit was Hitler's occupation of Prague and the rest of Czechoslovakia.

Henderson's statements show that Runciman, who was sent to Czechoslovakia as an arbitrator, was a judge who had decided to bring about an agreement between the parties in dispute even before he began to examine the issue. From these statements, however, one can also conclude that the circle round Chamberlain were less concerned to repair the injustice done to Czechoslovakia in the Paris Peace Treaties than to eliminate Czechoslovakia as a democratic bulwark against fascism. This circle, which was hostile to all democratic movements, rightly realized that the future of the British, German and Czechoslovak democracies were closely bound up with one another.

[1] Ibid.

It was, therefore, not so much the fear of Soviet Russia as the threat to the supremacy of the English aristocracy which inspired these ultra-conservative circles to support Hitler. Furthermore, Hitler could also employ against them the deception technique which he had used successfully against the German conservatives. It took the German-Soviet Pact of 1939 to shake their belief in Hitler and Himmler as crusaders and champions of the upper classes.

## PART FOUR

### The Cultural Ideological Factor

Our relationship with other people is often considerably modified by personal acquaintance. Our class prejudices, our beliefs, our ethical principles and our code of behaviour act as a brake on this process, perhaps somewhat less in urban than in rural society. These processes by which human relationships are modified are called 'classifications' or 'identifications'.[1]

Where the relationship concerns particular groups, states or nations, the number of 'stereotypes', simplifications and prejudices tends to increase. Our opinion of another nation depends on the knowledge and feeling which we have imbibed at home, at school, at church and from all our primary and secondary personal contacts. Our view of a nation which we do not know very well is determined by the past or present behaviour of its government, how we have heard of it and by the effect of this knowledge on our original attitude.

Each group within a nation will have its own specific collective attitude to other nations.[2] The Czech working class's idea of Russia was very different from that of the Czech middle class. The Irish Catholic attitude to Italy will differ from that of the Irish Protestant. Collective judgements, therefore, are modified by group loyalties of this kind, which cut across national frontiers.

It could be argued with some justification that collective judgements are really *not* judgements at all but a heterogeneous jumble of other people's experiences relayed to persons, groups or nations by the experiences of the primary group and by books, films, the theatre and the radio. Modern communications media have widened people's intellectual horizons and reinforced irrational sentiments, and this has had a considerable effect on the mechanism of man's social life. The

[1] Lasswell, *World Politics and Personal Insecurity*, op. cit., pp. 165 f.
[2] Georg Simmel, *Soziologie*, 'Excurs über den Fremden', op. cit., pp. 509–12.

modern press, cinema and radio have profoundly affected the popular mind. It might be assumed that the improvement in communications and information would promote human contacts generally. But the human mind has not kept pace with this development and has failed to adapt itself to the demands of modern life, preventing full use of the opportunities opened up by technology, although the persistent and widespread applications of primary ideals to secondary groups and associations favours the growth of democracy. The socio-psychological climate of mass society, however, is such that it is impossible for people to assimilate in their subconscious the knowledge which they have about other nations.

In Europe, particularly in central Europe, collective prejudices arise in an environment which is completely different from the one encountered in America. There the European immigrant cannot apply his ready-made prejudices, which are based on his intellectual heritage. He soon comes to realize that they are so much ballast, which he must jettison if he wants to prosper. In Europe traditional prejudices are stubbornly maintained among different linguistic groups often living in the same state and mostly geographically closer to one another than happens with corresponding groups in the American States.

At first sight it might seem that these prejudices could be overcome by travel, but Robert Michels has shown that this does not invariably produce the desired result. As a rule the traveller seldom sheds the ingrained impressions acquired in his original environment and he will tend to assess his new environment in the light of the old one. In a foreign country he will, of course, probably in the first instance perceive the defects and only longer acquaintance will provide the balanced judgement necessary for him to emphasize the similarities rather than the differences. Yet a change of attitude towards another country brought about by personal contact is not necessarily a change for the better. The result can often be revulsion.[1] It often happens that members of a national group A, on meeting members of a national group B, identify the members of the B group positively, without, however, revising their general attitude to the B group. If, however, they identify a member of the B group negatively, this will only serve to reinforce their anti-B feelings. We may assume that the reason for this lies in the connection between collective prejudices and the system of loyalties, whose basic features we have already described.

In central and south-east Europe with its collection of linguistically heterogeneous regions and communities, deeply-rooted national prejudices are evident everywhere (cf. Chap II). As long as communications

[1] G. M. Stratton, *Social Psychology of International Conduct*, New York 1929, and C. H. Cooley, *Social Organization*, New York 1912, pp. 80, 107 ff.

had not reached the present technical level, these prejudices could easily be controlled and localized. However, since the advent of greater travel facilities and more news media the areas of friction and their consequent tensions have greatly increased. The extension of the franchise for the Austrian and Hungarian parliaments before 1914 suddenly sharpened people's awareness of the existence of national conflicts, as the press and the growing number of political meetings brought home to the nationalities of Austria-Hungary the collective prejudices and bias of their partners. In 1918 the separating and segregating of the conflicting parties was tried as an experiment. But this naturally did not relieve the tensions born of national prejudice and antagonism. News and information spread even more rapidly than before the war and the newly created frontiers were intended to provide a protective belt for the collective beliefs and prejudices.

Nazi policy revealed a profound knowledge of the most important group prejudices. The manipulation of loyalties, ideologies and hatreds became the main weapon for furthering their policy, the principle of *divide et impera* their most important rule. We ought to describe how the National Socialists were able to explore and exploit the most popular views, prejudices and behaviour stereotypes prevailing throughout the world. They not only discovered contemporary clashes of interest which they could utilize to set nation against nation; they also unearthed disagreements and conflicts which had been major factors in shaping the various national histories (cf. Chaps. VI–VIII). They set to work in the belief that every nation has some unhealed wound and they realized the advantage any reopening of these old wounds would bring to totalitarianism in general and to Nazism in particular.

The creation and exploitation of conflicts – already described – produced especially useful dividends for the Nazis in the international sphere. There was not a single conflict between the nations of Europe which they did not exploit. Their propaganda acted like a powerful reflector which throws such an intense light on one particular problem that all the rest remain plunged in darkness. The cruelties inflicted on the Austrians of the South Tyrol by the Italian fascists constituted a permanent sore for all the German-speaking people of Europe. Yet Nazi propaganda successfully diverted European public attention from the South Tyrol even while Nazi Germany was loudly claiming the right to integrate all the Germans in Europe. At the same time national socialism incited even the German-speaking populations of Yugoslavia and Romania to put pressure on these countries to modify their foreign policy. The Nazis turned a spotlight on the Teschen territory in order to disrupt Czech-Polish relations. They supported the Ukrainian independence movement in Poland to effect a temporary improvement in their relations with Russia. They attempted to play the Frisian section of the Dutch population off against Holland and the Flemish areas of Belgium against the Walloons.

How was it possible for the Nazis, under the conditions of modern communications, to plot in secret in so many different places at once without their network of agents being discovered and without common measures being taken against the universal threat which they represented?

We shall see that the reason lies in the state of mind which had gained the ascendancy among the ruling classes and public opinion. This consisted of a narrow-minded nationalism coupled with an intellectual inertia which spiritually isolated its own group from its neighbours – an attitude which has been described as 'ethnocentrism' – but is nevertheless unable to prevent relations with them.

This attitude enabled national socialism to harness for its own purposes sympathies and antipathies which were deeply rooted in the history and social structure of nations. It achieved its aim because, for one thing, it understood how to exploit the irreconcilability of desirable aims and collective prejudices and because, for another, it was able to apply, on the international plane, various propaganda techniques which were based on a knowledge of mass psychology. Nazi manipulation and exploitation of the mentality prevalent in these countries can be assessed as 'inventive thinking',[1] as defined by Karl Mannheim, and their methods of disruption and *Gleichschaltung* (enforced co-ordination) might be described as 'behaviourist planning'.

Thus, in the post-war period, all over Europe a pattern of conflicts had sprung up between those who held materialistic and atheistic views and those who believed in the traditional religions. The defenders of religion in various countries with no first-hand knowledge of national socialism, because of the Nazis' anti-bolshevik propaganda, fell victim to the fallacy that new and energetic defenders of religion had risen from the dead. As we have already pointed out, after he had won the war Hitler intended to declare war on all Christian denominations, but he disclosed his plans only to a close circle of associates. Although Alfred Rosenberg's anti-Christian views were notorious, the opponents of national socialism allowed themselves to be taken in. On the other hand the revolutionary side of national socialism appealed to many freethinkers. They were fascinated by the Nazi creed of 'beyond good and evil' and by the harsh treatment meted out to the various religious communities in Germany.

One of the typical phenomena of the sociology of struggle is that the conflicting parties lose sight of the relationship between their struggle

[1] Karl Mannheim, *Man and Society*, op. cit., pp. 193–6, 199–235.

and world politics. The history of mankind is rich in examples of the sudden appearance of divergencies between loyalties and interests. Thus in France during the Thirty Years War national sentiment and interests unexpectedly gained ascendancy over religious attachments. Catholic France allied herself with Protestant powers against Catholic Austria and Spain. Again, in 1620, the Protestant England of James I ruthlessly abandoned the Protestants of Bohemia, whose Queen was a daughter of James.

It was only to be expected that totalitarianism would try to exploit these trends in social behaviour. If there were no existing conflicts smouldering, age-old animosities lost and buried in the mists of time were dug up and unscrupulously used for political ends. Thus Haushofer put forward a plan for reconstituting the state of Catalonia from the French and Spanish territories formerly inhabited by Catalans. Old traditions of the troubadours were revived and new loyalties artificially created for reasons of political propaganda. The exploitation of minority problems is also part and parcel of this activity. The following quotation is very illuminating:

'In the direction of the Indian Ocean, Nazi Germany need only help the Shah of Persia if he wished to take over his own oil wells again, and should Turkey play false, Germany could march through Armenia to Kirkuk to liberate the Armenians!'[1]

Totalitarianism benefited from the fact that people were still unaware how distances had shrunk. In Prague a man could read in the paper every day that Germany was about to do this or that, hardly realizing how near the car and the aeroplane had brought Germany to him. In the same way in England, Neville Chamberlain, in speaking about Czechoslovakia could refer to it as a far off and unknown country; for although many people may have heard that any aeroplane can fly 700 miles in three hours, very few had grasped the military consequences of this.

As we said at the beginning the Nazis' programme of action was geared to the differences between the political and social structures of western and central Europe. In central Europe there were enough groups in existence to give active help in carrying out this plan. There were similar groups in the Western democracies too; but because of the older democratic tradition there these groups were less numerous. Pro-fascists in the West were assigned a passive rather than an active role in this plan. Their aim was to create a state of mind which was summed up by the phrase: 'The business of everybody is the business of nobody'.

[1] Karl Haushofer, 'Geopolitischer Neujahrs-Ausblick 1940', in *Zeitschrift für Geopolitik*, XVII Year, 1st half-volume 1940, p. 5.

Those people in the West whose reaction to every political measure taken by the authoritarian regime was one of approval were bound to be more valuable to Hitler than fascists who attempted to make democratic countries go fascist. Concentration camps and Jew-baiting might be regrettable; but they were, after all, the Germans' own affair. The ruthless suppression of all democratic parties was glossed over with the euphemism that 'the Third Reich had finally put an end to communism and the class struggle'. Most of the Western press ignored German rearmament. Instead, it praised the Nazis' magnificent achievement in solving the unemployment problem but failed to mention that the German unemployed were in fact absorbed by the armaments industry.

Several groups in the West openly supported some national brand of fascism, for example the Dutch National Socialists, the Belgian Rexists, the followers of the Action Française and the *Croix de Feu*, or Sir Oswald Mosley, the leader of the British fascists. If they failed in their primary aim they were ready to accept German national socialism as the next best thing. Although occasionally influential, these groups were only minor agents in the fascist plan.

Nazism could count much more on the various prejudices, the habits of mind and the stereotyped reactions in international relations.[1] In this connection the 'time lag' was of major importance. This helped national socialism to utilize the most diverse groups and bodies as involuntary collaborators. Although retaining their outward form, these groups were fundamentally changed by the process of integration. Most of them had in the past maintained links with similar groups in Germany. For instance all over the world there were Roman Catholics and Protestants who could not conceive that German Catholicism and Protestantism had in any way changed since 1933. They, too, might be dismayed by the fate of their co-religionists; but they never really grasped that thousands of Catholics and Protestants were being forced to accept extreme nationalism as the supreme value. Leaders of active resistance like the Archbishops Faulhaber, von Galen, Preysing or Pastor Niemöller could not alter the fact that many Protestants and Catholics had drifted away from from the Christian faith and Christian principles – Bishop Müller and Cardinal Innizer were symptomatic of this drift.

There were still people in the West who, in speaking about Germany, thought in terms of pre-1933 Germany. Nazi musicians and artists were still invited to democratic countries and Germans travelling abroad were regarded primarily as Germans and not as Nazis. We must not

[1] Stratton, op. cit., pp. 131 f., observes that misunderstanding and enmity between nations is due less to lack of knowledge than to lack of adjustment.

forget that conservative, liberal and socialist groups continued their intellectual exchanges with like-minded groups in other countries. Everything depended on whether these German groups could put up a spiritual resistance to Nazism – in other words whether they could remain so loyal to their own values that the Nazi ideology would be unable to alter these to any marked extent. But where the groups acquiesced in their integration into the totalitarian scheme without making any show of resistance the danger of contagion was immediate.

The European and American bureaucracies still had vivid memories of the efficient and incorruptible German civil service of the pre-Hitler period. This was exploited by Nazi propaganda, which now assured the world that under the New Order every kind of progress would be speeded up. Moreover, German science and technology, although deprived of many brilliant pioneers by Nazi policy, found their way into those central-European countries which were essentially hostile to democracy in theory and practice, to socialism and communism or which were strongly anti-Semitic.

The National Socialists *transferred* the ideas about democracy which they had acquired in the struggle against Weimar to *democracy in general*. If, because of their reactionary outlook, the German bureaucracy and judiciary had helped the Nazis, perhaps fellow-travellers were also to be found in France, Belgium, Holland and even as far away as Scandinavia. There were ambitious officers in the German Army. Why should there not be similar types in the armies of France, Belgium, Holland, Norway, Yugoslavia and, to come nearer home, in Austria? The army and the bureaucracy in many European countries were fertile soil for plans of this kind. Imbued with traditional ideas these institutions were suspicious of any sort of progress. If the proselytes were not sufficiently high-ranking, this was easily remedied by creating the necessary rank.

To help in disseminating their doctrines the Nazis made use of social ambition, interest in sport, films and the business connections of a number of politically uncommitted people abroad. A well-known industrialist, politician or sportsman, for example, would receive an invitation to attend a Nazi Party Congress or a drama festival, or to joint a hunting party in Germany.[1] If all the casual remarks he made while in Germany were reported it simply made him feel that much more important.

In this and similar ways democratic politicians and other men and women in public life as well as large numbers of social scientists,

[1] Thus Lord Halifax, master of the famous Middleton Hunt, received an invitation from Göring as the titular head of hunting in the Reich to go shooting foxes with him in Germany—and incidentally to meet Hitler as well. Rowse, op. cit., p. 64.

historians and journalists were persuaded to take a 'dispassionate and realistic' view of Hitler's seizure of power, the murder and arrest of German democrats, the persecution of the Jews, June 30, 1934, German rearmament, the occupation of the demilitarized zone and the massacres of Badajoz and Guernica. The prevalence of this particular kind of misplaced tolerance in democratic states needs to be analysed systematically as it is still by no means dead, but merely dormant.

## Pacifism and Neutrality

Many nationalists of the traditional continental type took kindly to the suppression of the parties by the Nazis. For political reasons they might not approve of the way the integration process was carried out in Germany. But although they doubtless detested such methods, there were always people who were ready to support the crushing of democracy if they could feel sure that this would be repeated in a more suitable manner in their country. In any case, they approved in principle the ruthless persecution of German pacifists if, like Carl von Ossietzky, they were socialists as well. The pacifists in the West, on the other hand, sought to continue their appeasement policy at all costs and welcomed any peace proposal Hitler was prepared to make. They went on insisting that pacifism had to work for peace in every country whether the German pacifists were allowed to continue their work or not. Thus pacifism posed a grave threat to democracy's very existence by mobilizing part of the democratic ideology against democracy's own interests. There were also many people who although not pacifists themselves, could not or would not recognize the real intentions of the Nazi rulers.

Yet it is still a moot point how far this widespread blindness to Hitler's policy of deception was due to men's hopes of peace and how far it was due to deliberate benevolence towards national socialism. Trevor-Roper[1] mentions the astonishing fact that the significance of *Mein Kampf* 'as an authentic account of the well-considered and concrete war aims which Hitler already had in mind even in 1923' was overlooked.

Trevor-Roper argues that Hitler, who would have used his copyright to prevent the publication of an unabridged translation of his book in English, was himself to blame for the fact that 'English, like other politicians and political writers, did not listen to the unmistakable language of *Mein Kampf*; perhaps they entertained the fond hope that

[1] Hugh Trevor-Roper, 'Hitlers Kriegsziele', in *Vierteljahrshefte für Zeitgesschichte*, Vol. 8, 1960, p. 124.

Hitler did not mean what he said or that he could not translate his aims into fact'. In the light of this account, in which he contrasts Hitler's repeatedly expressed war aims with Hitler's deception manoeuvres, the credulity of western Europe and especially of the influential British circles round Stanley Baldwin and Neville Chamberlain seems all the most astonishing.

This apparent credulity becomes explicable only in connection with the interest – mentioned above and expressed by Sir Nevile Henderson – of a small but extremely influential circle round Chamberlain who, until the conclusion of the German-Russian Pact in 1939, were convinced that, provided Britain showed enough understanding of Hitler's pan-German plans, his war aims might be confined to the East.

Thus, on November 9, 1937, Woermann, the Minister at the German Embassy in London, reported to the Foreign Office in Berlin on Konrad Henlein's visit to London, where the Sudeten leader had talks with Sir Robert Vansittart, then Under Secretary of State at the Foreign Office:[1]

'Concerning Henlein's London talks with Sir Robert Vansittart, I hear further confidentially that Vansittart is supposed to have shown himself extremely ready to support Sudeten German wishes for autonomy. This is in accordance with the British policy of eliminating points of friction in Europe in such a way as to avoid raising the major problems which lie behind them.

'A further subject of the conversations is said to have been the Austrian question. According to my informant's statement, Vansittart wished in this matter to hear from Henlein what further developments were expected in Germany. He gave him to understand that Britain considered a union of Germany and Austria inevitable in the long run, but pointed out the dangers which would arise if the union were attempted by means of a *putsch*. In doing so he is alleged to have stated that it seemed to him to be a better solution if one day Austria were to be militarily occupied by Germany, rather than if a *putsch* were attempted.'

Although Woermann suspected Vansittart's statements to be a trap it must not be forgotten that Vansittart was fully conscious of his duty to follow the procedure laid down by the Foreign Office and to interpret clearly the policy of his Prime Minister and Foreign Secretary to Henlein. It is obvious that the mere idea that Vansittart might have been speaking with his Prime Minister's voice was bound to be enough to strengthen Hitler's determination to overrun Austria and Czechoslovakia. In any case, Vansittart's remarks to Henlein were not that

---

[1] *Documents on German Foreign Policy*, Series D, Vol. 2, op. cit., No. 14.

decisive: they merely hardened Hitler's conviction that the Western press would stand passively by while the Third Reich attacked Austria and Czechoslovakia. We now know that no less a person than Lord Halifax had assured Hitler personally that as far as Austria, Czechoslovakia and Danzig went, Britain would not lift a finger to maintain the *status quo* – and that the British people were only concerned to secure the avoidance of such treatment of them as would be likely to cause trouble.[1]

Here we must point out that four months later Austria was occupied in the way Vansittart had suggested and that when the Munich Agreement was being arranged Chamberlain advocated that the Sudetenland should be occupied by German forces gradually and in order to maintain public law and order.[2]

Totalitarianism, both in its nationalist and communist form, always showed great skill in exploiting pacifism and the universal desire of the peoples of the world for peace for its own particular purposes. False protestations of peace and a mendacious pacifism were among the characteristic deceptions which were part of the Nazi preparations for war before the Second World War was launched. A policy deliberately designed to lull people's fears was to paralyse the democratic nations' will to resist. Konstantin Hierl, leader of the national socialist regimented Labour Service, wrote:

'This [simulated] pacifism is a political weapon and is a deliberate measure in our preparations for war. By lulling the enemy's suspicions with phrases about peace it seeks to make him neglect his defences. The soporific fog in which the enemy is enveloped also hides one's own rearmament.'[3]

Characteristic of this policy of concealment were the declarations of peace which Hitler[4] and other leaders of the Third Reich repeatedly made to France and which were completely belied by the new strategic roads and railways east of the frontier of Alsace-Lorraine.[5] This technique of lulling fears and suspicions while German rearmament was proceeding was helped by the repeated offers of non-aggression pacts and the non-aggression pact concluded with Poland.

It was the war-veteran associations in the West which were the constant target of this particular approach and the result was very

---

[1] Rowse, op. cit., p. 65.

[2] Cf. *Documents on German Foreign Policy 1918–1945*, Series D, Vol. 2, op. cit., Map 2 (appended to the Munich Agreement).

[3] *Das Braune Netz*, op. cit., p. 9.

[4] In *Mein Kampf* Hitler had spoken of the inevitable clash with France, Vol. 2, p. 765.

[5] *Das Braune Netz*, op. cit., p. 132.

successful. Thus the congresses held by Nazi camouflage organizations like the *Internationale Arbeitsgemeinschaft der Nationalisten* (The Nationalist International) were attended by the President of the British Legion, Major-General Sir Frederick Maurice, who spoke in favour of understanding between all war-veterans.[1] By exploiting this idea of understanding among old front-line enemies, national socialism was able to paralyse much of the will to resist among those were opposed of pacifism. In a contribution to the report of the Nazi-financed Academy for the Rights of Nations, Major-General J. F. C. Fuller, Chief of the British General Staff in the First World War, attacked the League of Nations and the system based on the rule of law. In this way, he said, every member of the British Empire would be pulled in two opposite directions – on the one hand towards independence, on the other towards a uniform world government.

In comparing the aims of this quisling academy with the principles of the British Empire,[2] Major-General Fuller completely misunderstood the true aims of this fifth-column organization. The motto of both, he thought, was unity in diversity, based on honour not right – a unity which comes about through the mutual recognition of the members. Therefore Fuller condemned the League of Nations which, with its articles providing for sanctions, assumed that every nation is a potential gangster and not a member of a community of free and respectable nations. The French General Pouderoux also took part in the first Nationalist Inernational Congress.

Closely connected with the problem of pacifism was the role played by defensive philosophies in undermining the democratic will to resistance. Thus about 1930 the General Staffs of the former Allies had already forgotten that the First World War had been more or less decided in Flanders and on the Marne by the tank. The West also had its own equivalent of the German Langemarck spirit, which was associated with memories of the battlefields of Verdun and Ypres. This defensive outlook was the German version of the Western illusion about the Maginot Line, which, in spite of General de Gaulle's timely warnings about armoured warfare, enjoyed the confidence of the French and English nations until its uselessness was demonstrated by the German armoured thrust in 1940.

As they paid tribute to the Unknown Soldier at the annual armistice services, millions of people in France, Britain, America, Poland and Czechoslovakia thought in the first place of the lonely infantryman who had fought in the trenches. After 1918 every little village memorial gave the impression that modern wars are infantry affairs.

[1] 'Akademie für die Rechte der Völker', op. cit., p. 78.     [2] Ibid., p. 77.

The successful dissemination of pacifist ideas by the League of Nations became the very reason for its failure when authoritarians and militarists seized the reins of power in some of its member states. The official and widely accepted doctrine among the League's member states had been that defensive wars were barely tolerable, apart from the agreement about military sanctions in Articles 16 and 17. If, however, defensive wars were only just tolerable, the natural reaction of the democratic states in face of the aggressiveness of the totalitarian states was bound to be to re-examine the question of the right of self-defence – and this at a time when the only effective policy would have been to launch a preventive war against the aggressors.

As we have already mentioned, the socialists adopted the ideas of pacifism, which had originated in western Europe, and presented them to the nations of central Europe as the essence of democracy. This principle was preached not only to the people at large but also to Social Democratic Party members and élite cadres. Within social democracy, however, there was a group of 'militant socialists' who realized the danger of this mentality before it was too late. The concept of the French Popular Front under Léon Blum was the Western counterpart of the Iron Front and the *Hammerschaften* of the Weimar Republic as well as Austria's *Republikanischer Schutzbund*. But even here the pacifist mentality within the French socialist movement proved strong enough to sacrifice Spanish democracy to an illusory hope of peace by embracing the policy of 'non-intervention'. Léon Blum, the Popular Front premier, gave pacifism as the reason for his behaviour. He feared that active intervention in Spain might lead to civil war in France. Albertini rightly points out that 'non-intervention' in the Spanish civil war was due to Léon Blum's weakness and that this was primarily due to the opposition of the left-middle-class Radical Socialist group and the negative attitude of the British government, whose support Léon Blum did not want to lose. This defensive mentality finally culminated in a readiness to accept peace 'at any price'.

The popularity of the French and the Belgian capitulation in 1940 was the corollary of this defensive outlook. It made it impossible to convince the masses that it was essential to fight for freedom. The remarkable volte-face of groups with unequivocal democratic and pacifist ideas is associated with the names of Gustave Hervé in France and with Hendrik de Man in Belgium. In the case of Hervé his pacifism was stronger than his socialism and he published pamphlets in support of national socialism as far back as 1934. In Britain the Prime Minister of the time, Stanley Baldwin, admitted he had not told the British public about German rearmament and the consequent need for defence measures by Britain because he knew that pacifist feeling was so strong that a realistic defence policy might have resulted in electoral defeat for the Conservatives.

The wave of pacifism went on rising until the outbreak of the Second World War. Throughout all these years the reaction to Nazi Germany's rearmament and increased military preparedness was a greater readiness for peace among numerous groups – on the Right as well as the Left – in the Western democracies. The more threatening and aggressive Hitler became, the more pacific was the behaviour of men like Baldwin, Chamberlain and Daladier.

After the Second World War the same thing happened when the Soviet Union began to develop atomic weapons. The mere fear that Russia would start a war – a most unlikely possibility – weakened the Western will to resistance. Again, this fear-based pacifism was common to both the Right and the Left, except that this time right-wing pacifism was exemplified in the capitulation of the American Secretary of State, Foster Dulles, in the face of Soviet aggression in Hungary and of Nasser's neo-fascist dictatorship during the Suez crisis in 1956. Just as the pacifism of the French Left complemented the capitulation of the French Right (Pétain and Laval) in 1940, the pacifism of the British Labour Party in 1956 complemented Dulles' and Eisenhower's fear-inspired pacifism.

The idea of pacifism, as it was understood thirty years ago and is still generally understood today, is due to a misunderstanding about the nature of peace. The pacifists, who want to preserve peace by unilateral disarmament by their own nation regardless of whether other nations disarm or not, start from an assumption which is strongly influenced by Rousseau's theory of the 'noble savage' who has been spoiled by society. The pacifist philosophy ignores the fact that peace can only be secured by the application of the law of a state or a supra-national power set up by common consent. It therefore believes that the weak or unarmed must not challenge any aggressive action by the strong. This is a dubious maxim, as other motives can be all-important in making a decision whether or not to embark on aggressive action. Moreover, it condemns countries which are unarmed to a slave existence *vis-à-vis* the armed. For it is this very limitation of the wilfulness natural to everyone – a limitation implicit in the fact of the consensus – which secures the freedom of all, which is now protected by the law. Pacifism must therefore be regarded as a transference of the naïve romanticism of the late eighteenth century and early nineteenth centuries to the sphere of international relations.

Fear is a sound reason for pursuing peace, provided the evil causing this fear is imminent, general and visible to all concerned. When the impending disaster strikes all those involved in the same way a general love of peace is born. The universal spectre of a nuclear war which underlies a balance of terror of this kind is what inspired the efforts which were made to improve American–Soviet relations after the Cuba crisis of 1962. However, pacifism which is rooted in fear leads to a state of peace only because the balance of terror creates a situation which is analogous to the peace 'determined by a state which is based on the rule of law'. The state based on the rule of law creates peace by *positively* enforcing law-abiding behaviour on the citizens under political obligations to that state. In contrast to this, the peace arising out of the 'balance of terror' is, for example, due to the fact that American nuclear striking power limits the power of the Soviet state and *vice-versa*, with the result that law now operates positively. In this case a positive is created from the mutual elimination of two negatives.

Nevertheless, it created a special climate of its own, exemplified by the terror which spread in countries like Holland, Belgium, Denmark and Norway under the impact of the sudden German attack in 1940, and induced people to imagine that the priests, nannies and chocolate-sellers they saw were fifth-columnists. It amounts to the sudden collapse of a view of life which no longer corresponds to the technological and cultural facts of the twentieth century. The counterpart to this sudden collapse of the real Maginot Line in France was the collapse of a mental Maginot Line behind which these countries had long been sheltering, namely the legal concept of national sovereignty which had assumed the form of neutrality on the plane of international law.

For hundreds of years neutrality had been a practice of international law to ensure the preservation of peace. If within the legal systems of states the legal institutions and practices depend on the social structures and relationships which these practices create, maintain, modify and destroy, this is much more true of the effect which inter-state structures and relationships have on international law. The growth of interdependence had altered the status of neutrality. In many states certain institutions of international law, including neutrality, had been incorporated into the law of the land, or at least had become an integral part of national custom and prescriptive law. Thus in Switzerland neutrality is an institution which ranks with the Federal Constitution itself. Neutrality has played a similar role in Holland and the Scandinavian countries. As an institution it dated from the time when small countries possessing an efficient national army could easily check the undisciplined and unreliable mercenary armies of the Great Powers. But it lost its importance in the age of mechanized and conscripted armies.

In the previous chapters we showed how the Nazis suppressed original associations and groups in Germany and provided substitute symbols to replace the aims and ideals of the past. In a similar way they utilized institutions of international law which no longer corresponded to contemporary social and political facts. Under the conditions and techniques of modern war the attitude of the neutral states to fascist preparations for acquiring world power was almost exactly that which the Weimar Republic adopted to national socialism; but whereas the German democrats went into exile and revised their views, the governments of the neutral states still clung to the outdated institution of neutrality. Nothing could have been more convenient for the Nazis' programme of conquest, which included those very countries. The tenacity of the system of neutrality is something which is quite astounding. Despite the clear evidence of the Nazi treatment of neutrals, other prospective victims obstinately refused to see through the Nazis' methods.

The Nazis also exploited the possibilities of international law on the subject of land and sea warfare. The tactic employed by Frederick the Great, and later by the Japanese in the Russo-Japanese War – beginning a war without making any prior declaration of war – was brought to perfection by the dictators ruling Germany, Italy and Japan in the decades after 1918. They even used the exchange of prisoners and the protected status of hospital ships to further their aims. These methods owe their success to the exaggerated emphasis which was placed on the legal aspect of international agreements and to the lack of research into the national and social background of these institutions.

In 1919 and 1920 people came generally to the conclusion that the world must never again be plunged into such a disastrous war. The preamble to the Covenant of the League of Nations stated that the new institution was intended to replace the institutions of international law which were obsolete and quite inadequate for coping with the new situation in the world. However, by clinging to the institutions with which they had hitherto settled their international relations, the member states gave the League of Nations an experimental character from the start. In other words, in international politics there is no place for a central international organization and traditional international law to coexist and yet work independently of each other.

States can either settle their external relations within the framework of an international organization or outside it by means of bilateral treaties, alliances, etc. To employ both methods at the same time is detrimental to international law and order. The two systems come down to us from very different epochs and very different historical situations and therefore presuppose very different social, economic and technical structures.

If one asks how far the Covenant provided a safeguard for the maintenance of democratic principles, the answer is that, apart from the inadequacy of its judicial and executive powers, perhaps the greatest mistake of the League of Nations was its underlying assumption that all governments – whether member states or non-member states – were *a priori* infallible. The fiction was held to be sacrosanct that, no matter what its methods and no matter how it had come to power, a government had to be recognized as the legal representative of that particular nation. The unanimity required by the Covenant was merely the consequence of this fiction.

## PART FIVE

*Totalitarianism's Forms and Techniques on the International Plane*

### Four Degrees of Totalitarian Rule

From what has been said so far it is obvious that it is quite impossible to reduce all the fascist movements to one common denominator. Likewise, their diffusion and impact cannot be traced to any one cause. The impact which they made is partly due to normal social processes and can be explained by the international repercussions of a technological-economic and ideological-cultural kind such as we have already mentioned. But a decisive change took place when totalitarianism in its national socialist form was able to make a highly industrialized strongly armed, financially powerful and scientifically advanced country like Germany the base from which to embark on its plans for conquest.

This is not to argue that totalitarianism represents a system which is essentially different from other forms of authoritarianism. What we are dealing with in the case of Germany is a system which, given the technical, scientific and cultural aids which were available to it, logically thought out and perfected the possibilities potential in all tyrannies. This does not, of course, mean that there was not some change in essence. Therefore, before describing totalitarianism's organizational and operative forms in the international sphere it seems advisable to take a brief look at other related but inferior authoritarian systems.

The first degree of modern dictatorship is traditional authoritarian rule derived from absolutism and based on the normal powers available to the state executive, such as the army and the police. In most countries in the world this form of rule had always been the commonest. In Europe it first appeared due to the Arab influence in the Sicilian bureaucratic state set up by the Holy Roman Emperor Frederick II. Then, after the fifteenth century, it spread over the whole European continent and was forced to retreat only after the French Revolution. We have already said that the central-European revolution of 1918 was just as unsuccessful as the Revolution of 1848 in its attempt to overcome this form of government. Furthermore, there were large numbers of authoritarian systems in existence; for example in the Balkans, where the Turkish Ottoman Empire had created a tradition of authoritarianism, or Russia with her deeply rooted tradition of despotism, and Sicily and Spain where the Islamic state system continued to influence the political system and the style of government for centuries.

Let us imagine that a country with this kind of political organization and tradition has temporarily adopted a democratic constitution and then, two years after fascism has seized power in Italy, is plunged into a crisis. The young democracy may perhaps get into difficulties, as in Austria, or parliament and the ruling dynasty may be at loggerheads, as in Yugoslavia. The important thing to note is that before the rise of fascism in Italy very different steps would have been taken in an attempt to meet this crisis. The monarch would have dissolve parliament, new elections would have been held or he might have taken over the reins of government himself for the time being or, perhaps, set up a military dictatorship. The fact that an authoritarian regime had been formed in Italy only a few years before was bound to turn the thoughts and ambitions of the ruling class to examine the possibilities of totalitarianism. The instigators of an authoritarian *coup d'état* did not at first consciously take Italy as a model. They followed the normal tradition of using the army and the bureaucracy. This was the kind of pattern adopted by Primo de Rivera in Spain, Pilsudski in Poland, and by King Alexander in Yugoslavia.

The second degree consists of this mixture of traditional authoritarian and fascist elements (for instance, propaganda support and proscription of democratic politicians).

The case of Austria belongs to the third degree. As a direct consequence of the victory of a totalitarian movement in another country the supporters of reactionary and dictatorial systems consciously set up a similar regime for a future struggle or to improve their negotiating position with the main totalitarian power.[1] Authoritarian governments like the Vichy government in France before the unoccupied zone was taken over by the Germans, and the governments in Romania, Bulgaria and Hungary during the first phase of the Second World War, fall into

---

[1] In the case of Austria, the main totalitarian power was Germany; after the Second World War, in the case of Yugoslavia as well as Egypt, it was the Soviet Union.

this category. Those in power in these countries knew full well that they owed their position to Nazi rule and that they were dependent on it. Outwardly, however, they were still protected by the symbols of the unified national state and they were reluctant to consider themselves as direct agents of the chief totalitarian power.

Finally, there is a fourth degree, namely when the totalitarian movement in a country is the direct agent of another country In most cases the third degree is only a prelude to the fourth, which includes the various quisling movements.[1] The picture is further complicated by the fact that socio-psychological attitudes which correspond to all four degrees of authoritarian rule can co-exist within a single state. In a society with an authoritarian structure there may be people who are ready to accept a temporary dictatorship or others who welcome an independent authoritarian regime. Others, again, would perhaps support an authoritarian regime in order to fight totalitarianism and, finally, others might be willing to act as fifth-columnists. The more variations there are and the more blurred the lines demarcating the four degrees, the more effective are the totalitarian propaganda techniques. The Nazis made great use of this knowledge in their penetration and infiltration activities.

Once it became clear that the authoritarian groups in the various countries of Europe were ready to support the national socialists, the only problem left to solve was the technical one of how these different degrees of willingness could be reduced to a common denominator. From their experience in the struggle against the Weimar Republic and as a result of the successful integration of once democratic groups into the totalitarian system, the Nazis had evolved a special method of infiltrating foreign countries, comparable with the methods they used for subverting groups and providing substitute symbols inside Germany.

This variation of the deception technique is also called the 'palliative' method. Von Wiese describes the social processes of palliation as an attempt to make a thing appear acceptable and innocuous by concealing its defects and its doubtful aspects, thus presenting the imperfect as perfect. This method is like spotlighting one particular feature of an object so intensely that all its other aspects vanish into obscurity. Nazi infiltration methods were far more successful in central and south-eastern Europe than in western Europe. But here, too, authoritarian aspirations discovered collaborators and allies in all four degrees among small but powerful layers of society.

The final result of Nazi propaganda and the general susceptibility to

[1] Nolte, op. cit., p. 48, also distinguishes four degrees or stages of authoritarian rule; the pre-fascist, the early fascist, the normal central fascist position and the radical fascist stage.

totalitarian trends was to bring about a vast integration of the most diverse, even heterogeneous groups into the totalitarian scheme for dominating Europe and the world. By the use of concealment tactics it succeeded in neutralizing or integrating millions of democrats and bitter enemies of national socialism, even against their will.

The opportunities open to national socialism to disseminate its ideas and influence people in the old and new world were lucidly expounded by Karl Haushofer who, beginning as a supporter, later became an opponent of national socialism. As far back as 1933 he saw national socialism to be a world-wide movement, not merely a significant phenomenon local to one particular country.[1] He realized that the fascist uniform – the Black Shirts in Italy, the Brown Shirts (SA) in Germany, the Blue Shirts in China and Ireland, the Grey Shirts in Switzerland – was 'a leading symbol of spiritual affinity'. Haushofer predicted that no national splinter group 'which has still preserved its old cultural links with the old stock *would* be able to escape its appeal'.[2] 'Hence the depth of the movement in Austria, with her German cultural and racial links, hence the impossibility even for the German part of Switzerland which had been untouched by war and its spiritual upheaval of being able to escape its pressure'.[3] The Nazi emanations originated, according to Haushofer, from three main centres: the first was in central Europe, the second in the heart of the Mediterranean world and the third in the East, on the edge of the Pacific.[4] Haushofer realized that national socialism wore a Janus face 'one which viewing the whole world at once discounts the world's immense distances and one which can be understood only in every nation's native soil and also probably by individual groups, but not by the masses'.[5] Nolte, too, speaks of a 'remarkable intertwining of particular and universal tendencies in every fascist movement'.[6]

The underlying basis of this campaign was a practical division of the world into regions with and regions without a specified number of *Volksdeutsche* (ethnic Germans). In a speech made in the early summer of 1934 to representatives of Germans who were resident abroad, Hitler had personally outlined the future activities which he demanded be carried out in the interests of the Third Reich by Germans living abroad. Among other things, Hitler said:

'You have been entrusted with one of the most important tasks. You are needed not just to foster and maintain the German spirit as you have done so far. You must mould and train it into a fighting force.

[1] Karl Haushofer, *Der Nationalsozialistische Gedanke in der Welt*, Munich 1933, p. 8.　　[2] Ibid., p. 10.　　[3] Ibid., p. 11.
[4] Ibid., p. 19.　　[5] Ibid., p. 46.　　[6] Nolte, op. cit., pp. 50 f.

You are not therefore to win parliamentary rights and limited liberties for the German cause. Such rights might even be a hindrance rather than a help. You have therefore no longer to do your best according to your own lights . . . but to obey orders from above. The policy of the overseas German groups is no longer to be debated and voted upon: it will instead be decided here by me, or by my deputy, Party Comrade Hess. As the front line of our German fighting movement you will make it possible for us to take up our battle stations and launch our attack. You have all the functions which we older men carried out in the last war. You are our outposts. You will have to prepare enterprises far in advance of the main front. You will have to mask our own preparations for attack. Regard yourselves as being at war. You are subject to martial law. . . .'[1]

The *Auslandsorganisation* (AO) of the National Socialist Party was set up to further this design. It was responsible for organizing all people 'of German blood living outside the frontiers of the Reich who were conscious of their identity as Germans and who possess German nationality plus an Aryan racial status'.[2] The 700,000 German sailors on the high seas were also accounted as *Auslandsdeutsche* for organizational purposes. The head of the *Auslandsorganisation* was Ernst Wilhelm Bohle. Under a decree issued by Hitler on January 30, 1937, the vital duties which Germans resident abroad were directed to undertake included:

'7. To be not only a *member* but also a *fighter* . . .
8. To canvas and to strive day after day to make every honest German join our movement. To convince him of its superiority and its justice and of the need for our victory.
9. To read our party paper, our publications and our books.
10. To join the other party comrades in the countries where you live'.[3]

The *Auslandsorganisation* was organized as a *Gau* (district). It was based on the central and local groups abroad and on board German ships. Its leaders held an equivalent rank to the lowest officials in Germany. Above them were the Provincial Group or Provincial District leaders, who were personally responsible to the *Gauleiter* for the direction of Germanism in their countries. Bohle's organization had the most extensive ramifications. To help him in his capacity as *Gauleiter*

---

[1] Reproduced from Rauschning, *Gespräche mit Hitler*, op. cit., pp. 135 ff.
[2] Emil Ehrich, *Die Auslandsorganisation des NSDAP*, Berlin 1937, p. 7.
[3] Ibid., p. 11.

there were a Staff Department, a Personnel Branch and an Administrative Branch; his deputy was Alfred Hess, a brother of Rudolf Hess.[1]

As de Jong rightly remarks, their function in all countries was to destroy the enemy from within,[2] a task which was made more difficult by the fact that not all Germans residing abroad obeyed the orders issued by the *Auslandsorganisation*. The organisation's effectiveness, according to de Jong, was based on the fact that Hitler in principle made no distinction between *Auslandsdeutsche* (Germans resident abroad) and *Volksdeutsche* (ethnic Germans, people of German blood who were nationals of other countries). The organization's most effective weapon against *Reichsdeutsche* (Germans who were merely resident in a country) was the threat to deprive them of their citizenship. Abroad, the organization carried out certain functions on behalf of the Security Policy and in specific cases anti-Nazis were seized and, with the help of the organization, taken to Germany on German ships. Another of the organization's functions was to gather political, economic and military intelligence material.[3]

[1] Ibid., pp. 15 f.: 'The provincial group leaders, the provincial district leaders, the district leaders, the local group leaders and the community leaders. Bohle was in charge of eight provincial groups, divided up: 1. North and East Europe, 2. Western Europe (except Great Britain and Ireland), 3. South-East Europe, Austria and the Middle East, 4. Italy, Switzerland and Hungary, 5. Africa, 6. North America, 7. Latin America, 8. The Far East, Australia, Great Britain and Ireland, 9. Shipping department. Then there were 10. the German Labour Front of the *Auslandsorganisation*, to guarantee uniform leadership on board ships, etc. Social tasks of the *Auslandsorganisation*, 11. Civil Service department . . . of the *Reichsbund* (Reich Union) of Civil Servants, 12. the department for teachers . . . the National Socialist *Lehrerbund* (Teachers' Union), including teachers abroad . . . *Gaudozentenzund* (University Lecturers' Union), foreign branch, 14. *Gaustudentenbund* (Students' Union), foreign branch, the President of the National Socialist non-organized Cultural Society, 16. department of the National Socialist *Rechtswahrerbund* (Law–Preservation Union), 17. the Working Party of German Women abroad, 18. Youth Department, the foreign branch of the Hitler Youth, 19. the foreign trade bureau, subordinate to the commissioner for economic questions of the *Auslandsorganisation*, 20. the inspection bureau. This bureau prepared statistics on the organization achievements and institutions of Germanism abroad. Also subordinate to it are postal and registration departments. Responsible for transport, guarding, announcements in the management of the *Auslandsorganisation*, 21. the cultural department (ultimately the central department . . . of all the many organizations and offices for promoting intellectual and cultural exchanges with Germans living abroad); 22. the personnel branch, 23. the press department, 24. the Gau court, expulsions from the Nazi Party. Expulsions effective abroad can only be promulgated by this *Auslandsorganisation* court, 25. the legal branch; 26. the bureau for the provision of speakers and speaker supply generally, especially for national festivals and ceremonies in non-German countries in Europe, etc., 27. the re-immigration department, 28. the treasury department, under the direction of the Gau treasurer, 29. the training department, Reich school for *Auslandsdeutsche* and seamen in Donner Castle in Altona . . . 30. the department for racial welfare, 31. the technological department, 32. Hamburg branch of the *Auslandsorganisation*', op. cit., p. 15.

[2] Louis de Jong, 'Organisation and Efficiency of the German Fifth Column', in *The Third Reich*, London 1955, pp. 870 ff.　　　　　　　　　　[3] Ibid., p. 876.

The *Auslandsdeutsche* also enjoyed the attention of the *Auslands-institut*, headed by Dr R. Csaki, a *Volksdeutsche* from Romania and linked with the *Deutscher Schutzbund* (German Protection League) which looked after various German associations abroad.[1]

As far back as 1935 national socialism had spent 262 million marks on its work abroad[2] and 2,450 Gestapo agents were already operating outside Germany. Part of their job was the supervision of *Reichs-deutsche* abroad, especially the political *émigrés*. Even German embassy staffs were watched. Espionage, spying against democratic organizations abroad, even the kidnapping and murdering of refugees came into their province.[3]

National socialism used the state's instruments of power to enforce the recognition and toleration of the activities of the *Auslandsorganisa-tion* in other countries and in cases where, for instance, a democratic state like Czechoslovakia was suspicious of the organization. Thus in February 1938, the German Minister made the following demands of the Czechoslovak government:[4]

'Above all it [the *Auslandsorganisation*] is not, however, to be re-garded as an association or even as a party, and the legislation on associations is therefore not applicable to it. The *Auslandsorganisation* is rather a part of the NSDAP (National Socialist Party), which, as a public corporation of the Reich, has to maintain the internal unity of the population of the German State. As such a part, neither it nor its regional groups possess a legal personality of their own. . . . If it is generally recognized that foreigners may associate to form national colonies in their countries of residence for convivial, social, cultural and charitable activities, then Reich-Germans abroad must be per-mitted to participate in the *Auslandsorganisation* in the same way. This comprises:

> *Free adherence to the NSDAP, subordination to the leadership of the NSDAP and its branches in so far as these are active in the country of residence. Freedom of contact with the NSDAP in the Reich.*

. . . In view of the political conditions [in Czechoslovakia] it is neces-sary to create clear conditions from the outset. The NSDAP must refuse to negotiate concerning restrictions to this definition of its activities abroad. Nor will it be possible, during the negotiations regarding the

---

[1] *Das Braune Netz*, op. cit., pp. 69 f.   [2] Ibid., p. 84.
[3] Ibid., pp. 85 ff.
[4] *Documents on German Foreign Policy*, Series D, Vol. 2, op. cit., No. 63.

recognition of the *Auslandsorganisation*, to include in the discussions the programme of the NSDAP, which is a purely internal political question. So far as we are concerned there can only be recognition or prohibition.' (Author's italics)

Yet the reason for the Nazi insistence on the recognition of the *Auslandsorganisation* in 1938, particularly in Czechoslovakia with its large German minority, was explained by an article in the *Völkischer Beobachter* (1934) entitled 'National Socialism is an Ideology'. 'It takes hold of our fellow Germans,' says the article, 'and strengthens them in holding fast to the German nature and customs. It spreads out beyond the borders of the state and even beyond the space occupied by the German people; it has already taken hold of parts of foreign nations . . . The place for the practical application of this principle is the Foreign Organization of the NSDAP, which is directly subordinate to the deputy of the Führer, Reichsminister Rudolf Hess.[1]

The clear distinction which the Nazi Party made between *Auslands-deutsche* and *Volksdeutsche* disappeared in 1938. Thus in a speech on August 28, 1938, Hess declared that *Volksdeutsche* were now openly in the ranks of the Nazis. They would march proudly and happily in the ranks of the National Socialist movement past their Führer in Nuremberg, together with German citizens from the Reich. This speech referred specifically to the Sudeten Germans.[2]

It is obvious that Rudolf Hess's speech was a frank acknowledgement that the *Auslandsorganisation* was the nucleus of a fifth column. The West had nothing like it. It may be assumed that Bohle, who himself had a thorough knowledge of the British Empire, had adopted the machinery of the nineteenth-century British colonial government system in India and Africa. But how did this system have to operate if the *Auslandsorganisation* was organized on these lines in countries like Austria, Holland, Belgium or France?

The *Volksdeutsche* abroad came under the aegis of the *Volksbund für das Deutschtum im Ausland* (VDA) (League for Germanism Abroad) which in 1935 comprised 24,000 local groups[3] and a large number of affiliated associations in neighbouring countries, for example the *Bund Deutscher Osten* (League of Germans in the East), *Deutscher Memelbund* (League of Memel Germans), *Sudetendeutscher Hilfsverein* (Sudeten German Auxiliary Association) *Elass-Lothringen Hilfsverein* (Alsace-Lorraine Auxiliary Association) the *Ibero-Ameri-kanische Institut* (Latin-American Institute), the *Institut für Grenz- und Auslandsdeutschtum* (Institute for Germanism on the Frontiers and

[1] Nuremberg Document 3401–PS on the National Socialist *Auslandsorganisation*.
[2] Nuremberg Document 3258–PS.
[3] *Das Braune Netz*, op. cit., see table following p. 37.

Abroad), as well as the foreign departments of the German athletic clubs.

Dr Hans Steinacher, a radical Austrian National Socialist, was appointed Reich leader of the League for Germanism Overseas in 1933. De Jong, however, says that relations between this and the Nazi *Auslandsorganisation* left much to be desired because of petty jealousies between Bohle and Steinacher.[1] Steinacher was the one who was bound to lose the struggle against Bohle who, although not in Hitler's good books, nevertheless enjoyed the support of Rudolf Hess and the SS.

At the beginning of 1933 it became obvious that Nazi subversive activities and the exploitation of the German ethnic groups' devotion to the Reich had been reorganized on a completely different basis. But it was not until February 3, 1933, that Rudolf Hess announced that he had instructed SS Gruppenführer Lorenz to reorganize the whole scope of the work connected with Germanism and racialism in the countries along the frontiers. After that the *Volksbund für das Deutschtum im Ausland* was declared to be the sole authority handling racial activities outside the German frontiers. Karl Haushofer was put in charge, the administrative responsibility was given to Paul Hinke who was also a member of the *Volksdeutsche Mittelstelle* (Volksdeutsche Central Department) of the SS and 'administered the League for Germanism Abroad in accordance with the instructions of the leader of the *Volksdeutsche Mittelstelle*', Lorenz.[2]

Hess emphasized that from now on no further independent activities could be carried out by the *Auslandsorganisation* (VDA). The organization was now divided into provincial bodies corresponding to the regional *Gaue* (districts) of the National Socialist Party.

Rudolf Hess's decree provides an invaluable insight into the work of the Nazi fifth column, which had to be especially effective in countries with a large number of ethnic Germans, as in Czechoslovakia, Poland, Romania and Yugoslavia. It is characteristic that the *Volksdeutsche Mittelstelle* was founded as a cover-organization shortly before Hitler's attack on the Sudetenland, Czechoslovakia and Poland, and the extended powers given to it by Hitler's deputy must be regarded as a recognition of its invaluable work at the time of the Sudeten crisis in September 1938. Hess's decree declared, *inter alia*:

'I herewith forbid the Party, its organizations and affiliated associations from all racial work abroad. The only competent body for this task is the Agency for Racial Germans *and the VDA is its camouflaged tool.*

[1] See de Jong's contribution in *The Third Reich*, op. cit., p. 881.
[2] Nuremberg Document 837–PS, International Military Tribunal, Nuremberg 1947, Vol. XXVI.

Within the Reich the VDA, generally speaking, is responsible only for providing the means for racial work beyond the frontiers. The VDA must be supported in this and in every way by the Party offices. Any outward appearance of a connection with the Party is, however, to be avoided.

'5. The BDO [League of German in the East] is at the disposal of the Gauleiters of the frontier *Gaue* for political duties on the frontiers. In addition, the establishment of a frontier territory bureau (*Grenzlandamt*) for the following *Gaue* had been agreed to, in cases where such a bureau is not already in existence: East Prussia, Pomerania, Mark Brandenburg, Silesia, Sudetenland, Bavarian Ostmark, Upper Danube, Lower Danube. In all other *Gaue* special frontier bureaux or representatives would be superfluous ...

'The activity of the BDO and the VDA is to be supported in every way by the Party offices. The National Socialist leadership of both associations will ensure energetic co-operation on their part in all tasks assigned to them by the NSDAP.

'Their nature is determined by considerations of foreign policy and the associations must bear this in mind when representing them in public'.[1] (Author's italics)

By means of the *Volksdeutsche Mittelstelle* the SS achieved its ambition of exerting direct influence on the work of the fifth column. The SS Secret Service, the *Sicherheitsdienst* (SD), played a vital role in the disruption of Czechoslovakia. Thus two of Schellenberg's representatives had an all-important conversation with the Slovak leader, Tiso, on March 13, 1939, after which Tiso declared himself ready to subordinate Slovakia to the Third Reich.[2] On the other hand this decree was also based on the experience which the Nazi Party had gained while it was infiltrating Austria and the Sudetenland. As we shall show later the lack of any central direction in the subversion resulted in the exposure of the German ambassadors in Vienna and Prague as well as of the leading figures in the German cabinet. Furthermore, antagonisms and dissensions broke out within the national socialist groups active in Austria and Czechoslovakia and this had an unsettling effect, making it necessary, for instance, to invest the Reich Germans Habicht[3] and Keppler with complete authority within their movement. Apparently even such an ardent friend of the Third Reich as Seyss-Inquart was not completely trusted. Again, in the Sudetenland, there

[1] Ibid., p. 363.    [2] Schellenberg, op. cit., p. 58.
[3] Extract from the trials of the main war criminals before the International Military Tribunal, November 14, 1945–1 October 1948, Vol. 16, p. 408 (German edition). Statement by von Papen: 'Mr Prosecutor, Herr Habicht was not an agent. Herr Habicht had been appointed by Hitler as the leader of the Party in Austria.'

was an open breach between the leader of the Sudeten German Party, Konrad Henlein, and the leader of the radical wing of the National Socialists, Kaspar, a breach which compelled the German government to intervene and mediate through the person of the German Minister in Prague, Eisenlohr. The appointment of SS Obergruppenführer Lorenz to the post of leader of the *Volksdeutsche Mittelstelle* was an indication of the growing ascendancy of the SS in matters concerning the ethnic German groups abroad. Furthermore, the SS also strengthened its position by its direct employment of the *Sicherheitsdienst*.[1] The methods by which the Nazi plans for expansion were carried out in areas with a German-speaking population will shortly be described by looking at the cases of Austria and the Sudetenland.

## Totalitarian versus Authoritarian Dictatorship

In Chapter VI we described the collapse of Austrian democracy, how it was prepared by the authoritarian measures of the Austrian Chancellor Dollfuss and the *Heimwehr* financed by Mussolini. Dollfuss's dictatorship was often regarded as a 'preventive dictatorship' which was meant to forestall totalitarianism. Its ineffectiveness became clear in July 1934, when Dollfuss was murdered by the Austrian SS Standarte with the connivance of the Nazi Party. But it was left to Dollfuss's successor, Schuschnigg, to discover the impotence of the position of a traditional type of authoritarian dictator when confronted with the ruthless and deliberate strategy of totalitarianism.[2] After 1934 there had been a rapprochement between former pan-Germans and national socialism without the former actually joining the Austrian Nazi Party.

As we have already explained, the Austrian nationalists included a number of disillusioned supporters of the Habsburg regime from the upper ranks of society. The Nazi Party benefited from the pan-German sympathies of men like Dr Seyss-Inquart, who was not officially a member of the Nazi Party, but belonged to the Styrian *Heimwehr*, and Glaise-Horstenau, a retired Austrian general, who had not formally joined the Party either, and Chancellor Schuschnigg was urged to take these 'Trojan horses' into his government. When giving evidence in Nuremberg,[3] Glaise-Horstenau said he had first met Seyss-Inquart at the time of the agreement which Hitler and Schuschnigg concluded on July 11, 1936, and it was intended to include the Nazi

[1] Schellenberg, op. cit., pp. 58 f.
[2] Schuschnigg had meanwhile succeeded in subduing the *Heimwehr* but he was unable to win co-operation from the democratic forces in Austria.
[3] International Military Tribunal, Vol. 16, p. 130.

Party in the Austrian government led by the Patriotic Front not as a political organization but as the representatives of certain ideas.

Seyss-Inquart and he, Glaise-Horstenau, had sworn allegiance to the Austrian Constitution, to which Adolf Hitler had given his blessing. How, then, asked the prosecutor[1] in Nuremberg, had these Austrian 'patriots' behaved in the days of the *Anschluss* in 1938? Glaise-Horstenau's reply was that when the final crisis broke he had been in Germany 'quite by chance', to give a lecture on 'Central Europe in the Year One Thousand' in Stuttgart (the seat of the *Auslandsorganisation*). Then he had gone to see relatives in the Palatinate, where he had been visited by Bürckel – later *Reichsstatthalter* (Governor) in Austria – (presumably also 'by chance') and then while at Bürckel's home he had heard Schuschnigg's speech announcing a plebiscite on the position of Austria. After that he had been called to the Reich Chancellery by Hitler and – this much can be deduced from his cross-examination – instructed to go back to Austria.

On landing at Vienna airport he had been met by the Minister of the Interior, Seyss-Inquart[2] (presumably once again 'by chance') and at 11 o'clock had gone with him to Chancellor Schuschnigg, who was nearly in tears. Both men insisted on the Chancellor withdrawing his plan to hold a plebiscite to confirm Austria's independence of Germany. When Schuschnigg refused, at 1 o'clock, they had offered to resign. In the course of these negotiations Seyss-Inquart had been called to the telephone and Hitler had told him he must now demand the office of Chancellor as he, Hitler, could no longer work with Schuschnigg. But Glaise-Horstenau had also brought the draft of a telegram giving bogus reports of riots in Austria; this telegram was sent to Berlin a little later by Keppler. It contained a request for troops to be sent to Austria. At Nuremberg the prosecutor put this question to Glaise-Horstenau: 'When you received this false telegram and the draft of the radio speech for Seyss-Inquart, you surely did not think that, as far as Austria was concerned, you were acting in a peaceful and loyal way? . . . You were then Minister without Portfolio in the Austrian government. But you knew very well that it was a complete fraud. And yet you were ready to go back to Austria and to negotiate with Seyss-Inquart, knowing that such a telegram had been prepared and sent by a courier'. But Glaise-Horstenau regarded his activity only as a contribution to the normalization of German-Austrian relations.

Of the other 'good sort' in the Austrian cabinet, Dr Seyss-Inquart, the leader of the Austrian Nazis said in 1942[3] that he had always

---

[1] Ibid., pp. 131 ff.
[2] Hitler had forced Schuschnigg to give Seyss-Inquart this post.
[3] International Military Tribunal, Vol. 16, p. 151.

placed himself unconditionally under the political leadership of
Klausner, the political leader of the Austrian National Socialists. The
Austrian Nazis in Schuschnigg's camp had had agents everywhere.
Contacts had been maintained even with Schuschnigg's household staff
and the Austrian Nazi Party had reported to Ribbentrop and Himmler
on Hitler's go-between, Keppler.[1]

Thus Schuschnigg's visit to Berchtesgaden arranged for February 12,
1938 – about which Schuschnigg had said only von Papen on the
German side had been informed – was betrayed to the Austrian Nazi
leaders. Rainer, Gauleiter for Austria, stated:

'Papen had been expressly told to handle preparations for the conference confidentially. In Austria, only Schuschnigg, Schmidt and
Zernatto knew about it. They believed that on our side only Papen
was informed. Papen, too, thought that only he knew about it, but we
too were informed and had had conversations with Seyss about the
subject.'

Rainer added:

'We had already prepared the following. The last result of the conversation Seyss communicated to me in a shop in the Kärtnerstrasse. I
called the telephone number where Globus [that is, Globocznigg] was to
be reached in Berlin and told him of the negative result of the conversation. I could speak with Globus entirely freely. We had a secret
code for each name, and besides we both spoke a terrible dialect so
that not a soul would have understood us. . . . In the meantime,
Keppler had gone to Munich by sleeping car. . . . I then forwarded
instructions by Party member Mühlmann, who proved to be an excellent liaison man to government offices in the Reich. He left for
Salzburg on the same train as Schuschnigg. While Schuschnigg had his
car taken off at Salzburg and spent the night there before he went on by
car to Obersalzberg, Mühlmann stayed on the train and got out at
Berchtesgaden. Keppler and he went to the Führer before Schuschnigg
and were able to tell him everything. Schuschnigg arrived in the
morning, was received and experienced boundless surprise that the
Führer took up the negotiations where his own negotiations with Seyss
had been broken off without results the day before. The Führer did not
conduct the negotiations as Schuschnigg expected. He really let himself go. Schuschnigg was finished off that time, in a manner one can
hardly imagine. The Führer grabbed him, shook him and shouted at
him, reproaching him for all the dirty tricks he had committed during
the past years. Schuschnigg had become a heavy smoker. We knew

[1] Ibid., p. 151.

what went on even in his bedroom. We knew all about his way of life. Now he was smoking fifty, now sixty cigarettes. But in the presence of the Führer, he was not allowed to smoke. Schuschnigg could not even smoke.

'Ribbentrop told me he really pitied Schuschnigg. He merely stood at attention before the Führer, with hands held against the seams of his trousers, and all he could say was "Yes, sir. *Jawohl!*" '[1]

In Berchtesgaden Schuschnigg was confronted with the demand that Austrian foreign policy be brought into line with that of the Third Reich and that the two 'Trojan horses', Seyss-Inquart and Glaise-Horstenau, should be promoted, the former to become the Austrian Minister of the Interior and the latter to be Austrian Army Minister.[2] In future the National Socialists must be perfectly free to pursue their activities in Austria without let or hindrance[3] and a National Socialist, Dr Fischbock, was to be made Finance Minister to prepare plans for Austria's assimilation into the German economy. Large numbers of Nazis were also to be absorbed into the Austrian army. By making changes in the Austrian Army General Staff, Schuschnigg was able to avoid appointing Glaise-Horstenau as his Army Minister,[4] but the police and the security service remained directly under Seyss-Inquart's control.

The pledges which Schuschnigg had undertaken were to be implemented with all possible speed. And by February 17, 1938, five days after the Berchtesgaden Agreement, the new Austrian Minister of Security presented himself to the Führer at the Chancellery in Berlin, giving the Hitler salute, and there he received his instructions. The Berchtesgaden Agreement, it soon became evident, had not brought any relaxation in German-Austrian relations but, instead, an intensification of Nazi pressure on the Schuschnigg regime. The brown wave which was soon to submerge Austria was already visible.

On February 28, 1938, Seyss-Inquart informed Hitler's agent, Keppler, that 'the Soviet, French, British and Italian Missions in Vienna were doing their utmost "to sabotage the [Berchtesgaden] Agreement", that is, to prevent the undermining of the Austrian state apparatus by the National Socialists, or at least to slow it up'.[5] In these circumstances Schuschnigg decided to prove to the outside world that the majority of the Austrian people were against joining the Third Reich. On March 8, 1938, Schuschnigg received the Austrian President Miklas's permission to hold a plebiscite, which was to take place on

---

[1] Ibid., pp. 152 ff.  [2] Ibid., p. 156.
[3] Ulrich Eichstädt, *Von Dollfuss zu Hitler*, Wiesbaden 1955, pp. 298 ff.
[4] Ibid., p. 303.  [5] Ibid., p. 354.

March 13. But that very evening the Nazis knew what was afoot and Seyss-Inquart sent a letter of protest to Schuschnigg the next day. He gave a copy of this letter to the SS leader, Globocznigg, who flew to Berlin with it to inform Hitler of developments.[1] Hitler now believed the time was ripe to carry out plan 'Otto' – army mobilization in the event of a Habsburg restoration in Austria.

This detailed account of events has been given to show how the Nazi fifth column operated in areas inhabited by *Volksdeutsche*. The important thing to note here is that the Reich Nazi Party in Vienna appeared in a co-ordinating and directing role, while the actual act of treason in Austria was the work of Austrians themselves, for example Seyss-Inquart, Glaise-Horstenau, Globocznigg, Rainer, Klausner and their accomplices. This method was then to be applied to other European countries.

## The Henlein Movement as an Example of Totalitarian Penetration of *Volksdeutsche* Areas

The reader is already familiar with the fate of the Sudeten German minority in Czechoslovakia after 1918.[2] The rise of national socialism in neighbouring Germany was bound to awaken a very strong response in the Sudeten German areas for the reasons we have mentioned. It raised an equally intense hatred among the Sudeten German democratic groups, namely the German Social Democratic Workers' Party, the Christian Social Party and the Farmers' Union, all three of which were represented in the Czechoslovak government, as well as the German Democratic Party which, numerically, was very small at the time. The anger and horror which the German democrats felt at the fate of their political brothers in the Reich induced them to give increased support to Masaryk's and Beneš' democratic republic, although this did not move the Czechs to grant the Germans any greater concessions. Nevertheless, the German 'activists' (as the German democrats were known in Czechoslovakia) preferred to co-operate with the Czechoslovak government and the Western democracies rather than be forced to toe the Nazi line.

However, it must be emphasized that in these circumstances the Czech nationalists themselves proved to be totally blind to the danger looming over their country. Even at this juncture concessions on the

---

[1] Ibid., p. 360.
[2] Cf. in particular Chap. IV, pp. 152 ff., 169 ff., discrimination against the Sudeten German minority and the Czech policy of assimilation and suppression, and pp. 176 ff., on the economic neglect of Sudeten German areas.

part of the Czechs, such as the granting of linguistic equality or economic aid for the distressed Sudeten German areas, could have strengthened the Sudeten German democratic parties in their struggle against Nazism.[1] But the Czechoslovak government preferred to confine itself to taking repressive measures against national socialism. The German National Socialist Party had been the oldest Nazi party and was already well organized before Hitler founded his own party in Germany.[2] At the time of Hitler's rise and the Nazi seizure of power in the Reich this party could show a modest increase in polling strength and it tried to organize its semi-military organizations on the German pattern into SA detachments, which were described as 'Sport Detachments' to the outside world. In the autumn of 1933 there took place the so-called *Volkssportprozess* (national sport trial), which led to the dissolution of the German National Socialist Party and, unjustifiably, also the dissolution of the German Nationalist Party. The leaders of the National Socialists, Jung and Krebs, fled to Germany, where they became members of the Reichstag.

Before fleeing, however, Krebs had ordered the gymnast leader, Konrad Henlein, to form a movement to replace the one which had been dissolved.[3] Germany enjoyed the respect of all the middle-class groups in the Sudetenland and consequently Konrad Henlein was admirably suited to perform this particular task. At the time the Sudeten Germans thought him to be just the man to unite the whole population in a national, but democratic sense and thus effectively to represent the just demands of the Sudeten Germans *vis-à-vis* the Czechoslovak authorities. At first Henlein appeared to be reluctant to support national socialism. To what extent he himself was ever a genuine convert to the Nazi creed is uncertain. But it is an undoubted fact that as a former Austrian officer he had a certain feeling of solidarity with Austria and this was the spirit which inspired him and him *Kameradschaftsbund* (Union of Comrades).

The leading members of this Union and he together founded the *Sudetendeutsche Heimatfront* (Sudeten German Home Front),[4] which was strongly influenced by Othmar Spann's corporative doctrines. At first it followed a sort of 'middle course between Austrian corporative fascism and national socialism'.[5] Nevertheless it is certain that Konrad Heinlein's Sudeten German *Heimatfront* – called the *Sudetendeutsche Partei* (SdP) (Sudeten Germany Party) after 1935 – received definite

[1] Wenzel Jaksch, op. cit., p. 303.
[2] The party existed as far back as 1918 and, in embryo, even before the First World War. Hitler had adopted its name for his own party.
[3] *Jahrbuch der Auslandsorganisation der NSDAP*, 1st Vol., 1942, pp. 32–3.
[4] The very name *Heimatfront* is like an echo of the Austrian *Heimwehr* movement.
[5] Jaksch, op. cit., p. 302.

financial backing from the Third Reich. In 1933 the party paper received 120,000 Czech crowns and the same year, on instructions from Rudolf Hess, the League for Germanism Abroad gave the Henlein movement a subsidy of eight million crowns. After 1935 Henlein received from the German Foreign Office, through the German Legation in Prague, 12,000 Reichsmarks a month and 3,000 Reichsmarks for its office in Berlin, which was called 'Büro Bürger'.[1]

The Weizsäcker trial makes it clear that, despite all the financial assistance from Berlin, Henlein was not at first completely trusted by the Nazis, since he had too many contacts with the aristocracy and also laid great stress on the importance of parliamentary democracy.[2] But this mistrust was obviously misplaced. Had Henlein shown his true colours before 1938 and had he stated that the Sudeten German Party was taking the place of the dissolved German National Socialist Party, his work, meritorious from the Nazi point of view, would undoubtedly have been quickly nipped in the bud by the Czechoslovak government and he and his collaborators would have been expelled or arrested. Then there might never have been any Munich Agreement. But Henlein's activity is the best example of the fifth column's 'quisling' character. It is therefore fitting first to illustrate his effectiveness and his links with government and party circles in the Third Reich by quoting the authentic text of the documents before we make any comment about the significance of the facts or the conclusions to be drawn from them and the possibilities of making generalizations about the method used to ensure the diffusion of Nazism.

In 1937 Henlein ran into difficulties within his own movement. The radical wing of the disbanded National Socialist Party, the so-called *Aufbruch* (awakening) group, which had joined him under the leadership of the former Nazi deputy Kaspar, was dissatisfied because his intention was to work towards the final union with the Reich, taking one step at a time. In the Czechoslovak general election of 1937 Henlein's Sudeten German Party had polled 70 per cent of the votes cast. Yet the German 'activist' parties had remained in the government and Prague was still the chief haven for German democrat refugees. Kaspar was encouraged, especially by SS circles, to show more dash than Henlein. Henlein, who feared the influence Himmler had with Hitler, deemed it necessary to explain his aims and protest his loyalty to the Führer. At this juncture, however, he could not afford to seek a personal audience with Hitler; instead he had to maintain relations

<hr />

[1] Cf. de Jong's contribution to *The Third Reich*, pp. 878 ff. and *Jahrbuch der Auslandsorganisationen der NSDAP*, op. cit.

[2] A witness, Altenburg, in *The Proceedings of the Weizsäcker Trial, Documents on German Foreign Policy, 1918–1945*, Series D, Vol. 2, London 1950, pp. 52–62.

with his Führer through the German Legation in Prague. On November 19, 1937, he sent a secret report to Berlin 'for the Führer and Reich Chancellor on the urgent questions concerning German policy in the Czechoslovak Republic'. Because of its significance, the greater part of that report is reproduced here:[1]

1941/434970–96                                                    19th November 1937

*Report for the Führer and Reich Chancellor Dealing With Questions Of Immediate Interest to German Policy in the Czechoslovak Republic.*

SECRET
Under Section II

2. The policy hitherto pursued by the Sudeten German Party has made the following contribution to *the new order of Europe in the spirit of National Socialism* and of the policy of the Reich:

(a) The Sudeten German Party, which today numbers more than 600,000 organized members and which at the elections of May 19, 1935 was able to unite within its ranks actually more than 70 per cent of the Sudeten German voters, and is thus the legitimate spokesman of the Sudeten Germans, has become in its struggles the unequivocal proof of the injustices of the Versailles Treaty structure.

(b) By the mere fact of coming forward as the strongest party in Czechoslovakia, and at the same time as a party of opposition to the system of government and by its planned propaganda within the country and abroad, the Sudeten German Party has destroyed the fiction of the Czech National State; by its evolution it has refuted the claim of the Czech State to be politically consolidated on national, social and economic foundations and has materially weakened the political and military value of Czechoslovakia as an ally.

(c) As opposed to the attitude of the Sudeten German splinter parties, the Sudeten German Party has enlisted the strength of the Sudeten Germans *against* the anti-German foreign policy of Czechoslovakia. It has combated the one-sided policy of alliance alike with France and with Russia, and so deprived the Prague Government of the opportunity created by the Activist Movement of 1926 of playing off the Sudeten Germans against the policy of the Reich.

(d) Above all the Sudeten German Party has, by means of its struggles within the State and by its propaganda, drawn the attention of the interested States to Czechoslovakia as a State tainted with bolshevism and as providing a basis for bolshevist operations in central

[1] *Documents on German Foreign Policy*, Series D, Vol. 2, op. cit., No. 23.

Europe. On the other hand, however, it has been at pains to keep in check among the Sudeten Germans, and so in a region on the margin of the German world, the bolshevist fungoid growth in its possibilities of development. Today the Sudeten German Party represents the third greatest anti-bolshevist fighting party in Europe.

(e) The Sudeten German Party has by its work of political education and organization exorcised the danger of any 'Czechoslovakizing' of the Sudeten Germans, that is of treating them in accordance with the Swiss model and has imbued the racial group and their sphere of life with national socialist principles.

In the face of 'democratic' world opinion the Sudeten German Party has given proof that the national socialist order of leadership and following corresponds with the law of the inner life of the German people, for not only has it been called into existence among the Sudeten Germans by their own free will, but in the face of pressure by the Czech State.

3. The Sudeten German Party must camouflage its profession of national socialism as an ideology of life and as a political principle. As a party in the democratic parliamentary system of Czechoslovakia, it must, outwardly, alike in writing and by word of mouth, in its manifestoes and in the press, in parliament, in its own structure, and in the organization of the Sudeten German element, employ democratic terminology and democratic parliamentary methods. In consequence, it may appear to uninitiated German circles of the Reich to be disunited and unreliable. This disunion, however, cannot be avoided so long as there still exists the necessity of a legal party, and the existence of such a party in Czechoslovakia presupposes the profession of democratic principles.

The apparent lack of unity of the Sudeten German party is intensified by the circumstance that at heart it desires nothing more ardently than the incorporation of Sudeten German territory, nay of the whole Bohemian, Moravian, and Silesian areas, within the Reich, but that outwardly it must stand for the preservation of Czechoslovakia and for the integrity of its frontiers, and must try to display some apparently genuine aim in the sphere of internal politics to justify its political struggle.

4. As already set forth it will become increasingly difficult for the Sudeten German Party to put forward an internal political aim as the objective for the struggle and endeavour of the movement with even the semblance of a possibility of achievement.

This development entails: a strengthening of that outlook among the Sudeten Germans which starts from the conviction that in the conditions cited it will be increasingly senseless to assume the burdens of petty drudgery, the difficulties of internal construction work among the Sudeten Germans and the dangers of the everyday political struggle; and a strengthening in their attitude of those sections which are trying to establish the conviction that the time has come for illegal action.

This development receives encouragement from the Reich, as may be illustrated from two examples:

(a) by the fact that among the wide masses of the population of the Reich sympathy with the fate of the Sudeten Germans has become general. The Sudeten Germans, particularly in the frontier districts, are in respect of the manifold relations arising out of ties of blood and economic and social activities, strengthened in their belief that the whole German people stands behind them in their struggle for existence. Over and above this the opinion is stated generally and in plain language that the military liquidation of Czechoslovakia is only a question of months. As this view, however, is openly expressed alike by the lower and higher executive officials of the Party, of the fighting associations, and of the Reich, in dealing with Sudeten Germans without regard to their position in the Sudeten German Party or the racial group, wide sections of the membership of the Party are already invoking 'guarantors' among Reich-Germans. In this connection the fact should not be underestimated that for the Sudeten German in his faith in the Reich the humblest customs official, SA or SS man, appears in the character of a representative of the Reich and of the Führer's will.

(b) The comments upon the Teplitz-Schönau episodes in the press and on the radio have also confirmed the Sudeten Germans in their view of the definite interest felt by the Reich in their fate. It has, however, also given rise to the idea that the press campaign on the part of the Reich will be followed by definite action against Czecho-slovakia ...'

This document reveals a number of different facets which, taken together, fully illustrate the true nature of the Henlein movement. The first and most striking factor is the anti-Czech feeling, which must be recognized as the primary emotional force behind Sudeten German nationalism. As we explained in previous chapters, this attitude is a reaction to the upsurge and spread of Czech nationalism in the nineteenth century.

1918 presented the Czechoslovak Republic with an opportunity to work out a compromise between Czechs and Germans, for example by allowing the Germans to keep and enjoy cultural autonomy. Although the Sudeten Germans were absorbed into Czechoslovakia against their will and in spite of their opposition, their growing willingness to co-operate within the framework of Czechoslovak democracy showed that a compromise was feasible.

But by 1933, when Nazism came to power in Germany, it was already more or less too late for such compromise. The Henlein movement's anti-Czech attitude therefore reflected a feeling of resentment which was widespread among the Sudeten Germans. Ideologically these feelings had nothing in common with national socialism and the movement was only planned by the Nazis as a platform for agitation. And the emphasis laid on the role of the Sudeten German Party as a national front which was above party affiliations and harmonizing class and ideological differences fully satisfied the Sudeten German demand for unity. Camouflaging this essentially Nazi movement and passing it off as a supra-party national front served not only as a form of protection against the Czechoslovak authorities but also as a means of deceiving the vast majority of the Sudeten German population which, as the electoral statistics up to 1933 had shown, were overwhelmingly opposed to national socialism.

Secondly – and this emerges clearly from paragraphs 2(e) and 4 of the document – the Henlein party subscribed to the aims of national socialism, often admitting that its object was to prevent any possibility of a German-Czech compromise in the democratic sense of the word. Czechoslovakia must on no account develop along Swiss lines. This proves the extent to which Czech nationalism, by its disregard for the German democrats' efforts, merely played into the hands of the Third Reich; for it must be made quite clear that the Henlein fear of a Swiss-type solution in Czechoslovakia was totally unfounded. If, as Jaksch is undoubtedly right in saying, the majority of responsible Czech government circles were unable to win the confidence of the German democrats supporting them in this crisis, it is a moot point whether any such possibility had in fact ever existed. Certainly the Czech intellectuals in and around Czech social democracy striving for an understanding of this kind were in a dwindling minority. Nor can President Beneš himself be regarded as sincere in his desire for an understanding, although he supported the idea for a time as a matter of opportunism.

Thirdly, it is clear that the Henlein movement was a cover organization, refusing to allow its members to have or form a will of their own and motivated by the principle of the leader-partisan relationship and therefore ready to carry out instructions and orders given by national socialism's supreme leader, Adolf Hitler.

Fourthly, the Henlein Party was obviously also a 'Trojan horse' harbouring armed quislings in its belly until the day of reckoning dawned and they could strike not only at the Czechs but also at the Sudeten Germans, their racial kinsmen. This fifth-column character of the movement was also perfectly suited to its mission to weaken Czechoslovakia's political and military alliances and, inside the country itself, to hound German *émigrés* and left-wing movements, which were vilified and smeared as being purely bolshevist.

Fifthly, the Henlein movement's claim to pseudo-legality – a technique which it copied from Hitler – was used to camouflage all these activities; it pretended to be a democratic party recognizing the parliamentary principle and claimed to champion the cause of Czechoslovak independence and territorial integrity. It must, therefore, be recognized that the Henlein movement was a highly effective instrument for executing the totalitarian policy of diffusion.

Furthermore, the Henlein movement proved that it had not the slightest qualms about committing treason not only against the democratic state but to go further and also to sabotage any prospect of bringing about a greater degree of integration in central Europe by means of a Danubian federation.

This idea was advocated, on the Czech side, by a far-sighted statesman, Dr Milan Hodža, and in Austria by Dr Schuschnigg. The plan also had supporters in Slovakia, Hungary, and perhaps also in Poland. But it ran counter to Hitler's plans for conquest.

On January 12, 1938, the German Minister in Prague sent this report to the Foreign Office in Berlin:[1]

'Against this the further weakening of the League of Nations by Italy's withdrawal, and Germany's announcement that she would on no condition re-enter it, were heavy blows to Czechoslovakia, in so far as thereby the hope was finally wrecked that, under the aegis of the League of Nations, a new balance of power might evolve in Europe, within which this country, too, might find its secure place. The League of Nations, now so one-sided and weakened, could hardly continue to offer any stay or support to carry through a peaceful settlement in cases of international conflict. The thought may therefore suggest itself to the governments of the Danubian countries, including Bulgaria, to create a kind of substitute through closer union between themselves. There is no doubt that this idea plays a certain part in Beneš' deliberations and it represents, as it were, the foreign policy side of the, originally, purely politico-economic plans drawn up by Hodža. Here, it is true, there is no longer, as a year ago, any question of erecting a dam against German need for expansion towards the south-east, even though this aspect may be presented in Paris and London. The primary

[1] Ibid., No. 47.

condition for the realization of such ideas, however, was the bridging over of the antagonism between Hungary and the countries of the Little Entente, which has been attempted but so far could not be brought to fruition. The next equally important condition was approval by Germany and Italy.'

The leaders of the Sudeten German Party immediately adopted the Third Reich's new foreign policy line attacking the plan for a Danubian federation. First, on February 8, 1938, the deputies K. H. Franck, Kreissel and Karmasin visited Mgr Hlinka, the leader of the Slovak Volkspartei (Slovak People's Party), in Rosenberg[1] to propose concerted action between the Henlein party and the Slovak autonomists. Plans were made to hold a big Slovak independence rally in Pressburg in June. From Rosenberg K. H. Franck and Künzel drove to Budapest where they conspired with Hungarian ministers. They visited the Premier, Daranyi, and the Foreign Minister, Kanya. This conversation on February 19 took place in the knowledge of the imminent departure of the Austrian Chancellor Schuschnigg for Berchtesgaden for talks with Hitler, and Kanya assured Henlein's emissaries that 'all plans of an anti-German nature based on Hungary's collaboration with Czechoslovakia would break down in the face of Hungary's refusal'.

What now follows throws a striking light on the role which the Sudeten German Nazis played as the grave-diggers of the idea of a free Danubian state of a federative type, in which Austrians and Sudeten Germans could have lived with Czechs, Hungarians and Slovaks as equals and as economically thriving communities.

'In reply to a doubt which we expressed very cautiously as to the possible attitude of Chancellor Schuschnigg, Kanya said that he was definitely convinced that Chancellor Schuschnigg would be no party to an anti-German plan. *As we discovered later, Kanya must at the time of the discussions have been informed of the fact of the Chancellor's departure for Obersalzberg and must have been told of his probable attitude with regard to this.*

'According to information which reached us in Vienna from the Polish Legation, *Chancellor Schuschnigg had informed the Hungarian Minister*, after the French Minister in Vienna, of his decision to accept the Führer's invitation even before he had notified his own Cabinet.

'We already had the impression at the time that the representations of the Hungarian statesmen were mostly given on the hypothesis that we would pass them on to Berlin. When we left, Daranyi was extremely

[1] Ibid., No. 54.

cordial and referred to the coming visit of State Secretary Pfundner, whereupon Kanya, too, requested that contacts be maintained.'[1] (Author's italics.)

The Sudeten German Party's anti-Czech attitude still seems understandable when one takes into account the social, political, cultural and economic tradition of this region and it certainly reflected the feelings of the majority of the Sudeten German population. Seen in this context the Sudeten German Party's collaboration with the Third Reich can hardly be described as typical of a fifth column. But the subversive character of the Party became evident the moment it torpedoed the plan for a Danubian federation. If the Sudeten German Party had seriously considered its supporters' interest it could not point to having any such mandate: it acted purely and simply as the emissary of the Third Reich.

The Henlein movement's policy began to bear fruit even before the annexation of Austria. Even on February 4, 1938, the German Minister in Prague was already able to report to the Foreign Office in Berlin:[2] 'In domestic politics in Czechoslovakia excitement prevails at present, as is otherwise only normal before an election campaign.'

He reported enthusiastically on 'the deep-seated uneasiness, especially of the Czech Social Democrats and the German activist parties'. He believed that all this indicated 'the creation of the domestic political conditions for the revision of relations by the leaders of the state, and thus also of the relations between Czechs and Slovaks on the one hand and Sudeten Germans on the other'.

Eisenlohr remarked, with great satisfaction, that the reason for the Sudeten German democrats' uneasiness was a New Year article by the leader of the Czech Agrarian Party, Beran,[3] which had roused fears among the social democrats and the German activists that they might be thrown out of the government. It was only now that the true significance of the Sudeten German Party was to be revealed. The relevant document, makes it clear that this time Henlein and his collaborators were, in effect, the Nazi Party's agents.

The Minister further remarked:

'Today the Government needs the Sudeten German Party because, for reasons of foreign policy, the serious approach to the minority problem can no longer be shelved, and because the administration needs for this a partner capable of negotiating, and one whose word carries weight with the Sudeten German people. As things stand, this partner can only be Konrad Henlein.

[1] Ibid., No. 60.          [2] Ibid., No. 53.          [3] Ibid.

'. . . *I have had a long talk with Konrad Henlein on these points, and when I realized that he was not clear in his mind on any of these issues, I advised him to reflect on them so that he might be prepared and resolute for any eventuality which might arise. Henlein expressed to me his conviction that the Sudeten German people would follow him willingly, whatever his attitude to this or that case. But he needed support in the rear from the Reich* and therefore must be certain that his decisions harmonized with those of the Reich government. Above all, he must know whether we were still interested in maintaining the fissure between Germans and Czechs, or whether we concurred in the attempt at gradual conciliatory settlement.

'*I answered Henlein that he would probably always have sufficient time before taking any decisions of principle to address the necessary inquiry to Berlin, either through his representatives there or through myself. In general it might be said that all governments envisage at least two different types of policy for the attainment of their political aims, one based on peaceful means and the other as a last resort* . . .

'The negotiations with the Czechoslovak government on Sudeten German affairs must, when the time came, be conducted by him or his mandatory; they could not be conducted by us. We would advise, support, and privately help him, but this did not signify *carte blanche* to cry for the moon. It would be necessary to maintain close contact and keep each other informed about current developments and the ideas of both sides . . .

'*Henlein promised to come to Prague every week, and, apart from the contact already existing between the Legation and his deputy, K. H. Franck, and the fraction of the Sudeten German Party, also to maintain regular personal contact with me.* For his part, he expressed the wish that I should inform the Reich government of the present situation, and the possibilities which might sooner or later arise from it, so as to prepare and facilitate attitudes and decisions which might become necessary.

'*The foregoing exposition pursues this purpose.*' (Author's italics.)

After Austria's enforced union with Germany, the floodgates burst in the Sudetenland. Sudeten German social democracy was in a hopeless position; for the other activist parties had left the government and joined the Sudeten German Party. At this particular moment Sudeten German Social Democracy was the only German democratic party in the world. Its leaders Jaksch, Reitzner, Kessler and others, who were well aware of their exposed and perilous position, continued their struggle for peace and democracy, supported by the party militant group, the Republican Guard.

Henlein and his collaborators now received open recognition. On March 28, 1938, Henlein went for his first audience with Hitler. Rudolf Hess, Ribbentrop and Obergruppenführer Lorenz of the *Volksdeutsche Mittelstelle* of the SS were also present. At this meeting Hitler declared that he intended to settle the Czechoslovak problem in the not too distant future.[1] Henlein humbly professed that he was simply a substitute for Hitler in the Sudetenland, to which Hitler magnanimously replied: 'I will stand by you; from tomorrow you will be my viceroy.'

Hitler now began to increase the pressure on Czechoslovakia. Thus, for instance, he gave Henlein orders that 'the Sudeten German Party should make demands which are unacceptable to the Czech government'.

The following day the policy to be pursued by the Sudeten German Party was set down precisely by the German Foreign Minister in the Foreign Office in Berlin:[2]

F 18/352/354             Berlin, March 29, 1938.
                                     Pol. I 789(IV)

*Minute of the Discussion on Sudeten German Questions held in the Foreign Ministry at midday on March 29, 1938.*

TOP SECRET

A list of those who took part in the discussion is attached.

The Reich Foreign Minister emphasized at the beginning the necessity of keeping the appointed discussion strictly secret and then stated, with reference to the principles imparted to Konrad Henlein yesterday afternoon by the Führer personally, that there were two questions above all others which are important for the conduct of the policy of the Sudeten German Party:

1. The Sudeten German element must know that behind it stood a people of 75 millions who would tolerate no further suppression of the Sudeten Germans by the Czechoslovak government.
2. It was for the Sudeten German Party to present to the Czechoslovak government those demands, the fulfilment of which they considered necessary for the attainment of the freedom they desired.

In regard to this the Reich Foreign Minister said that it could not be the duty of the Reich government to make detailed suggestions to Konrad Henlein, who was the expressly recognized leader of the Sudeten German element, recently confirmed by the Führer, as to what demands should be put to the Czechoslovak government. It was

[1] Ibid., No. 107.                 [2] Ibid., No. 109.

a matter of drawing up a maximum programme. . . . *The final object of the negotiations to be conducted by the Sudeten German Party with the Czechoslovak government would be, by the scope and step-by-step specification of their demands, to avoid entry into the government.* It must be made clear in the negotiations that the Sudeten German Party alone, not the Reich government, was the negotiating party with the Czechoslovak government. The Reich government, on its part, must decline to appear *vis-à-vis* the Prague government, or London and Paris, as the representative or pacemaker of the Sudeten German demands . . . *For further collaboration, Konrad Henlein was advised to maintain closest possible contact with the Reich Foreign Minister and with the leader of the Volksdeutsche Mittelstelle, as well as with the German Minister in Prague, as representative there of the Reich Foreign Minister. The task of the German Minister in Prague would consist in supporting as reasonable the demands of the Sudeten German Party, not officially, but in more private talks with the Czechoslovak statesmen without directly influencing the extent of the Party's demands.*

In conclusion, the question of the appropriateness of the Sudeten German Party co-operating with the remaining minorities in Czechoslovakia, notably the Czechs, was discussed. The Reich Foreign Minister decided here that the Party must be left free to keep in loose touch *with the other minority groups,* whose parallel action might appear appropriate.

R[ibbentrop]

F    18/355                                                    [Appendix 2]
LIST OF THOSE PRESENT AT THE DISCUSSION ON SUDETEN
GERMAN QUESTIONS ON TUESDAY, MARCH 29, 1938, 12
O'CLOCK MIDDAY

*Present:*
  Reich Foreign Minister von Ribbentrop.
  State Secretary von Mackensen.
  Ministerial-Director von Weizsäcker.        } Foreign Ministry
  Minister Eisenlohr, Prague.
  Minister Sieve.
  *Legationsrat* von Twardowski.
  *Legationsrat* Altenburg.
  *Legationsrat* Kordt.

  *SS-Obergruppenführer* Lorenz.               } *Volksdeutsche*
  Professor Haushofer.                           *Mittelstelle*

| Konrad Henlein, Karl Hermann Franck, | ⎰ Sudeten German |
| Dr Künzel, Dr Kreissl. | ⎱ Party |

(Author's italics.)

In the summer of 1938 the Third Reich increased the pressure even more. An irrevocable decision was taken on May 30, 1938, to the effect that Czechoslovakia was to be eliminated[1] and that she must be smashed by military action in the immediate future. A propaganda war of threats was to intimidate Czechoslovakia and undermine her powers of resistance. Then the national groups would give instructions how the military action was to be supported.

The fifth-column line-up now began to take shape. As Nuremberg Document PS 388[2] clearly shows, it was believed that the success of the German military operations would depend on co-operation from the people living in the Sudeten German frontier areas, deserters from the Czechoslovak army, parachutists and sabotage groups.

Now, in accordance with the mission entrusted to him by Hitler, Henlein began to make so many demands of the Czechs that these could not possibly be met. Thus, on April 24, 1938, Henlein demanded full freedom for the Sudeten Germans to declare their allegiance to national socialism.

Hitler had considered the first days of October 1938 to be the latest possible deadline for a military operation in Czechoslovakia.[3]

At the same time Goebbels unleashed an all-out propaganda campaign against Czechoslovakia inside the Reich.

On September 12, 1938, at the Nazi Party Congress in Nuremberg, Hitler made an extremely aggressive speech in which he called on the Sudeten German population to rise up against the Czechoslovak government. Immediately afterwards clashes broke out between members of the Sudeten German Party and Czechoslovak units. When Czechoslovakia then proclaimed martial law, Henlein broke off negotiations with the government and extended his demands to include the cession of the Sudeten areas. He had moved his headquarters from Asch across the frontier into Germany the day before this development.[4] Broszat has rightly pointed out that the rupture of negotiations by Henlein, coinciding with Chamberlain's meeting with Hitler in Bad Godesberg on September 15, 1938, and the flight of thousands of Sudeten Germans, especially military conscripts, across the German

[1] Cf. de Jong's contribution, op. cit., p. 894.
[2] International Military Tribunal: Nuremberg Trials, Vol. 25.
[3] Cf. Martin Broszat, 'Das Sudetendeutsche Freikorps', in: *Vierteljahrschefte für Zeitgeschichte*, Vol. 9, 1961, pp. 30 f.
[4] Ibid., p. 32.

frontier made it easier for Hitler to confront Chamberlain with the threat of war against Czechoslovakia.[1]

But Henlein had hardly arrived in Germany when the mayors belonging to his party refused to obey his orders. This naturally did not fit in with Hitler's war plans, according to which they were to exhort the people to behave peacefully and obey orders. In these circumstances the Social Democrat Party, as the only German party actively working against Nazism, now had a last chance to go to the population with an appeal for peace and democracy, an appeal which, in view of the obviously mounting danger of war, had considerable force.

The attempted Nazi uprising collapsed. Efforts were therefore made to stir up unrest in Czechoslovakia from outside. This was done by Hitler setting up the Sudeten German *Freikorps* on September 17, 1938, against the advice of the Supreme Army Commander, Colonel General von Brauchitsch.[2]

Hitler declared the aim of the *Freikorps* to be: 'Protection of the Sudeten Germans and the *maintenance of further unrest and clashes*.'

The *Freikorps* was closely associated with the Nazi Storm Troops (SA): the army had to supply it with arms, but only arms of Austrian origin. The task of the *Freikorps* was to create a large number of incidents along the entire frontier by making attacks on Czechoslovak military posts, forming terror groups and so on.[3] On September 22, 1938, the Sudeten German *Freikorps*, whose strength was between 10,000 and 15,000 men,[4] advanced into Asch, Eger and the surrounding areas, so that the requisite *fait accompli*[5] was created for the talks between Hitler and Chamberlain taking place in Bad Godesberg the same day.

# PART SIX
## *National Internationalism and International Nationalism*

### The Nationalist International

An important centre of the schemes for totalitarian infiltration was the foreign policy department of the Nazi Party, headed by Alfred Rosenberg and coming under the sole, direct control of Adolf Hitler and his deputy.[6] The main office in Berlin was run by a staff of some 150

---

[1] Ibid., p. 33.   [2] Ibid., p. 37.
[3] International Military Tribunal, Vol. 36. E.C.–366.
[4] Broszat, op. cit., p. 40.   [5] Ibid., pp. 44 f.
[6] *Das Braune Netz*, op. cit., pp. 42 ff.

people but the organization employed hundreds of confidential contacts and agents abroad as well as commissars in all auxiliary organizations, associations and unions.[1] Connected with the foreign department were, for example the *Weltbund gegen die Kommunistische Internationale* (World Union against the Communist International) with its headquarters in London, the International Anti-Marxist Institute in Geneva, anti-Semitic organizations like the World Anti-Jewish League, the World Union of Anti-Semites, the Aryan-Christian Alliance, the Institute for the Study of the Jewish Question and the World Service, directed by Lt.-Col. Fleischhauer.

Associated with Rosenberg's departments there were, however, also organizations like the Nordic Society, the German-Japanese Society, the China Club, the Ukrainian Institute, the German-Foreign Academic Club, the Society of Foreign Friends, the Academy for German Law, the Russo-Nationalist Freedom Movement Rond, the League of National Socialist Confederates (Switzerland), the Baltic Legion and the Austrian Legion, as well as organizations whose purpose was the recovery of German colonies.

The Nationalist International merits special attention. This *Internationale Arbeitsgemeinschaft der Nationalisten* (International Working Party of Nationalists), of which the chairman was Dr Hans Keller, was set up by Hess, Rosenberg and their adherents. This organization gives us a clear picture of the way the most diverse groups of people, some unsuspecting, some merely Nazi sympathizers, in effect collaborated with the real quislings. After three successful congresses – held in Berlin in 1934, in London in 1935, and in Oslo in 1936 – the *Akademie für die Rechte der Völker* (Academy for the Rights of Peoples) was founded at the nationalist movement's Oslo congress. Professor Edgar Tatarin-Tarnheyden of Rostock described the nature of this movement in the following words:[2]

'The movement to establish contacts and meetings among the nationalists of the most important cultural nations in the world was born of the realization that international law today, like the "League of Nations" decided on in Versailles, are both based on a false outlook and false premises which no longer correspond to the realities of international life and are in themselves also contrary to the idea of a genuine peaceful order among nations . . . The Nationalist "International's" declaration of war was aimed at the great international organizations of formal egalitarian democracy, communism and romantic etatism.'

The speaker regretted that Norway's Nationalist Party *Nasjonal*

---

[1] Ibid., p. 44.     [2] *Akademie für die Rechte der Völker*, op. cit., pp. 15 ff.

*Samling* under the leadership of the former War Minister Vidkun Quisling preferred to confine itself to the role of a mere observer, and also wanted its paper *Fritt Folk* to promote the work of the Congress by printing favourable reports every day.

Even then some of the Belgians attending the congress made speeches which pointed to the creation of the future Belgian fifth column. Thus at the movement's second congress Louis de Coninch expressed this opinion:

'Two more things have to be extirpated from the European countries: the parliamentary system which is completely corrupted and that international financial power which is largely responsible for the hatred shown between the Nations of the World.'[1]

The Danish Nazi quisling, Dr Clausen, appeared for the first time at the congress held in London. And the presence of such prominent figures as SS-Oberführer Ministerialdirektor Professor Theodor Vahlen, then President of the Prussian Academy of Science, Secretary of State Professor Gottfried Feder, Professor Rudolf Jung, Dr Karl Lapper, Chief of the Propaganda Department of the Nazi Youth Movement, and, not least, the fact that, at a special ceremony, Alfred Rosenberg presented his book *Europe's Crisis and Rebirth* to the President of the Academy, showed the great interest which the Third Reich took in the organization.[2] Of the members of the British committee Lord Queensborough had apparently been misled about the organization's aims, as he naïvely imagined they could be compatible with his patriotism for Britain. In an article in the *Contemporary Review* in 1935 on his impressions of the London congress, the author Greenwood said literally:

'. . . interference by some nations in the domestic affairs of others. One of the most important reasons for modern nationalism is the desire of each nation to be left alone to hammer out the solution of the fundamental political, social and economic problems with which we are all confronted . . . The second issue was between what might be described as the static and dynamic conceptions of nationalism – security and revision.'[3]

Herbert Foster-Anderson, a supporter of Stanley Baldwin, attended all the congresses of the Nationalist International and spoke in support of Keller's conception of the antithesis between nation and state:[4]

'There are two features in a nation which are not present in the idea of a state. These are the land and the race. As the individual is a living synthesis of body and spirit, which only our reason analyses into two

[1] Ibid., p. 32.       [2] Ibid., pp. 58–67.       [3] Ibid., pp. 79 f.       [4] Ibid., p. 81.

abstractions of thought, with the result that it is at a loss to decide which governs the other, so the nation is a living synthesis of the land and the race, a synthesis which a state system, divorced from land and indifferent to race, splits up into land to be exploited and classes which fight each other for its control.'

An even more positive attitude to the Nazi ideology was taken by Viscount Lymington, who was associated with this International and who, in the first number of his periodical *The New Pioneer*, wrote in support of the idea of racial inequality,[1] and by Evelyn Wrench, also known to the reader as Geoffrey Dawson's biographer, who invited Dr Keller to the Oxford Congress of the All Peoples' Association.[2]

The congresses held by the Nationalist International several years before the outbreak of war provided a meeting place for all those elements outside the narrower German cultural circle who were sympathetic to the Third Reich's ideological aims and in this way they also helped to bring about the developments which took place between 1938 and 1940.

One notable contribution was that made by an Austrian Roman Catholic priest, Dr Simon Pirchegger, at the congress at which the Academy was founded. His views reflect the pan-German outlook and the latent anti-democratic, anti-Semitic sentiments prevailing among a section of the Austrian clergy:[3]

'The international powers of Western democracy and Jewish Marxism which sometimes secretly, sometimes openly, take a hand in the destinies of nations are joined by a third – political Catholicism.'

Pirchegger went even further than was then usual in this particular ideological group.

'This power [i.e. political Catholicism] must therefore also be studied very carefully by the International Academy of Nationalists if it is really to perform its task of moulding the destinies of all peoples according to their intrinsic nature and protecting them from every alien, uncharacteristic influence.'

He publicly denounced Mgr Alfredo Ottaviani's book *Institutiones Juris Publici Ecclesiastici* because Ottaviani supported Catholic political parties.[4] Pirchegger accused the Vatican of having tried 'to erect one "Catholic Bulwark" after another against the allegedly Godless Third Reich', and thus putting German Catholics in a difficult position.

---

[1] Ibid., p. 88.    [2] Ibid., p. 92.    [3] Ibid., pp. 237 f.    [4] Ibid., pp. 238 f.

He said he would be compelled 'to oppose the Vatican's political activity so that he could live at peace with his national and patriotic conscience.'[1]

The most important elements which were later to emerge as fifth-columnists and quislings (between 1938 and 1945) were already in evidence in the Nationalist International. There was Vidkun Quisling, who presented the International with a painting of himself for its Assembly Hall,[2] and the Danish national socialist Clausen, the Flemish and Walloon fascists in Belgium, the French collaborators, the Romanian fascists and the Hungarian revisionists. Prominent, though not connected with this group, were those elements among the reactionary, conservative classes in England, France and other countries, such as the Chamberlain-Halifax-Henderson-Runciman-Lothian group and the later Vichy regime of General Pétain – people who cannot possibly be described as Nazis, but whose anti-democratic, anti-liberal, anti-international and anti-Marxist views were of the greatest value when it came to spreading the idea of totalitarianism. The Dutch oil magnate Deterding,[3] on whom the Dutch national socialists depended for their finances, also had links with the Nationalist International.

All this shows that the Nazi Nationalist International was not a *spiritus rector* but simply a highly effective instrument and a framework for implementing the Nazi policy of infiltration. At the same time it served as a meeting place for foreign circles sympathetic to national socialism. Its peculiar intellectual climate provides important clues about the mental attitude of those men in the West who made the Nazis' war plans possible and helped to make them successful. First and foremost there were the appeasers, who were responsible for thwarting the German resistance group's last-minute attempt to bring down the Hitler regime with the help of a determined stand by the West. In spite of the change which his views underwent on the outbreak of war – a change which, in any case, was extremely belated – Lord Lothian[4] was one of the most dangerous of men. After Hitler had marched into Prague on March 15, 1939, the former Oxford Rhodes Scholar and member of the German resistance group, Trott zu Stolz, came to England on a secret mission. Lord Lothian, however, tried to advise Hitler through him to gloss over the rape of Czechoslovakia by

---

[1] Ibid., p. 244.    [2] Ibid., p. 151.    [3] Ibid., p. 142.
[4] Cf., for example, Hitler's negotiations with Lord Lothian and Conwell Evans on May 4, 1937, quoted as Appendix III in Butler, op. cit., pp. 337 ff. See also *History of The Times*, op. cit., p. 891 marginal note, about Lord Lothian's two visits to Hitler: 'Lothian had not the slightest doubt that this [German] attitude is perfectly sincere' although his ignorance of the German language is a somewhat extenuating circumstance.

allowing the Czechs to retain their cultural independence. On this incident Rowse remarks:

'It is ironic that, through von Trott, the German General Staff should have been sending us advice that might have stopped Hitler, while, also through von Trott, Lothian should have sent just the advice that would have enabled Hitler to get away with everything.'[1]

The opposition to Hitler's war plans which existed among senior German officers is also borne out by American sources.[2]

One can only agree with Rowse when he says of the appeasers who were Fellows of his College, Lord Lothian, Lord Halifax, Dawson and others, that, as a result of their activities, Nazi Germany achieved a dominating position of supremacy which represented a threat to the security and even the existence of the entire world and which could only be dispelled by war.[3]

What is incomprehensible, however, is that having made this analysis Rowse attributes to these men, who were appeasers and accomplices of national socialism, no more than minor responsibility, assigning the primary blame to the entire German nation – that is to say, including the Social Democratic Party, the Zentrum, the Liberals, Goerdeler, Beck, Stauffenberg and Trott. The Nationalist International proves conclusively that national socialism was an international conspiracy which was by no means confined to Germany alone but had its partisans in many countries. This is evident when one considers the figures of Trott and Lothian and their eventual fate: Trott met his death fighting with the German resistance in Plötzensee while Lothian finished up in the respectable post of British Ambassador in Washington.

## Particularism and Universalism in the New Order of Europe

Although Hitler had spoken of the Germanic State of the German Nation in *Mein Kampf*, the idea of a pan-Germanic empire extending in circles centred round the 'Third Reich' only really took shape with the conquest of Denmark, Norway, Holland, Belgium and France.[4]

---

[1] Rowse, op. cit., p. 99.

[2] In a conversation between General Beck and Col. Truman Smith the American Military Attaché in Berlin at the time, Beck is said to have appealed for a stand against Hitler in the following words: 'Can't you do anything to help my poor country?' Allen Dulles, *Germany's Underground*, New York 1947, p. 39.

[3] Rowse, op. cit., p. 117.

[4] Since the Second World War there have been signs of attempts to claim that Hitler's concept of a pan-Germanic Empire was the precursor and pioneer of a European ideology. Kluke has rightly pointed out that no idea could be more mistaken than this, which not only falsifies history but is also bound to discredit ideas of

As far back as 1937, in a secret speech to future Nazi leaders at the *Ordensburg* at Sonthofen, Hitler had hinted at his plans for a war of conquest, plans which were inseparably bound up with his idea of German universalism.[1] According to this speech, totalitarian Nazi Germany was to serve as a basis for claims with which Nazism would soon confront the world. 'The fact is', Hitler declared, 'that ultimately might is always right.' Hitler's historical survey re-echoed with the pain felt over the vanished greatness of the Holy Roman Empire of the German Nation: 'We once possessed Europe. We only lost it because we lacked the vigorous leadership which – taking the long view – was essential not only to maintain but to improve our position.'[2]

However, for national socialism 'Germanic' and 'European' were frequently synonymous terms. For Hitler, of course, Europe was not a geographical concept but one which was determined by blood relationships. This came out clearly in his attitude to the United States and his regret that so many Norwegians, Swedes, Danes and Dutch, whom he needed for settling the East, had emigrated to America.[3] The New Order of Europe was to be set up in accordance with pan-Germanic principles, which meant removing the Germanic elements from the Belgian, French, Czech and Polish nations. Loock points out that by doing this the Nazis in fact made pan-Germanic and pan-German to mean one and the same thing. According to Himmler, the aim of Germanic policy would have been to turn the Dutch 'into conscious Germanic and German citizens'.[4]

In making this analysis of Hitler's idea of Europe we must refer back to the facts mentioned in Chapter VIII. It is clear that for Hitler it was simply a question of extending spatially his totalitarian domination, his racial ideas and his policy of deception. As in the area of Germany proper, his procedure in this sphere also was to apply his habitual techniques for disrupting pluralistic social structures, as, for example, exploiting existing group conflicts and resurrecting old ones and using neo-medieval forms of organization. Thus his 'pan-Germanic Empire of the German Nation', which he wanted to rule as 'Elected Emperor', takes the form of an extended German Reich, on a racial basis. However, because of its totalitarian structure, national socialism was unable to give expression to the ideas and forms of the Holy Roman

a united Europe among all nations outside Germany. Paul Kluke, 'Nationalsozialistische Europaideologie', in *Vierteljahrshefte für Zeitgeschichte*, Vol. 3, 1955, pp. 240 f. and p. 270.

[1] Adolf Hitler, *Mein Kampf*, op. cit., p. 362.
[2] Picker, op. cit., pp. 443 ff.
[3] Ibid., p. 45.
[4] Quoted by Hans-Dietrich Loock, 'Zur "Grossgermanischen Politik" des Dritten Reiches', in *Vierteljahrshefte für Zeitgeschichte*, Vol. 8, 1960, p. 40.

Empire, even under a modern guise. For the universalism of the Holy Roman Empire had been based, not least, on Christianity and natural law, on a vast diversity of peoples, races and cultural communities speaking many different languages, on a political and historical unity based on superior juridical concepts. Fundamental to this was the tolerance shown by the Roman-German Emperor towards the racial, cultural and linguistic differences of, for example, Italy, Spain, the Netherlands, Bohemia and Poland. The aristocratic, corporative hier-archical structure of the old Empire had given people but little equality; nevertheless it provided a fair measure of liberty, which made life pleasant for its privileged classes and at least generally tolerable for everybody.

Hitler, however, was only capable of thinking in terms of the old, intolerant frontier mentality of Austria-Hungary, bent on levelling all racial differences.[1] Thus shortly after seizing power he declared:

'In the centre I will set the steel core of a Greater Germany, welded into an indissoluble unity. Then Austria, Bohemia and Moravia, western Poland. The block of one hundred million, indestructible, without a flaw, without any foreign nation. The firm foundation of our power. Then an Eastern alliance – Poland, the Baltic States, Hungary, the Balkan States, the Ukraine, the Volga basin, Georgia. An alliance, but not of equal partners; it will be an alliance of vassal states, with no policy, no economy of its own. And I have no intention of mak-ing concessions on sentimental grounds, as, for instance, restoring Hungary. I make no distinction between friends and foes. The time of small states is past. There will also be a Western Union, of Holland, Flanders, Northern France. And a Northern Union of Denmark, Sweden, Norway.'[2]

Leadership can be learned only by ruling over foreign peoples; only a master race can do that. 'The Czechs would have lost their sense of inferiority if they had shown themselves superior to the other nations bordering on Austria.'[3] After a self-contemplation of several centuries the German must now learn to act. They had proved themselves cap-able of ruling over others. Austria was the best example. If the Habs-burgs had not been allied with the enemy, the nine million Germans would have finished off the fifty million others in the Habsburg empire.

Hitler reveals his ignorance of the evolutionary aims of the British Empire time and time again. Why, he thought, should not others fight

[1] Cf., on this point, Picker, op. cit., p. 47.
[2] Quoted by Hermann Rauschnigg, *Gespräche mit Hitler*, op. cit., p. 118.
[3] Picker, op. cit., p. 48.

for the Germans, if Indians fought for the British? If the English ruling class came from Lower Saxony, England could also provide the SS with a reservoir of leaders.[1]

How was the political order which the Nazis planned for the areas they occupied to be created? In no case were the conquered provinces to have the right to raise an army or an air force of their own;[2] for self-government leads to independence. What was seized could not be kept by democratic institutions. The inhabitants of these regions were to be forced to relapse into illiteracy. Above all, German teachers must not be sent to the eastern regions. Hitler would have let them have music, but no sort of intellectual activity. There would have been no hospitals or inoculations to protect people against disease. 'The Russians don't get old. They only live to fifty or sixty. Why inoculate them? We must put our lawyers and doctors in their place: no inoculations, no washing! They can have as much vodka and tobacco as they like.'[3]

Germanic provinces, like the low-lying Dutch and Flemish lands, he wanted as far as possible to avoid by making them Reich *Gaue* and letting them retain their individual character. Even the Hungarians, whom he respected for being '*hard-boiled* nationalists', he wanted either to rule over or to take out the German minority. He disagreed with Himmler's idea of picking out the Germanic nucleus from France. (Author's italics.)

Detailed plans had been worked out for annexing northern and eastern France and the annexation of Alsace-Lorraine was already in hand.[4] The setting up of a Burgundian state[5] under German rule and as a model SS state was also considered, on historical grounds. Even Brittany was to become independent from France. Only the need to keep France more or less on his side during the war stopped Hitler from making these part of his peace conditions in 1940.

Belgium and Holland were also meant to enjoy a special relationship, which would allow them independence and assign a modest role to the fascist and Nazi quisling groups of Degrelle, Staf de Clercq and Mussert. In any case, Belgium and Holland were to be part of the pan-Germanic Reich. So, too, were Denmark and Norway and, after final victory had been achieved, Sweden as well. Hitler intended to give these countries such a highly centralized form of government that any 'separatist tendency' would be stifled.

---

[1] Ibid., p. 48. This shows Hitler's ignorance of history. The English ruling class did not originate from Lower Saxony but from the Norman barons whose wild warrior hordes, before their conversion to Christianity in the tenth century, had razed, plundered and pillaged German towns in Wotan's name.

[2] Ibid., p. 49.        [3] Ibid., pp. 50 f.

[4] Cf., for example, Lothar Gruchmann, *Nationalsozialistische Grossraumordnung*, Stuttgart 1962, pp. 76 f.        [5] Ibid., pp. 77 f.

Differences soon broke out between the quisling movements and the rulers appointed by the Third Reich, whose methods were increasingly influenced by Himmler's SS. Thus Hitler mentioned that he had asked Mussert 'whether he believed that he [Hitler] had found it easy to divide up Austria, his native land, into a lot of small districts to eliminate separatist tendencies and to be able to incorporate her more easily into the Germanic Reich'.[1] This is a further proof of Hitler's deceit in his dealing with the Germanic member states in the New Order. Thus the Dutch Frisians were to be separated from their mother country and united with the Frisians on the other bank of the river Ems. Reich schools, whose pupils were to be one-third Dutch or Norwegians and two-thirds German, were to provide the education of the future Dutch and Norwegian national socialist leaders.[2]

And so the policy of deception was also applied to the Germanic parts of the New Order. For instance, Hitler stressed:

'It is necessary to go carefully with the Dutch and Norwegians. It must always be remembered that Bavaria would not have been ready to join Prussia in 1871 either; she had simply been persuaded to be incorporated in the great blood-related union of Germany by Bismarck. Nor did I tell the Austrians in 1938 that I wanted to make them part of Germany; instead I had always hinted that I wanted them to unite with Germany to form the pan-Germanic Reich. And so one must always make it clear to the Germanic people of north and northwest Europe that the "Reich" always means the Germanic Reich and that Germany is simply its strongest ideological and military source of power.'[3]

In practice, therefore, the pan-Germanic policy amounted to 'annexing' and 'co-ordinating' the German-occupied areas. Thus Vidkun Quisling gave vent to his disappointment that Terboven was appointed *Reichskommissar* in Norway over his head. As in Norway, Hitler tried to get rid of the independent royal dynasties and parliamentary governments in Denmark and transform these countries into mere provinces of the Third Reich. The Dutch national socialist Mussert was also annoyed that the *Reichsstatthalter*, Seyss-Inquart, refused to treat him as a figure of importance.

In the meantime, however, the quislings had to learn that the SS, who mistrusted them as separatists and particularists, came on to the scene as rivals for power in their own countries.[4] The SS went into the occupied areas because they were a police force and because the SS

---

[1] Picker, op cit., p. 67.　　　[2] Ibid., pp. 67 f.　　　[3] Ibid., p. 67.
[4] Cf. Trost von Tonningen to Brand on April 15, 1943. Nuremberg Document 2740. Analysis of the document by the prosecution, March 28, 1947.

Central Office was also the Reserve Office of the Waffen SS (SS military units). In Oslo, Copenhagen and The Hague reserve commands were set up as early as 1940. During the war 'by appealing to the "blood concept" which it had turned into reality, the SS leaders claimed for themselves an ever-increasing political influence in the "Germanic countries".'[1] The SS had begun 'to build the German Reich for the Führer'.

The Chief of the SS Head Office, Gottlob Berger, complained to the Office of the Reich leader of the SS that *Reichskommissar* Seyss-Inquart himself had failed to grasp the idea of the Germanic Central Department. It was proposed 'to register all persons in the Nordic countries who are prepared to come to the Reich, depending upon a later decision by the Führer. To register young people in the countries concerned and to see to it that – without using compulsion – they are indoctrinated in accordance with Reich policy and that they do not pursue any separatist course. To train these young people further, in close collaboration with the Reich Labour Service, in order to make them full-blooded members of our Reich by means of service in the Waffen SS.'[2]

On this occasion Berger stressed the point that in all these matters he had been an obedient disciple of Himmler's and would never have told him lies.

Cracks in the structure of the Greater Germanic Reich were already clearly visible. In an outburst of uninhibited hostility towards the growing influence of Austrians in the Nazi Party and the SS, Berger declared: 'And those gentlemen will have to get rid of one idea: We are not more unskilled or more stupid where political matters are concerned than the gentlemen from the Ostmark.'

Even in 1942 tension grew up not only between Germans and Austrians but also between the German officers and the volunteers in the Flanders Legion who came under their command. Thus the leader of the Flemish national socialists, Staf de Clercq, complained that the young volunteers were 'insulted with the worst abuses for most trifling incidents; they are even beaten up'.[3] Complaints could not be handed in and those who complained were often punished. The Flemings were insulted and abused in the vilest terms, which could only end in destroying morale and belief in national socialist ideas.

In 1943, at Himmler's suggestion, Hitler had authorized the setting up of a Germanic corps under SS Gruppenführer Steiner, a Waffen SS General. As Reitlinger says,[4] the European SS was in no way the prod-

[1] Loock, op. cit., p. 56.

[2] Nuremberg Document N.O. 1340.

[3] Nuremberg Document N.O. 765, Office of the Chief Counsel for War Crimes.

[4] Gerald Reitlinger, *Die SS-Tragödie einer deutschen Epoche*, Vienna–Munich, Basle 1956, p. 155.

uct of any ideological concept. Hitler would have been opposed to a united Europe, except as an enlarged economic region for Germany, without bothering to find ideological reasons. His motive in agreeing to the expansion of the SS had been the hope that an army of young foreigners would fight for him and thus be kept from joining resistance movements in France, the Netherlands and Scandinavia. The number of men enrolled in the 'Germanic' SS and the 'European Volunteers' taken into the Waffen SS reached its peak in December 1944 when, after the failure of the July 20 revolt, Himmler had become Commander in Chief of the Reserve Army. The Germanic SS units consisted of the French 'Charlemagne' Division, the Belgian 'Flanders' and 'Walloon' Divisions, the Dutch 'Netherland' Division and the Scandinavian 'Northland' Division.[1] These divisions were flung ruthlessly into battle at the end of the war when the German troops were already showing signs of war-weariness. The fighting value of the foreign divisions was high, since their members were afraid of being shot as quislings if they were taken prisoner.

It was already obvious that the Greater Germanic Reich was meant not so much to realize the aims of a *Grossraumordnung* (order for a large geographical complex), the New Order of Europe, as to bolster up the increasingly desperate plight of the German armies locked in mortal combat with the Great Powers.

'The Germanic Corps will comprise the present division "Viking" and the division "Waraeger", which will be newly organized; 6,000 Germanic volunteers will have to be enlisted. In an ever-increasing degree the replacement situation within the Reich makes it exigent to draw on the Germanic countries for volunteers for the Waffen SS. Through the organization of the Germanic Corps the unification of *all* Germanic volunteers under *one* command will be attained. Furthermore, the Führer approved the organization of a Germanic French regiment "Charlemagne" (*Karl der Grosse*). In addition, a Croatian SS division is to be activated if political conditions permit.'[2]

And so the pan-Germanic Reich already had French and Croatian SS units, although the Slavs were regarded as an inferior breed.

Hitler and Himmler clearly never took the 'Greater Germanic Reich' idea with any real seriousness, as is proved by the raising of a Mohammedan SS division, the 13th 'Handschar' Division, consisting of 20,000 Muslims. Another Mohammedan SS division was recruited in the Balkans in 1944. It was known as the SS 'Kama' Division.[3]

[1] Ibid., p. 157.
[2] Nuremberg Document N.O. 1783, Report on the third session of the Germanic Working Party of January 12, 1943.                [3] Reitlinger, op. cit., p. 199.

These SS troops wore the Turkish fez as well as their SS insignia; and, unlike the 'six godless division' set up in 1941, each battalion had a Muslim chaplain or Imam. While training in France the division came under the spiritual care of the Mufti of Jerusalem.[1] This 'purely Germanic' politician and theologian, whose appearance was strongly reminiscent of the traditional Christian conception of Caiaphas, the high priest, was promoted by Hitler to the ranks of SS Gruppenführer. After the occupation of the northern Caucasus in 1942, 110,000 Turkomans and 35,000 Tartars from the Crimea as well as Kalmuks were enlisted. According to Himmler, among the Russian peoples only the Slavs and the Russian Jews were 'sub-human'; the Mongols, from whom Attila, Genghis Khan, Tamerlane, Lenin and Stalin had sprung were a superior element.[2] However, from 1943 onwards Himmler began to recruit Slav SS divisions and did so in increasing numbers.[3] This explains how the Russian General Vlassov finally came to hold such an important position.

In these circumstances it was hardly surprising that the Nordic nations, who still cherished the Germanic tradition of liberty, never showed the slightest desire to serve as spies and policemen for the Greater Germanic Reich. And so the Racial Office[4] complained that Quisling was increasingly losing the confidence of the Norwegian National Socialist Party and that anti-German feeling was gathering momentum in Norway, as in all the other Germanic countries. And Quisling was also treating the freemasons with respect and had been able to send the Führer only 200 instead of the 1,200 men he had promised. As to Denmark, the Racial Office observed that the behaviour of the Danish national-socialist leader, Clausen, left much to be desired. In the Netherlands, the complaint goes on, Seyss-Inquart had prematurely declared Mussert 'Führer' of the Dutch nation. In Flanders, where the leader of the Flemish SS had been shot by reactionaries, the situation was particularly bad, Degrelle, the leader of the Walloon fascists, had indeed proved his worth in battle and was also politically valuable, but, unfortunately, he was a practising Catholic and therefore had to be handled carefully. And, the complaint continues, 'in future in the field of our political work the expression "Germanic Reich" or "Greater Germanic Reich" shall be avoided and merely the expression "Reich" shall be used. The conception "nation" (i.e. union with a purpose) shall step into the background. The conceptions "nation" and "national" shall be used with respect to Germania as a whole, and not in connection with individual Germanic countries. For instance, when referring to Norway, the

---

[1] Ibid.  [2] Ibid., p. 201.  [3] Ibid., p. 375.
[4] Nuremberg Document N.O. 1783, op. cit.

words "Norwegians" or "Norwegian population" are, too, used exclusively. In general the expression "Germanic" and "Germanic blood" are to be used, the word "Germanic" to replace the expression "Nordic" from now on.'[1]

Gradually, however, the non-Germanic concept developed into the European concept. The theme of one SS pamphlet,[2] for example, was ideological war and the Waffen SS were described as fighters and heralds of the New Europe. 'For America and England, Europe is only a colony, for the Jews and bolsheviks only an object for exploitation. For the peoples of Europe, Europe is the heart of the world. If the heart stops beating, the body dies. Hence, he who fights in the ranks of the Waffen SS must know why he defends his homeland against the assault of an ideology alien in race and character to Europe and that he fights for a New Order for Europe. The SS has grown from the German to the greater German, from the Greater German to the Germanic, from the Germanic to the European assignment as "Shock Troops for a New Europe".'

And so a feeling of hostility slowly grew up between the national socialist parties in the occupied countries and the SS, which wanted to set up its own organization in those countries. The counter-state of the SS did everything possible to take over both the Reich and the Nazi Party, not only in Germany but in the occupied territories as well. 'The foreign members of the SS had sworn the SS oath to Hitler and thereby entered the sphere 'where the Führer constitution founded on Hitler's personal sovereignty began to be realized'. When they assumed political functions in their native countries they did so as representatives of the order pledging allegiance to Hitler alone.'[3] This meant that local Nazi parties in the occupied territories were merely propaganda agents and the order of the SS was to supply the leadership for all the Germanic countries.

This shows that underlying Hitler's idea of Europe was an utter contempt for the individuality and the cultural and historic heritage of the European peoples, and a lack of anything like recognition of their equality. Had he been able to carry out his plan, the Slavs would have been excluded from Europe and made into a subject race[4] and the Latin peoples would have been assigned an inferior status. But even the Germanic peoples would have lost their individuality in the process of ideological *Gleichschaltung*, the ideological conformity enforced on them by National Socialism and some would have been resettled to carry out police duties for the Third Reich in the East.[5] The SS took

[1] Ibid.  [2] Nuremberg Document N.O. 772.
[3] Loock, op. cit., pp. 62 f.  [4] Cf. Gruchmann, op. cit., pp. 261 ff.
[5] Cf. also Kluke, op. cit., pp. 261 ff.

over control of the *Grossraum* (large geographical bloc) order because they could be employed as ruthless police units. It was only after Stalingrad that Nazi publicists began to speak of the 'European' order as a cause worth defending against bolshevism, plutocracy and Judaism.[1]

## The 'Crown Jurists' and the *Grossraum* Order

Parallel to the Nazi plan to enslave Europe and the world under its totalitarian tyranny was an unsuccessful attempt to justify the New Order in the sphere of political theory. After Carl Schmitt had applied his undoubted talents to the task of destroying the Weimar Republic he also offered – not unconditionally, of course – to justify the Nazi *Grossraum* order. He now discovered that the traditional idea of the state and the concept of the sovereignty and equality of all states had become outdated and no longer corresponded to the facts of international relationships.[2]

Schmitt argued that this concept of the state had been destroyed by the concept of the *Volk* (a people of racial homogeneity and the same blood), thus making things easy for the Nazi expansion policy which was then at the beginning of its pan-German stage. But just as the concept of the state had envisaged a spatial order involving 'a territorially-limited and territorially-closed unit', so the state disappeared in the concept of the 'Reich', which, in its turn, would be embodied in a concrete large geographical area.[3]

Consequently Schmitt also regarded international law as outdated. He rightly recognized that the traditional concepts of international law, like neutrality,[4] which was based on the legal fiction of the equality of sovereign states, were obsolete.

Yet he undoubtedly went too far when he regarded even universalism as out of date. By universalism Schmitt understood 'the transformation of a spatially conceived non-intervention principle into a non-spatial, general intervention system'.[5] This had happened because 'Woodrow Wilson put the ideological concept of liberal democracy and its related ideas, in particular the ideas of "international free trade" and "the free world market", in place of the original and genuine Munroe doctrine'.[6] The League of Nations which, by reason of Article 16 in its

---

[1] Ibid., p. 270.
[2] Carl Schmitt, 'Der Reichsbegriff im Völkerrecht' in *Positionen und Begriffe*, Berlin 1939, pp. 303 ff.
[3] Car Schmitt, *Völkerrechtliche Grossraumordnung*, Berlin, Vienna 1939, p. 7.
[4] Carl Schmitt, 'Das neue Vae Neutris!' in *Positionen und Begriffe*, op. cit., pp. 251 ff.
[5] Carl Schmitt, 'Grossraum gegen Universalismus', ibid., p. 297.      [6] Ibid.

covenant, had destroyed neutrality, had expressed universalist claims,[1] just like the British Empire.[2]

Looked at from the standpoint of the Nazi leadership, Schmitt was guilty either of a misunderstanding or of 'shooting a line'. He endeavoured to establish a distinction between the British Empire and the concept of 'Reich'. While, according to Schmitt, the concept of Empire was symptomatic of 'methods of economic, capitalist colonization and expansion', the concept of the 'Reich' had remained free from this taint.[3] Schmitt conceives of the 'Reich' as something purely racial and embracing all national racial life. But in doing so he had exposed Hitler and his plans for incorporating the west Slav areas of Czechoslovakia and Poland.

A further divergence from the pet fantasies of Germany's political rulers at the time was his emphasizing of the distinction between this racial concept of 'Reich' and that underlying the Holy Roman Empire, which he considered to come into the same category as the British Empire. On the other hand Schmitt held the view that 'not international law but a general world law and human law' applies to a world empire such as the British Empire. The existence of this world empire showed him that the 'traditional' concept of the state no longer corresponds to the truth and reality.[4] The Anglo-Saxon countries had hypocritically made the change to world empire and world law by attacking the concept of sovereignty – here Schmitt becomes extremely aggressive, since the central thesis of his master, Thomas Hobbes, is impugned – while making extravagant protestations of humanitarian and pacifist ideals on the occasion of German's defeat in the First World War.

Furthermore, underlying traditional international law is the doctrine of 'the balance of power', which is, in turn, based on the idea of a weak central Europe in which British foreign policy can chop and change as it fancies. The Third Reich, so thought Schmitt and other constitutional lawyers, had put an end to this false universalism with its Anglo-Saxon claims, which were to guarantee the impotence of central Europe. It is interesting to note that Schmitt cited the declaration which Hitler made in the Reichstag on February 20, 1936 – in effect the opening shot in the aggression against Austria and Czechoslovakia – in which he claimed 'Germany's right to protect the German racial groups who possessed foreign nationality' and described this as establishing a true international *Grossraum* principle for a large territorial bloc embracing the region of central and eastern Europe, 'inhabited by many peoples and racial groups which are not alien to

[1] Carl Schmitt, 'Völkerrechtliche Neutralität und völkische Totalität', ibid., p. 258.
[2] Carl Schmitt, 'Der Reichsbegriff im Völkerrecht', ibid., p. 303.
[3] Ibid., pp. 303 f.                    [4] Ibid., p. 306.

one another'.[1] A *Grossraum* order for such a large geographical area was therefore the *conditio sine qua non* of the concept of the ethnic Reich and nullified the principle of non-intervention. Within this bloc the Reich had a leading and determinative role and 'radiated' its political ideas throughout its own particular domain. To achieve this it must on principle exclude intervention by extraneous powers.[2]

This, of course, assumed the existence of second- and third-class states and communities which have no option but to accept this hierarchical arrangement if they are 'irradiated' by the political ideas of the Reich. While, according to Schmitt, under the old systems of international law, war had been 'a relation of order to order and not of order to disorder', which corresponded to civil war, only the latter relationship was possible in the *Grossraum* bloc. Thereby, however, Schmitt had deprived all peoples within the central and east European *Grossraum* of the right of defence against national socialism. In time of war this was bound to mean that all central and east Europeans would be treated not as combatants but as rebels and outlaws, without any rights of their own.

The Nazi policy of expansion and subjugation thus acquired the sanction of 'international law'. Lidice and the outrages in the general government, in Croatia etc. received the absolution of 'international law'. Even constitutional lawyers like Triepel, whose ideas were still rooted in the constitutional values of the German Empire and the Weimar Republic, endeavoured to establish the concept of 'hegemony',[3] but at the same time to limit it by including it in the Western cultural and constitutional heritage. Above all, Schmitt's concepts of international law, according to which the Nazi *Grossraum* was to be confined to the *Volksdeutsche* (ethnic German) groups (Schmitt's intention being to allow the Slav peoples living in the German and Austrian region before 1914 to retain their cultural autonomy) were bound to displease the Nazi leaders, who were laying plans for the conquest of the world. Had the much-read Carl Schmitt not studied *Mein Kampf* closely enough? In any case his and Triepel's theories could not provide even a juridical justification for 'the Greater Germanic Empire of the German Nation', to say nothing of the New Order of Europe.

Constitutional lawyers like Werner Daitz[4] and Georg Hahn, who spoke of the 'equality' of the European peoples,[5] were more pliant. Hahn understood this 'equality' as a 'recollection of the eternal basic

---

[1] Carl Schmitt, *Völkerrechtliche Grossraumordnung*, op. cit., p. 64.

[2] Ibid., p. 69.

[3] Cf. Heinrich Triepel, *Die Hegemonie. Ein Buch von führenden Staaten*, Stuttgart 1938.

[4] Cf. Kluke's description of him, op. cit., p. 271.

[5] Georg Hahn, *Grundfragen europäischer Ordnung*, Berlin, Vienna 1959, p. 57.

values of itself' and its 'realization in a characteristic constitution'. What, however, this 'characteristic constitution' was to mean was made clear by Hitler's declaration – cited by Hahn – that Germany wanted nothing for herself which she was not also ready to give to others – totalitarian dictatorship.

As the *Grossraum* is organized according to biological principles it was bound, Daitz thought, to be a 'family law of peoples', in which the Third Reich would naturally be the paterfamilias.[1] Apart from this undisputed leading role the other 'members of the family', irrespective of their biological merits or demerits, were to be graded according to their economic contribution to the whole family – particularly for the paterfamilias. There is no need to emphasize that the rights of this paterfamilias over the life, physical safety and property of the members of the family under his wing were modelled on the rights of the pater-familias of archaic Rome.

In the ever-increasing tensions between nationalism and *Grossraum* ideas, particularism and universalism, *Volkstum* (folkdom, the racial character and heritage of the German *Volk*) Reich and Europa, race and world dominion, the paradox inherent in national socialism becomes increasingly obvious. As we explained in the early part of the book, nationalism spread from one people to another. This happened largely because it bred resistance in the peoples attacked, inspiring rival nationalist sentiments among both these and other peoples. As nationalism, by its very nature, must play a specific role this means that a nation can only embark on an expansionist policy at the expense of rival nationalisms. But this is only conceivable in terms of the conquest and subjugation of other peoples. The effective integration of these peoples in the name of nationalism is, however, impossible in the long run as the education in nationalism imbibed from the leading power in the bloc inevitably leads to nationalist revolt and therefore to the break-up of the entire complex.

This shows the intensification, the exaggeration of integral nationalism which springs from its inner dynamism, leads to its eventual destruction, not only among the subject peoples but also in the leading power itself, which has to try to justify its supremacy by invoking the international and universalist principles which are alien to its ideology. In point of fact the European peoples subjugated in the name of nationalism easily saw through universalistic catch-phrases like the 'Greater Germanic Reich' or the 'New Order of Europe', knowing them to be merely camouflage for an egoistical, racial and nationalist jingoism; and therefore they reacted characteristically with their own nationalist sentiments.

[1] Kluke, op. cit., p. 272.

The evidence provided by documents quoted in this chapter clearly show that the 'Greater Germanic Reich' and the 'New Order of Europe' had already dissolved even before the British and American troops landed in Normandy.

For the peoples of central Europe, however, the monster of the *Grossraum* order proved profoundly tragic. In their negotiations in Teheran and Yalta the Allies adopted the Nazi principle underlying this order, but restricted its application to central Europe. Consequently the peoples living there were assigned to the Soviet sphere of influence, partly as Carl Schmitt had conceived it, so that the racially and ethnically heterogeneous Slavs together with Russia formed the nucleus of the *Grossraum* bloc 'irradiated' by the Kremlin, with the defeated Germans, Hungarians and Romanians attached to it as 'protected' peoples. After the conclusion of the *Staatsvertrag* (State Treaty), Austria was the only country allowed to 'evolve' further as a 'neutral' country within the frontiers of the Austrian Republic of 1918, in so far as her geographical, economic and cultural circumstances would allow.

## Outlook For the Future

It is now two and a half decades since the end of the Second World War and the shape of future social, cultural and political development is beginning to emerge. Tendencies hitherto blurred by post-war economic distress and ideological conflict and therefore largely obscured are gradually coming into focus.

There is an irreconcilable antithesis between two of the main elements of democracy, liberty and equality. The West has placed the main emphasis on liberty while the communist world endeavours to impose equality by means of totalitarian terror. Since Stalin's death and because mankind is in danger of annihilation in a nuclear holocaust the hostility between the two worlds has somewhat abated.

In the West, the recognition of equality has been so closely associated with the principle of liberty that it is almost impossible to speak of a paradox. It has, in fact, become clear that the basic socialist demand – for the abolition of social inequality and for working-class prosperity – have come significantly nearer to being realized in the West than in the East. On the other hand the Khrushchev era – in a limited context to be sure – also saw the introduction of certain human rights in the communist world.

Looked at from an economic standpoint, it might be said that the age of individualistic capitalism which began in the sixteenth century is coming to an end and that society is claiming an ever greater control over industry and trade, which was left to private enterprise in the eighteenth and nineteenth centuries. In the name of social progress we are striving to create a situation which, by enshrining economic rights and duties in various systems of basic law, seems in many ways to be very similar to the Middle Ages.

As every community has an inherent tendency to strike a compromise between liberty and authority, it is natural for people to want more personal and political liberty. If these liberties are to be safeguarded, however, they must be legalized and written into the constitution.

If *sacro egoismo* is no longer accepted as an absolute virtue in economic relationships, the same applies to national sovereignty, considered from the point of view of constitutional law. Another of the more enduring results of the Second World War is that only three or four sovereign states actually survived with their sovereignty undiminished. The growing membership of the United Nations cannot conceal this fact.

A tendency which is becoming increasingly evident is the evolution of the national state into the continental state, organized as a single administration, defence and economic unit. Few people had foreseen this at the beginning of the Second World War. Any such notion would have been dismissed then as unrealistic, although the most extreme form of nationalism, in the guise of national socialism, was compelled by the inexorable laws of war to develop in the direction of the continental state. That the goal was pursued with unsuitable methods – that is to say in an amateurish way – by resorting to deceit and brutality, in no way alters the fact that this trend became discernible during the course of the Second World War. It conjures up the alarming bogy of a great state run on totalitarian lines – one which is perhaps more rational, subtle and less overtly addicted to brutality and naked force than Hitlerism and Stalinism, but, instead, infinitely more technocratic, bureaucratic and scientific and therefore much more difficult to defeat.

While Aristotle's theories were already being superseded in the realm of natural science as long ago as the sixteenth century, Aristotle still dominates social and political thinking. The best proof of the slowness of the evolution of political science is the fact that again and again one must perforce go back to re-examine Plato's *Republic* and Aristotle's *Politics* in connection with almost every controversial constitutional and political issue.

Thus the domination of economic and political life by the class struggle between the noblity, the middle class and the proletariat reflected the basic ideas of Plato and Aristotle, which were translated by

Karl Marx and his disciples into a utilitarian language more comprehensible to the modern world.

Maciver reminds us that even in our own times the Aristotelian principle of community expansion still applies. Cities and villages had once been independent communities, which had later lost their autonomy to the national community. In the course of the evolution of society the community has constantly grown in size. But the larger group cannot take shape until the smaller one has been completed. Thus the town community could not replace the family; it could only give it substance – just as the national community did not take the place of the town community, but defined it more clearly. Even today many of the elements in Maciver's analysis are true, but some have been overtaken by technological and political developments. However, it raises the whole question as to whether Aristotle's doctrine of the struggle between rich and poor can be considered valid for our contemporary concept of community. For if the possibility, indeed the vital necessity for democratic controls in view of the evolution of various new forms of community, is taken into account, Maciver's views need to be modified. This was proved not only by the League of Nations after the end of the First World War, but is proved even more clearly now by the progressive decline in the authority of the United Nations, which over twenty years ago held out real hope that the ideal of a 'family of nations' would become a reality. Many of the disasters which mankind suffered and is still suffering spring from the repugnance which nations feel against absorption into a higher unit. Until the industrial revolution the slow, unsystematic growth of society meant that the gradual integration of small communities into larger ones passed more or less unnoticed.

But the development of modern mass media and economic planning makes it highly unlikely that there can again be the sort of crisis-free evolution which comes from the spontaneous co-operation of all social groups.

In Europe it was the national, not the international community which first benefited from modern developments in all spheres. For the mark of the national state is not merely its dislike of international co-operation. By pursuing a policy of centralization within its own national frontiers it always attempted to destroy the regions from which it had originally sprung and by tightening up internal order – supported by an ever-mounting wave of nationalist sentiment – it sought to make 'technocratic' use of the new developments. By its misuse of the state, however, nationalism impedes the development of the larger community and Limanowski believed it would be possible to effect a synthesis between nationalism and internationalism. The League of

Nations was the result of this belief. Its collapse showed that such a synthesis was not feasible.

Yet after the Second World War the United Nations Organization was founded on the same beliefs, although the Great Power predominance in the Security Council was already an indication that the evolution of the continental state was under way. The all-important question now is how and when this will happen. In Europe, for example, developments in the last twenty years point to a dwindling of enthusiasm for pan-European ideas and a resurgence of narrow-minded nationalism. This is equally true of eastern Europe, where countries like Poland, Hungary, Romania and Czechoslovakia stubbornly seek to preserve their national identity against the Russian continental state. It is certain, however, that even if medium and smaller national states adopt common consultative assemblies and bureaucratic institutions they cannot possibly succeed in founding continental states to compare with the existing giants – the United States of America, the Soviet Union and Red China. On the contrary, if these institutions and offices cease to develop along these lines there is a real danger that the very idea and the formative power of international communities will at least be weakened, if not destroyed by the fact of traditional racial policy. For that nations would need to have a feeling of common statehood. But are national states yet mature enough to instil such a supra-national consciousness in their populations?

Yet even if such a sentiment is engendered and the territorial question is solved in accordance with the dictates of pluralistic society, this is still no answer to the crucial question, namely whether in the continental states – which we must regard as the actual stones from which to build the world state – the democratic way of life and the democratic form of government can continue to exist as a reality, or develop in the East. Although we have already drawn attention to the grave threat to democracy posed by large-scale society, we must never forget that there are ways and means of meeting these dangers. Mass society, as exemplified for instance in the modern American megalopolis, London, Tokyo or Calcutta does not confirm the Cassandra-like cry of Nietzsche, Spengler or Orwell about the supine herd which needs the Superhuman Leader or the Big Brother. In large-scale society successful democracy is simply a matter of having the courage to break free from the limitations which Aristotle placed on politics in order to break new ground and pioneer new paths.

Geiger is right when he writes:

'Recent critics of the state of contemporary politics see indifference and passivity on the part of citizens as the greatest danger. Democracy needs the citizen's participation in the business of politics, otherwise the state merely becomes the prey of confidence tricksters with a lust for power. In this connection people are fond of pointing out that fascist dictators have come to power not so much as a result of the active zeal of their adherents as of the political lethargy and stupidity of the middle class. Democracy's salvation depends on the citizen taking an active part in politics.'[1]

This apathy is especially dangerous in the Welfare State, where the immemorial struggle between rich and poor – which neither Plato nor Aristotle could imagine would ever be absent from politics – has been abolished.

The question now confronting modern democracy is how twentieth-century man, who is provided with adequate food, housing, clothing, leisure, transport and health services by the state, is to be kept interested in his civic responsibilities – a question beyond the imagination of the ancients. One must agree with Geiger, who rejects the doctrine of the herd-like nature of mass man and speaks instead of man's 'unique mixture of intrinsic indolence and emotional revolt'.[2]

Ortega y Gasset holds the same view. Modern mass man, he maintains, has the mentality of a spoiled child, who is ignorant of the limitations to which his will is subject and believes he has no obligations and who yet wants to have a finger in every pie.

But it is mass man's intensive interest in social and cultural life which is the real hope of democracy. This is no way contradicted by Erich Fromm's theory of the 'fear of freedom' which always drives the unimportant elements in society to run away from or rebuff the giants.

Even if one agrees with Riesmany[3] that a sense of loneliness, insecurity and helplessness drives mass man to despair and that he feels he has become a mere cog in a machine, this still does not mean that his only solution must be to seek refuge in dictatorship. Victory of authoritarianism's many variants will be possible when democracy ceases to withdraw into itself and, instead, takes the offensive and sets out to put into practice the ideals which have inspired all those who fought for the cause of liberty in the past few centuries. Democracy will triumph over the forces of technocratic and bureaucratic nihilism if it can fill men with the belief in truth and liberty as a means of ennobling the human soul and realizing its potential. In practice this means that the future of democracy depends on the further evolution of the humanitarian forms of individualism. The triumph of liberty is

---

[1] Theodor Geiger, *Arbeiten zur Soziologie*, Neuwied, Berlin 1962, p. 180.
[2] Ibid., p. 181.        [3] Riesmany, op. cit.

only possible if the democratic state concerns itself not merely with satisfying the wants of the animal side of human nature but fosters man's higher development by encouraging education and culture. Moreover, the right to vote and civil liberties must not only be consolidated and maintained but refined and extended. Forms of living must be discovered which will liberate man from his sense of loneliness and insecurity. He must be offered alternatives – a hand in shaping the economy and a voice in deciding policy.

# BIBLIOGRAPHY

## PART I

Berlin Documents Centre, Main Archives of the National Socialist Party, Munich, Ordner 106.

Case No. 5, Military Tribunal, U.S.A. (Friedrich Flick) p. 4005.

*Das Braune Netz*, Paris 1935.

*Deutschland und der Dawes-Plan*, Report of the Generalagent, Berlin 1926.

*Documents on German Foreign Policy 1918–45*, Series D, Vol. II, London 1950, 'Germany and Czechoslovakia'; No. 23; No. 47; No. 53; No. 54; No. 59; No. 60; No. 63; No. 107; No. 109; No. 482.

*Economic Development in South Eastern Europe*, published by the Organization for Political and Economic Planning, 1945.

Extract from the proceedings against the main war criminals before the International Military Tribunal, November 14, 1945–October 1, 1946, Nuremberg 1948.

Federal German Archives P 135/6266; R 43/12682.

International Military Tribunal, Vol. 16.

International Military Tribunal, Nuremberg 1947, Vols. 25, 26, 36.

Minutes of the Constitutional Committee of the Austrian Reichstag 1848–1849, Ed. Anton Springer, Leipzig 1885.

Minutes of the Görlitz Congress of the German Social Democratic Party, Berlin 1921.

Nuremberg Documents N.O. 765, Office of the Chief Counsel for War Crimes; N.O. 772; 837–PS; 1340; N.O. 1783, Report on the third session of the Germanic Arbeitsgemeinschaft of January 12, 1943; 2740, Analysis of the documents by the prosecution March 28, 1947; 3258–PS; 3401–PS on the Nazi Auslandsorganisation.

Proceedings of the Weizsäcker Trial. *Documents on German Foreign Policy 1918–45*, Series D, Vol. II, London 1950.

Statistics of the German Reich, Vol. 232.

*Statistical Yearbook* of the Czechoslovak Republic, published by the State Statistical Office, Prague 1938.

*Statistical Yearbook* for the German Reich, Berlin 1926.

*Yearbook* of the Auslandsorganisation of the National Socialist Party.

## PART II

Acton-Dalberg, Lord, *Essays on Freedom and Power*, Boston, Mass., 1949.

Ahlers, Johannes, *Polen, Volk, Staat, Kultur, Politik und Wirtschaft*, Berlin 1935.

Akademie für die Rechte der Völker, *Der Kampf um die Völkerordnung*, Berlin 1939.

Albertini, Rudolf von, 'Zur Beurteilung der Volksfront in Frankreich 1934–1938', in: *Vierteljahrshefte für Zeitgeschichte*, Vol. 7, Stuttgart 1959.

Allport, Gordon W., *Treibjagd auf Sündenböcke*, Berlin, Bad Nauheim 1951.

Anschütz, G., *Die Verfassung des Deutschen Reiches vom 11. August 1919*, Berlin 1933.

Aquinas, Thomas, *Summa Theologica*, Salzburg 1933–39.

Arendt, Hannah, *Elemente und Ursprünge totalitärer Herrschaft*, Frankfurt 1955.

—, *Fragwürdige Traditionsbestände im politischen Denken der Gegenwart*, Frankfurt 1957.

—, 'What was Authority', in: *Authority*, Ed. Carl J. Friedrich, Cambridge, Mass., 1958.

Aretin, Karl Othmar Freiherr von, *Die Konfessionen als politische Kräfte im Ausgang des alten Reiches*, Baden-Baden 1957.

Aristotle, *Politics*, translated by Ernest Barker, Oxford 1952.

Asch, Bruno, 'Der Kampf gegen die Arbeitslosigkeit', in: *Die Gesellschaft*, Vol. II, Berlin 1926.

Augustine, Saint, *De Civitate Dei*, Kempten, Munich 1911–16.

Baernreither, Joseph M., *Fragmente eines politischen Tagebuches*, Ed. Prof. Joseph Redlich, Berlin 1928.

Bahr, Hermann, *Dalmatinische Reise*, Berlin 1909.

—, *Tagebuch*, Berlin 1909.

Bardolff, Carl von, *Soldat im alten Österreich*, Jena 1938.

Barker, Ernest, *Reflections on Government*, Oxford 1945.

—, *Greek Political Theory*, London 1952.

—, *The Politics of Aristotle*, Oxford 1952.

Basch, Antonin, *The Danube Basin and the German Economic Sphere*, London 1944.

Bausch, Hans, *Der Rundfunk im politischen Kräftespiel der Weimarer Republik 1923–1933*, Tübingen 1956.

Beckerath, Herbert von, *Das Reparationsproblem*, publications of the Friedrich-List-Gesellschaft, Berlin 1929, Vol. I.

Beckerath, Erwin von, *Wesen und Werden des faschistischen Staates*, Berlin 1927.

Beer and Ulam, *Patterns of Governments, The Major Political Systems of Europe*, New York 1958.

Benedikt, Heinrich, Ed., *Geschichte der Republik Österreich*, Munich 1954.

Beneš, Eduard, *Le Problem autrichien et la question tchèque*, Paris 1908.

—, *Der Aufstand der Nationen*, Berlin 1928.

—, *Democracy Today and Tomorrow*, London 1939.

—, *Demokratie Heute und Morgen*, Zürich, New York 1944.

—, *Memoirs*, London 1954.

Bergsträsser, Ludwig, *Geschichte der Politischen Parteien in Deutschland*, Munich 1960.

Berlau, J., *The German Social Democratic Party 1914–1921*, New York 1949.

Bernstein, Eduard, *Sozialismus und Demokratie in der grossen englischen Revolution*, Stuttgart 1919.

Beust, Count, *Aus Drei Viertel Jahrhunderten*, Stuttgart 1887.

Bierschenk, Theodor, *Die Deutsche Volksgruppe in Polen 1934–1939*, Kitzingen am Main 1954, published as Supplement X to the Albertus University Yearbook, Königsberg.

Boicher, M., *Le sentiment national en Allemagne, 1750–1815*, Paris 1948.

Bracher, K. D., *Die Auflösung der Weimarer Republik*, Villingen 1960. Stuttgart, Düsseldorf 1955.

Bracher, K. D., W. Sauer, G. Schulz, *Die nationalsozialistische Machtergreifung*, Cologne, Opladen 1962.

Brandeis, Louis D., *Essays*, Ed. Felix Frankfurter, New Haven Yale 1932.

Brandenburg, Erich, *Die Ursachen des Weltkrieges*, Leipzig 1925.

Braun, Otto, *Von Weimar zu Hitler*, New York 1940.

Brecht, Arnold, *Vorspiel zum Schweigen*, Vienna 1948.

Brockelmann, Carl, *Geschichte der islamischen Völker und Staaten*, Oldenburg, Munich, Berlin 1943.

Broszat, Martin, *Der Nationalsozialismus, Weltanschauung, Programm und Wirklichkeit*, Stuttgart 1960.

—, 'Das Sudetendeutsche Freikorps', in: *Vierteljahrshefte für Zeitgeschichte*, Vol. 9, Stuttgart 1961.

Brügel, J. W., *Ludwig Czech, Arbeiterführer und Staatsmann*, Vienna 1960.

Brüning, Heinrich, 'Ein Brief', in: *Deutsche Rundschau*, Ed. Rudolf Pechel, Berlin, 70th Year, Vol. 7, July 1947.

Bryce, James, *Modern Democracies*, 2 vols., London 1923.

Buchheim, Hans, *Totalitäre Herrschaft*, Munich 1962.

Bullock, Allan, *Hitler, A Study in Tyranny*, London 1950.

Burckhardt, Jacob, *Weltgeschichtliche Betrachtungen*, Berlin, Stuttgart 1910.

Bussenius-Hubatsch, *Urkunden und Akten zur Geschichte der preussischen Verwaltung in Südpreussen und Neuostpreussen*, Frankfurt am Main, Bonn 1961.

Butler, J. R. M., *Lord Lothian, (Philip Kerr) 1882–1940*, London, New York 1960.

Butler, Nicolas Murray, *Liberty, Equality, Fraternity*. Address delivered in the Parish Memorial Art Museum, Southampton, Long Island, 31.8.1941.

Cahen, Claude, 'The Body Politic', in: *Unity and Variety in Muslim Civilisation*, Ed. G. E. von Grünebaum, Chicago 1955.

Caspar, Gustav Adolf, 'Die Deutsche Sozialdemokratie und die Entstehung der Reichswehr 1918–1921', *Wehrwissenschaftliche Rundschau*, Frankfurt am Main, April 1958.

—, 'Die Sozialdemokratische Partei und das deutsche Wehrproblem in den Jahren der Weimarer Republik', Supplementary Vol. XI der *Wehrwissenschaftlichen Rundschau*, Frankfurt am Main, October 1959.

Carr, E. H., *The Future of Nations*, London 1941.

—, *International Relations between the Two World Wars 1919–1933*, London 1963.

—, *German–Soviet Relations 1919–1939*, Oxford 1952.

Catlin, G. E. G., Systematic Politics: *Elementa Politica et Sociologica*, Toronto 1962.

Charmatz, Richard, *Österreichs innere Geschichte von 1848 bis 1907*, Part I, Leipzig 1905.

—, *Vom Kaiserreich zur Republik*, Vienna 1947.

—, 'Ein konservativer Sozialpolitiker. Karl Freiherr von Vogelsang', in: *Lebensbilder aus der Geschichte Österreichs*, Vienna 1947.

Churchill, W., *The Second World War*, Vol. I, London, Toronto, Melbourne, Sydney, Wellington 1948.

Cicero, *De re publica*, Zürich 1955.

—, *De Legibus*, Berlin–Schöneberg 1907–10.

Clark, R. T., *The Fall of the German Republic*, London 1935.

Cobban, Alfred, *National Self-determination*, Chicago 1944.

—, *Dictatorship*, London 1939.

Cole, G. D. H., *The Second International*, Part II, London 1956.

Collingwood, R. G., *The New Leviathan*, Oxford 1942.

Cooley, Charles Horton, *Social Organization*, New York 1912.

Corwin, E., *Twilight of the Supreme Court*, New Haven 1934.

Craig, Gordon A., *The Politics of the Prussian Army*, Oxford 1955.


Dahrendorf, R., *Gesellschaft und Freiheit*, Munich 1961.

Daim, Wilfried, *Der Mann, der Hitler die Ideen gab*, Munich 1958.

Dawson, W. H., *Germany and the Germans*, Vol. I, London 1896.

Decker, G., *Das Selbstbestimmungsrecht der Nationen*, Göttingen 1955.

Deutsch, Julius, 'Zwischen Faschismus und Demokratie', in: *Neue Blätter für den Sozialismus*, First Year, Vol. 5, Potsdam, May 1930.

—, *Der Bürgerkrieg in Österreich*, Karlsbad 1934.

—, *Ein weiter Weg*, Zürich, Leipzig, Vienna 1960.

Dicey, A. V., *Law of the Constitution*, London 1962.

—, *Lectures on the Relation between Law and Public Opinion in England during the Nineteenth Century*, London 1914.

Dmowski, Roman, *Mysli Nowoczesnege Polaka* (Thoughts of a modern Pole), London 1903.

Dulles, Allen, *Germany's Underground*, New York 1947.

—, *The Craft of Intelligence*, New York 1963.


Ebert, Friedrich, *Schriften, Aufzeichnungen, Reden*, Dresden 1926.

Eder, Karl, *Der Liberalismus in Altösterreich*, Vienna, Munich 1955.

Ehrich, Emil, *Die Auslandsorganisation der NSDAP*, Berlin 1937.

Eichstädt, Ulrich, *Von Dollfuss zu Hitler*, Wiesbaden 1955.

Eisenmann, Louis, *Le Compromis Austro–Hongrois de 1867*, Paris 1904.

Emerson, Rupert, *From Empire to Nation. The Rise to Self-Assertion of Asia and Africa*, Cambridge, Mass., 1960.

Engels, Friedrich, *Die Lage der arbeitenden Klasse in England*, Stuttgart 1921.

Ensslin, Wilhelm, 'The Emperor and the Imperial Administration', in: *Byzantium*, Ed. H. Baines and H. Moss, Oxford 1948.

d'Entrèves, A. P., *Natural Law*, London 1951.

Eötvös, Baron, *Der Einfluss der herrschenden Ideen des 19. Jahrhunderts auf den Staat*, Vol. II, Leipzig 1854.

Erbe, René, *Die nationalsozialistische Wirtschaftspolitik 1933–1939 im Lichte der modernen Theorie*, Zürich 1958.

Ermacora, F., *Der Verfassungsgerichtshof*, Graz, Vienna, Cologne 1956.

Eschenburg, Theodor, *Der Beamte in Partei und Parlament*, Frankfurt 1952.

—, *Die improvisierte Demokratie der Weimarer Republik*, Laupheim 1955.

—, 'Tocquevilles Wirkung in Deutschland', in: Alexis de Tocqueville, *Werke und Briefe*, Vol. I, Stuttgart 1959.

Esmein, A., *Eléments du Droit Constitutionnel Français et Comparé*, Paris 1927.

Eyck, Erich, *A History of the Weimar Republic*, London 1962.

Fabricius, Hans, *Geschichte der Nationalsozialistischen Bewegung*, Berlin 1936.

Faul, E., *Der moderne Macchiavellismus*, Cologne 1961.

Federal German Supreme Court, 'Statusbericht', in: *Jahrbuch des Öffentlichen Rechts*, N. F. (1957), Vol. 6.

Fichte, Johann Gottlieb, *Reden an die deutsche Nation*, Hamburg 1955.

Fisher, H. A. L., *Bonapartism*, London 1957.

Flechtheim, Ossip K., *Die KPD in der Weimarer Republik*, Offenbach 1948.

Foerster, Wolfgang, *Generaloberst Ludwig Beck*, Munich 1952.

Forst de Battaglia, *Zwischeneuropa*, Frankfurt 1954.

Forsthoff, Ernst, *Der totale Staat*, Hamburg 1933.

Fraenkel, Ernst, *The Dual State*, New York, London, Toronto 1941.

Frank, Hans, *Im Angesicht des Galgens*, Munich–Gräfeling 1953.

Franz, Georg, *Liberalismus. Die deutschliberale Bewegung in der habsburgischen Monarchie*, Munich 1955.

Frauendorfer, Max, *Der ständische Gedanke im Nationalsozialismus*, Munich 1933.

Frick, Wilhelm, *Die Nationalsozialisten im Reichstag 1924–1931*, Munich 1932.

Friedjung, Heinrich, *Der Kampf um die Vorherrschaft in Deutschland 1859–1866*, Vol. 2, Stuttgart 1900.

Friedrich, Carl J., *Authority*, Cambridge 1958.

—, *Constitutional Government and Politics*, New York, London 1937; revised edition published under the title of *Constitutional Government and Democracy*, Boston, New York, Chicago, London 1950.

—, *Foreign Policy in the Making*, New York 1938.

—, *The New Belief in the Common Man*, Brattleboro 1942.

—, *Totalitäre Diktatur*, Stuttgart 1951.

—, *Der Verfassungsstaat der Neuzeit*, Berlin, Göttingen, Heidelberg 1953.

—, *Die Philosophie des Rechts in historischer Perspektive*, Berlin, Göttingen, Heidelberg 1955.

—, *Demokratie als Herrschafts- und Lebensform*, Heidelberg 1959.

Friesenhahn, Ernst, 'Die Staatsgerichtsbarkeit des Deutschen Reiches', in: Anschütz-Thoma, *Handbuch des Deutschen Staatsrechts*, Tübingen 1932, Vol. II.

—, 'Die Verfassungsgerichtsbarkeit in der Bundesrepublik Deutschland', in: *Verfassungsgerichtsbarkeit in der Gegenwart*, Ed. H. Mosler, Cologne, Baden-Baden 1962.

Fromm, Erich, *Die Furcht vor der Freiheit*, Zürich 1945.

Gathorne-Hardy, G. M., *A Short History of International Affairs 1920–1939*, London, New York, Toronto 1960.

Geiger, Theodor, *Die soziale Schichtung des deutschen Volkes*, Stuttgart 1932.

—, *Arbeiten zur Soziologie*, Neuwied/Rh., Berlin–Spandau 1962.

Gessl, Josef, *Seipels Reden*, Vienna 1926.

Gessler, Otto, *Reichswehrpolitik in der Weimarer Zeit*, Stuttgart 1958.

Gierke, Otto von, *Das deutsche Genossenschaftsrecht*, Berlin 1863–1913, see in particular Vol. III (1881): Die Staats- und Korporationslehre des Altertums und des Mittelalters und ihre Aufnahme in Deutschland.

Gilbert, Martin and Gott, Richard, *The Appeasers*, London 1963.

Gilson, Etienne, *Introduction à l'étude de Saint Augustin*, Paris 1929.

Glaise-Horstenau, Edmund von, *Die Katastrophe*, Zürich, Leipzig, Vienna 1928.

Glum, Friedrich, *Das parlamentarische Regierungssystem in Deutschland, Grossbritannien und Frankreich*, Berlin 1950.

Goebbels, Joseph, *Wesen und Gestalt des Nationalsozialismus*, Berlin 1934.

—, *Vom Kaiserhof zur Reichskanzlei, Eine historische Darstellung in Tagebuchblättern*, Munich 1934.

Goguel, François, *France under the Fourth Republic*, Ithaca 1951.

Goldinger, Walter, 'Der geschichtliche Ablauf der freignisse in Österreich 1918 bis 1945', in: *Geschichte der Republik Österreich*, Ed. H. Benedikt, Munich 1954.

—, *Geschichte der Republik Österreich*, Vienna 1962.

Gough, J. W., *John Locke's Political Philosophy*, Oxford 1956.

Graham, Malbone W., *New Governments of Eastern Europe*, London 1929.

—, 'Polish Politics, 1918–1938', in: Bernadotte E. Schmitt, *Poland*, Berkeley, Los Angeles 1945.

—, 'Parties and Politics', in: *Czechoslovakia*, Ed. R. J. Kerner, Berkeley, Los Angeles 1949.

Gruchmann, Lothar, *Nationalsozialistische Grossraumordnung*, Stuttgart 1962.

Grunberger, Bela, 'Der Antisemit und der Ödipuskomplex', in: *Psyche*, Stuttgart, August 1962.

Grzezinski, Albert, *Im Kampf um die Deutsche Republik*, Bundesarchiv (typewritten manuscript in German of: La Tragi-Comédie de la République Allemande, Paris 1934).

Gumbel, Emil J., *Verschwörer*, Vienna 1924.

Gumbel, Emil J., *Denkschrift des Reichsjustizministers zu 'Vier Jahre Politischer Mord'*, Berlin 1924.

—, 'Landesverratsstatistik', in: *Die Menschenrechte*, Organ of the German League for Human Rights, Year III, No. 4, Berlin, 15.5.1928.

—, *Vom Fememord zur Reichskanzlei*, Heidelberg 1962.

Hadamovsky, Eugen, *Der Rundfunk im Dienste der Volksführung*, Leipzig 1934.

Haffner, Sebastian, *Germany: Jekyll and Hyde*, London 1940.

Hagen, Walter, *Die geheime Front*, Stuttgart 1950.

Hahn, Georg, *Grundfragen europäischer Ordnung*, Berlin, Vienna 1939.

Hallgarten, G. Wolfgang, *Hitler, Reichswehr und Industrie*, Frankfurt am Main 1955.

Hantsch, Hugo, *Die Nationalitätenfrage im alten Österreich*, Vienna 1953.

Hartenstein, Wolfgang, 'Die Anfänge der Deutschen Volkspartei (1918–1920)', in: *Beiträge zur Geschichte des Parlamentarismus und der politischen Parteien*, Vol. 22, Düsseldorf 1962.

Hartung, F., 'Studien zur Geschichte der Preussischen Verwaltung', in: *Staatsbildende Kräfte der Neuzeit*, Berlin 1961.

Hassinger, Hugo, *Die Tschechoslowakei*, Vienna, Leipzig, Munich 1925.

—, Österreichs Wesen und Schicksal', in: *Wiener Geographische Studien*, No. 20, 1949.

Haushofer, Karl, *Der Nationalsozialistische Gedanke in der Welt*, Munich 1933.

—, Geopolitischer Neujahrs-Ausblick 1940, in: *Zeitschrift für Geopolitik*, XVII Year, 1st half volume 1940.

Hayes, C. J., *The Historical Evolution of Modern Nationalism*, New York 1931.

—, 'The Novelty of Totalitarianism in the History of Western Civilization', in: *Symposium on the Totalitarian State*, Philadelphia 1940.

Heidegger, Hermann, *Die deutsche Sozialdemokratie und der nationale Staat 1870 bis 1920*, Göttingen 1956.

Heiden, Konrad, *Adolf Hitler*, 2 vols., Zürich 1937.

Heller, Hermann, *Rechsstaat oder Diktatur*, Tübingen 1930.

Henderson, Nevile, *Failure of a Mission*, London 1941.

Herder, J. G., *Ideen zur Philosophie der Geschichte der Menschheit*, Vol. 4, Karlsruhe 1790–94.

Hermens, F. A., *Demokratie oder Anarchie*, Frankfurt am Main 1951.

—, *Parteien, Volk und Staat*, Karlsruhe 1960.

—, *Verfassungslehre*, Frankfurt am Main, Bonn 1964.

Herrfahrdt, Heinrich, 'Die Kabinettsbildung nach der Weimarer Verfassung unter dem Einfluss der politischen Praxis', in: *Öffentlichrechtliche Abhandlungen*, Ed. Triepel, Kaufmann, Smend, Berlin 1927.

Hertz, Frederick, *The Economic Problem of the Danubian States*, London 1947.

Herweg (E. Diehl), *Georg Schönerer und die Entwicklung des Alldeutschtums in der Ostmark*, Vienna 1921–35.

Heuss, Theodor, *Friedrich Naumann*, Stuttgart 1937.

Himmler, Heinrich, *Die Schutzstaffel*, Munich 1937.

Hippel, Ernst von, 'Das Richterliche Prüfungsrecht', in: *Handbuch des Deutschen Staatsrechts*, Vol. II, pp. 49 ff., Tübingen 1932.

Hirsch, Julius, *Die deutsche Währungsfrage*, Jena 1924.

Hitler, Adolf, *Mein Kampf*, Munich 1933.

Hobbes, Thomas, *The Leviathan*, with an Introduction by Michael Oakeshott, Oxford 1962.

Hodža, Milan, *Federation in Central Europe*, London, New York, Melbourne 1942.

Hoetzel, Jiri, *Ceskoslovenské Správní Právo*, Prague 1934.

Högner, Wilhelm, *Die verratene Republik*, Munich 1958.

Höltje, Christian, *Die Weimarer Republik und das Ostlocarno-Problem 1919–1934*, Würzburg 1958.

Hornung, Otto, *Neu Österreich*, Zürich 1890.

Horthy, Miklos, *Ein Leben für Ungarn*, Bonn 1933.

Horwill, George, *Proportional Representation*, London 1925.

Hubatsch, W., *Das Zeitalter des Absolutismus*, Brunswick 1962.

Hume, David, *Essays and Treatises on Several Subjects*, Edinburgh 1793.


Jaksch, Wenzel, *Europas Weg nach Potsdam*, Stuttgart 1958.

Jaspers, Karl, *Die geistige Situation unserer Zeit*, Berlin, Leipzig 1931.

Jászi, Oskar, *The Dissolution of the Habsburg Monarchy*, Chicago 1961.

Jellinek, Walter, *Verwaltungsrecht*, Berlin 1928.

Jones, William T., *Masters of Political Thought*, Vol. 2, London 1947.

Jong, Louis de, *Die deutsche Fünfte Kolonne im Zweiten Weltkrieg*, Stuttgart 1959.

—, 'The Organisation and Efficiency of the German Fifth Column', in: *The Third Reich*, London 1955.

Jouvenel, Bertrand de, *Sovereignty*, Cambridge 1957.

Jung, C. G., *Integration of the Personality*, London 1940.

—, *Psychologie und Religion*, Zürich 1947.


Kann, Robert A., *The Multinational Empire*, 2 vols., New York 1950.

Kaufmann, Erich, *Autorität und Freiheit*, Göttingen 1960.

Kavka, F., *An Outline of Czechoslovak History*, Prague 1960.

Keller, H., *Volksgemeinschaft und Völkerfriede*, Berlin 1935.

Kelsen, Hans, *Vom Wesen und Wert der Demokratie*, Tübingen 1920.

Kern, F., *Gottesgnadentum und Widerstandsrecht im früheren Mittelalter*, 2nd Edition, Münster, Cologne 1934.

Kersten, Felix, *Totenkopf und Treue*, Hamburg 1952.

Keynes, J. M., *The Economic Consequences of the Peace*, London 1920.

—, *Ein Traktat über Währungsreform*, Munich, Leipzig 1924 (*A Tract on Monetary Reform*, London, New York 1923).

—, *Vom Gelde*, Berlin 1955 (*A Treatise on Money*, London 1930).

Kirschbaum, S. Joseph M., *Slovakia, Nation at the Cross Roads of Central Europe*, New York 1960.

Kiszling, Rudolf, *Die Kroaten*, Graz, Cologne 1956.

Klopp, Wiard (Ed.), *Die sozialen Lehren des Freiherrn Karl von Vogelsang*, St. Pölten 1894.

Kluckhohn, Paul (Ed.), *Die Idee des Volkes im Schrifttum der deutschen Bewegung von Möser und Herder bis Grimm*, Berlin 1934.

Kluke, Paul, 'Nationalsozialistische Europaideologie', in, *Vierteljahrshefte für Zeitgeschichte*, Vol. 3, Stuttgart 1955.

Knabe, Lotte, 'Die Gelasianische Zweigestaltentheorie bis zum Ende des Investiturstreites', in: *Historische Studien*, Berlin 1935.

Knoll, August M., 'Karl von Vogelsang und der Ständegedanke', in: *Die soziale Frage und der Katholizismus*, published at the Görresgesellschaft, Paderborn 1931.

Koellreuter, Otto, *Der Sinn der Reichstagswahlen vom 14. September 1930 und die Aufgaben der deutschen Staatslehre*, Tübingen 1930.

Kogon, Eugen, *Der SS-Staat*, Düsseldorf 1946.

Köhler, B., *Die zweite Arbeitsschlacht*, Munich 1936.

Kohn, Hans, *Die Idee des Nationalismus*, Frankfurt am Main 1962.

Krasinski, Valerian, *Panslavism and Germanism*, Edinburgh 1849.

Kraus, Herbert, *Crisis of German Democracy*, Princeton 1932.

Krockow, Christian Count von, *Die Entscheidung*, Stuttgart 1958.

Kuczynski, Jürgen, *Studien zur Geschichte des staatsmonopolistischen Kapitalismus in Deutschland 1918–1945*, Berlin 1963.

Kühn, Johannes, *Toleranz und Offenbarung*, Leipzig 1923.


Lasswell, Harold D., *Psychopathology and Politics*, Chicago 1930.

—, 'Strategy of Revolutionary and War Propaganda', in: *Public Opinion and World Politics*, New York, London 1943.

—, 'World Politics and Personal Insecurity', in: *A Study of Power*, Glencoe, Illinois 1950.

—, 'Politics: Who Gets What, When, How', in: *The Political Writings*, Glencoe, Illinois 1951.

—, The World Revolutionary Situation', in: *Totalitanism*, Ed. Carl J. Friedrich, Cambridge, Mass. 1954.

—, *Politik und Moral*, Stuttgart, Düsseldorf 1957.

Leber, Julius, *Ein Mann geht seinen Weg, Schriften, Reden, Briefe*, edited by his friends, Berlin, Frankfurt am Main 1952.

Lederer, Ivo J., *Jugoslavia at the Paris Peace Conference*, New Haven 1963.

Leibholz, G., *Die Auflösung der liberalen Demokratie und das autoritäre Staatsbild*, Munich, Leipzig 1933.

—, *Strukturprobleme der modernen Demokratie*, Karlsruhe 1958.

Lelewel, Joachim, *Betrachtungen über den politischen Zustand des ehemaligen Polen*, Brussels, Leipzig 1845.

Lemberg, Eugen, *Geschichte des Nationalismus in Europa*, Stuttgart 1950.

Liebe, Werner, 'Die Deutschnationale Volkspartei 1918–1924', in: *Beiträge zur Geschichte des Parlamentarismus und der politischen Parteien*, Vol. 8, Düsseldorf 1956.

Liebknecht, W., *Robert Blum und seine Zeit*, Nuremberg 1882.

Limanowski, *Socialism, Democracy, Patriotism,* published by the Polish Socialist Party, Josef Kaniowski, 67 Colworth Road, Leytonstone, London E. 1902.

Lindsay, A. D., *Christianity and Economics,* London 1933.

—, *The Modern Democratic State,* New York 1962.

—, *The Essentials of Democracy,* Oxford 1940.

Lloyd George, David, *The Truth about Reparations and War-Debts,* London 1932.

—, *The Truth about the Peace Treaties,* London 1938.

Locke, John, *Two Treatises of Civil Government,* London, New York 1955.

—, *Vier Briefe über die Toleranz (Epistola de Tolerantia,* Gouda 1689), Darmstadt 1963.

Loock, Hans-Dietrich, 'Zur "Grossgermanischen Politik" des Dritten Reiches', in: *Vierteljahrshefte für Zeitgeschichte,* Vol. 8, Stuttgart 1960.

Lowell, L. H., *The Government of England,* Vol. II, New York 1919.

—, *Public Opinion and Popular Government,* New York, London, Bombay, Calcutta, Madras 1919.

—, *Public Opinion in War and Peace,* Cambridge, Mass., 1926.

Löwenstein, Karl, 'Zur Soziologie der parlamentarischen Repräsentation in England nach der grossen Reform', in: *Archiv für Sozialwissenschaft und Politik,* Tübingen 1924.


Macartney, C. A., *National States and National Minorities,* London 1934.

Maček, Vladko, *In the Struggle for Freedom,* translated by E. and S. Gazi, New York 1957.

Maciver, R., *Community,* London 1928.

—, *The Web of Government,* New York 1947.

Maciver, R. M., and Charles H. Page, *Society,* London 1950.

Maine, Sir Henry, *Popular Government,* London 1909.

Mannheim, Karl, *Man and Society,* London 1940.

—, *Mensch und Gesellschaft im Zeitalter des Umbaus,* Darmstadt 1958.

—, *Diagnose unserer Zeit,* Zürich, Vienna, Constance 1951.

Markert, Werner (Ed.), *Ost-Europa-Handbuch,* 'Yugoslavia', Cologne, Graz 1954.

Marx-Engels, Works, Vols. 5 and 8, Berlin 1960.

Masaryk, T. G., *Das neue Europa,* Berlin 1922.

—, *The Making of a State,* London 1927.

—, *Die Weltrevolution,* Berlin 1925.

Mathiot, André, *The British Political System,* London 1958.

Matthias, Erich, and Morsey, Rudolf (Ed.), *Das Ende der Parteien 1933,* Düsseldorf 1960.

Mazzini, I., *Royalty and Republicanism in Italy,* London 1850.

McT. Kahin, George (Ed.), *Major Governments in Asia,* Cornell 1958.

Mehring, F., *Geschichte der deutschen Sozialdemokratie,* Part II, Berlin, 1960.

Meinecke, Friedrich, 'Liberalism and Nationality in Germany and Austria', in: *Cambridge Modern History,* Vol. IX, Cambridge 1909.

—, *Weltbürgertum und Nationalstaat,* 3rd Edition, Munich 1915.

Meinecke, Friedrich, *Die deutsche Katastrophe*, Wiesbaden 1946.

Merriam, Charles Edward, *The Making of Citizens, A Comparative Study of Civil Training*, Chicago 1931.

—, *The New Democracy and the New Despotism*, New York 1939.

—, *Political Power*, Glencoe, Illinois 1950.

Michels, Robert, *Zur Soziologie des Parteiwesens in der modernen Demokratie*, Leipzig 1925.

—, *Der Patriotismus*, Munich, Leipzig 1929.

Mill, J. S., *On Liberty*, Oxford 1948.

—, *Considerations on Representative Government*, London 1861.

Mitscherlich, Alexander, *Auf dem Weg zur vaterlosen Gesellschaft*, Munich 1963.

Möller van den Bruck, *Das Dritte Reich*, Hamburg 1931.

Mohler, Armin, *Die Konservative Revolution in Deutschland 1918–1932. Grundriss ihrer Weltanschauungen*, Stuttgart 1950.

Molisch, Paul (Ed.), *Geschichte der deutschnationalen Bewegung in Österreich*, Jena 1926.

Mommsen, Hans, *Die Sozialdemokratie und die Nationalitätenfrage im habsburgischen Vielvölkerstaat*, Vienna 1963.

Mommsen, W., *Max Weber und die deutsche Politik*, Tübingen 1959.

Montesquieu, *Vom Geist der Gesetze*, Tübingen 1951. (*De l'Esprit des lois*, Geneva 1748.)

Morrison, Herbert, *Government and Parliament*, London 1954.

Morstein Marx, Fritz (Ed.), 'Totalitarian Politics', in: *Symposium on the Totalitarian State*, Philadelphia 1940.

Mosler, H. (Ed.), *Verwaltungsgerichtsbarkeit in der Gegenwart*, Cologne, Berlin 1962.

Mosca, Gaetano, *The Ruling Class*, New York, Toronto, London 1939.

Münch, Hermann, *Böhmische Tragödie*, Brunswick, Berlin, Hamburg 1949.

Naphtali, Fritz, *Wirtschaftsdemokratie*, Berlin 1928.

Naumann, Friedrich, *Mitteleuropa*, Berlin 1915.

Neumann, Franz, *Behemoth, The Structure and Practice of National Socialism*, London 1942.

Neumann, Franz L., *Angst und Politik*, Tübingen 1954.

Neurohr, J., *Der Mythos vom Dritten Reich – Zur Geistesgeschichte des Nationalsozialismus*, Stuttgart 1957.

Newman, Karl J., 'Papst, Kaiser, Kalif und der Basileus', in: *Politische Vierteljahrsschrift*, Vol. I, Cologne and Opladen 1963.

—, 'Tyranny and Group Loyalties', in: *Philosophy*, Vol. 18, No. 70, London 1943.

—, 'Georg Simmel and Totalitarian Integration', in: *American Journal of Sociology*, Vols. L, VI, Chicago 1951.

—, 'Pakistan's Preventive Autocracy and its Causes', in: *Pacific Affairs*, Vol. XXXII, No. 1, New York, March 1959.

—, 'The New Monarchies of the Middle East', in: *Journal of International Affairs*, New York 1959, No. 2.

—, 'The Dyarchic Pattern of Government and Pakistan's Problems', in: *Political Science Quarterly*, New York, March 1960.

—, 'The Constitutional Evolution of Pakistan', in: *International Affairs*, London, July 1962.

—, *Die Entwicklungsdiktatur und der Verfassungsstaat*, Frankfurt am Main 1963.

Nicolson, Harold, *Peacemaking 1919*, London, New York 1933.

Niekisch, Ernst, 'Revolutionäre Politik', in: *Das Dritte Reich für Freiheit und Gemeinschaft*, III, Nuremberg 1926.

Nolte, Ernst, *Der Faschismus in seiner Epoche*, Munich 1963.

Obermann, Emil, *Soldaten, Bürger, Militaristen*, Stuttgart 1958.

Odegard, P., *Pressure Politics. The Story of the Anti-Saloon League*, New York 1928.

Ortega y Gasset, José, *The Revolt of the Masses*, London 1951.

Ostrogorski, M., *Democracy and the Organisation of Political Parties*, 2 vols., London 1902.

Paetel, Karl O., 'The Reign of the Black Order', in: *The Third Reich*, London 1955.

Pareto, V., *Mind and Society*, New York 1938.

Park, Robert E., *The Immigrant Press and its Control*, New York 1922.

—, and Herbert A. Miller, *Old-World Traits Transplanted*, New York, London 1921.

Picker, Henry, *Hitler's Tischgespräche im Führerhauptquartier 1941/42*, Bonn 1951.

Plato, *Republic*.

Pobjedonostsev, Konstantin, *Reflections of a Russian Statesman*, London 1898.

Pohle, Heinz, *Der Rundfunk als Instrument der Politik*, The History of German Radio from 1923/38, Hamburg 1955.

Popovici, A., *Die Vereinigten Staaten von Gross-Österreich*, Leipzig 1906.

Popper, Karl, *The Open Society and its Enemies*, London 1948.

Preuss, Hugo, *Das Deutsche Volk und die Politik*, Jena 1915.

—, *Um die Reichsverfassung von Weimar*, Berlin 1924.

Rabl, Kurt, *Staatsbürgerliche Loyalität im Nationalitätenstaat*, Munich 1959.

Radbruch, Gustav, 'Die politischen Parteien im System des deutschen Verfassungsrechts', in: *Handbuch des Deutschen Staatsrechts*, Ed. Anschütz and Thoma, Vol. I, Tübingen 1930.

Raschhofer, Hermann, *Die Sudetenfrage*, Munich 1953.

Rauchberg, H., *Bürgerkunde der tschechoslowakischen Republik*, Reichenberg 1925.

Rauschning, H., *Make and Break with the Nazis*, London 1941.

—, *Die Revolution des Nihilismus*. Zürich, New York 1938.

—, *Gespräche mit Hitler*, Zürich 1940.

Redlich, Josef, *Das österreichische Staats- und Reichsproblem*, Vol. I, Leipzig 1920.

—, *Kaiser Franz Joseph von Österreich*, a biography, Berlin 1928.

—, Diary, *Österreichs Schicksalsjahre 1908–1919*, Graz, Cologne 1953.

Renner, Karl (under the pseudonym of Rudolf Springer), *Der Kampf der österreichischen Nationen um den Staat*, Vienna, Leipzig 1902.

—, *Grundlagen und Entwicklungsziele der Österreich-Ungarischen Monarchie*, Vienna, Leipzig 1906.

—, *Österreich von der Ersten zur Zweiten Republik*, 2 vols., Vienna 1953.

Reimann, Gunter, *The Vampire Economy*, New York 1939.

Reitlinger, Gerald, *Die SS, Tragödie einer deutschen Epoche*, Vienna, Munich, Basle 1956.

Riesman, D., Denney, R., Glazer, N., *The Lonely Crowd*, New York 1954.

Rogers, Lindsey, *Crisis Government*, New York 1934.

Rose, W. J., 'Russian Poland in the 19th Century', in: *The Cambridge History of Poland from Augustus II to Pilsudski (1697–1935)*, Cambridge 1941.

Rosenberg, Alfred, *Der Deutsche ördensstaat*, Munich 1934.

Rosenberg, Arthur, *Entstehung und Geschichte der Weimarer Republik*, Ed. Kurt Kersten, Frankfurt am Main 1955.

Rosenstock, E., *Die europäischen Revolutionen*, Jena 1931.

Rosenthal, E. I. J., *Political Thought in Medieval Islam*, Cambridge 1958.

Roucek, Joseph, 'Minorities', in: *Poland*, Ed. Bernadotte E. Schmitt, Berkeley, Los Angeles 1945.

Rousseau, Jean Jacques, *Considérations sur le Gouvernement de Pologne*, 1772.

—, *Contrat Social ou Principes du droit politique*, Paris 1933.

Rowse, A. L., *All Souls and Appeasement*, London, New York 1961.

Royal Institute of International Affairs, Chatham House, *Report on South Eastern Europe*, Oxford 1939.

Ruggiero, Guido de, *Geschichte des Liberalismus in Europa*, Munich 1930.

Russell, Bertrand, *Power, a New Social Analogy*, London 1948.

—, *Authority and the Individual*, London 1949.

—, *The Impact of Science on Society*, London 1952.


Salomon, Ernst von, *Der Fragebogen*, Hamburg 1951.

Schacht, Hjalmar, *Das Ende der Reparationen*, Oldenburg 1931.

Schätzel, Walter, 'Entstehung und Verfassung der Polnischen Republik', *Jahrbuch des Öffentlichen Rechts der Gegenwart*, Vol. XII, Tübingen 1923/24.

Scheidemann, Philipp, *Memoiren eines Sozialdemokraten*, 2 vols., Dresden 1928.

Scheler, Max, *Krieg und Aufbau*, Leipzig 1916.

—, *Schriften zur Soziologie und Weltanschauungslehre*, Berne, Munich 1963.

Schellenberg, Walter, *Memoiren*, London 1956, Cologne 1959.

Schieder, Theodor, *Staat und Gesellschaft im Wandel unserer Zeit*, Munich 1958.

Schlesinger, R., *Central European Democracy and its Backgrounds*, London 1953.

Schmidtmayer, Alfred, *Geschichte der Sudetendeutschen*, Karlsbad, Leipzig 1936.

Schmitt, Carl, *Politische Theologie*, Munich 1922.

—, *Die geistesgeschichtliche Lage des heutigen Parlamentarismus*, Munich, Leipzig 1926.

—, *Der Begriff des Politischen*, Hamburg 1933.

—, *Der Leviathan in der Staatslehre des Thomas Hobbes*, Hamburg 1938.

—, *Völkerrechtliche Grossraumordnung*, Berlin, Vienna 1939.

—, *Positionen und Begriffe*, Berlin 1939.

—, *Verfassungsrechtliche Aufsätze*, Berlin 1958.

—, *Die Diktatur*, Munich, Leipzig 1928.

—, *Gespräche über die Macht und den Zugang zum Machthaber* (no date).

Schüddekopf, Otto-Ernst, *Das Heer und die Republik*, Hanover, Frankfurt am Main 1955.

—, *Linke Leute von Rechts*, Stuttgart 1960.

Schramm, Percy E., *Hitler als militärischer Führer*, Frankfurt am Main, Bonn 1962.

Schröder, Arno, *Hitler geht auf die Dörfer*, Detmold 1938.

Schulz, Gerhard, 'Der Begriff des Totalitarismus und der Nationalsozialismus', in: *Soziale Welt*, Vol. XII, Part 2, Göttingen 1961.

Schuschnigg, Kurt von, *Dreimal Österreich*, Vienna 1938.

Selznick, Philip, *The Organizational Weapon, A Study of Bolshevik Strategy and Tactics*, New York, Toronto, London 1952.

Seton-Watson, Hugh, *Eastern Europe between the Wars*, Cambridge 1962.

Seton-Watson, R. W., *Slovakia Then and Now*, London 1931.

—, *A History of the Czechs and Slovaks*, London, New York, Melbourne 1943.

—, *Masaryk in England*, Cambridge 1943.

Severing, Carl, *Mein Lebensweg*, Cologne 1950.

Sforza, Carlo, *Europe and the Europeans*, Sydney 1936.

Shepherd, Gordon, *Die österreichische Odyssee*, Vienna 1958.

—, *Engelbert Dollfuss*, Graz, Vienna, Cologne 1961.

Shirer, William L., *The Rise and Fall of the Third Reich*, New York, London 1960.

Sidgewick, H., *The Elements of Politics*, London, New York 1897.

Sieghart, Rudolf, *Die letzten Jahrzehnte einer Grossmacht*, Berlin 1932.

Silagi, Denis, *Ungarn und der geheime Mitarbeiterkreis Kaiser Leopolds II*, Munich 1960.

Simmel, Georg, *Soziologie*, Munich, Leipzig 1923.

Sington, Derrick, and Weidenfeld, Arthur, *The Goebbels Experiment*, London 1942.

Smend, Rudolf, Die Verschiebung der konstitutionellen Ordnung durch die Verhältniswahl, in: *Festgabe für Karl Bergbohm*, Bonn, 1919.

Sorokin, P., and Zimmermann, C. C., *Principles of Rural Urban Sociology*, New York 1928.

Soulier, A., *L'Instabilité Ministérielle sous la Troisième République (1871–1938)*, Paris 1939.

Spann, Othmar, *Der wahre Staat*, Jena 1931.

—, *Gesellschaftslehre*, Leipzig 1923.

Spengler, Oswald, *Untergang des Abendlandes – Umrisse einer Morphologie der Weltgeschichte*, 2 vols., 1st edition, Munich 1918.

—, *Preussentum und Sozialismus*, Munich 1924.

Spitmüller, Alexander, '. . . *und hat auch Ursach', es zu lieben*', Vienna 1955.

Springer, Anton, *Protokolle des Verfassungsausschusses im österreichischen Reichstage 1848–1849*, Leipzig 1885.

Stampfer, Friedrich, *Erfahrungen und Erkenntnisse*, Cologne 1957.

Steed, Henry Wickham, *The Habsburg Monarchy*, London, Edinburgh 1914.

Stern, Carola, *Ulbricht – eine politische Biographie*, Cologne, Berlin 1963.

Stratton, G. M., *Social Psychology of International Conduct*, New York 1924.

Strauss, Leo, *The Political Philosophy of Hobbes*, Öxford 1936.

Stresemann, Gustav, *Vermächtnis*, Ed. Henry Bernhard, Vols. I–III, Berlin 1932/33.

Szász, Zsombor de, *The Minorities in Rumanian Transylvania*, London 1933.


Tarn, W. W., *Alexander the Great and the Unity of Mankind*, London 1933. Proceedings of the British Academy, Vol. XIX.

Taylor, A. J. P., *The Habsburg Monarchy*, London 1941.

—, *The Origins of the Second World War*, London 1961.

Thoma, Richard, 'Das Reich als Demokratie', in: *Handbuch des deutschen Staatsrechts*, Ed. Anschütz and Thoma, Tübingen 1930.

—, Abhandlung über das richterliche Prüfungsrecht in der Weimarer Republik, in *Archiv des Öffentlichen Rechts*.

Thomas, Hugh, *The Spanish Civil War*, London 1961.

Tocqueville, Alexis de, *Democracy in America*, 2 vols., New York 1948.

—, 'L'ancien Régime et la Révolution', in; *Œuvres complètes*, Vol. III, Paris 1877.

Töannies, Ferdinand, *Gemeinschaft und Gesellschaft*, Leipzig 1887.

Trevor-Roper, Hugh Redwald, 'Hitlers Kriegsziel (Hitler's War Aims)', in: *Vierteljahrshefte für Zeitgeschichte*, Vol. 8, Stuttgart 1960.

Triepel, Heinrich, *Die Staatsverfassung und die politischen Parteien*, Berlin 1928.

—, *Die Hegemonie – Ein Buch von führenden Staaten*, Stuttgart 1938.

Turner, Henry A., *Stresemann and the Politics of the Weimar Republic*, New Haven 1963.


Valentin, Veit, *Geschichte der deutschen Revolution von 1848 bis 1849*, 2 vols., Berlin 1930/31.

—, *Geschichte der Deutschen*, Berlin 1947.

Vaughan, C. E., *The Political Writings of J. J. Rousseau*, Cambridge 1915.

Veblen, Thorstein, *Imperial Germany and the Industrial Revolution*, London 1934.

Vigneau, Jean, 'The Ideology of the Egyptian Revolution', in: *The Middle East in Transition*, Ed. W. Z. Laqueur, London 1958.

Vleugels, Wilhelm, *Die Kritik am wirtschaftlichen Liberalismus in der Entwicklung der deutschen Volkswirtschaftslehre*, Munich, Leipzig 1935.

Vocras, Baron Henry de, *Memoirs of Count Beust*, London 1887.

Voegelin, Eric, *The New Science of Politics*, Chicago 1952.

Vogelsang, Thilo, *Reichswehr, Staat und NSDAP*, Stuttgart 1962.

Wandruszka, 'Die Männer von 1848', in: *Wort und Wahrheit*, Vol. 10, Vienna 1947.

—, 'Österreichs politische Struktur, Die Entwicklung der Parteien und politischen Bewegungen', in: *Geschichte der Republik Österreich*, Ed. H. Benedikt, Munich 1954.

—, 'Die historische Schwäche des Bürgertums', in: *Wort und Wahrheit*, Vol. 10, Freiburg in Breisgau 1956.

Warren, Earl, *The Supreme Court in United States History*, 3 vols., Boston 1924

Waugh, Martin, 'Psychoanalytische Betrachtungen zur Dynamik und Genese des Vorurteils, des Antisemitismus und des Nazismus', in; *Psyche*, XVIth Year, No. 5, 1962.

Weber, Alfred, *Die Krise des modernen Staatsgedankens*, Stuttgart 1925.

Weber, Max, *Wirtschaft und Gesellschaft*, Tübingen 1925.

—, *Die protestantische Ethik und der Geist des Kapitalismus*, Tübingen 1934.

—, *Gesammelte Politische Schriften*, Tübingen 1958.

Weinberg, Gerhard L., *Hitlers Zweites Buch*, Stuttgart 1961.

Westarp, Count, Kuno, *Am Grabe der Parteiherrschaft*, Berlin 1932.

Weyer, F., *Jahrbuch des Öffentlichen Rechts der Gegenwart*, Vol. II, Tübingen 1922.

Wiese, Leopold von, *System der Allgemeinen Soziologie*, Munich, Leipzig 1933.

—, *System der Allgemeinen Soziologie*, Leipzig 1938.

Willey, Malcolm M., and Stuart A. Rice, *Communication Agencies and Social Life*, Vol. I, New York, London 1933.

Winkler, Franz, *Die Diktatur in Österreich*, Zürich, Leipzig 1935.

Wrench, John Evelyn, *Geoffrey Dawson and our Times*, London 1955.

Ziegler, H. O., *Autoritärer oder totaler Staat?*, Tübingen 1932.

Zimmern, Sir Alfred, *Nationality and Government*, London 1918.

Zolger, Iwan, 'Die Verfassung Jugoslawiens', *Jahrbuch des Öffentlichen Rechts der Gegenwart*, Vol. XI, Tübingen 1922.

Zürcher, A., *The Experiment with Democracy in Central Europe*, New York 1933.

# GLOSSARY

*Auslandsorganisation der NSDAP:* the organization whose purpose was to propagate Nazi doctrines among Germans abroad and to control their economic, political and cultural activities.

*Freikorps:* armed bodies raised and commanded by former German army officers in the early years of the Weimar Republic to take decisive action against left-wing revolutionaries.

*Gleichschaltung:* the compulsory regimentation of all phases of German life to conform to the pattern established by the Nazi Party.

*Grossraum:* a large geographical block or complex.

*Hammerschaften:* groups of working-class activists in Austria.

*Heimwehr:* a small fascist group in Austria, formed as a result of frontier fighting with Yugoslavia and Hungary and later inspired and partly financed by Mussolini.

*Ordensburgen:* the special SS castles where SS leaders were trained. Trainees went through a six-year course, successively attending the four castles where there was a deliberate atmosphere of the Order of Teutonic Knights of the fourteenth and fifteenth centuries.

*Reichsbanner:* the para-military organization of the German Social Democratic Party.

*Reichsdeutsche:* German nationals; if living abroad merely resident in a country.

*Reichswehr:* the professional armed forces of the state.

*Republikanischer Schutzbund:* the para-military organization of the Austrian Social Democratic Party.

*Stahlhelm:* one of the main German war veterans' associations.

*SA (Sturmabteiling):* the brown-shirted Nazi storm troops, led by Ernst Röhm, who were the political shock troops of the Nazi Party in Germany.

*SS (Schutzstaffel):* the black-shirted élite guard of the Führer; the armed force of the Nazi Party, commanded by Heinrich Himmler.

*Volk:* a people of racial homogeneity and the same blood – the underlying concept of the Nazi state.

*Volksdeutsche:* people of German blood living abroad but of non-German citizenship.

*Volksgemeinschaft:* general racial community.

*Volkstum:* the racial character and heritage of the German *Volk.*

*Vaterländische Front:* formed by Dollfuss after he had dissolved all the Austrian political parties and intended as a new dynamic forum in which Austrians of all creeds and beliefs could rally behind him in his struggle against the Nazis.

# INDEX

Abbt, Thomas, 41
Action Française, 370, 382
Activist parties (in Sudetenland), 406, 408, 415–16
Acton-Dalberg, Lord, 39, 50, 137, 193, 281
Adande, Alexander, 19
Adler, Max, 262
Adler, Victor, 63, 259
Administration (monocratic organization), 40, 107, 110
Agrarian Party of Czechoslovakia, 103, 158, 176, 250
Agricultural Labour decrees (in Austria 1921–2), 261
Ahlers, Johannes, 102, 111, 167
*Akademie für die Rechte der Völker*, 371 ff., 387 ff., 421 ff.
Albania, 15
Albertini, Rudolf von, 386
Alexander the Great, 114
Alexander, King of Yugoslavia, 93, 173, 393
Allport, Gordon W., 285
Alsace-Lorraine Auxiliary Association, 309
Althusius, Johannes, 197–8
Alvensleben-Neugattersleben, Count Bodo von, 376
American revolution, 270
Anabaptists, 204
Anschütz, Gerhard, 120, 131 ff.
Antimarxism (in *Heimwehr*), 261
Anti-Semitic organizations, 421
Anti-Semitism, 258, 284, 286, 330, 371 ff., 424–5
Apis, Colonel (Dimitryervič Dragutin, Serbian terrorist), 81
Appeasers (in Austria), 265
Aquinas, Thomas, 195, 197, 199, 266, 331
*Arcana imperii*, 27
Archetypal symbols, 328, 335 ff.
Arendt, Hannah, 107 ff., 157, 203, 221–2, 310, 322
Aretin, Karl Ottomar Freiherr von, 86
Aristocracy (concept and forms), 282 ff., (in Austria) 283
Aristotle, 14, 25, 31, 105, 138, 143, 161–2, 193–4, 201, 205, 208, 210, 217, 219, 222, 353–4, 439 ff.
Armenians, 391

Arndt, Ernst Moritz, 48
Artamanen (branch of German Youth Movement), 345
Asch, Bruno, 186
Ashantahene (tribal chief of the Ashantis), 46
Association of German Industry, 304
Athelstane (in *Ivanhoe*), 149
*Auslandsorganisation der NSDAP*, 396 ff.
Austria, Hitler's occupation of, 180
Austria-Hungary (pre-1914 economic progress), 174 ff.
Austrian Communal Law (1848), 56
Austrian Constituent Assembly (1848–9), 109
Austrian Republic:
  Constitution, 259 ff.
  Enabling law, 314
  Foreign policy, 180
  General strike (1934), 266
  Parliamentary crisis (1933), 264
  Promulgation of corporative-type Constitution, 265
  Unemployment and economic depression, 178 ff.
Autarchy in Succession States, 175 ff., (in Third Reich), 302
Authoritarianism, 209, 321 ff.
Authority, 201, 222 ff.

Babylonian captivity of Popes, 198
Badeni, Count K., 75
Bagehot, Walter, 85, 130
Bahr, Hermann, 42, 69
Bakunin, 201
Baldwin, Stanley, 191, 371 ff., 385, 388–389, 422
Balkan Union, 174
Bardolff, Carl von, 238
Barker, Ernest, 104–5, 162, 195
Barrès, Maurice, 210
Barrington-Ward, 372
Basch, A., 175
Basileus (Byzantine autocrat), 345
Bauer, Otto, 47, 60, 259 ff.
Baumann, SS Unterstursturmführer, 375 ff.
Bausch, Hans, 298
Bavarian People's Party, 223
Bebel, August, 67
Beck, Colonel Josef (Polish Foreign Minister), 313, 320